PLANNING SUSTAINABLE CITIES

PLANNING SUSTAINABLE CITIES
GLOBAL REPORT ON HUMAN SETTLEMENTS 2009

United Nations Human Settlements Programme

publishing for a sustainable future

London • Sterling, VA

First published by Earthscan in the UK and USA in 2009

United Nations Human Settlements Programme (UN-Habitat)
PO Box 30030, GPO Nairobi 00100, Kenya
Tel: +254 20 762 3120
Fax: +254 20 762 3477 / 4266 / 4267
Web: www.unhabitat.org

DISCLAIMER

The designations employed and the presentation of the material in this publication do not imply the expression of any opinion whatsoever on the part of the Secretariat of the United Nations concerning the legal status of any country, territory, city or area, or of its authorities, or concerning delimitation of its frontiers or boundaries, or regarding its economic system or degree of development. The analysis, conclusions and recommendations of the report do not necessarily reflect the views of the United Nations Human Settlements Programme, the Governing Council of the United Nations Human Settlements Programme or its Member States.

HS Number: HS/1192/09E (paperback)
                      HS/1193/09E (hardback)

ISBN: 978-1-84407-899-8   (paperback)
                      978-1-84407-898-1   (hardback)
                      978-92-113-1929-3   (UN-Habitat series)
                      978-92-113-2162-3   (UN-Habitat paperback)
                      978-92-113-2163-0   (UN-Habitat hardback)

Typeset by MapSet Ltd, Gateshead, UK
Cover design by Susanne Harris

For a full list of publications please contact:

Earthscan
Dunstan House
14a St Cross St
London, EC1N 8XA, UK
Tel: +44 (0)20 7841 1930
Fax: +44 (0)20 7242 1474
Email: earthinfo@earthscan.co.uk
Web: **www.earthscan.co.uk**

22883 Quicksilver Drive, Sterling, VA 20166-2012, USA

Earthscan publishes in association with the International Institute for Environment and Development

A catalogue record for this book is available from the British Library

Library of Congress Cataloging-in-Publication Data
Planning sustainable cities : global report on human settlements 2009 / United Nations Human Settlements Programme.
      p. cm.
   Includes bibliographical references.
   ISBN 978-1-84407-898-1 (hbk.) — ISBN 978-1-84407-899-8 (pbk.) 1. City planning—Environmental aspects. 2. Urban ecology (Sociology) 3. Sustainable development. I. United Nations Human Settlements Programme. II. Title: Global report on human settlements 2009.
         HT166.P5424 2009
   307.1'2—dc22
                                                                                                                  2009022390

At Earthscan we strive to minimize our environmental impacts and carbon footprint through reducing waste, recycling and offsetting our CO_2 emissions, including those created through publication of this book. For more details of our environmental policy, see www.earthscan.co.uk.

This book was printed in Malta by Gutenberg Press.
The paper used is FSC certified
and the inks are vegetable based.

Mixed Sources
Product group from well-managed forests, and other controlled sources
www.fsc.org Cert no. TT-CoC-002424
© 1996 Forest Stewardship Council

The paper used for this book is FSC-certified and totally chlorine-free. FSC (the Forest Stewardship Council) is an international network to promote responsible management of the world's forests.

FOREWORD

The major urban challenges of the twenty-first century include the rapid growth of many cities and the decline of others, the expansion of the informal sector, and the role of cities in causing or mitigating climate change. Evidence from around the world suggests that contemporary urban planning has largely failed to address these challenges. Urban sprawl and unplanned peri-urban development are among the most visible consequences, along with the increasing vulnerability of hundreds of millions of urban dwellers to rising sea levels, coastal flooding and other climate-related hazards.

Planning Sustainable Cities: Global Report on Human Settlements 2009 looks at the widespread failure to meet the needs of the majority of urban inhabitants, especially those in the rapidly growing and predominantly poor cities of the developing world, and identifies ways to reform urban planning.

The report identifies a troubling trend in most cities in developed and developing countries: the growth of up-market suburban areas and gated communities, on the one hand, and the simultaneous increase in overcrowded tenement zones, ethnic enclaves, slums and informal settlements, on the other. Strong contrasts have also emerged between technologically advanced and well-serviced economic production and business complexes such as export processing zones, and other areas defined by declining industry, sweatshops and informal businesses.

This report documents many effective and equitable examples of sustainable urbanization that are helping to define a new role for urban planning. I commend its information and analysis to all who are interested in promoting economically productive, environmentally safe and socially inclusive towns and cities.

Ban Ki-moon
Secretary-General
United Nations

INTRODUCTION

Planning Sustainable Cities: Global Report on Human Settlements 2009 assesses the effectiveness of urban planning as a tool for dealing with the unprecedented challenges facing 21st-century cities and for enhancing sustainable urbanization. There is now a realization that, in many parts of the world, urban planning systems have changed very little and are often contributors to urban problems rather than functioning as tools for human and environmental improvement. Against this background, the Global Report's central argument is that, in most parts of the world, current approaches to planning must change and that a new role for urban planning in sustainable urban development has to be found.

The Global Report argues that future urban planning must take place within an understanding of the factors shaping 21st-century cities, including:

- the environmental challenges of climate change and cities' excessive dependence on fossil fuel-powered cars;
- the demographic challenges of rapid urbanization, rapid growth of small- and medium-sized towns and an expanding youth population in developing nations, and, in developed nations, the challenges of shrinking cities, ageing and the increasing multicultural composition of cities;
- the economic challenges of uncertain future growth and fundamental doubts about market-led approaches that the current global financial crisis have engendered, as well as increasing informality in urban activities;
- increasing socio-spatial challenges, especially social and spatial inequalities, urban sprawl and unplanned peri-urbanization; and
- the challenges and opportunities of increasing democratization of decision-making as well as increasing awareness of social and economic rights among ordinary people.

An important conclusion of the Global Report is that, even though urban planning has changed relatively little in most countries since its emergence about 100 years ago, a number of countries have adopted some innovative approaches in recent decades. These include strategic spatial planning, use of spatial planning to integrate public-sector functions, new land regularization and management approaches, participatory processes and partnerships at the neighbourhood level, and planning for new and more sustainable spatial forms such as compact cities and new urbanism. However, in many developing countries, older forms of master planning have persisted. Here, the most obvious problem with this approach is that it has failed to accommodate the ways of life of the majority of inhabitants in rapidly growing and largely poor and informal cities, and has often directly contributed to social and spatial marginalization.

There are a number of key messages emerging from the Global Report, all of them contributing towards finding a new role for urban planning in sustainable urban development. One important message is that governments should increasingly take on a more central role in cities and towns in order to lead development initiatives and ensure that basic needs are met. This, to a large extent, is a result of the current global economic crisis, which has exposed the limits of the private sector – in terms of its resilience and future growth as well as the ability of the 'market' to solve most urban problems. It is clear that urban planning has an important role to play in assisting governments to meet the urban challenges of the 21st century.

As the world becomes numerically more urban, it is important that governments accept urbanization as a positive phenomenon and an effective means for improving access to services, as well as economic and social opportunities. If urban planning is to play a more effective role as a consequence of this policy orientation, countries need to develop overall national urban strategies.

With respect to the reconfiguration of planning systems, the Global Report's message is that careful attention should be given to identifying opportunities that can be built on, as well as factors that could lead to the subversion and corruption of planning institutions and processes. In particular, urban planning needs to be institutionally located in a way that allows it to play a role in creating urban investment and livelihood opportunities through responsive and collaborative processes as well as coordination of the spatial dimensions of public-sector policies and investment.

To ensure that participation is meaningful, socially inclusive and contributes to improving urban planning, a number of minimum conditions need to be satisfied, including: a political system that allows and encourages active citizen participation; a legal basis for local politics and planning that specifies how the outcomes of participatory processes will influence plan preparation and decision-making; and mechanisms for socially marginalized groups to have a voice in both representative politics and participatory planning processes.

The Global Report identifies a number of promising trends for bridging the green and brown agendas, including:

- the development of sustainable energy in order to reduce cities' dependence on non-renewable energy sources;
- the improvement of eco-efficiency in order to enable the use of waste products to satisfy urban energy and material needs;
- the development of sustainable transport in order to reduce the adverse environmental impacts of dependence on fossil fuel-driven cars; and
- the development of 'cities without slums' so as to address the pressing challenges of poor access to safe drinking water and sanitation as well as vulnerability to natural hazards.

The report recommends a three-step process for effectively responding to urban informality: first, recognizing the positive role played by urban informal development; second, adopting revisions to policies, laws and regulations to facilitate informal-sector operations; and, third, strengthening the legitimacy of planning and regulatory systems. Two aspects are particularly important in this process: embracing alternatives to the forced eviction of slum dwellers and informal entrepreneurs, for example regularization and upgrading of informally developed areas; and the strategic use of planning tools such as construction of trunk infrastructure, guided land development and land readjustment.

Strategic spatial plans linked to infrastructure development can promote more compact forms of urban expansion focused around public transport. In this context, linking major infrastructure investment projects and mega-projects to strategic planning is crucial. An infrastructure plan is a key element of such strategic spatial plans. In this, transport–land-use links are the most important ones and should take precedence, while other forms of infrastructure, including water and sanitation trunk infrastructure, can follow.

Most urban planning systems do not have monitoring and evaluation as an integral part of their operations. The Global Report suggests that urban planning systems should integrate monitoring and evaluation as permanent features, along with clear indicators that are aligned with plan goals, objectives and policies. Urban plans should also explicitly put in plain words their monitoring and evaluation philosophies, strategies and processes. The outcomes and impacts of many large-scale plans are difficult to evaluate because of the many influences and factors that are at play in cities over time. For this reason, it makes more sense to focus on site plans, subdivision plans and neighbourhood plans, all of which are smaller in scale and more conducive to monitoring and evaluation.

A final message of the Global Report is that curricula in many urban planning schools need to be updated. This is particularly the case in many developing and transition countries where curricula have not been revised to keep up with current challenges and issues. Planning schools should embrace innovative planning ideas, including the ability to engage in participatory planning, negotiation and communication, understanding the implications of rapid urbanization and urban informality, and the ability to bring climate change considerations into planning concerns. In addition, it should be recognized that planning is not 'value-neutral' – for this reason, urban planning education should include tuition in ethics, the promotion of social equity and the social and economic rights of citizens, as well as of sustainability.

The Global Report is published at a time when there is keen global interest in the revival of urban planning, within the context of sustainable urbanization. I believe the report will not only raise awareness of the role of urban planning in striving for sustainable cities, but also offer directions for the reform of this very important tool.

Anna Kajumulo Tibaijuka
Under-Secretary-General and Executive Director
United Nations Human Settlements Programme (UN-Habitat)

ACKNOWLEDGEMENTS

MANAGEMENT TEAM

Director: Oyebanji O. Oyeyinka.
Chief editor: Naison D. Mutizwa-Mangiza.

AUTHORS: UN-HABITAT CORE TEAM

Ben C. Arimah (also Task Manager, Overall Report); Inge Jensen (also Task Co-manager, Statistical Annex); Naison D. Mutizwa-Mangiza; and Edlam Abera Yemeru (also Coordinator, International Advice).

AUTHORS: EXTERNAL CONSULTANTS

Vanessa Watson, University of Cape Town, South Africa (Chapters 1, 3 and 11); Ambe Njoh, University of South Florida, US (Chapters 2 and 3); Simin Davoudi, Patsy Healey and Geoff Vigar, with Michael Majale, Newcastle University, UK (Chapter 4); Carole Rakodi, University of Birmingham, UK (Chapters 5 and 7); Peter Newman, Curtin University, Australia (Chapter 6); Alison Todes, with James Duminy, WITS University, South Africa (Chapter 8); Mark Seasons, University of Waterloo, Canada (Chapter 9); Bruce Stiftel, Georgia Institute of Technology, US, with Juan Demerutis, University of Guadalajara, Mexico; Andrea I. Frank, School of City and Regional Planning, Cardiff University, UK; Thomas Harper, University of Calgary, Canada; Daniel Kweku Baah Inkoom, University of Science and Technology, Ghana; Lik-Meng Lee, University Sains Malaysia, Malaysia; Jose Julio Lima, Federal University of Para, Brazil; Ali Memon, Lincoln University, New Zealand; Terence Milstead, Appalachian State University, US; Izabela Mironowicz, Wroclaw University of Technology, Poland; Tumsifu Nnkya, ARDHI University, Tanzania; Didier Paris, University of Lille, France; Christopher Silver, University of Florida, US; and Neil G. Sipe, Griffith University (Australia) (Chapter 10).

PREPARATION OF STATISTICAL ANNEX (UN-HABITAT)

Inge Jensen; Gora Mboup (Task Co-manager); Julius Majale; Philip Mukungu; and Wandia Riunga.

TECHNICAL SUPPORT TEAM (UN-HABITAT)

Beatrice Bazanye; Nelly Kan'gethe; Pamela Murage; and Naomi Mutiso-Kyalo.

INTERNATIONAL ADVISERS
(HS-NET ADVISORY BOARD[1] MEMBERS)

Samuel Babatunde, Agbola, Department of Urban and Regional Planning, University of Ibadan, Nigeria; Louis Albrechts, Institute for Urban and Regional Planning, Catholic University of Leuven, Belgium; Marisa Carmona, Department of Urbanism, Delft University of Technology, The Netherlands; Nowarat Coowanitwong, School of Environment, Resources and Development, Asian Institute of Technology, Thailand; Suocheng Dong, Institute of Geographic Sciences and Natural Resources Research, Chinese Academy of Sciences, China; Alain Durand-Lasserve, Sociétés en Développement dans l'Espace et dans le Temps, Université Denis Diderot, France; József Hegedüs, Metropolitan Research Institute, Varoskutatas Kft, Hungary; Alfonso Iracheta, Programme of Urban and Environmental Studies, El Colegio Mexiquense, Mexico; A. K. Jain, Delhi Development Authority, India; Paula Jiron, Housing Institute, University of Chile, Chile; Vinay D. Lall, Society for Development Studies, India; José Luis Lezama de la Torre, Centro de Estudios Demográficos, Urbanos y Ambientales, Mexico; Om Prakash Mathur, National Institute of Public Finance and Policy (IDFC), India; Winnie Mitullah, Institute of Development Studies (IDS),

University of Nairobi, Kenya; Aloysius Mosha, Department of Architecture and Planning, University of Botswana, Botswana; Peter Newman, Institute for Sustainability and Technology Policy, Murdoch University, Australia; Peter Ngau, Department of Regional and Urban Planning, University of Nairobi, Kenya; Tumsifu Jonas Nnkya, Institute of Housing Studies and Building Research, University of Dar es Salaam, Tanzania; Deike Peters, Centre for Metropolitan Studies, Berlin University of Technology, Germany; Carole Rakodi, International Development Department, University of Birmingham, UK; Gustavo Riofrio, Centro de Estudios y Promoción del Desarrollo (DESCO), Peru; Nelson Saule Junior, Instituto de Estudios Formacao e Assessoria em Politicas Socials (POLIS), Brazil; Elliott Sclar, Centre for Sustainable Urban Development, Columbia University, US; Mona Serageldin, Centre for Urban Development Studies, Harvard University Graduate School of Design, US; Dina K. Shehayeb, Housing and Building National Research Centre, Egypt; Richard Stren, Cities Centre, University of Toronto, Canada; Graham Tipple, School of Architecture, Planning and Landscape, Newcastle University, UK; Luidmila Ya Tkachenko, Research and Project Institute of Moscow City Master Plan, Russia; Willem K. T. van Vliet–, College of Architecture and Planning, University of Colorado, US; Patrick Wakely, Development Planning Unit (DPU), University College of London, UK; and Belinda Yuen, School of Design and Environment, National University of Singapore, Singapore.

OTHER INTERNATIONAL ADVISERS

Michael Cohen, New School University, US; Jenny Crawford, Royal Town Planning Institute, UK; Rose Gilroy, Institute for Policy and Planning, Newcastle University, UK; Suzanne Gunn, Newcastle University, UK; Cliff Hague, Secretary General, Commonwealth Association of Planners, UK; Colin Haylock, Urban Design Group Leader, Ryder HKS, UK; Jean Hillier, Global Urban Research Centre, Newcastle University, UK; Ted Kitchen, Sheffield Hallam University, UK; Nina Laurie, School of Geography, Politics and Sociology, Newcastle University, UK; Scott Leckie, Director, Displacement Solutions, Switzerland; Ali Madanjpour, Global Urban Research Centre, Newcastle University, UK; Roberto Monte-Mor, Federal University of Minas Gerais, Brazil; John Pendlebury, Global Urban Research Centre, Newcastle University, UK; Christopher Rodgers, Research Newcastle Law School, Newcastle University, UK; Maggie Roe, Institute for Policy Practice, Newcastle University, UK; Richard H. Schneider, Department of Urban and Regional Planning, University of Florida, US; Robert Upton, Secretary General, Royal Town Planning Institute, UK; and Pablo Vaggione, Secretary General, International Society of City and Regional Planners (ISOCARP).

ADVISERS (UN-HABITAT)

Claudio Acioly; Subramonia Ananthakrishnan; Christine Auclair; Daniel Biau; Filiep Decorte; Mohamed El-Sioufi; Szilard Fricska; Angelique Hablis; Mohamed Halfani; Cecilia Kinuthia-Njenga; Lucia Kiwala; Ansa Masaud; Cecilia Martinez; Joseph Maseland; Jossy Materu; Eduardo Moreno; Teckla Muhoro; Claude Ngomsi; Laura Petrella; Lars Reutersward; Frederic Saliez; Wandia Seaforth; Paul Taylor; Raf Tuts; Brian Williams; and Nick You.

AUTHORS OF BACKGROUND PAPERS

Jamal Husain Ansari, School of Planning and Architecture, New Delhi, India ('Revisiting urban planning in Southern Asia'); Koffi Attahi, National Bureau for Technical and Development Studies, Abidjan, Côte d'Ivoire; Appessika Kouame, National Bureau for Technical and Development Studies, Abidjan, Côte d'Ivoire; and Hinin-Moustapha Daniel, National Bureau for Technical and Development Studies, Abidjan, Côte d'Ivoire ('Revisiting urban planning in sub-Saharan Africa 'Francophone' countries'); Ken Breetzke, Engineering Department of the eThekwini Municipality, South Africa ('From conceptual frameworks to quantitative models: Spatial planning in the Durban metropolitan area, South Africa – the link to housing and infrastructure planning'); Xiaoyan Chen, School of Planning, University of Waterloo, Canada ('Monitoring and evaluation in China's urban planning system: A case study of Xuzhou'); Laurence Crot, University of Neuchâtel, Switzerland ('The characteristics and outcomes of participatory budgeting: Buenos Aires, Argentina'); Anne Nicole Duquennois, Environmental Design and Arts and Sciences at the University of Colorado, US; and Peter Newman, Curtin University, Australia ('Linking the green and brown agendas: A case study on Cairo, Egypt'); Andrea I. Frank, School of City and Regional Planning, Cardiff University, UK; and Izabela Mironowicz, Wroclaw University of Technology, Poland ('Planning education in Poland'); Pietro Garau, University of Rome, Italy ('Revisiting urban planning in developed countries'); Patsy Healey, Newcastle University, UK ('Developing neighbourhood management capacity in Kobe, Japan: Interactions between civil society and formal planning institutions'); Sonia Hirt, Virginia Polytechnic Institute and State University, US; and Kiril Stanilov, University of Cincinnati, US ('Revisiting urban planning in the transitional countries'); Uche Cosmas Ikejiofor, Federal Ministry of Environment, Housing and Urban Development, Nigeria ('Planning within a context of informality: Issues and trends in land delivery in Enugu, Nigeria'); Daniel Kweku Baah Inkoom, University of Science and Technology, Ghana ('Planning education in Ghana'); Clara Irazábal, University of Southern California, US ('Revisiting urban planning in Latin America and the Caribbean'); Paul Lecroart, Urban Planning and Development Agency for IAU Île-de-France, France ('The urban regeneration of Plaine Saint-Denis, Paris region, 1985–2020: Integrated planning in a large "urban project"'); Michael Majale, Newcastle University, UK ('Developing participatory planning practices in Kitale,

Kenya'); Mostafa Modbouly Nassar, Housing and Building National Research Center, Cairo, Egypt ('Revisiting urban planning in North Africa and the Middle East'); Ambe Njoh, University of South Florida, US ('Self-help, a viable non-conventional urban public service delivery strategy: Lessons from Cameroon'; 'New urbanism, an alternative to traditional urban design: The case of celebration, Florida, US'; 'Community-based and non-governmental organizations in urban development in Mexico City: The case of San Miguel Teotongo'; and 'The state as enabler in urban policy-making in Colombo, Sri Lanka'); Don Okpala, executive coordinator of Idoplin Limited, Lagos, Nigeria ('Revisiting urban planning in sub-Saharan Africa 'Anglophone' countries'); Cameron Owens, Department of Geography, Simon Fraser University, Canada ('Challenges in evaluating liveability in Vancouver, Canada'); Carole Rakodi, University of Birmingham, UK ('The politics of urban regeneration in Cardiff, UK'); Carole Rakodi, University of Birmingham, UK; and Tommy Firman, School of Architecture, Planning and Policy Development, Institute of Technology in Bandung (ITB), Indonesia ('Planning for an extended metropolitan region in Asia: Jakarta, Indonesia'); Dory Reeves and Bonnie Parfitt, School of Architecture and Planning, University of Auckland, New Zealand; and Carol Archer, Faculty of the Built Environment, University of Technology, Jamaica ('Gender and urban planning'); Jan Scheurer, Australian Housing and Urban Research Institute, RMIT University, Melbourne, Australia; and Peter Newman, Curtin University, Australia ('Vauban: A European model bridging the green and brown agendas'); Belinda Yuen, National University of Singapore, Singapore ('Revisiting urban planning in East Asia, South-East Asia and the Pacific').

PUBLISHING TEAM (EARTHSCAN LTD)

Jonathan Sinclair Wilson; Hamish Ironside; Alison Kuznets; and Andrea Service.

NOTE

1   The HS-Net Advisory Board consists of experienced researchers in the human settlements field, selected to represent the various geographical regions of the world. The primary role of the Board is to advise UN-Habitat on the substantive content and organization of the Global Report on Human Settlements.

CONTENTS

PART I
CHALLENGES AND CONTEXT

PART II
GLOBAL TRENDS: THE URBAN PLANNING PROCESS (PROCEDURAL)

PART III
GLOBAL TRENDS: THE CONTENT OF URBAN PLANS (SUBSTANTIVE)

PART IV
GLOBAL TRENDS: MONITORING, EVALUATION AND EDUCATION

PART V
FUTURE POLICY DIRECTIONS

PART VI
STATISTICAL ANNEX

LIST OF FIGURES, BOXES AND TABLES

FIGURES

BOXES

TABLES

LIST OF ACRONYMS AND ABBREVIATIONS

AESOP	Association of European Schools of Planning
APERAU	Association for the Promotion of Education and Research in Management and Urbanism
BOT	build–operate–transfer
BRT	bus rapid transit
CAP	community action planning
CBO	community-based organization
CCTV	closed-circuit television
CDS	City Development Strategy
CO_2	carbon dioxide
CSO	civil society organization
EPM	environmental planning and management
ESPON	European Spatial Planning Observation Network
EU	European Union
FDI	foreign direct investment
g	gram
GDP	gross domestic product
GIS	geographic information systems
GNI	gross national income
GPEAN	Global Planning Education Association Network
GPN	Global Planners Network
GTZ	Deutsche Gesellschaft für Technische Zusammenarbeit
GUO	Global Urban Observatory
ha	hectare
HDI	Human Development Index
HIV-AIDS	human immunodeficiency virus–acquired immunodeficiency syndrome
ICLEI	International Council for Local Environmental Initiatives
ILO	International Labour Organization
IMF	International Monetary Fund
IPCC	Intergovernmental Panel on Climate Change
ITDG	Intermediate Technology Development Group
km	kilometre
kWh	kilowatt hour
LECZ	low-elevation coastal zone
LRT	light rail transit
m	metre
MDG	Millennium Development Goal
MW	megawatt
NGO	non-governmental organization
OECD	Organisation for Economic Co-operation and Development
PPP	purchasing power parity
PUA	participatory urban appraisal
SCP	Sustainable Cities Programme
SDF	spatial development framework
SUDP	Strategic Urban Development Plan
TOD	transit-oriented development

UK	United Kingdom of Great Britain and Northern Ireland
UMP	Urban Management Programme
UN	United Nations
UNCED	United Nations Conference on Environment and Development
UNCHS	United Nations Centre for Human Settlements (Habitat) (now UN-Habitat)
UNDESA	United Nations Department of Economic and Social Affairs
UNDP	United Nations Development Programme
UNEP	United Nations Environment Programme
UN-Habitat	United Nations Human Settlements Programme (formerly UNCHS (Habitat))
UNICEF	United Nations Children's Fund
US	United States of America
WHO	World Health Organization

KEY FINDINGS AND MESSAGES

KEY FINDINGS: CURRENT AND FUTURE URBAN CHALLENGES

Future urban planning must take place within an understanding of the factors shaping 21st-century cities, especially the demographic, environmental, economic and socio-spatial challenges that lie ahead. It also needs to recognize the changing institutional structure of cities and the emerging spatial configurations of large, multiple-nuclei or polycentric, city-regions.

Demographic challenges

The global urban transition witnessed over the last three or so decades has been phenomenal and is presenting planning and urban management with challenges that have never been faced before. While the period 1950–1975 saw population growth more or less evenly divided between the urban and rural areas of the world, the period since has seen the balance tipped dramatically in favour of urban growth. In 2008, for the first time in history, over half of the world's population lived in urban areas and, according to current projections, this will have risen to 70 per cent by 2050. Almost all of this growth will take place in developing regions. Between 2007 and 2025, the annual urban population increase in developing regions is expected to be 53 million (or 2.27 per cent), compared to a mere 3 million (or 0.49 per cent) in developed regions.

It is predicted that many new megacities of over 10 million people and hypercities of over 20 million will emerge during the next few decades. The bulk of new urban growth, however, will occur in smaller, and often institutionally weak, settlements of 100,000–250,000 people. In contrast, some parts of the world are facing the challenge of shrinking cities. Most of these are to be found in the developed and transitional regions of the world. But more recently, city shrinkage has occurred in some developing countries as well.

A key problem is that most of the rapid urban growth is taking place in countries least able to cope – in terms of the ability of governments to provide, or facilitate the provision of, urban infrastructure; in terms of the ability of urban residents to pay for such services; and in terms of resilience to natural disasters. The inevitable result has been the rapid growth of urban slums and squatter settlements. Close to 1 billion people, or 32 per cent of the world's current urban population, live in slums in inequitable and life-threatening conditions, and are directly affected by both environmental disasters and social crises, whose frequency and impacts have increased significantly during the last few decades.

Environmental challenges

One of the most significant environmental challenges at present is climate change. It is predicted that, within cities, climate change will negatively affect access to water and that hundreds of millions of people will be vulnerable to coastal flooding and related natural disasters as global warming increases. Moreover, it will be the poorest countries and people who will be most vulnerable to this threat and who will suffer the earliest and the most. High urban land and housing costs currently are pushing the lowest-income people into locations that are prone to natural hazards, such that four out of every ten non-permanent houses in the developing world are now located in areas threatened by floods, landslides and other natural disasters, especially in slums and informal settlements. Significantly, such disasters are only partly a result of natural forces – they are also products of failed urban development and planning.

A second major concern is the environmental impact of fossil fuel use in urban areas, especially of oil, and its likely long-term increase in cost. The global use of oil as an energy source has both promoted and permitted urbanization, and its easy availability has allowed the emergence of low-density and sprawling urban forms – suburbia – dependent on private cars. Beyond this, however, the entire global economy rests on the possibility of moving both people and goods quickly, cheaply and over long distances. An oil-based economy and climate change are linked: vehicle emissions contribute significantly to greenhouse gas emissions and hence global warming. Responding to a post-oil era presents a whole range of new imperatives for urban planning, especially in terms of settlement density and transportation.

Economic challenges

Processes of globalization and economic restructuring in recent decades have impacted in various ways on urban settlements in both developed and developing countries, and will continue to do so. Particularly significant has been the impact on urban labour markets, which show a growing polarization of occupational and income structures (and hence growing income inequality) caused by growth in the service sector and decline in manufacturing. There have also been important gender dimensions to this restructuring: over the last several decades women have increasingly moved into paid employment, but trends towards 'casualization' of the labour force (through an increase in part-time, contract and home-based work) have made them highly vulnerable to economic crises. In developed countries, the last several decades have also seen a process of industrial relocation to less developed regions as firms have attempted to reduce labour and operating costs.

The global economic crisis that began in 2008 has accelerated economic restructuring and led to the rapid growth of unemployment in all parts of the world. One important result of these economic and policy processes on urban labour markets has been rapid growth of the urban informal economy in all regions of the world, but particularly in developing countries. Here, informal sector jobs account for more than 50 per cent of all employment in Africa and the Latin America and Caribbean region, and a little lower in Asia. There are also important gender dimensions to informality: women are disproportionately concentrated in the informal economy and particularly in low-profit activities. Among the most significant challenges that urban planning has to address in the next few decades, especially in developing countries, are increasing poverty and inequality, as well as to the rapidly expanding urban informal sector.

Socio-spatial challenges

Urban planners and managers have increasingly found themselves confronted by new spatial forms and processes, the drivers of which often lie outside the control of local government. Socio-spatial change seems to have taken place primarily in the direction of the fragmentation, separation and specialization of functions and uses within cities, with labour market polarization (and hence income inequality) reflected in growing differences between wealthier and poorer areas in both developed and developing country cities. Highly visible contrasts have emerged between up-market gentrified and suburban areas with tenement zones, ethnic enclaves and ghettos, as well as between areas built for the advanced service and production sector, and for luxury retail and entertainment, with older areas of declining industry, sweatshops and informal businesses. While much of this represents the playing out of 'market forces' in cities, and the logic of real estate and land speculation, it is also a response to local policies that have attempted to position cities globally in order to attract new investment through 'competitive city' approaches.

In some parts of the world, including in Latin American and Caribbean cities, fear of crime has increased urban fragmentation as middle- and upper-income households segregate themselves into 'gated communities' and other types of high-security residential complexes. 'Gated communities' have multiplied in major metropolitan areas such as Buenos Aires, São Paulo, Santiago, Johannesburg and Pretoria.

In many poorer cities, spatial forms are largely driven by the efforts of low-income households to secure land that is affordable and in a location close to employment and other livelihood sources. This process is leading to entirely new urban forms as the countryside itself begins to urbanize. The bulk of rapid urban growth in developing countries is, in fact, now taking place in unplanned peri-urban areas, as poor urban dwellers look for a foothold in the cities and towns in locations where land is more easily available, where they can escape the costs and threats of urban land regulations, and where there is a possibility of combining urban and rural livelihoods.

Institutional challenges

Formal urban planning systems are typically located within the public sector, with local government usually being the most responsible tier. Within the last three decades, and closely linked to processes of globalization, there have been significant transformations in local government in many parts of the world, making them very different settings from those within which modern urban planning was originally conceived about 100 years ago.

The most commonly recognized change has been the expansion of the urban political system from 'government' to 'governance', which in developed countries represents a response to the growing complexity of governing in a globalizing and multilevel context, as well as the involvement of a range of non-state actors in the process of governing. In developing countries, the concept of governance has been promoted as a policy measure, along with decentralization and democratization, driven largely by multilateral institutions such as the World Bank and United Nations agencies. These shifts have had profound implications for urban planning, which has often been cast as a relic of the old welfare state model and as an obstacle to economic development and market freedom.

In addition, urban planning at the local government level has also had to face challenges from shifts in the scale of urban decision-making. As the wider economic role of urban centres and their governments has come adrift from their geographically bounded administrative roles, so the need to move towards rescaling to the city-region level and introducing multilevel and collaborative governance has become increasingly apparent in many parts of the world.

Another global trend has been in the area of participation. Since the 1960s, there has been a growing unwillingness on the part of communities to passively accept the planning decisions of politicians and technocrats that impact on their living environments. However, within cities in both developed and developing countries, 'delivering consensus' is becoming more difficult, as societal divisions have been increasing, partly as a result of international migration and the growth of ethnic minority groups in cities, and partly because of growing income and employment inequalities that have intersected with ethnicity and identity in various ways. In developing countries, urban crime and violence have also contributed to a decline in social cohesion and an increase in conflict and insecurity in many cities.

KEY FINDINGS: URBAN PLANNING RESPONSES AND TRENDS

Emergence and spread of contemporary urban planning

Contemporary urban planning systems in most parts of the world have been shaped by 19th-century Western European planning, commonly known as master planning, or modernist urban planning. Its global diffusion occurred through several mechanisms, especially colonialism, market expansion and intellectual exchange. Professional bodies and international and development agencies also played an important role. Frequently, these imported ideas were used for reasons of political, ethnic or racial domination and exclusion, rather than in the interests of good planning.

In many developed countries, approaches to planning have changed significantly. However, in many developing countries, the older forms of master planning have persisted. In some countries, master planning is still found to be useful, sometimes due to the very rapid rate of state-directed city-building, and sometimes because it serves the interests of elites who often emulate modern Western cities and whose actions inevitably marginalize the poor and the informal in cities.

The most obvious problem with modernist planning is that, being based on spatial interventions that assume a far higher level of social affluence than is the case in most developing countries, it fails to accommodate the way of life of the majority of inhabitants in rapidly growing, and largely poor and informal cities, and thus directly contributes to social and spatial marginalization. Furthermore, it fails to take into account the important challenges of 21st-century cities such as climate change, oil dependence, food insecurity and informality; and to a large extent, it fails to acknowledge the need to meaningfully involve communities and other stakeholders in the planning of urban areas.

A number of new and sometimes overlapping approaches to urban planning have been identified in the Global Report, the principal ones being:

- *Strategic spatial planning*, which does not address every part of a city but focuses on only those aspects or areas that are strategic or important to overall plan objectives;
- *Use of spatial planning to integrate public-sector functions*, including injection of a spatial or territorial dimension into sectoral strategies;
- *New land regularization and management approaches*, which offer alternatives to the forced removal of informal settlements, ways of using planning tools to strategically influence development actors, ways of working with development actors to manage public space and provide services, and new ideas on how planning laws can be used to capture rising urban land values;
- *Participatory processes and partnerships at the neighbourhood level*, which include 'participatory urban appraisal', 'participatory learning and action' and 'community action planning', including 'participatory budgeting';
- *New forms of master planning*, which are bottom up and participatory, oriented towards social justice and aim to counter the effects of land speculation; and
- *Planning aimed at producing new spatial forms*, such as compact cities and new urbanism, both of which are a response to challenges of urban sprawl and sustainable urbanization.

These new approaches to planning have many positive qualities, but also aspects that suggest the need for caution in terms of their wider use. There is still too much focus on process, often at the expense of outcomes. There is also a strong focus on the directive aspect of the planning system and neglect of the underlying regulatory and financing systems, and how these link to directive plans. Planning is still weak in terms of how to deal with the major sustainable urban challenges of the 21st century: climate change, resource depletion, rapid urbanization, poverty and informality.

Institutional and regulatory frameworks for planning

A variety of new agencies have become involved in urban planning – for example, special 'partnership' agencies that focus on particular development tasks, metropolitan and regional development agencies, as well as agencies created through initiatives funded by external aid programmes. This has been partly in response to decentralization of authority from national governments to cities, regions and quasi-governmental organizations, as well as to different forms of privatization.

The legal systems underpinning planning regulation are being modified in many countries to allow greater flexibility and interactions. This situation is encouraging two related responses. One is an increase in litigation as a way of resolving planning disputes. The other is a counteracting movement to avoid litigation through developing negotiation and collaborative practices.

The presence of large-scale land and property developers (often linked to competitive city policies) is expanding substantially, creating challenges for national and local planning practices that are seeking to promote greater equity and environmental sensitivity in urban development.

In many large urban complexes that have resulted from metropolitanization and informal peri-urbanization processes, there is an increasing mismatch between administrative boundaries and the functional dynamics of urban areas, leading to problems in coordinating development activity and integrating the social, environmental and economic dimensions of development.

Approaches to the formulation and implementation of plans have moved from assuming that a planning authority could control how development takes place, to recognizing that all parties (including the private sector and civil society organizations) need to learn from each other about how to shape future development trajectories.

Participation, planning and politics

In most developed countries, formal procedures for public participation in planning decisions have long existed. Well-established representative democratic political systems in these countries enable citizen participation in urban planning processes. Yet this remains tokenistic in some developed and transition countries.

A technocratic blueprint approach to planning persists in many developing countries, inhibiting the direct involvement of citizens or other stakeholders in decision-making. Attempts to adopt participatory planning processes and revise planning legislation accordingly have been minimal in many developing countries.

In spite of this, a growing number of cities are adopting participatory approaches to planning due to the widespread recognition that technocratic approaches have been largely ineffective in dealing with the challenges of urbanization. A variety of innovative approaches for participatory planning, from the local to city level, have been developed in recent years, often with support from international programmes, such as the UN-Habitat-supported Urban Management, Sustainable Cities and Localizing Agenda 21 programmes.

At the local/community level, *participatory urban appraisal* (PUA), which draws on tools and methods of participatory rural appraisal, has been used to identify needs and priorities. PUA provides information inputs into decision-making rather than itself being a decision-making tool. It has therefore been complemented by *community action planning* (CAP), which develops actionable ideas and implementation arrangements based on the information generated through PUAs. A good example of CAP is the *women's safety audit*, which has been employed to address the safety of women in the planning and design of safer neighbourhoods.

At the city level, *participatory budgeting* has enabled citizen participation in municipal budgeting and spending, while *city development strategies* (CDSs) have enabled communities to participate in the prioritization of urban development projects. A CDS uses participatory processes to develop an action plan for equitable urban growth. To date, over 150 cities worldwide have been involved in developing CDSs.

Bridging the green and brown agendas

Rapid urban growth in the past 50 years has meant that managing the built (or human) environment, while coping with environmental pollution (especially waste) and degradation, has become a significant challenge in the cities of developed countries and has overwhelmed many cities in the developing world. Fewer than 35 per cent of the cities in developing countries have their wastewater treated; worldwide 2.5 billion and 1.2 billion people lack safe sanitation and access to clean water, respectively; and between one third and one half of the solid waste generated within most cities in low- and middle-income countries is not collected. Most of this deprivation is concentrated in urban slums and informal settlements.

Innovations to achieve green and brown agenda synergies are under way all over the world. These are manifest in the following overlapping trends identified in the Global Report:

- developing renewable energy in order to reduce cities' dependence on non-renewable energy sources;
- striving for carbon-neutral cities so as to significantly cut and offset carbon emissions;
- developing small-scale, distributed power and water systems for more energy-efficient provision of services;
- increasing photosynthetic spaces as part of green infrastructure development in order to expand renewable sources of energy and local food;
- improving eco-efficiency in order to enable the use of waste products to satisfy urban energy and material resource needs;
- increasing sense of place through local sustainable development strategies so as to enhance implementation and effectiveness of innovations;
- developing sustainable transport in order to reduce the adverse environmental impacts of dependence on fossil fuel-driven cars; and
- developing 'cities without slums' so as to address the pressing challenges of poor access to safe drinking water and sanitation as well as environmental degradation.

Although the sustainable urban development vision has been embraced by cities all over the world, none are yet able to simultaneously and comprehensively address the different facets of the sustainable urban development challenge and to fully demonstrate how to integrate the green and brown agendas.

Urban planning and informality

The effectiveness of urban planning is a key determinant of the prevalence of informality in cities. Accordingly, urban informality in developed countries is limited, given their well-developed planning systems. In contrast, a substantial and increasing proportion of urban development in developing countries is informal due to limited planning and governance capacities.

Affordable serviced land and formal housing remains inaccessible to most urban residents in cities of developing countries, especially low- and middle-income groups. Therefore a significant number of them live in housing that does not comply with planning regulations. A staggering 62 per cent of the urban population in sub-Saharan Africa lives in slums, compared to 43 per cent in South Asia. Much of future urban growth in developing country cities is expected to take place in peri-urban areas and expanded metropolitan regions where informal development is widespread.

About 57 per cent of all employment in the Latin America and Caribbean region is informal. About 60 per cent of all urban jobs in Africa are in the informal sector and, in francophone Africa, 78 per cent of urban employment is informal, while the sector currently generates 93 per cent of all new jobs. In Central Asia, the informal sector is responsible for between 33 and 50 per cent of the total economic output. Even in the countries of the Organisation for Economic Co-operation and Development (OECD), the informal economy accounts for about 16 per cent of value added.

In many countries, informality is regarded as both undesirable and illegal, leading to ineffective government responses such as elimination and neglect. However, because of the failure of such policies to either eliminate the sector or improve the livelihoods of informal entrepreneurs, there has been some rethinking and renewed attempts to develop alternative policy responses to informality. For instance, legal provisions against evictions, regularization and upgrading of informal settlements and land-sharing arrangements are some of the approaches that have been used to avoid the harmful effects of forced eviction of both informal settlement/slum dwellers and informal economic entrepreneurs.

Strategic use of planning tools, including public investment in trunk infrastructure to influence patterns of development, guided land development using strategic planning, land pooling or readjustment and the gradual extension of detailed planning and development control, have also enhanced the effectiveness of responses to informality.

Partnerships with informal economic actors to manage public space and provide services have helped to address the challenges of informality in some cities. This involves recognizing informal entrepreneurs' property rights, allocating special-purpose areas for informal activities and providing basic services.

Planning, spatial structure of cities and provision of infrastructure

Since the late 1970s, the 'unbundling' of infrastructure development – through forms of corporatization or privatization of urban infrastructure development and provision, and developer-driven urban development – has tended to drive patterns of urban fragmentation and spatial inequality in many countries. The period since the 1980s has seen a major growth of urban mega-projects, including infrastructure projects. This has been linked to the new emphasis on urban competitiveness and urban entrepreneurialism.

Although the private sector has tended to focus on more profitable aspects of infrastructure development, privatized provision of services has also occurred in poorer communities. While these processes sometimes extend services to areas that would not otherwise have them, they also impose considerable costs on the poor.

The structure of road networks and public transport systems shapes the spatial organization of many cities, and has been a crucial element in attempts to restructure cities spatially. However, the accessibility–value relationship has meant that lower-income groups have had little choice of where to live and work. In addition, the availability of trunk lines for water and sewerage and transmission lines for electricity in particular areas reduces development costs and has also influenced patterns of growth. This type of bulk infrastructure is also increasingly seen as a key element in shaping patterns of spatial development, after road and public transport networks.

Monitoring and evaluation of urban plans

Monitoring and evaluation of the implementation of urban plans has become part of practice in the more progressive planning departments of cities and regions in developed countries. However, in the transitional and developing countries, very little progress has been made so far in embracing monitoring and evaluation as integral parts of the urban planning process.

In developing countries, the most extensive application of monitoring and evaluation has occurred as part of development programmes that are funded by international agencies, managed by state organizations and implemented by local authorities. There is less evidence of community/official urban plan-level monitoring and evaluation in developing countries. There are typically few resources for planning generally, and especially for plan enforcement or monitoring.

Because the importance of monitoring and evaluation can be difficult to appreciate in local governments that face complex, energy-sapping urban challenges, not many urban authorities have fully embraced this important management tool. In addition, monitoring and evaluation can produce negative as well as positive results. The latter situation is often embraced by local decision-makers, while the former is frequently ignored, downplayed or even rejected.

Planning education

There are about 550 universities worldwide that offer urban planning degrees. About 60 per cent (330 schools) of these are concentrated in ten countries. The remaining 40 per cent (220 schools) are located in 72 different countries. In total, there are at least 13,000 academic staff in planning schools worldwide. While developing countries contain more than 80 per cent of the world's population, they have less than half of the world's planning schools.

Urban planning education in most countries has moved from a focus on physical design towards an increased focus on policy and social science research. Graduates from planning schools focusing on physical design find themselves increasingly marginalized in a situation where planning processes progressively require knowledge of issues related to sustainable development, social equity and participatory processes.

Despite awareness of the importance of gender in planning practice, it is not a core part of the syllabus in many urban planning schools. While about half of all planning schools teach social equity issues in their curricula, only a minority of these specifically teach gender-related issues.

There are significant regional variations in terms of the relative importance given to technical skills, communicative skills and analytic skills in planning curricula. The variations are linked to the prevalence of policy/social science approaches, as opposed to physical design. For example, while planning schools in Asia rate analytical skills as most important, followed by technical skills and then communication skills, the focus varies substantially in Latin America. Overall in Latin America, technical, rationalist perspectives are the norm, with skills such as master planning, urban design and econometric modelling being more common than those of participation or negotiation.

KEY MESSAGES: TOWARDS A NEW ROLE FOR URBAN PLANNING

Broad policy directions

Governments, both central and local, should increasingly take on a more central role in cities and towns in order to lead development initiatives and ensure that basic needs are met. This is increasingly being recognized and, to a large extent, is a result of the current global economic crisis, which has exposed the limits of the private sector in terms of its resilience and future growth as well as the ability of the 'market' to solve most urban problems. Urban planning has an important role to play in assisting governments and civil society to meet the urban challenges of the 21st century. However, urban planning systems in many parts of the world are not equipped to deal with these challenges and, as such, need to be reformed.

Reformed urban planning systems must fully and unequivocally address a number of major current and emerging urban challenges, especially climate change, rapid urbanization, poverty, informality and safety. Reformed urban planning systems must be shaped by, and be responsive to the contexts from which they arise, as there is no single model urban planning system or approach that can be applied in all parts of the world. In the developing world, especially in Africa and Asia, urban planning must prioritize the interrelated issues of rapid urbanization, urban poverty, informality, slums and access to basic services. In developed, transition and a number of developing countries, urban planning will have to play a vital role in addressing the causes and impacts of climate change and ensuring sustainable urbanization. In many other parts of the world, both developed and developing, urban planning should play a key role in enhancing urban safety by addressing issues of disaster preparedness, post-disaster and post-conflict reconstruction and rehabilitation, as well as urban crime and violence.

A particularly important precondition for the success of urban planning systems is that countries should develop a national perspective on the role of urban areas and challenges of urbanization, articulated in some form of national urban policy. This is not a new idea, but, as the world moves to a situation in which urban populations dominate numerically, it is more important than ever before that governments accept that urbanization can be a positive phenomenon and a precondition for improving

access to services, economic and social opportunities, and a better quality of life. In this context, a reformed urban planning will have to pay greater attention to small- and medium-sized cities, especially in developing countries where planning often focuses on larger cities. Countries will also need to integrate various aspects of demographic change in their urban planning policies, particularly the youth bulge observed in many developing countries, shrinking or declining cities, as well as the rapidly ageing population and increasingly multicultural composition of cities in developed countries.

Capacity to enforce urban planning regulations, which is seriously lacking in many developing countries, should be given very high priority and should be developed on the basis of realistic standards. The regulation of land and property development, through statutory plans and development permits, is a vitally important role of the urban planning system. Yet, in many countries, especially in the developing world, outdated planning regulations and development standards are, paradoxically, one of the main reasons underlying the failure of enforcement. They are based on the experience of the much more affluent developed countries and are not affordable for the majority of urban inhabitants. More realistic land and property development standards are being formulated in some developing countries, but this effort must be intensified and much more should be done to improve enforcement as well as the legitimacy of urban planning as a whole.

Specific policy directions

■ Institutional and regulatory frameworks for planning

In the design and reconfiguration of planning systems, careful attention should be given to identifying investment and livelihood opportunities that can be built on, as well as pressures that could lead to the subversion and corruption of planning institutions. In particular, urban planning needs to be institutionally located in a way that allows it to play a role in creating urban investment and livelihood opportunities, through responsive and collaborative processes. In addition, corruption at the local-government level must be resolutely addressed through appropriate legislation and robust mechanisms.

Urban planning can and should play a significant role in overcoming governance fragmentation in public policy formulation and decision-making, since most national and local development policies and related investments have a spatial dimension. It can do this most effectively through building horizontal and vertical relationships using place and territory as loci for linking planning with the activities of other policy sectors, such as infrastructure provision. Therefore, regulatory power needs to be combined with investment and broader public-sector decision-making.

To command legitimacy, regulatory systems must adhere to the principle of equality under the law, and must be broadly perceived as doing so. It is important to recognize that regulation of land and property development is sustained not just by formal law, but also by social and cultural norms. In designing planning systems, all forms of land and property development activity, formal and informal, must be taken into account and mechanisms for protecting the urban poor and improving their rights and access to land, housing and property must also be put in place.

The protective as well as developmental roles of planning regulation must be recognized in redesigning urban planning systems. Statutory plans and permit-giving regulate the balance between public and private rights in any development project, as well as providing the authority for conserving important community assets. Protective regulation is necessary for safeguarding assets, social opportunities and environmental resources that would otherwise be squeezed out in the rush to develop. Regulation with a developmental intent is necessary for promoting better standards of building and area design, enhancing quality of life and public realm, and introducing some stabilization in land and property development activity, particularly where market systems dominate.

■ Participation, planning and politics

Governments need to implement a number of minimum but critical measures with respect to the political and legal environment as well as financial and human resources, in order to ensure that participation is meaningful, socially inclusive and contributes to improving urban planning. These measures include: establishing a political system that allows and encourages active participation and genuine negotiation, and is committed to addressing the needs and views of all citizens and investment actors; putting in place a legal basis for local politics and planning that specifies how the outcomes of participatory processes will influence plan preparation and decision-making; ensuring that local governments have sufficient responsibilities, resources and autonomy to support participatory processes; ensuring commitment of government and funding agents to resource distribution in order to support implementation of decisions arising from participatory planning processes, thus also making sure that participation has concrete outcomes; and enhancing the capacity of professionals, in terms of their commitment and skills to facilitate participation, provide necessary technical advice and incorporate the outcomes of participation into planning and decision-making.

Governments, both national and local, together with non-governmental organizations, must facilitate the development of a vibrant civil society and ensure that effective participatory mechanisms are put in place. The presence of well-organized civil society organizations and sufficiently informed communities that can take advantage of opportunities for participation and sustain their roles over the longer term is vitally important if community participation in urban planning is to be effective. Mechanisms for socially marginalized groups to have a voice in both representative politics and participatory planning processes must also be established.

■ Bridging the green and brown agendas

In order to integrate the green and brown agendas in cities, urban local authorities should implement a comprehensive set of green policies and strategies covering urban design, energy, infrastructure, transport, waste and slums. These policies and strategies include: increasing urban development density, on the broad basis of mixed land-use strategies; renewable energy and carbon-neutral strategies, principally to reduce greenhouse gas emissions, as part of climate change mitigation measures; distributed green infrastructure strategies to expand small-scale energy and water systems, as part of local economic development that is capable of enhancing sense of place; sustainable transport strategies to reduce fossil fuel use, urban sprawl and dependence on car-based transit; eco-efficiency strategies, including waste recycling to achieve fundamental changes in the metabolism of cities; and much more effective approaches to developing 'cities without slums', at a much larger scale, focusing on addressing the challenges of poor access to safe drinking water and sanitation and environmental degradation in cities of the developing world.

Many green innovations can, and should, be comprehensively integrated into statutory urban planning and development control systems, including planning standards and building regulations. Introducing strategies for synergizing the green and brown agenda in cities will not be possible without viable and appropriate urban planning systems. Recent experience has also demonstrated the effectiveness of combining such a regulatory approach with partnerships between government, industry and communities in the development and implementation of local sustainability innovations and enterprises.

■ Urban planning and informality

Governments and local authorities must, unequivocally, recognize the important role of the informal sector and ensure that urban planning systems respond positively to this phenomenon, including through legislation. A three-step reform process is required for urban planning and governance to effectively respond to informality: first, recognizing the positive role played by urban informal development; second, considering revisions to policies, laws and regulations to facilitate informal sector operations; and third, strengthening the legitimacy and effectiveness of planning and regulatory systems on the basis of more realistic standards.

More specific innovative and tried approaches to land development and use of space should be adopted and implemented if urban policy and planning are to effectively respond to informality. The first approach is pursuing alternatives to the forced eviction of slum dwellers and forced removal or closure of informal economic enterprises. For example, regularization and upgrading of informally developed areas is preferable to neglect or demolition. The second approach is the strategic use of planning tools such as construction of trunk infrastructure, guided land development and land readjustment. The third approach is collaborating with informal economic actors to manage public space and provide services, including through recognizing informal entrepreneurs' property rights, allocating special-purpose areas for informal activities and providing basic services.

■ Planning, spatial structure of cities and provision of infrastructure

Strategic spatial plans linked to infrastructure development can promote more compact forms of urban expansion focused around accessibility and public transport. This will lead to improved urban services that are responsive to the needs of different social groups, better environmental conditions, as well as improved economic opportunities and livelihoods. The importance of pedestrian and other forms of non-motorized movement also requires recognition. Linking major infrastructure investment projects and mega-projects to strategic planning is also crucial.

To enhance the sustainable expansion of cities and facilitate the delivery of urban services, urban local authorities should formulate infrastructure plans as key elements of strategic spatial plans. Transport–land-use links are the most important ones in infrastructure plans and should take precedence, while other forms of infrastructure, including water and sanitation trunk infrastructure, can follow. The involvement of a wide range of stakeholders is essential to the development of a shared and consistent approach, but the infrastructure plan itself also needs to be based on credible analysis and understanding of trends and forces. The plan should also provide the means for protecting the urban poor from rising land costs and speculation, which are likely to result from new infrastructure provision.

Regional governance structures are required to manage urban growth that spreads across administrative boundaries, which is increasingly the case in all regions of the world. Spatial planning in these contexts should provide a framework for the coordination of urban policies and major infrastructure projects, harmonization of development standards, comprehensively addressing the ecological footprints of urbanization, and a space for public discussion of these issues.

■ The monitoring and evaluation of urban plans

Urban planning systems should integrate monitoring and evaluation as permanent features. This should include clear indicators that are aligned with plan goals, objectives and policies. Urban plans should also explicitly explain their monitoring and evaluation philosophies, strategies and procedures. Use of too many indicators should be avoided and focus should be on those indicators for which information is easy to collect.

Traditional evaluation tools – such as cost–benefit analysis, cost-effectiveness analysis and fiscal impact assessment – are still relevant, given the realities of local government resource constraints. Recent interest in performance measurement, return on investment and results-based management principles means that the use of these quantitative tools in urban planning practice should be encouraged.

All evaluations should involve extensive consultation with, and contributions by, all plan stakeholders. This can be achieved through, for example, participatory urban appraisal methods. Experience has shown that this can enhance plan quality and effectiveness through insights and perspectives that might otherwise not have been captured by the formal plan-making process.

Most routine monitoring and evaluation should focus on the implementation of site, subdivision and neighbourhood plans. The outcomes and impacts of many large-scale plans are difficult to evaluate because of the myriad of influences and factors that are at play in communities over time. It therefore makes more sense for monitoring and evaluation to focus on plans at lower spatial levels, i.e. site, subdivision and neighbourhood plans.

■ Planning education

There is a significant need for updating and reform of curricula in many urban planning schools, particularly in many developing and transition countries where urban planning education has not kept up with current challenges and emerging issues. Planning schools should embrace innovative planning ideas. In particular, there should be increased focus on skills in participatory planning, communication and negotiation. Updated curricula should also enhance understanding in a number of areas, some emerging and others simply neglected in the past, including rapid urbanization and urban informality, cities and climate change, local economic development, natural and human-made disasters, urban crime and violence and cultural diversity within cities. Capacity-building short courses for practising planners and related professionals have an important role to play in this.

Urban planning schools should educate students to work in different world contexts by adopting the 'one-world' approach. Some planning schools in developed countries do not educate students to work in different contexts, thus limiting their mobility and posing a problem for developing country students who want to return home to practice their skills. The 'one-world' approach to planning education is an attempt to remedy this and should be encouraged. A complementary measure is the strengthening of professional organizations and international professional networks. Such organizations and associations should be inclusive, as other experts with non-planning professional backgrounds are significantly involved in urban planning. **Finally, urban planning education should include tuition in ethics and key social values, as planning is not 'value-neutral'.** In this context, tuition should cover areas such as the promotion of social equity and the social and economic rights of citizens, as well as sustainable urban development and planning for multicultural cities.

Recognition and respect for societal differences should be central to tuition in ethics and social values, since effective urban planning cannot take place and equitable solutions cannot be found without a good understanding of the perspectives of disenfranchised and underserved populations.

PART I

CHALLENGES AND CONTEXT

1

URBAN CHALLENGES AND THE
NEED TO REVISIT URBAN PLANNING

Urban settlements in all parts of the world are being influenced by new and powerful forces that require governments to reconsider how they manage urban futures. Urban areas in both developed and developing countries will increasingly feel the effects of phenomena such as climate change, resource depletion, food insecurity and economic instability. These are all factors that will significantly reshape towns and cities in the century ahead and all of them need to be effectively addressed if cities are to be sustainable, that is, environmentally safe, economically productive and socially inclusive. Many developing countries, in addition, will continue to experience rapid rates of urbanization. With over half of the world's population currently living in urban areas,[1] there is no doubt that the 'urban agenda' will increasingly become a priority for governments everywhere.

Since the earliest days of human settlement, people have consciously and collectively intervened in the nature and form of urban areas to achieve particular social, political or environmental objectives. This activity has been known as planning. Over the last century, urban planning[2] has become a discipline and profession in its own right, has become institutionalized as a practice of government as well as an activity of ordinary citizens and businesses, and has evolved as a complex set of ideas which guides both planning decision-making processes and urban outcomes. There are now important and highly contested debates on what forms of urban planning are best suited to dealing with the problems of sustainable development that urban settlements currently face, and will face in the future.

At certain times in the last century, planning has been seen as the activity that can solve many of the major problems of urban areas, while at other times it has been viewed as unnecessary and unwanted government interference in market forces, with the latter able to address urban problems far more effectively than governments. More recently, it has been argued that systems of urban planning in developing countries are also the cause of many urban problems, and that by setting unrealistic standards of land and urban development, and by encouraging inappropriate modernist urban forms, planning is promoting urban poverty and exclusion. This argument was strongly made at the joint meeting of the UN-Habitat World Urban Forum and the World Planners Congress in Vancouver in June 2006, where

it was suggested that the profession of urban planning needs to be reviewed to see if it is able to play a role in addressing issues in rapidly growing and poor cities. To do this, however, governments, urban local authorities and planning practitioners have to develop a different approach that is pro-poor and inclusive, and that places the creation of livelihoods at the centre of planning efforts.

This issue of the *Global Report on Human Settlements* considers the importance of urban planning as a significant management tool for dealing with the unprecedented challenges facing 21st-century cities and attaining the goals of sustainable urbanization (see Box 1.1). There is now a realization that the positive management of urban change cannot be left only to the market or governments. Governments, together with other important urban stakeholders, will have to jointly agree on the long-term objectives of urban change. These objectives will need to include ways of achieving socio-spatial equity, environmental sustainability and economic productivity in urban areas. But if planning is to play a role in addressing the major issues facing urban areas, then current approaches to planning in many parts of the world will have to change. A key conclusion to emerge from this Global Report is that while the forces impacting upon the growth and change of cities have changed dramatically, in many parts of the world planning systems have changed very little and are now frequent contributors to urban problems rather than functioning as tools for human and environmental improvement. However, this does not necessarily need to be the case: planning systems can be changed so that they are able to function as effective and efficient instruments of sustainable urban change. Given the enormity of the issues facing urban areas in the coming decades, there is no longer time for complacency: planning systems need to be evaluated and, if necessary, revised; the training and education of planners need to be re-examined; and examples of successful urban planning need to be found and shared worldwide.

This introductory chapter outlines the main issues of concern and summarizes the contents of the rest of the Global Report. The chapter first sets out the key urban challenges of the 21st century that will shape a new role for urban planning. This in turn lays the basis for the question, in the third section, which asks if and how urban planning

At certain times in the last century, planning has been seen as the activity that can solve many of the major problems of urban areas

This issue of the Global Report on Human Settlements considers urban planning as a significant management tool for dealing with the unprecedented challenges facing 21st-century cities

Box 1.1 The goals of sustainable urbanization

Environmentally sustainable urbanization requires that:

- greenhouse gas emissions are reduced and serious climate change mitigation and adaptation actions are implemented;
- urban sprawl is minimized and more compact towns and cities served by public transport are developed;
- non-renewable resources are sensibly used and conserved;
- renewable resources are not depleted;
- the energy used and the waste produced per unit of output or consumption is reduced;
- the waste produced is recycled or disposed of in ways that do not damage the wider environment; and
- the ecological footprint of towns and cities is reduced.

Only by dealing with urbanization within regional, national and even international planning and policy frameworks can these requirements be met.

Priorities and actions for economic sustainability of towns and cities should focus on local economic development, which entails developing the basic conditions needed for the efficient operation of economic enterprises, both large and small, formal and informal. These include:

- reliable in infrastructure and services, including water supply, waste management, transport, communications and energy supply;
- access to land or premises in appropriate locations with secure tenure;
- financial institutions and markets capable of mobilizing investment and credit;
- a healthy educated workforce with appropriate skills;
- a legal system which ensures competition, accountability and property rights;
- appropriate regulatory frameworks, which define and enforce non-discriminatory locally appropriate minimum standards for the provision of safe and healthy workplaces and the treatment and handling of wastes and emissions.

For several reasons, special attention needs to be given to supporting the urban informal sector, which is vital for a sustainable urban economy.

The social aspects of urbanization and economic development must be addressed as part of the sustainable urbanization agenda. The Habitat Agenda incorporates relevant principles, including the promotion of:

- equal access to and fair and equitable provision of services;
- social integration by prohibiting discrimination and offering opportunities and physical space to encourage positive interaction;
- gender and disability sensitive planning and management; and
- the prevention, reduction and elimination of violence and crime.

Social justice recognizes the need for a rights-based approach, which demands equal access to 'equal quality' urban services, with the needs and rights of vulnerable groups appropriately addressed.

Source: Partly adapted from UN-Habitat and Department for International Development (DFID), 2002, Chapter 4, pp18–27.

needs to change to address these new issues effectively. Section four considers the factors that have led to a revived interest in urban planning, and indicates the numerous positive roles which planning can play. This section provides examples of how planning has been used successfully to meet new challenges. The fifth section summarizes some of the most important new approaches to urban planning that have emerged in various parts of the world, while the sixth section offers a definition of urban planning and a set of normative principles against which current or new approaches might be tested. The seventh section summarizes the contents of the main chapters of the Global Report, and the final section concludes the chapter.

URBAN CHALLENGES OF THE 21ST CENTURY

Future urban planning needs to take place within an understanding of the factors that are shaping the socio-spatial aspects of cities and the institutional structures which attempt to manage them. It also needs to recognize the significant demographic and environmental challenges that lie ahead and for which systems of urban management will have to plan. The overarching global changes that have occurred since the 1970s are first considered, and then the ways in which these impact upon demographic, socio-spatial and institutional change in urban areas and their implications for planning. There are also new forces and views that will impact upon a revised role for urban planning, such as environmental threats and climate change, oil depletion and costs, food security, and post-disaster and post-conflict demands. In all cases, local context shapes the impact of these forces.

Main forces affecting urban change

Over the last several decades, global changes in the environment, in the economy, in institutional structures and processes and in civil society have had significant impacts upon urban areas. These trends in the developed, developing and transitional regions of the world are reviewed below.

Future urban planning needs to take place within an understanding of the factors that are shaping the socio-spatial aspects of cities

■ Environmental challenges

The Brundtland Commission's report – *Our Common Future* – which called for 'development that meets the needs of the present without compromising the ability of future generations to meet their own needs', placed the issue of sustainable development at the core of urban policy and planning concerns (see Chapter 6). The most important environmental concern now is climate change. The authoritative Stern Report[27] on the economics of climate change concludes that it will 'affect the basic elements of life for people around the world – access to water, food production, health and the environment. Hundreds of millions of people could suffer hunger, water shortages and coastal flooding as the world warms.' Moreover, it will be the poorest countries and people who are most vulnerable to this threat who will suffer the most. Current forms of urbanization are pushing the lowest-income people into locations that are prone to natural hazards, such that four out of every ten non-permanent houses in the developing world are now located in areas threatened by floods, landslides and other natural disasters.[28]

A second major environmental concern is oil supply and the likely long-term increase in the cost of fossil fuels. The global use of oil as an energy source has both promoted and permitted urbanization, and its easy availability has allowed the emergence of low-density and sprawling urban forms – suburbia – dependent upon private cars. Beyond this, however, the entire global economy rests on the possibility of moving both people and goods quickly, cheaply and over long distances. An oil-based economy and climate change are linked: vehicle and aircraft emissions contribute significantly to greenhouse gas emissions and, hence, global warming. One reason for the current global food crisis is unpredictable spikes in the cost of oil. Responding to a post-oil era, in the form of public transport- and pedestrian-based movement systems, more compact and integrated cities, and more localized food and production systems (reducing the ecological footprint of cities) all present new imperatives for planning.

While climate change and oil depletion will fundamentally change the nature of life on this planet, urbanization and city growth are also causing, and are subject to, a multitude of environmental impacts. The 2007 UN-Habitat Global Report – *Enhancing Urban Safety and Security*[29] – makes the point that cities are inherently risk prone due to the concentrated nature of settlements and the interdependent nature of the human and infrastructural systems. Urban settlements are increasingly becoming 'hot spots' for disaster risk. Urban development also results in negative environmental impacts through the consumption of natural assets and the overexploitation of natural resources. Urbanization modifies the environment and generates new hazards, including deforestation and slope instability, thus resulting in landslides and flash flooding. Vulnerability to natural disasters is differentiated: cities with lower levels of economic development and disaster preparedness are more at risk, as are women, children, the aged and the disabled. The world's 1 billion urban slum dwellers are also far more vulnerable, as they are usually unprotected by construction and land-use planning regulations.

> ### Box 1.2 Effects of economic restructuring on older cities in developed countries: Chicago, US
>
> Walk down 63rd Street in Woodlawn, on the south side of Chicago, within a stone's throw of the University of Chicago campus, along what used to be one of the city's most vibrant commercial strips, and you will discover a lunar landscape replicated across the black ghettos of the US – in Harlem and the Brownsville district of Brooklyn in New York, in north Philadelphia, on the east side of Cleveland and Detroit, or in Boston's Roxbury and Paradise Valley in Pittsburgh. Abandoned buildings, vacant lots strewn with debris and garbage, broken sidewalks, boarded-up store-front churches and the charred remains of shops line up miles and miles of decaying neighbourhoods left to rot by the authorities since the big riots of the 1960s.
>
> On the morrow of World War II, 63rd Street was called the 'Miracle Mile' by local merchants vying for space and a piece of the pie. The neighbourhood counted nearly 800 businesses and not a single vacant lot in an 18-by-4 block area. Woodlawn was overflowing with life as people streamed in from the four corners of the city, comprising throngs so dense at rush hour that one was literally swept off one's feet upon getting out of the elevated train station. Here is the description of the street given to me by the only white shopkeeper left from that era in August 1991:
>
> *It looks like Berlin after the war and that's sad. The street is bombed out, decaying. Seventy-five per cent of it is vacant. It's very unfortunate, but it seems that all that really grows here is liquor stores. And they're not contributing anything to the community: it's all 'take, take, take!' Very depressing [sighs heavily]. It's an area devoid of hope; it's an area devoid of investments. People don't come into Woodlawn.*
>
> Now the street's nickname has taken an ironic and bitter twist for it takes a miracle for a business to survive on it. Not a single theatre, bank, jazz club or repair shop outlived the 1970s. The lumber yards, print shops, garages and light manufacturing enterprises that used to dot the neighbourhood have disappeared as well.
>
> *Source:* Wacquant, 2008, pp53–54

Significantly, such disasters are only partly a result of natural forces. They are also the products of failed urban development and planning. It is therefore important to take a risk-reduction approach which views such disasters as problems of development, requiring new approaches to the planning of urban growth and change. This is the case not only for large-scale environmental hazards, but also for what are known as 'small hazards', such as traffic accidents, which kill 1.2 million people per annum.[30] Pedestrian and vehicle movement networks in cities are a central concern of urban planning.

Women are disproportionately concentrated in the informal economy and particularly in low-profit activities

■ Economic change

Processes of globalization and economic restructuring in recent decades have affected urban settlements in both developed and developing countries in various ways, although the form of impact has been strongly determined by local factors and policies. Particularly significant has been the impact upon urban labour markets, which show a growing polarization of occupational and income structures caused by growth in the service sector and decline in manufacturing. There have been important gender dimensions to this restructuring: over the last several decades women have increasingly moved into paid employment, but trends towards 'casualization' of the labour force have made them highly vulnerable to economic crises.[3] In developed countries, the last several decades have also seen a process

Urban planning in both developed and developing countries will be taking place in a context of inequality and poverty and with high levels of informal activity

of industrial relocation as firms attempted to reduce labour and operating costs. Firms have sought lower land costs, cheaper labour pools and lower unionization levels by relocating to developing countries, to less developed regions within the developed world, or even from inner-city areas to suburbs.

Urban residents are disproportionately affected by international economic crises. The current global economic crisis that began in 2008 has accelerated economic restructuring and rapid growth of unemployment in all parts of the world. Box 1.1 provides an example of how economic restructuring has affected older working-class areas in Chicago. Here the number of working residents dropped by 77 per cent over past decades as manufacturing industries relocated or closed, and upwardly mobile residents left the area,[4] and this was prior to the major job losses that have affected the US since late 2008. This kind of restructuring has been occurring in the larger 'global' cities of the world and in older industrial regions, but is equally true in smaller urban centres and in those parts of the world, largely in developing countries, which have not been subject to significant foreign direct investment. Phnom Penh, in Cambodia, for example, has undergone dramatic social and spatial restructuring in recent years despite low levels of foreign direct investment and little industrial growth.[5]

One important effect of these economic and policy processes on urban labour markets has been the rapid growth in the informal economy in all urban centres, but particularly in developing countries. In Latin America and the Caribbean, four out of every five new jobs are in the informal sector, which currently employs 57 per cent of the region's workers.[6] In Mexico City, 60 per cent of residents work in the informal sector, and the number of street vendors increased by 40 per cent from 2000 to 2005. In Central Asia,[7] the informal sector is responsible for between one third and one half of the total economic output. In Africa, where the formal economy has always been relatively weak, 78 per cent of urban employment in the Francophone region is informal, and this sector generates 93 per cent of all new jobs.[8] The concept of economic informality is by no means new; yet there are strong indications that its nature has changed and its scale has increased over the last few decades, particularly during 2008. There are also important gender dimensions to informality: women are disproportionately concentrated in the informal economy and particularly in low-profit activities.[9]

Recent writings on the topic of globalization and cities stress the point that while there are few parts of the world that have not felt the effects of these processes, there is much diversity in the nature of these impacts, with actual outcomes strongly influenced by pre-existing local conditions and local policies. The dramatic increases in income inequality that result from changing urban labour market structures are also not inevitable: a number of East Asian cities have been strongly influenced by the actions of 'developmental states' which have channelled resources into urban industrial growth, and into public-sector spending on urban infrastructural projects and programmes. In these

cases, job and income polarization have been less dramatic. By contrast, in some parts of the world, international and national policy interventions have exacerbated the effects of globalization. For example, those countries that were subjected to International Monetary Fund (IMF) and World Bank structural adjustment programmes have been more severely affected.

Future urban planning in both developed and developing countries will therefore be taking place in a context of inequality and poverty and with high levels of informal activity, a significant proportion of which is survivalist in form.

■ Institutional change

Formal urban planning systems are typically located within the public sector, with local government usually being the most responsible tier. Within the last three decades, and closely linked to processes of globalization, there have been significant transformations in local government in many parts of the world, making them very different settings from those within which planning was originally conceived (see Chapter 4).

The most commonly recognized change has been the expansion of the urban political system from 'government' to 'governance', which in developed countries represents a response to the growing complexity of governing in a globalizing and multilevel context, as well as the involvement of a range of non-state actors in the process of governing. In developing countries, the concept of governance has been promoted along with decentralization and democratization, driven largely by multilateral institutions. During the 1980s, a mainly economic perspective dominated, with World Bank–International Monetary Fund sponsored structural adjustment programmes providing the framework for public-sector change across developing countries. The principal ideas were privatization, deregulation and decentralization. By the end of the 1980s, however, key World Bank officials had accepted that *good governance* was the key issue and, by 1997, the shift was firmly entrenched when the World Development Report emphasized the importance of strong and effective institutions, rather than rolling back the state, as in the past.

From the late 1990s, 'good governance' became the mantra for development in developing countries, and planning was supported to the extent that it promoted this ideal. The term has come to mean different things, however. The World Bank, for example, has been associated with a mainly administrative and managerialist interpretation of good governance, while United Nations agencies such as the United Nations Development Programme (UNDP) have emphasized democratic practice and human and civil rights. UN-Habitat's *Global Campaign on Urban Governance*,[10] launched in 2000, sought to advocate good urban governance worldwide and to increase the capacity of local/municipal governments and other stakeholders to put this into practice. UN-Habitat's concept of good governance is characterized by three strategies: decentralizing responsibilities and resources to local authorities; encouraging the participation of civil society; and using partnerships to achieve common objectives.

Urban planning is highly reliant on the existence of stable, effective and accountable local government, as well as a strong civil society, in order to play a positive role

The most important environmental concern now is climate change

These shifts have had profound implications for urban planning, which has often been cast as a relic of the old welfare state model and as an obstacle to economic development and market freedom. In fact, the emergence of planning can be closely linked to a Keynesian approach to development, which was state led and strongly reinforced in Europe by the requirements of post-war reconstruction. In a context in which the power of governments to direct urban development has diminished with the retreat of Keynesian economics, and in which the new central actors in urban development are real estate investors and developers, whose activities are often linked to economic boosterism, planning has found itself to be unpopular and marginalized. It has also found itself at the heart of contradictory pressures on local government to promote urban economic competitiveness, on the one hand, while on the other dealing with the fall-out from globalization in the form of growing social exclusion, poverty, unemployment and rapid population growth, often in a context of unfunded mandates and severe local government capacity constraints.[11]

In addition, urban planning at the local government level has also had to face challenges from shifts in the scale of urban decision-making. As the wider economic role of urban centres and their governments has come adrift from their geographically bounded administrative role, so decision-making about urban futures has rescaled and introduced ideas of multilevel and collaborative governance.[12] The idea of urban decision-making framed by the concept of 'city-regions'[13] is becoming more common.

The issue of planning's relationship to the market has been particularly difficult in those regions of the world undergoing a shift from socialist to democratic political systems. In East Europe,[14] urban land was privatized, thus reducing the power of local governments to control urban development, but at the same time all planning powers were transferred to local institutions that had no capacity, expertise or funds to implement new, and often poorly developed, local planning laws. One expert from Sofia, Bulgaria, commented: 'our city grows on auto-pilot'. While functioning on 'auto-pilot', the capital city lost about 15 per cent of its public green spaces in just 15 years, as they were taken by private developments legalized later.[15] In other parts of the world, government is decentralizing far more slowly. In East Asia, there are few urban local governments with power and finances.[16] In China, there is a gradual increase in decision-making power at lower levels of the administrative system, but it is still highly constrained. Planning laws favour a technical approach to urban planning, with regulatory structures intended to promote a largely depoliticized decision-making environment.[17]

Generally, urban planning is highly reliant on the existence of stable, effective and accountable local government, as well as a strong civil society, in order to play a positive role. Many developing countries simply do not have these.[18] Under such conditions, urban planning will continue to be ineffective or, alternatively, will be used in opportunistic ways by those with political and economic power.

■ Changes in civil society

Since the 1960s, there has been a growing unwillingness on the part of communities to passively accept the planning decisions of politicians and technocrats that impact upon their living environments. In turn, planners have come to recognize that planning implementation is more likely to be effective if it can secure 'community support'. The notion of public participation in planning (see Chapter 5) has developed considerably since this time, with a plethora of methods and techniques put forward to 'deliver consensus'. However, successful participatory planning is largely conditioned by broader state–civil society relations, and the extent to which democracy is accepted and upheld. This is highly uneven across the globe. Even where participatory planning is accepted, and where civil society can be drawn into planning processes, it is recognized that global economic and social change has, in turn, impacted upon civil society and has often made the ideal of participatory planning far harder to achieve.

In cities in both developed and developing countries, societal divisions have been increasing, partly as a result of international migration streams and the growth of ethnic minority groups in cities, and partly because of growing income and employment inequalities which have intersected with ethnicity and identity in various ways. A wide-ranging review of the literature on social movements in developing countries[19] found that despite the growth of social movements and moves to democratization, participation is still mediated more typically by patron–client relations rather than by popular activism. Other researchers point to the extent to which urban crime and violence have brought about a decline in social cohesion and an increase in conflict and insecurity.[20] Growth in violent crime, often supported by increasingly organized and well-networked drug and arms syndicates and fuelled by growing poverty and inequality, have eroded the possibilities of building social capital in poorer communities. Conducting participatory planning in situations such as these can be extremely difficult.

There has been a tendency in planning to assume a one-dimensional view of civil society and the role it might play in planning initiatives. The ideal of strong community-based organizations, willing to debate planning ideas, may be achievable in certain parts of the world, but civil society does not always lend itself to this kind of activity. While organized civil society has been a characteristic of Latin America,[21] it takes very different forms in Africa, the Middle East and much of Asia, where 'social networks which extend beyond kinship and ethnicity remain largely casual, unstructured and paternalistic'.[22] Resistance tends to take the form here of 'quiet encroachment' rather than proactive community organization. In many parts of the world as well, civil society is being inspired more by popular religious movements than by organized demands for better infrastructure or shelter, given that efforts to secure the latter have so often failed.[23] In China, contrary to the West, governance does not derive from an acknowledged separation of state and society, but rather from an attempt to maintain their integration.[24]

However, recent literature[25] makes the point that urban residents will have to find a way in which to engage

Cities and towns in all parts of the world are very different places from what they were when planning first emerged as a profession – over 100 years ago

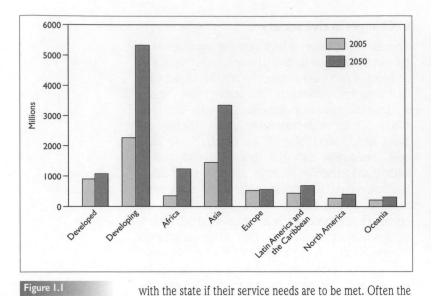

Figure 1.1

Urban population by region, 2005–2050

Note: Asia does not include Japan.

Source: UN, 2008

with the state if their service needs are to be met. Often the strategies that seem to work are not explicitly political, but come about as a result of the imperative for some kind of collective action on the part of the poor as a way of meeting basic service needs. As residents 'fill the space' which the state is unable to occupy, negotiated arrangements with the state emerge that involve neither formal participation processes nor partnerships, nor organized confrontations. These 'in-between' processes are termed 'co-production' and are seen as a more realistic way in which state–society engagement can take place.[26]

Urban change

Changes in economic and governmental systems, in the nature of civil society, and in the nature and scale of environmental and conflict-related challenges have all had major impacts upon processes of urbanization and urban growth, and socio-spatial dynamics in urban settlements.

■ Urbanization and urban growth

Cities and towns in all parts of the world are very different places from what they were when planning first emerged as a profession – over 100 years ago. And while the 20th century as a whole was a time of major urban transformation, the last few decades, coinciding with the global restructuring of economy and society, have seen new and particular impacts upon urban growth and change (see Chapter 2). The global urban transition witnessed over the last three or so decades has been phenomenal. While the period of 1950 to 1975 saw population growth more or less evenly divided between the urban and rural areas of the world, the period since has seen the balance tipped dramatically in favour of urban growth. In 2008, for the first time in history, over half of the world's population lived in urban areas and by 2050 this will have risen to 70 per cent.[31] It is significant to note that the bulk of this growth will be taking place in developing regions.

Between 2007 and 2025, the annual rate of change of the urban population in developing regions is expected to be 2.27 per cent, and 0.49 per cent in developed regions.[32] Figure 1.1 indicates urban population growth projections by region.

This transition is presenting urban management and planning with issues that have never been faced before. Urban growth will be less rapid in developed regions, in Latin America and the Caribbean and in transitional countries of East Europe, all of which are already highly urbanized, but rapid in Africa and Central, South and East Asia, which are currently less urbanized. China is expected to double its urban population from about 40 per cent of its national population during 2006 to 2030 to more than 70 per cent by 2050.[33] Furthermore, certain cities will attain sizes that have not been experienced before: new megacities of over 10 million and hypercities of over 20 million are predicted. The bulk of new urban growth, however, is predicted to occur in smaller settlements[34] of 100,000 to 250,000 which have absorbed much of the rural labour power made redundant by post-1979 market reforms[35] and continuing adverse terms of world trade in the agricultural sector. While megacities present management problems of their own, it is the smaller cities that suffer particularly from a lack of planning and services to cope with growth.

By contrast, some parts of the world are facing the challenge of shrinking cities. Most of these are to be found in the developed and transitional regions of the world. For example, cities in Latvia, Estonia, Armenia and Georgia have lost 17 to 22.5 per cent of their urban population.[36] In the US, 39 cities have faced population loss between 1990 and 2000.[37] Such shrinkage occurs when regional economies are in decline and populations migrate elsewhere, or when satellite cities draw a population away from a historically dominant urban core.[38]

In those parts of the world experiencing rapid urban growth, a key problem is that it is taking place in countries least able to cope: in terms of the ability of governments to provide urban infrastructure; in terms of the ability of urban residents to pay for such services; and in terms of coping with natural disasters. These countries also experience high levels of poverty and unemployment. The inevitable result has been the rapid growth of slums and squatter settlements – often characterized by deplorable living and environmental conditions. In the developing world, close to 37 per cent of the urban population currently live in slums in inequitable and life-threatening conditions, and are directly affected by both environmental disasters and social crises. In sub-Saharan Africa, 62 per cent of the urban population live under such conditions.[39] Such informal settlements are often built in high-risk areas such as steep hill slopes, deep gullies and flood-prone areas that are particularly susceptible to extreme weather conditions.

The issue of urbanization of poverty is particularly severe in sub-Saharan Africa, given that the bulk of urbanization is taking place under different economic conditions than those that prevailed in Latin America and parts of Asia. Here urbanization is occurring for the most part in the absence of industrialization and under much lower rates of economic growth. Urban growth rates are also more rapid here than elsewhere – between 2000 and 2005, Africa's average urban growth rate was 3.4 per cent per annum, compared to Asia at 2.6 per cent per and Latin America at 1.8 per cent.[40] The inevitable consequences are that urban poverty and unemployment are extreme, living conditions and urban services are particularly bad (see Box 1.2), and survival is supported predominantly by the informal sector, which tends to be survivalist rather than entrepreneurial.

A significant feature of urbanization in both Africa and parts of Asia is the high level of mobility of the population. In Africa strong urban–rural ties still exist and keep many people in perpetual motion between urban and rural bases. This strategy of spatially 'stretching the household'[41] functions as an economic and social safety net, allowing access to constantly shifting economic opportunities as well as maintaining kinship and other networks. In China, a massive 'floating population' has emerged in which some 90 million to 125 million people are migrant workers, moving between urban and rural areas or between urban areas.[42] One implication of this phenomenon is that conceptualizing cities and towns as self-contained entities, which can be planned and managed accordingly, becomes questionable; another is that the commitment of people to particular urban locales and what happens in them becomes more tenuous. These factors have important implications for planning.

■ Urban socio-spatial change

The issue of how global economic change in the last few decades has impacted upon socio-spatial change in towns and cities has received much attention, along with the qualification that both local and global processes have shaped these changes. In essence, however, planners and urban managers have found themselves confronted with new spatial forms and processes, the drivers of which often lie outside the control of local government.

Socio-spatial change seems to have taken place primarily in the direction of the fragmentation, separation and specialization of functions and uses in cities, with labour market polarization (and, hence, income inequality) reflected in growing differences between wealthier and poorer areas. This is the case in both developed and developing countries. It is possible to contrast upmarket gentrified and suburban areas with tenement zones, ethnic enclaves and ghettos; and areas built for the advanced service and production sector, and for luxury retail and entertainment, with older areas of declining industry, sweatshops and informal businesses.[43] While much of this represents the playing out of 'market forces' in cities, and the logic of real estate and land speculation, it is also a response to local policies that have attempted to position cities globally in order to attract new investment. 'Competitive city' approaches to urban policy, most frequently found in developed countries, aim to attract global investment, tourists and a residential elite through upmarket property developments, waterfronts, convention centres and the marketing of culture and heritage.[44]

However, urban policies have also tried to control the negative effects of profit-driven development through the surveillance of public spaces, policing and crime-prevention efforts and immigration control. For example, in Latin American and Caribbean cities, fear of crime has increased urban fragmentation as middle- and upper-income households segregate themselves into 'gated' and high-security residential complexes. 'Gated' communities have multiplied

> **Box 1.3 Failure of public service provision in a rapidly growing metropolis: Lagos, Nigeria**
>
> The intense social polarization and spatial fragmentation since the mid 1980s have led to a scenario in which many households – both rich and poor – attempt to provide their own water supply, power generation and security services. As night falls, the drone of traffic is gradually displaced by the roar of thousands of generators that enable the city to function after dark. Many roads in both rich and poor neighbourhoods become closed or subject to a plethora of *ad hoc* checkpoints and local security arrangements to protect people and property until the morning. In the absence of a subsidized housing sector, most households must struggle to contend with expensive private letting arrangements often involving an upfront payment of two years' rent and various other fees, while the richest social strata seek to buy properties outright with vast quantities of cash. A self-service city has emerged in which little is expected from municipal government and much social and economic life is founded on the spontaneous outcome of local negotiations.
> *Source:* Gandy, 2006, p383

in major metropolitan areas such as Buenos Aires, São Paulo and Santiago. In Buenos Aires alone, the number of gated communities along its northern highway tripled in the 1990s, reaching 500 by 2001. Some of these have now become 'gated cities', providing full urban amenities for their residents with 'private highways' linking them together.[45]

Urban fragmentation has also been linked to economic development. An analysis of spatial change in Accra (Ghana) and in Mumbai (India)[46] shows how in each city three separate central business districts (CBDs) have emerged for local, national and global businesses, each differentially linked to the global economy. In South Asian cities, service-sector investments have been attracted to cities by the construction of exclusive enclaves with specialized infrastructure. In India, software technology parks cater for the business and social needs of internet technology and related enterprises. 'Pharma City' for the biotechnology industry and 'High Tech City' for the technology sector are similar initiatives, usually with special planning and servicing standards.[47] Significantly, the growth of investment in real estate and mega-projects in cities across the globe, often by large multinational companies, has drawn attention to the need for planning as a tool for local authorities to manage these pressures and to balance them with social and environmental concerns.

In many poorer cities, spatial forms are largely driven by the efforts of low-income households to secure land that is affordable and in a reasonable location. This process is leading to entirely new urban forms as the countryside itself begins to urbanize, as in vast stretches of rural India, Bangladesh, Pakistan, China, Indonesia, Egypt, West Africa, Rwanda and many other poorer countries and regions.[48] The coast of Benin (West Africa) is now a densely populated area stretching 125km through the three historical towns of Ouidah, Cotonou and Porto Novo. Around Porto Novo, population densities exceed 400 people per square kilometre.[49] Similarly, large cities have spread out and incorporated nearby towns, leading to continuous belts of settlement, such as the corridor from Abidjan to Ibadan, containing 70 million people and making up the urban agglomeration of

The bulk of rapid urban growth in developing countries is now taking place in the peri-urban areas

'Modern' urban planning emerged in the latter part of the 19th century, in response to rapidly growing, chaotic and polluted cities in Western Europe, brought about by the Industrial Revolution

Lagos. In Latin America, the coastal corridor in Venezuela now includes the cities of Maracaibo, Barquisimeto, Valencia, Caracas, Barcelona-Puerto La Cruz and Cumana, and the corridor in Brazil is anchored by São Paulo and Rio de Janeiro. Some mega-regions are transnational, such as Buenos Aires-Montevideo.[50]

The bulk of rapid urban growth in developing countries is now taking place in the peri-urban areas as poor urban dwellers look for a foothold in the cities and towns where land is more easily available, where they can escape the costs and threats of urban land regulations, and where there is a possibility of combining urban and rural livelihoods. For example, it is predicted that 40 per cent of urban growth in China up to 2025 will be in peri-urban areas, with this zone extending 150km or more from the core city.[51] It is these sprawling urban peripheries, almost entirely unserviced and unregulated, that make up the bulk of what is referred to as informal settlements. These kinds of areas are impossibly costly to plan and service in the conventional way, given the form of settlement, and even if that capacity did exist, few could afford to pay for such services. In fact, the attractiveness of these kinds of locations for poor households is that they can avoid the costs associated with formal and regulated systems of urban land and service delivery. Because of this, however, it is in these areas that environmental issues are particularly critical, both in terms of the natural hazards to which these settlements are exposed and the environmental damage that they cause.

WHY DOES URBAN PLANNING NEED TO CHANGE?

The planning of urban settlements has been taking place since the dawn of civilization. The first known planned settlement of Old Jericho was dated at 7000 BC and Catal Hüyük, in present-day Turkey, was already well developed in terms of its urbanity by 6000 BC (see Chapter 3). The urban settlements of Mohenjo-Daro and Harappa in the Indus Valley (in present-day Pakistan), dating back to 3500 BC, show evidence of planned street networks, drainage and sewage systems, and the separation of land uses.[52] Chinese settlements from 600 BC were planned to align with cosmic forces.[53] In Latin America and the Caribbean, ancient civilizations such as the Aztec civilization in modern Mexico, the Maya civilization in modern Mexico, Guatemala and Belize, and the Inca civilization in modern Peru and the Andean regions of modern Ecuador, Bolivia, Colombia, Chile and Argentina developed sophisticated systems of urban planning.[54] Several pre-colonial towns in Africa exhibited some form of rudimentary planning as well. Within the last century, however, planning has taken on a rather different form.

Modern urban planning

'Modern' urban planning emerged in the latter part of the 19th century, largely in response to rapidly growing, chaotic and polluted cities in Western Europe, brought about by the Industrial Revolution (see Chapter 3). The adoption of urban planning in this part of the world as a state function can be attributed to the rise of the modern interventionist state and Keynesian economics. Urban 'visions' put forward by particular individuals[55] in Western Europe and the US in the late 19th century were to shape the objectives and forms of planning, which in turn showed remarkable resilience through the 20th century.

There are several characteristics of this modern approach to planning.[56] First, planning was seen as an exercise in the physical planning and design of human settlements, with social, economic or political matters lying outside the scope of planning. Planning was a technical activity to be carried out by trained experts with relatively little involvement of politicians or communities. Second, it involved the production of master plans, blueprint plans or layout plans, showing a detailed view of the built form of a city once it attained its ideal end-state. While the master plan portrayed an ideal vision of the future, the primary legal tool for implementing these visions was the land-use zoning scheme. This legal concept – justified on the basis of the rational need for separating conflicting land uses – originated in Germany and was adopted with great enthusiasm across the US and Europe in the early part of the 20th century, particularly by the middle- and high-income groups who were able to use it as a way of maintaining property prices and preventing invasion by 'less desirable' lower-income residents, ethnic minorities and traders. The idea that planning can be used as a means of social and economic exclusion is not new.

Over the years, a range of different terms have been used to describe plans, with some terms specific to certain regions of the world. Table 1.1 lists the main terms in use, with a broad definition of each. In this chapter, the term *directive plan* is used to refer to that aspect of the planning system that sets out future desired spatial and functional patterns and relationships for an urban area.

The ideal urban forms that master planning promoted were specific to the time and place from which they emerged (see Box 1.3). For example, Ebenezer Howard's Garden City attempted to recreate English village life through bringing 'green' back into towns and through controlling their size and growth. The objectives were social: the preservation of a traditional way of life that was essentially anti-urban. The objectives were also aesthetic: bringing the beauty of the countryside into the towns.[57] In France, the ideas of architect Le Corbusier in the 1920s and 1930s established the ideal of the 'modernist' city,[58] which came to be highly influential internationally and still shapes planning in many parts of the world. Le Corbusier held that the ideal city was neat, ordered and highly controlled. Slums, narrow streets and mixed-use areas should be demolished and replaced with efficient transportation corridors, residences in the form of tower blocks with open space 'flowing' between them, and land uses separated into monofunctional zones. In the early 20th-century US, architect Frank Lloyd Wright promoted ideal cities in the form of low-density and dispersed urban forms, with each family on its own small plot. Some have argued that the seeds of later suburbia are to be found in these ideas.

'Modern' urban planning emerged in the latter part of the 19th century, largely in response to rapidly growing, chaotic and polluted cities in Western Europe

Type of plan	Description
Master plan	These are spatial or physical plans that depict on a map the state and form of an urban area at a future point in time when the plan is 'realized'. Master plans have also been called 'end-state' plans and 'blue-print' plans.
Comprehensive plan	Reflects the belief that the planning system should plan towns (or large parts of them) as a whole and in detail. In the past, this term also suggested that wholesale clearance of the existing city should occur in order for the new comprehensive plan to be realized.
Comprehensive City Plan	Term used in China to describe an urban master plan (1989 City Planning Act).
General plan	Another term for a master plan, indicating uses and building norms for specific plots. Usually underpinned by a zoning system.
Layout plan or local plan	These are physical plans, often at a local scale, depicting details such as roads, public spaces and boundaries.
Destination plan or building plan	A plan for a specific area where substantial change is anticipated, usually in the context of a wider strategic or 'structure' plan or 'scheme'.
Strategic spatial plan	The terms 'structure plans' and 'strategic plans' are closely related, and the latter term is now more commonly used. A strategic plan is a broader-level selective (or prioritizing) spatial plan, usually showing, in a more conceptual way, the desired future direction of urban development. Particular decision-making processes accompany the production of a strategic plan.
Directive or development plan	A more generic term referring to structure or strategic plans.
Land-use zoning	Detailed physical plans or maps showing how individual land parcels are to be used, and assigning to the landowner (which may also be the state) certain legal rights and conditions pertaining to the use and development of the land. Ideally the zoning plan aligns with the master plan.
Regulatory planning	Refers to the rights and conditions set out in the zoning plan, along with legal requirements pertaining to the process of allocating or changing land-use rights, buildings and space use.

Table 1.1

Definitions of various types of urban plans

While the origins of master planning were strongly influenced by values in developed countries, this did not prevent these forms of planning from spreading to almost every part of the world in the 20th century through processes of colonialism, market expansion and intellectual exchange (see Chapter 3). Frequently, these imported ideas were used for reasons of political, ethnic or racial domination and exclusion rather than in the interests of good planning. Colonialism was a very direct vehicle for diffusing planning systems. In these contexts, planning of urban settlements was frequently bound up with the 'modernizing and civilizing' mission of colonial authorities, but also with the control of urbanization processes and of the urbanizing population. Most colonial, and later post-colonial, governments also initiated a process of the commodification of land within the Western liberal tradition of private property rights, with the state maintaining control over the full exercise of these rights, including aspects falling under planning and zoning ordinances.

The idea of master planning has been subject to major critique in the planning literature, and in some parts of the world it has been replaced by processes and plans that are more participatory, flexible, strategic and action oriented. But in many regions, and particularly in developing countries, the early 20th-century idea of master planning and land-use zoning, used together to promote modernist urban environments, has persisted to date. In many parts of the world, citizens are still excluded from the planning process or informed only after planning decisions have been made.

The 'gap' between outdated planning approaches and current urban issues

As a result of the persistence of older approaches to urban planning, there is now a large disjuncture between prevailing planning systems and the nature of 21st-century cities. As the previous section has indicated, urban areas are now

---

Box 1.4 Most influential urban forms from the early 20th century

The most influential urban forms have been:

- *The garden city*, circa 1900 (UK): small, self-contained satellite towns, detached dwellings, large plots of land, low densities, separation of incompatible land uses, radial road networks and aesthetic, curving routes.
- *Greenbelts*, circa 1900 (UK): wide buffers of open space surrounding a town or city to prevent it from expanding outwards, and to separate it from new satellite towns (garden cities or new towns) beyond the belt.
- *The neighbourhood unit*, 1920s (US): low-density expanses of open space, focused on community facilities, minimizing conflict between cars and pedestrians by confining arterial routes to the periphery and discouraging through-traffic; assumption that this layout will create social communities.
- *Radburn layout*, 1928 (US): closely related to garden cities, this layout is characterized by cul-de-sacs and superblocks free of traffic; cars and pedestrians are separated from each other, public facilities and shops are located on pedestrian networks and embedded in open space.
- *Urban modernism*: new urban developments following Le Corbusian ideas of tower-blocks 'floating' in open space and connected by parkways.
- *Urban renewal* (1930s onwards): 'slum' clearance and rehousing projects following Radburn or neighbourhood unit layouts, and urban modernism.
- *Road hierarchies*, 1960s (UK): informed by the 1963 report by Colin Buchanan (traffic in towns). Provides a rationale for urban traffic management and the problems of traffic congestion by creating a hierarchy of roads with different functions. At the lowest level of the hierarchy an environmental cell (or residential area) carries only local traffic on 'local distributors'. At higher levels, district and primary distributors (freeways) carry passing and longer-distance traffic. The assumption is that every household will eventually own a car and all urban movement will be car based. These ideas fitted well with urban modernism and the two strands became closely interlinked.
- *New towns*, (war and post-war UK): as a regional response to a perception of problems of growth in major cities (de-concentration), but also seen as a tool of development in lagging regions.
- *Suburbia*, 1920s onwards: undefined and extensive areas of residential development on the urban periphery, single-family units, low densities and large plots of land, structured around car movement systems, serviced with community facilities and shopping malls. Assumes very high levels of car ownership and affluence.

Sources: Hall, 1988; Taylor, 1998

highly complex, rapidly changing entities, shaped by a range of local and global forces often beyond the control of local plans and planners. Many cities in developing countries now display the relics of planned modernist urban cores, surrounded by vast areas of informal and 'slum' settlement together with elite, developer-driven, commercial and residential enclaves. Older forms of modernist planning have little relevance for either of these forms of development. Moreover, with the process of decentralization in many parts of the world, there is a growing expectation from civil society and business groups that they should be involved in planning processes; but processes and practices of modernist planning preclude this.

It is surprising, therefore, that these outdated forms of planning persist in so many parts of the world, and are often strongly defended by governments. One reason might be that planned modernist cities are associated with being modern, with development and with 'catching up with the West', and have thus been attractive to governments and elites who wish to be viewed in this way. Another is that as long as the planning provisions are in place, they can be selectively mobilized to achieve particular sectional or political interests, or to influence the land use and development of some parts of cities in ways that may exclude the poor. Planning laws have sometimes been used to evict political opponents or as justification for land grabs.[59] In some parts of the world, urban informality is condoned by governments as it allows them to avoid the responsibility of providing services or land rights.[60] There are, however, additional problems with the persistence of older approaches to planning, as the following section indicates.

Problems with previous (modernist) approaches to urban planning

The most obvious problem with master planning and urban modernism is that they completely fail to accommodate the way of life of the majority of inhabitants in rapidly growing, largely poor and informal cities, and thus directly contribute to social and spatial marginalization. The possibility that people living in such circumstances could comply with zoning ordinances designed for relatively wealthy European towns is extremely unlikely. Two outcomes are possible here. One is that the system is strongly enforced, and people who cannot afford to comply with the zoning requirements are excluded to areas where they can evade detection – which would usually be an illegal informal settlement in the peri-urban areas. Alternatively, the municipality may not have the capacity to enforce the ordinance, in which case it will be ignored as simply unachievable.

With the first alternative, inappropriate and 'first world' zoning ordinances are instrumental in creating informal settlements and peri-urban sprawl, which have highly negative impacts upon the people who have to live under such conditions, upon city functioning and upon the environment. In effect, people have to step outside the law in order to secure land and shelter due to the elitist or exclusionary nature of urban land laws.[61] It could be argued, therefore, that city governments themselves are producing social and

spatial exclusion, and environmental hazards, as a result of the inappropriate laws and regulations which they adopt. The problem is an obsession with the physical appearance of cities rather than valuing and building on the social capital that is frequently created in poor or low-income communities.

A further aspect of planning that needs to change in many parts of the world is the way in which it has been located institutionally. In many countries, urban planning is not well integrated within governance systems and tends to operate in isolation from other line-function departments, and from the budgeting process. Its potential to coordinate the actions of other line-function departments in space has thus been missed, as well as the potential to influence the direction of those departments concerned with urban infrastructure. There is a further tendency for the directive aspects of planning to be de-linked from the regulatory or land-use management system, with the two often in different departments, making the implementation of directive spatial plans very difficult. Significantly, attempts to reform planning systems – for example, through urban management approaches – have often focused only on the directive aspects of planning, leaving the land-use management system to continue business as usual. Institutionally, modernist planning also finds itself out of synchrony with shifts to 'governance', decentralization and democratization. The top-down, technical and expert-driven approach that often still drives master planning can leave it at odds with community priorities and can impede implementation.

In sum, in many parts of the world, older and conventional forms of urban planning persist. These forms of planning are not only inappropriate for addressing the new, complex and rapidly changing factors that are affecting urban areas, but in some circumstances may be directly contributing to the exacerbation of poverty and spatial marginalization. Unrealistic planning regulations can force the poor to violate laws in order to survive.

WHY IS THERE A REVIVED INTEREST IN URBAN PLANNING?

Over the last century, the 'popularity' of planning has waxed and waned in various parts of the world. In China, it was abolished under Mao Tse-tung, but was formally rehabilitated in 1989 with the City Planning Act, which required the production of master plans to guide the growth of China's burgeoning cities.[62] In Eastern Europe, urban master planning was a central pillar of communist ideology. Planning suffered a severe crisis of legitimacy in the post-communist neo-liberal era, but the resultant chaotic growth of cities and environmental crises compelled the re-establishment of planning across the region in the post-2000 period.[63] In territories affected by Western colonization, urban planning was introduced as a central function of government by colonial powers; and in most places planning legislation was retained in the post-colonial era. Inappropriate and outdated planning legislation, low capacity to implement plans, and a growing gap between plan and reality in rapidly growing and

Colonialism was a very direct vehicle for diffusing planning systems

Master planning has been subject to major critique, and in some parts of the world it has been replaced by processes and plans that are more participatory, flexible, strategic and action oriented

poor cities turned planning into a generally discredited function – a situation that still persists in some countries.

In the developed countries of Western Europe and North America, the 'golden age' of planning in the post-war and Keynesian era was replaced by attempts to weaken and sideline planning under the New Right politics of the 1970s and 1980s. Policies designed to 'roll back' the state and give more control to markets saw planning reorganized to promote the interests of business, finance and property speculators.[64] But this was to change again in the late 1990s as it became clear that unplanned and market-led urban development was having serious and negative environmental and social impacts. Planning is now again seen as important in this part of the world, although countries have responded differently to the need to reorganize, reshape and refocus planning systems so that they respond to current urban priorities.

Undoubtedly, however, it is the major new challenges of the 21st century that are currently leading to a worldwide return to an interest in planning: rapid urbanization, climate change, and resource shortages and costs – particularly of fuel and food. These are all issues that have significant implications for the spatial structure and functioning of cities and towns, and for their servicing, and are issues which 'the market' will not resolve. Essentially, they demand state intervention to fundamentally change the nature of cities; and this implies the need for planning. The next sections show how planning can be an important tool in addressing some of the issues that cities will have to confront.

The role of planning in addressing rapid urbanization, urban poverty and slums

Rapid urbanization, urban poverty and the growth of slums have also refocused attention on planning. The finding that 193,107 new urban dwellers are added to the world's urban population each day, resulting (in the case of developing countries) in a new city the size of Santiago or Kinshasa each month, has given cause for great concern. The fact that 17 per cent of cities in the developing world are experiencing annual growth rates of 4 per cent or more suggests that significant land and infrastructure development will have to take place to accommodate this growing population.[65]

Moreover, the bulk of these new urbanites will be poor and therefore will not be able to meet their accommodation and service needs through formal mechanisms. Governments will have to take the lead in directing service and shelter delivery for the growing urban population. The failure of governments to do this in the past has resulted in close to 1 billion slum dwellers worldwide. This figure is expected to double in the next 30 years if no firm action is taken. Given that the upgrading of slums is a more expensive process than planning ahead of development, there is no question that new urban growth should be planned. Urban planning can play a key role in achieving Target 11 of the Millennium Development Goals (MDGs), which seeks to substantially improve the lives of at least 100 million slum dwellers by 2020 through alternatives to new slum formation.

Addressing the slum challenge requires a new approach to planning. A key question that arises is: how can urban planning contribute to improving the living conditions of current slum dwellers by providing adequate alternatives to new slum formation? Planning can ensure that slum upgrading programmes are participatory. This requires identifying the existing and potential roles of the various stakeholders, who include the poor, national and local authorities, the private sector and civil society groups, as well as the international community. Apart from the technical aspects of slum upgrading, a key role of planning would be to 'assess ways in which the relative strengths of each stakeholder group can be combined to maximize synergies between their contributions'.[66] Planning can also ensure that slum upgrading programmes are community led, negotiated and participatory in order to avoid conflicts and safeguard the livelihoods of the poor. Too often, slum upgrading programmes in developing countries involve little meaningful dialogue with those affected.

Planning will have to play a significant role in providing alternatives to the formation of new slums, given the anticipated doubling of urban population over the next generation. To this end, cities need to apply the principle of planning before development by focusing on the future needs of low-income populations.[67] This will entail improving the performance of city authorities to manage the process of urbanization and future urban growth through effective land-use planning, and mobilization of resources and capacity-building. The first of these will require making land and trunk infrastructure available for low-income housing in agreed locations, as well as the provision of education, healthcare, access to employment, and other social services within these areas. This would also require enacting realistic and enforceable regulations that reflect the culture and lifestyle of the community. The second will entail leveraging a variety of local/domestic and international sources to facilitate community financing and the mobilization of local action.

The role of planning in addressing sustainable urban development and climate change

Worries about the environmental impacts of urban development were behind the revival of interest in planning in the 1990s, with the United Nations Conference on Environment and Development (UNCED) introducing the concept of sustainable development into planning primarily through the Agenda 21 frameworks. As countries rapidly urbanize, the issue of sustainable urbanization becomes crucial since unplanned urbanization will constrain the sustainable development of cities. Urban planning can play a vital role in ensuring sustainable urbanization. The goal of sustainable urbanization is liveable, productive and inclusive cities, towns and villages. Achieving sustainable cities and contributing to climate protection requires planned change to the way in which cities are spatially configured and serviced. Both adaptation and mitigation measures to respond to the effects of climate change require that cities

In many parts of the world, older and conventional forms of urban planning persist

Rapid urbanization, urban poverty and the growth of slums have also refocused attention on planning are planned differently.

Climate change is a global phenomenon, but a deeply local issue. Urban areas contribute to climate change through resource use in urban activities. But they can also play a pivotal role in climate change mitigation and adaptation strategies. Urban planning can help mainstream climate change considerations into urban development processes. Responding to climate change has important implications for urban planning: steering settlement away from flood-prone coastal areas and those subject to mudslides; protecting forest, agricultural and wilderness areas and promoting new ones; and developing and enforcing local climate protection measures. In Latin America and the Caribbean, the planning system plays an important role in determining building codes and materials specifications, protective devices such as dikes, and the retrofitting of existing structures to make them more hazard resistant.[68] Planning also plays a role in identifying hazard-prone areas and limiting their use through land-use zoning, tax incentives and the relocation of residents from hazard-prone areas.

Ideas about compact and public transport-based cities are ways in which cities could impact less upon climate change. Retrofitting existing car-based cities with public transport- and pedestrian-based movement systems would go a long way towards reducing fuel demands. It has also been suggested that cities planned in this way are more equitable in terms of providing good accessibility to both wealthier and poorer urban residents and overcoming spatial marginalization.[69] However, the possibility of controlling urban development this way in many cities in developing countries remains a challenge.

The role of planning in addressing urban crime and violence

While there are numerous social and economic factors that give rise to crime and violence in cities, poor planning, design and management are also contributing causes.[70] At the design level, it is important to promote human surveillance of public spaces and the design of parks and public spaces so that they are well lit and well integrated with other activity-generating uses. Large mono-functional areas such as open-space parking and industrial areas are likely to be deserted at certain times and, hence, unsafe. High blank walls and buildings without active street frontage can also encourage crime. Mixed-use higher-density developments with integrated public space systems are preferable.

Experience has shown that it is important for safety principles to be factored into all urban design and planning. For instance, in the UK, police architectural liaison officers are available to advise planners and designers.[71] There are also advisory documents available at both national and local government level, setting out the goals of the planning system in relation to urban safety. UN-Habitat, as part of its Safer Cities Programme in African cities, has developed a number of planning and design suggestions. These include planning for mixed use and activity in public places; signage and lighting; access to help; CCTV surveillance and patrols, particularly by communities; cleaning and waste removal;

management of markets and public ways; and urban renewal schemes.[72] Besides, urban planning can contribute to crime prevention through better management of the urbanization process. This entails providing basic services and infrastructure and improving the living conditions of city dwellers.

The role of planning in addressing post-conflict and post-disaster situations

Urban planning can play a crucial role in post-conflict situations. Post-conflict societies are characterized by weak institutional capacity to plan; absence of a strong rule of law, which results in chaotic and inefficient development; dysfunctional land management and land administration systems; invasion of land by the poor, homeless, internally displaced persons, returnees and refugees; conflicting claims over the same plot of land or house; large-scale destruction of buildings and infrastructure that might have to be reconstructed outside formal channels; and large-scale ambiguity and gaps in the regulatory framework.[73] Introducing urban planning in post-conflict situations is a crucial step for sound urban development and can contribute to creating a more stable, peaceful and prosperous society. It also allows for effective coordination of donor assistance, as well as more efficient use of limited local physical, human, technical and financial resources. The UN-Habitat *urban trialogues* approach, illustrated in Somalia, used spatial planning to help reintegrate conflict-displaced communities back into cities.[74]

Post-disaster situations offer urban planning a unique opportunity to rethink past development practices, improve the sustainability of human settlements and effectively prepare communities against threats and risks. Urban planning can contribute to post-disaster rehabilitation of human settlements. Planning can also strengthen the capacity to manage natural and human-made disasters, increase the capacity for disaster prevention and mitigation, and strengthen coordination and networking among communities, non-governmental organizations (NGOs), governments and external support organizations in addressing disaster-related activities. Furthermore, urban planning can ensure that programmes and projects undertaken after disasters address the long-term development objectives and needs of the affected areas, and ensure an effective transition to sustainable development.

It is clear that urban planning has an important role to play in addressing major urban issues of the 21st century. Rapid urbanization, urban poverty, growth of slums, climate change, urban crime, conflicts, as well as natural and human-made disasters, are some of the most important of these. A realization of this potential role is part of the reason for a revived interest in urban planning. UN-Habitat has played a central role in drawing the attention of governments to the need to address these issues, with all six of the Global Reports published to date focusing on the escalating urban crisis and the need for intervention. These reports have called for good urban governance, appropriate urban planning and management policies, and in the most recent report, appropriate urban policy, planning design and gover-

Urban planning can help mainstream climate change considerations into urban development processes

Urban planning can play a crucial role in post-conflict situations nance to address urban safety and security. This Global Report, which focuses on urban planning, places this management tool firmly at the top of the global urban agenda, while recognizing that planning approaches have to change significantly in order to meet this challenge.

POTENTIALS OFFERED BY NEW APPROACHES TO URBAN PLANNING

While conventional master planning continues in many parts of the world, there has been extensive criticism of this approach and, consequently, attempts to find new approaches to urban planning (see Chapter 3). There is also a new tendency for concerns such as gender, crime and safety, health, heritage and environment to be incorporated within urban planning approaches as 'cross-cutting' programmes, often with the encouragement of international development agencies. In some cases, new planning ideas are still experimental or have only been tried out in a limited number of places. Most of these new planning initiatives have elements in common, and they try to address what have been clear problems in traditional master planning systems. These common elements:

- are strategic rather than comprehensive;
- are flexible rather than end-state oriented and fixed;
- are action and implementation oriented through links to budgets, projects and city-wide or regional infrastructure;
- are stakeholder or community driven rather than only expert driven;
- are occasionally linked to political terms of office;
- contain objectives reflecting emerging urban concerns – for example, city global positioning, environmental protection, sustainable development, achieving urban-related MDGs, social inclusion and local identity;
- play an integrative role in policy formulation and in urban management by encouraging government departments to coordinate their plans in space; and
- focus on the planning process, with the outcomes being highly diverse and dependent upon stakeholder influence or local policy directions.

This section briefly reviews the most important of these approaches. To a large extent they have been shaped by the regional context from which they have emerged, although it is possible to discern international borrowing of these ideas. The new approaches are grouped under seven broad categories:

1   strategic spatial planning and its variants;
2   new ways of using spatial planning to integrate government;
3   approaches to land regularization and management;
4   participatory and partnership processes;
5   approaches promoted by international agencies and addressing sectoral urban concerns;

6   new forms of master planning; and
7   planning aimed at producing new spatial forms.

There is considerable overlap between these categories; some emphasize planning process and others outcomes, and sometimes these are combined.

Strategic spatial planning and its variants

Strategic spatial planning emerged in Western Europe during the 1980s and 1990s[75] partly in response to the problems of master planning. A strategic spatial planning system commonly contains a directive, a long-range spatial plan consisting of frameworks and principles, and broad and conceptual spatial ideas, rather than detailed spatial design. The plan does not address every part of a city – being strategic means focusing on only those aspects or areas that are important to overall plan objectives. The spatial plan is linked to a planning scheme or ordinance specifying land uses and development rights. The spatial plan also provides guidance for urban projects, which in the context of Europe are often 'brownfield' urban regeneration projects and/or infrastructural projects.

Strategic spatial planning has since found its way to other parts of the world. It has been adopted by several cities in Eastern Europe[76] and a number of Latin American cities. One problem has been that the new strategic plan is often abandoned when a new political party or mayor comes into power because to continue it might be seen as giving credibility to a political opposition. Where the strategic plan is not integrated with the regulatory aspect of the planning system, and does not affect land rights, as is usually the case, then there may be little to prevent the strategic plan from being frequently changed or discontinued.[77]

In Barcelona (Spain), a variant of strategic spatial planning claimed significant success and represented an important shift away from master planning. A city-wide strategic plan promoted a 'compact' urban form and provided a framework for a set of local urban projects which had a strong urban design component. However, some see this approach to strategic planning as largely corporate planning around economic development goals with certain social and environmental objectives attached.[78] The 'Barcelona Model' has since been 'exported' to other parts of the world, with an attempt to apply it in Buenos Aires[79] highlighting the need for caution when transferring planning ideas to very different contexts.

Spatial planning as a tool for integrating public-sector functions

The problem of integrating different functions of urban government has become a common one, and this is seen as a potentially important role for spatial planning. The new UK planning system,[80] which introduces regional spatial strategies and local development frameworks, aims to replace conventional land-use planning with spatial planning. The new approach focuses on decentralized solutions, as well as a desire to integrate the functions of the public sector and

Post-disaster situations offer urban planning a unique opportunity to rethink past development practices

New planning ideas are still experimental or have only been tried out in a limited number of places inject a spatial or territorial dimension into sectoral strategies. There is also recognition that achieving environmental sustainability will require sectoral interests to work together and cut across traditional disciplinary and professional boundaries.[81] As a result, the purpose of the new spatial plans – 'shaping spatial development through the coordination of the spatial impacts of sector policy and decisions' – is very different from the purpose of the previous land-use plans – 'regulating land use and development through designation of areas of development and protection, and application of performance criteria'. An unresolved issue, however, is exactly how the new spatial plans align with the development control system. In South Africa, departmental integration has been a central goal of the new integrated development planning (IDP) system in local government.[82] The IDP is a medium-term municipal plan linked to a five-year political cycle, although aspects of the plan, including the vision and the spatial development framework, have a longer-term horizon.

Approaches to land regularization and management

The most challenging issue for urban planning in terms of land regularization and management has been how to address the issue of informality. The expanding informal areas of cities in developing and transitional regions, especially the peri-urban areas, are usually regarded as undesirable and in need of eradication and/or planning control. Yet it is now well recognized that such an approach simply worsens poverty and exclusion. New regularization approaches require an attitudinal shift in government to recognize the potentially positive role of informality; require policies, laws and regulations that are adapted to the dynamics of informality; and require efforts to improve the support for, and legitimacy of, the planning system by those involved in informality. New planning ideas suggest alternatives to the removal of informal settlements, ways of using planning tools to strategically influence development actors, and ways of working with development actors to manage public space and provide services.

Participatory processes and partnerships in planning

Participation and public–private partnerships have become important elements in all of the innovative planning approaches discussed in this Global Report. Potentially, participation in planning can empower communities and build social capital, can lead to better design of urban projects and can allow for participants' concerns to be incorporated within strategies. Successful participation is, however, dependent upon certain preconditions relating to the political context (a political system that encourages active citizenship and that is committed to equity and redress), the legal basis for participation (processes and outcomes are legally specified) and available resources (skilled and committed professionals, well-resourced and empowered local governments, and informed and organized communities and stakeholders).

At the neighbourhood scale, there has been some success with participatory urban appraisal and the more inclusive participatory learning and action, followed by community action planning. At the city scale, one of the best-known innovative participatory approaches is participatory budgeting, which first occurred in Porto Alegre in Brazil and has since been attempted in other parts of the world. Citizens participate and vote on the municipal budget in either regional or thematic 'assemblies', and form local forums to discuss how the budget should be spent in their areas. Research shows that this is not a simple solution which can be imposed everywhere[83] and is not a technical process that can be detached from local political culture.

A rather different form of participation, but nonetheless very prevalent, is public–private partnerships. In developing countries these have often developed around public infrastructure provision when municipalities lack resources or skills to provide this. In developed countries, they often take the form of private-sector planning and investment in urban projects. Frequently these involve redeveloping urban brownfield sites, where the profit-oriented aims of the developer are aligned with the aims of municipalities for modernization, economic restructuring and physical regeneration. Urban regeneration in Cardiff[84] is a good example of how a coalition between the political elite and private-sector commercial property development interests was central to explaining the success achieved. However, as in Cardiff, this approach can neglect social inclusion, equality and sustainability objectives, everyday service delivery and the achievement of high-quality urban design.

Approaches promoted by international agencies: The Urban Management Programme and sector programmes

The Urban Management Programme (UMP), established in 1986 by the Urban Development Unit of the World Bank in partnership with the United Nations Centre for Human Settlements (UNCHS, now UN-Habitat) and funded by UNDP, is the largest global urban programme to date. The objective was to promote socially and environmentally sustainable human settlements and adequate shelter, and to reduce urban poverty and social exclusion. It focused on providing technical assistance and capacity-building in five key areas: urban land, urban environment, municipal finance, urban infrastructure and urban poverty. In common with other recent ideas in planning, and particularly with the 'urban management' approach, it attempted to shift the responsibility for planning and development to the whole of local government rather than being the responsibility of only one department, attempted to promote participatory processes in local government decision-making, to promote strategic thinking in planning, and to tie local government plans to implementation through action plans and budgets. In 2006 UN-Habitat disengaged from the programme and transferred the work to local anchor institutions.[85]

Over the last couple of decades, there have been attempts, largely by international development agencies, to promote particular sectoral, or issue-specific, concerns in urban plans. The most important of these have been:

Strategic spatial planning has since found its way to other parts of the world

Participation and public–private partnerships have become important elements in innovative planning approaches

- *The Localizing Agenda 21 Programme*: this emerged from the 1992 Earth Summit agreements. It offers a multi-year support system for selected secondary cities as the means to introduce or strengthen environmental concerns in their plans.
- *The Sustainable Cities Programme*: a joint initiative by UN-Habitat and the United Nations Environment Programme (UNEP), designed to build capacities in environmental planning and management through urban local authorities.
- *The Safer Cities Programme*: initiated by UN-Habitat to tackle the escalating problem of urban crime and violence by developing the crime prevention capacities of local authorities.
- *The Disaster Management Programme*: established by UN-Habitat to assist governments and local authorities to rebuild in countries recovering from war or natural disasters.
- *The Healthy Cities Programme*: initiated by the World Health Organization (WHO) for the purpose of improving, promoting and maintaining conducive urban environmental health conditions by involving all actors within the city.
- *The Global Campaign on Urban Governance*: launched by UN-Habitat in 1999, it attempted to encourage urban planning to be pro-poor and inclusive. Its vision was to realize the inclusive city – a place where everyone, regardless of wealth, status, gender, age, race or religion, is enabled to participate productively and positively in the opportunities that cities have to offer. It specifically promoted the involvement of women in decision-making.
- *The Global Campaign for Secure Tenure*: launched by UN-Habitat in 2002, it aimed to improve the conditions of people living and working in slums and informal settlements by promoting security of tenure. It encouraged negotiation as an alternative to forced eviction, and the establishment of innovative systems of tenure that minimize bureaucratic lags and the displacement of the urban poor by market forces.
- *City Development Strategy (CDS)*: promoted by the Cities Alliance – a joint World Bank–UN-Habitat initiative – and encourages local governments to produce inter-sectoral and long-range visions and plans for cities.
- *Gender responsiveness*: the promotion of gender mainstreaming issues in local government and planning. Gender-specific participatory governance tools such as gender budgeting, women's safety audits and women's hearings have been developed.[86]

In addition to these agency-driven, issue-specific programmes, there are further issues that have gained some prominence in the planning literature. The linking of urban planning with infrastructure is the subject of Chapter 8 of this Global Report. How to conduct planning in the peri-urban areas of developing countries has become an important new concern,[87] and ways of using planning to address climate change is likely to become increasingly important in the future.

New forms of master planning

In some parts of the world, traditional master planning and regulatory systems continue; but these instruments are being used in innovative ways. In Brazil, 'new' master plans are seen as different from the old ones in that they are bottom up and participatory, oriented towards social justice and aim to counter the effects of land speculation. The view is that while conventional urban planning strives to achieve an ideal city, from which illegality and informality are banned, new urban master planning deals with the existing city to develop tools to tackle these problems in just and democratic ways.[88] One important new regulatory tool has been the special zones of social interest. This is a legal instrument for land management applied to areas with a 'public interest': existing *favelas* and to vacant public land. It intervenes in the dynamics of the real estate market to control land access, secure social housing, and protect against down-raiding and speculation that would dispossess the poor.

New urban forms: The 'compact city' and 'new urbanism'

During recent years, there has been a reaction against urban modernist forms[89] and urban sprawl. While low-density, sprawling cities are the norm in most parts of the world, there is growing support for the 'compact city' and 'new urbanist' forms (see Chapters 6 and 8).[90] At the city-wide scale, the 'compact city' approach argues for medium- to high-built densities. Mixed-use environments and good public open spaces are important, especially as places for small and informal businesses. Urban containment policies are common, often implemented through the demarcation of a growth boundary or urban edge designed to protect natural resources beyond the urban area and to encourage densification inside it.

New urbanism adheres to similar spatial principles but at the scale of the local neighbourhood. This position promotes a vision of cities with fine-grained mixed use, mixed housing types, compact form, an attractive public realm, pedestrian-friendly streetscapes, defined centres and edges, and varying transport options.[91] Facilities such as health, libraries, retail and government services cluster around key public transport facilities and intersections to maximize convenience. These spatial forms have been strongly promoted in the US, and have been implemented in the form of neighbourhoods such as Celebration Town[92] and Seaside.

To conclude, it is worth noting that most of these ideas focus on procedural aspects and new ways in which planning can be integrated within governance processes. There has been far less attention paid to the urban forms that result from these planning processes, or the nature of the regulatory frameworks underpinning them, although there are some exceptions. Yet, the new objectives that are informing strategic planning, particularly those relating to social inclusion, can only be realized through changes in regulatory frameworks and systems of land rights.

Over the last couple of decades, there have been attempts, by international development agencies, to promote issue-specific concerns in urban plans

In some parts of the world, traditional master planning and regulatory systems continue; but these are being used in innovative ways

DEFINING URBAN PLANNING AND IDENTIFYING NORMATIVE PRINCIPLES

This section undertakes two tasks. It puts forward a definition of urban planning that attempts to capture the newly emerging conception of planning as well as the varied nature of the activity across the globe. It then proposes a set of normative principles or criteria, against which planning systems in various parts of the world can be assessed. The reason for this is to avoid putting forward any new or revised 'model' of planning that could supposedly be applied anywhere. This Global Report seeks to stress that urban conditions and dynamics are highly variable in different parts of the world (see Chapter 2), and new planning systems and approaches must be fully embedded in the institutional and socio-economic contexts within which they operate.

Definitions of planning

While urban planning as a form of governmental practice can be found in most parts of the world, its role and form, and perceptions of what it should achieve, vary significantly and there are debates on this within regions and countries. Even the term used to describe the activity of planning varies: spatial planning, land-use planning, physical planning, city planning, town (and regional) planning, and development planning are English-language terms in use. The French term *urbanisme* and the Spanish *urbanization* (to make urban) refer more broadly to economic and social relations rather than just physical factors and are closer to the term development planning. And in China the terms master plan, comprehensive city plan and detailed plan are in current use.

More recently, attempts to change conventional physical planning to be a more strategic and integrated activity of government have resulted in terms such as 'urban (public) management', now including the activity of urban planning. To complicate matters further, the emergence of environment as an important concern of government has resulted in the term 'environmental planning/management', sometimes referring to environment in the broadest sense, to include both the natural and built environment.

Earlier definitions of urban planning which described it as an activity of government also require modification in some parts of the world. The change from 'government' to 'governance' in liberal democracies has meant that urban planning is now often initiated and carried out in the context of partnership between the state, the private sector and civil society organizations. In many cities, property developers now play a bigger role in urban planning than does the state. Also possible, where states are weak and ineffective, are situations in which communities and households plan, service and develop their own areas. By contrast, in countries such as China where state, civil society and economic actors are highly integrated, urban planning can still be described as an activity of government.

The following definition is put forward as a reflection of the concept of urban planning[93] that has been used in this Global Report (see Box 1.4).

Normative principles to guide revised approaches to urban planning

While the activity of urban planning is recognized and practised in most parts of the world, the contexts within which it operates vary greatly. Different urban issues, different political, economic and institutional systems, and different cultures and value systems all shape the planning system in different ways. It would therefore be incorrect to assume that a single new model or approach to planning could be developed, which could then be introduced in all parts of the world. Rather, the approach taken here is to suggest a list of normative principles against which all planning systems can be assessed. Planning systems in different parts of the world may meet these principles in different ways, using different institutional structures and processes, and different methodologies and outcomes. Some of these principles may be more appropriate in certain contexts than in others. Some cities or regions may have particular priorities or values not reflected here. This set of principles also coincides closely with those recently put forward by the Global Planners Network (GPN): a network of 25 professional planning institutes (see Box 1.5).

In this Global Report the following principles are posed as questions that can be used to interrogate urban planning systems:

- Does the planning system recognize, and have the ability to respond to, current and impending environmental and natural resource issues and natural hazards and threats in ways that promote sustainability? Does it provide for the recognition of the ecological consequences of all urban projects?
- Does the planning system recognize, and have the ability to promote social justice – in particular, to be participatory, pro-poor, redistributive, gender sensitive and inclusive and to acknowledge the important role of informality? Linked to this, does it have the ability to promote global charters such as the MDGs?
- Is the planning system backed up by, and aligned with, progressive national constitutions and international agreements on human and environmental justice? Can it recognize the 'rights' of urban dwellers to the city?
- Does the planning system fit within the constitutional allocation of powers and functions?
- Does the planning system recognize, and have the ability to respond to, cultural, socio-economic and spatial diversity at all scales?
- Does the planning system facilitate and encourage open and ongoing public dialogue between various partners and groupings on planning processes and outcomes? Are the outcomes of such dialogues clearly translated into planning documents and regulations?
- Does the planning system facilitate urban built forms and infrastructural systems that are environmentally

sustainable and supportive of local livelihoods and social inclusion? Can the system recognize and support the making of 'places' that reflect local identity, cultures and needs?

- Does the planning system acknowledge the important role played by informality, including slums and informal settlements, in many cities? Is it able to be sufficiently flexible to act on the opportunities presented by informal practices and groups and by community-based organizations (CBOs) and NGOs?
- Is there sustained support for the planning system from government, from politicians, from the business sector and from both wealthy and poor communities? Has it been adopted for sound reasons and not because it has been imposed by outside donor or aid agencies, or international consultants?
- Can the planning system cope with the need for both greater and lesser degrees of flexibility – for example, to be able to implement firm controls where the need for protection (of the environment, heritage, etc.) and social inclusion exist, or where market externalities occur, and to be more flexible where population and economic factors are rapidly changing?
- Does the planning system have the ability to promote (e.g. achieve local economic development and slum upgrading) as well as control? This implies that it does not just present a future vision, but can also take steps to reach it?
- Does the planning system consider plan and implementation as interrelated processes, linked to budgets and decision-making systems (i.e. it does not just present a future vision but can also take steps to reach it)?
- Is there alignment and synergy between directive and strategic spatial plans and the system of land laws and land-use management? Is there a mechanism for this linkage?
- Is there alignment and synergy between urban plans and broader institutional visions that may be captured in public documents such as a CDS?
- Is the planning system institutionally located and embedded so that it can play an effective role in terms of spatial coordination and promotion of policies, and implementation?
- Is there recognition that urban planning systems have limitations in terms of achieving all of the above, and that properly aligned and integrated national and regional plans and policies are extremely important in terms of achieving well-performing urban areas?
- Does the planning system include an approach to monitoring and evaluating urban plans, including clear indicators of plan success? Do institutions have the capacity and resources to undertake this task?
- Are there close linkages between planning practice, the professional organizations of planning, and the planning education systems? Do the planning education systems have the capacity and resources to produce sufficient skilled graduates, who are in touch with current issues and practices?

Box 1.5 A definition of urban planning

Definitions of planning have changed over time and are not the same in all parts of the world. Earlier views defined urban planning as physical design, enforced through land-use control and centred in the state. Current perspectives recognize the institutional shift from government to governance (although in some parts of the world planning is still centred in the state), the necessarily wider scope of planning beyond land use, and the need to consider how plans are implemented.

Urban planning is therefore currently viewed as a self-conscious collective (societal) effort to imagine or re-imagine a town, city, urban region or wider territory and to translate the result into priorities for area investment, conservation measures, new and upgraded areas of settlement, strategic infrastructure investments and principles of land-use regulation. It is recognized that planning is not only undertaken by professional urban and regional planners (other professions and groupings are also involved); hence, it is appropriate to refer to the 'planning system' rather than just to the tasks undertaken by planners. Nonetheless, urban (and regional) planning has distinctive concerns that separate it from, for example, economic planning or health planning. At the core of urban planning is a concern with space (i.e. with 'the where of things', whether static or in movement; the protection of special 'places' and sites; the interrelations between different activities and networks in an area; and significant intersections and nodes that are physically co-located within an area).

Planning is also now viewed as a strategic rather than a comprehensive, activity. This implies selectivity, and a focus on that which really makes a difference to the fortunes of an area over time. Planning also highlights a developmental movement from the past to the future. It implies that it is possible to decide between appropriate actions now in terms of their potential impact in shaping future socio-spatial relations. This future imagination is not merely a matter of short-term political expediency, but is expected to be able to project a transgenerational temporal scale, especially in relation to infrastructure investment, environmental management and quality of life.

The term 'planning' also implies a mode of governance (a form of politics) driven by the articulation of policies through some kind of deliberative process and the judgement of collective action in relation to these policies. Planning is not, therefore, a neutral technical exercise: it is shaped by values that must be made explicit, and planning itself is fundamentally concerned with making ethical judgements.

Source: adapted from Healey, 2004

Box 1.6 The principles of the Global Planners Network: New urban planning

The Global Planners Network (GPN) puts forward the following ten principles for new urban planning:

1 promote sustainable development;
2 achieve integrated planning;
3 integrate with budgets;
4 plan with partners;
5 meet the subsidiarity principle;
6 promote market responsiveness;
7 ensure access to land;
8 develop appropriate planning tools;
9 be pro-poor and inclusive;
10 recognize cultural variation.

Source: www.globalplannersnetwork.org/

ORGANIZATION OF THE REPORT

This Global Report is divided into six parts. Parts I to V consist of 11 chapters while Part VI is the Statistical Annex. It is useful at this stage to introduce the chapters in the report and to summarize the issues they cover.

Part I – Challenges and context

The purpose of Part I of the Global Report is to provide an introduction and background to the need to revisit urban planning. This chapter has explained the important new forces that are affecting urban settlements in all parts of the world and, hence, the reason for a review of urban planning to see if current approaches are able to address new urban challenges. Planning systems in many parts of the world are in need of change, and this chapter has summarized some of the emerging new approaches. The rest of this chapter has outlined the definition of planning used in this report, and finally proposed a set of normative principles against which current urban planning systems can be assessed.

Chapter 2 describes the very different urban conditions that are to be found in various parts of the world. An important premise of this Global Report is that traditional approaches to planning have often failed to consider, or respond to, the very different contexts for planning. These differences are partly regional: both urban conditions and socio-political systems are remarkably different in developed and developing parts of the world (and within these categories as well). There are also important differences within urban settlements that planning needs to take account of: differences structured by levels of development, poverty, inequality, etc., and differences in forms of human settlement. Chapter 2 highlights these differences in order to emphasize the point that there can be no one model of planning which can apply in all parts of the world.

Part II – Global trends: The urban planning process (procedural)

The purpose of this part of the Global Report is to provide a background to the emergence of urban planning and new approaches. It then examines trends in institutional and political forces that have shaped planning systems, and the processes of decision-making in planning.

Chapter 3 explains the emergence and spread of contemporary forms of urban planning. It considers how a technical, expert-led and top-down form of planning emerged in developed countries at the end of the 19th century. This approach to planning then spread to other parts of the world. More recently, there has been a shift from this earlier form of planning to new forms that emphasize participatory decision-making processes and the need for flexible plans that can respond to changing economic and social forces. However, in many parts of the world, traditional forms of planning still persist. This chapter aims to explain these processes and differences and to identify the innovative approaches to planning that appear to hold promise.

Chapter 4 examines the complex and highly variable institutional contexts within which the activities of planning take place. It examines the main purposes of planning, the tasks it performs and the tools available to implement these tasks. It provides a framework for understanding the institutional contexts of planning, and the tensions that can arise within these. The important issue of the legal context of planning activity is explored, and how the different institutions undertaking land and property development operate in relation to this context. The chapter examines the issue of urban governance capacity and the different arrangements that have emerged to undertake planning: these affect plan formulation and implementation in important ways. A key point of emphasis in this chapter is that the institutional and regulatory frameworks which shape planning are highly variable, given that they, in turn, are part of a wider governance context influenced by history and place.

Chapter 5 examines the issue of participation and politics in planning. The shift from a view of planning as a technical and expert-driven activity to one which views it as a process of societal consultation, negotiation and consensus-seeking has been profound. This chapter explains trends in urban politics and how these provide a framework for government, and the relationships between government and non-governmental actors in policy formulation and implementation. It examines debates on the difficult issue of public participation in planning, drawing on experiences documented in both the planning and development fields. The chapter examines what might be more appropriate and pro-poor approaches to planning, and how the potentials of participation might be achieved while avoiding its pitfalls.

Part III – Global trends: The content of urban plans (substantive)

Over the past decades there have been important shifts in approaches to planning and the kinds of urban issues which urban plans deal with. Older and traditional approaches tended to focus on the separation of land uses, regulating built form, promoting 'aesthetic' environments, and achieving efficient traffic flow. More recently, different issues have required attention in planning. Three of the most important issues – environment, informal urban activity and infrastructure planning – are dealt with in this part.

Chapter 6 links planning and sustainable urban development. The emergence of environment and natural resource availability as key issues for cities and urban planning are increasingly important. This chapter discusses how urban planning can promote sustainable urbanization by responding to global and local environmental challenges. In this new area of urban planning, the institutional, regulatory and technical preconditions are still being developed. Planning and environmental management often operate in different government silos and with different policy and legal frameworks, and there are frequent tensions between the 'green' and 'brown' agendas in cities. This chapter shows many ways in which the two agendas can be reconciled if sustainable urban development is to be realized.

An important premise of this Global Report is that traditional approaches to planning have often failed to consider, or respond to, the very different contexts for planning

Chapter 7 considers the fact that urban settlements, particularly (but not only) in developing countries, are becoming increasingly informal. By contrast, planning takes place within the formal structures and legal systems of government, and often does not cater for, or support, the majority of city-builders and operators, who are informal. Many of the urban poor in developing countries cannot afford to live in planned areas or conform to the requirements of planning regulations. This exclusion of large proportions of the urban population in developing countries has given rise to new urban forms, as many informal urban dwellers now live in the peri-urban areas. These fragmented, sprawling and un-serviced areas are now some of the fastest growing parts of cities, but are also the most difficult to service and plan. This chapter examines the issues which these trends raise for a revised urban planning.

Chapter 8 links planning with the spatial structure of cities and the provision of urban infrastructure. Urban settlements everywhere are spatially shaped by their infrastructural systems, and the nature and form of these contribute significantly to the degree of marginalization of the urban population and the sustainability of urban ecological systems. Transport, water, sewerage, electricity and telecommunications systems play key roles in the development of efficient, healthy and sustainable cities. Other amenities (schools, health services, etc.) are also important for the development of liveable cities. Compact, mixed-use and public transport-based urban forms support urban efficiency and liveability far more than low-density car-dependent forms. More recently, urban development has been driven by 'mega-projects' that impact upon infrastructural systems and urban change in important ways. This chapter concludes that a much closer connection between spatial planning and infrastructure provision is crucial to achieve efficient, sustainable and inclusive cities.

Part IV – Global trends: Monitoring, evaluation and education

This part of the Global Report discusses two areas that potentially give support to planning and help it to be more effective: monitoring and evaluation, and planning education.

Chapter 9 considers the monitoring and evaluation of urban plans. Urban planning is often at a disadvantage as there is a poorly developed tradition of plan monitoring and evaluation. Planners find it difficult to argue that their work is having a positive impact as they are often uncertain about the effectiveness or efficiency of their interventions. This chapter explains the evolution of programme and policy evaluation in the public sector, as well as the concepts, principles and models of evaluation. Evaluation systems are common in most developed countries and larger urban centres; but in developing countries there are obstacles that preclude planning evaluation. However, there is growing interest in the development and use of indicators to enhance urban policy decision-making and performance measurement.

Chapter 10 discusses planning education. Planning effectiveness is strongly influenced by the expertise of the trained professionals who manage and produce planning processes and products, although newer approaches recognize that planning activity depends upon the inputs of many sectors, groups and professionals. This chapter examines whether planning education is attuned to changing urban contexts, and the degree to which planning schools worldwide have the capabilities needed to lead the next generation of planning practice in the light of changes under way. It notes that in some parts of the world, planning education has not kept pace with changing urban conditions and demands on professionals. The chapter documents the development of tertiary-sector urban planning education worldwide, and lays out the key philosophical and practical debates that framed planning education as it grew in the 20th century. It assesses the capacity of educational and professional institutions and suggests directions for change.

Part V – Future policy directions

Building on the previous chapters, the final part of the Global Report explores the future policy directions necessary to make urban planning more effective.

Chapter 11 is the concluding chapter. Its purpose is to outline a new role for urban planning. It suggests that in many parts of the world a 'paradigm' shift in urban planning is required if life in urban settlements is to be tolerable through the next century. The chapter first summarizes the key findings of the report. It then draws out what the main elements of a more positive urban planning might be. It identifies the main principles of innovative planning that might stimulate ideas elsewhere, although the actual form they would take will always be fundamentally influenced by context. Finally, it examines the changes that would need to be in place or the initiatives that might be supportive to promote new approaches to planning.

CONCLUDING REMARKS

This chapter has introduced the idea of revisiting urban planning. It explains why it has become necessary to reconsider the future of urban settlements, and it documents the main factors that are now affecting urban settlements in all parts of the world. It notes that while many of these factors affect settlements globally, they are still not producing homogeneous urban places. Global factors interrelate with local particularities, and local histories, to produce very different urban places facing different kinds of urban issues. Understanding these recent urban changes highlights the gap that has emerged between current urban dynamics and planning legal and institutional systems, which, in many parts of the world, have changed very slowly. This gap between early 20th-century Western European and North American ideas about ideal urban environments, on the one hand, and the realities of rapid urbanization, slum growth, informality and environmental change, on the other, has rendered many planning systems ineffective and sometimes destructive.

The serious nature of all of these urban challenges requires action, and urban planning presents a potential tool

> Over the past decades there have been important shifts in approaches to planning and the kinds of urban issues which urban plans deal with

> Urban planning is often at a disadvantage as there is a poorly developed tradition of plan monitoring and evaluation

that can be reformed, where necessary, to contribute to finding solutions to these problems. With this in mind, this chapter has emphasized the potentials of urban planning and the cases where it has been used to good effect. It has also discussed some of the new approaches that have emerged in recent years, not because they offer themselves as 'models' that can be imposed on any context, but because they contain ideas which can be useful in different kinds of urban areas with different kinds of problems. An important conclusion is that there is no single model or approach to urban

planning that can solve urban problems. Unless new approaches to planning are deeply embedded in the institutional culture and norms of a place, and articulate closely with accepted practices of urban management, they will have little effect. For this reason, this chapter has not attempted to set out an 'answer' to the question of what should urban planning be like? Rather, it has offered a set of normative criteria against which existing planning systems can be tested; how they meet these criteria may vary considerably.

> There is no single model or approach to urban planning that can solve urban problems

NOTES

1   UN-Habitat, 2008b.
2   The term 'urban planning' has the same meaning in this Global Report as 'city planning' and 'town planning', and is used throughout to refer to planning in large cities as well as medium-sized and small urban places.
3   UN, 1999.
4   Wacquant, 2008.
5   Shatkin, 2006.
6   Irazábal, 2008a.
7   Hirt and Stanilov, 2008.
8   Attahi et al, 2008.
9   UN, 1999.
10 Details of the Global Campaign on Urban Governance can be found in UNCHS (2000) and UN-Habitat (2002a).
11 Beall, 2002.
12 Brenner, 1999.
13 Noting that this idea has a long pedigree in planning, and particularly in the work of Geddes, Mumford, Abercrombie and the Regional Planning Association.
14 Hirt and Stanilov, 2008.
15 Hirt and Stanilov, 2008.
16 Logan, 2002.
17 Leaf, 2005a.
18 Devas, 2001.
19 Walton, 1998.
20 National Research Council, 2003.
21 Irazábal, 2008a.
22 Bayat, 2004, p85.
23 Davis, 2004.
24 Leaf, 2005b.
25 Mitlin, 2008.
26 Mitlin, 2008.
27 HM Treasury, 2006, pvi.
28 Sheuya, 2008, p9, cited in Irazábal, 2008a.
29 UN-Habitat, 2007a, Section IV.
30 UN-Habitat, 2007a.
31 UN, 2008.
32 UN, 2008, Table 1.1.
33 Yuen, 2008.
34 This is not the case everywhere. Beauchemin and Bocquier (2004) show that secondary towns in West Africa are hardly growing as people migrate to larger settlements.
35 Davis, 2004.
36 Hirt and Stanilov, 2008.
37 UN-Habitat, 2008b.
38 UN-Habitat, 2008b.
39 UN-Habitat, 2008b.
40 UN, 2008.
41 Spiegel et al, 1996.
42 Yuen, 2008.
43 Marcuse, 2006.
44 Kipfer and Keil, 2002; UN-Habitat, 2004a.
45 Irazábal, 2008a; UN-Habitat, 2007a.
46 Grant and Nijman, 2006.
47 Ansari, 2008.
48 Qadeer, 2004.
49 Attahi et al, 2008.
50 Irazábal, 2008a.
51 Yuen, 2008.
52 Ansari, 2008.
53 Yuen, 2008.
54 Irazábal, 2008a.
55 Hall, 1988.
56 Taylor, 1998.
57 Taylor, 1998.
58 The Charter of Athens, initiated in 1928 and later strongly influenced by Le Corbusier, was an important document (by 1944) in terms of establishing modernist urban principles.
59 Berrisford and Kihato, 2006.
60 Yiftachel, 2003.
61 Fernandes, 2003.
62 Friedmann, 2005a.
63 Hirt and Stanilov, 2008.
64 Healey, 1992.
65 UN-Habitat, 2008b.
66 Payne, 2005, p136.
67 UN Millennium Project, 2005.
68 Irazábal, 2008a.
69 See Fainstein (2000) on the 'Just City'.
70 UN-Habitat, 2007a, p239.
71 UN-Habitat, 2007a, pp89, 241.
72 UN-Habitat, 2007a, p241.
73 Augustinus and Barry, 2004.
74 UN-Habitat, 2006i.
75 Albrechts, 2001a.
76 Hirt and Stanilov, 2008.
77 Steinberg, 2005.
78 Marshall, 2000.
79 Crot, 2008.
80 Reflected in the Planning and Compulsory Purchase Act of 2004.
81 Nadin, 2007.
82 Harrison et al, 2008.
83 Crot, 2008.
84 Rakodi, 2008 and Chapter 5.
85 UN-Habitat, 2005.
86 UN-Habitat, 2002b.
87 Allen, 2003; Kyessi, 2005.
88 Souza, 2003, p194.
89 See Jacobs (1963) for one of the earliest critiques of these forms.
90 Jenks et al, 1996; Jenks and Burgess, 2000; and Williams et al, 2000.
91 Grant, 2006.
92 Njoh, 2008a.
93 Derived from Healey, 2004.

CHAPTER 2

UNDERSTANDING THE DIVERSITY OF URBAN CONTEXTS

The urban contexts in which planning occurs differ signifi-cantly from one region to another. This chapter examines the nature of these differences, focusing on the consequent challenges that urban planning should address. As briefly indicated in Chapter 1 and elaborated upon in Chapter 3, the view of urban problems as being essentially uniform across the world partly underlies efforts to create universal urban planning approaches and models. Evidence in this Global Report suggests that this view is flawed and partly accounts for the failure of urban planning in many countries. The underlying premise of this chapter is that urban planning initiatives are unlikely to succeed without an adequate understanding of the diversity of urban contexts. Collectively, demographic, size, spatial and economic factors, mediated by globalization and location, are of paramount importance in revisiting urban planning and determining the ways in which it should be reoriented and strengthened in order to make it more relevant.

In light of the above observations, the following dimensions of urban diversity are examined in this chapter: urbanization and demographic trends; city size and spatial forms; level of economic development and poverty; and vulnerability to natural and human-induced hazards. Each of these dimensions of urban diversity and its planning implica-tions are discussed with respect to developed, transitional and developing countries.

URBANIZATION AND DEMOGRAPHIC TRENDS

Less than 5 per cent of the world's population lived in cities a century ago.[1] The world began experiencing unprece-dented rates of urbanization in the early 20th century.[2] Urban growth rates averaged 2.6 per cent per year between 1950 and 2007. This period witnessed a quadrupling of the world's urban population from 0.7 billion to 3.3 billion, thus increasing the level of urbanization from 29 per cent in 1950 to 49 per cent in 2007 (see Table 2.1). Perhaps more noteworthy is that in 2008, the proportion of the world's population living in urban areas exceeded 50 per cent.[3] This trend is expected to continue as 6.4 billion people, or about 70 per cent of the world's population is expected to live in urban areas by 2050.

The world's urban population growth rates have, in recent years, slowed down to the current average annual rate of 1.8 per cent. While the level of urbanization in devel-oped countries had reached 50 per cent more than half a century ago, this level will not be attained in developing countries until 2019.[4] Levels of urbanization remain low in developing regions when compared to developed regions. The only exception is Latin America, where urbanization levels compare favourably with those of developed countries. As shown in Figure 2.1, urban growth rates are higher in Africa and Asia than in other regions of the world.

The urban contexts in which planning occurs differ signifi-cantly from one region to another

Region	Urban population (million)					Percentage urban				
	1950	1975	2007	2025	2050	1950	1975	2007	2025	2050
World	737	1518	3294	4584	6398	29.1	37.3	49.4	57.2	69.6
More developed region	427	702	916	995	1071	52.5	67.0	74.4	79.0	86.0
Less developed region	310	817	2382	3590	5327	18.0	27.0	43.8	53.2	67.0
Africa	32	107	373	658	1233	14.5	25.7	38.7	47.2	61.8
Asia	237	574	1645	2440	3486	16.8	24.0	40.8	51.1	66.2
Europe	281	444	528	545	557	51.2	65.7	72.2	76.2	83.8
Latin America and the Caribbean	69	198	448	575	683	41.4	61.1	78.3	83.5	88.7
North America	110	180	275	365	402	63.9	73.8	81.3	85.7	90.2
Oceania	8	13	24	27	31	62.0	71.5	70.5	71.9	76.4

Source: UN, 2008, pp3–5

Table 2.1

Global trends in urbanization (1950–2050)

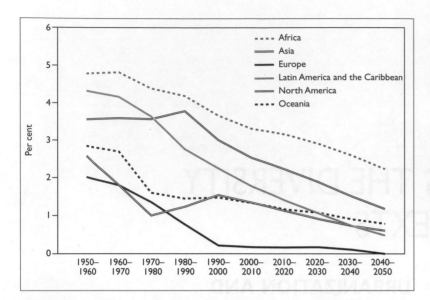

Figure 2.1

Average annual rate of
change of urban
population

Source: UN, 2008

Developed and transitional countries

The process of urbanization is much more advanced in the developed regions of the world. Here, about 74 per cent of the population live in cities (see Table 2.1). This trend is expected to continue, albeit slowly, as 86 per cent of the population is expected to be urban by 2050. While the level of urbanization in developed countries is high, the rate of urban population growth is low. The average growth rate between 1975 and 2007 was 0.8 per cent, and this is expected to decline to 0.3 per cent between 2025 and 2050.

Current and expected urban growth in the developed world will be due mainly to international migration from developing or poorer countries – on average, 2.3 million people migrate to developed countries each year.[5] International migration thus accounts for about one third of urban growth in developed countries.[6] This presents new urban planning challenges in developed countries with respect to multicultural urban contexts.

■ Western Europe

Western Europe began experiencing significant levels of urbanization between the mid 18th century and 1914, partly as a consequence of the Industrial Revolution and the growth of colonial empires.[7] Europe witnessed an increase of towns, with at least 100,000 inhabitants from about a dozen at the beginning of the 19th century to more than 150 in 1900.[8] Major factors explaining this growth include the concentration of workers in industrial centres, which were typically raw material sites; the concentration of people in port cities, specializing in the domestic and international distribution of finished goods; and the need for some cities to serve as national political/administrative capitals, and as international financial centres for the new industrial age.[9]

Urban population growth in Western Europe has been declining since 1950, dropping from 1.84 per cent between 1950 and 1975 to 0.54 per cent between 1975 and 2007.[10] International migration from Eastern Europe and developing countries now accounts for a sizeable proportion of population growth in the region.

International migration ... accounts for about one third of urban growth in developed countries

■ North America

Currently, 81 per cent of North Americans reside in urban areas – making it the most urbanized region in the world (see Table 2.1). Urban population growth is, however, declining, as indicated in Figure 2.1. Major cities in the US such as New York, Chicago, Philadelphia and Detroit, experienced an 'urban explosion' in population between 1910 and 1950. However, between 1970 and 2000, many cities experienced population decline. Examples of such cities include St Louis, which lost 59 per cent of its population, as well as Pittsburgh, Cleveland and Detroit, which lost between 48 and 51 per cent of their population.[11]

The exodus from cities, in significant numbers, did not result in a corresponding decline in North America's urban population as there were enough immigrants to replace departing urban residents. However, the exodus resulted in the erosion of the tax base of many cities, given that immigrant incomes are generally low. For example, Los Angeles County lost 1.2 million of its population during the first half of the 1990s. However, while the county received enough international migrants to offset this loss and register a net gain of more than 960,000 people, its municipal revenue suffered a decline.[12] Multicultural composition is now a significant and very visible feature of many North American cities.

■ Oceania and Japan

The pace of urbanization in Oceania declined sharply from 1950 to 1990, and stabilized thereafter (see Figure 2.1). The overall trend of urban growth in Australia and New Zealand has been slow, with nearly half of the cities in both countries growing at less that 1 per cent annually. Currently, the level of urbanization stands at 71 per cent and is projected to reach 76 per cent in 2050. Japan experienced rapid rates of urbanization following the end of World War II. Rates of urbanization in Japan have, like those in Australia and New Zealand, been declining since the 1960s.

International migrants account for a significant proportion of Oceania's urban growth. In 2000, Australia's immigrant stock was 5.8 million, or 18 per cent of the country's population.[13] The contribution made to population growth by immigration (59.5 per cent) in 2008 was higher than that of natural increase (40.5 per cent).[14] An important but often ignored group in Australia's and New Zealand's diverse population consists of the indigenous Australians (or Aboriginal Australians) and the Maori indigenous people, respectively. These groups were confined to the rural areas for a long time. However, since the 1930s, the population of indigenous people in cities has been increasing as cities expand and incorporate previously rural areas or as the indigenous people pursue urban-based opportunities.[15]

■ Transitional countries

Prior to the 1970s, Eastern Europe experienced significant rates of urban growth, with as many as two-thirds of the cities in the region growing at rates exceeding 3 per cent.[16] The 1980s witnessed a rapid deceleration in urban growth. By 2000, the urban growth rate had plummeted to 0 per cent for most cities. More recent accounts reveal that

Eastern European cities have actually been declining during the last half decade.[17] Although emigration to Western Europe has increased significantly since the 1990s, a considerable amount of international migration occurs within the region.

Two related demographic trends are noteworthy in transitional countries.[18] First is the negative population growth rate experience by several cities. It has been observed that 75 per cent of Eastern European cities witnessed a decrease in their population between 1990 and 2005.[19] Figure 2.2 presents a sample of such cities. The decline in urban population was a result of increased migration to the European Union, negative economic trends, rising rates of mortality and decreasing fertility rates. The collapse of the Soviet Union contributed to the decline in urban population and affected many aspects of urban living.[20] The second remarkable demographic trend experienced by the region during the last few decades is the rapidly ageing population, as manifested in the increasing proportion of people aged over 60.[21] These two demographic trends have serious implications for urban planning in transitional countries.

Developing countries

With the exception of the Latin America and Caribbean region, the level of urbanization is much lower in developing countries. About 44 per cent of the population of developing countries lives in urban areas (see Table 2.1). This is expected to grow to 67 per cent by 2050. The average annual growth rate was 3.1 per cent between 1975 and 2007. This is, however, expected to decline to 2.3 per cent for the 2007 to 2025 period, and 1.6 per cent for 2025 to 2050. Developing countries are thus experiencing the fastest rate of urbanization worldwide. This can be attributed to high levels of natural increase and an increase in rural–urban migration.

■ Latin America and the Caribbean

Urbanization has been remarkable in Latin America and the Caribbean, where the urban population increased from 41 per cent in 1950 to 78 per cent in 2007, making it the most urbanized region in the developing world. Between 1950 and 1975, the region's urban growth rate stood at 4.2 per cent. This decreased to 2.6 per cent between 1975 and 2007. A further decrease of 1.4 per cent is envisaged between 2007 and 2025. Most of the urban growth in the region occurred between 1930 and 1970.

Countries within the region differ remarkably in the extent and rate of urbanization. Countries such as Argentina, Chile and Uruguay were already highly urbanized by 1950, while countries such as Cost Rica, Guatemala and Guyana are still less than half urban.[22] While the region's four largest countries – Brazil, Mexico, Colombia and Argentina – are about 80 per cent urbanized, the smaller ones are only about 45 to 60 per cent urbanized.[23] The largest number of international migrants (500,000 – about 6 per cent of the total population) is concentrated in the Dominican Republic – most of the migrants come from its poorer neighbour:

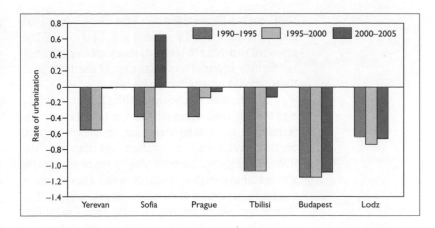

Haiti.[24] In Mexico, international migrants are typically transient since the country serves as a gateway for migrants seeking entry into the US.

■ Asia

Asia is home to approximately 3.7 billion people, or more than 60 per cent of the world's population, and constitutes one of the most rapidly urbanizing regions of the world. The urban population of Asia increased fivefold during the last 27 years: from 237 million (17 per cent) in 1950 to 1.65 billion (41 per cent) in 2007.[25] By 2050, it is expected that more than two-thirds of the population will be living in urban areas. Urban population growth in the region has been declining since the 1990s, from an annual average of 3.13 per cent to the present rate of about 2.5 per cent (see Figure 2.1). The process of urbanization in Asia is driven mainly by rural–urban migration. Urbanization is also linked to economic transition and increasing levels of globalization, as many countries have become the recipients of foreign direct investment, mainly in the form of the outsourcing of manufacturing of consumer goods by parent companies in developed countries.

There are three specific trends that have implications for urban planning in the region.[26] First, an increasing trend towards ageing already marks the demographic profile of some countries. For example, 24 per cent of the Chinese population will be 65 or older by 2050.[27] Second is the accentuation of socio-economic class disparities and the emergence of a strong middle class. This trend has been accompanied by a change in consumption habits, particularly in increasingly wealthy cities such as Shanghai, Shenzhen, Zhuhai and Shantou (China), Mumbai, New Delhi, Jakarta, Bangkok and Seoul. This has resulted in heightened demand for private cars, air-conditioning units, new forms of housing and retail space, among others. All of these pose major challenges, ranging from environmental pollution to urban sprawl and traffic congestion in large urban centres.

■ Sub-Saharan Africa

Sub-Saharan Africa is the least urbanized, but most rapidly urbanizing, region in the world. During the 1950s, only 11 per cent of the region's population lived in urban areas, but this had increased to 35 per cent by 2005.[28] It is projected that by 2030 and 2050, the region will be 48 and 60 per cent urbanized, respectively.[29] Urban growth rates have

Figure 2.2

Shrinking cities in transitional countries

Source: UN, 2008

With the exception of the Latin America and Caribbean region, the level of urbanization is much lower in developing countries been equally high, averaging over 5 per cent between 1955 and 1970, and currently standing at 3.3 per cent. While projected to decline in the years ahead, urban growth will remain high. Levels of urbanization are diverse throughout the region, and so are urban growth rates.

Urbanization in sub-Saharan Africa is driven mainly by high levels of rural–urban migration, natural increase, the reclassification of rural areas, and, in some countries, negative events such as conflicts and disasters. The HIV/AIDS pandemic currently ravaging the region has also affected urban growth in various countries. The epidemic is also robbing countries of their most productive population, contributing to increasing levels of urban poverty and placing a severe burden on the limited health infrastructure within cities.

In many countries in sub-Saharan Africa, rapid urbanization is taking place within the context of economic stagnation or low economic growth, poor agricultural performance, rising unemployment, financially weak municipal authorities incapable of providing basic services, poor governance, and the absence of coherent urban planning policy.[30] Such conditions have led to the widespread urbanization of poverty – typically manifested in the proliferation of slums and informal settlements. These are some of the issues that will dominate the region's urban planning agenda for some years to come.

■ Middle East and North Africa

Urbanization in the Middle East and North Africa is characterized by considerable diversity. For example, while Bahrain, Kuwait and Qatar were already 80 per cent urbanized during the 1970s, most of the other countries were still predominantly rural.[31] Between 1950 and 2000, the region's level of urbanization increased from 27 to 58 per cent.[32] While urban growth is projected to decline, the level of urbanization is expected to reach 70 per cent by 2030.[33]

A prominent demographic feature of the region is the youth bulge: about 65 per cent of the region's population is under the age of 30.[34] While countries within the region have invested more in education than most developing

regions, this has not led to higher levels of youth employment, as youth unemployment currently stands at 25 per cent.[35] Such high levels of unemployment among young people are often associated with various negative consequences, including crime and general delinquency. Another demographic feature relates to international migration. Migrants constitute a significant proportion of the region's population.[36] In Kuwait, Qatar and the United Arab Emirates, international migrants significantly outnumber the local population (see Figure 2.3). This calls for ingenuity in planning for multicultural contexts.

Planning implications of urbanization and demographic trends

There are significant planning implications associated with the urbanization and demographic trends identified in the preceding sections, including the ways in which the urbanization process as a whole is viewed, the rapidly increasing demand for housing and urban services, and the specific and very pressing needs of the youth and the aged.

■ Urbanization as a positive phenomenon

A total of 193,107 new city dwellers are added to the world's urban population daily. This translates to 5 million new urban dwellers per month in the developing world and 500,000 in developed countries.[37] The task of providing for such large numbers is quite daunting. Emphasis on these dynamics has, in some quarters, given rise to the impression that urbanization is a negative process that should, in some way, be curbed or halted. This has not worked. Even the most severe of anti-urbanization measures from an earlier period of Chinese history were not able to stem the flow of people to the cities. In China, despite the enforcement of residency permits (*Hukou*) for those wishing to reside in cities, a floating population of about 80 million to 120 million resided in cities 'illegally' in 2000.[38] Against this background, urbanization is increasingly being seen as a positive phenomenon and a precondition for improving access to services, economic and social opportunities, and a better quality of life for a country's population.

■ Planning for urban growth

Closely related to the foregoing is the imperative that urban planning in developing countries, particularly in Africa and Asia, needs to respond to the rapid pace of urbanization. Urban planning within the context of rapid urbanization is not a luxury, but a necessity.[39] High levels of urban growth in the absence of adequate planning have resulted in spiralling poverty, proliferation of slum and squatter settlements, inadequate water and power supply, and degrading environmental conditions.

Thus, among the most significant challenges of urban planning today and in the next few decades is how to address the housing, water supply and sanitation needs of a rapidly urbanizing population. As will be shown in Chapters 6, 7 and 8, this requires delivery of urban land at scale, linked to networks of public infrastructure, in ways that address both the mitigation and adaptation demands of environmental

There are significant planning implications associated with ... urbanization and demographic trends

---

Figure 2.3

Middle East and North Africa countries with more than 10 per cent immigrant population, 2005

Source: UN, 2006b

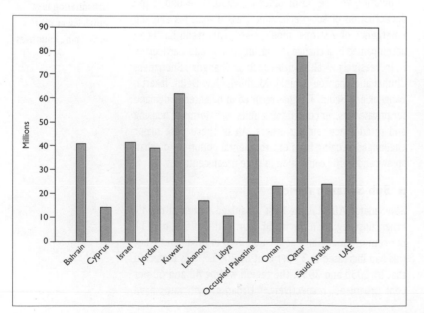

change. Urban planning will also need to devise ways of adequately managing the urban development process as a whole, as unmanaged or chaotic urban growth is a significant obstacle to the sustainable development of towns and cities.

■ Urban planning and the youth

An important demographic trend in developing countries that has implications for urban planning is the relatively large proportion of the youth population. It is predicted that by 2030, 60 per cent of those living in urban areas of developing countries will be under the age of 18.[40] Urban planning will have to pay particular attention to the needs of this segment of the population. This is particularly the case in Africa, the Middle East, South America, Central Asia and the Pacific Islands, where the youth account for a sizeable proportion of the population. While the youth can form the most energetic and innovative segment of the population, if unemployed, they can be a source of social disruption. Planning for a youthful population places particular demands on urban development in terms of the need for education and training facilities, as well as investment in sports and recreational facilities.

■ Planning, urban shrinkage and ageing

The demographic trends with the most far-reaching implications for planning in transitional and developed countries are urban population decline and an ageing population. For transitional countries, these factors present problems of dealing with deteriorating buildings and infrastructure in a context where the local tax base is severely eroded.

In the case of developed countries, international migration renders the features of shrinking cities and ageing less extreme when compared to transitional countries. Nonetheless, industrial restructuring and offshore relocation have left many older industrial and mining towns without a viable economic base. In such settings, planning has to address the challenges of population outflow, abandoned homes and areas, and a declining support base for commercial activities and public facilities.

The planning challenges arising from urban shrinkage in both developed and transitional country contexts range from determining how to meet the cost of underused infrastructure, to identifying alternative uses for abandoned social facilities, huge swathes of vacant housing units, as well as commercial and industrial facilities. Planning for an ageing urban population requires innovation[41] as a rapidly ageing population places increased demand on healthcare, recreation, transportation and other facilities for the elderly.

■ Urban planning and cultural diversity

Increasing waves of international migration have meant that urban areas in all parts of the world are increasingly becoming multicultural. People from different ethnic, cultural and religious backgrounds now live together in cities. If not properly managed, this could trigger anti-immigrant resentment and violence. There is the possibility that cultural diversity could also make participatory processes around planning issues more difficult, as different socio-cultural groups have different expectations and demands of cities

(see Chapter 5). Cultural diversity has important implications for how built environments are managed. Urban planning will need to seek the right balance between cultural groups seeking to preserve their identity in cities and the need to avoid extreme forms of segregation and urban fragmentation. Cultural mix also places new demands on urban planning to mediate between conflicting lifestyles and expressions of culture. Conflicts around religious buildings, burial arrangements, ritual animal slaughter and building aesthetics are issues that urban planners increasingly have to tackle.

CITY SIZE AND SPATIAL FORMS

The world's urban population of 3.3 billion is unevenly distributed among urban settlements of different sizes.[42] 52 per cent of the world's urban population resides in cities and towns of less than 500,000 people. A similar picture is painted for developed and developing countries, as 54 and 51 per cent of their urban population, respectively, live in such cities. Despite the attention they command, megacities – cities with over 10 million people – are home to only 9 per cent of the world's urban population.

As cities experience demographic growth, they tend to expand spatially. One consequence of this process is the merging of previously non-adjoining towns and cities, resulting in metropolitanization in some cases, or uncontrolled peri-urbanization (which often appears chaotic) in others. Metropolitanization entails the conversion of rural land into urban uses and the engulfment of adjacent municipalities by large cities to constitute new metro-areas. Cities such as Bangkok, Beijing, Jakarta, Kolkata, Lagos, Manila and São Paulo have expanded spatially to engulf swathes of neighbouring rural land and previously independent municipalities.[43] The physical expansion of urban areas either through metropolitanization, peri-urbanization or urban sprawl presents a major challenge for urban planning in all parts of the world.

Developed and transitional countries

Collectively, about 63 per cent of the urban population in developed countries is concentrated in intermediate and small-sized cities, with just 9.8 per cent residing in megacities. A common thread running through cities in developed countries is that urban densities have been declining, thus contributing to the problem of urban sprawl. For instance, between 1960 and 1990, Copenhagen's population density declined by 13 per cent, while its area increased by 25 per cent.[44] During the same period, Amsterdam experienced a 10 per cent reduction in its population density, but expanded its land area by more than 60 per cent.

One factor that accounts for urban sprawl in developed countries is economic prosperity. The problem of urban sprawl has been more severe in North America, where, as far back as the early 1900s, a significant segment of the population owned cars. The problem is less severe in Western Europe, where rates of car ownership that had been attained

The demographic trends with the most far-reaching implications for planning in transitional and developed countries are urban population decline and an ageing population

Cultural diversity has important implications for how built environments are managed

in the US during the 1930s were not reached until the 1970s.[45] Another determinant of urban sprawl is government policy, which has been more tolerant in North America, but more stringent in Western Europe. The development of the core areas of many Western European and Japanese cities before the era of the automobile explains their relative compactness, in comparison to Australia, New Zealand, Canada and the US.

■ Western Europe

Western Europe does not have any megacities. Most cities in Western Europe contain between 500,000 and 1 million inhabitants. Despite the absence of megacities and the slow growth of cities and towns, Western Europe is experiencing problems associated with urban expansion. The need to commute – a consequence of sprawl – is a feature of many Western European cities. For example, in Munich, 56 per cent of new commuting between 1998 and 2006 was to jobs outside the Munich metro-area.[46]

The imperatives of globalization have dictated a degree of spatial restructuring, fuelling a trend toward metropolitanization in some areas of the region. In general, economic growth facilitated the development of functional transportation systems, which made suburban living affordable. Furthermore, population growth has intensified the density of some inner-city areas, prompting the well-off to relocate to suburbs. Consequently, countries or regions such as Belgium, The Netherlands, eastern, southern and western Germany, northern Italy, the Paris region, Ireland, Portugal and the Madrid region have significant sprawl problems.[47] The main adverse effects of urban sprawl have been air pollution, traffic congestion and inefficient use of land.

■ North America

In North America, only two cities – New York and Los Angeles – qualify as megacities. These cities contain about 12 per cent of the urban population of the US. A greater proportion of the urban population resides in agglomerations of less than 5 million people, with small-sized cities of less that 500,000 accounting for 37 per cent of the urban population (see Figure 2.4). A major feature of North American cities is urban sprawl, which has been attributed to permissive land-use planning and the growth of affluent households. By 2000, urban sprawl was increasing at twice the rate of urban population growth in the US, with Las Vegas being the fastest growing metropolitan area.[48] Canada currently has three of the world's ten urban areas with the most extensive sprawl – Calgary, Vancouver and Toronto.[49]

Urban sprawl has contributed to the high number of cars, distances travelled, length of paved roads, fuel consumption and alteration of ecological structures in North America over the past two decades.[50] Urban sprawl also entails territorial expansion through annexation. For instance, in 1982, the city of Edmonton in Canada annexed a number of adjacent jurisdictions, thereby doubling its land area and increasing its population by 100,000.[51] The challenge for urban planning is complicated by the fact that some of the factors, such as population growth, that were previously deemed to cause sprawl now seem insignificant.[52] For example, several US cities – Akron, Cincinnati and Cleveland – lost population but grew spatially between 1970 and 1990.

■ Oceania and Japan

Australia has no city of more than 5 million inhabitants. The largest city – Sydney – has a population of 4.3 million people.[53] Japan is the only country in the region with megacities: Tokyo (35.7 million) and Osaka (11.3 million). The blueprint that guided modern city development in Australia, New Zealand and Japan after World War II adhered more to North American, as opposed to Western European, principles of urban design. Throughout the region, urban sprawl has become a major planning concern, as traffic congestion and pollution have worsened. In New Zealand, cities are expanding and blurring urban–rural boundaries as the population living in peri-urban areas grows. This tends to complicate municipal governance.[54] In Australia, annexation and consolidation are resulting in the 'disappearing towns syndrome'.[55] For example, Hurstbridge, Bellbowie, Adinga Beach and Golden Bay-Singleton disappeared and became parts of Melbourne, Brisbane, Adelaide and Mandurah, respectively.[56]

■ Transitional countries

The transitional countries have only one megacity – Moscow (10.4 million) – and no urban agglomeration with a population between 5 million and 10 million. St Petersburg, Russia, was in this category up until 1995, but became a casualty of the shrinking city syndrome. Moscow is dominant and constitutes a primate city in the region. The concentration of political and economic power in this city and, to some extent, in Leningrad during the Soviet era prevented metropolitanization.[57]

The centralized decision-making structure permitted the state to establish compact, highly dense cities with functional public transport systems.[58] The absence of real estate markets ensured the allocation of land use by the state instead of free market mechanisms. Collectively, these features produced densely packed and highly regulated cities

Despite the absence of megacities and the slow growth of cities and towns, Western Europe is experiencing problems associated with urban expansion

A major feature of North American cities is urban sprawl, which has been attributed to permissive land-use planning and the growth of affluent households

Figure 2.4

Distribution of urban population by city size in North America

Source: UN, 2008, p229

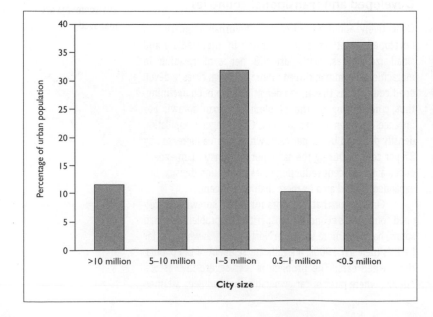

with dominant centres, public housing, retail shopping facilities, and an abundance of recreational facilities.[59] The political and economic reforms initiated during the 1990s are gradually altering this structure in several ways.[60] First is the displacement of low-income families and lower-level retail business from the inner city to low-cost neighbourhoods on the urban fringes. Second is the trend towards suburbanization and sprawl, as private investors develop exclusive high-income suburban enclaves. The reforms have also led to the privatization of public housing, and this has heightened socio-spatial stratification of urban space.

Developing countries

While developing countries contain 14 of the world's 19 megacities, only 8.4 per cent of their urban population reside in such cities.[61] A greater proportion of the urban population (61.4 per cent) lives in cities of less than 1 million inhabitants. Developing countries are also experiencing problems related to peri-urbanization. In particular, peri-urbanization has contributed to the escalation of infrastructure and service delivery costs. Core areas of cities in developing countries have been decreasing demographically while their suburbs continue to expand spatially.[62] The case of Mexico City, whose core wards have lost 45 per cent of their population as the suburbs have increased since the 1960s, is illustrative. Similar phenomena have been occurring in Mumbai, Buenos Aires, Seoul and Manila since 1981.[63]

■ Latin America and the Caribbean

A major feature of Latin American urbanization is the gigantic nature of cities in the region.[64] The region has four of the world's largest megacities – Mexico City, São Paulo, Buenos Aires and Rio de Janeiro – which collectively accommodate 14.1 per cent of the region's urban population (see Figure 2.5). Despite the relatively high concentration of the region's urban population in megacities and the high level of urban primacy, 59 per cent of the urban population reside in cities of less than 1 million inhabitants (see Figure 2.5). Cities in this category have experienced remarkable growth. For instance, cities of less than 500,000 inhabitants not only recorded the fastest urban growth in the region (2.6 per cent per year), but were the destinations of nearly half of all new urban residents from 1990 to 2000.[65]

A noticeable feature of the region's urban agglomerations is that they have expanded beyond their established boundaries, sometimes into different provinces.[66] For example, Mexico City has encroached upon municipalities in two states, while Buenos Aires covers 30 different municipalities. Another phenomenon with implications for municipal governance and planning in the region is the internal structure of urban areas. There has been an increasing relocation of population, industries and services from city centres to the periphery since the 1990s.[67] This has contributed to low-density suburban growth, which, in turn, has escalated the cost of public infrastructure provision and service delivery.

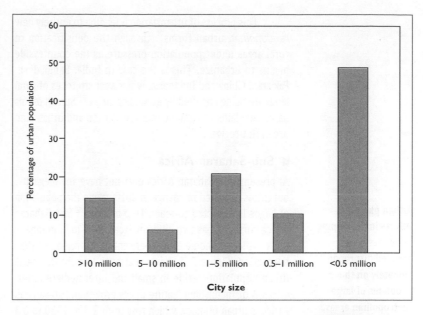

■ Asia

Asia is the region with the most megacities (eight if Japan is excluded and ten if included). Despite this, 60 per cent of the region's urban population live in cities of less than 1 million people, while 10 per cent reside in megacities (see Figure 2.6). What this portends is a need for the urban planning agenda within the region to focus on the key issues relating to small- and medium-sized cities, in addition to those of megacities.

A significant trend in Asia is that urbanization is occurring beyond metropolitan borders, leading to the formation of enormously extended mega-urban regions that have developed along infrastructure corridors radiating over long distances from core cities.[68] These include the Shanghai mega-urban region, occupying an area of over 6340 square kilometres; the Beijing mega-urban region, extending over 16,870 square kilometres; and the Jakarta mega-urban region, which occupies an area of 7500 square kilometres.[69] These new spatial configurations have created complex planning and governance problems within the region.

Figure 2.5

Distribution of urban population by city size in Latin America and the Caribbean

Source: UN, 2008, p227

Figure 2.6

Distribution of urban population by city size in Asia

Source: UN, 2008, p224

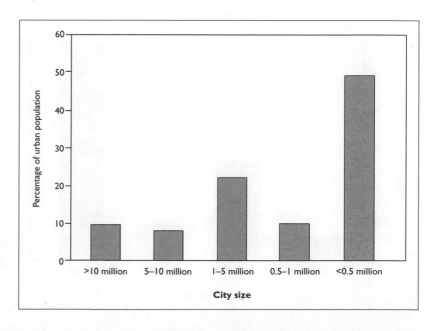

This process of urbanization is leading to entirely new *ruralopolitan* urban forms[70] through the densification of rural areas under population pressure as the countryside begins to urbanize. This is the case in India, Bangladesh, Pakistan, China and Indonesia, where vast stretches of rural lands are being engulfed by expanding cities.[71] Sprawl of this nature explains the unique mixture of rural and urban land use in this region.

■ Sub-Saharan Africa

At present, sub-Saharan Africa does not have any megacity; but this is expected to change in 2010, when the population of Lagos is expected to reach 10.6 million.[72] Sub-Saharan Africa currently has two cities in excess of 5 million inhabitants, which are home to 5.9 per cent of the region's urban population. Figure 2.7 shows that over two-thirds of the urban population reside in small and intermediate cities.

A distinguishing feature in city growth in sub-Saharan Africa is urban primacy, which rose from 2.8 in 1950 to 6.3 in 2000.[73] This is indicative of the disproportionate concentration of people, activities, investment and resources in the largest city of a country, to the detriment of other towns and cities. Urban primacy poses complex planning challenges, particularly because of its tendency to contribute to problems such as urban sprawl, congestion and environmental degradation.

The second feature is towards increasing levels of peri-urbanization. Many large cities are spreading out at a remarkable pace and, in the process, are engulfing surrounding rural land and adjacent towns, leading to continuous belts of settlements. This process is largely informal and is driven by the efforts of low-income households to secure land that is affordable and in a reasonable location. This process has led to the emergence of new settlement forms, which neither the existing structures of government or current regulatory frameworks are able to respond to effectively. It is these sprawling urban peripheries, almost entirely un-serviced and unregulated, that make up the bulk of unregulated settlements. It is also in these areas that most urban growth is taking place.

■ Middle East and North Africa

The Middle East and North Africa contain two megacities – Cairo and Istanbul – with 11.9 million and 10.1 million inhabitants, respectively. In 2000, the region had 16 cities with a population of over 1 million people, which increased to 19 in 2005. It is projected that the region will contain at least 24 cities with more than 1 million inhabitants by 2010, and at least 6 cities with a minimum of 5 million inhabitants by 2015.[74] As part of what has come to be known as 'oil urbanization', which started in the 1950s, previously traditional human settlements have been dramatically transformed. In some cases, the transformation has entailed the private development of public urban places,[75] producing, in the process, a variety of novel urban forms. In the United Arab Emirates, whole cities have been developed on artificial islands configured in the likeness of palm trees and the world map. In other cases, the process has been rather spontaneous, as in metro-Cairo, Rabat and Sana'a, where traditional walled settlements coexist with modern districts and squatter settlements.

Rapid urban growth has produced large urban agglomerations and metropolises.[76] For example, Mecca, Jeddah and Riyadh have developed into urban agglomerations with populations of between 1 million and 5 million residents. Similarly, the cities of Izmit (0.22 million) and Bursa (1.2 million) are gradually becoming part of a large metro-area around Istanbul. In the case of Cairo and Alexandria, which are 200km apart, metropolitan growth of both cities is resulting in outward sprawl from their respective centres. If this continues, there is a real possibility that the two cities will merge in the foreseeable future to constitute a single gigantic Nile metropolis.[77]

Planning implications of city size and spatial form

The main planning implications associated with the size and spatial structure of cities discussed in the preceding sections include the need to pay greater attention to small- and medium-sized cities; the necessity of arresting or directing the spatial expansion of cities, especially sprawl and unplanned peri-urbanization; and the need to recognize and build upon urban informality.

■ Small and intermediate urban centres

The discussion in the preceding section shows that more than half of the urban population in both developed and developing countries live in cities of less than 500,000 inhabitants. In addition, small and medium cities are urbanizing faster than the large metropolises. Despite the demographic importance and potential role of such cities, urban planning efforts in developing countries have focused disproportionately on the problems of large metropolitan areas, thereby further fuelling the problem of urban primacy. If small and medium cities are to fulfil their potential, then they should form part of the urban planning agenda for developing countries in the 21st century. Specific areas where urban planning could play a major role could include making such cities more attractive for its inhabitants and

Urban planning efforts in developing countries have focused disproportionately on the problems of large metropolitan areas, thereby further fuelling the problem of urban primacy

Figure 2.7

Distribution of urban population by city size in sub-Saharan Africa

Source: UN, 2008, p222

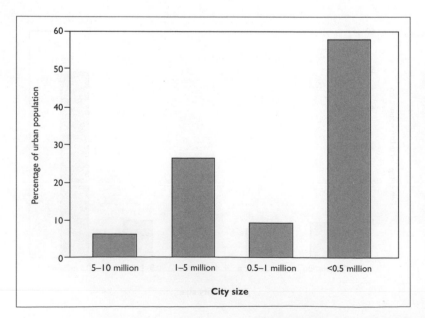

investors[78] by improving transport, communication and other forms of infrastructure, as well as improving municipal governance, including decentralization and strengthening of local democracy and civil society.

■ Planning and urban expansion

The spatial expansion of cities is an inevitable consequence of urban population growth. Some forms of spatial expansion, especially urban sprawl, invariably lead to the inefficient utilization of scarce resources, particularly land and energy. The challenge for planning is not to prevent urban growth, but to devise mechanisms for directing or controlling the timing, rate and location of such growth. Urban sprawl – whether suburbanization in North America, peri-urbanization in Africa or metropolitanization in Asia and Latin America – are all products of either inappropriate or ineffective planning regulations.

Urban agglomerations provide opportunities for socio-economic development and for maximizing the utility of scarce resources through economies of scale. However, these opportunities are often outweighed by the problems arising from the unplanned nature of contemporary urbanization, especially in developing countries. Under these circumstances, planning is faced with the challenge of addressing the many social, economic and physical problems, including upgrading of informal peri-urban settlements, provision of public transport and other trunk infrastructure, as well as effective planning and governance in cooperation with adjoining local authorities and in the context of different land tenure systems. These challenges are addressed in Chapters 6, 7 and 8.

■ Planning and urban informality

A key issue that 21st-century urban planning in developing countries will have to contend with is the increasing levels of informality associated with contemporary urban patterns. The process of city growth in many developing countries is taking on forms that are largely informal. Various key aspects of urban development – extensive peri-urban development of informal settlements, housing construction and the allocation of land, and provision of urban services – are informal. On the other hand, urban planning takes place within the realm of the formal sector and, in most countries, only caters for a small segment of the urban population. This creates a huge gap between actual urbanization outcomes and the orderly ideals prescribed by conventional urban planning.

Informality is, therefore, a reality confronting cities in developing countries, and efforts to formalize the informal sector have largely been unsuccessful. Formalization processes often have destroyed livelihoods and shelter, and have exacerbated exclusion, marginalization and poverty in developing world cities. For urban planning in developing countries to be relevant and serve the greater good, it must identify innovative ways of dealing with informality, given that the informal is often the norm rather than the exception. The issue of urban informality is discussed in greater detail in Chapter 7.

URBAN ECONOMIC CONTEXTS

Global urbanization is taking place within the context of the worst economic recession since 1945. The year 2008 witnessed the virtual collapse of the global financial system. Although the current economic crisis had its roots in the subprime mortgage markets in the US, the damage quickly spread to financial institutions in other developed countries.[79] By October 2008, the crisis had erased around US$25 trillion from the value of stock markets globally.[80]

The current global recession has several implications for urban areas. First, global economic growth is expected to shrink by 1.3 per cent in 2009.[81] This implies that less funding will be available for urban development and capital projects. Second, higher levels of unemployment are envisaged in various sectors of the economy, but particularly in finance, construction, automotive and manufacturing for export industries, as well as in the tourism, services and real estate sectors – all of which are closely associated with the economic well-being of cities and towns. The global unemployment rate for 2008 was 6 per cent, up from 5.7 per cent in 2007. This is expected to increase to 7.1 per cent in 2009.[82] Third, following the increase in the rate of unemployment, poverty levels are expected to rise and will be compounded by rising food prices. Indeed, the World Bank estimates that the number of poor people increased by between 130 million and 150 million on account of the increase in food prices in 2008.[83] Furthermore, the global economic crisis could exacerbate the rise in income inequality being witnessed in many parts the world.

Developed and transitional countries

Although a far cry from the conditions that existed during the Industrial Revolution, problems such as poverty, homelessness, crime, and other social pathologies are re-emerging in developed countries.[84] Moreover, the effects of globalization have varied remarkably. Some cities have benefited from their role as major financial hubs in a global economy. Others have suffered gravely following the late 20th century de-industrialization of North America and Europe. In addition, developed countries are suffering their worst recession since World War II, as economic growth is expected to contract by 3.8 per cent in 2009.[85] The worsening economy has seen unemployment in many developed countries rise to its highest level in recent times, with very negative consequences on the economies of urban areas.

Income inequality within developed countries has been widespread and significant since the mid 1980s.[86] This has affected most countries, with large increases observed in Canada and Germany. Consequently, social exclusion, urban segregation and persistent pockets of destitution and poverty are increasingly common in cities of developed countries.

■ Western Europe

Urbanization in Western Europe, which is driven mainly by international migration, is occurring within the context of

Urban planning in developing countries will have to contend with the increasing levels of informality associated with contemporary urban patterns

The current global recession has several implications for urban areas

deep economic recession characterized by negative economic growth, rising unemployment and stringent financial conditions. Economic growth within the region is expected to contract by 4.2 per cent in 2009, with Germany, Italy and the UK experiencing negative growth rates of 5.6, 4.4 and 4.1 per cent, respectively.[87] The contraction in economic growth will have far-reaching implications for urban areas. The unemployment rate for the Euro area is predicted to reach 10.1 per cent in 2009, and 11.7 per cent in 2010.[88] For many migrants from developing and transitional countries who reside in the region, the rising levels of unemployment will affect their ability to make remittances to their home countries.

While the levels of inequality across Western Europe have been widening since the 1980s, the region remains the most egalitarian in the world. The average Gini coefficient for Western Europe is 0.30, indicating universal access to public goods and services. As shown in Figure 2.8, countries such as Demark, Sweden, Luxembourg, Austria, Finland, The Netherlands and Belgium have the lowest levels of inequality, indicative of the effectiveness of regulatory, distributive and redistributive capacity of the national and local welfare states.[89] Countries with high levels of inequality include Portugal, the UK, Italy, Ireland, Greece and Spain.

■ North America

Following the recent financial crisis in the housing and banking sectors, the US economy has entered its deepest recession since the Great Depression. In Canada, the economic downturn, which commenced in 2007, turned into a full-fledged recession towards the end of 2008.[90] The economic recession in both countries will affect urban areas in many ways. Economic growth in 2009 is expected to decline by 2.8 and 2.5 per cent in the US and Canada, respectively[91] and, with urban areas contributing disproportionately to gross domestic product (GDP), cities are expected to be hardest hit. For instance, investment in urban housing, which constitutes a mainstay of the US economy, had fallen by 20 per cent at the end of 2008.[92] In addition, house prices had dropped by 19 per cent at the end of March 2009.

In the US, unemployment is rising at an accelerating pace. A total of 633,000 jobs were lost in March 2009, by which time the unemployment rate had reached 8.5 per cent.[93] Since December 2007, 5.1 million jobs have been lost, with 3.3 million or approximately two-thirds of this loss occurring between October 2008 and March 2009. Unemployment rates are higher among minority groups: blacks (13.3 per cent) and Hispanics (11.4 per cent), as compared to whites (7.9 per cent).[94] Unemployment is also significantly higher among teenagers of working age (21.7 per cent). With rising unemployment, an increasing number of urban households are unable to meet their mortgage commitments. For instance, close to 12 per cent of US mortgages were in arrears or in foreclosure by the end of 2008,[95] thus, exacerbating the problem of homelessness and destitution in urban areas.

The US has one of the highest levels of income inequality among developed countries. Large metropolitan areas such as Atlanta, New Orleans, Washington, DC, Miami and New York experience the highest levels of inequality, similar to those of developing country cities such as Abidjan, Nairobi, Buenos Aires and Santiago – with Gini coefficients of around 0.50.[96] Canada's level of inequality is moderate, with a Gini coefficient of 0.32.[97] Inequalities are, however, increasing in most urban areas. Race is an important determinant of the level of inequality in North America, with black and Hispanic households often earning less than white households and residing in inner-core, squalid, run-down and segregated neighbourhoods characterized by higher levels of unemployment, crime and other social pathologies.

■ Oceania and Japan

Two major outcomes of the global economic crisis in this region are the decline in economic growth and rising levels of unemployment, both of which have implications for urban areas. Economic growth in Japan, Australia and New Zealand is expected to contract by 6.2, 1.4 and 2.0 per cent, respectively, in 2009.[98] The effects of rising levels of unemployment occasioned by the slump in the mining industry on the sustainability of the livelihoods of urban communities in Australia are vividly described in Box 2.1.

While the levels of inequality across Western Europe have been widening, the region remains the most egalitarian in the world

The US has one of the highest levels of income inequality among developed countries

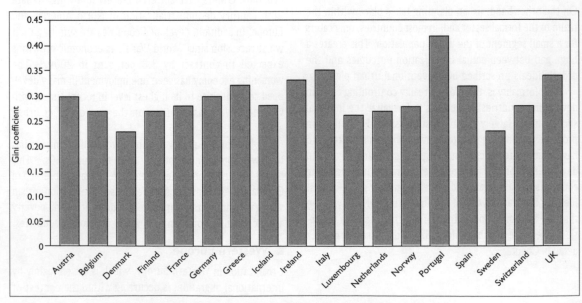

Figure 2.8

Gini coefficient of income inequality in Western Europe, mid 2000s

Source: OECD, 2008, p51

The region is also characterized by economic disparities. The Gini coefficient for urban areas in Australia ranges from 0.31 in small cities to 0.33 in major cities.[99] In New Zealand, the Gini coefficient is 0.34[100] and 0.33 in Tokyo.[101] Economic disparities in Oceania vary remarkably by race. For instance, in New Zealand, the unemployment rate for the indigenous Maori population was 9.6 per cent in 2008, which is twice the national average and three times the rate for the white population.[102] Some of the implications of this are spatially manifested. In New Zealand, urban areas are characterized by residential segregation, resulting in the confinement of the Maori to low-income neighbourhoods.[103] In Australia, while migrants from Asia and Africa are increasingly becoming victims of socio-economic discrimination, Aboriginals constitute the traditional victims of marginalization since they have limited access to land, housing and employment.[104]

■ Transitional countries

The period of transition from centrally planned to market-based economies has been associated with dramatic increase in the levels of poverty, unemployment and inequality within former communist countries.[105] Unemployment rates in the region peaked in the mid and late 1990s, hitting the urban areas particularly hard. With the start of the economic recovery, unemployment rates began to decline in 2000. These gains could be eroded by the current global economic crisis. For instance, in the Commonwealth of Independent States and Baltic states, economic growth is expected to shrink by 5.1 and 10.6 per cent, respectively, in 2009. Negative GDP growths are anticipated for Russia, Ukraine, Lithuania and Latvia.[106] This has major implications for state-funded urban development programmes in these countries. Unemployment across the region is also on the rise. In Latvia and Lithuania, the unemployment rate for February 2009 was 14.4 and 13.7 per cent, respectively.[107] With an unemployment rate of 8.1 per cent in January 2009, Russia is facing its highest rate since March 2005.[108] Such high levels of unemployment will definitely exacerbate urban poverty in these countries.

At the beginning of the millennium, the share of residents living below nationally established poverty lines in Moldova, Armenia, Georgia and the Kyrgyz Republic included nearly half of their population. Moreover, in some countries of the former Soviet Union and former Yugoslavia, there is a trend towards unprecedented levels of inequality, continuously declining living standards and a sharp increase in the number of households living in slum conditions.[109] The processes of rising income differentiation within urban areas are generating a mosaic pattern of spatial inequality, as some communities have begun to enjoy significant improvements in the quality of their built environment while others are experiencing economic, social and environmental decline.

Developing countries

Rapid urban growth in developing countries, particularly in Africa and Asia, will be taking place within a context of a

---

Box 2.1 Australia hit hard by mining slump

Few Australians had even heard of Ravensthorpe until two months ago, but now it is synonymous with the end of the country's resources boom. In January, the Anglo-Australian mining giant BHP Billiton announced the closure of its nickel mine. Remarkably, it had only been operational for eight months. BHP Billiton blamed the slump in global commodities prices. The price of nickel, which is used to make stainless steel, has nose-dived since its high in 2007. Then it commanded a price of AU$51,000 per tonne. Now it can be bought for one fifth (AU$10,200) of that amount. The closure of Raventhorpe has meant 1800 jobs losses among BHP staff and contractors.

But its knock-on effects on the local communities are incalculable. The nearest towns are Ravensthorpe itself, a once-tranquil country town, and the unfortunately named Hopetoun on the coast. Both communities bought the BHP Billiton pitch hoping that the mine would generate profits for at least the next 25 years. They had planned and, more importantly, invested accordingly. New suburbs sprung up, their cul-de-sacs lined with expensive homes, as well as boutique cafés, shops, a state-of-the-art car wash, a pharmacy, wind turbines to provide electricity, and a brand, spanking new school.

But with no alternative employment in these towns, people drawn here by the promise of prosperity are now trying to flee. As a result, property prices have fallen by up to 50 per cent and their hard-pressed owners are saddled with debts. Some businesses have reported a 70 per cent drop in turnover, and others have shut down. The number of pupils at the new school is expected to drop from 195 to 50.

We have heard a lot in recent months about toxic assets. Ravensthorpe and Hopetoun are in danger of becoming toxic communities. The entire community is now going to be dismantled. Hopetoun is in danger of becoming a ghost town, with phantom suburbs. Ravensthorpe is in a remote corner of a remote country; but neither distance nor its abundant resources have offered it any protection from the global downturn.

Source: Bryant, 2009

---

relatively weakened economy. Although the global economic crisis has its roots in developed countries, its impacts will be felt upon the urban economies of developing countries in various ways. To start with, economic growth in developing countries is expected to fall from 6.1 per cent in 2008 to 1.6 per cent in 2009.[110] Apart from exacerbating unemployment and poverty, the slump in economic growth could severely reduce the availability of financial resources for state-initiated urban development programmes. In this regard, slum upgrading and prevention programmes, urban regeneration and poverty reduction initiatives, which traditionally rank low on the priority lists of many developing countries even in times of relative economic prosperity, will be affected. The decline in economic growth could affect the ability of developing countries to achieve the Millennium Development Goals (MDGs) and to address pressing environmental issues such as climate change. Economic recession in developed countries may affect the flow of foreign direct investment, official development assistance and remittances to developing countries.

Urbanization in developing countries is taking place amid increasing levels of urban poverty. Table 2.2 shows that the number of people below the US$1 per day extreme poverty line in urban areas of developing countries increased from 236 million in 1993 to 283 million in 2002. The urban poverty rate has been relatively stagnant over time: declining from 13.5 to 12.8 per cent between the two periods (see Table 2.2). However, if China is excluded, the incidence of urban poverty for the developing countries increases from

Rapid urban growth in developing countries will be taking place within a context of a relatively weakened economy

The decline in economic growth could affect the ability of developing countries to achieve the MDGs and to address pressing environmental issues such as climate change

Table 2.2

Urban poverty measures for 1993 and 2002 using the US$1 per day poverty line

Region	Number of poor (millions)		Percentage below the poverty line		Urban share of the poor (%)	Urban share of population (%)
	Urban	Total	Urban	Total		
1993						
East Asia Pacific	28.71	435.88	5.55	26.17	6.59	31.09
China	10.98	342.36	3.33	29.05	3.21	29.77
Eastern Europe and Central Asia	6.12	12.49	2.06	2.65	48.98	63.06
Latin America and the Caribbean	26.07	54.62	7.82	11.85	47.73	72.33
Middle East and North Africa	0.77	5.07	0.61	2.01	15.29	52.82
South Asia	107.48	490.78	35.30	41.43	21.90	25.70
India	94.28	418.83	40.06	46.57	22.51	26.17
Sub-Saharan Africa	66.42	273.15	40.21	49.24	24.32	29.78
Total	235.58	1271.99	13.50	27.78	18.52	38.12
Total excluding China	224.60	929.63	15.86	27.34	24.16	41.64
2002						
East Asia Pacific	16.27	239.50	2.28	13.03	6.79	38.79
China	4.00	179.01	0.80	13.98	2.24	37.68
Eastern Europe and Central Asia	2.48	7.42	0.83	1.57	33.40	63.45
Latin America and the Caribbean	38.33	64.93	9.49	12.26	59.03	76.24
Middle East and North Africa	1.21	6.09	0.75	2.11	19.87	55.75
South Asia	125.40	519.74	32.21	37.15	24.13	27.83
India	106.64	423.06	36.20	40.34	25.21	28.09
Sub-Saharan Africa	98.84	327.61	40.38	47.17	30.17	35.24
Total	282.52	1165.29	12.78	22.31	24.24	42.34
Total excluding China	278.52	986.28	16.28	25.02	28.24	43.40

Source: Chen and Ravallion, 2007, p1676

15.9 per cent in 1993 to 16.3 per cent in 2002. A noticeable feature is that urban poverty is increasing faster than national poverty. Indeed, the share of urban poverty in relation to national poverty increased from 19 per cent in 1993 to 25 per cent in 2002. Table 2.2 broadly shows that the urban share of poverty increases with increasing levels of urbanization. This has been referred to as the *urbanization of poverty*, in which the concentration of poverty moves from rural areas to urban centres.[111]

One of the spatial manifestations of urban poverty is the proliferation of slums. Table 2.3 provides an overview of the extent of slums by region in 2005. Over one third (37 per cent) of the urban population in developing countries live in slums or housing conditions that suffer from one or more of the following: lack of access to improved water; lack of access to sanitation; non-durable housing; insufficient living area; and insecurity of tenure. The regional pattern in the prevalence of slums to a large extent reflects the nature of access to basic services such as water and sanitation. From the foregoing, it is clear that issues of urban poverty and slums should constitute a major agenda for urban planning in developing countries.

A major urban economic trend in the developing world is increasing inequality. Between 1990 and 2004, the share of income by the poorest one fifth of the population dropped from 4.6 to 3.9 per cent.[112] Regionally, the highest levels of inequality are in Africa and Latin America, with many countries and cities experiencing widening disparities between the rich and the poor. In both regions, the poorest 20 per cent of the population consume just 3 per cent of national consumption.[113] Inequalities are also observable at the city level.

■ Latin America and the Caribbean

Following the ongoing economic crisis, and close links to the US economy, economic growth in Latin America and the Caribbean is expected to contract by 1.5 per cent in 2009.[114] For a region that is highly urbanized and grappling with a host of urban problems – crime and violence, inequality and poverty – the global economic crisis presents major challenges. The unemployment rate for the region is expected to increase from 7.2 per cent in 2008 to between 7.6 and 8.3 per cent in 2009.[115] These are likely to be conservative estimates, given that unemployment statistics in developing countries often underestimate the problem. The region already experiences high levels of youth unemployment – a factor associated with the proliferation of youth gangs and high rates of urban crime and violence. Therefore, the anticipated increase in unemployment is also likely to aggravate existing levels of crime and violence.

Latin America and the Caribbean is the only region in the developing world where a greater proportion of poor

A major urban economic trend in the developing world is increasing inequality

Table 2.3

Proportion of urban population living in slums, 2005

Major region	Urban population (thousands)	Number of slum dwellers (thousands)	Percentage of urban population living in slums
North Africa	82,809	12,003	14.5
Sub-Saharan Africa	264,355	164,531	62.2
Latin America and the Caribbean	434,432	117,439	27.0
Eastern Asia	593,301	216,436	36.5
Southern Asia	468,668	201,185	42.9
South-Eastern Asia	243,724	67,074	27.5
Western Asia	130,368	31,254	24.0
Oceania	2153	519	24.1
Total developing countries	2,219,811	810,441	36.5

Source: UN-Habitat (2008b, p90)

people live in urban areas. Table 2.2 shows that by 2002, the urban share of the poor had increased to 59 per cent from 48 per cent in 1993.[116] In Latin America and the Caribbean, 27 per cent of the urban population reside in slums – making it one of the regions with the lowest incidence. This is a reflection of the proactive steps taken by various governments since the 1980s to address the problem of slums and squatter settlements.

Latin America and the Caribbean region is characterized by high levels of inequality. The richest 5 per cent of the population receive 25 per cent of the regional income, while the poorest 30 per cent receive 7.5 per cent.[117] The average Gini coefficient for the region is well above 0.50. Table 2.4 shows that the region's income inequality has increased over the last two decades. The disparities in income inequality are also reflected in urban areas (see Figure 2.9). The cities with the highest levels of inequality are to be found mainly in Brazil: Goiania, Brasilia, Belo Horizonte, Fortaleza and São Paulo, where the Gini coefficient is above 0.60. Other cities with relatively high levels of inequality include Bogotá, Rio de Janeiro, Curitiba, Buenos Aires and Catamarca (Argentina), Santiago, Quito, Guatemala and Mexico City. Relatively low levels of inequality are found in Caracas, Montevideo and Guadalajara, where the Gini coefficient was below 0.45 in 2002.[118] Inequality often divides cities spatially along socio-economic, ethnic or racial lines. For instance, in Cayenne, the capital of French Guiana, residents are spatially distributed along ethnic lines: the wealthy, mainly French, residents live in exclusive communities, while the poor, mainly immigrants from Brazil, Suriname, as well as indigenous South Americans, are crowded in shanty-towns dotted on the city's fringes.[119]

■ Asia

Being the second fastest urbanizing region after Africa, and home to 50 per cent of the world's urban population, the current economic crisis will have far-reaching implications for urban living in Asia. The gains made in poverty reduction and economic growth within the last two decades risk being eroded by the current global recession. With the contraction in global demand for exports, and external financial constraints, economic growth in Asia is expected to decline from 6.8 per cent in 2008 to 3.3 per cent in 2009.[120] The recession will be felt most in the newly industrialized economies, where negative growth rates have been predicted. The slump in economic growth is expected to negatively impact upon government revenue, which forms the basis for expenditure on urban development and capital projects.

The global recession will lead to a massive loss of jobs in urban areas. About 23 million people in the region are expected to lose their jobs in 2009 – resulting in an unemployment rate of 5.4 per cent, or 113 million jobless people.[121] This is aptly demonstrated in China, where the reduced demand for exports led to the closure of about 7000 factories

Countries	Early 1990s	Mid 1990s	Early 2000s	Change (%)
Argentina	0.426	0.458	0.504	7.7
Bolivia	0.543	0.558	0.559	1.6
Brazil	0.595	0.583	0.572	-2.3
Chile	0.547	0.549	0.561	1.4
Colombia	0.559	0.543	0.558	-0.1
Costa Rica	0.439	0.440	0.446	0.8
El Salvador	0.505	0.494	0.518	1.3
Honduras	0.556	0.541	0.530	-2.6
Jamaica	0.496	0.515	0.490	-0.6
Mexico	0.539	0.525	0.527	-1.2
Nicaragua	0.542	-	0.541	-0.1
Panama	0.547	0.540	0.544	-0.3
Peru	0.457	0.464	0.477	2.0
Uruguay	0.408	0.409	0.425	1.7
Venezuela	0.417	0.445	0.455	3.8
Average (non-weighted)	0.505	0.507	0.514	0.9
Average (weighted)	0.519	0.512	0.514	-0.4

Source: Gasparini, 2003

Table 2.4

Gini coefficients trends for selected countries in the Latin America and the Caribbean region

The current economic crisis will have far-reaching implications for urban living in Asia

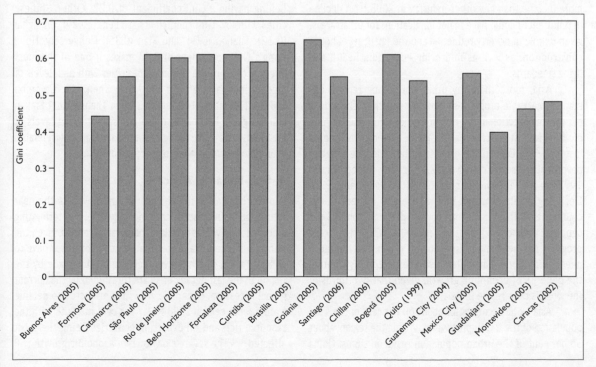

Figure 2.9

Gini coefficients for selected cities in Latin America

Source: UN-Habitat, 2008b, p69

Figure 2.10

Gini coefficients for selected cities in Asia

Source: UN-Habitat, 2008b, p75

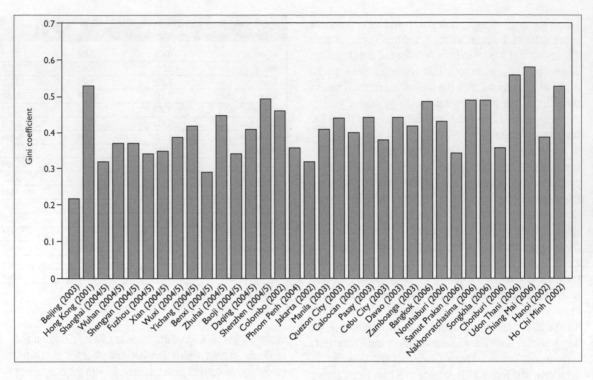

in the southern special economic zone of Shenzhen and Guangdong in 2008, leading to millions of migrant workers being laid off.[122] The return of these workers and their families to the countryside has served to exacerbate poverty, unemployment and underemployment in the rural areas.

Asia will be hard hit by a reduction in the flow of remittances on account of the global recession. Countries such as India, China, the Philippines, Bangladesh and Pakistan are among the top ten remittance-recipient countries, receiving US$30 billion, US$27 billion, US$18.7 billion, US$8.9 billion and US$7.1 billion, respectively, in 2008.[123] In these countries, remittances account for the largest source of external income, after foreign direct investment. In Bangladesh for instance, remittances generated more income than any other industry in 2008.[124] A decline in remittances could have major implications for urban areas, given its role in poverty reduction and the financing of house construction, as well as improving education, health and living standards.

Asia, more than any other developing region, has made remarkable progress in poverty reduction. The extent of poverty reduction in the region has been described as 'one of the largest decreases in mass poverty in human history'.[125] In East and Central Asia, the incidence of urban poverty decreased from 5.6 and 2.1 per cent, respectively, in 1993, to 2.3 and 0.8 per cent in 2002 (see Table 2.2). Declining levels of urban poverty are also evident at the country level. In China, urban poverty declined from 3.3 per cent in 1993 to 0.81 per cent in 2002. While significant progress has been made in reducing urban poverty, more needs to be done, particularly with respect to distributing the benefits of economic growth, given that two-thirds of the world's poor reside in Asia.[126]

Asia alone accounts for about 60 per cent of the slum population of the developing world. Within the region, about 36 per cent of the urban population reside in slums. China

and India account for about 55 per cent of the region's slum population. The countries with high incidence of slums include Afghanistan, Lao PDR, Cambodia, Bangladesh and Nepal, while those with a low prevalence include Hong Kong, Thailand, Korea and Indonesia. Variations in the prevalence of slums are indicative of the nature of housing and urban development policies, rates of urbanization, economic growth, poverty and instability.

Asia has one of the lowest levels of inequality in the developing world. The urban Gini coefficient for the region (0.39) is remarkably lower than that of sub-Saharan Africa (0.46) and Latin America and the Caribbean (0.50).[127] Figure 2.10 shows remarkable variation across cities within the region. Chinese cities appear to be the most egalitarian, with Beijing having a Gini coefficient of 0.22. Other Chinese cities with low Gini coefficients are Benxi (0.29), Shanghai (0.32), Fuzhou (0.34) and Xian (0.35). Conversely, Hong Kong's Gini coefficient of 0.53 makes it one of the most unequal cities in the region. Other cities with high levels of income inequality are Ho Chi Minh, Shenzhen, Colombo and the Thai cities of Chang Mai, Udon Thani, Samut Prakan and Bangkok. In most of these cities, increasing levels of inequality have occurred against the backdrop of accelerated economic growth in their respective countries.

■ Sub-Saharan Africa

Rapid urbanization in sub-Saharan Africa will, in the near future, be taking place within the context of a deteriorating global economy. This will have major ramifications, given the numerous urban challenges that African countries have to contend with. The hard-won economic gains made by the region in the last decade or so are threatened by the current global recession. Economic growth is projected to decline from 5.5 per cent in 2008 to 1.7 per cent in 2009, with the resource-rich and oil-exporting countries being the most affected.[128] The severe slowdown in economic growth will

Asia will be hard hit by a reduction in the flow of remittances on account of the global recession

Asia has one of the lowest levels of inequality in the developing world

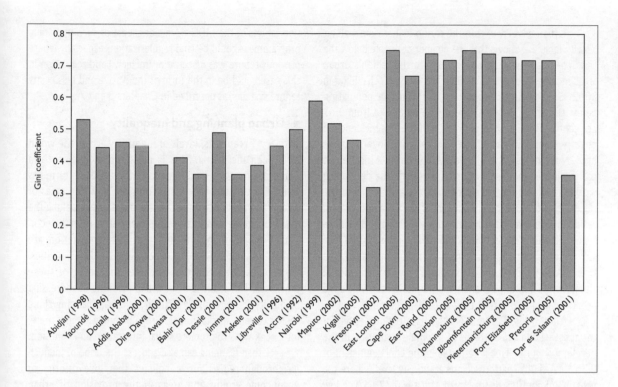

Figure 2.11

Gini coefficients for selected cities in Africa

Source: UN-Habitat, 2008b, p72

affect the ability of many countries to meet their urban development objectives, including the MDGs, many of which are urban related.

Besides job losses in urban areas, the ongoing economic meltdown will exacerbate the existing high levels of urban poverty in the region, causing the poor to fall more deeply into poverty. Table 2.2 reveals that the number of people below the US$1 per day extreme poverty line in urban areas increased from 66 million in 1993 to 99 million in 2002, while the incidence of urban poverty is 40.4 per cent – the highest in the world. Although rural poverty is still pervasive in sub-Saharan Africa, the share of urban poverty in relation to national poverty is increasing.

The problem of urban poverty in sub-Saharan Africa manifests itself in the proliferation of slum and squatter settlements. The region has the highest incidence of slums – with 62 per cent of the urban population living in slums. Countries with a very high incidence of slums include Angola, Chad, Central African Republic, Ethiopia, Guinea Bissau, Madagascar, Niger, Sierra Leone, Sudan and Uganda. The high prevalence of slums in these countries is a reflection of their low levels of income, high levels of poverty and rapid pace of urbanization. Indeed, urbanization and slum formation in sub-Saharan Africa are closely intertwined. Between 1990 and 2000, slum areas in the region grew at an average annual rate of 4.5 per cent, while urban growth was 4.6 per cent.[129] What this implies is that much of the future growth in African cities and towns will take place in slums and informal settlements.

Sub-Saharan Africa has the second highest level of income inequality after Latin America. The average Gini coefficient for urban areas in sub-Saharan Africa is 0.46.[130] Figure 2.11 shows the levels of income inequality for a selection of African cities. South African cities have extremely high levels of income inequality, ranging from 0.67 in Cape Town to 0.75 in Johannesburg, which are significantly higher

than in many Latin American cities. Cities with moderately high levels of inequality are Abidjan, Nairobi, Maputo and Accra. The most egalitarian cities are Dar es Salaam, Freetown, Yaoundé, and the Ethiopian towns of Dire Dawa, Awasa, Bahir Dar, Jimma and Mekele. From the foregoing, it can be surmised that the most unequal cities, in terms of income distribution, are those located in high- and middle-income countries.

■ Middle East and North Africa

The fall in oil prices and external financial constraints are hitting the region hard. Consequently, economic growth is projected to decline from 5.9 per cent in 2008 to 2.5 per cent in 2009, while oil-exporting countries such as the United Arab Emirates, Kuwait and Saudi Arabia are expected to record negative growth rates.[131] This is likely to impact upon urban areas, given the highly urbanized nature of most of the countries in the region. The United Arab Emirates is noteworthy in this regard. Besides being an oil-exporting country, it serves as a major financial hub. So, in addition to the loss of revenue from lower oil prices, the country has suffered from the reversal of capital inflow and contraction in global finance. This, in turn, has affected the construction industry, which has been booming since 2002, as building projects worth US$582 billion have been suspended.[132]

Levels of unemployment have traditionally been high in the region, and will be aggravated by the ongoing global crisis. The rate of unemployment in North Africa and the Middle East is expected to increase from 10.3 and 9.04 per cent, respectively, in 2008, to 11.2 and 11 per cent in 2009.[133] In a region where 65 per cent of the population is under the age of 30,[134] high levels of unemployment will disproportionately affect the youth. Rising levels of unemployment could also affect millions of migrant workers in Saudi Arabia, the United Arab Emirates, Kuwait, Oman, Qatar and Bahrain.

Sub-Saharan Africa has the second highest level of income inequality after Latin America

Rising levels of unemployment could affect millions of migrant workers in Saudi Arabia, the United Arab Emirates, Kuwait, Oman, Qatar and Bahrain

Urban poverty within the region is increasing, albeit slowly. Table 2.2 shows that the number of people below the US$1 per day extreme poverty line in the region's urban areas increased from 0.77 million in 1993 to 1.21 million in 2002. Similarly, the proportion of the urban population below the US$1 per day poverty line increased from 0.61 per cent in 1993 to 0.78 per cent in 2002. The incidence of poverty is much higher if the US$2 per day poverty line is used. Nonetheless, the Middle East and North Africa region has the lowest incidence of urban poverty in the developing world. The incidence of slums is also relatively low in the region. In North Africa, 15 per cent of the urban population reside in slum-like conditions. In the Middle East, the prevalence of slums is generally low and varies across the sub-region. Countries such as Bahrain, Kuwait, Israel, the United Arab Emirates and Qatar have a very low incidence of slums, while Yemen, Lebanon and Iraq have relatively large proportions of their urban population living in slums.

The Middle East and North Africa region has one of the most egalitarian patterns of income distribution in the developing world. This is reflected in the Gini coefficient of 0.36.[135] A similar pattern occurs at the city level, where the urban Gini coefficient for North Africa is 0.37.[136] The low levels of inequality within the region have been attributed to the strong cohesive social system and the emphasis on social redistribution polices in Islamic countries.[137]

Planning implications of urban economic context

In the foreseeable future, urban planning will need to address a number of economic challenges, especially the following: urbanization of poverty and the prevalence of slums; income inequality and the resultant social exclusion; uncertain economic growth; and poor urban employment prospects.

■ Urban planning, poverty and slums

The twin problems of urban poverty and the proliferation of slums should be at the top of the planning agenda in many developing countries. The magnitude of these problems has been described in the preceding sections. Some countries have tried to exclude the poor from cities by implementing anti-urban policies or by focusing on rural poverty in the hope that this will discourage rural–urban migration. Because of the failure of these policies, it is now clear that urban planning should strive to reduce poverty through pro-poor programmes that emphasize equity, participation and social justice.

Planning can address the problem of slums and informal settlements through upgrading programmes, which entail the provision or improvement of infrastructure and basic services such as water, sanitation, garbage collection, storm drainage, street lighting, paved footpaths and streets. Besides the physical improvement of these settlements, the provision of such infrastructure can deliver major benefits in economic growth, poverty reduction and environmental sustainability, reduce the health burden faced by residents, as well as contribute to achieving the slum, water and sanita-

tion targets of the MDGs. A major aspect of such upgrading programmes should be land regularization, especially where previous tenure was insecure or unclear. Land regulation in this case could be in the form of innovative and less costly tenure systems, as described in Chapters 3 and 7.

■ Urban planning and inequality

With few exceptions, levels of inequality across the world have been increasing. This is most remarkable in Latin America, Africa and transitional countries. This, in turn, has given rise to cities with stark contrasts between areas of wealth and poverty, with escalating crime levels fuelling the desire by the wealthy to segregate themselves from the poor. Thus, income inequality and spatial fragmentation are mutually reinforcing, leading to segregated and violent cities. Women, children and the aged feel the brunt of these processes. The challenges for urban planning in addressing inequality are particularly difficult, as urban planning alone cannot counter market forces. Urban planning should, therefore, seek ways to promote social integration and cohesion.

Urban planning can also address the issue of inequality through redistributive policies that give priority to low-income groups and areas in the provision of urban services. The provision of schools, basic health services, water supply and sanitation in poor neighbourhoods will, in the long run, contribute to reducing the level of inequality within cities. In cities of developed countries, a key issue that urban planning will have to contend with involves the spatial manifestations associated with the various forms of social exclusion and marginalization that migrants and other minority groups face.

■ Urban planning and economic uncertainty

Although the current global economic crisis had its roots in the subprime mortgage markets in the US, all countries – developed, developing and transitional – have been affected in various ways. Many countries are experiencing decline in economic growth. This implies that less funding will be available for state-initiated urban development programmes. In developing countries, urban development programmes such as slum upgrading and prevention projects, as well as urban regeneration and poverty reduction initiatives, will be adversely affected. So, too, will the achievement of the MDGs. All of this reinforces the need for governments to act in partnership with civil society and private-sector actors – both formal and informal – on urban planning issues. It also underlines the need for a developmental role for governments, as opposed to a neo-liberal approach which assumes that the market can solve most urban problems.

■ Urban planning and employment

In an era where formal employment opportunities across the world are dwindling due to the global economic recession, urban planning can play a key role in facilitating livelihoods through local economic development. Over the last two decades, local economic development has increasingly become an important development strategy in both developed and developing countries due to the economic challenges that cities face. Local economic development is a

The twin problems of urban poverty and the proliferation of slums should be at the top of the planning agenda in many developing countries

Urban planning can address the issue of inequality through redistributive policies that give priority to low-income groups and areas in the provision of urban services

community-empowering participatory process in which local governments, local communities, civil society, as well as the private and public sectors work together to stimulate and improve the local economy of a given area.[138] Local economic development seeks to enhance economic competitiveness; to increase sustainable growth; to ensure that growth is inclusive; and to produce tangible benefits for participating local communities.[139] Besides stimulating economic growth and creating employment, a key component of local economic development is poverty reduction. Urban planning could also create the enabling conditions for employment to thrive by adopting more flexible land-use management or zoning systems that allow for mixed land uses, as opposed to mono-functional zoning that seeks to segregate different activities. The former will allow income-generating or economic activities to take place within residential areas or any other favourably located sites.

LOCATION AND VULNERABILITY TO NATURAL AND HUMAN-MADE DISASTERS

Cities are highly vulnerable to the effects of natural and human-made disasters due to a complex set of interrelated processes, including the location and rapid growth of major urban centres in coastal locations; the modification of the built and natural environment through human actions; the expansion of settlements into hazard-prone locations; and the failure of authorities to regulate building standards and land-use planning strategies.

Since 1975, there has been a fourfold increase in the number of recorded natural disasters. Each of the three years with the highest number of recorded disasters has been during the current decade, with 801 disasters in 2000, 786 in 2002 and 744 in 2005.[140] Between 1996 and 2005, disasters accounted for over US$667 billion in material loss.[141] While all continents report more natural disaster events, on average, the rate of increase has been highest for Africa, where a threefold increase in natural disaster events has been experienced in the last decade alone.[142] Human-made disasters have seen a tenfold increase from 1975 to 2006, with the greatest rates of increase in Asia and Africa.

Geographic location is a major determinant of the type and frequency of natural hazards that a city may experience. Eight of the ten most populous cities are located on earthquake faults, while 90 per cent of these cities are in regions vulnerable to destructive storms (see Table 2.5). The low-elevation coastal zone (LECZ) – the contiguous area along the coast that is less than 10m above sea level – is highly vulnerable to natural hazards. This zone accounts for 2 per cent of the world's land area, but contains 10 per cent of its total population and 13 per cent of its urban population.[143] Due to their favourable location, coastal areas are densely populated and have large concentrations of economic activities. Indeed, coastal areas account for 53 per cent of the world's GDP.[144] However, populations within coastal areas are at risk from sea-level rise, extreme weather events such as tropical cyclones, flooding and other hazards associated with climate change.

Developed and transitional countries

Floods, windstorms, earthquakes and volcanoes are the most common forms of natural disasters affecting developed countries. The human impacts of natural disasters vary remarkably between developed and developing countries. While economic loss in absolute terms is high in developed countries, human loss is low. This is a result of the very high levels of capital investment, as well as high levels of investment in disaster mitigation. Developed countries account for less than 10 per cent of the world human loss due to natural disasters.[145] In 1999, the US reported two to three times as many natural disasters as Bangladesh; yet, Bangladesh experienced 34 times more deaths.[146] The distinguishing characteristic is the high technical capacity for early-warning systems, disaster preparedness and risk reduction in the developed world, and the ability to effectively manage pre- and post-disaster situations, all of which are lacking in many developing countries.

In the developed world, 10 per cent of the total urban population live in the low-elevation coastal zone, with 86 per cent of the entire population of the zone being urban dwellers. In Europe, North America, Japan, Australia and New Zealand, the low-elevation coastal zone is highly urbanized: between 79 and 94 per cent of the population are urban (see Table 2.7). Such high levels of urbanization along coastlines render large numbers of people vulnerable to

Cities are highly vulnerable to the effects of natural and human-made disasters

Geographic location is a major determinant of the type and frequency of natural hazards that a city may experience

City	Population (million)	Disaster risk					
		Earthquake	Volcano	Storms	Tornado	Flood	Storm surge
Tokyo	35.2	X		X	X	X	X
Mexico City	19.4	X	X	X			
New York	18.7	X		X			X
São Paulo	18.3			X		X	
Mumbai	18.2	X		X		X	X
Delhi	15.0	X		X		X	
Shanghai	14.5	X		X		X	X
Kolkata	14.3	X		X	X	X	X
Jakarta	13.2	X				X	
Buenos Aries	12.6			X		X	X

Source: Chafe, 2007, p116

Table 2.5

Ten most populous cities and associated disaster risk, 2005

flooding and extreme weather conditions associated with climate change.

■ Western Europe

Floods constitute the most frequent form of natural disaster in Western Europe. Between 1990 and 2006, a total of 1483 events affecting over 42 million people and causing 98,119 deaths, with an estimated economic cost of over US$168 billion, occurred.[147] Vulnerability and human loss are highest for extreme temperature events, compared to other world regions. Between 1996 and 2005, Europe experienced 47 per cent of all extreme temperature events, but 81 per cent of all mortalities. The heat wave of 2003 resulted in about 35,000 deaths.[148] Western Europe has a strong capacity for resilience. It is also a region with relatively low levels of hazard exposure. The role played by high levels of economic development and political stability in shifting the impact of disasters from human to physical assets is evident in this region. This is exemplified by volcanic eruptions, where Europe suffers the highest economic losses of any region, but with very few people being killed or affected.

■ North America

Windstorms, including hurricanes and tornadoes, are the most frequent type of disaster affecting the greatest number of people and causing the highest total economic costs in North America. Windstorms can trigger flooding and landslides. North America experiences the greatest economic loss from natural disasters. In 2005, Hurricane Katrina alone caused US$125 billion in economic loss (see Table 2.6). The impacts of volcanic eruptions have been limited, suggesting good levels of resilience to this hazard type. Neo-liberal policies, particularly in the US, have scaled down state responsibilities for risk reduction and response and placed greater emphasis on the role of private citizens and companies. This has had mixed results for urban resilience to natural and human-made hazards, as was seen in the failed state response and recovery efforts during Hurricane Katrina in 2005.

■ Oceania and Japan

Between 1996 and 2005, Oceania recorded the lowest incidence of disasters for any region and hazard type, with the exception of volcanic eruption.[149] The region also has the lowest economic losses and absolute number of people killed and affected by all disaster types. Within the region, disasters are most commonly associated with windstorms, and these result in the greatest economic losses. Earthquakes and tsunamis account for the highest levels of mortality. The natural cycle of weather patterns, aided by human activities such as overstocking, vegetation loss, dams, groundwater and irrigation schemes, underlie many natural disasters in New Zealand and Australia. In 2007 alone, New Zealand experienced four major storms with an economic loss of about NZ$131.3 million.[150] Japan's location in one of the world's most active crustal zones puts its cities at risk of many natural hazards, including earthquakes, storms and floods (see Tables 2.5 and 2.6). For low-lying small island states within the region, sea-level rise due to climate change poses major challenges.

■ Transitional countries

Some of the countries in East and Central Europe have difficult topographies and are located in areas that place them at risk to natural and human-induced disasters. Many of the countries are landlocked, sit on, or are surrounded by steep mountains that are frequently disturbed by seismic activity, heavy rains, avalanches, landslides and earthquakes. Serbia, Montenegro and Kosovo suffered from serious flooding in November and December 2007. Human-induced disasters, such as the massive explosion at an arms depot in Albania in March 2008, also tend to occur more frequently in this region.[151] Disasters of this genre are often a function of ineffective governance.

During the Soviet era, authorities paid very little attention to environmental issues. Environmentally damaging agricultural, mining and manufacturing practices went unchecked, while large quantities of untreated toxic and hazardous waste were inappropriately disposed of. Besides, substandard nuclear plants, such as Kozloduy in Bulgaria, were allowed to operate with no safety procedures in place. The plant, which is located near the Danube River, has leaking pipes and obsolete reactors, and is considered to be the most dangerous reactor in the world. Residents of cities close to the plant have undoubtedly been exposed to unsafe levels of radiation.

Developing countries

Developing countries have experienced the fastest rate of increase in the incidence of natural and human-made disasters over the last three decades. Since these countries are rapidly urbanizing, they face increased risks in the future from natural disasters. Cities in developing countries suffer disproportionately from the impacts of natural disasters – this is evident in Tables 2.5 and 2.6. This is a function of the inability on the part of authorities to manage pre- and post-disaster situations. Consequently, natural disasters tend to claim more lives than in developed countries. Indeed, 98 per cent of the 211 million people affected by natural disasters between 1991 and 2000 resided in developing countries.[152] While economic losses in absolute terms are low in compari-

---

Floods constitute the most frequent form of natural disaster in Western Europe

Cities in developing countries suffer disproportionately from the impacts of natural disasters

Table 2.6

Selected urban disasters, 1906–2006

Year	City	Disaster	Deaths (estimated number)	Economic loss (US$ billion, 2005)
2005	New Orleans	Hurricane	1800	125.0
2005	Mumbai	Flood	400	0.4
2003	Bam, Iran	Earthquake	26,300	1.1
2003	Paris	Heat wave	14,800	4.7
2001	Bhuj (India)	Earthquake	19,700	5.5
2000	Johannesburg	Flood	100	0.2
1999	Istanbul/Izmit	Earthquake	15,000	14.1
1995	Kobe, Japan	Earthquake	6400	128.2
1985	Mexico City	Earthquake	9500	7.3
1976	Tangshan, China	Earthquake	242,000	19.2
1970	Dhaka	Flood	1400	10.1
1923	Tokyo	Earthquake	143,000	31.8
1906	San Francisco	Earthquake	3000	10.9

Source: Chafe, 2007, p117

son to developed countries, they are 20 times greater as a percentage of GDP.[153]

One factor accounting for the magnified impact of natural disasters in developing countries is the lack of development itself, which makes it impossible not only for citizens to adhere to building regulations, but also for authorities to enforce them. In addition, the scarcity or high cost of buildable land has left many with no choice but to settle in disaster-prone areas.

Table 2.7 indicates that 14 per cent of the urban population of developing countries live in the low-elevation coastal zone, while 54 per cent of the coastal zone is urban. The high level of urbanization in the low-elevation coastal zone vis-à-vis the entire developing world (44 per cent) presents major challenges, given the low capacity and weak infrastructure to deal with rising sea levels.

■ Latin America and the Caribbean

Earthquakes, hurricanes, tropical storms and floods are the main natural hazards in this region. During the three decades leading up to the 21st century, the region experienced 32 disasters that accounted for about 7500 deaths per year, on average.[154] The economic loss arising from these disasters varies between US$700 million and US$3.3 billion.[155] The incidence of natural disasters differs by sub-region. For instance, 50 per cent of all disasters, 65 per cent of fatalities, 75 per cent of the affected population and 53 per cent of the total destruction were in South America. These statistics may overstate South America's vulnerability to natural disasters compared to other sub-regions. The effective exposure to risk, measured in terms of occurrence per thousand square kilometres, is more informative. The effective exposure to risk for the Caribbean is 10.1 against 0.3 for South America.[156] While the cumulative losses resulting from natural disasters from 1970 to 1999 represented 4 per cent of the GDP of South American countries, it amounted to 43 per cent for the Caribbean.[157] This suggests that smaller countries are, in economic terms, more vulnerable to natural disasters.

In Latin America and the Caribbean, 8 per cent of the population reside in the low-elevation coastal zone (see Table 2.7). Countries such as the Bahamas, Suriname, Guyana and Belize rank among the top ten in the world that have the highest proportion of their urban population living in the coastal zone.[158] In most of the Caribbean, 50 per cent of the population reside within 2km of the coast.[159] This, coupled with urbanization patterns and processes in low-income areas, have, in part, contributed to making the Caribbean highly vulnerable to rises in sea levels and extreme weather conditions.

■ Asia

The incidence of disasters associated with avalanches or landslides, earthquakes or tsunamis, floods, windstorms and industrial accidents is higher in Asia than in any other region. The high population density means that mortality is highest in this region for all disaster types, with the exception of volcanic eruptions. The number of people affected is also high. Economic loss is similarly high for all disasters,

Region	Population in LECZ (000s)	Urban population in LECZ (000s)	Percentage urban population in LECZ	Level of urbanization in LECZ (%)
Africa	55,633	32,390	12	58
Sub-Saharan Africa	24,911	16,845	9	68
North Africa	30,723	15,545	18	51
Asia	449,845	235,258	16	52
Eastern Asia	159,969	109,434	15	68
Southern Asia	140,964	56,023	14	40
South-Eastern Asia	137,245	61,201	36	45
Western Asia	11,472	8482	8	74
Commonwealth of Independent States Asia	194	119	0.3	61
Latin America and the Caribbean	33,578	24,648	8	73
Oceania	852	442	22	52
Developing countries	539,908	292,738	14	54
Europe (including Commonwealth of Independent States Europe)	50,200	39,709	8	79
North America	24,217	21,489	8	89
Japan	29,347	27,521	27	94
Australia and New Zealand	2846	2421	14	85
Developed countries	106,519	91,140	10	86
World	646,519	383,878	13	59

Source: UN-Habitat, 2008b, p142

Table 2.7

Urban population in the low-elevation coastal zone (LECZ), 2000

except for extreme temperatures, volcanic eruptions, industrial accidents and miscellaneous accidents.[160] Flooding is the most frequent natural hazard affecting the largest number of people and causing the greatest economic losses. Between 1996 and 2005, a total of 472 floods resulted in 42,570 deaths, affected 1.3 billion people and caused an economic loss of US$129 billion.[161] Tsunamis and earthquakes cause the greatest mortality, with the 2004 Indian Ocean Tsunami accounting for around 230,000 deaths, in which the province of Aceh lost capital stock worth 97 per cent of its GDP.[162] The Kashmir earthquake of 2005 caused an estimated loss of US$5 billion to Pakistan.[163] In the Chinese province of Sichuan, the earthquake of 12 May 2008 resulted in 69,000 deaths, 370,000 injured, 17,000 missing and 4.8 million homeless.[164]

Asia alone accounts for 61 per cent of the urban population of the entire low-elevation coastal zone, and has 16 per cent of its urban population within the zone (see Table 2.7). What this means is that with more than 235 million people living in the LECZ, Asia has the highest number of urban dwellers at risk from flooding, with the poor being most affected, given the poor quality and hazardous location of their homes. Many cities, such as Shanghai, Bangkok, Karachi, Kolkata, Chennai, Hanoi, Mumbai and Dhaka, are at risk from sea-level rise.

■ Sub-Saharan Africa

Flooding is the most frequent natural disaster in Africa and results in the highest mortality.[165] Earthquakes, floods and storms cause the greatest economic loss, and drought affects the most people. Food insecurity resulting from drought can affect urban areas indirectly through price fluctuations and the in-migration of refugees. Economic loss to disasters is low for Africa, compared to other world regions, but is high

In most of the Caribbean, 50 per cent of the population reside within 2km of the coast

Asia alone accounts for 61 per cent of the urban population of the entire low-elevation coastal zone as a proportion of GDP. Between 1996 and 2005, more people were killed or affected by volcanic eruptions in Africa than in any other region, despite the low incidence of volcanic eruption events.[166] The high loss-to-event ratio indicates low resilience, and this was demonstrated in the volcanic eruption of Mount Nyiragongo, which destroyed 40 per cent of the buildings and displaced 250,000 people in Goma (Democratic Republic of Congo) in 2002.[167]

Table 2.7 shows that 9 per cent of the urban population of sub-Saharan Africa live within the low-elevation coastal zone. While this appears relatively low, the level of urbanization in the coastal zone is 68 per cent, making it the most urbanized ecosystem within the region. Coastal cities in sub-Saharan Africa are by far the most developed and are likely to be adversely affected by rising sea levels. Such cities include Abidjan, Accra, Cape Town, Dakar, Lagos, Libreville, Mombasa and Port Louis. Many of these cities do not have the necessary infrastructure and preparedness to withstand the effects of extreme weather conditions.

■ Middle East and North Africa

The natural factors that have provided the foundation for the wealth of cities in the Middle East and North Africa also threaten their survival. For instance, the desert exposes them to droughts and extreme problems of water shortage. The projected water availability per person for the region for the next two decades is 500 cubic metres, while the current world average per capita is 7000 cubic metres.[168] Other natural disasters known in the region are flash floods, earthquakes, landslides and desertification. Examples of recent episodes of these include the following: an earthquake in Morocco in February 2004 claimed 600 lives and rendered 30,000 homeless; in May 2003, an earthquake in Algeria killed 538 and injured 4600; and in October 2008, floods claimed 90 lives and left about 25,000 people homeless in Yemen.[169] Extended dry seasons – a common problem in the region – destroy land cover and lead to desertification.

Planning implications of vulnerability to natural and human disasters

With increasing extreme weather events associated with climate change, cities are facing mounting and often inter-related environmental challenges, to which urban planning must respond with innovative solutions. These will include more appropriate land-use planning; more appropriate building codes and disaster-resistant construction; protection of critical infrastructure; more effective post-disaster rehabilitation; and implementation of effective climate change mitigation and adaptation measures.

■ Land-use planning and disasters

Given the occurrence of natural disasters in cities across the world, land-use planning can serve as a valuable tool for mainstreaming disaster risk reduction into urban development processes. Land-use planning provides a framework within which interventions to partner local actors for risk mapping and community resilience building can be undertaken. This includes partnerships between municipal governments, community groups and the private sector. Familiar planning tools such as zoning, community participation, geographic information systems (GIS), and information and education programmes are all essential to mainstreaming risk reduction within the land-use planning process.

Mainstreaming risk reduction within strategies that underpin land-use planning is challenging, particularly for authorities in developing countries with limited resources. Designing and implementing comprehensive land-use planning also poses a major challenge for many smaller cities, where municipal capacity for urban planning is limited. Planning to manage risk systems in their entirety further complicates land-use planning. Human settlements of all sizes are situated within larger socio-ecological systems that include environmental features as well as social and cultural systems. These systems are interdependent, expressed, for example, through migration and economic exchange between rural and urban areas or across urban centres. Planning for risk management will need to consider not only the internal, but also the external environment.

■ Building codes and disaster-resistant construction

Urban planning can play an integral role in developing building codes that ensure safety standards in components of the built environment. Most countries have building codes aimed at ensuring that construction meets a minimum standard of disaster resilience. However, in some cases, codes might not be as appropriate as they should be. In order to be effective, the building codes proposed by urban planning should meet the following criteria specified by the United Nations International Strategy for Disaster Reduction:[170]

- realistic, given economic, environmental and technological constraints;
- relevant to current building practice and technology;
- updated regularly in light of developments in knowledge;
- understood fully and accepted by professional interest groups;
- enforced in order to avoid the legislative system being ignored or falling into disrepute;
- adhered to, with laws and controls based more on a system of incentives rather than punishment; and
- integrated fully within a legal system that takes account of potential conflicts between the different levels of administration and government.

A major challenge that planning is likely to face is enforcing adherence to building codes, particularly in developing countries. Failure to comply with codes is a major cause of vulnerability in buildings. Too often, perverse incentives make it more attractive for administrators, architects, builders, contractors and even house owners to circumvent construction standards. The potential for regulation of building codes to be undertaken by the private sector has been explored. While it might be cost efficient for the private sector to undertake site inspections, it is unclear if it would

---

Coastal cities in sub-Saharan Africa are by far the most developed and are likely to be adversely affected by rising sea levels

Urban planning can play an integral role in developing building codes that ensure safety standards in the built environment

be any less open to the perverse incentives that distort public-sector inspection and enforcement.[171]

■ Protecting critical infrastructure

Urban planning can play a major role in protecting critical infrastructure and services such as electricity, water and sanitation, telecommunications, transportation systems and health services. Protecting such vital infrastructure and services will influence response and reconstruction capacity and minimize secondary and indirect losses, such as the disruption in the flow of goods and services during the period after a disaster has struck a city. The potential for cascading events to affect multiple infrastructure systems makes it paramount that critical infrastructure and services be protected and, where possible, managed independently of each other to prevent contagion effects. It should be emphasized that protecting critical infrastructure and services against all conceivable sources of harm is prohibitively expensive, especially so for countries and cities with weak and small economies.

■ Planning and post-disaster rehabilitation

Urban planning can contribute to post-disaster rehabilitation of human settlements since municipal authorities and local governments are best placed to coordinate relief and reconstruction efforts. Partnerships with community groups and international development and humanitarian agencies are necessary in post-disaster planning. Post-disaster situations, particularly in Asia and Africa, offer urban planning a unique opportunity, or clean slate, to rethink past development practices, improve the sustainability of human settlements, and effectively prepare communities against risks. Planning can also strengthen the capacity to manage natural and human-made disasters, increase the capacity for disaster prevention and mitigation, and strengthen coordination and networking among communities, non-governmental organizations (NGOs), governments and external support organizations in addressing disaster-related activities. Furthermore, urban planning can ensure that programmes and projects undertaken after disasters address the long-term development objectives and needs of the affected areas, and ensure an effective transition to sustainable development.

■ Urban planning and climate change

In order to cope with the effects of climate change through rising sea levels, cities all over the world, but especially in developing countries, will need to implement innovative adaptation and mitigation strategies. Some of these strategies are discussed in Chapter 6. Urban planning can contribute to implementing some of these strategies. Adaptation for cities entails such diverse actions as increasing the resilience of infrastructure, changing the location of settlements and implementing practices that enhance sustainable development. There are, however, several challenges. Adapting now to future climate change is difficult because of the uncertainty in forecasting and a tendency for conservative estimates of future change. Besides, cities in developing countries face financial and technical constraints and limited adaptive capacity.

Mitigating climate change through reduction of greenhouse gas emissions in cities requires immediate and aggressive action, alongside adaptation. There is great scope for future work in enabling mitigation through improved urban design. One direction might be in those areas where mitigation also offers a financial opportunity. Examples include improved building materials and energy efficiency to reduce costs; transport demand management to reduce congestion and the health impacts of transport; and the promotion of renewable or alternative energy generation, such as methane recuperation from landfills for use in local energy generation schemes. These are areas where urban planning holds good promise.

CONCLUDING REMARKS

This chapter has examined the urban contexts across various regions. The diversity of the urban contexts across the world has major implications for urban planning. Levels of urbanization are high in developed and transitional countries, as well as in Latin America and the Caribbean, but much lower in Africa and Asia. Conversely, the pace of urbanization is faster in Africa and Asia. In both developed and developing countries, more than half of the urban population live in small and intermediate cities; and much of future population growth will take place in these cities.

The phenomenon of shrinking cities is most prevalent in the developed and transitional countries. An important demographic trend with implications for planning in developing countries is the high proportion of young people, especially in Africa, the Middle East, South America, Central Asia and the Pacific Islands. On the other hand, cities in developed countries have to contend with an increasingly ageing population and multiculturalism. In developing countries, the peri-urban fringe holds a significant proportion of the urban population, and is often the fastest growing area of cities, with informality being a dominant phenomenon.

The current global recession has affected cities in developed, transitional and developing countries alike. In developed countries, it has led to contraction in economic growth, rising levels of unemployment and, in some cases, massive falls in housing prices. For developing countries, the economic crisis has the tendency to exacerbate poverty, inequality and the prevalence of slums, and to undermine the implementation of urban development programmes, including those related to the MDGs.

For urban planning to respond effectively to the issues identified in the preceding paragraphs, it is important that urbanization itself is viewed as a positive phenomenon. Besides planning for rapid urban growth, planning will have to pay greater attention to small- and medium-sized cities, particularly in developing countries where the focus is often on large cities. Urban planning will need to respond to the youth bulge observed in many developing countries, shrinking cities, rapidly ageing population and multiculturalism in cities of developed and transitional countries. In developing countries, 21st century urban planning will have to address

Urban planning can play a major role in protecting critical infrastructure and services

Mitigating climate change through reduction of greenhouse gas emissions in cities requires immediate and aggressive action, alongside adaptation the twin problem of poverty and slums, as well as contend with increasing levels of informality. A consequence of the current economic recession is that funding for state-initiated urban and infrastructural projects will become scarce. This, in turn, underlines the need for governments to act in partnership with civil society and private-sector actors on urban development. Finally, in all parts of the world, but especially in developing countries, urban planning can serve as a valuable tool for mainstreaming disaster risk reduction within urban development processes.

NOTES

1   Njoh, 2003a.
2   UN, 2008.
3   UN, 2008, p2.
4   UN, 2008, p2.
5   UN-Habitat, 2008b.
6   UN-Habitat, 2008b.
7   Le Galès, 2006; Lees and Lees, 2007.
8   Le Galès, 2006.
9   Ecology.com, undated.
10   UN, 2008, pp114–122.
11   Demographia, undated.
12   UN-Habitat, 2004a.
13   GCIM.org (undated).
14   Australian Government, 2009.
15   *New Zealand Yearbook*, 2006.
16   Mykhnenko and Turok, 2007, p16.
17   UN, 2008; Hirt and Stanilov, 2008.
18   Hirt and Stanilov, 2008.
19   Mykhnenko and Turok, 2007, p2.
20   National Research Council, 2003.
21   Hirt and Stanilov, 2008, p12.
22   National Research Council, 2003.
23   Irazábal, 2008a, p2; Cerruti and Bertoncello, 2003; UN, 2008, p5.
24   Irazábal, 2008a.
25   UN, 2008, p5.
26   Yuen, 2008.
27   UNFPA, 2007, p33.
28   UN, 2008, pp74–75.
29   UN, 2008, p74–75.
30   Cheru, 2005.
31   UN-Habitat, 2004a.
32   World Bank, 2002.
33   Cohen, 2006.
34   Middle East Youth Initiative (undated).
35   Middle East Youth Initiative (undated).
36   Nassar, 2008.
37   UN-Habitat, 2008b, p11.
38   Angel et al, 2005; BBC News, 2000.
39   Bloom and Khanna, 2007, p13.
40   UNFPA, 2007, p27.
41   UNFPA, 2007.

42   UN, 2008, p8.
43   UN-Habitat, 2004a.
44   Demographia (undated).
45   Cox, 2009.
46   Cox, 2009.
47   EEA, 2006.
48   UNEP, 2007.
49   UNEP, 2007.
50   UNEP, 2007.
51   Porter and Hecht (undated).
52   Macionis and Parrillo, 2004.
53   UN, 2007.
54   Statistics New Zealand, 2001.
55   Slater, 2008.
56   Slater, 2008.
57   UN-Habitat, 2004a.
58   EEA, 2006, p15.
59   Hirt and Stanilov, 2008.
60   Hirt and Stanilov, 2008.
61   UN, 2008.
62   Demographia (undated).
63   Demographia (undated).
64   Cerrutti and Bertoncello, 2003.
65   UN-Habitat, 2008b.
66   Rojas, 2006.
67   Rojas, 2006.
68   UN-Habitat, 2004a, p62.
69   UN-Habitat, 2004a.
70   Qadeer, 1999, 2004.
71   Yuen, 2008; Van Grusven, 2000.
72   UN, 2008.
73   Africapolis, 2008.
74   UN, 2008.
75   Daher (undated) ; Al-Asad (undated).
76   UN-Habitat, 2004a.
77   UN-Habitat, 2004a.
78   Bolay and Rabinovich, 2004.
79   Commission for Social Development, 2009.
80   Naudé, 2009.
81   IMF, 2009.
82   ILO, 2009.
83   Commission for Social Development, 2009.
84   UN-Habitat, 2004a.
85   IMF, 2009.
86   OECD, 2008.
87   IMF, 2009.
88   OECD, 2009.

89   OECD, 2008.
90   OECD, 2009.
91   IMF, 2009.
92   OECD, 2009.
93   BBC News, 2009a.
94   Bureau of Labor Statistics, 2009.
95   OECD, 2009.
96   UN-Habitat, 2008b.
97   OECD, 2008.
98   IMF, 2009.
99   UN-Habitat, 2008b.
100 OECD, 2008,
101 UN-Habitat, 2008b.
102 Statistics New Zealand, 2009.
103 Johnston et al, 2005.
104 Colic-Peisker and Tilbury, 2008.
105 EBRD, 2006; Hirt and Stanilov, 2008.
106 IMF, 2009.
107 BBC News, 2009b.
108 *Russia Today*, 2009.
109 UN, 2007; UN-Habitat, 2004a; Clapham et al, 1996.
110 IMF, 2009.
111 UN-Habitat, 2003; Chen and Ravallion, 2007.
112 UN-Habitat, 2008b.
113 UN-Habitat, 2008b.
114 IMF, 2009. GDP growth for 2009 in major economies such as Argentina, Brazil, Mexico and Argentina is expected to shrink by 2.0, 1.3, 3.7 and 2.2 per cent, respectively.
115 ILO, 2009.
116 Chen and Ravallion, 2007.
117 UN-Habitat, 2008b; Irazábal, 2008a.
118 UN-Habitat, 2008b.
119 Irazábal, 2008a.
120 IMF, 2009. In China and India, GDP growth in 2009 is projected to fall to 6.5 and 4.5 per cent, respectively, representing half the rate recorded in 2007.
121 *Economic Times*, 2009.
122 Commission for Social Development, 2009.
123 Ratha et al, 2008.
124 Dummet, 2009.

125 UNESCAP, 2003.
126 UN-Habitat, 2004a.
127 UN-Habitat, 2008b.
128 IMF, 2009.
129 UN-Habitat, 2008b.
130 UN-Habitat, 2008b.
131 IMF, 2009.
132 ABS-CBN News, 2009.
133 ILO, 2009.
134 Middle East Youth Initiative (undated).
135 UN-Habitat, 2004a.
136 UN-Habitat, 2008b.
137 UN-Habitat, 2004a.
138 UN-Habitat and EcoPlan, 2005.
139 UN-Habitat and EcoPlan, 2005.
140 IFRCRCS, 2003.
141 IGE, 2007.
142 IFRCRCS, 2003.
143 McGranahan et al, 2007.
144 IGE, 2007.
145 Chafe, 2007.
146 UNEP, 2002.
147 WHO-Europe, 2007.
148 Bhattachatya, 2003.
149 UN-Habitat, 2007b.
150 *The Dominion Post*, 2008.
151 IFRCRCS, 2008.
152 IFRCRCS, 2003.
153 IGE, 2007.
154 Chevériat, 2000.
155 Chevériat, 2000, p9.
156 Chevériat, 2000, p35.
157 Chevériat, 2000, p35.
158 McGranahan et al, 2007.
159 UN-Habitat, 2008b.
160 UN-Habitat, 2007b.
161 UN-Habitat, 2007b.
162 See www.oxfam.org.au/world/ emergencies/asia_tsunami.html.
163 UN-Habitat, 2007b.
164 Yuen, 2008.
165 UN-Habitat, 2007b.
166 UN-Habitat, 2007b.
167 See www.volcanolive.com/ news16.html.
168 World Bank, 2007b.
169 Nassar, 2008; IRIN, 2008.
170 ISDR, 2004.
171 www.proventionconsortium.org.

PART II

GLOBAL TRENDS: THE URBAN PLANNING PROCESS (PROCEDURAL)

CHAPTER 3

THE EMERGENCE AND SPREAD OF CONTEMPORARY URBAN PLANNING

This chapter deals with the emergence and spread of modernist urban planning, and the reasons for its persistence in many parts of the world. It then turns to the various innovative approaches to urban planning that are being attempted in both developed and developing countries, and examines the extent to which these meet the normative criteria for planning systems set out in Chapter 1.

The term 'modernist planning' refers to the approach to urban planning that developed in the post-1850 urban industrial period in Western Europe and other advanced capitalist countries. While there are many variations of modernist planning, it generally involves a particular process of producing plans (which was 'top down' and expert led, and regarded as solely a function of government); a particular form of plan (generally known as a master plan, underpinned by a land-use regulatory system); and the promotion of a particular urban form (urban modernism, characterized by mono-functional use areas, low-built densities, movement systems based on the private car, tower blocks and quantities of green open space).

The planning of urban settlements has been taking place since the dawn of civilization, and the first section refers to the evidence in this regard. However, in the latter part of the 19th century a new set of ideas about planning settlements emerged, originally to deal with the negative health consequences associated with the Industrial Revolution. During the first part of the 20th century, planning became, for the first time, an accepted function of government, and planning developed into an organized profession. The second part deals with this new development of planning. The notion of what constitutes a well-planned urban environment, which was shaped by a particular time and place, was then spread through a range of different mechanisms to other parts of the world. The third part discusses this diffusion of modernist planning. Significantly, the modernist approach has proved resistant to change in recent decades. As the fourth section argues, modernist planning still persists in many parts of the world, despite the fact that the urban issues and problems that it is meant to address have changed considerably. This section reviews this persistence of the approach, why it has occurred and why this can be regarded as a problem. The fifth section of the chapter recognizes that in many parts of the world

there are also shifts towards new or contemporary approaches to urban planning. While these are highly varied, they nonetheless have elements in common that bring them closer to the normative criteria for planning identified in Chapter 1. This section deals with the new approaches.

The chapter emphasizes the point that these new approaches should not be viewed as models that can be applied in all contexts. An important lesson from the experience of modernist planning is that planning approaches, which have been shaped by a particular context, should not be considered as models and imposed uncritically on very different contexts. While planning has common purposes, tasks and types of tools throughout the world, the form these take will always be shaped by the social and cultural norms of particular places.

EARLY FORMS OF URBAN PLANNING

Urban planning is as old as human settlement itself, and archaeologists have uncovered evidence of urban planning in the Middle East and North Africa, Latin America, Asia and sub-Saharan Africa. The purpose of briefly reviewing these findings here is to emphasize the point that whether or not settlements are planned is not optional: they have always been planned, although not always by governments and not always according to the tenets of modernist planning. A main premise of this Global Report is not whether there should be urban planning, but rather what form it should take.

Middle East and North Africa

The Middle East is home to some of the oldest cities in the world, and Old Jericho is believed to be the first city on Earth.[1] A considerable degree of planning competence was necessary to produce materials such as the sun-dried bricks that were used to construct the houses, the large trench, tower and other structures found within Jericho, as well as the wall that enclosed and protected the town from external threats. The ancient cities of the Fertile Crescent of Mesopotamia (present-day Iraq) attained the peak of their development about 2800 BC. One of the best known of

> The planning of urban settlements has been taking place since the dawn of civilization

> A main premise of this Global Report is not whether there should be urban planning, but rather what form it should take

these, Uruk, covered an area of about 445ha and contained as many as 50,000 inhabitants.[2] Another ancient city, Catal Hüyük, in present-day Turkey, was already well developed in terms of its urbanity by 6000 BC. Istanbul has ancient origins, and served as the capital of three historic empires: the Eastern Roman (324–395 AD), the Byzantine (395–1453 AD) and the Ottoman (1453–1923 AD). It was a leading socio-economic and cultural centre in the Middle East and has been classified as a 'world city' as a result of its historical heritage.[3] The ancient cities of Egypt emerged not long after urbanization had begun in the Mesopotamian region. Memphis and Hierakonopolis were established by 3100 BC during the reign of Menes, the first paramount pharaoh of a united Egypt.

Western Europe

Cities in Greece and Italy show the earliest evidence of urban planning in Western Europe. The location and physical structure of towns in these two civilizations were largely influenced by military concerns. For instance, Athens, which evolved from a small farming village from about the end of the fourth and beginning of the third millennium BC, was located on an isolated fortified hilltop. In addition to the encircling wall, there was the Acropolis, which was a large citadel, and the Agora, which served as the centre of socio-political and economic life, a central meeting place, and a market. Streets in Greek cities prior to the advent of the 'Hippodamian grid', which later became a dominant feature of cities in the Greco-Roman world, were irregular. The streets were deliberately made to meander for military reasons, as this rendered navigation difficult for invading forces. It was not until the 7th century BC that the gridiron street pattern was introduced in human settlements in Greek colonies.

Rome initially developed as a village of shepherds in the 8th century BC. The Etruscans inhabited the city during the early days of the Roman Empire and laid out its earliest system of public infrastructure, including streets, sewers and municipal buildings. To facilitate effective administration, the city was divided into four distinct districts during the 5th century BC. Julius Caesar (49–55 BC) had an interest in spatial design and developed an elaborate plan for the city. The plan divided the city into 14 districts, and created a street pattern dominated by two major streets. The plan included paved streets, schools and libraries.

Latin America

Latin America had urban civilizations of great antiquity, such as the Maya, Aztec and Inca civilizations. Located in the Yucatan, the Mayans became prominent around 250 AD in present-day southern Mexico, Guatemala, western Honduras, El Salvador and northern Belize. The Mayans were already living in urban settlements by 2600 BC. Some of these settlements had populations in excess of 300,000 by the late 1400s when Christopher Columbus arrived in the region. The Aztec Empire was located in Central Mexico on the site currently occupied by Mexico City. The empire's capital, Tenochtitlan, was built on raised islets in Lake Texcoco. The Inca Empire stretched for about 4020km from Quito in present-day Ecuador to the Maule River in Chile. Archaeological research has uncovered evidence of an elaborate ancient architecture, including temple-pyramids, palaces and observatories. The urban infrastructure of the Incas includes 22,530km of well-planned and maintained footpaths.

East and South-East Asia

Cities dating back to about 3500 BC existed in Mohenjo-Daro in the Indus Valley and at Harappa in the Punjab. These cities had sophisticated spatial design structures, public bathrooms, well-designed systems of covered drainage laid at depths of up to 0.6m below the street level, and broad paved streets.[4] There is a striking similarity between these historic urban settlements and what was later introduced in the region under the banner of modernity. The ancient towns of the Indus Valley in the north-western region of present-day Pakistan assumed a compartmentalized spatial structure with distinct areas for different land-use activities.

In ancient China, cities were typically constructed around a gridiron street pattern, criss-crossing at right angles and often punctuated by six avenues. Cities were often enclosed within walls, in the same manner as ancient Greek cities. The street pattern in these cities bore a striking resemblance to what was to be introduced by European colonial authorities. European colonial authorities employed the gridiron street pattern not only to facilitate the mobility of people, goods and services, but also as an instrument of social control and acculturation. Until the Tang Dynasty (618–907 AD), urban planning in ancient China was rigid and highly centralized. A more decentralized form of planning emerged following the demise of the Tang Dynasty and with the rise of the Song Dynasty (960–1279 AD).

Sub-Saharan Africa

Many towns and cities flourished in Africa prior to the colonial era. These include Meroë, Axum, Kumbi-Saleh, Timbuktu, Djenne, Ife and Gao in North and West Africa, and Great Zimbabwe, Kilwa, Sofala, Mombasa and Zanzibar in South and East Africa.[5] Meroë was established in about 560 BC and served as the capital of the Black Kingdom of Kush. Some of these cities were surrounded by walls of stone or earth.[6] Walls surrounding these ancient cities had three main purposes: defining the settlements, controlling growth and protecting the inhabitants from external threats.

Often, the towns were intersected by avenues and alleyways, which opened onto broad thoroughfares. In the more politically centralized polities such as Asante, Yoruba, Hausa and Ganda, the towns were configured in radial concentric formations with roads that originated at the ruler's compound or a central marketplace, and radiated to various provincial centres. In south-western Nigeria, the planning process adopted was one that enhanced the realization of aspirations and protected socio-economic and political interests.[7] For instance, the location of the main market in close proximity to the king's palace was meant to facilitate easy access to a wide variety of goods, especially food items by the king's household. Similarly, safety and security were the major considerations in the road network design and social institutions surrounding the palace. 'Planning activities' such as the construction of roads and markets, drainage clearance and digging of waste disposal sites were often undertaken under the supervision of family heads and local chiefs who in turn reported back to the king.[8] The towns remained essentially agrarian, regardless of their size. This meant that ancient African towns successfully maximized the use of urban space while minimizing the feeling of congestion.

East and Central Europe

East and Central Europe also has a history of urbanization dating back thousands of years. Nesebar is one of Europe's oldest cities. The ancient city's spatial structure was largely influenced by the Greeks who colonized the region at the beginning of the sixth century BC. This explains typical ancient Greek urban design features such as the acropolis, a temple of Apollo, an agora and a wall with Thracian fortifications. Dubrovnik, also known as Ragusa, is a historic city founded in the seventh century and located on the Adriatic Sea in Croatia. One remarkable aspect of Dubrovnik is that as far back as 1272, it had well-developed local governance statutes, which included urban planning regulations. The regulations included elements specifically addressing matters of general welfare, health and sanitation. A third ancient planned city, Novgorod, dates back to the tenth century.[9] The city benefited from its first formal planning initiative in 1530, when the authorities made conscious effort to replan its streets. In 1723, Peter the Great replanned the city, and present-day Novgorod has since developed around the framework that was established during this time.

In sum, urban planning has been practised by all regions and cultures since the earliest times. It represented a collective effort by societies to organize their living spaces in ways that were most suited to their environments, economies and political structures, although this sometimes expressed imbalances in power and wealth. In the 21st century there are parts of the world where planning is no longer a useful tool through which societies can organize their living spaces; but there is no reason why it cannot be reformed to play this role.

THE EMERGENCE OF MODERNIST PLANNING

Modernist planning emerged in the latter part of the 19th century, largely in response to rapidly growing, chaotic and polluted cities in Western Europe, brought about by the Industrial Revolution. From the outset, it was influenced by two sets of factors: technical and ideological.[10] The first set of factors accounted for planning's effort to combat the negative externalities of industrialization and urbanization.

In this regard, planning and health officials collaborated to contain contagious and deadly diseases such as cholera and other epidemics. Accordingly, planning and public health were linked, with ancestry in the English sanitary movement of the 1840s.[11] Urban planners, most of whom were civil engineers and health professionals, were required to design schemes to improve sanitation conditions in residential areas and work places. Other efforts sought to separate land-use activities, especially residential, from industrial zones. Yet others were designed to separate those infected by contagious diseases from the rest of the population.

Planning has also been described as a tool for attaining political and ideological goals of the state or ruling class. It was not uncommon, therefore, for middle- and higher-income groups to use planning as a way of maintaining their property prices and excluding 'less desirable' lower-income residents, ethnic minorities and traders from their areas.[12] In this regard, 20th-century developments in European urban planning are characterized as 'essentially a political, social, cultural, professional and technical response to a blend of circumstances which marked the years at the turn of the century'.[13] Technical and ideological factors collectively produced a number of urban 'visions' put forward by particular individuals. These were to shape the objectives and forms of planning, which in turn showed remarkable resilience through the 20th century.

Three essential components characterized planning for most of the 20th century.[14] The first was that it was seen as an exercise in the physical planning and design of human settlements; hence, while it responded to social, economic or political matters, it was not seen as the task of planning to intervene in these matters. Planning was therefore perceived as a technical activity to be carried out by trained experts without the involvement of politicians or communities. Second, planning involved the production of master plans, blueprint plans[15] or layout plans, showing a detailed view of the built form of a city once it attained its ideal end-state. Third, planning was viewed as a normative task that should be driven by a particular set of values which described the ideal living environment and, in the view of planners, reflected the 'public good'. Broadly, these values tended to be quite specific to the time and place in which they were formulated. Hence, early British town planning was strongly influenced by the radical and utopian socialism of the time and a nostalgic longing for the village life of medieval England. One of the most influential planning forms of the time, the Garden City, developed by Ebenezer Howard, represented an attempt to recreate this village life through bringing 'green' back into towns made up of winding roads and separate cottage residences, and through controlling the size and growth of the town. The objectives here were twofold: social – the preservation of a traditional way of life which was essentially anti-urban; and aesthetic – bringing the beauty of the countryside into the towns.[16]

In other countries where the concept of planning emerged to counter the 'horrors' of the industrial city, other normative visions prevailed. In France, the ideas of Le Corbusier during the 1920s and 1930s established the ideal of the 'modernist' city,[17] which came to be highly influential

Early British town planning was strongly influenced by the radical and utopian socialism and a nostalgic longing for the village life of medieval England

In France, the ideas of Le Corbusier during the 1920s and 1930s established the ideal of the 'modernist' city internationally and still shapes planning in many parts of the world. Le Corbusier held that the ideal city was neat, ordered and highly controlled. Slums, narrow streets and mixed-use areas were to be demolished and replaced with efficient transportation corridors, residences in the form of tower blocks with open space 'flowing' between them and land uses separated into mono-functional zones.[18]

In the US, early 20th-century visions of the ideal city were different. Frank Lloyd Wright's solution to the problems of rapid industrialization in New York took the form of low-density, dispersed cities with each family on its own small plot, but using the modern technologies of the time (such as the car) to access other urban functions. Some argued that the seeds of later suburbia are to be found in these ideas. Other elements of American urban idealism were drawn from Europe: Le Corbusian modernism inspired skyscraper development and the City Beautiful movement drew on the boulevards and promenades of the great European capitals. The political agenda underlying these ideas should not be lost: for the middle class 'the planner's first aim was to eliminate the breeding places of disease, moral depravity, discontent and socialism'.[19]

But while the spatial forms promoted in the planning visions tended to vary, the nature of the plans that produced them had more in common. The *master plans* which carried these urban visions were based on a number of key assumptions that:

- Planners possessed particular design expertise, much like architects, but that once the design was complete it was then up to other professionals to implement it.
- Planners were the custodians of the 'public good', which they were entrusted to promote, through their plans. The UK planning system has generally accepted a state interpretation of aggregated individual preferences, which sets the goals of amenity, convenience and efficiency as standards to define the best use of land. But in the US, much land-use policy has been driven by a market-related ethic which holds that the right decision is the one which creates the greatest aggregate level of social benefit, indicated by the price signals of a free market economy in land.
- Through the design of physical space it would be possible to shape the nature of societies which occupied it. The assumption that the 'neighbourhood unit' planning model could create social communities was a good example of this.
- Plans should be comprehensive. The modernist assumption here is that planners can envisage new and better urban worlds, and plan for them.
- It was possible to predict both the scale and nature of population and economic growth over the long term and plan for this.
- Cities were amenable to manipulation in terms of these plans: that local governments as the implementers of plans had sufficient control over the use of each land parcel to ensure that the plan would eventually be realized.

- It was possible to envisage a future ideal state for each city and to achieve this through the plan, and that thereafter no further change would occur.

The close partner to the master plan was the development control system, or zoning scheme. If the master plan was the 'creative' and forward-looking vision of the city, then the zoning scheme was the primary legal tool through which it would be implemented. This took various forms. In the UK, development rights are nationalized. Local plans give an indication of future land use but no automatic rights, giving wider discretionary powers to planners when faced with a development application. In the US, the forward plan (comprehensive plan) plays a less important role in most cities and may be disregarded. The important planning tool is the zoning scheme,[20] giving property owners with particular land-use rights almost unlimited right to exercise them, with any challenge to this taking place through the courts rather than being adjudicated by the forward plan.[21]

The concept of land-use zoning originated in Germany and was adopted with great enthusiasm across the US and Europe in the early part of the 20th century. In the US, it was declared a general police power in 1926[22] and 754 communities had adopted zoning ordinances by 1929. In the UK, the 1932 Town and Country Planning Act carried forward ideas of master planning and development control, and provided a model for much colonial planning. These ideas were also reflected in European planning of the time, where the concept of detailed land-use zoning and master plans has been even more resilient.[23]

This modernist concept of planning, which emerged in response to a very particular time and set of regional circumstances, spread throughout the world in the following decades. The next section examines why and how this occurred.

THE GLOBAL SPREAD OF MODERNIST PLANNING

A central observation in this Global Report is that in many parts of the world, planning systems are in place that have been imposed or borrowed from elsewhere. In some cases, these 'foreign' ideas have not changed significantly since the time they were imported. Planning systems and urban forms are inevitably based on particular assumptions about the time and place for which they were designed; but these assumptions often do not hold in other parts of the world and thus these systems and ideas are often inappropriate in the context to which they have been transplanted. Frequently, these imported ideas have also been drawn on for reasons of political, ethnic or racial domination and exclusion rather than in the interests of good planning. This section first examines the mechanisms through which these planning ideas were transferred from one part of the world to another, and then the form which they took in the adopting region.

In the US, early 20th-century visions of the ideal city took the form of low-density, dispersed cities with each family on its small plot

In many parts of the world, planning systems are in place that have been imposed or borrowed from elsewhere

Mechanisms for the transfer of planning ideas

Urban planning ideas were spread in a number of different ways. Planning historians[24] have offered a typology of the transfer of planning ideas: the first category being 'imposition' (through authoritarianism, contestation or consensus) and the second category being 'borrowing' (through synthesis, selection or uncritical reception). Historians have argued that the nature of the power relationship between exporting and importing country is a major determining factor, with colonialism and conquest giving rise to imposition of foreign planning systems, while a more equal relationship between countries sees planning ideas transported through other means: travelling planning consultants, politicians or other influential people, or scholarly articles and books. This process of diffusion was never smooth or simple: the ideas themselves were often varied and contested, and they articulated in different ways with the contexts to which they were imported.

The main conduits for the transfer of planning ideas have been colonial governments, educational and scientific institutions (including lecture tours and international conferences), professional associations and journals, and international development agencies and consultancies.

■ Colonial governments

Colonialism was a very direct vehicle for diffusing planning systems, particularly in those parts of the world under colonial rule when planning was ascendant. In these contexts planning of urban settlements was frequently bound up with the 'modernizing and civilizing' mission of colonial authorities, but also with the control of urbanization processes and of the urbanizing population. Military officers-cum-colonial administrators, engineers, surveyors, architects and contractors were instrumental in efforts in this regard. Colonial authorities confidently assumed that European models of planning would be effective in colonized territories. A British colonial officer in India, referring to British Garden Cities, was quoted as saying:

> I hope that in New Delhi we shall be able to show how those ideas which Mr Howard put forward ... can be brought in to assist this first Capital created in our time. The fact is that no new city or town should be permissible in these days to which the word 'Garden' cannot be rightly applied.[25]

In the years after independence, many foreign professionals left; but a significant number remained to work under post-colonial governments, in most cases implementing planning legislation inherited from colonizing powers. In this way institutionalized modernist planning approaches retained influence in governments well after the colonial era.

■ Educational and scientific research institutions

The university education of planners did not begin until the early 20th century. The University of Liverpool (UK) offered the first course beginning in 1907, and Harvard University (US) claims the earliest North American degree course dating from 1928 (see Chapter 10). Planning programmes in developing countries only emerged later, often with curricula, texts and staff originating in developed countries, particularly where colonial linkages existed. Modernist planning was therefore taught for decades in planning schools in the developing world, and in many countries this is still the case. There was also a flow of students from developing countries to study in institutions in developed countries. This was based on the assumption that degrees from such institutions were of higher quality and more prestigious. Many universities in developed countries began to offer 'international' planning programmes to students from the developing world. While these considered developing contexts in a general way, the teaching philosophies, approaches and tools were usually derived from a developed world context. All of these mechanisms served to diffuse planning approaches from the developed to the developing world.

Lecture tours and international conferences have formed a further mechanism for the transfer of modernist planning ideas. The organization with a record for extensive use of this strategy is the Garden Cities Town Planning Association (GCTPA) (see Box 3.1).

■ Professional associations and journals

Professional associations and the journals that they produce were, and continue to be, instrumental in transmitting Western planning ideas and schemes to other parts of the world. Prominent here was the French *Revue Générale de l'Architecture et des Travaux Publics*. This has been characterized as 'one of the leading architectural journals on both sides of the Atlantic during the 19th century'.[26] César Daly, the journal's editor from 1839 to 1888, is best remembered for his articulation of the nature of the city in the modern industrial age. His research on the principal determinants of the underlying infrastructure of industrial cities was modelled on Second Empire Paris. This research constitutes one of the main pillars of urban reforms in the French capital as well as other major cities throughout France and its dependencies.

Several professional organizations, including the Royal Institute of British Architects (1834), the American Institute of Architects (1857) and the Royal Institution of Chartered Surveyors (1868), were already propagating Western concepts of physical structures and spatial organization across

The main conduits for the transfer of planning ideas have been colonial governments, educational and scientific institutions, professional associations and journals and international development agencies

Lecture tours and international conferences have formed a further mechanism for the transfer of modernist planning ideas

> **Box 3.1 The Garden Cities Town Planning Association and the spread of Eurocentric planning models**
>
> The Garden Cities Town Planning Association (GCTPA) was spun off from the parent organization – the Garden Cities Association – as a means of casting a more encompassing net to capture interest and membership from all over the world. In 1913 alone, the organization dispatched over 21,000 information packets around the world. To achieve its desire to spread and universalize the Western planning model, the GCTPA created a colonial unit in 1912, with the purpose of drawing attention to the planning needs of the newly emerging countries. In 1913, GCTPA Secretary Ewart Culpin embarked on a three-month tour of Canada and the US.
> Source: Freestone, 1998, p161

the world before Ebenezer Howard founded the Garden Cities Association in 1899.[27] Following this, several associations became actively involved in urban affairs and planning. These included the Royal Town Planning Institute (1914), the Canadian Institute of Planners (1919), the American City Planning Institute (1917) (which later became the American Institute of Planners in 1939 and then the American Planning Association in 1978) and the Planning Institute of Australia (1951). These professional associations have always operated international chapters through which they are able to spread Western planning concepts and ideology. Newer professional planning associations such as the Commonwealth Association of Planners and Global Planners Network have been less dogmatic in the promotion of Eurocentric planning models and more attentive and receptive to developments in the planning field in non-Western regions.

■ International development agencies and consultancies

Western urban planning consultants have been active in transmitting Eurocentric planning models to other regions since the colonial era in Africa and Asia. Colonial governments, most of which operated on very tight budgets, needed professionals with expertise in architecture and urban planning but could not afford them on a full-time basis. Hiring these professionals as consultants was therefore a logical alternative. The use of Western consultants continued after colonial rule. Since the end of World War II, there has been a steady increase in the number of Western-based planning and architectural firms executing projects in foreign countries. In this regard, the *Bureau Central d'Etudes pour les Equipement d'Outre-Mer* has been instrumental in transplanting European ideas and concepts in urban planning and public infrastructure development to the French-speaking world.[28]

The influence of modernist planning in various parts of the world

As noted earlier, modernist planning ideas were imposed upon, or adopted in, countries in developing and transitional regions. The point has been made that the transfer of ideas is never a simple process, and imported concepts interact in various ways with local conditions.

■ Transitional countries: Eastern and Central Europe

Industrialization and urbanization came later in Eastern Europe than it did in the West. But by the early 20th century, countries in Eastern Europe were looking to the West for planning solutions to address their growing cities. The Soviet Union was keen to avoid the uncontrolled urban growth seen in the West and planning ideas which offered 'decentralization, low density and even shrinkage were perceived as desirable alternatives'.[29] Ebenezer Howard's Garden City model was therefore particularly attractive. A Russian translation of Ebenezer Howard's classic, *The Garden Cities of Tomorrow*, was released in 1911. Shortly after, a Russian Garden City Association was established.[30] Although this

association was short lived due to the Russian Revolution of 1917, Howard's ideas, particularly the idea of designing more spacious, airy and well-ventilated cities, lived on in the Soviet Union. Making the built environment green became a popular term in Soviet urban planning vocabulary.

The Garden City model was not the only Western concept adopted in the Soviet Union. The comprehensive planning scheme developed by Patrick Geddes and the master plan were adopted as well. The absence of speculation and free market forces in the Soviet Union contributed to making Soviet planners relatively more successful than their Western counterparts in master planning. Under Stalin, master planning was linked to the need for post-war reconstruction, and rebuilding took the form of 'socialist realism' projects with classical architectural styles, public squares and perimeter blocks. Attempts by local architects to introduce urban modernism during this period were suppressed.[31]

In the region previously known as Yugoslavia, a centralized planned economic system was introduced during the communist era beginning in 1946. The first decade of the post-war era witnessed a barrage of criticisms being levelled against bourgeois architecture and urbanism. At the same time, efforts were made to implement the principles of egalitarian and planned urbanization through industrial decentralization. At the city level, a number of planning principles were promoted through the mechanisms of standardization, proper city size, the role of the city centre and the neighbourhood unit.[32] Planners in the region were increasingly turning to the West for answers to the region's urban problems, and they moved swiftly to embrace the functional ideas of Le Corbusier and CIAM.[33] These ideas were implemented throughout Yugoslavia during the post-war era, and CIAM 10 was held in Dubrovnik in 1956.

■ Latin America

In Latin American cities, past colonial links played a role in transferring European planning ideas to this part of the world; but more general intellectual exchange did this as well. Latin American authorities of the republican consolidation era viewed major European cities as emblematic of modernity. Consequently, they undertook massive urban renewal projects in an effort to replicate European cities in the region.

The authorities were particularly drawn to the designs that constituted part of Georges-Eugène Haussmann's *grand travaux* projects in Paris. Two distinct waves of Haussmannian planning in the region occurred during the second half of the 19th century. The first wave led to the 'systematization' of the structure of the capital cities within the colonial-era city limits. The second resulted in expanding the capital cities beyond these limits. The modernization efforts were physically manifested through the superimposition of wide tree-lined boulevards on the colonial urban layouts. Despite borrowing generously from the West, authorities saw the projects as a means of ridding the colonial cities of all vestiges of their history. This was especially the case in the capital cities of Argentina, Chile and Brazil, which were the most rapidly expanding economies in the region at that time.

In general, French planning ideas had the most influence on the form and structure of major Latin American cities during the last century. For instance, traces of Le Corbusier's ideas are visible in many urban structures in the region. This is despite the fact that Le Corbusier's proposals had become the object of criticisms by a new generation of Latin American urban design professionals at the turn of the century. One of the best-known projects influenced by Le Corbusier was Lucio Costa's plan for Brasilia, which incorporated a division of city space into functional zones, the use of superblocks and tower blocks, the generous provision of green space, and the priority accorded to motorized vehicular traffic. As a practising architect and urban planner, Costa incorporated the ideas of Le Corbusier into the design of the Gustavo Capanema Palace (*Palacio Gustavo Capanema*) located in downtown Rio de Janeiro, and his plan for Brasilia.[34]

From the 1900s, the cities of Latin America were expanding at an alarming rate, and sprawling suburbs developed as the middle class sought new residential locations. This expansion was exacerbated by the advent of the motor car in the region. To remedy the situation, authorities imported the Garden City model and modified it to take the form of the 'garden suburb', located within cities rather than outside them. Rio de Janeiro was extensively affected by European engineering, architecture and planning models. This was especially the case during Francisco Pereira Passos's tenure (1902–1906) as mayor.[35] An engineer, Passos studied in Paris from 1857 to 1860 and, thus, was familiar with the works of Georges-Eugène Haussmann. As mayor of Rio, Passos oversaw the city's massive urban renewal project. The project was one of Latin America's most extensive during the first half of the 20th century. The project had two ostensibly contradictory aims: to rid Rio de Janeiro of all vestiges of its colonial heritage, and to endow it with features characteristic of major European cities. There is little doubt that the street-widening and similar projects attained their objective of improving spatial aesthetics. However, the project in Rio de Janeiro caused enormous collateral damage. For example, about 3000 buildings, most of which provided housing for the city's poor families, were destroyed. Besides, the resultant large streets were not pedestrian friendly as they encouraged speedy automobile traffic.

■ **South-East and East Asia**

While most diffusion of Western urban planning models to this region occurred during the colonial era, some of the more important influences came through countries that were not colonizing powers. Prominent in this regard is the US. Although not a traditional colonial power, the US has historically been present in, and maintained ties with, territories and countries in Asia and the Pacific region. Any meaningful discussion of the impact of imported ideas upon urban planning in this region must therefore take account not only of the role of the traditional colonial powers such as Britain, France, The Netherlands, Spain and Portugal, but also that of other culturally and politico-economically influential nations such as the US, Canada, Russia and Japan. Occasionally, these countries acted not as emissaries of their

own models and principles, but those of their allies. For example, the urban planning models that the Japanese planners promoted during their occupation of China were not of Japanese but of American or other Western origin.

The City of Baguio (the Philippines) was the first major human settlement with design roots in the US to be established in Asia. It was designed by the famous Chicago architect Daniel Hudson Bunham, the founder of the City Beautiful movement. The city's axial orientations and panoramic vistas stand in stark contrast to the Hispanic-American designs characteristic of the surrounding Filipino lowlands. Baguio served as the summer capital of colonial Philippines between 1909 and 1913. Another American urban planning invention, the neighbourhood unit, which was originally formulated in the 1920s, later found its way to China.[36] However, it was first employed on a significant scale in China not by Americans but by Japanese colonial urban planners. This shows how the international diffusion of planning ideas is not a linear trajectory but a complex process involving 'local appropriations, (mis)interpretations, reinventions and resistances'.[37] Following Japan's military occupation of Manchuria in 1931, and subsequent to renaming the city Xinjing (Shinkyo) in 1931, the Japanese produced a five-year plan (1932–1937) that sought to reconstitute the city based on the principles of Eurocentric urban planning, particularly the neighbourhood unit concept.[38]

While the Japanese were persuaded by Western concepts of urban design, their ability to adopt such concepts in Japan was constrained by several forces, not least of which were Japan's land tenure system and its weak planning powers. Therefore, Japanese planners saw in their occupation of China an opportunity to experiment with the barrage of Western planning ideas that had become internationally prominent, especially during the period leading up to World War II and immediately thereafter. Later in the 1940s, indigenous Chinese urban planners followed in the footsteps of their Japanese colonial predecessors by employing not only the neighbourhood unit but also other Western models of planning in their human settlement development projects. For instance, the first draft of the new Greater Shanghai plan incorporated many standard features of Western spatial design. This is a function of the fact that Western-trained Chinese designers, planners and architects dominated the municipal commission that produced the 1946 plan. Features usually associated with Euro-American planning include zoning, the self-contained satellite city and the neighbourhood unit.

British colonialism had a significant impact upon physical structures, institutional reforms and urban planning education in Asia. British colonial authorities established new human settlements and influenced the development of existing ones in India, Sri Lanka, Malaysia and the Maldives. The imperative for trade dictated a need to concentrate most colonial urban development projects in port cities. Thus, for instance, Chennai (formerly Madras), Mumbai (formerly Bombay) and Kolkata (also known as Calcutta) in India, and Karachi (Pakistan), Colombo (Sri Lanka), Singapore and Hong Kong emerged as the leading beneficiaries of colonial urban development efforts in South-East and East Asia. The British

French planning ideas had the most influence on the form and structure of major Latin American cities during the last century

British colonialism had a significant impact upon physical structures, institutional reforms and urban planning education in Asia introduced urban forms that were previously unknown in the region. Thus the concept of racial spatial segregation, which sought to separate Europeans from 'racial others', was foreign in the region, even in societies such as India that practised caste-based segregation.

In Singapore, the plan designed by Sir Stamford Raffles went beyond the 'whites' versus 'others' nomenclature that was a standard feature in British colonial town planning elsewhere.[39] British colonial Singapore contained six main ethnic groups (European, Chinese, Malay, Indian, Arab and Bugis), which were assigned to different districts within the urban centre. Zoning provided justification for implementing apparently racist spatial planning schemes. A typical example is the implementation of policies that guaranteed Europeans exclusive rights to picturesque hilltop locations, the so-called 'hill stations'. Before the end of the colonial era in India, the British had developed as least 80 hill stations throughout the country.

Institutionally, the British contributed to the development of urban planning in the region by introducing British legal and institutional frameworks for formulating and implementing planning policies. British colonial authorities are credited with the following developments that still exist to date: municipal governance structures; formalization of the land development process; a system for cataloguing and storing data on land, land uses and users; zoning regulations; and building control regulations.

A series of cholera outbreaks in the late 1800s and early 1900s gave colonial authorities the opportunity to introduce strategies recommended in Edwin Chadwick's report to combat the health consequences of the Industrial Revolution almost half a century earlier in England. The health officer for Calcutta Municipal Corporation recommended health policies for colonial India that were rooted in British public health practice. The policies sought to improve ventilation for housing units, develop good drainage systems and supply potable water to the burgeoning urban populations of the region. The same policies were subsequently recommended for Hong Kong and Singapore, and later throughout British colonies in Asia and Africa.

The Dutch also influenced planning in this region. Dutch structural engineer H. Thomas Karsten was influential in this regard.[40] Karsten, who possessed no formal training in urban planning, exhibited antipathy towards Western civilization and adopted a radical approach to spatial organization. He favoured urban planning principles that integrated Western with indigenous elements and displayed a concern for the preservation of native culture that was unusual among colonial authorities. Despite his aversion for the colonial dogma of the time, Karsten's spatial design constructs remained essentially European, as demonstrated in his planning proposals and projects.

■ Middle East and North Africa

Traces of European influence on spatial and physical structures are visible everywhere in the Middle East and North Africa. By 1914, most of the region, including all of North Africa, Cyprus and Aden, were under the occupation of European imperial powers, and the Persian Gulf states were under the control of Britain as protectorates. At the same time, Britain and Russia were closely involved with the internal affairs of Iran and Afghanistan. These powers were responsible for attempts to 'modernize' the region, including in the area of urban planning and municipal governance. Measures to reform or build key institutions, including the land tenure systems, municipal governments, building codes, public infrastructure, and spatial (planning and urban design) and physical structures (architecture and construction materials and techniques) were instituted.

Legislation dealing with urban land use, regulatory measures and spatial design structures based on the European model are commonplace throughout the region. For instance, building codes and regulations defining relationships between buildings and streets were directly imported from Europe. The increasing influence of the West, coupled with wealth from oil revenue, particularly in Saudi Arabia, Kuwait and Iraq, have accelerated the supplanting of traditional building materials such as mud and stone by Western varieties such as cement, plywood, aluminium and glass. In addition, urban planning authorities adopted the gridiron pattern of streets in new subdivisions in the region.

European colonial powers were largely responsible for introducing Western urban planning concepts and models in North Africa. Here, they encountered well-developed densely populated Islamic walled cities with no room for expansion. Accordingly, colonial urban planners had one specific mission: develop new planned spacious layouts based on European principles to serve as exclusive European enclaves.[41] In Algeria, Tunisia and Morocco, colonial urban planners developed new layouts that reflected French urban planning style as well as urban features. The new towns contained broad, straight boulevards separating city blocks, minor feeder streets and plots dividing the blocks and high-density multi-storey buildings concentrated in terraces within the centre. The inclusion of these features constituted an attempt to replicate Haussmann's design of Paris in colonial North Africa and the new layouts stood in stark contrast to the Islamic towns. Italian and British colonial planners developed plans that were less elaborate than those of their French counterparts. Nevertheless, they were successful in making indelible imprints on the urban spatial structures of Libya and Egypt.

These Western urban planning models usually resulted in the emergence of two self-contained urban sectors in cities throughout North Africa. The Islamic towns (*medinas*) continued to function in many respects as they had prior to the European conquest,[42] and the new layouts, or what the French referred to as *villes nouvelles* or *villes européennes* (European towns), functioned as independent units to serve the European settler community. This brought about *de facto* racial residential segregation. As the *medinas* grew increasingly overcrowded, they were seen as a health and security threat and the response was to build new *medinas* along traditional Islamic lines but employing Western organizational methods and principles. With rapid urbanization, informal settlements (*biddonvilles*) began to develop. In some cases these were demolished, but in others

---

Margin notes:

Zoning provided justification for implementing apparently racist spatial planning schemes

European colonial powers were largely responsible for introducing Western urban planning concepts and models in North Africa

basic services were provided in a series of rectangular layouts or cités in suburbs of the major cities.[43]

Until the end of World War II, Western planning laws and regulations were applicable exclusively in the European towns, and were extended to the *medinas* only when public health and safety was an issue. After World War II, colonial government intervention in urban planning became more forceful through the establishment of more elaborate urban planning machinery and the creation of unified urban planning systems.

■ Sub-Saharan Africa

In sub-Saharan Africa, diffusion of planning ideas occurred mainly through British, German, French and Portuguese colonial influence, using their home-grown instruments of master planning, zoning, building regulations and the urban models of the time – garden cities, neighbourhood units and Radburn layouts, and later urban modernism. Most colonial and later post-colonial governments also initiated a process of the commodification of land within the liberal tradition of private property rights, with the state maintaining control over the full exercise of these rights, including aspects falling under planning and zoning ordinances. Some of the impacts of colonial urban planning on the structure and pattern of African cities are presented in Box 3.2.

However, it is significant to note that imported planning systems were not applied equally to all sectors of the urban population. For example, towns in colonized territories in sub-Saharan Africa[44] were usually zoned into low-density residential areas for Europeans (these areas had privately owned large plots, were well serviced and were subject to European-style layouts and building codes); medium-density residential areas for African civil servants (with modest services, some private ownership and the enforcement of building standards); and high-density residential areas (for the indigenous population who were mostly involved in the informal sector, with little public infrastructure, and few or no building controls). In East African colonies, the Asian population was placed in the medium-density zone. Spatially, the low-density European areas were set at a distance from the African and Asian areas, apparently for health reasons. Many master plans and zoning schemes today maintain this density distinction and also define single-use areas: residential, business, industrial and public. Planning laws and zoning ordinances in many cases are exact copies of those developed in Europe or the UK in the early 20th century and subsequently enforced under colonial rule.

Planning, therefore, was, and still is, used as a tool of social segregation and exclusion in many colonized territories. This reached epic proportions in South Africa where planning became the central mechanism for the apartheid government (post-1948) to achieve racially segregated cities.

Many African countries still have planning legislation based on British or European planning laws from the 1930s or 1940s, which have been revised only marginally. Post-colonial governments tended to reinforce and entrench colonial spatial plans and land management tools, sometimes in even more rigid form than colonial governments.[45]

Enforcing freehold title for land and doing away with indigenous and communal forms of tenure was a necessary basis for state land management, but also a source of state revenue and often a political tool to reward supporters. Frequently, post-colonial political elites who promoted these tenure reforms were strongly supported by former colonial governments, foreign experts and international policy agencies. In Cameroon, for example, a 1974 legislation required people to apply for a land certificate for private landownership. However, the procedures were complex and expensive and took about seven years to complete. Few people applied; yet in 1989 the certificate became the only recognized proof of landownership and all other customary or informal rights to land were nullified.[46]

Controls over land were also extended to housing in the post-colonial period. The master plans were used (and mostly still are) in conjunction with zoning ordinances that stipulated building standards and materials for housing as well as tenure requirements. For example, without an official building permit, an approved building plan and land title, a house in Cameroon is regarded as informal.[47] Yet, securing these involves five different government agencies and is a long, circuitous and expensive process which most poor people cannot understand or afford. Inevitably, the bulk of housing in African cities is deemed as informal.

Important and capital cities in Africa were often the subject of grand master planning under colonial rule, or involving prominent international planners or architects. Remarkably, in many cases, these plans remain relatively unchanged and some are still in force. Some examples include the urban plan of Mogadishu, Somalia, drawn up between 1928 and 1930 and last revised between 1944 and 1948; the plan for Banjul, Gambia, drawn up in 1943 and used until the late 1970s; the 1944 plan for Accra, revised in 1957 and still in force; the plan for Lusaka drawn up by Doxiadis in 1968; and the master plan for Abuja, Nigeria,

In sub-Saharan Africa, diffusion of planning ideas occurred mainly through British, German, French and Portuguese colonial influence

Many African countries still have planning legislation based on British or European planning laws from the 1930s or 1940s

drawn up by US consultants in the 1970s and currently being implemented.[48] The guiding 'vision' in these plans has been that of urban modernism, based on assumptions that it has always been simply a matter of time before African countries 'catch up' economically and culturally with the West.

THE PERSISTENCE OF MODERNIST URBAN PLANNING

The preceding sections have discussed the historical emergence of particular approaches to urban planning (termed modernist planning) and how these approaches came to be adopted in large parts of the world. The section that follows discusses how and why these older forms of planning have persisted in many countries, what the reasons for this persistence might be, and what the impacts have been.

Extent of persistence of older approaches to urban planning

In recent times, growing criticism of modernist planning has emerged from the same part of the world in which it originated (Western Europe and the US), and in some countries concerted effort has been made to develop alternative approaches. Yet, modernist planning is still practised throughout the world,[49] including in countries where it has been strongly criticized. It is probably true to say that modernist planning remains the dominant form of planning worldwide. This section examines where modernist planning has persisted, why this has been the case, and what the effects of this have been.

In general, while it is possible to argue that modernist urban planning has persisted in much of the world, in individual countries and cities, the pattern is often more complex. While a broad modernist approach may have been maintained, national and local governments in many places have amended their planning systems to suit local demands, and have sometimes reformed parts of their systems and not others. It is also not unusual for innovative planning approaches to be adopted in parallel with older approaches: examples of this in Africa and Eastern Europe are cited below. Sometimes, older terminology (e.g. the term 'master plan') has been retained, but the form and process of planning may have changed considerably. Plans are often the result of highly contested political processes and there can be major differences between original intentions and final outcomes. Finally, the built urban form of cities in most parts of the world is determined only partially by planning and far more by the property development industry and private individuals: urban modernist built forms are often favoured by these sectors as well.

■ Developed regions

Much of the critique of master planning and modernist urban forms has come from the planning and architectural literature in the developed regions of the world,[50] and in

practice there has been a significant shift away from it and towards strategic planning. In many European countries, strategic spatial plans now provide a framework for local redevelopment and regeneration projects, which are usually private-sector led or delivered through partnership arrangements.[51] Plans often encourage urban forms that are more compact, mixed use and sustainable. In the US, public incentives and investment are used to guide private development projects, although most cities retain a comprehensive plan and zoning scheme. In Australia, city-wide strategic plans attempt to encourage urban compaction and sustainable urban forms.[52] There have been suggestions, though, that a form of master planning has been revived in many of the new regeneration and redevelopment projects, but that this is now market-led rather than state-led master planning, with the architect and developer primarily in charge.[53] The new master plans are three-dimensional urban designs usually for prestige property developments, such as waterfronts, conference centres or shopping malls; but in all other respects they retain the qualities of old-style and discredited master planning. Modernist architectural styles still frequently prevail.

■ Transitional regions

Under communism, master planning was the dominant form of urban planning in the East European transitional countries. In the post-communist neo-liberal era, planning suffered a crisis of legitimacy; but the resultant chaotic growth of cities and environmental crises resulted in the re-establishment or revival of master planning across countries in the region after 2000. For example, the current master plan for Tbilisi (Georgia) is dated 1975; but even recent plans, such as the 2007 plan for Sofia (Bulgaria), is termed a master plan.[54] In part, this persistence has been because of a lack of resources and capacity at local government level, which has prevented innovative planning, and in part because of bureaucratic inertia. With few exceptions, such as plans involving environmental issues, citizen/stakeholder participation continues to be low throughout the region. Some planners in the region oppose citizen and stakeholder participation, contending that it is unnecessary and cumbersome. Even in the rare instances of participation, as in the Sofia master plan, only token public participation was tolerated.[55] In essence, post-communist planning in Sofia has followed the master plan approach, thereby displaying very little break from past planning traditions.[56]

There are indications of change, however. Some cities are adopting Agenda 21 processes, and some are producing strategic plans with stakeholder involvement. Authorities in Slovenia have used surveys, interview sessions, workshops and collective mapping exercises to elicit the input of citizens and other stakeholders in the planning process. In the Slovenian town of Komenda, for example, the final product has been described as a genuinely citizen-driven plan. In Serbia, civic urban networks have set up informal city websites dedicated to the public discussion of urban problems and the channelling of public concerns to municipal authorities. In Budapest, buildings in the city's older areas had deteriorated significantly during the communist era, and during the 1970s had been marked for demolition and modernist renewal. But in the 1980s, a new rehabilitation plan was prepared, preserving the buildings, and this was successfully implemented by the district government. Most importantly, the authorities were proactive and successful in enlisting the support of private developers.[57]

■ **Developing regions**

Modernist forms of planning have shown the strongest persistence in the developing world, and have sometimes been the approach of choice in countries setting up new planning systems (China). However, there is mounting evidence suggesting that master planning is not always an appropriate management tool to deal with the kinds of problems faced by cities in the developing world.

Modernist planning remains particularly strong in those countries which were once under European colonial rule: much of Africa and parts of Asia. Many African countries still have planning legislation based on British or European planning laws from the 1930s or 1940s, and which has been revised only marginally. Planning systems in many African countries are highly centralized, top down, and non-participatory, producing rigid end-state master plans underpinned by traditional zoning schemes. As mentioned earlier, important and capital cities in Africa were often the subject of grand master planning under colonial rule, sometimes involving prominent international planners or architects. Remarkably, in many cases, these plans remain relatively unchanged and some are still in force. For example, the master plan for Abuja, Nigeria, drawn up by US consultants in the 1970s, is currently being implemented. In Francophone Africa, French planning documents that were transferred to the colonies in the 1960s have hardly been changed. For example, the last revision of the terms of reference for the preparation of urban planning documents in Côte d'Ivoire was in 1985. It was obvious that these terms of reference were not in harmony with the new constitutional context or with modern urban development practices.[58]

Planning in the sub-continent of India has had strong parallels with the African experience, given the common factor of British colonial rule. Limited health and safety measures at the start of the 20th century gave way to master planning and zoning ordinances, introduced under British rule but persisting in post-colonial times. Some 2000 Indian cities now have master plans, all displaying the problems that caused countries such as the UK to shift away from this approach, and yet the main task of municipal planning departments is to produce more such plans.[59] Bangladesh and Pakistan are also still under the sway of master planning. Recently, the growing criticism of the master plan in India led the Ministry of Urban Development to organize a national conference on the theme of Alternatives to the Master Plan. After extensive discussions and debates extending over three days, the meeting concluded that the only alternative to the master plan is a 'better' master plan.[60]

In other parts of the world, institutionalized urban planning came much later, but followed familiar patterns. In China, the City Planning Act of 1989 set up a comprehensive urban planning system based on the production of master plans to guide the growth of China's burgeoning cities. These master plans appear to have learned from some of the critiques of Western master planning. The more positive aspects of these plans, which distinguish them from old-style master plans, are that they are concerned with implementation and with social and economic aspects of cities as well as physical aspects. Furthermore, the urban forms that accompany them, although conforming to urban modernism, also incorporate new ideas about sustainable environments. As indicated earlier, other parts of South and South-East Asia were colonized by Europe and inherited their planning systems, many of which are still in existence.[61]

Countries in Latin America initially followed European modernist approaches to planning; but in recent years they have shifted away from master planning, or reformed it, to a greater extent than other developing regions. Many urban areas have attempted strategic and participatory forms of planning, master plans have been used in new and innovative ways, and some cities have successfully linked their urban plans to infrastructure development (Curitiba, Brazil).[62] Some important and innovative forms of planning and urban management (participatory budgeting and new regulatory approaches) had their origins in this region.

Why modernist approaches to urban planning have persisted

It has been noted that modernist planning (its top-down processes, the rigid end-state form of plans – master plans, and the mono-functional and sterile urban environments produced) has been strongly criticized for some decades. It has been accused of being outdated, inappropriate and, above all, ineffective, especially in cities experiencing rapid growth and change, and the pressures of globalization. It has also been argued that this approach to planning is no longer compatible with the changing role of local governments as the latter have shifted to include a wider range of stakeholders in decision-making and to be facilitative and to promote rather than act as conduits for state-led intervention. The most common criticism of master plans is that they bear so little relation to the reality of rapidly growing and poor cities, or are grounded in legislation that is so outdated, that they are not implemented or are ignored.[63] Yet, in many parts of the world, and particularly in developing countries where modernist planning was frequently inherited from colonial powers, it persists. Governments appear to be reluctant or unable to reform their planning systems. This section puts forward some reasons as to why this might be the case.

In some countries there has been a lack of capacity and skills to reform the planning system. This seems to have been one reason for the persistence of modernist planning in many of the transitional countries.[64] Here the shift away from a communist political system was recent and abrupt, and many aspects of policy had to be transformed in a short period of time. There was almost no experience in local governments of handling planning issues, and little knowledge of participatory or strategic planning processes. At the same time, communism gave way to a strong neo-liberal

Modernist forms of planning have shown the strongest persistence in the developing world

The most common criticism of master plans is that they bear so little relation to the reality of rapidly growing and poor cities

ethos, in which planning was seen as a remnant of older systems of state control. Until very recently, therefore, there has been little support for state involvement in urban planning.

In other parts of the world, and particularly countries in Asia, political systems are highly centralized and there is little tradition of citizen involvement in public decision-making. In China for example, contrary to the West, governance is not based on a separation of state and society, but rather from an attempt to maintain their integration.[65] The concept of central state control over all aspects of urban growth and change through master plans fits well into these kinds of political systems and into situations where most land is in state ownership. Some countries in this region have largely done without institutionalized planning systems.[66] Local governments in these countries have been weak, and cities have been shaped by national economic development policies and rampant market forces. National governments have invested in large productive urban infra-structure projects, but have made almost no effort to attend to welfare needs or environmental issues, or to rationalize spatial development and land release.

It has been suggested that it may not always be in the interests of governments to reform their planning systems, as modernist planning places a great deal of power in the hands of government officials and politicians who might be reluctant to give this up. Modernist approaches are often land dependent, and authorities in many developing countries would not be willing to give up their control over land-related matters, as this would seriously weaken their position. Planning can be used as a 'tactic of marginalization',[67] where particular ethnic or income groups are denied access to planning services and are then marginalized or stigmatized because they live in informal or unregulated areas. Another scenario is that urban areas are covered by rigid and outdated planning regulations that are only partially or intermittently enforced, and this opens the door to bribery and corruption.[68] Master planning has been used (opportunistically) across the globe as a justification for evictions and land grabs. An example is the mass eviction and demolition, which occurred in Zimbabwe in May 2005, under the Town and Country Planning Act of 1976 (Chapter 29, section 12), which authorizes the state to demolish structures and evict people. The planning machinery was effectively mobilized to evict and demolish vendors' structures, informal businesses and homes labelled as illegal by the government.[69] Estimates show that 700,000 people either lost their homes, their source of livelihood or both, with a further 2.4 million people or 18 per cent of the Zimbabwean population being affected to varying degrees.[70]

The built and architectural forms promoted by modernist planning have also shown remarkable resistance to change, and continue to shape urban environments in the building of new capital cities (such as Abuja, Nigeria) and in new city construction in China, Dubai and elsewhere. It appears that the ideas of French architect Le Corbusier and his followers are still strongly associated with being modern, with development and with 'catching up with the West', and have thus been attractive to governments and elites who

wish to be viewed in this way. The aggressive promotion of these forms by developers, consultants and international agencies has also played a key role.

Why modernist approaches to planning are problematic

The most obvious problem with modernist planning is that it completely fails to accommodate the way of life of the major-ity of inhabitants in rapidly growing, and largely poor and informal cities, and thus directly contributes to social and spatial marginalization or exclusion. Furthermore, it fails to take into account the important challenges of 21st-century cities (e.g. climate change, oil depletion, food insecurity and informality), and fails to acknowledge the need to involve communities and other stakeholders in the planning and management of urban areas.

The regulatory aspects of modernist planning (land-use zoning and building regulations) have usually required people to comply with particular forms of land tenure, build-ing regulations, building forms and construction materials, usually embodying European building technologies and imported materials, and requirements for setbacks, minimum plot sizes, coverage, on-site parking, etc. Complying with these requirements imposes significant costs and is usually complex and time consuming. In a study of nine cities in Africa, Asia and Latin America, it was found that most had planning and building standards that were unsuited to the poor.[71] The official minimum plot size in many developing countries is considerably higher than the size of plots regularly occupied in informal settlements and costs more than what many households can afford. Similarly, official standards for road reservations are far more generous in terms of land area than in capital cities of Europe where car ownership is significantly higher than in suburban areas of developing countries.[72] Those adversely affected by such unrealistic standards are the urban poor and low-income households in that they are left out of the planning arena, ending up in unplanned and un-serviced areas where poverty is endemic.[73]

The objectives of regulations relating to safety and health and ensuring access (important for fire and ambulance services at least) are necessary. However, the majority of populations in cities in developing countries live in informal settlements and survive off informal work, and on precarious and unpredictable incomes. The possibility that people living in such circumstances could comply with a zoning ordinance designed for relatively wealthy European towns is extremely unlikely. One of two outcomes is possible here. One is that the system is strongly enforced and people who cannot afford to comply with the zoning requirements are forced to move to areas where they can evade detection – which would usually be an illegal informal settlement, probably in the peri-urban areas. Alternatively, the munici-pality may not have the capacity to enforce the ordinance, in which case it will be ignored as simply unachievable. A common pattern in many cities is that there are core areas of economic and governmental significance that are protected and regulated, while the rest are not. In effect, people have

---

Planning can be used as a 'tactic of marginalization', where particular groups are denied access to planning services

Master planning has been used (oppor-tunistically) across the globe as a justifi-cation for evictions and land grabs

to step outside the law in order to secure land and shelter due to the elitist nature of urban land laws.[74] It could be argued, therefore, that city governments themselves are producing social and spatial exclusion as a result of the inappropriate laws and regulations which they adopt.

A characteristic of master plans is that they are usually drawn up by experts as end-state blueprint plans, and without consultation with communities. They are also usually underpinned by regulatory systems that are applied inflexibly and technocratically. These features impact negatively in a number of ways. In cities in developing countries, it is not uncommon that architects of master plans are either consultants who are based in developed countries or who have been trained there. Many have little understanding of the dynamics of poverty and the peculiar nature of urbanization in cities in developing countries, or alternatively adhere to the older modernist belief that these cities will soon catch up economically with those in developed countries. Consultation processes could, of course, potentially allow such foreign experts to gain an understanding of what it means to be a poor urban dweller in the 21st century. But many such experts believe little is to be gained from consultation processes and that they know best. The result is usually that such experts generalize an understanding of values, lifestyles, priorities, etc. from their own part of the world to the rest. They imagine employed, car-owning, nuclear families living in formal houses with full services, in cities which are growing relatively slowly and which have strong and well-resourced local governments – when the reality in cities in developing countries is entirely different.

A further problem with physical master plans prepared by outside experts is that neither the plan nor the process of implementing it is embedded in the local institutional culture. Chapters 4 and 5 describe plan preparation and implementation as institutional learning processes that need to involve not only the 'town and regional planners' in government, but a range of other professionals, departments and actors in government, as well as other civil society-based stakeholders. Institutional arrangements need to shape themselves around the plan and its implementation, achieving at the same time the building of capacity in government and society, and this cannot occur when the plan is drawn up by an outside expert who delivers a finished product and then departs.

The urban modernist spatial and architectural forms that are usually supported by modernist planning tend to reinforce spatial and social exclusion, and produce cities which are not environmentally sustainable. In many cities, modernization projects involved the demolition of mixed-use, older, historic areas that were well suited to the accommodation of a largely poor and relatively immobile population. These projects displaced small traders and working-class households, usually to unfavourable peripheral locations. But most importantly, they represented a permanent reallocation of highly accessible and desirable urban land from small traders and manufacturers to large-scale formal ones, and to government. Where attempts to reoccupy these desirable areas by informal traders and settlers has occurred, their presence is sometimes tolerated,

sometimes depends upon complex systems of bribes and corrupt deals, and is sometimes met with official force and eviction. The development of new planned urban areas has also tended to exclude lower-income groups. Cities planned around car-based movement systems ensure that those with a car have high levels of mobility and accessibility, while those without cars – the majority in developing cities – often find themselves trapped in peripheral settlements, unable to access public facilities and work opportunities. This is made worse by the low-built density developments and green buffers or wedges characteristic of modernist city forms. Low-income households, which have usually been displaced to cheaper land on the urban periphery, thus find themselves having to pay huge transport costs if they want to travel to public facilities or jobs.

The separation of land uses into zoned monofunctional areas also generates large volumes of movement, and if residential zoning is enforced, leads to major economic disadvantage for poorer people who commonly use their dwelling as an economic unit as well. Mono-functional zoning never reflected or accommodated the realities of urban life anywhere in the world, and still does not. The separation of income groups in many cities through plot size, or density, zoning is also a major drawback for poorer groups. Those who survive from the informal sector – by far the majority in developing cities – find themselves trapped in bounded areas with low purchasing power. It is precisely access to wealthier people that they need to make businesses viable. Income separation also exacerbates levels of crime in poor areas. One study in American cities[75] found that spatial segregation was the most significant of all factors, which accounted for the homicide rate in black urban areas. High crime rates lock poorer areas into a downward spiral of low property values and limited private-sector investment, and, hence, greater poverty and deprivation.

The problems associated with modernist planning discussed above, and the changing urban, economic and environmental contexts have, in part, led to the emergence of more innovative or contemporary approaches to urban planning. The next section identifies some of these newer approaches, highlighting their strengths and weaknesses.

INNOVATIVE APPROACHES TO URBAN PLANNING

New innovative approaches to urban planning have emerged in response to recent changing economic and environmental imperatives, and, in some ways, meet the normative criteria for planning systems set out in Chapter 1. While each of the approaches reviewed here has been shaped by a particular regional context, some international 'borrowing' has already occurred. An important lesson from the master planning experience is the danger of transplanting planning systems and approaches from one context to another, given the highly varied nature of urban societies across the world (see Chapter 2). The purpose of presenting the approaches below, therefore, is not to suggest models or solutions that

A characteristic of master plans is that they are usually drawn up by experts without consultation with communities

The problems associated with modernist planning, and the changing urban, economic and environmental contexts have, in part, led to the emergence of more innovative approaches to urban planning can be taken 'off the shelf' for implementation. Rather, they offer ideas generated from 'situated' experiences that can be considered in relation to the specific urban planning issues in other places.

The new approaches are grouped under seven broad headings (see Table 3.1), dealing first with the main aspects of planning systems (directive planning and regulatory planning), then with new planning processes, and finally with new ideas about spatial forms. The seven categories are:

Strategic spatial planning emerged in developed countries and has also been adopted in certain developing contexts

1 strategic spatial planning and its variants;
2 new ways of using spatial planning to integrate government;
3 approaches to land regularization and management;
4 participatory and partnership processes;
5 approaches promoted by international agencies and addressing sectoral urban concerns;
6 new forms of master planning; and
7 planning aimed at producing new spatial forms.

There is considerable overlap between these categories; some emphasize process and others outcomes, and sometimes these are combined. This section does not claim to be comprehensive in terms of capturing all of the very many innovative planning ideas that have emerged in the last couple of decades. The aim here is to focus on what appears to be the most important innovations that are being implemented in different contexts or settings.

Strategic spatial planning

Strategic spatial planning emerged in developed countries and has also been adopted in certain developing contexts. A variant of strategic spatial planning termed the Barcelona Model has also emerged.

Table 3.1

New approaches to urban planning

Category	Type	Characteristics
Strategic spatial planning	• Strategic spatial planning in developed countries • Strategic spatial planning in developing regions • The Barcelona model of strategic spatial planning	Implications for planning processes and the nature of the directive plan; Barcelona model has implications for urban form: large, well-designed urban projects.
Spatial planning as institutional integration	• The new British planning system • Integrated development planning	Implications for planning processes and the nature of the directive plan. Planning's role in government is important.
Land regularization and management	• Alternatives to evictions • Influencing development actors • Managing public space and services	New approaches to regulatory aspects of planning; focus on accommodating informality.
Participatory and partnership processes	• Participatory planning • Partnerships	Focus on planning processes and state–community relations.
International agency approaches and sectoral concerns	• The Urban Management Programme • Sector programmes	Implications for planning processes and institutional location. Sector programmes are issue specific.
New master planning		New processes and regulatory approaches; implications for land market processes.
New spatial forms	• The 'compact city' • New urbanism	Focus on urban form, less on process. Reaction to modernist and unsustainable cities.

■ Strategic spatial planning in developed countries

Strategic spatial planning emerged in Western Europe during the 1980s and 1990s[76] partly in response to an earlier disillusionment with master planning, but also due to a realization that the project-based approach to urban development, which had become dominant in the 1980s, was equally problematic in the absence of a broader and longer-term spatial framework.[77] It has since spread to other developed countries such as the US, Canada and Australia, as well as to some developing countries. To date, strategic spatial planning is more prominent in the planning literature than it is in practice, but it appears to be enjoying growing support as it meets the requirements of cities in the developed world for a form of urban planning which:

• is responsive to strong civil-society (and business) demands for involvement in government and planning;
• can coordinate and integrate economic, infrastructural and social policies in space in the interests of a city's global economic positioning;
• can take a strong stand on resource protection and environmental issues, as well as on heritage and 'quality of place' issues; and
• is implementation focused.

Box 3.3 on the recently produced strategic spatial plan for Toronto is an example of a plan that contains many of these elements.

Strategic spatial planning often focuses on a process of decision-making: it does not carry with it a predetermined urban form or set of values. It could just as easily deliver gated communities, suburbia or new urbanism, depending upon the groups involved in the implementation process. However, in practice, many of the current plans promote sustainability, inclusiveness and qualities of public space. In the context of Western Europe, which is culturally and climatically highly diverse and contains a large range of different urban forms that have emerged over a long history, it is appropriate that new developments fit in with the old. Advocates of strategic spatial planning[78] argue that the place-making elements of strategic planning must be a social process involving a range of people and groups. Without this, there would be the danger of 'outside experts' delivering inappropriate urban forms, as was the case with urban modernism.

The typical strategic spatial planning system contains a 'directive' or forward, long-range spatial plan that consists of frameworks and principles, and broad spatial ideas, rather than detailed spatial design (although it may set the framework for detailed local plans and projects). The plan does not address every part of a city – being strategic means focusing on only those aspects or areas that are important to overall plan objectives. Usually these general planning goals are sustainable development and spatial quality.[79] The spatial plan is linked to a planning scheme or ordinance specifying land uses and development norms to indicate restrictions that apply to development rights. Decisions on land-use change are guided by the plan: many European systems have three levels of policy guidance – national, regional and local. The spatial plan also provides guidance for urban projects (state or partnership led), which in the context of Europe are often 'brownfield' urban regeneration projects and/or infrastructural projects.

Strategic spatial planning also has a crucial institutional dimension. Proponents argue that the actual process of formulating the plan is as important as the plan itself. It is an active force which needs to bring about changed mindsets of those participating, as well as the development of new institutional structures and arrangements, within and between levels of governance, to carry the plan. Coordination and integration of policy ideas of line-function departments is essential (because planning is not just about the functional use of land), and the plan itself cannot achieve this coordination: new institutional relationships must evolve to do this. The plan must therefore be institutionally embedded and must act to build social capital in governance structures.[80] In theory, this could include the participatory budgeting processes that have become popular in Brazil. This is very far removed from the idea of a foreign consultant delivering a plan document and then departing.

As a process, strategic spatial planning addresses many of the problems of old-style master planning. However, much will depend upon the actual ethics and values that the plan promotes, the extent to which the long-term vision is shared by all, and the extent to which a stable and enduring consensus on the plan can be achieved. Guiding urban development is a long-term process and there is little chance of success if the plan is changed with each new election. In practice, strategic spatial planning may be seen as an ideal; but is not easy to put into practice, and there have been criticisms that economic positioning is taking precedence over addressing issues of socio-spatial exclusion. As cultural conflict increases in multicultural cities of the developed world, achieving real consensus also becomes difficult. There have also been criticisms of planning through shared governance arrangements: that it can weaken government's ability to implement local climate protection policies[81] and that it allows business interests to have undue influence in urban development.[82]

Strategic spatial planning in developed countries has emerged in a context characterized by strong, well-resourced and capacitated governments with a strong tax base, in stable social democracies, where control through land-use management systems is still a central element in the planning system, made possible through state control over how development rights are used. Cities in many developed regions are growing slowly, and while poverty and inequality are increasing, the majority are well off and can meet their own basic urban needs. It would be very problematic, therefore, to imagine that the planning problems of the cities of developing countries could be solved simply by importing strategic spatial planning.

■ Strategic spatial planning in developing regions

Strategic spatial planning has since found its way to other parts of the world, and these experiences offer further

> Box 3.3 The 2007 Strategic Plan for Toronto, Canada

The 2007 Strategic Plan for Toronto contains many elements of the strategic approach to planning. The plan is 'the broadest expression of the type of city we envision for the future'. It is based on the goal of sustainability, which promotes 'social equity and inclusion, environmental protection, good governance and city-building'. The concept of integration is evident in its statement that 'sustainability helps us to broaden our vision by considering economic, environmental and social implications together, rather than using a single perspective'. Its shift away from top-down technocratic processes is indicated by its statement that the plan 'encourages decision-making that is long range, democratic, participatory and respectful of all stakeholders'. The strategic nature of the plan is suggested in the following: 'Toronto is a big, complex and fully urbanized city. Its future is about re-urbanization and its continuing evolution will involve a myriad of situations and decisions. This plan provides a general guide; but it cannot encompass or even imagine every circumstance.' The plan also connects future urban development closely to transport infrastructure: new growth will be steered towards areas well served by transit and road networks.

Source: www.toronto.ca/planning/official_plan/pdf_chapter1-5/chapters1_5_aug2007.pdf

lessons and cautions. A number of Latin American cities adopted the strategic urban planning approach in the late 1990s, with the more successful cases occurring in Cordoba, La Paz, Trujillo and Havana. Strategic urban planning is still relatively new in Latin American, with many attempts seemingly 'borrowed' from the European experience through the involvement of various think-tank agencies. One problem has been that the new strategic planning process adopted by a city administration is often abandoned when a new political party or mayor comes into power because to continue it might be seen as giving credibility to the political opposition.[83] The fact that a plan can be dropped also suggests that neither business nor civil society see it as sufficiently valuable to demand its continuation. The Bolivian approach of introducing a national law (1999 Law of the Municipalities) requiring all municipalities to draw up an urban plan based on the strategic-participatory method is one way of dealing with this, but does not prevent the content of the plan changing with administrations.

Where the strategic plan is not integrated with the regulatory aspect of the planning system, and does not affect land rights, as is usually the case, then there may be little to prevent the strategic plan from being frequently changed or discontinued (see Table 3.2). In Latin American, the very different approach required by strategic planning often encounters opposition:[84] from politicians and officials who use closed processes of decision-making and budgeting to insert their own projects and further their own political interests, and from planners who are reluctant to abandon their comfortable role as the 'grand classical planner' and take on roles as communicators and facilitators.

In Francophone African cities, strategic planning has proved useful where the Millennium Development Goals (MDGs) were linked to planning, as in the city of Tiassalé in Côte d'Ivoire.[85] With support from UN-Habitat and the African Network of Urban Management Institutions, strategic plans based on the MDGs were drawn up. Integrating the MDGs within planning made it possible to rectify certain major shortcomings encountered in master planning. The approach made available a strategic spatial framework with

As a process, strategic spatial planning addresses many of the problems of old-style master planning

In Francophone African cities, strategic planning has proved useful where the MDGs were linked to planning

City	Year initiated	Present status	Comment
Cordoba, Argentina	1996	Stopped in 2000	Due to change in administration
Rosario, Argentina	1998	Ongoing	Good international positioning
Buenos Aires, Argentina	?	Ongoing	Political delays, slow
Bogotá, Colombia	1997	Stopped in 1998	Due to change in administration
Santiago, Chile	?	Stopped in 1998	Due to change in administration
La Paz, Bolivia	2000	Ongoing	Strategic plans mandatory
Trujillo, Peru	1999	Ongoing	Local Agenda 21 framework
Comas District, Lima, Peru	2000	Ongoing	Effective, inclusive
Havana, Cuba	1994	Ongoing	Three updates, inclusive, help from foreign experts

Source: Steinberg, 2005

Table 3.2

Status of strategic urban planning in Latin American cities

time horizons and indicators of objectives; gave an understanding of the realities and trends in the implementation of the MDGs at the urban level; made it possible to acquire information to identify the actions to take in order to improve living conditions and access to basic social services at the urban level; and made available indicators for monitoring the strategic plan and, thus, strengthened public accountability.

■ The Barcelona model of strategic spatial planning

In Barcelona (Spain), a variant of strategic spatial planning has claimed significant success, representing an important shift away from master planning. A city-wide strategic plan promoted a 'compact' urban form and provided a framework

---

Box 3.4 Harnessing resources for delivery in Middlesbrough, UK

Middlesbrough is one of the top ten most deprived boroughs in the UK. Much of its infrastructure is outdated – an environment often dominated by a 'Victorian' economy, which has since declined. The town has a poor image and high levels of out-migration and has faced low demand for housing. The existing housing stock is unbalanced, with concentrations of social and terraced housing in particular neighbourhoods, limiting range and choice, especially in the fringe around the town centre. The quality of the environment is poor, particularly around the River Tees where the degraded landscape covers an extensive area. In Middlesbrough there is a real need to create wealth, jobs, opportunity and a better standard of physical development.

Within Middlesbrough the delivery landscape for spatial planning was influenced by planning being perceived as a service rather than a useful mechanism for change. The range of public-sector bodies and their interrelationships were very complex and have not assisted the delivery. One of the components of Middlesbrough Council's success has been the realignment of its directorates, making sure that there is open dialogue between those leading different departments, not least between housing and planning. The first step in this was to increase the visibility of staff at the highest levels of management and to ensure an open dialogue was forthcoming, enabling barriers to be overcome. In addition, there has been strong political alignment and support, and an increasing professionalization of members, working across party. Middlesbrough has used a multidisciplinary approach, identifying areas of skills cross-over between different departments and highlighting how they can be used to further the town's development proposals.

How is this effective? The approach:

• has developed an organization which is fit for purpose;
• has engaged political leadership;
• has worked across the local authority to achieve change; and
• has led a proactive approach.

Source: UCL Deloitte, 2006, p3

---

for a set of local urban projects which had a strong urban design component. However, some see this approach to strategic planning as largely corporate planning around economic development goals (the global positioning of Barcelona) with certain social and environmental objectives attached.[86] Local projects have been driven by more pragmatic and market-related needs. Commentators on the approach[87] argue for a closer connection between strategic spatial plans and large-scale, multifunctional urban projects. But there is doubt that this will deal with the problem of elite capture of these processes and, hence, may worsen urban inequalities. This is almost inevitable under a prevailing neo-liberal ideology in Europe and very likely in developing countries with their more unequal and volatile political processes. It has been argued that the linking of these plans and projects to a strong, progressive urban politics is the only way to counter this danger.[88]

The 'Barcelona Model' has since been 'exported' to other parts of the world, with an attempt to apply it in Buenos Aires[89] highlighting the need for caution when transferring planning ideas to contexts that are very different from their place of origin. In this case, politically induced instability meant that the institutional setting for strategic planning was not conducive to its implementation.

Spatial planning tools for integrating public sector functions

There are two innovative forms of planning that aim to achieve institutional integration and coordination as an important function of the urban planning system. The first is the new British planning system and the second is the South African integrated development planning system.

■ The new British planning system

The problem of integrating different functions of urban government is a common one, and this is seen as a potentially important role for spatial planning. The new British planning system,[90] which introduces regional spatial strategies and local development frameworks, aims to replace conventional land-use planning with spatial planning. It responds to arguments that the previous system was slow, cumbersome, legalistic, out of touch with institutional, economic and social change, insufficiently inclusive, overconcerned with process at the expense of outcomes, and inadequately grounded in defensible analysis. The new approach focuses on decentralized solutions, as well as a desire to 'join up' or integrate the functions of the public sector from the perspective of the user and to inject a spatial or territorial dimension into sectoral strategies. Box 3.4 indicates how the new approach has been adopted in Middlesbrough. There is also recognition that achieving environmental sustainability will require sectoral interests to work together and cut across traditional disciplinary and professional boundaries.[91]

Hence, the purpose of the new spatial plans (shaping spatial development through the coordination of the spatial impacts of sector policy and decisions) is very different from the purpose of the previous land-use plans (regulating land use and development through designation of areas of development and protection, and application of performance criteria). An unresolved issue, however, is exactly how the new spatial plans align with the development control system.

■ **Integrated development planning**

In post-apartheid South Africa, departmental integration has been a central goal of the new integrated development planning (IDP) system in local government.[92] Although the IDP has a peculiarly South African genealogy, it was also shaped within the emergent international discourse on governance, planning and urban management, and there appear to be elements in common with the new UK approach. The IDP is a medium-term municipal plan linked to a five-year political cycle, although aspects of the plan, including the vision and the spatial development framework (SDF), have a longer-term horizon. The SDF is a city-wide directive plan, similar to strategic spatial plans, and can indicate specific projects at the local level. The IDP manager's office in each municipality is charged with the task of needs assessment, vision development, and aligning the plans and projects of each line-function department to the urban vision.[93] The strategic spatial plan has the role of spatially coordinating these sectoral plans, as in the UK, rather than spatial goals feeding into these other plans.[94] Spatially 'harmonized' projects are then intended to direct the budget.

There is general consensus that the idea of IDPs is positive and certainly an advance on previous forms of urban management. There is also the recognition that it will take a long time for municipalities to get accustomed to this very different way of operating, and efforts must be sustained. So far, there are modest successes, but still many problems.[95] Line-function departments, including the planning department, still operate in isolation from each other with the IDP attempting to integrate the products of these functions but not their processes. Integration is therefore not yet institutionally embedded. The capital budget in many places is still shaped by the relative power of departments and by the politicians of the day, rather than by the norms of sustainability and equity. There are very few linkages between the SDFs and the land-use management system – in many places the latter dates from days of apartheid, while the SDFs are new. There is therefore a disjuncture between the zoning ordinances, many of which promote urban modernism and social exclusion, and the SDFs, which try to promote a different urban form, but lack the tools to do so. There is still no consensus at national level about how the land-use management system should operate; given the vacuum, individual provinces and cities have been attempting their own partial reforms.

Participation has come to be seen as 'professional participation', involving different departments and levels of government rather than citizens and stakeholders. In many cities, the latter takes very limited forms of participation, such as presenting the results of the IDP for public comment. Over time, the managerialist and technocratic dimensions of policy-making and planning have come to dominate, and participation remains only rhetorically impor-

tant. A recent study suggests that despite the emphasis given to good governance, the everyday reality in many municipalities is of patronage in appointments and tendering, institutional conflict, poor delivery records and financial crisis.[96]

The IDP has good intentions, which have not yet been realized. But it may still be too early to pass final judgement. What is clear to date is that it is a complex and sophisticated system, and many municipalities, and particularly politicians, lack the capacity or motivation to understand and fully implement it. Given that South Africa is a relatively well-resourced and well-governed developing country, this should provide a cautionary note regarding simplistic borrowing of the approach in less well-resourced regions.

New approaches to land regularization and management

The most challenging issue for urban planning in terms of land regularization and management has been how to address the issue of informality (see Chapter 7). The ever-expanding informal areas of cities in developing and transitional regions, and especially the peri-urban areas, are usually regarded as undesirable and in need of eradication and/or planning control. It is now recognized that such an approach simply worsens poverty and exclusion. A number of innovative alternatives to the removal of informal settlements, ways of using planning tools to strategically influence development actors, and ways of working with development actors to manage public space and provide services have emerged.[97] All of them require an attitudinal shift that recognizes the potentially positive role of informality; policies, laws and regulations which are adapted in relation to the dynamics of informality; and efforts to improve the support for, and legitimacy of, the planning system by those involved in informality.

International agreements and conventions on housing rights[98] require governments to take certain steps relating to consultation, information, the right of appeal and compensation before or during evictions. In principle, evictions should not occur at all unless they can be justified in terms of environmental or 'public good' requirements. In some parts of the world, the consultation process with slum dwellers has given rise to innovative solutions such as land-sharing, redevelopment, collaborative management of public spaces, or alternative ways of handling essential evictions.

■ **Regularization and *in situ* upgrading**

The regularization and *in situ* upgrading of informal settlements is always preferable to neglect or demolition. Giving household secure tenure is an important part of this, with a growing recognition that this does not need to be freehold title, which is the most costly and complex form of tenure. Alternative innovative forms of tenure in informal settlements include group tenure, usufruct or 'adverse possession'. The latter can entitle a person or community in possession of land owned by another to acquire rights to the land provided that certain legal requirements are satisfied (e.g. that the claimant does not own any other land) and that

Participation has come to be seen as 'professional participation', involving different departments and levels of government rather than citizens and stakeholders

The most challenging issue for urban planning in terms of land regularization and management has been how to address the issue of informality

The initial priority for improving tenure security in Phnom Penh, Cambodia, was to stop the forced evictions that the authorities had been undertaking on a regular basis.

An initial proposal was to provide all households in informal settlements with a temporary occupation licence. Given that the administrative burden of identifying eligible families and issuing them all with temporary occupation licences would have been excessive, it was proposed that the authorities announce a moratorium on relocations and evictions for a provisional period of six months. It was hoped that this would be sufficient to allow people to go to work in the morning secure in the knowledge that their homes and possessions would still be there when they returned.

Within the moratorium period, it was proposed that communal land rights be provided in all settlements selected for upgrading. Feedback from local communities and non-governmental organizations (NGOs) suggested that this option would be acceptable and would minimize the administrative burden on land management agencies. It would also allow such areas to receive services and environmental improvements through a participatory process of physical and socio-economic development, as proposed by the government's ambitious upgrading programme. Finally, it was hoped that communal land rights would increase security without stimulating rapid increases in land prices, which could attract downward raiding by higher-income groups.

For unauthorized settlements on private land, land-sharing was proposed, under which settlers could be provided with long-term communal land leases on part of their site, leaving the landowner free to develop the remainder.

The duration of such forms of tenure was discussed with key stakeholders, and a period of three to ten years was proposed. It was suggested that during this period, communities should be encouraged to form representative organizations that would meet specified standards of good governance. Those communities able to demonstrate this would then be eligible to apply for communal land titles, which would provide permanent security of tenure. Those that failed to meet the criteria would be entitled to renew their communal land right for a further period.

Source: Payne, 2005

date topography and steer development away from unsuitable areas. Phased construction of roads and water supply will guide developers to appropriate grid superblocks, within which detailed planning regulation may be phased in. An experiment with this approach is under way in Ecuador.[99]

This suggests a strategic approach to the application of planning regulation. Where many poorer cities lack the resources to carry out effective land-use management, it is better to concentrate efforts on the public realm and areas where development has major environmental and safety implications, while limiting intervention (especially detailed development regulation) in other areas, particularly middle- and low-density residential areas. Detailed planning and regulation should therefore focus on urban centres and commercial zones, public spaces, public markets and clusters of public buildings. In China and Viet Nam, this approach demonstrated that governments were reasserting their control incrementally, following a period of informal development during which the demands on governments forced them to prioritize needs other than regulating development.[100]

■ Working with informal economic actors

A third innovative approach involves working with informal economic actors to provide services and manage spaces, rather than either forced eviction of street traders or relocation to formal markets. Operators need to become organized to present their needs, and municipalities need to be flexible and willing to use collaborative approaches. Since many informal businesses operate from homes, a mixed-use zoning category needs to replace single-use residential zoning, as in the 2007 Delhi Master Plan. Dedicated market spaces should be provided for street trading. These need careful location at points of high accessibility and should offer spaces with a range of rental costs and other facilities (storage, electricity, etc.). The Warwick Junction market in Durban, South Africa[101] provides a successful solution to inner-city street trading but has required dedicated management and the involvement of a range of municipal departments. In peri-urban areas, where the provision of public services is poor, there is value in an incremental approach to service provision using community-based and informal service providers, managed by local committees, and with technical advice from city administrations.[102]

■ Capturing rising land values

Finally, there is growing interest in land laws that can capture rising urban land values (through property and capital gains taxes) by governments for redistributive purposes. The concept of *value capture* has been used in parts of the US, Canada and Latin America. Colombia introduced a new tax law in 1997 (Law for Territorial Development) that set out several ways in which local authorities could participate in rising land values: property owners could negotiate a cash payment to the municipality, could pay in kind through transfer of part of the land, or could participate in the formation of an urban development partnership.[103] Value capture is seen as an effective way to link forward planning and land-use regulations, and serves to

Value capture is seen as an effective way to link forward planning and land-use regulations

the occupier has been in possession continuously, without challenge from the legal owners for a specified term. Where an informal settlement is on land informally subdivided by landholders with legal ownership rights (either title or customary tenure), then registration can be based on a combination of the written evidence of transactions and the testimony of witnesses such as village elders or local officials. The experience of Phnom Penh (Cambodia) with such innovative forms of secure tenure is documented in Box 3.5. The general trend in upgrading approaches is to focus on incremental infrastructure improvements as a means of enhancing tenure security and encouraging investment in housing, rather than tenure security being regarded as a necessary precursor to other improvements.

■ Public investment in trunk infrastructure

A second innovative planning approach to informal settlement involves the use of public investment in trunk infrastructure to influence the pattern of development. A strategic plan should guide land development, and this is followed by land pooling and land banking, and the gradual extension of detailed planning and development control. It is suggested that expansion areas sufficient for 20 to 30 years ahead should be identified and defined by a grid of secondary roads for access, public transport and main infrastructure provision. Adaptations to the grid can be used to accommocontrol land use, finance urban infrastructure, and generate additional local revenue. One positive outcome of urbanization and urban growth is that it increases urban land values, and this potential needs to be socially harvested rather than only benefiting the private sector.

To conclude, regulation and land-use management are the most powerful aspects of urban planning; yet most reforms have concentrated on directive planning. The regulatory system is probably the most difficult to change because of entrenched legal rights and interests; but without reform in this sphere it will be extremely difficult to use planning to promote urban inclusion and sustainability.

Participatory processes and partnerships in planning

Participation and partnerships in planning emerged in liberal democracies during the 1960s, and have subsequently been the focus of criticism and refinement in planning and urban development literature (see Chapter 5). From the 1970s, participation has been strongly promoted in the developing world by non-governmental organizations (NGOs) and international development agencies. Participation and partnerships have, to a greater degree, become important elements in all of the innovative planning approaches discussed in this section.[104]

Potentially, participation in planning can empower communities and build social capital, lead to better design of urban projects and allow for participants' concerns to be incorporated within strategies. Physical planning is often accused of neglecting the social and economic dimensions of projects, and participation is a mechanism for addressing this. The general conclusion is that participation is important and necessary, but that, in practice, much of it is consultative or instrumental, providing participants with little real influence over decision-making.

Lessons from experience suggest that successful participation is dependent upon certain preconditions relating to the political context, the legal basis for participation and available resources. Successful cases of participation indicate that the following are necessary:

- measures to ensure that socially marginalized groups have a voice in both representative politics and participatory processes;
- overcoming resistance by elected political representatives by ensuring that wider participation has win–win outcomes for them;
- combining direct participation with decision-making by political representatives to resolve conflicting priorities and interests;
- overcoming resistance by professionals, including planners, through professional education and peer exchanges;
- learning from innovative participatory approaches in other sectors to improve approaches to land-use planning;
- enhancing participation at the city/strategic level by providing for direct engagement (e.g. referendums) or

indirect participation (e.g. advisory councils) to complement the representative political system; and
- support for civil society organizations to enhance the ability of poor people and marginalized social groups to exercise voice.

Innovative participatory planning approaches have occurred at the neighbourhood and at the city scale. At the neighbourhood scale there has been some success with participatory urban appraisal (PUA),[105] more inclusive participatory learning and action (PLA) (for problem identification) and community action planning (CAP). PUA/PLA has been used in many parts of the developing world and is considered an effective way of supplementing professional views by allowing people to identify and prioritize their own needs. Methods involve mapping, modelling, diagramming, pile sorting, or scoring with seeds, stones or other counters, often in small groups (see Box 3.6). CAP depends upon the formation or existence of some kind of community organization, followed by collaborative planning with experts and organizations. This approach aligns well with the notion of 'co-production', in which residents 'fill the space' which the state is unable to occupy. Negotiated arrangements with the state emerge that involve either formal participation processes or partnerships, not organized confrontations. These processes have been termed 'co-production' and are being seen as a more realistic way in which state–society engagement can take place.[106]

At the city level, one of the best-known innovative participatory approaches is participatory budgeting, which was first implemented in Porto Alegre in Brazil and has since been attempted in many other parts of the world. By 2006, it had been introduced in over 1000 municipalities in Latin America and in over 100 Western European cities.[107] While details vary from city to city; broadly, citizens participate and vote on the municipal budget in either regional or thematic 'assemblies', and form local forums to discuss how the budget should be spent in their areas. Forum delegates are involved at the council level to make final allocation decisions. Research shows that this is not a simple solution that can be imposed anywhere[108] and is not a technical process that can be detached from local political culture. The main preconditions are grassroots democracy through open local assemblies; social justice through a formula that allocates a larger share of resources to the most disadvantaged districts; and citizen control through an ongoing participatory budgeting council that monitors implementation.

Other innovative participatory processes have been linked to wider development planning approaches, rather than to spatial planning. The Kerala People's Campaign for Decentralized Planning (India) was initiated by a state government. Here, ward-level assemblies identify local needs, and these are appraised and considered by government and politicians. Projects are prioritized by locally elected institutions and incorporated within a local plan for implementation. A further approach that involves wider development issues is the CDS process, introduced by UN-Habitat and the Cities Alliance. In this process, stakeholders participate in problem identification, prioriti-

Physical planning is often accused of neglecting the social and economic dimensions of projects, and participation is a mechanism for addressing this

One of the best-known innovative participatory approaches is participatory budgeting, which was first implemented in Porto Alegre in Brazil zation, visioning and development planning for the entire city.

A rather different form of participation is public–private partnerships. In developing countries, these have often developed around public infrastructure provision when municipalities lack resources or skills to provide this. In developed countries, they often take the form of private-sector planning and investment in urban projects. Frequently, these involve redeveloping urban brownfield sites, where the profit-oriented aims of the developer are aligned with the aims of municipalities for modernization, economic restructuring and physical regeneration. Urban regeneration in Cardiff (Wales)[109] is a good example of how a coalition between the political elite and private-sector commercial property development interests was central to explaining the success achieved. However, this approach, as in the case of Cardiff, tends to sideline social inclusion, equality and sustainability objectives, everyday service delivery and the achievement of high-quality urban design.

Approaches promoted by international agencies: The Urban Management Programme and sector programmes

Over the past two decades, several international development agencies have attempted to address the problems of modernist urban planning in developing and transitional countries by introducing special programmes and processes into local government systems. The aim of these programmes has been to attempt to make local authorities more responsive to other urban stakeholders, and to address particular urban issues which are considered important. In recent years, some of these 'sector action plans' have focused on poverty, gender, crime and safety, health, heritage and the environment, among others.

■ The Urban Management Programme (UMP)

Regarded as one of the largest global urban programmes, the Urban Management Programme (UMP) was established in

Over the past two decades, several international development agencies have attempted to address the problems of modernist urban planning in developing and transitional countries

1986 by the Urban Development Unit of the World Bank in partnership with the United Nations Centre for Human Settlements (UNCHS) (now UN-Habitat) and funded by the United Nations Development Programme (UNDP). The Cities Alliance organization also emerged from this grouping.[110] The UMP operated in 120 cities in 57 countries, with the overall mission of promoting socially and environmentally sustainable human settlements and adequate shelter for all, and the objective of reducing urban poverty and social exclusion. In order to achieve this objective, the UMP sought to provide technical assistance in five key areas: urban land; urban environment; municipal finance; urban infrastructure; and urban poverty. The UMP also sought to strengthen the capacity of urban managers to cope with the challenges associated with rapid urban growth.[111]

In common with other recent and innovative ideas in planning, and particularly with the 'urban management' approach, the UMP attempted to shift the concept of planning and development to the whole of local government rather than belonging to one department; to promote participatory processes in local government decision-making; to promote strategic thinking in planning; and to tie local government plans to implementation through action plans and budgets. The more recent CDS, promoted particularly by the Cities Alliance, encourages local governments to produce inter-sectoral and long-range visions and plans for cities.

Observations on the success of this programme are mixed. A key contribution of the UMP is that it placed urban issues on the international agenda by creating a forum for donors and aid-related institutions to discuss urban-related issues.[112] This is particularly important in that the UMP was established at a time when urban issues and urban planning, in general, were increasingly marginalized among donor agencies. The UMP also placed issues such as urban poverty, urban environment and sustainability, and participatory governance through the inclusive mechanism of city consultations at the forefront of the development agenda of many countries and local authorities. Several weaknesses of the UMP, particularly of the participatory processes, have been identified.[113] These include difficulty with measuring the impact of the participatory processes on the performance of local authorities, and on the well-being of the poor; follow-up to city consultations has been weak; city consultations have not always brought about changes in the way in which local authorities conduct their affairs; the inability of UMP partners to remain engaged with the same city for a long period of time; and the overambitious nature of plans generated through city consultation processes have meant that there was no follow-up investment to ensure implementation. All of these problems provide further signposts for a new approach to urban planning. In 2006, UN-Habitat disengaged from the programme and transferred the work to local anchor institutions.[114]

The UMP has been extensively implemented in Dar es Salaam, Tanzania (see Box 3.7). Here, more basic problems were evident. The UMP appeared to be successfully changing one part of the planning system – directive planning – but left untouched the regulatory system, which

---

Box 3.7 The Urban Management Programme in Dar es Salaam, Tanzania

In 1990, the Government of Tanzania requested technical assistance from the United Nations Development Programme (UNDP) to review the Dar es Salaam Master Plan. This coincided with the launch of the Sustainable Cities Programme (SCP) – an initiative of UN-Habitat in partnership with the United Nations Environment Programme (UNEP).

Regarding the location of the initiative, the Urban Development Division (UDD), as the organization responsible for preparation of master plans, wanted it to be located in the division. However, the SCP's main goal of capacity-building in local authorities meant that the initiative was placed under the minister responsible for local government in the Prime Minister's Office. This decision later adversely affected the technical support from the UDD, which also had professional planners who would later be needed for the SCP initiative.

Developing a Strategic Urban Development Plan (SUDP) had three intermediate objectives:

1   Develop a strategic development plan for Dar es Salaam, including environmental management strategies, sector investment strategies, spatial planning, financial planning and administrative/legal requirements.
2   Develop priority actions identified in the strategic development plan into fully prepared technical assistance projects and 'bankable' investment packages.
3   Strengthen local capacity to plan, coordinate and manage urban development and growth with emphasis on improved multi-sectoral coordination and community-based participation.

UN-Habitat envisioned a Strategic Urban Management Framework that is not a 'plan' as such since it does not set out a specific growth pattern that should be observed rigidly (as would a master plan). Instead, it provides options and development 'rules and principles' that need to be taken into account when making project and site-specific or area-wide investment decisions. UN-Habitat guidelines also state that the framework should not replace other plans or urban management instruments.

The process involved extensive consultations and stakeholder working groups on strategic issues, drawing on a wide spectrum of groups and actors in government and civil society. The product, the SUDP, provides development rules and principles and three alternative options for various parcels of land. Beyond this, the SUDP prescribes preferred land uses and 'a dynamic framework in which urban development activities can be coordinated via exchange of information, leveraging of resources and purposeful partnerships'. It was intended to replace the General Planning Scheme for Dar es Salaam (the old master plan) and guide general and detailed land-use plans to guide spatial development at city and district or neighbourhood levels. Due to the lengthy participation process, it was only presented to the Ministry of Lands, Housing and Settlement Development (responsible for urban and regional planning) for approval in early 2006 and has still not been approved.

Source: Nnkya, 2006a

---

forms a crucial part of plan implementation. The inherited land regulation system continued to entrench the inequalities. In effect, the UMP set up a parallel planning system, requiring developers first to apply to the local stakeholder committee for application approval in terms of the strategic plan, and then to submit it to the usual development control department.[115] While the real power lies with those administering the land regulations, there appears to be little advantage to developers to follow both processes, and little chance of a strategic plan being implemented. There was no clear evidence to suggest that the Dar es Salaam UMP process had been fully institutionalized.[116]

■ Sector programmes

The last two decades also witnessed attempts by international development agencies to promote particular sectoral or issue-specific concerns in urban plans. Some of the most important of these are:

• *The Localizing Agenda 21 programme (LA21)*: this programme was developed by UN-Habitat in 1992 following the Earth Summit in Rio de Janeiro. It offers a multi-year support system for selected secondary cities as the means to introduce or strengthen environmental concerns in their plans and operations. The specific objectives of LA21 include:

–   the development and implementation of broad-based environmental action plans, focusing on context-specific aspects of municipal planning and management, and incorporating incipient and ongoing settlement improvement initiatives;
–   enhancing the capacity of local authorities to integrate these action plans within strategic structure plans to stimulate inter-sectoral synergy and fulfil its pivotal role between local development actors; and
–   the achievement of tangible results and visible impact for low-income communities in selected pilot towns, leading to more sustainable and equitable urban development.

• *The Sustainable Cities Programme*: this joint initiative by UN-Habitat and UNEP was established during the early 1990s as a facility to package urban environmental planning and management (EPM) approaches, technologies and know-how through urban local authorities. The programme is founded on broad-based stakeholder participatory or city consultation approaches. The first phase was concluded in 2001, and the second phase from 2002 to 2007. Currently, the SCP operates in over 30 countries worldwide. The approach adopted by the programme entails:

–   strengthening local capacities to address urban

Box 3.8 Using planning to reintegrate displaced communities

The UN-Habitat 'urban trialogues' approach uses spatial planning to help reintegrate communities displaced by conflict back into cities. In Somalia, this implied three levels of action: a spatial structure plan, strategic projects and enabling conditions for development. The spatial structure plan provided an integrative framework so that short-term actions could contribute to long-term goals of development. Strategic projects happened immediately, in parallel with the long-term plan, to make a visible difference on the ground and to provide a way of integrating sectoral aid and actions. Enabling conditions required assistance to local government, infrastructure delivery and reviewing the legal framework to ensure rights for the poor.

The issue of land rights is a crucial one in these situations as this may have been a core reason for conflict and there are often competing or overlapping claims to land post-conflict. It has been argued that the establishment of a land management system in post-conflict context is urgent as it can help to create social and economic stability, forestall land grabs, deal with returning displaced persons, and help to restore the functions of government. However, the cadastre must be designed to cope with a highly fluid and changing situation, as well as one where claims to land are largely informal. This means that the first step is to adjudicate local land claims through community-based processes and then, instead of moving directly to a (Torrens) titling programme, to retain a deeds system since the deed is an affirmation of land rights but does not constitute them as a title does. Deeds provide evidence of rights in land that can be later rebutted by other evidence, which is crucial for restitution processes.

Source: Augustinus and Barry, 2004; UN-Habitat, 2006i

environmental priority issues;
- enabling replication and scaling-up of EPM activities; and
- mobilizing anchoring institutions for EPM support.
• *The Safer Cities Programme*: this programme, which was initiated by UN-Habitat in 1996, tackles crime and violence as issues of good urban governance. The programme recognizes that crime and insecurity have been strongly affected by the impact of urbanization and, as such, have become a major preoccupation for many cities in Africa, Asia, Latin America and the Caribbean, and the Pacific. It addresses the escalating problem of urban crime and violence by developing the crime prevention capacities of local authorities. The programme's initial focus was on Africa, at the request of a group of African city mayors who were concerned about the extent of violence in their cities and wanted help with the development of prevention strategies. This provided a learning ground upon which the programme adapted, piloted and tested various tools within an internationally recognized municipal framework. To date, Safer Cities initiatives are well under way in several African cities and have been extended to Latin America, Asia and Port Moresby (Papua New Guinea) to cater for an increasing need for exchange of information, knowledge and good practice.
• *The Disaster Management Programme*: this was established by UN-Habitat to assist governments and local authorities to rebuild in countries recovering from war or natural disasters. It attempts to bridge the gap between relief and development by combining technical expertise, normative understanding and experience. In post-conflict situations, urban planning has had an important role to play in re-establishing settlements. Recent positions argue for linking relief to development

and introducing development-oriented emergency aid. The UN-Habitat *urban trialogues* approach,[117] illustrated in Somalia, used spatial planning to help reintegrate conflict-displaced communities back into cities (see Box 3.8).

• *The Healthy Cities Programme*: this programme was initiated by the World Health Organization (WHO) in 1986 for the main purpose of improving, promoting and maintaining conducive urban environmental health conditions by involving all relevant actors and agencies within a city.
• *The Global Campaign on Urban Governance*: launched by UN-Habitat in 1999, the campaign attempted to encourage urban planning to be more pro-poor and inclusive. Its vision was to realize the inclusive city – a place where everyone, regardless of wealth, status, gender, age, race or religion, is enabled to participate productively and positively in the opportunities that cities have to offer. It specifically promoted the involvement of women in decision-making. In seeking to realize the inclusive city, the Global Campaign on Urban Governance proposed seven normative principles: sustainability; subsidiarity; equity; efficiency; transparency and accountability; civic engagement and citizenship; and security. These norms, which are interdependent and mutually reinforcing, hold good promise for making urban planning more effective, as they introduced new ways of planning and managing cities.
• *The Global Campaign for Secure Tenure*: launched by UN-Habitat in 2002, the campaign aimed to improve the conditions of people living and working in slums and informal settlements by promoting security of tenure. It encouraged negotiation as an alternative to forced eviction, and the establishment of innovative systems of tenure that minimize bureaucratic lags and the displacement of the urban poor by market forces. The campaign provided an innovative rights-based approach to urban planning and management, as it was directly linked to urban citizenship, since security of tenure can solidify the right of slum dwellers to exist in the city, make claims on resources, and be active participants in settlement improvement programmes.
• *City Development Strategy (CDS)*: this approach is promoted by the Cities Alliance and encourages local governments to produce inter-sectoral and long-term visions and plans for cities in a participatory manner. This strategy can provide a framework for spatial urban plans. The essentials of a CDS are:[118]
- assess the state of the city and its region;
- develop a long-term vision;
- focus on short-term results and accountability;
- value the contributions of the poor;
- encourage local business growth;
- engage networks of cities;
- focus on implementation;
- concentrate on priorities; and
- foster local leadership.
• *Gender responsiveness*: the UN-Habitat UMP programme considered various ways of mainstreaming

gender issues in local government and planning. Gender-specific participatory governance tools such as gender budgeting, women's safety audits and women's hearings were developed.[119] Box 3.9 provides examples of gender-aware planning in some European cities.

These sector programmes have been important in terms of raising particular urban issues and ensuring that they find a place in the urban planning process. The extent to which they have been successful on the ground in changing planning and management practices, and improving the lives of their target groups, varies remarkably. Usually success depends upon a range of contextual factors, including the presence of a champion organization or individual. One problem appears to have been that these programmes can easily complicate the policy environment in situations where local government capacity is already low. They may also require new forms of intra-governmental coordination that are difficult to achieve in practice. For example, in Francophone Africa, the UMP took the form of 'sector action plans' (focusing on HIV/AIDS, security or poverty); but the proliferation of these proved to be institutionally confusing and frustrating for citizens who wanted a more comprehensive range of needs addressed.[120]

A further problem is the extent to which these programmes become institutionally embedded. If local governments simply 'add them on' to their conventional planning and regulatory systems, which is usually the case, then programmes are unlikely to be sustainable or implementable. At the same time, it needs to be recognized that any such new programme can be an immediate stimulus for political manoeuvring. In the case of post-conflict and post-disaster initiatives, there are almost inevitably political issues around which groups are assisted, and whose norms and standards shape new urban developments.

In addition to these agency-driven, issue-specific programmes, there are further issues that have gained some prominence in the planning literature and are likely to be the subject of concern for planning in future years. The first is the linking of urban planning with urban development and infrastructure (see Chapter 8). A second issue is how to conduct planning in the peri-urban areas of developing countries.[121] Third is how to use urban planning to promote environmentally sustainable cities and find ways of linking the 'green' and 'brown' urban agendas,[122] as well as addressing the problem of climate change (see Chapter 6). The environmental issue has already received some attention in planning systems through Local Agenda 21 processes; but new and more far-reaching ideas and processes are required for 21st-century challenges.

New forms of master planning

In some parts of the world, traditional master planning continues, but is being used in innovative ways. In Brazil, two principles were included in the 1988 Constitution aimed at democratizing access to the city: the social function of property; and popular participation in the definition and administration of urban policies. The campaign Participatory

Master Plan: City for All (*Plano Director Participativo: Cidade de Todos*) aimed to have 1700 cities with these plans by October 2006.[123] 'New' master plans are seen as different from the old ones in that they are bottom up and participatory, oriented towards social justice and aim to counter the effects of land speculation. While conventional urban planning strives to achieve an ideal city, from which illegality and informality are banned, the new urban planning approach deals with the existing city to develop tools to tackle these problems in a just and democratic way.[124]

One important new regulatory tool within the master plans has been the Special Zones of Social Interest, first attempted in Belo Horizonte and Recife in the 1980s, and subsequently in other *favelas*. The Special Zones of Social Interest is a legal instrument for land management that can be applied to areas with a 'public interest', to existing *favelas* and to vacant public land. It is designed to ensure rights as well as access of the poor to land. It does this by facilitating the process of regularizing land rights and entitlements, protecting against speculation and other problems that can inhibit the poor's access to land. The principle behind the Special Zones of Social Interest is that in Brazil, landownership is a condition for access to many other rights (justice, credit, housing finance) and that the right of all to land is the basis for the extension of urban citizenship. The zones intervene in the dynamics of the real estate market to control land access, secure social housing, and protect against downraiding and speculation that would dispossess the poor.

New urban forms: 'New urbanism' and the 'compact city'

During recent years, there has been a reaction against urban modernist forms[125] and urban sprawl, both of which are highly car dependent, unfriendly for pedestrians and environmentally unsustainable. While low-density, sprawling

Sector programmes have been important in terms of raising particular urban issues and ensuring that they find a place in the urban planning process

In some parts of the world, traditional master planning continues, but is being used in innovative ways cities are the norm in most parts of the world, there is a growing support for new urbanist and compact city forms, and, increasingly, planning policy documents refer to these principles (see Chapter 8).[126]

■ The compact city approach

At the city-wide scale, the 'compact city' approach argues for medium- to high-built densities, enabling efficient public transport and thresholds to support concentrations of economic activity, services and facilities (see Chapters 6 and 8). Mixed-use environments and good public open spaces are important, especially as places for small and informal businesses. Urban containment policies are common, often implemented through the demarcation of a growth boundary or urban edge, which will protect natural resources beyond the urban area and will encourage densification within it. Curitiba, in Brazil, has certain of these elements and is often cited as a good example of a planned, sustainable and public transport-based city. However, these ideas may be difficult to implement in many developing regions where strong and effective local governments are not in place, and where an extensive and growing peri-urban area makes the implementation of growth boundaries difficult and detrimental to the poor and the informal.

■ New urbanism

The new urbanism approach reflects many of the spatial principles of the compact city and the sustainable city approaches, but at the scale of the local neighbourhood. This position promotes local areas with fine-grained, mixed-use, mixed housing types, compact form, an attractive public realm, pedestrian-friendly streetscapes, defined centres and edges, and varying transport options.[127] Facilities such as health, libraries, retail and government services cluster around key public transport facilities and intersections to maximize convenience. These spatial forms have been strongly promoted in the US and have been implemented in the form of neighbourhoods such as Celebration Town[128] and Seaside. What projects such as these demonstrate is that while the intentions of new urbanism may be sound, and while alternatives to car-dependent sprawl are essential, there is a danger that they can become elite and over-planned enclaves that are not in tune with diverse and dynamic urban areas.

Most of the new and innovative approaches to urban planning discussed above are moving in the direction of the normative principles for urban planning set out in Chapter 1. Most are attempting to address what have been clear problems in traditional modernist planning approaches. It is also possible to identify some areas of commonality across the various new approaches, with most attempting to:

- be strategic rather than comprehensive;
- be flexible rather than end-state oriented and fixed;
- be action and implementation oriented through links to budgets, projects and city-wide or regional infrastructure;
- be stakeholder or community driven rather than only expert driven;
- be linked to political terms of office;

- contain objectives reflecting emerging urban concerns – for example, city global positioning, environmental protection, sustainable development, and achieving urban-related MDGs, social inclusion and local identity;
- play an integrative role in policy formulation and in urban management by encouraging government departments to coordinate their plans in space;
- focus on the planning process, with highly diverse outcomes (urban modernism, gated communities, new urbanism, compact city models) and dependent upon stakeholder influence or local policy directions; and
- shift in the direction of new urban forms that are very different from those of urban modernism: these are forms which take account of environmental and resource issues, and the need to create quality urban public spaces.

However, in many respects, planning approaches which meet all of the normative criteria have still not emerged. Some approaches meet certain criteria, but not others. Often the aims of new approaches are laudable; but their implementation remains a problem. Implementation is often dependent upon broader socio-political factors lying outside the control of the planning system. There is still a great deal of focus in the new approaches on process, often at the expense of outcomes (the nature of the urban environment produced), and a strong focus on the directive aspect of the planning system and neglect of the underlying regulatory system, and how this links to directive plans. Furthermore, planning is still weak in terms of how to deal with the major issues of the 21st century: climate change, resource depletion, rapid urbanization, poverty and informality.

CONCLUDING REMARKS

This chapter has examined the emergence of urban planning from ancient times, when it was first used to shape human settlements, to the Industrial Revolution, when it came to be seen as a tool to manage rapidly growing and industrializing cities, through its spread to the rest of the world, and into the current period when it is undergoing significant debate and change. It is clear that human beings have always acted to consciously plan and organize their settlements, and will no doubt continue to do so for the foreseeable future. However, over the last 100 years or so, a particular problem has emerged in that planning has been bound up with global processes of colonialism and imperialism, and has been used for purposes other than the creation of well-functioning and sustainable urban centres. One result of this has been that inappropriate models of planning have been adopted in various parts of the world, and for particular reasons are now very hard to change. It is generally acknowledged that planning is inevitably a political process, and cannot be detached from local and global political forces. Yet, the nature of the challenge to urban environments in the 21st century is of such seriousness that it is now imperative that planning, which is potentially a tool to address these challenges, is revised in order to play a role in the future of towns and cities.

In many respects, planning approaches which meet all of the normative criteria have still not emerged

Planning is still weak in terms of how to deal with the major issues of the 21st century: climate change, resource depletion, rapid urbanization and informality

A central focus of this chapter has been a review of innovative approaches to planning from various parts of the world, not in order to suggest new universal solutions that can be applied in all contexts, but rather to see if there are common ideas that are emerging from various parts of the world. This chapter suggests that there are such commonalities, and that city governments in all parts of the world can consider whether or not these may be useful in their particular context. Many of these new approaches are also moving closer to the normative criteria for good planning systems, set out in Chapter 1. Some of these innovative planning ideas are dealt with in greater detail in the chapters that follow.

NOTES

1   Macionis and Parrillo, 2004, p33.
2   Macionis and Parrillo, 2004, p33.
3   Ayataç, 2007.
4   Rosen, 1993.
5   Hull, 1976.
6   Hull, 1976.
7   Arimah and Adeagbo, 2000.
8   Arimah and Adeagbo, 2000.
9   'Novgorod', www.novgorod1150.com/history/spravka/.
10   Benevolo, 1967.
21   Ashworth, 1954; Peterson, 1979; Herbert, 1999.
32   Hall, 1988.
34   Cherry, 1979, p306.
14   Taylor, 1998.
15   The term 'blueprint' is borrowed from architecture and refers to the final and fully detailed design that an architect would produce for a building.
16   Taylor, 1998.
17   The Charter of Athens (initiated in 1928) and later strongly influenced by Le Corbusier was an important document (by 1944) in terms of establishing modernist urban principles.
18   Hall, 1988.
19   Hall, 1988, p176.
20   The relationship between planning systems and property rights is highly varied. In the UK development rights are nationalized. By contrast, in the US, France and South Africa there is constitutional support for private property rights (although a recent court case has recognized the right of US local government to acquire compulsorily private property in the interests of economic regeneration).
21   Cullingworth, 1993.
22   Hall, 1988.
23   Taylor, 1998.
24   Ward, 2002.
25   King, 1980, p203.
26   Papayanis, 2006.
27   The year in which each organization was established appears in parenthesis. The Garden Cities Association later became the Town and Country Planning Association.
28   The BCEOM is a semi-public company that was established in 1949 by the Ministry of French Overseas Territories specifically to execute planning and engineering projects in French overseas dependencies.
29   Rieniets, 2005.
30   Block, 1954.
31   Strobel, 2003.
32   Nedovic-Budic and Cavric, 2006.
33   CIAM stands for Congrès Internationaux d'Architecture Moderne, founded in 1928.
34   Macionis and Parrillo, 2004.
35   Hardoy, 1992.
36   Lu, 2006.
37   Lu, 2006, p370.
38   Lu, 2006.
39   Home, 1997.
40   Dutch Architects, online.
41   Christopher, 1984.
42   Christopher, 1984, p177.
43   Christopher, 1984.
44   Njoh, 1999.
45   Njoh, 2003b.
46   Njoh, 2003b.
47   Njoh, 2003b.
48   Njoh, 1999.
49   See Chapter 4 for discussions of the institutional variations that affect planning.
50   For an early critique, see Jacobs (1963). For subsequent critiques and alternative approaches to master planning, see collaborative and communicative planning (Innes, 1995; Healey, 1997); pragmatic planning (Forester, 1993); equity planning (Krumholz and Forester, 1990); strategic spatial planning (Albrechts, 2001b); multicultural planning (Sandercock, 1998). For a collection of key articles and chapters covering the development of these ideas in planning, see Hillier and Healey (2008).
51   Rakodi, 2008.
52   Garau, 2008.
53   Giddings and Hopwood, 2006.
54   Hirt and Stanilov, 2008.
55   Hirt and Stanilov, 2008.
56   Hirt, 2005.
57   Hirt and Stanilov, 2008.
58   Attahi et al, 2008.
59   Ansari, 2004.
60   Ansari, 2008.
61   Yuen, 2008.
62   Irazábal, 2008a.
63   Arimah and Adeagbo, 2000.
64   Hirt and Stanilov, 2008.
65   Leaf, 2005a.
66   Logan, 2002.
67   Yiftachel, 2003.
68   Devas, 2001.
69   Kamete, 2007.
70   Tibaijuka, 2005; Berrisford and Kihato, 2006.
71   Devas, 2001.
72   Payne, 2005.
73   Kironde, 2006.
74   Fernandes, 2003.
75   Rolnick, 1999.
76   Although it has a much longer pedigree in planning history – see Albrechts, 2001b.
77   Albrechts, 2001b; Healey et al, 1997.
78   Healey et al, 1997.
79   Albrechts, 2001b.
80   Albrechts, 2001b; Healey et al, 1997.
81   Bulkleley and Kern, 2006.
82   Swyngedouw, 2005.
83   Steinberg, 2005.
84   Steinberg, 2005.
85   Attahi et al, 2008.
86   Marshall, 2000.
87   Borja and Castells, 1997.
88   Marshall, 2000.
89   Crot, 2008.
90   Reflected in the Planning and Compulsory Purchase Act of 2004.
91   Nadin, 2007.
92   Harrison et al, 2008.
93   An example of an IDP (for metropolitan Cape Town) is available at www.capetown.gov.za (links from five-year plan).
94   Vigar and Healey, 1999.
95   Harrison et al, 2008.
96   Harrison et al, 2008.
97   This section summarizes the innovative approaches discussed in detail in Chapter 7.
98   International Covenant on Economic, Social and Cultural Rights adopted by the United Nations in 1966; and the International Covenant on Civil and Political Rights which allows appeal to the United Nations Human Rights Committee.
99   Angel, 2008.
100   Waibel, 2008.
101   See Chapter 7.
102   Kyessi, 2005.
103   Rojas and Smolka, 1998.
104   This section summarizes innovative planning ideas discussed in detail in Chapter 5.
105   A refinement of participatory rural appraisal, developed by Chambers (2004).
106   Mitlin, 2008.
107   Cabannes, 2006; Sintomer et al, 2008.
108   Crot, 2008.
109   Rakodi, 2008; see also Chapter 5.
110   Local Agenda 21 processes, which emerged from 1992 Earth Summit Agreements, followed a similar direction to the UMP and were later linked to the UN-Habitat urban agenda (see Allen and You, 2002).
111   Drakakis-Smith, 2000.
112   Cohen, 2005; Mehta, 2005.
113   Mehta, 2005, p7.
114   UN-Habitat, 2005.
115   Halla, 2002.
116   Nnkya, 2006a.
117   UN-Habitat, 2006g.
118   Cities Alliance, 2005.
119   UN-Habitat, 2002b.
120   Attahi et al, 2008.
121   Allen, 2003; Kyessi, 2005.
122   Scheurer and Newman, 2008.
123   Irazábal, 2008a.
124   Souza, 2003, p194.
125   See Jacobs (1963) for one of the earliest critiques of these forms.
126   Jenks et al, 1996; Jenks and Burgess, 2000; Williams et al, 2000.
127   Grant, 2006.
128   Njoh, 2008b.

4

THE INSTITUTIONAL AND REGULATORY FRAMEWORK FOR PLANNING

This chapter sets out the institutional and regulatory frameworks in which planning systems are currently situated and to which they contribute. Such frameworks vary enormously, derived as they are from the wider governance context and its particular history. Nevertheless, it is possible to identify some general trends in the contemporary development of planning systems and the activities related to them.

The purposes of planning and how it is undertaken are shaped by the wider context of governance. This wider context reflects the way in which a society thinks about issues such as how urban areas should develop; how the benefits of urban development should be distributed; and what the balance between individual rights and collective concerns should be as development proceeds. It is rare for institutional contexts and conceptions of development trajectories to be unified in some smoothly working integrated system. Instead, there are usually substantial tensions and conflicts between different sections of any society about how urban development should proceed and who should benefit from it. There are also significant disjunctions between the activities of different segments of a society's governance structure. Such tensions and conflicts are particularly acute where major changes are under way in economic, social and political conditions and in the dynamics of urban areas. Urban planning in such situations is not only tossed and turned by these changes, but its institutions and practices are themselves often active players in ongoing struggles. Planning agencies may resist evolving directions, but they may also promote new possibilities. Similarly, they may undermine opportunities for social progress and environmental sustainability, although they may also promote them.

In this chapter, urban planning processes and activities are set in this recognition of the complex, highly variable institutional contexts in which they take place. The chapter consists of seven main sections. The first section, on the relationship between planning and governance, sets the scene for the subsequent discussion on the institutional context of planning and planning agencies. The second

> The purposes of planning and how it is undertaken are shaped by the wider context of governance

> Urban planning ... institutions and practices are themselves often active players in ongoing struggles

section, which elaborates upon the role of planning institutions and the institutionalization of planning practices, introduces the two meanings of 'institutions': one refers to wider societal norms and practices and the other to specific planning agencies and organization. These are further elaborated upon in the three following sections. The third and fourth sections discuss the significance of the legal and the land and property systems that underpin urban planning, while the fifth section focuses on the regulatory power of planning and its role in the formal government structures. The sixth section discusses the significance of regulatory roles, resources, arenas and stakeholders in the implementation of plans and planning policies. The concluding section presents a number of lessons for policy-makers.

PLANNING AND GOVERNANCE

This section is about the relationships between planning and governance. It begins by clarifying the concept of governance and how it differs from the formal structures of government. It then focuses on the challenge of achieving collective action in the realm of public affairs at a time when there is a global trend towards proliferation of actors, institutions and interests in decision-making processes. One such public activity is the management of urban change, in which planning systems, in all countries where such a system exists, make an important contribution. Within this context, planning is seen as a form of urban/place governance and, as such, is embedded in wider power relations.

Urban governance and government

The ways in which cities are governed and organized both reflect and reinforce changes in the social, economic and spatial structure of urban areas. The enormous differences between the performance of cities and countries around the world can be explained, at least partially, by differences in governance.[1] Such diversity is not a new phenomenon.

However, there is widespread recognition that the government institutions inherited from the mid 20th century need substantial change to address the challenges of contemporary urban life. Modern urban systems are characterized by complex patterns of interdependencies between actors, institutions, functional activities and spatial organizations. One key trend has been to rethink the relation between formal government and wider society. The term *governance* has come to be used to refer to this enlarged scope.

However, the term governance is understood in two different ways: in a *descriptive* sense, it refers to the proliferation of institutions, agencies, interests and regulatory systems.[2] In a *normative* sense, it refers to an alternative model for managing collective affairs. It is seen as 'horizontal self-organization among mutually interdependent actors',[3] of whom government is only one and with only 'imperfect control'.[4] Proponents argue that such a new form of governance becomes necessary because of profound restructuring of the state. In recent decades, the restructuring trends have been reflected in a number of ways, such as:

- a relative decline in the role of formal government in the management of social and economic relationships;
- the involvement of non-governmental actors in a range of state functions at a variety of spatial levels;
- a change from hierarchical forms of government structures to more flexible forms of partnership and networking;
- a shift from provision by formal government structures to sharing of responsibilities and service provision between the state and civil society; and
- the devolution and decentralization of formal governmental responsibilities to regional and local governments.

In today's complex urban systems, controlling, managing or even steering the fragmented and often competing societal interests is beyond the capacity of the state as an agent of authority. Thus, formal governments are no longer the key locus for integration of urban relationships, but merely one of many actors competing for access to resources and control of urban planning agendas. Thus, UN-Habitat has defined urban governance as:

> *The sum of the many ways individuals and institutions, public and private, plan and manage the common affairs of the city. It is a continuing process through which conflicting or diverse interests may be accommodated and cooperative action can be taken. It includes formal institutions as well as informal arrangements and the social capital of citizens.*[5]

The challenge of urban governance

The trends in urban governance mentioned above have led to the expansion of policy-making space to engage a wider range of actors. However, at the same time, it has led to institutional fragmentation, multiplication of agencies,

complex webs of relationships, reconfiguration of networks, disparity of powers and responsibilities across different tiers and departments of governmental and non-governmental institutions, increasing role of market forces, and confusion over 'who does what'.[6] In urban planning processes, for example, actors are drawn from beyond the boundaries of the formal institutions of government, spread among public, private and civil society sectors, and straddle jurisdictional boundaries.[7] These actors represent diverse, and sometimes conflicting, policy objectives and interests.

In this context, and irrespective of whether a normative or descriptive interpretation of governance is adopted, a key concern is how to meet the challenge of these governance situations. This challenge is about 'achieving collective action in the realm of public affairs, in conditions where it is not possible to (merely) rest on recourse to the authority of the state'.[8] It is about how collective action can emerge from a diverse set of interests; how new forms of integration can be created out of fragmentation; and how new forms of coherence can emerge out of inconsistency, in the realm of public affairs.[9] One such public affair is the management of urban change and development, to which planning systems aspire to play a central role. Such a role is implemented through both specific planning actions and the creation of ground rules and instruments for actions by other stakeholders in urban futures.

Planning, urban governance and power relations

Given the diversity of actors and interests involved in managing urban futures, it becomes evident that planning is not just about formulating ideas, policies and programmes, but also about implementing these through collective actions. It is in this context that planning is seen as a form of urban (or place) governance; as a result, planning is embedded in power relations. Power in this context refers to power *to* act as much as power *over* the action of others.[10] In the social relations of governance processes, both forms of power exist and remain in tension.[11]

The significance of power *to* act (or enabling power) stems from the move from a traditional model of hierarchical authority related to the formal structure of a political system to a situation where the power is diffused between those in formal political positions and other stakeholders. These actors exercise different forms of power. Those with access to either resources such as information, expertise and finance (e.g. planning professionals and experts), or rules and accountability (e.g. elected politicians) may have *command-and-control power*. Others with key positions in the social and economic structures (e.g. landowners, developers and infrastructure/property investors) may have *systemic power* (e.g. through access to substantial financial resources or ownership of land). A third group with the ability to lobby and mobilize effective local campaigns (e.g. environmental and community groups) may have *bottom-up power*. This latter is illustrated by Kobe (see Box 4.3) where, despite the centralized government structure in Japan, a kind of bottom-up design of planning institutions emerged

Formal governments are no longer the key locus for integration of urban relationships, but merely one of many actors competing for access to resources and control of urban planning agendas

Planning is not just about formulating ideas, policies and programmes, but also about implementing these through collective actions

from civil society protest in the 1960s called *machizukuri*. This later shaped the Japanese government decentralization efforts and the building of capacity in local government and civil society.

This dispersion of power among various actors means that although those with systemic and command power may have an advantage in urban governance relations, they can only make use of their position if they turn that power into *enabling* power. This is the power to achieve collective action. Hence, the effectiveness of urban planning and governance depends not only upon the assumed command-and-control power of a master plan, but upon the persuasive power that can mobilize actions of diverse stakeholders and policy communities to contribute to collective concerns.[12] The likelihood of such enabling power to emerge is higher in the societies where power is more diffused and is transparently exercised so that checks and balances can be put in place. On the contrary, in the societies where power is concentrated, and exercised through corruption and coercion, such consensual processes pose a formidable challenge. In these circumstances, where local government is either non-existent or lacks accountability and transparency and the civil society is weak, the tensions between 'power to' and 'power over' are often resolved in favour of the latter. Worse than that, planning systems often become the instrument for exercising power *over* the weak, the less vocal and the poor, whether explicitly considered or through unthinking practices.[13] In such situations, settlement planning becomes an instrument of repression rather than accommodation. So, for enabling power to flourish from governance processes, it is paramount that checks and balances are in place to promote transparency, accountability and inclusive participation in planning processes,[14] all of which are the main ingredients of good governance, as elaborated upon below.

Promoting 'good governance'

The normative perspective on governance has provided a way of promoting policy measures aimed at decentralization, privatization and democratization of government functions. During the 1980s, driven largely by multilateral organizations such as the World Bank and United Nations agencies, this agenda was strongly pursued as a way of unblocking the institutional and governance barriers to socio-economic development. However, by the end of the 1980s, the emphasis began to shift away from the rolling back of the state towards promoting 'good governance' in which formal government structures, particularly at the local level, were to play an important role in meeting the challenge of collective action. This was based on the idea that, in both developed and developing countries, formal government (if elected through democratic processes) continues to play a significant role in shaping the governance processes at various spatial levels.[15] This recognition is particularly important in urban planning since rights to the use and development of land are significantly affected by formal law.

Thus, since the late 1990s, 'good governance' has become the mantra for development in developing countries, with planning being seen as a key promoter of such an ideal. However, it has come to mean different things. In general, there has been a tendency to see urban governance simply in terms of urban management (i.e. the operation and maintenance of a city's infrastructure and services). However, it is increasingly recognized that urban governance processes are not merely managerial processes and are, indeed, heavily politicized struggles over distribution of resources and quality of places. This is particularly clear in relation to urban planning.[16] Hence, for many multilateral organizations, including the United Nations, good governance is about a desired standard of practice for which common values or norms can be identified, with emphasis being placed on human and civil rights, and democratic and participatory practices. UN-Habitat, for example, defines good governance as an efficient and effective response to urban problems by accountable local governments working in partnership with civil society. The main characteristics of good urban governance are:

* *sustainability* – balancing the social, economic and environmental needs of present and future generations;
* *subsidiarity* – assigning responsibilities and resources to the closest appropriate level;
* *equity of access* to decision-making processes and the basic necessities of urban life;
* *efficiency in delivery* of public services and in promoting local economic development;
* *transparency and accountability* of decision-makers and all stakeholders;
* *civic engagement and citizenship* – recognizing that people are the principal wealth of cities, and both the object and the means of sustainable human development; and
* *security* of individuals and their living environment.[17]

Applied to the urban level, these normative ideas provide encouragement to a trend towards urban governance processes that are able to integrate social, economic and environmental agendas and relate these to people's daily life experiences. However, whether and how such a trend is able to evolve, and how urban planning practices develop, depends upon the institutional dynamics of particular contexts.

What matters is that the development of urban governance capacities helps to promote effective urban planning. However, the relation between governance capacity and the capacity for effective planning works both ways. Efforts to improve planning systems and practices can help to strengthen governance capacity. It is clear that planning practices and institutions are active players in shaping urban futures; yet they are, at the same time, shaped by the wider social and institutional context within which they operate.[18]

The effectiveness of urban planning and governance depends ... upon the persuasive power that can mobilize actions of diverse stakeholders and policy communities to contribute to collective concerns

Urban governance processes are ... heavily politicized struggles over distribution of resources and quality of places

PLANNING INSTITUTIONS AND THE INSTITUTIONALIZATION OF PLANNING PRACTICES

Urban planning, as a field of governance, is performed through, and has effects on, a wide range of institutions in society. These may be both formal government agencies and less formalized ways of undertaking and regulating development. More broadly, specific agencies are shaped by the wider institutions in society through which, for example, land and property rights are established, the legitimacy of governance action secured and the distribution of material resources achieved. Given the contemporary challenge to urban planning to integrate diverse agendas in contexts where governance power is fragmented and diffused,[19] it is important to consider the institutional context for urban planning at both the specific and the broader level. This section first sets out a general approach to understanding institutions and then considers the implications for, and trends in, urban planning institutions. This is done first at the broad governance level and then at the specific level of planning agencies and organizations. The section concludes by commenting on the challenges for the design of planning systems.

Institutions as wider norms and practices

Earlier generations of planners gave only limited attention to the institutional context for urban planning. However, experiences since then have highlighted the significance of institutional contexts and their dynamic evolution for any public policy area, including urban planning. It is thus important to understand the broader norms and practices that frame the ways in which, for example, conflicts are dealt with, resources are allocated and action is taken in the realm of public affairs – in other words, how things get done.

All societies have norms and practices that govern specific areas of activity, but these can be very different from one place to another. Figure 4.1 attempts to summarize the range of possible institutions, understood in this broad sense. At a very broad level are the interacting spheres of formal government systems and public agencies, markets and other processes driven by economic considerations, and the worlds of civil society, including all kinds of voluntary agencies and informal practices.[20] Within these, various specific institutions may play a significant part in how urban development occurs. Economic activity may be pursued by large international corporations, substantial businesses, small- and medium-sized enterprises and all kinds of forms of production and exchange that operate below the radar of formal recognition. Within the state sphere, formal government and legal structures may coexist with all kinds of informal political practices that may undermine the declared logic and values of formal systems. Within civil society, often considered as less formalized, powerful institutions may exist, reflecting family loyalties, cultural and religious traditions, and older political and legal systems suppressed by, for

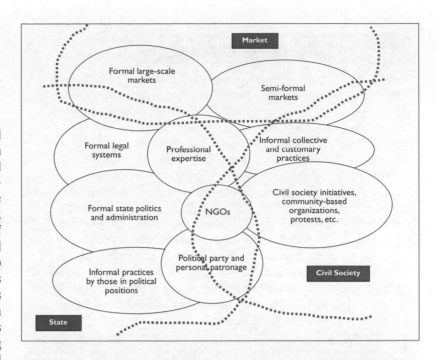

Figure 4.1

Broad-approach institutional contexts

example, former colonial regimes.[21] Political activists and professional experts often find themselves negotiating between sets of institutions and the wider spheres of the state, economy and civil society. Each of these has its own particular set of norms and practices, although affected by interaction with other systems. These not only structure the distribution of access, rights of redress, and the relation between individual and collective considerations, but also establish the legitimacy of specific practices, such as those related to urban planning.

Figure 4.1 suggests a way of 'scoping' the broad institutional context for urban planning. A key issue for effective urban planning at present is the capacity to integrate a range of social forces in an urban area and mobilize them to address actions to improve daily life conditions. Examples where this has been achieved suggest that such capacity is promoted where formal government and legal systems are respected and considered legitimate, where there are a plurality of groups in civil society and among economic actors demanding governance attention to the quality of the urban environment, and where there are rich linkages between the spheres of the state, economy and civil society. Such a situation helps to keep all spheres co-evolving with each other as conditions change. Here, formal planning systems may play a constructive role so long as attention and respect is continually given to how formal organizations and procedures interact with the often less formal ways of organizing within civil society and the variety of forms which economic activity can take. Within developed countries, such institutional conditions are found in, for example, The Netherlands, and in cities such as Portland, US,[22] and Vancouver, Canada,[23] which have an international reputation for the quality of their urban environments and the contribution made to these by their urban planning systems.[24] But examples can also be found where respect for civil society initiative is slowly won after years of campaigning, as in Kobe, Japan (see Box 4.3), or where participatory initiatives undertaken with international aid slowly grow to transform a

Urban planning, as a field of governance, is performed through, and has effects on, a wide range of institutions in society

Box 4.1 Developing participatory urban planning practices in Kitale, Kenya

Kitale is a rapidly expanding secondary town about 380km north-west of Nairobi, Kenya. By 2001, the town's annual population growth rate of 12 per cent had outstripped the capacity of the local authority to plan and manage the town's development effectively, and to provide land, infrastructure, housing and other services. As a result, 65 per cent of the 220,000 population lived in slums and informal settlements. Thus, the international non-governmental organization (NGO) Intermediate Technology Development Group (ITDG) designed and implemented a participatory action research project to address these problems.

The project sought to develop, test and disseminate a partnership approach to the planning of urban space with local institutions, with the overall goal being to enhance the effectiveness of city and municipal planning and management. In aiming to achieve economically, socially and environmentally sustainable local development, as well as an effective participatory governance framework for urban planning and management, the project brought together three methodologies: participatory planning, partnership and local development. Three slums areas were selected, through a participatory process, as sites to pilot innovative institutional frameworks through which sustainable slum and urban upgrading interventions could be developed and implemented.

In carrying out the project, ITDG adopted the multiplicative strategy in which NGOs achieve results through deliberate influence, training, networking and policy reform. Hence, the project has had a significant impact upon the institutional and regulatory framework for urban planning and service delivery in Kitale town. The experience from Kitale has also influenced urban planning practice more widely in Kenya.

Source: Majale, 2008

Box 4.2 Struggles between formal land rights and customary land rights in Moshi, Tanzania

Moshi is a major town in Tanzania, designated in national government strategy during the 1970s as a 'growth pole'. Following this, national government planners prepared a master plan to show how land should be used and developed over a 20-year period. Much of this had already experienced some development intensification under the system of customary land rights. Local communities in and around Moshi knew little about the existence of the plan until their land came to be affected by urban expansion projects. In one instance, residents of a village discovered accidentally some years later that their village was designated for urban extension. The implication was that they would lose their customary rights, with little compensation. As various village groups checked out the situation more carefully, the scale of urban expansion became clearer. Protest built up, which the national government tried to suppress.

At the heart of the protest was the question of who should have the right to appropriate the land value arising from urban development. In both the formal system of land rights, which is normally applied in urban areas, and in the customary tenure system, plots could be bought and sold. As the scale of the urban area grew, and despite the formal view that land had only 'use value', not exchange value, plots were bought and sold under both systems. As the struggle between the two tenure systems developed, it sometimes took the form of direct action, with plot boundary markers positioned according to the master plan being removed by local people. The protesters were able to exploit legal loopholes in the status of the master plan to lodge a court action against the plan's provisions and the national government's actions. They were eventually successful; but the legal process took a long time, by which time many residents had experienced displacement of some kind. In addition, the climate of uncertainty as to which land allocation practice would prevail was exploited by well-placed influential people, who were able to get hold of well-positioned plots and thus benefit from the land value uplift generated by urbanization.

Source: Nnkya, 1996, 1999

previously weak local governance capacity, as in the case of Kitale, Kenya (see Box 4.1).

However, in some contexts, formal government and law may have little respect and legitimacy. In many parts of sub-Saharan Africa, such institutions are sometimes seen as a colonial inheritance, often subverted into a mechanism to promote the personal and political interests of elites.[25] In this context, pre-existing ways of organizing how urban land is used and developed may jostle with formal urban planning arrangements introduced in colonial and post-colonial times, creating uncertainty and confusion as to where the authority to resolve conflicts over access to urban resources lies.[26] In such situations, customary governance traditions have sometimes grown in importance as a way of organizing access to urban resources and opportunities.[27]

However, neither political patronage nor customary practices are likely to promote equity[28] or give consideration to the complexity of the way in which development and infrastructure relate to each other, and social, environmental and economic issues interact in urban environments. This is well illustrated by the case of urban fringe development in Enugu, Nigeria, where customary and formal state practices together controlled access to plots.[29]

Many urban initiatives, especially those directed to improve living conditions in slums, have sought to introduce different ways of working to counteract tendencies towards exploitation by dominant elites or confused struggles over the control of ownership and access to key urban resources. A number of developing countries have adopted policies to convert illegal occupancy of land into formal legal land rights, thereby enabling access to formal finance.[30] This evolution, however, has not been welcomed by all. Sometimes communities rightly fear 'gentrification': the process whereby more affluent groups displace the original residents. In other situations, people's poverty is such that formal ownership and access to loan finance has little relevance.[31] Instead, they may feel that customary and informal systems provide more secure tenure, as the example of Moshi in Box 4.2 shows.

A focus on institutions in this broad sense (i.e. as norms and procedures) thus implies that, whenever planning is promoted, attention should be paid to 'competing rationalities'[32] of the various institutions involved. The agencies of planning 'systems' are themselves active agents in these evolutions, promoting some sets of norms and resisting others. It is also important to recognize that these institutions are not static. They are themselves in continuous evolution as they interact with each other and with the challenges of dealing with a changing world. These institutional complexities are increasingly being recognized and creative ways are sought to move towards fairer, more transparent, inclusive and integrative institutions for allocating key urban resources.

Institutions as specific agencies and organizations

The narrower meaning of institutions refers to specific configurations of agencies and organizations that operate within the parameter of wider norms and practices. A 'planning system' and its specific agencies and organizations fall within this meaning of institutions. Formal planning systems consist of bundles of public and private rights, agency authority, coordination mechanisms and procedural protocols that are defined by formal political and legal authorities. This, however, is not to suggest that informal planning systems do not exist.[33]

Many of today's planning systems in developed countries were designed in the mid 20th century.[34] During this time it was common to assume that nation states had a hierarchical arrangement of government responsibilities. The national level provided a framework of laws governing land-use regulation, powers of land assembly and the balance between public and private rights in land and property development activity. The national level also articulated key national policy objectives and provided grants and subsidies to promote particular kinds of development. These then might be further developed at an intermediate level, perhaps by provinces or other regional or intermediate bodies. Municipalities were charged with preparing plans to encapsulate their development policy in the light of higher-tier policies and the local conditions of their areas. They were also expected to carry out development and regulatory activity within the framework set by national and regional levels of the system. It was then assumed that development would occur as defined in formally agreed plans.

In some countries, this arrangement really did work as expected. This was especially so where levels of government worked in cooperative partnership, where the wider institutional context encouraged an integrated governance landscape, and where formal institutions were accepted as the dominant legitimate sources of authority. This is the case in most of the countries in North-West Europe. In many other countries, however, all kinds of disjunctions appeared. Here, implementation problems ranged from tensions between levels and sectors of government, to tensions between competing institutions and agencies for developing and regulating urban development processes.[35] This has sometimes led to the creation of special agencies to bypass difficulties with the existing arrangements. For example, agencies have been created to deal with particular projects, such as new town development coordination and special partnerships for major development projects or a major area reconfiguration project.[36] Designing the agency structure of a planning system cannot therefore be readily approached with some kind of ideal template. Instead, attention should be paid to how, in a specific institutional context, different government agencies may relate to the different tasks that are central to the guidance and management of urban development futures.

Formal planning systems are inserted into an array of pre-existing arrangements, derived from one or more of the broad institutions outlined above. They provide ground rules for proactive development (managing urban extension, redevelopment and reconfiguration), and for regulating the flow of change in the built environment. By extension, they may also have a role in managing change in less-urbanized landscapes. They may or may not be part of a larger project

focused on the social, economic and environmental development of urban areas. Furthermore, they may operate at various spatial levels from neighbourhood to transnational levels.

The variety in agency forms and relations implies that there is no one 'model' of the agency structure of a planning system. What is an appropriate structure needs to be worked out in specific contexts, in relation to the evolving wider governance landscape.[37] However, irrespective of the diversity, there are a number of critical issues that can make or break an effective planning system. These are the:

- nature of the political and legal systems that underpin urban planning activities, and the cultures of respect for the legal system and trust in its impartiality;
- local specificity of land and property markets;
- location of planning agencies within formal government structures;
- degree of vertical and horizontal policy integration and institutional coordination;
- extent to which power and responsibilities are devolved and decentralized;
- appropriateness of planning tools and resources for planning tasks; and
- quality of human and intellectual capital.

These will be further elaborated upon in the subsequent sections of this chapter. First, however, it is important to highlight the significance of institutional design in urban planning.

The institutional design and redesign of urban planning systems

A key factor in the promotion of effective governance capacity is the design of formal planning systems. These structure what legal and administrative powers and instruments are available to formal government agencies to shape development processes and which agencies are given the formal powers to define how instruments are to be used to pursue specific planning tasks. These tasks centre on the:

- ongoing management of built environment change;
- promotion of development – physical, social, environmental and economic – and the relation between development and infrastructure provision;
- protection of environmental resources; and
- preparation of strategies and policies to guide how the other three tasks are performed.

Current planning systems vary in the emphasis given to each of the above, and in the breadth given to each task. In many countries, formal planning systems have been narrowed down into land-use allocation frameworks, allocating sites to specific uses and, frequently, formal development rights to owners. This practice is referred to in European debates as 'land-use planning' in contrast to a more developmentally focused 'spatial planning'.[38] In many developing countries with a British colonial inheritance, such site-allocation

Formal planning systems are inserted into an array of pre-existing arrangements

The design of formal planning systems ... structure what legal and administrative powers and instruments are available to formal government agencies to shape development processes

planning is known as 'master planning', as opposed to an active form of development planning.[39] In Latin America and Mediterranean Europe, planning systems require the preparation of a 'general municipal plan', which assumes that the site allocation and developmental objectives of urban planning can be combined. The result has been a very cumbersome system that is frequently bypassed or modified by *ad hoc* 'variations'.[40]

How urban planning is actually practised, however, is the result of the way in which the formal institutional design of a planning system interacts with other dimensions of governance dynamics, both formal and informal. There is repeated criticism that planning practices fail to achieve what system designers expected. Often, this is because the designers failed to pay attention to the wider institutional context, and the tensions and struggles within it. System designers have also often overemphasized a top-down hierarchical structure. More recently, following the general trend towards more decentralized governance arrangements, some system designers have sought to give more flexibility for local autonomy. Such an approach has been energetically pursued in Brazil.[41] However, there is an ever-present danger in decentralized systems that the wider impacts of local action will be neglected.

A widespread global trend in recent years has been to redesign planning systems to make them more relevant to contemporary urban conditions. In these efforts, increasing attention is being paid to institutional contexts and how to encourage more active and inclusive governance capacity within them. Such redesign initiatives may arise where new regimes come to power, determined to make a difference to urban conditions, as in Brazil, and earlier in Barcelona, Spain.[42] Alternatively, they may be driven by social movements, concerned about daily life conditions and environmental consequences, or by a government facing new pressures, and thus realizing that the planning system needs to be reconfigured.[43] What is important in any initiative to redesign a planning system, however, is to pay careful attention to the institutional context within which it is situated and to how planning system initiatives will interact with the evolution of that context.

LEGAL SYSTEMS AND THE DISTRIBUTION OF RIGHTS AND RESPONSIBILITIES

Formal legal systems are central in defining the extent, nature and location of the regulatory powers of planning systems. They not only define such rights but also legitimate the limitation of such rights, often for public purposes. In the context of urban development, legal systems have far-reaching implications. They define the system of urban government, they establish the system of urban planning and regulation of land development, and they delimit the powers of urban planners and managers.[44] Legal systems thus define rights and responsibilities with respect to access to, and the enjoyment of, urban opportunities. Commonly, these are understood as access to housing, land and property, rights to

the 'use and development' of a property, and rights to resources held 'in common'. But there are also wider considerations, such as the right to satisfy basic needs (rights to adequate housing; work opportunities; clean water; education, health and social welfare; safety and security; good air quality; and freedom from polluting nuisances); the right of access to the ambiences and opportunities that a city offers; the right to participate in the governance of one's place of living; and the right to safeguard assets considered important not only for current well-being but for that of future generations. Indeed, social movements, non-governmental organizations (NGOs), local authorities and others have been promoting 'the Right to the City'.[45] In recent years, international covenants on human rights and national human rights law have come to have a significant impact upon planning law.[46]

Urban planning systems and regulatory planning practices are significantly shaped by the prevailing legal system. This happens, in part, through the use of the legal system to resolve planning-related disputes. In some countries, such as the US, it is often said that the legal system has become the primary arena where urban planning policies are defined.[47] In other countries, the legal system exerts its influence by the judgements made in various courts (supra-national, national and sub-national), and the enforcement practices which these judgements legitimate. People conform in expectation of such judgements, unless policy frameworks and the formation of legal judgements become unstable, arbitrary or irrelevant to people's situation. Then recourse to the courts, typically more available to the more affluent and powerful, becomes more common.

For poorer people, formal institutions may fail to make provision for their needs and/or may not be seen as legitimate or effective. For instance, in many African countries, it is increasingly being suggested that the regulatory framework governing the delivery of residential land plots is so encumbered by bureaucratic procedures and regulatory norms and standards that areas allocated in formal plans for housing become unaffordable and unavailable for low-income settlements.[48] If this is the case, informal (often formally illegal) practices for accessing needs and opportunities may develop, such as land invasion, property subdivision, and acquisition for private purposes of spaces intended for public uses. These practices may be backed locally by informal institutions that develop their own norms and standards.[49]

Throughout the world, there are different principles which govern legal systems. These derive from cumulative histories and lead to diverse forms of constitutions, political representation and policy-making traditions.[50] For example, in Western Europe, some countries draw on public administrative law developed in Napoleonic times (e.g. France, Germany and Austria). This is based on creating a complete set of abstract rules and principles prior to decision-making. In contrast, the British legal family (which includes Britain and Ireland) has evolved from English Common Law and the principle of precedent, which is based on the accumulation of case law over time. It offers far fewer rules and those that exist have been built up gradually by individual law cases.

A widespread global trend in recent years has been to redesign planning systems to make them more relevant to contemporary urban conditions

What is important in any initiative to redesign a planning system, however, is to pay careful attention to the institutional context within which it is situated and to how planning system initiatives will interact with the evolution of that context

This has allowed greater administrative discretion and improvisation. These differences in legal styles have had ramifications for the administrative systems and the relationships between central and local governments, as well as for planning systems.[51]

From an international perspective, there are many more legal traditions. One classification identifies seven different traditions of law that have some influence in the world today.[52] However, there has been little work relating these general legal traditions to their expression in planning law in different parts of the world. If there is a general tendency in formal planning law, it is towards more precise specification of rights and responsibilities. On the one hand, this helps to advance the rights of neglected groups, such as women and children, the disabled, and specific minorities, and to enshrine environmental standards into planning system requirements. On the other hand, such legal specification builds rigidities into planning systems and expands opportunities for litigation.

Litigation over planning issues itself seems to be an emerging global trend. This is most clearly the case in developed countries; but the opportunity for legal challenge has also been important in situations where customary law challenges formal law. This was the case on the rural–urban periphery in Moshi, Tanzania (see Box 4.2).

In addition to substantial variation in legal systems, there are major differences in the cultures of respect for legal systems, too. In the US, for example, citizens are very proud of their legal system. They see it as an important safeguard of the individual rights of every American. In other places, formal legal systems are often perceived as something 'outside', remote and unable to appreciate the worlds in which low-income people live their lives.[53] In this context, recourse to illegal land subdivision may often be judged more efficient and equitable than the cumbersome processes of an underfunded and sometimes corrupted planning system.

The legal system of a country and the cultural context in which it is used and abused has a significant impact upon the design of a country's planning system and upon how its practices evolve. The legal assumptions underpinning a planning system and its practices are often not recognized, especially where the design of a planning system has been imported from elsewhere. This often leads to problems in transferring an imported practice into a new context. Japan provides an interesting historical case. German ideas for managing the control of development and land assembly were influential among early 20th-century planners in Japan; but the political power of individual property owners was such that they were resisted within Japan itself. However, they were actively developed in the areas that Japan colonized, notably Korea and parts of north China.[54]

In designing or redesigning planning systems, therefore, it is important to note that the regulatory power of planning is underpinned by legal systems that define a number of key areas, including:

- Who holds the right to develop land and the institutional location of this right?

- What provisions are made for the appropriation of land for urban development purposes?
- What provisions are made to enable affected stakeholders to participate in and object to planning decisions?
- How and how far are public realm benefits (betterment) extracted from private development initiatives?
- How are disputes resolved?

Rights to develop land are sometimes held by the state. This is the case in many socialist regimes where land is formally nationalized. In the UK, the 1947 Town and Country Planning Act was considered innovative at the time because it 'nationalized' the right to development land. Since then, the right to develop has been granted by local planning authorities in the form of a planning 'permission'. In many other countries, the right to develop is lodged formally in a zoning ordinance or planning scheme, which specifies land uses and building norms. Once this is agreed upon, landowners have a right to develop according to the scheme. This last arrangement appears to give considerable certainty and transparency to stakeholders. However, preparing and agreeing such plans may take a long time, and development activity may rapidly overtake such schemes once agreed. Such plans are thus often criticized and bypassed as too inflexible and out of date for contemporary conditions.

Most planning systems contain provisions for the *appropriation of land for planning purposes*, such as providing public facilities and infrastructures, and to assist in assembling sites for major projects. These are likely to remain important tools where, for example, land resources are needed for major infrastructures. How and how frequently these provisions are used depends upon the political context. In countries where governments are trusted to promote public welfare, such 'compulsory purchase' of 'eminent domain' may be seen as legitimate. The only issue may be arriving at a fair price. But in countries where the ownership of a plot of land is seen to be a primary expression of individual liberty and/or where government is regarded as continually infringing individual liberty, as in the US, then such compulsory purchase, often termed 'expropriation', may be resented and resisted. Such a situation applies in Japan, where site assembly in major urban reconfiguration projects has to proceed by the consent of all affected owners through *land readjustment* mechanisms.[55] Most developing countries have legislation that enables governments to purchase or appropriate land in the interest of the public at large, either at or below market prices.[56]

The legal underpinnings of a planning system are also important in defining *rights to participate in and to object to planning strategies, policies and decisions*. Since restricting an individual owner's right to develop as they wish and purchasing a property for a public purpose against an owner's will are major limitations of property rights, most systems contain provisions for the owner to object to a decision made. These objections may be heard in some form of semi-judicial enquiry or directly in the courts. But there is also always the question about the rights to object of other affected parties, such as neighbours, or those concerned about the wider economic, social and environmental impacts of a policy. Many

Litigation over planning issues ... seems to be an emerging global trend

The legal underpinnings of a planning system are also important in defining rights to participate in and to object to planning strategies, policies and decisions

planning systems contain provisions for these 'third parties' (i.e. after the planning authority and the property owner) to object to a plan or to a permit decision. Such objections may then be heard in enquiry processes and the courts.

A major issue in urban development is the way in which the *costs and benefits of the value created by development are distributed*. Where land is publicly owned, in theory the state incurs both costs and benefits. This was the case until recently in Sweden and The Netherlands, where urban development land was held in public hands. However, the experience of having land in public ownership does not always inspire confidence that such objectives will be achieved. Public agencies which come to be landowners may fail to consider its value to an urban area generally. They may become mired in patronage politics, distributing access to plots to party supporters, friends and relations. Publicly owned sites may also be vulnerable to invasion. But in contexts where developers are private owners, the issue of who pays for the wider development impacts of a project becomes very important. This has led to the specification of requirements under planning law for 'developers' contributions' to urban infrastructures. There is a trend in developed countries to enlarge the scope of these contributions, although these are generally negotiated rather than specified in formal law.[57] It is an impossible task to keep track of all current mechanisms that attempt to ensure that public realm benefits and return value created by the urbanization process lead to public realm improvements for an urban community as a whole. The mechanisms provided need to reflect the taxation system in play, and the way in which infrastructures and other community facilities are provided and managed in any situation. But they must also reflect the extent to which value in urban land and property accumulates and how patterns of value play out in different parts of an urban area.

Resolving disputes over rights and responsibilities in the urban planning field may lead to formal appeals to legal courts, although planning systems may have semi-judicial or less formal mechanisms for dispute resolution. In countries where informal institutions and corrupted formal systems are actively present in urban development processes, any kind of formal redress for injustices is not easy to achieve. This is particularly the case in developing countries where urbanization is proceeding apace. Affected parties then have to resort to political action or some form of direct action. The result is that many poorer residents can find that their rights to occupancy and to the public realm are threatened. Even where the formal planning system is well established and reasonably respected, it may prove so complex, costly and time consuming that many find it difficult to access.

LAND AND PROPERTY OWNERSHIP AND DEVELOPMENT INSTITUTIONS

The regulatory practices associated with planning systems lie at the intersection between public purposes, the institutions of land and property ownership, and property development activity. Sometimes, as in some socialist contexts, these are all represented by public agencies, but not necessarily in coordination with each other. In societies where land is held in private ownership, this intersection is primarily between 'public' and 'private' interests, or, more widely, the relation between state action and market action. How planning systems operate, in practice, and how far the legal underpinnings of systems are brought into the forefront of attention depends upon political will and governance cultures, as discussed in the previous section. To understand the practices associated with urban planning in any situation thus requires paying attention to, first, specific institutional structures of land and property ownership and, second, the dynamics of property development activities. Both of these vary from place to place, both within countries and between countries. This is particularly important as it is these structures which are often responsible for major inequalities in a society.

For example, in the UK, large landowners played a major role in urbanization during the 19th century. Indeed, the relations that built up between landowners and developers came to shape the country's development industry in the late 20th century.[58] In Sweden and The Netherlands, in contrast, urbanization in the mid 20th century was a state activity, with all development land held in public ownership. This not only had a major impact upon the form of urbanization, but also shaped the building companies which evolved to deliver housing policy.[59]

In urban contexts, property rights may develop into very complex bundles. Most cities and towns, in both developed and developing countries, contain a range of land tenure and property rights systems. In the latter, in addition to formal rights (freehold, leasehold, public and private rental), there may also be customary and religious tenure options, and various types of unauthorized/informal tenure.[60] In addition, there may be competition between different 'institutions' within a society over which system of defining rights should prevail.[61] Working out such ownerships can be enormously complex, creating difficulties for urban reconfiguration projects.

Urban property development is also affected by whether land units are held in small or large lots. In many countries, land units are small, sometimes because of pre-urban subdivision to provide plots for owners' children, sometimes as a result of land reform movements. In Japan, urban land has typically been owned in small plots. In older areas, this has led to an urban form of single buildings, often several storeys high and closely packed together along narrow streets, as each owner has maximized the value of their plot. In newer areas, development has sprawled out across rural areas on individual small farm plots. A similar sprawling can be found in the urban agglomerations of northern Italy and is appearing around many expanding urban agglomerations in China. In contrast (and as noted above), until recently, all undeveloped land around urban areas allocated for future development in The Netherlands and Sweden was held in public ownership. Municipalities then provided large serviced sites to developers, who then built blocks of dwellings to plan specifications. One outcome of

[margin note] A major issue in urban development is the way in which the costs and benefits of the value created by development are distributed

[margin note] In countries where informal institutions and corrupted formal systems are actively present in urban development processes, any kind of formal redress for injustices is not easy to achieve

this process was the formation of what subsequently became quite large housing associations (managing rental properties) and major housing development companies.[62]

Increasingly, in developed countries, a large-scale development industry has emerged, including builders of individual houses, large construction companies, land developers, real estate agencies, financial investors and mortgage lenders. Some of these companies have gone on to become major global players, developing residential, commercial and leisure projects all over the world. In such situations, the fortunes of the industry may have a major impact upon national economies, as has become all too clear in the global financial crisis that started in 2008. This investment orientation may also be found in informal housing markets, where development institutions on a considerable scale may emerge. The challenge for planning systems is then to extract public realm benefits from the activities of very powerful players, both economically and politically. In this regard, the 2004 London Spatial Development Plan established a policy that all residential developments over a certain size should ensure that 50 per cent of the dwellings provided were 'affordable'.[63] It has also been argued that planning systems should play a role in 'smoothing' market cycles by stabilizing expectations, creating an adequate flow of sites for development, and perhaps even acting 'counter-cyclically' to the primary economy.[64]

An important dimension of understanding the context for any kind of urban planning is, then, a grasp of locally specific land and property development dynamics. This is sometimes referred to as the need to understand land and housing markets, and the markets for other forms of property development, such as offices, retail projects, industrial parks and tourist enclave developments. However, it is only recently that attention has been given to the dynamics of local urban development markets, to the existence of multiple layers of property market in any locality, and to the relation between marketized and non-marketized property (i.e. property in public ownership and property that has no value). Many now argue that the economic discussion of land and housing markets needs to give more attention to the institutional dimensions through which market players and market practices are constructed.[65]

In many rapidly urbanizing contexts in developing countries, poorer people struggle to find any place to 'dwell'. Their orientation is towards 'use' value. However, in such situations, some places are much better situated than others in relation to opportunities to make a living or to services. Demand for such locations may be huge, but supply very limited. This may indicate that planning strategies should seek to expand not only the provision of housing but the provision of well-located places within the urbanizing area, and of the infrastructure required to move between them. It also means that those interested in making money out of the urban development process (landowners, property developers and investors) will seek to find and exploit the development potential of such sites. This can lead to serious displacement effects.[66]

In such contexts, too, individual owners as well as major companies may come to think of their property as an investment. They may store their savings in acquiring more dwellings, which they rent out. Or they may modify existing dwellings to create rental space. Any planning policy that proposes a lowering of value in some parts of a city to achieve changes in spatial arrangements of some kind is then likely to be fiercely resisted. In areas where upgrading projects are pursued (to improve the living conditions of residents), poorer residents often find it worthwhile to sell their dwelling in order to realize immediate returns, to pay off debts or just to release more fluid capital, and move somewhere less well located and provided for. This is one reason why such upgrading often leads to the 'gentrification' of low-income neighbourhoods.

These experiences all raise challenges for urban planning and for the designers of planning systems to find ways to 'manage' land and property markets and development processes generally; to reduce exploitative effects; to distribute 'rights to the city' more equitably; to provide more and better located neighbourhoods; and to negotiate for public realm benefits. The way in which urban planning is approached may thus come to have a significant 'market-shaping' role.[67]

PLANNING SYSTEMS, AGENCIES AND REGULATION

As mentioned above, planning systems and their specific agencies and organizations belong to the narrower meaning of institutions. What have become known as 'planning systems' refer to a collection of agencies, procedures, instruments and protocols that are often sanctioned by the formal state, backed by formal law, and linked especially to rights to develop and use housing, land and property. Hence, there is no one 'model' of the agency structure of a planning system that applies to all contexts. Yet, as noted above,[68] there are a number of critical issues that can make or break an effective planning system. The following sub-sections elaborate upon these issues.[69]

Planning regulation

Urban planning involves both proactive interventions in the way in which urban areas are developed, and regulatory interventions which aim to shape how others undertake their own activities. Although often portrayed as negative restriction, regulatory interventions may have both protective and developmental intent. *Protective* regulation is justified on the basis of safeguarding assets, social opportunities and environmental resources that would otherwise be squeezed out in the rush to develop. The justification for regulation with a *developmental* intent is to promote better standards of building and area design, enhancing quality of life and public realm, and introducing some stabilization in land and property development activity, particularly where market systems dominate.

Notwithstanding the diversity of planning regulation, a key issue for the design of planning systems centres on

Planning systems should play a role in 'smoothing' market cycles ... and perhaps even acting 'counter-cyclically' to the primary economy

The economic discussion of land and housing markets needs to give more attention to the institutional dimensions through which market players and market practices are constructed where regulatory 'power' is situated in a wider governance context and how it is practised. It is often assumed that such power resides in formal government decisions and the legal support of judicial systems. But another source of regulatory power is social acceptance. In some countries, enforcement action against those who flout planning regulations is sometimes initiated as a result of the protests of neighbours, who ask their local planning authority to take up a case. In such circumstances, a plan and its regulatory provisions become 'owned' by a community. But regulations change the balance of private, collective and public rights in development. They alter rights to develop land and property in particular ways. This may have major consequences on land and property values and on who can get access to land and property. In effect, such regulations may come to structure land and property development 'markets' and development processes. Such effects on land and property rights are therefore intensely political.

The location of planning agencies and formal responsibilities

Planning systems operate at various spatial levels ranging from national to neighbourhood levels. The 'agencies' of planning systems are commonly thought of as located in formal government authorities. There is, however, significant variation in which level of government is given formal responsibility for which activity. There is also variation in the institutional location of the 'checks and balances' on planning agencies. For example, in the highly centralized systems of China, the UK, Japan and some transitional countries, national government has strong planning powers and can rule over the final approval of local plans. Unlike Europe and Japan, Canada and the US lack a national body of legislation regulating local and urban planning. Instead, such responsibilities rest with states and provinces with a high level of autonomy assigned to municipalities. However, even here, national (or federal) governments may play a key role through controlling substantial budgets for urban development purposes. The experience of a successful urban regeneration project in Paris provides a good example (see Box 8.6).

The distribution of formal responsibilities within planning systems has an important structuring effect on planning practices. For example, formal systems specify in law who has the power to use the different planning tools, to change them and to oversee how they are used by others.[70] While there are significant variations between different countries, the patterns of responsibilities often involve more than one level of government and spread to other public and private agencies. At one end – in countries such as Australia, Canada and the US – the national level merely provides enabling legislation or adjudication, allowing municipal- or regional-level governments to develop their approaches. At the other end – in countries such as Cambodia, China, Japan and the UK – national governments keep tight control over the planning system and its practices. Similarly, in Anglophone sub-Saharan countries, the institutional and regulatory framework for urban planning rests, in most cases, at the national government level, or in countries with

a federal government structure, concurrently at the federal and state government levels. Local governments are expected to operationalize the policies that are mainly formulated at the upper levels. While many countries in Eastern and South-Eastern Asia (such as Malaysia and the Philippines) have adopted decentralization, others have remained highly centralized (such as Cambodia, China and Mongolia).[71] Most European planning systems seem to have achieved a balance somewhere between the two extremes.[72] These divisions of responsibilities matter because they serve to generate the formal arenas where planning strategies are legitimized, decisions about the use of regulations and the allocation of resources for public investment and responsibilities are confirmed, and conflicts are adjudicated upon.[73]

A major criticism of top-down systems of planning is that national government planners often have no access to place-specific knowledge and, hence, ignore specific local conditions and assets. Plans may reflect a static universal template that fails to adjust to changing local conditions. It is reported that physical urban growth in Chengdu, China, has taken place in the opposite direction to that foreseen and planned for in its master plan.[74] While Viet Nam has embraced the decentralization of plan preparation to the provincial and city levels, in practice plans are drafted by national government planning institutes. Similarly, in Belarus, regional and municipal plans may be prepared by a national body rather than by local authorities, resembling a rigid style of planning.[75]

In cases where the local level of government has considerable autonomy, a municipality and its planning office take a leading role. The energetic transformation of Barcelona, Spain, is such a case, as is the well-known case of the introduction of 'participatory budgeting' in Porto Alegre, Brazil.[76] In many developing countries, a municipal planning office will rely on the advice of a higher tier of government. Alternatively, it may draw on consultancy advice or work through a 'planning commission'.[77] Where municipalities aim to coordinate their activities in a form of 'integrated area development', then the planning department of a municipality may become part of the central municipal executive, as in Durban, South Africa.[78]

Aside from formal statutory planning agendas, a widespread global trend has been the formation of special 'partnership' agencies focused on particular development tasks.[79] These may take very many different forms, and vary significantly in their autonomy and transparency. They also tend to raise questions as to their formal legitimacy. In some cases, informal agencies created through neighbourhood or other civil society initiative may be acknowledged as a *de facto* 'planning agency' (see Box 4.3). Agencies may also be created through initiatives funded by external aid programmes.[80] These may or may not find a future once aid has been withdrawn, depending upon how relations with other parts of the governance 'landscape' develop.

Decentralization and local capacity

Despite variations, local responsibility is a feature of most urban planning systems. It is at the local level that the inter-

Planning systems operate at various spatial levels ranging from national to neighbourhood levels

Formal systems specify in law who has the power to use the different planning tools, to change them and to oversee how they are used by others relationship of different factors and initiatives becomes most visible as these affect urban environments. The local level is also significant in the implementation of planning policies. However, the framework for local planning policies and practices is often shaped by wider policy priorities that are set at international, national and regional levels. The relationships between these levels and the extent of national control over local urban planning vary considerably across the world.

In many parts of the world, emphasis has been put on decentralization of power and responsibilities to the local level. Empowering local government has been considered a basis for democratization, which, along with accountability and markets, made up the three 'development themes' of the 1990s across developing countries. The desire for local empowerment was partly driven by an emerging consensus that local government is best placed to seek urban solutions and urban participation.[81]

A study undertaken in the early 1990s showed that, of a sample of 25 developing and transitional countries with populations of more than 5 million, most claimed to be undertaking decentralization efforts.[82] In Africa, in countries such as Botswana, Ethiopia, Kenya, Tanzania and Uganda, legislation during the 1990s enacted devolution of functions, power and services.[83] In Nigeria, all urban planning responsibilities were devolved to the local government level in the late 1980s. In Asia, the Philippines 1991 Local Government Code is considered as one of the most revolutionary government reform laws, transferring power to local government and providing for more active participation of people at the local level.[84] Indonesia launched its 'big bang' decentralization policy in 2001, effectively devolving almost all government functions to local governments.[85] Lebanon has recently experienced a review of its municipalities to examine the extent to which they have been capable of efficient service delivery and post-war reconstruction.[86]

In Latin America, the debt crisis and structural adjustments coincided to produce a new relationship between state, local government, civil society and markets. Less exclusive, more grassroots-oriented groups, based on neighbourhood mobilization, women's movements and environmental lobbies emerged.[87] Europe, too, saw a new regional movement in the 1990s, with devolution of power to regional governments taking place in countries such as France, Italy, Spain and the UK, albeit with different degrees of autonomy.

This devolution has highlighted the issue of the capacity of local administrations to meet the challenges they face. The motivation for, and the pattern of, decentralization initiatives differ considerably in different countries, leading to various degrees of local empowerment. For example, in Ghana, local political authorities were mostly created as a concession to demands for decentralization; but the elected local councils were not given the power to appoint the municipal executives and heads of department.[88] In Brazil, however, decentralization was part of a general process of more democratic government and constitutional reform, and municipalities became responsible for providing local services, land-use planning and control.[89]

Box 4.3 Civil society planning initiatives in Kobe, Japan

In Japan, local government and urban planning capacity have been underdeveloped until very recently. Civil society struggles over Kobe's neglected inner-city neighbourhoods in the 1960s – triggered by serious environmental deterioration – were maintained over two decades, and led to innovative practices in local area management in which citizens took the initiative in developing local area guidelines for managing change. Such initiatives have come to be known in Japan as *machizukuri*, or 'community development', activities. In this way, a kind of bottom-up design of planning institutions has emerged. In Kobe, such initiatives produced informal master plans, which later became formalized as new national legislation provided the powers to make use of them.

These experiences influenced emerging local government practices from the 1980s onwards, both in Kobe itself and in Japan more widely. The Kobe experience helped to shape new planning legislation, and the city became one of the earliest to make use of these new powers. These initiatives became a valuable resource in the aftermath of the 1995 earthquake. By 2007, Kobe was one of 17 cities in Japan designated to have a higher degree of municipal autonomy in policy areas, including social welfare, public health and urban planning.

Source: Healey, 2008

However, decentralization of authority has often taken place without any accompanying strengthening of the resources available to local governments. Decentralization by itself is not sufficient for effective urban planning.[90] It is paramount that local responsibilities go hand in hand with adequate resources in terms of finance and human capital. For example, in many sub-Saharan countries, local governments are receiving fewer resources at a time when urbanization rates are increasing, unemployment is rising and informal settlements spreading.[91]

Policy integration and institutional coordination

Institutional structures and mechanisms for decision-making, cooperation and power partitioning can significantly influence the successful implementation of urban planning tasks. Given the complexity of contemporary urban systems, the capacity for effective urban planning depends upon coordination of interdependent actors within and beyond the formal structure of government.[92] The fragmentation of governance institutions has already been underlined. Today, formal government functions relevant to urban development are typically spread across the tiers of government or departments within local government and between local and national governments. They may even involve relations across regional and national borders. Creating horizontal and vertical coordination between various levels of government, as well as between government and NGOs, and achieving integration between disparate responsibilities and different policies have become a key challenge for effective governance. What this involves is illustrated in the *European Spatial Development Framework*, which considers such coordination as a prerequisite for effective urban planning and development (see Figure 4.2).[93]

Vertical coordination refers to coordination of policies and programmes between different tiers of governments, ranging from the supra-national level to national and sub-national levels. Such coordination is particularly pertinent in

Decentralization of authority has often taken place without any accompanying strengthening of the resources available to local governments

Figure 4.2

**Ways of coordination
for spatial development**

Source: adapted from CEC,
1999, p36, Figure 7

The need for ...
coordination under-
pinned a raft of
partnership initia-
tives during the
1980s and 1990s

the context of emerging devolution and decentralization of power and responsibilities. It encourages a form of multi-level governance. This is defined as the existence of overlapping competencies among multiple levels of governments and the interaction of political actors across these levels. In many countries, multilevel governance includes public, private and civil-society actors. The private sector is often involved as a result of privatization policies, particularly with respect to infrastructure and services, such as water supply, waste management, energy and transport. NGOs may be involved through an implicit transfer of responsibilities from the state. Civil society organizations may be involved as representatives of the people, and also because of their knowledge of local problems.[94]

Horizontal coordination involves two aspects. One concerns policy integration across different policy sectors at any given spatial level. The other is about institutional coordination, particularly between constituent municipalities of a given city-region. The organization of policy into separate functions (such as health, education, transport, economic development, etc.) has a useful logic but also presents a major obstacle for effective urban governance. In Eastern and South-Eastern Asian countries, for example, planning, budgeting and economic development tend to fall under the remit of separate government ministries. In Indonesia, spatial planning occurs independently of budgetary programmes and economic development plans. This greatly reduces the effectiveness of urban planning and often leads to implementation problems. In Viet Nam, the planning process is highly fragmented, with three plans (namely, the spatial, the socio-economic and the development plans) that each fall under a different ministry.[95] Furthermore, there is little communication or teamwork between these ministries during the planning process. As a result, 'paper plans' are formulated that are never implemented.[96]

Various initiatives have been put in place in different countries to achieve better policy coordination at the urban level. Many countries have sought to promote agencies with political and executive powers at the level of metropolitan

regions in order to meet the challenges presented by growing megacities. But these have often encountered resistance.[97] Experiences from Brazil suggest that, with time, it may be possible to overcome such resistances.[98]

The second aspect of horizontal coordination is about cooperation and coordination between different municipalities on strategic issues that cut across administrative boundaries (see Figure 4.2). Within these institutionalized forms of cooperation, voluntary participation of municipalities is seen as an added value. The aim is to produce and implement coordinated strategies that cut across the administrative boundaries to overcome potential conflicting approaches from each municipality and to capture any synergies from collaborative working.[99] In some cases such collaboration even cuts across national boundaries. For example, following the construction of Øresund Bridge, Malmö and Copenhagen work together on strategic planning to address issues that do not respect national borders. In countries such as Latvia and Estonia, legal mandates have been put in place for horizontal coordination between neighbouring regions. This means that all urban development plans must be in concordance with those of their neighbours.[100]

Indeed, the need for (or the rhetoric of) coordination underpinned a raft of partnership initiatives during the 1980s and 1990s. Amongst the multiple benefits of such partnerships, building consensus and capacity and creating synergy are frequently mentioned.[101] In some cases, national governments and supra-national bodies have attempted to actively steer processes of coordination and create the conditions for positive-sum partnerships. At the local level, municipalities have an important role to play in promoting new forms of governance and enhancing local institutional capacities for urban planning. This is because they are situated at the crossing point between the traditional vertical axis of power and public administration and the horizontal axis of partnership between government, private sector and civil society that is being promoted worldwide.

However, there are still difficulties in achieving such coordination and consequent integration of urban development initiatives. One is the mismatch between administrative and functional boundaries. There have been some attempts to create administrative areas around *city-regions* and *metropolitan areas*. A famous instance from the US is Portland's metropolitan region.[102] Often, it is transport and water management issues that encourage such a perspective, although concerns about urban sprawl may be another motivation.[103] However, given that such functional boundaries are multifaceted and dynamic, formal restructuring of municipalities may not be the right course of action.[104] Instead, a more flexible and voluntary cooperation among the constituent municipalities of the city-region may be more productive. This, however, has to be encouraged and incentivized by national government. Such a practice has emerged in France.[105] The current reform of the UK planning system encourages the development of multi-area agreements among the constituent municipalities of eight major city-regions as a way of addressing cross-boundary strategic planning and policy issues. In South Africa, the Gauteng provincial government is taking advantage, and also mitigating the effects, of 'the fact that a continuous polycentric urban region in the province will soon be equivalent to some of the largest cities in the world'.[106]

Despite the difficulties, instances where urban governance arrangements that promote policy integration and institutional coordination focused on place qualities have emerged. Place and territory become mechanisms around which the spatial consequences of policies and proposals in various policy sectors can be considered. The strategic role of planning in integrating other policy areas as well as linking urban development ideas to urban investment programmes is increasingly recognized by governments and other stakeholders. In the UK, for example, a major reform of the planning system was instituted in 2004, in parallel with wider decentralization initiatives, to promote a more integrated and developmentally focused approach to planning.[107] An example of planning's integrative and coordinative role is the Strategic Plan of Riga (Latvia), which functions as the key umbrella document providing conceptual guidance for other planning and regulatory documents.[108] Elsewhere – for example, in South Africa (see Box 4.4) – integrated development planning has been introduced as a way of overcoming the lack of intergovernmental coordination, with varying degrees of success.

But in many situations, planning offices and the plans that they produce struggle to perform such a role. Government departments often compete for ministerial favour. The urban planning function may be a weak part of local government, and local government itself may be weak and disregarded by those actually engaged in urban development processes. Nevertheless, there is an increasing recognition that the spatial dimension and a focus on place (over which planners claim some expertise) provide a valuable integrating opportunity.

PLAN FORMULATION AND IMPLEMENTATION

The traditional view of the relation between plan and implementation saw it as a linear process of survey and evidence-gathering, policy formulation and, finally, implementation. This presents the relationship between evidence and policy and between policy and action as unproblematic and straightforward. In practice, however, as stressed throughout this chapter, the process is far more complex. Notwithstanding such complexities and the political nature of planning processes, strategies and plans are only useful if they are likely to be implemented, in the sense of having effects on urban development processes in line with intentions. Thus, planning must be about conceiving urban strategies alongside a consideration of the governance capacity to deliver them.

Urban planning has been much criticized for failing to adequately consider implementation issues. There is a considerable legacy from the 20th century of grand plans with little actual realization on the ground. Implementation has often proved particularly problematic when plans were developed out of obligation, statutory or otherwise, or from

---

Box 4.4 Integrated development plans in South Africa

In 2000, a new form of local government transformed the role of local authorities in South Africa, from one with limited service provision and regulatory powers to a broad developmental one. A key element of this was the introduction of integrated development plans that reorient the planning and budgeting functions of local authorities towards addressing local development needs. In addition to balancing basic economic priorities between local needs and strategic opportunities, integrated development plans were also aimed at overcoming historic racial divisions and inequalities, and the deep social rifts and functional dislocation inherited from the apartheid past.

Every municipality must produce five-year strategic plans that promote integration by balancing the three pillars of sustainability – economic, social and environmental – and coordinating actions across sectors and spheres of government. Integrated development plans do this by linking and integrating: equal spheres of government (vertical coordination); sectors (horizontal coordination); and urban and rural areas. The plans must articulate a vision for the development of the municipal area, as well as development objectives, strategies, programmes and projects. They are reviewed annually through a participatory process involving local communities and stakeholders.

Source: www.communityplanning.net/makingplanningwork/mpwcasestudies/mpwCS07.htm

---

an overambitious political project. However, traditional master planning and the rational-comprehensive planning tradition tended to see implementation as synonymous with the *control* of urban systems, often with military precision. If that did not happen, the process of plan formulation was seen as a failure and plans were ridiculed as 'paper tigers'. However, this limited view of planning processes fails to recognize the role of fine-grained adjustments and intangible processes of change over time in implementation. A wider view of planning processes considers implementation as a social learning process for all parties involved. Within this perspective, tools of implementation are not limited to regulatory and fiscal measures, but also include other modes, such as collaborative practices. In such interactive learning processes, the process of formulating and expressing planning policies is seen itself as part of the process of putting policies into effect.[109] Based on this interactive view of the planning process, this section focuses on current and emerging planning tools and resources, policy communities, stakeholders and planning arenas.

Planning tools and resources

In order to undertake the key tasks of urban planning listed above,[110] planning effort needs to be directed at mobilizing and coordinating a range of tools and resources. Table 4.1 summarizes, in a general way, the tools and resources needed to pursue each task. The tools indicated may be consolidated into five types: plans; regulatory measures; resource mobilization; human capital; and consultation and collaborative practices. The first four of these are discussed in this sub-section, while the last is discussed in Chapter 5.

■ Urban plans

Planning is commonly associated with the formulation and implementation of plans for neighbourhood areas, cities, city-regions and regions at national and, indeed, transnational and supra-national levels.[111] The term 'plan' (in

The strategic role of planning in integrating other policy areas ... is increasingly recognized by governments and other stakeholders

Planning must be about conceiving urban strategies alongside a consideration of the governance capacity to deliver them

Task	Tools
Ongoing management of built environment change	Restrictions (i.e. specification of limits, etc.) Requirements (i.e. specification of contributions to the public realm) 'Street-level' management
Development promotion	Direct development by the public sector Acquisition of development land and property by government Encouragement by financial incentives Coordination and mobilization efforts
Strategies, policies and plans	Knowledge and information Specification of key principles and criteria Plans and visions Production of plans with 'statutory' power Coordination activities

Source: derived in part from Lichfield and Darin-Drabkin, 1980

Table 4.1

Planning tasks and tools

The power of a plan has a lot to do with the authority accorded to it in formal law

relation to urban planning work) refers to a statement, diagram, written policies and perspectives, or other document expressing intentions for the future development of an area. The form and contents of urban plans are often shaped by higher-tier plans, either as part of a traditional hierarchical planning system or within a more 'multilevel' form of coordination. Some countries produce national spatial plans and policy statements. Others have regional, sub-regional or sectoral plans and strategies that are expected to frame urban plans. These are almost always merely part of the governance apparatus applicable in a territory, leading to the necessity of coordination both horizontally and vertically.

Plans may come in different forms and may be expected to perform one or more of the following tasks:

- Provide a list of actions to be undertaken (an agenda).
- Provide principles or rules to guide subsequent actions (a policy statement).
- Provide an image of what could come about (a vision).
- Provide a fully worked out development scheme (a design).
- Provide guidance on sets of interrelated decisions about action now, linked to specific contingencies anticipated in the future (a strategy).[112]

Box 4.5 Planning system reform in Lombardy, Italy

During the early 1990s, after major corruption scandals involving payments by developers to political parties, efforts were made across Italy to introduce a new, more policy-focused and technically informed approach to urban planning. Powers to define planning instruments were devolved to regions, and municipalities were strengthened by the introduction of elected mayors. There had been much discussion among the planning community in Italy about how to overcome the rigidity of the main planning tool, the *piano generale regolatore*, which combined both a strategic view of how an area should develop and a specific land-use zoning function.

Working in parallel, the Lombardy region and the Commune of Milan evolved a new suite of planning instruments. These separated the expression of a strategic framework (since 2005 called a *documento di piano*) from the formal specification of development rights and constraints to be specified in a *piano delle regole* (plan of regulations). These were complemented by a *piano dei servizi*. The purpose of this third plan was to indicate infrastructure requirements, both physical and social. These provided the basis for making transparent demands on developers for service contributions. These three documents provided the basis for a new type of overall plan, the *piano di governo del territorio*, which would finally replace the old *piano generale regolatore*.

Source: Healey, 2007, pp110–113; see also Mazza, 2004

The power of a plan has a lot to do with the authority accorded to it in formal law, through national government advice or through customary practices.[113] The importance of plans in guiding individual decisions over plots of land derives directly from this. In planning systems where the right to develop is enshrined in a zoning ordinance (such as parts of the US), the plans that express this carry a lot of weight in deciding what can take place on an individual plot. In more discretionary systems (such as in the UK), a plan is more an information tool, a statement of what the city government wishes to see happen in a place. This may then become an important point of reference for those involved in urban development, shaping their own decisions. As discussed above,[114] planning systems across the world vary in the relation between the granting of development rights and the role of a plan. There is also substantial variation in the extent to which formally approved plans are given attention and enforced.

Early attempts at planning were often very top down, led by a single planner sometimes with a very singular vision of what the future city should look like. In developing countries, this was typified by the importation of ideas from developed countries,[115] often led by an expatriate 'celebrity planner'.[116] During the latter half of the 20th century, urban plan-making became a more complex process – the product of the ideas of professional teams rather than individuals. However, they often took a great deal of time to prepare and were out of date by the time they were finalized. As a consequence, many critics became concerned that the production of such plans had become overly complex both in procedural terms, through consultation processes and the like, and in terms of the data considered necessary to predict future needs and to provide for them. A further problem was that monitoring the performance of plans becomes more important, but more difficult to do in transparent ways. The development of performance indicators has, in recent years, become an important accompaniment to such plans.[117]

Partly as a consequence, there has been a significant shift from large-scale master planning to more action-oriented participatory planning, often focused on specific urban areas or projects – as highlighted in Chapter 3. Such efforts can encompass accommodating growth through the provision of new settlements or urban extensions, or it could involve the regeneration of specific small urban areas. These experiences have led to two developments in urban plan-making. The first is to separate indicative strategies for urban areas from plans that grant specific development rights. This practice is well established in North-West Europe. Box 4.5 provides an interesting case from Italy, where such a separation is being attempted in a country with a tradition of general municipal plans where city-wide strategies and the allocation of development rights were previously merged.

The second development is to focus on making plans to mobilize and encourage action with respect to specific parts of an urban area. Such plans are often prepared through stakeholder partnerships and provide both a 'development framework' for specific actions and a proto-contract for agreements on specific projects. The emerging framework for an emerging 'edge city' at an infrastructure node in Amsterdam, The Netherlands, provides such an example (see Box 4.6). This case underlines the importance of connecting such development frameworks to the wider context and ensuring that attention to the integration of social, environmental and economic issues with such major projects is maintained.[118]

The move away from grandiose master planning reflects a view that narrowing the complexity of the plan can help to focus attention on what is really of most significance to a city at a given time. This often means that hard choices have to be made in the light of available resources. This may mean that a city-wide plan focuses on a few key actions, such as the laying of an infrastructure grid.[119]

■ Regulatory measures

As noted above, planning regulations are vital tools for planning systems.[120] Such regulations fall into a number of different areas. Where property rights are nationalized, they revolve around managing issues, such as where particular forms of development may take place; the particular mix of land uses on a site; and the quality of building expected there (design, energy, efficiency, etc.). Such development regulations are often combined with building regulations. The latter are increasingly important, both in encouraging more sustainable building practices and in recognizing the role of appropriate building technologies in less developed countries. Here, regulations are used in tandem with a development plan in which development locations are determined. But regulation has a flip-side. Without being able to limit development in other parts of the city, plans to develop in specific, wanted places may not be realized. In Cork, Ireland, a city-region plan sought to direct development from the congested east to the less developed west of the region. But without sufficient power to regulate development in the east, this ambition was only partially achieved.[121] Many countries suffer from this situation, especially where urban planning regimes do not extend beyond urban area boundaries established before major bursts of urbanization.

City governments also typically have other important legal powers.[122] One set of powers relates to the *assembly of land* for major development and redevelopment projects. Where land is mostly owned by the private sector, compulsory purchase and land-assembly powers are very common.[123] In India, for example, the Delhi Development Authority owns a significant proportion of the land, which it has acquired through compulsory large-scale land acquisition policies that have been implemented since 1957. However, the 'compulsory purchase' or 'expropriation' of land by state agencies often leads to substantial conflict and injustice.[124] Some countries (e.g. Brazil) lack such instruments altogether.[125]

Another important mechanism, usually linked to the granting of a development permit, allows the negotiation of *developer contributions* to infrastructure and other community development objectives. These are considered in the sub-section below.

> **Box 4.6 'It ain't what you do, it's the way that you do it': Creating new sustainable centralities in the Amsterdam city-region, The Netherlands**
>
> During the 1990s, Amsterdam city planners tried to maintain the city centre as the prime area for business development. However, the commercial property market decided otherwise and – in order to escape the planning framework – began to try to locate in less congested areas in the south of the city (Zuidas). The planners decided to follow the market pressure and diverted their attention here instead. While in many contexts this could have been a recipe for an unsustainable 'edge city' development, Amsterdam drew on its rich history of thinking through the social and ecological consequences of new development to shape the development through a design master plan and regulatory tools. These tools ensured a variety of uses beyond the commercial driver, making the area more self-contained in relation to the mix of floor space. Ground-floor uses were retail or community uses, keeping the area lively at different times of the day and ensuring that residents and workers did not have to travel for certain services. They also connected this new part of the city to the public transport network and provided an extensive network of bicycle lanes to prevent the new area from becoming car dependent.
>
> *Source:* Majoor, 2008

The ability to *appeal* against the above regulatory decisions is also an area with considerable global variation. Where appeals are allowed, the right to appeal may be limited to the developer and not to 'third parties'. In other systems, appeals are allowed only on the grounds of a failure of due process. Some appeals are heard in legal courts. In some planning systems, semi-judicial processes have been established, as in the British public enquiry and the French *enquete publique*.[126] Both processes tend to be slow; but the latter also provide important arenas in which issues are aired publicly, contributing to the long-term social learning processes that can be so important in creating good public policy.[127]

■ Resource mobilization

A critical issue in effective urban planning is to relate strategies, policies and specific proposals to the resources that could achieve them. The range of fiscal measures deployed in planning systems is constantly evolving. For a considerable time governments have used financial inducements and disincentives to direct development to particular parts of a country, region or city. Such incentives are often used alongside the relaxation of planning restrictions in a particular area, as in the example of employment zones in the US, enterprise zones in the UK and special economic zones in Southern Asia.[128] The creation of zones where certain uses are permitted without recourse to the normal regulatory planning regime is often accompanied by incentives for business to consider locating in such a place. While such policies can improve the conditions in the immediate area, they are often criticized for displacing activity from other areas and failing to create additional economic activity. Therefore, there have to be good reasons – for example, high levels of unemployment in an area – to deploy such policies. Otherwise municipalities may compete with each other for scarce inward investment, offering larger and larger incentives. Continual relaxation of regulatory frameworks may also lead to degraded environmental conditions.

Planning regulations are vital tools for planning systems

Building regulations … are increasingly important

'Compulsory purchase' or 'expropriation' of land by state agencies often leads to substantial conflict and injustice

Financial measures can also be deployed to extract community benefits from a development. During the mid 20th century, it was often assumed that formal government (the state) should pay for public infrastructures. Sometimes private developers were required to pay charges for hook-ups to infrastructures (UK and US) or a general 'urbanization' charge (Italy). In large developments, they might be expected to provide buildings for schools, community centres and health facilities. But, in good times (i.e. when urbanization was proceeding apace and property values were rising), the landowner and developer typically captured the increase in land value resulting from well-serviced urbanization. For cash-strapped municipalities dealing with deficiencies in community facilities, physical infrastructures and low-cost housing, this has always seemed unjust.

As a result, in situations where development activity is mostly undertaken by private developers of some kind, negotiation practices have evolved through which agreements are reached about who should pay for what. These are variously called development exactions, developers' contributions, planning gain, betterment and 'value capture'.[129] It is sometimes thought that these are underhand negotiations, leading to the 'buying' of authority to develop. Where patronage politics prevails, this eventuality is quite likely. However, if the negotiation process is transparent and the beneficiaries known, developers will be more accepting of planning authorities' demands, and include this when calculating the price to pay for land they have to purchase. In other words, such negotiation practices have evolved reasonably well where governance policies have some coherence and stability, and are conducted in a transparent way. Clearly, they also require personnel with a grasp of development situations and who are skilled in negotiating for the public realm. However, if such coherence and stability is lacking, and if what developers provide for public realm benefits becomes diverted to some kind of patronage, then the legitimacy of the practice may be called into question.

The potential for 'underhand' dealing and for strong developers to exploit weak municipalities in negotiations over public realm benefits may lead to arguments for the use of an alternative tool in the form of a standard payment related to the size and scale of a development project in some way. This may be taken as a tax, in which case it is likely to flow into national treasuries or general municipal funds. Or it may be taken as an earmarked charge, allocated for specific public realm assets. It is often argued in the UK that the general gains from property development are best collected through the 'capital gains' that are part of the general tax paid by any development project. But most developers acknowledge that claims for contributions to address specific adverse impacts upon a community are justified. In this way, they become 'shaped' by planning expectations.[130]

Thus, given the right governance context, developer contributions are a useful way to address the externalities that arise from particular developments. This can be difficult in conditions of rapid urban growth where the provision of infrastructure and services often lags behind the pace of physical change. Such contributions typically require careful case-by-case negotiation. The transparency and certainty of the parameters of such negotiations can be greatly enhanced if these are stated in authoritative plans. Linking such financial measures to spatial plans can help in ensuring fairness and in responding to the pace of change.[131]

There are thus several measures that can be used to provide resources for urban development activities. What makes the difference to the effectiveness of urban planning strategies is the careful linkage between actions indicated in plans and strategies, the use of regulatory instruments, and the provision of resources to carry a strategy forward. Many plans and strategies become discredited where such linkages are weak.

■ Human capital

Undertaking the coordinative and integrative work that is at the heart of effective urban planning is a complex task, demanding considerable expertise. As highlighted in Chapter 10, lack of adequately trained personnel with necessary knowledge and expertise is reported as a major constraint for effective urban planning in many parts of the world. An extreme example is Cambodia, where the absence of expert knowledge and personnel has culminated in what is effectively the suspension of urban land-use planning after the cessation of international funding during the late 1990s. In many other developing countries, the shortage of skilled staff at the local level and the brain drain are a major obstacle in effective urban planning.[132]

The absence of planning skills, in many developing and transitional countries, has sometimes led to the importation of consultancies and practitioners from developed nations to devise plans and policies. Historically, there was much transfer from developed to developing countries.[133] As emphasized in Chapter 3, such externally prepared master plans often missed the critical issues for a city. Today, international consultancies are much more likely to have local offices and to work with planners in the places they are employed. But they also often work from a limited palette of ideas, and with a narrow understanding of the implementation potential of these ideas, given questions of understanding and institutional capacity in particular places.

Furthermore, cities themselves are keen to emulate the success of other cities, looking to transfer ideas without enough attention as to whether they may work when removed from their particular situation. This is not to say that places should not learn from each other, but that this learning should not seek to copy exactly from another situation in the manner of a recipe.

Policy communities, stakeholders and planning arenas

Throughout this chapter, the importance of relating planning interventions to a good understanding of local conditions has been stressed. Urban areas, even in one region of one country, vary in their geography and economic possibilities. They also vary in the specific configuration of their institutional dynamics, as expressed through the actors, agencies, networks and arenas where urban issues that need policy attention are identified and addressed. In designing a

Given the right governance context, developer contributions are a useful way to address the externalities that arise from particular developments

Lack of adequately trained personnel with necessary knowledge and expertise is ... a major constraint for effective urban planning

planning system and in working in a particular urban context, it is important to give attention to:

- the *networks and policy communities* that form around particular policy activities, development tasks and implementation activities;
- the *stakeholders* whose actions, interests and values are affected by urban development issues; and
- the *arenas* available for interaction between stakeholders and networks.[134]

In many cases, planners find themselves part of a national 'community' of planners, as well as of local communities of municipal or community development workers. In the past, planners have sometimes tended to insulate themselves within their professional communities or within a wider '*policy community*',[135] including stakeholders such as larger developers and energetic pressure groups. Such policy communities can develop their own 'silo' mentalities, making interaction with other groups difficult. Recent trends towards more interactive forms of planning have underlined the importance of a more externally oriented way of interacting with and drawing together the many 'communities' and networks that are involved in creating urban development futures.

If urban planning is to be inclusive, it is paramount that wider groups of *stakeholders*, including those who may not recognize that they will be affected, are identified and engaged in decision-making processes.[136] These include a wide range of people, but may be categorized as follows:

- those whose interests are affected by urban planning processes (i.e. households, businesses, community or neighbourhood associations, and landholding/owning interest groups);
- those who control relevant implementation interests (i.e. politicians, planners, major investors and implementation agencies drawn from a wide variety of governmental, non-governmental and private-sector organizations); and
- those who possess relevant information and expertise needed for dealing with the wide spectrum of issues to be addressed and the variety of instruments to be applied (i.e. NGOs, business organizations, academics and other experts).[137]

Inclusive processes, however, do not necessarily lead to consensus. While the enlarged network of social relations enhances planners' access to knowledge resources, new ideas, and human and social capital, it may also generate tensions and conflicts over power and responsibilities. The outcome of such interactive processes among this wider network may lead in different directions. It may lead certain policy community members to become defensive of their own policy territory and competencies and, hence, to either withdraw from the network or to act against it. Or it may lead to the emergence of new and innovative ideas and solutions to urban problems. Once again, steering the process towards the latter to achieve some degree of agree-

ment among a wider group of stakeholders, rather than a small group of policy elites, has become an important part of the planners' toolkit. With this aspiration in mind, the late 1980s laid the foundations for a new approach across Africa by focusing on the themes of accountability, markets, democratization and decentralization.[138] Several countries in sub-Saharan Africa – including Kenya, Mozambique, South Africa, Tanzania and Uganda – have responded in varying degrees to these pressures by opening up and broadening the urban planning process to an increasingly wide spectrum of stakeholders or popular participation through supportive legislative frameworks.[139] However, such participation is still limited primarily to forms of consultation. In practice, NGOs are incorporated within the formal decision-making processes on planning matters only in very limited cases.[140]

Policy arenas are the institutional sites where members of policy communities come together to develop ideas and actions for urban futures. They act as nodal points for stakeholders and are places where critical decisions are made. Sometimes, they are fixed in time and space and are formally defined by planning rules, or they may be fluid and *ad hoc*. Such arenas may be a local council chamber, the office of a planning authority, a law court, a semi-judicial enquiry process, an informal community development group, or a business association. Such arenas occur at various locations and over time – for example, at different levels of formal government and/or in less formal *ad hoc* arrangements between key stakeholders.

The critical point to recognize about arenas is that they vary in who gets *access* to them, both in terms of presence and voice. Differentiated access can be due to:

- formal codes of engagement as defined by law (e.g. in the UK, the 'examination in public' of plans is only open to those invited to it);
- cultural norms and social codes (traditional hierarchies);
- implicit internal practices (style and language, user-friendliness); or
- power relations.

In the Balkan region, for example, the primary formal planning arena continues to be the formal hearing, which is relatively open; but the input of private parties in plan implementation often subverts formal plans through the bribing of politicians and planning officials.[141] In countries such as the Czech Republic, the establishment of regional development agencies in the early 1990s, which involved public–private partnerships in urban planning and development, is considered to be a welcome departure from the above practices.[142]

Given the differentiated access to planning arenas, there is always potential for struggle over which arena to use for which issue and at what stage in the development of that issue. In Brazil, for example, attempts to establish a Metropolitan Parliament with political authority to integrate the work of municipalities in large cities such as Curitiba were strongly resisted by a number of municipalities who were concerned about losing their power over their own jurisdiction.[143]

> In the past, planners have sometimes tended to insulate themselves within their professional communities or within a wider 'policy community'

> It is paramount that wider groups of stakeholders ... are identified and engaged in decision-making processes

Another important issue to consider is the relationship between different types of arenas and the weight that they carry in the decision-making processes. Far too often, two trends can be observed. First, the more 'open-access' arenas become segmented off from the main nodes for urban policy development. This implies that the discussion in the wider forums has less leverage in the final decisions made. Hence, the voices of citizens, less-organized environmental groups and small businesses do not get heard in the main nodes of policy development. Second, the agenda is set by the public sector and the participants are 'the usual suspects' (i.e. the same group of people appearing in different arenas in slightly different combinations and compositions). Participation of any 'outside' stakeholders is marginal and policy is made, often behind closed doors, by a small, yet powerful, group of government officials and a few large businesses. Such marginalization of informal forums and their late inclusion in the process leads to a sense of democratic deficit and distance between governments and citizens in urban policy processes.

CONCLUDING REMARKS

Throughout this chapter, it has been stressed that the institutional context for urban planning has a significant effect on its forms and outcomes. It has also been underlined that institutional contexts are highly variable to specific times and places. Hence, in 'learning from the experience of others', it is important to appreciate such specificities. Because of this variety, identifying general trends is a difficult challenge and may serve to mask important local specificities in the institutional and regulatory frameworks for urban planning. With these reservations, it is nevertheless possible to identify the following *key trends* that are widely shared in different parts of the world:

- Many countries and regions are attempting to reconfigure their formal government structures, and the urban planning systems that operate within them, to make them more relevant to the dynamics of contemporary circumstances.
- Such initiatives tend to emphasize the decentralization of authority from nation states to cities and regions, less hierarchical ways of working, and greater involvement of actors from outside formal government, supported by more interactive ways of working.
- This is resulting in increasing variety in the form of agencies involved in urban planning, and presents difficult challenges of accountability and legitimacy.
- The legal systems underpinning planning regulation are being modified in many countries to allow greater flexibility and interactions; but at the same time new rigidities are appearing, introduced through national and international initiatives in environmental and human rights law.
- This situation is encouraging two related responses. One is an increase in litigation as a way of resolving planning disputes. The other is a counteracting

movement to avoid litigation through developing negotiation and collaborative practices.
- While much land and property development is still carried out by state agencies, and/or individuals and small operators, the presence of large-scale land and property developers, some working on a global scale, is expanding substantially. These create challenges for national and local planning practices that are seeking to promote greater equity and environmental sensitivity in urban development.
- In large urban complexes, there is an increasing mismatch between administrative boundaries and the functional dynamics of an urban area, which leads to major problems in coordinating development activity and integrating the social, environmental and economic dimensions of development.
- In this context, approaches to the formulation and implementation of plans have moved from assuming that a planning authority could control how development takes place, to recognizing that all parties need to learn from each other about how to shape future development trajectories.
- These trends not only require sufficient skilled people able to undertake the complex work of formulating and implementing plans and projects, but also mean that existing planners may need to shift their skills towards more interactive and collaborative ways of working. This adds to a general shortage of people, especially outside the developed world, with skills in planning work.

Given the general trends above, and recognizing the importance of understanding the institutional specifics of each situation, the following *general policy lessons* should be highlighted:

- Initiatives to improve planning systems need to pay careful attention to the specific institutional dynamics of particular nations, regions and cities. Successful experiences elsewhere cannot easily be transferred, although much can be learned from them.
- It is important to consider how planning agencies are related to formal and *de facto* government structures, particularly the degree of decentralized power and the potential for horizontal and vertical policy coordination.
- Planning systems need to be surrounded by checks and balances on the use of investment and regulatory resources in order to limit the arbitrary use of planning measures by powerful groups. Without building general trust in the probity of planning systems, it is difficult to build up societal support for planning institutions and instruments.
- While planning systems need the support of a legal framework that defines rights and responsibilities with respect to land and property development and contributions to the public realm, it is helpful to resist over-legalization and the rigidities and time-consuming processes that accompany this.

Marginalization of informal forums ... leads to a sense of democratic deficit and distance between governments and citizens in urban policy processes

- Planning measures, where they have material effects, play a significant role in shaping land and property market behaviour. It is helpful to focus explicitly on this role in relation to local conditions.
- Planning systems' regulatory power needs to be combined with investment power, in an integrated and proactive way, in order to release the potential of many different kinds of actors to contribute to the urban development process.

- Where planning systems and practices lack strength, respect and trust, it is helpful to focus initially on actions that bring clear benefits to many and build the ground for greater respect in the future. Such positive experiences help to build local capacity to address more complex issues.

NOTES

1   World Bank, 1997; UNCHS, 2001a.
2   Le Galès, 1998; Cars et al, 2002.
3   Jessop, 2000, p15.
4   Rhodes, 1997, p8.
5   UN-Habitat, 2002a, p14.
6   Batley, 1993; Davoudi and Evans, 2005.
7   See sub-section on 'Policy integration and institutional coordination'.
8   Stoker, 2000, p93.
9   Davoudi, 2005.
10 Dyrberg, 1997; Healey, 2007.
11 Davoudi and Evans, 2005.
12 See sub-section on 'Policy communities, stakeholders and planning arenas'.
13 See Attahi et al, 2008; Irazábal, 2008a.
14 See Chapter 5.
15 Brenner, 2000.
16 See sections on 'Planning institutions and the institutionalization of planning practices', 'Legal systems and the distribution of rights and responsibilities' and 'Land and property ownership and development institutions'.
17 UN-Habitat, 2002a.
18 See section on 'Planning institutions and the institutionalization of planning practices'.
19 See earlier section on 'Planning and governance'.
20 This is a widely used broad grouping to describe the overall composition of a society; see, for example, Urry, 1981.
21 See Attahi et al, 2008; Irazábal, 2008a.
22 See Abbott, 2001; Ozawa, 2004.
23 See Punter, 2003; Sandercock, 2005.
24 See also the case of Freiburg (Germany) in Scheurer and Newman (2008).
25 Gilbert and Healey, 1985; Payne, 1997; UN-Habitat, 2004b.
26 For an example, see Box 4.2.
27 Glenn, 2007, p87.
28 Equity is here referred to as 'equity of treatment', bearing in mind people's diverse life situations and capacities.

29 See Ikejiofor, 2008.
30 de Soto, 2000; Gilbert, 1998. See also UN-Habitat, 2007b, pp140–143.
31 See UN-Habitat, 2007b, pp140–143.
32 Watson, 2003; Geertz, 1983.
33 See Box 4.2.
34 See Chapter 3.
35 See sub-section on 'Policy integration and institutional coordination'.
36 See Salet and Gualini, 2007.
37 See earlier section on 'Planning and governance'.
38 See Albrechts, 2001a; Faludi and Waterhout, 2002.
39 Okpala, 2008.
40 See Irazábal, 2008a; Healey, 2007, Chapter 4.
41 See Irazábal, 2008a; also Petersen, 2008.
42 See Marshall, 2004.
43 Devas, 1993. See also the case of Kenya in Yahya (2002).
44 McAuslan, 1993.
45 Mitchell, 2003; UN Millennium Project, 2005. See also www.hic-net.org.
46 See, for example, the International Covenant on Economic, Social and Cultural Rights, and the General Comments prepared by the United Nations Committee on Economic, Social and Cultural Rights; UN-Habitat and OHCHR, 2002; UN-Habitat, 2002c, 2007b (Chapters 6 and 11), 2008a.
47 Cullingworth and Caves, 2003.
48 See Kironde, 2006; Payne, 2005; Payne and Majale, 2004.
49 See earlier section on 'Planning institutions and the institutionalization of planning practices'.
50 Glenn, 2007.
51 See Newman and Thornley, 1996; Davies et al, 1989.
52 Glenn, 2007. He calls these the Chthonic (or orally based), the Talmudic, Civil Law, Islamic, Common Law, Hindu and Asian.
53 Fernandes and Varley, 1998; Payne, 2005; Kironde, 2006; Glenn, 2007.
54 Sorensen, 2002. See also Chapter 3.

55 See Sorensen, 2002. A similar practice has been reported in Zhuhai, China (see Li, 2008).
56 However, UN-Habitat (2007b, p127) has earlier noted that:
    The power of states to expropriate carries with it several fundamental preconditions. When housing, land or property rights are to be limited, this can only be done: subject to law and due process; subject to the general principles of international law; in the interest of society and not for the benefit of another private party; if it is proportionate, reasonable and subject to a fair balance test between the cost and the aim sought; and subject to the provision of just and satisfactory compensation. Once again, if any of these criteria are not met, those displaced by such expropriation proceedings have a full right to the restitution of their original homes and lands.
    See also UN-Habitat, 2008a.
57 See European experience in this area in Healey et al (1995); Campbell and Henneberry (2005); CEC (1997).
58 Ball, 1983; Healey, 1998.
59 Needham et al, 1993.
60 UN-Habitat, 2004b, 2007b (Chapter 5), 2008a.
61 See the Moshi case in Box 4.2.
62 Needham et al, 1993.
63 Mayor of London, 2004; Bailey, 2009.
64 See Barras, 1987; Harvey, 1985; Webster and Lai, 2003.
65 Mattingly, 1993; Buckley and Kalarickal, 2005.
66 UN-Habitat, 2007a, 2007b.
67 See Healey, 1992.
68 See the section on 'Planning institutions and the institutionalization of planning practices'.
69 Issues surrounding the appropriateness of planning tools and resources are discussed in the section on 'Plan formulation and implementation'.
70 See the earlier section on 'Legal systems and the distribution of rights and responsibilities'.
71 Yuen, 2008.
72 See sub-section on 'Urban governance and government'.

73 Vigar et al, 2000.
74 Yuen, 2008.
75 Hirt and Stanilov, 2008.
76 Abers, 1998; Baiocchi, 2003; Marshall, 2004.
77 The US 'planning commission' is a group of appointed citizens who review and advise local governments (see Hopkins, 2001, p167).
78 See Breetzke, 2008.
79 See earlier sub-section on 'Institutions as specific agencies and organizations'.
80 See the case of Kitale (Kenya) in Majale (2008).
81 It was also driven by regional traditions, tribal wishes for autonomy, demand for self-control and growing self-confidence of local voters (Hall and Pfeiffer, 2000).
82 Dillinger, 1994, p1.
83 UN-Habitat, 2002b.
84 Tapales, 1996; Hall and Pfeiffer, 2000.
85 Yuen, 2008.
86 Nassar, 2008.
87 Irazábal, 2008a.
88 Dillinger, 1994, p9.
89 World Bank, 1998, cited in Hall and Pfeiffer, 2000.
90 See the sub-section on 'Planning tools and resources'.
91 Okpala, 2008.
92 Jessop, 1997, p96. See also earlier section on 'Planning and governance'.
93 CEC, 1999, para 74–76.
94 UNCHS, 2001a.
95 Yuen, 2008.
96 See section on 'Plan formulation and implementation'.
97 See, for example, Salet et al (2003) for the European experience.
98 Irazábal, 2008a.
99 See, for example, the experience of French inter-communal initiatives in Motte (2007).
100 Garau, 2008; Hirt and Stanilov 2008.
101 See Chapter 5.
102 See Abbott, 2001; Ozawa, 2004.
103 See Salet and Gualini (2007) for European experiences; see also Owens (2008).

104 For a critical review of the concept of the city-region, see Davoudi (2008).

105 Motte, 2007.

106 South African Cities Network, 2004, p167.

107 See Office of the Deputy Prime Minister, 2004; RTPI et al, 2007.

108 Hirt and Stanilov, 2008.

109 Good examples of such interactive strategy formation can be found in the Welsh Spatial Plan (see Welsh Assembly Government, 2003; Harris and Thomas, 2009), and in the development of neighbourhood development guidelines in Vancouver (Punter, 2003).

110 See earlier sub-section on 'The institutional design and redesign of urban planning systems'.

111 The *European Spatial Development Perspective* is a good example (CEC, 1999).

112 This is adapted from Hopkins (2001, Chapter 3).

113 See section on 'Planning systems, agencies and regulation'.

114 See Chapter 3 and the earlier section on 'Legal systems and the distribution of rights and responsibilities'.

115 See, for example, Jenkins et al, 2007.

116 See Chapter 3.

117 See Chapter 9.

118 See Moulaert et al, 2000; Salet and Gualini, 2007.

119 Mabogunje, 1990.

120 See section on 'Legal systems and the distribution of rights and responsibilities'.

121 See Haughton et al, forthcoming.

122 See section on 'Legal systems and the distribution of rights and responsibilities'.

123 See Alterman, 1988.

124 See note 56 above.

125 UN-Habitat, 2006b.

126 See CEC, 1997.

127 Owens and Cowell, 2002.

128 Ansari, 2008; Allmendinger and Thomas, 1998.

129 Alterman, 1988; Healey et al, 1995.

130 This emerges very clearly in the development of design regulation in Vancouver (Punter, 2003).

131 See, for example, Breetzke, 2008.

132 Yuen, 2008, p37.

133 Ward, 2002; Jenkins et al, 2007. See also Chapter 3.

134 After Vigar et al, 2000.

135 Marsh and Rhodes, 1992.

136 See Chapter 5.

137 UNCHS, 1995.

138 Hall and Pfeiffer, 2000.

139 Matovu, 2006.

140 See Wekwete, 1997, p540.

141 Hirt and Stanilov, 2008.

142 Hirt and Stanilov, 2008.

143 Irazábal, 2008a.

PLANNING, PARTICIPATION AND POLITICS

One of the most important shifts in planning during the last few decades has been from a view of it as an expert-driven technocratic activity to one that is inclusive of relevant stakeholders and communities (see Chapter 3). This fits with the shift from government to governance and its implications for the role of local/municipal government, which is also affected by moves to strengthen democracy and a concomitant wave of decentralization. However, there are many debates and tensions in the notions of governance and participatory planning. For example, there are debates about how participatory planning can be in the context of deep socio-economic differences and power imbalances.

The focus of this chapter is on participation and politics as it relates to planning. It begins by reviewing forms of citizen participation and then the characteristics of participatory urban planning. Given the centrality of gender to the ideals of citizen participation in urban planning, this is briefly examined next. Subsequently, the extent and nature of participation in urban planning in different parts of the world and political contexts are reviewed. The factors that influence approaches to participation in urban planning and their outcomes, as well as some of the pitfalls and challenges, are identified. Specific examples of innovative participatory urban planning experiences are then presented and their wider applicability reviewed. Finally, lessons from these experiences, as well as challenges, are taken into account in identifying ways to enhance participation in urban planning.

CHARACTERISTICS AND FORMS OF PARTICIPATORY URBAN PLANNING

Participation implies that planning is not a purely technocratic exercise in which policies and decisions are made by professionals in conjunction with authoritarian political power holders or even by elected representatives alone. It incorporates voice, responsiveness and accountability. Voice refers to the expression of citizen preferences and opinions through both the electoral process and other channels. Without responsiveness, consultation and the expression of

views may not influence plan proposals and planning decisions. Policies and plans mean little unless they determine the allocation of resources and decision-making; therefore, ways of ensuring that views are heard and acted upon – accountability – are also essential.

Attempts to develop a more sophisticated conceptual basis for participatory approaches have drawn on theories of democratic politics and urban planning theory to distinguish between *communicative* and *collaborative* approaches. Communicative (or deliberative) planning is based on a belief that better decisions are reached if they emerge out of a process of knowledge-sharing and dialogue between those concerned. Collaborative planning implies a process of debate, deliberation and consensus-building (i.e. joint decision-making). The underlying rationale for these approaches can be traced to democratic theory, which holds that active citizenship has intrinsic value. It suggests that participation provides an education in democratic practice, fosters a sense of belonging, leads to acceptance of collective decisions, encourages bureaucratic responsiveness and accountability, and brings collective knowledge and new ideas to bear on decision-making. Rather than a technocratic exercise carried out by experts, planning is conceived of as an interactive communicative activity. The result is considered to be more appropriate policy and fewer implementation problems.

Participation is an umbrella term for a variety of approaches and it is useful to distinguish between different forms and purposes of participation. A typology is suggested in Table 5.1 to illustrate this. However, even this more detailed typology simplifies the reality, and it should be borne in mind that actors' motivations for permitting or engaging in participation are mixed and different approaches can coexist.

The typology suggests a continuum from 'weak' to 'strong' forms of participation. Citizen control over decision-making is generally regarded as the most transformative and empowering form of participation. It is based on interactive processes of learning and self-mobilization, in which local groups take control over decisions and actions independent of external organizations, while developing links to obtain resources and technical assistance and keeping control over these resources.[1]

Citizen control over decision-making is generally regarded as the most transformative and empowering form of participation

Table 5.1

The form, meaning and purpose of citizen participation

Form	The purpose of participation	What 'participation' means to the implementing agency	What 'participation' means for those involved	Potential approaches
Nominal	Display, manipulation	Legitimization to show that it is doing something; pre-empt opposition	Inclusion, in the hope of gaining access to potential collective or individual benefits	Token representation on decision-making bodies
Consultative	Assembling useful information	Better informed decision-making with no loss of control	Policies and plans that are more appropriate, but with no guarantee that the outcomes of consultations are taken into account	Information collection through systematic data collection, consultative processes, responses to proposals
Instrumental	A means of increasing effectiveness and stretching external resources further	Efficiency to draw on beneficiaries' resources, increase cost effectiveness, and improve the prospects for successful operation and maintenance	Access to facilities and services that are normally provided only to those that can afford to pay	Contributions to costs (money, labour, etc.)
Representative	To give people a say in decision-making through the political system or specific channels	Sustainability; established systems are used for the expression of voice, improving responsiveness and ensuring accountability; provides a means of organizing and aggregating different views	Leverage, direct or indirect influence	Representative electoral political system (national and local government; decision-making and advisory bodies at city or local level)
Transformative	Both a means and an end	Partnership with non-governmental actors; collaborative decision-making and implementation	Joint analysis and development of plans; empowerment to enable people to define objectives, make their own decisions, control resources and take action	Governance arrangements that involve partnerships or 'contracts' between government and citizen groups; devolution of powers, responsibilities and resources

Source: based on Pretty, 1995; White, 1996, pp7–9; Cornwall, 2008, p273

Consultative and instrumental forms of participation are commonly associated with efficiency and effectiveness arguments – planners and project initiators provide for participation in order to improve the information available to them, reduce costs and ensure the achievement of project objectives. Consultation is essential and can improve transparency and responsiveness, resulting in more appropriate policies and plans that take the needs of different actors into account. Likewise, the need to stretch government resources and address affordability issues, as well as to ensure the 'ownership' and maintenance of services provided, may justify instrumental approaches.

However, consultation implies that the main decisions are taken by external agents (including officials, funding agencies and elected representatives), who may or may not take into account all of the views expressed, especially those of socially marginal groups. Moreover, in both developed and developing countries, consultation is widely used to legitimate decisions that have already been made and its outcomes are used selectively or potentially disregarded by those in power.[2] Thus, in addition to its functional value, participation may be used purely as a tokenistic legitimizing device.

Whether government offers substantive or only nominal opportunities for citizen participation, the outcomes are unpredictable. Even strong forms of participation do not necessarily challenge existing distributions of wealth and power and ensure that the interests of the marginalized are taken into account, while weak forms may both improve planning and provide opportunities for more meaningful approaches to be gradually introduced.[3] To ensure that citizens' views are taken into account during policy formulation *and* implementation, ways of ensuring accountability are also needed, including transparent modes

Even strong forms of participation do not necessarily challenge the existing distributions of wealth and power

of decision-making, answerability to both those affected and the electorate at large, and the ability to sanction state institutions if necessary.

Citizen participation in urban planning can take a variety of forms:

- It occurs at different levels, including local, city-wide and supra-city levels.
- It can be initiated by different actors, including government agencies, elected politicians, communities and other actors.
- It occurs at different stages in the planning process, including identification of needs, preparation of plans or formulation of policies, implementation and evaluation.
- It relates to a variety of planning and decision-making processes, including the formulation of a broad vision, policy or plan-making, proposals for particular activities or areas, and periodic resource allocation through budgeting processes.
- It varies depending upon stakeholders' capacities (e.g. time, resources, awareness of rights and opportunities to participate) and identity. This is especially so with regards to gender, as elaborated upon subsequently.

Many of the innovative participatory practices adopted in towns and cities do not relate specifically to the preparation of land-use and spatial plans. Rather, they influence the preparation and implementation of multi-sectoral economic and social development strategies, as well as annual budgeting processes and local projects focusing on improvements in services and housing. Although general development programmes, sectoral policies and municipal budgeting do, of course, have spatial dimensions, they are not always dealt with systematically.

GENDER IN PARTICIPATORY URBAN PLANNING

A key objective of participatory planning is to ensure that all concerned stakeholders, including socially marginalized groups, are able to influence decision-making. In doing so, planners need to consider the differences in stakeholders' capacity to engage in participatory processes. One of the most fundamental shortcomings of planning in this regard has been the unequal manner in which men and women have been incorporated within the planning process both as professionals as well as stakeholders. This has been a major focus of participatory urban planning in recent times.

Since the early beginnings of classical planning traditions in the late 19th century in Western Europe (see Chapter 3), a male-oriented model has been persistent. The dominance of men in the profession during these early times impacted upon the way in which planning was conceptualized and developed. The approach to planning that emerged was homogeneous, tended to favour 'white males' and made patriarchal assumptions about women. Women were seen to be limited to the private realm (i.e. the home), while the public realm was designed for men's use. What resulted was a built environment favouring the male citizen and one that reinforced stereotypical gender roles, including that of women as housewives. This approach became ingrained in planning education, theory and practice, including the development of modern planning in the 20th century. These models were further dispersed worldwide primarily through colonial imposition, but also through voluntary adoption by countries (see Chapter 3). Male-oriented planning models remained largely unchallenged until the second wave of feminism in North America during the 1960s and the resultant women's liberation movement.[4]

Since the 1960s, a growing body of research has highlighted the limitations of a male-oriented planning model and emphasized the importance of women's interactions with the built environment.[5] An increasing number of women entered the planning profession and, in time, their work influenced the development of approaches and tools for enhancing the gender-sensitivity of planning processes and outcomes.[6]

The general critique of blueprint approaches to urban planning during the 1970s gave further credence to those lobbying for the inclusion of women's concerns in planning. Early approaches to planning were critiqued for having failed to improve the lives of disadvantaged social groups and even having adverse impacts upon them. This led to a rethinking of policy-making and planning, and in particular pointed to the need for wider participation at both national and local levels. There were attempts to develop 'bottom-up' approaches to planning as an alternative or complement to 'top-down' planning in order to make decision-making more responsive and effective. The new approach to planning practice was to be 'people centred', less technocratic, more culturally sensitive and more explicitly pro-poor.

By the 1980s local governments and international bodies, unable to ignore the concerns of women, began to consider how to integrate their needs within planning. The United Nations, for example, actively promoted the importance of women in development through major conferences, conventions and campaigns, including the United Nations Decade for Women from 1976 to 1985. The concept of gender mainstreaming was also introduced during this period, arguing for the need to integrate gender within every stage of the policy-making process.

These developments have had far-reaching effects on current thinking on the design of urban environments, transport systems and housing. The need to provide opportunities for both men and women to participate equally in plan-making is also widely accepted. However, there remains a gap between policy and practice in many countries. Procedurally, women in urban areas are often significantly under-represented in decision-making processes.[7] The challenges that men and women face in their day-to-day lives in cities and therefore the priorities that they would like to be addressed through planning are different. This is the case in terms of employment (see Chapter 7), land and housing (see Chapter 7), and infrastructure (see Chapter 8). The employment status and average earnings of men and women vary greatly; women are often disadvantaged with regards to land and housing ownership rights, while physical infrastructure provision often excludes consideration of women's needs and priorities. Thus contemporary urban planning is still critiqued for failing to address such specific needs of women and men. Participatory approaches, especially those that are more transformative, offer much potential to address gender imbalances with regards to both the procedural and substantive aspects of urban planning.

Women in urban areas are often significantly under-represented in decision-making processes

GLOBAL TRENDS IN URBAN PLANNING, PARTICIPATION AND POLITICS

The extent to which bureaucratic and technocratic approaches to planning have been replaced or complemented by participatory approaches varies across the world. In this section, global trends in urban planning and participatory practice are summarized and some of the factors that explain differences between regions and countries identified.

Formal procedures for allowing the public to participate in planning decisions have long existed in developed countries

Developed countries

Formal procedures for allowing the public to participate in planning decisions have long existed in developed countries, as mentioned in Chapter 4. They generally involve rights to object to or appeal against proposals or development decisions, and public hearings prior to plan approval.[8] Civil law systems are generally associated with zoning approaches to planning, in which there is scope for participation in plan preparation; but decisions on applications for development permission that comply with the zoning provisions are purely administrative (e.g. France). In contrast, common law systems (e.g. the UK) are associated with discretionary approaches to development control, in which the plans are guidance documents, which constitute only one of the factors taken into account in decisions. In such a system, there is scope for participation in both plan preparation and development regulation.[9]

Developed countries invariably have representative democratic political systems, although the distribution of planning powers and responsibilities between levels of government varies. The power to make planning decisions typically lies with local elected politicians, subject to rights reserved by central governments to approve plans, decide on major or contentious planning proposals, and provide or withhold funds. Elected representatives have a responsibility to take the views of their constituents into account and to balance conflicting interests. Levels of citizen participation are generally higher at the local level, although sometimes as part of urban renewal programmes or in opposition to proposed construction projects rather than as part of forward planning. For example, in the US, participation has been mandated in urban renewal programmes since the 1960s, although the emphasis has often been on improving communication rather than sharing power.[10]

In addition to the voice and accountability exercised through periodic elections, lobbying and advocacy play an important role. In some countries, such as the UK, this is generally relatively low key and small scale. In others, such as the US, it is large scale and highly organized, while in some countries a few highly organized formal interests are very close to government (e.g. big business and trade unions).

In recent years, a great variety of tools and techniques for sharing information and consulting with citizens have been widely applied at both city and local levels. Despite this, it is not always easy to secure wide citizen participation in urban planning, with the result that specific organized interests exert more influence to advance their own interests. Some social groups are under-represented (women, youth, ethnic minorities and mobile groups), and this under-representation has been addressed in various ways, such as quotas and proportional representation. Some governments also provide technical and financial support for ordinary communities and citizens to participate in public review processes (e.g. Canada, some states in the US and parts of Australia). Elsewhere, professional planning organizations provide such support on a largely voluntary basis (e.g. the Planning Aid service in the UK).

Research shows that both elected politicians and planners in developed countries may have reservations about participatory approaches to planning. The former may feel threatened, both because of their conception of their own role as elected representatives with delegated power and because of the need to balance various interests and priorities. The latter sometimes feel that participation takes too long, slows up decision-making and adds to the cost of planning. Therefore, more extensive and radical participation in decision-making remains exceptional, and the agenda rarely goes beyond the 'organization of consensus'.[11] In practice, of course, consensus cannot always be reached and some groups are more influential than others.

In transitional countries of Europe the nature of citizen participation in urban planning has evolved differently. On paper, some participation was a legal requirement in most communist countries (especially Yugoslavia[12]). However, in reality, state and regional economic plans were prepared by political elites who supposedly represented the interests of all citizens. Political goals were then turned into urban spatial projects by built environment professionals. Participation was therefore merely a formality, taking the form of pseudo-open public hearings, which attracted mostly technocratic elites, and ceremonial exhibitions during which the public was allowed to see master plans.

Since 1989, in contrast, most transitional states have introduced new legislation that includes provision for participation. Participatory mandates stem from new constitutional provisions, as well as spatial planning laws that resemble those in many Western European countries. Broad participation often occurs in environmental planning (e.g. in hearings following environmental impact assessments of particular projects). In the Czech Republic, for example, active environmental non-profit organizations have promoted participation in environmental planning hearings.[13] Nevertheless, even when attempts are made to increase the scope for participation, it is frequently tokenistic.[14] Furthermore, planners (most of whom are architects and engineers) continue to advance technical solutions to urban problems. As such, master planning, with its pursuit of an idealized urban future at a city-wide scale, persists and, unlike local plan proposals and specific construction projects, generates little citizen interest.

An additional obstacle is the underdevelopment of civil society or its dominance by a few large, often Western-funded, non-governmental organizations (NGOs). Where governments permit civil society participation, they often prefer to deal with a few large non-profit organizations that are easier to interact with and less likely to be perceived as threatening.[15] In those countries that have opted for a market economy but maintained strong centralized government, notably Russia, significant obstacles to participation remain. Even where the old urban regimes have been replaced by ostensibly democratic ones, many continue to be dominated by members of the communist elite[16] and participation occurs mainly through government-approved non-profit organizations.[17] Where a settlement has not yet been reached with respect to the form of democracy and governance, including Ukraine, Albania and other countries marked by political and ethnic conflicts, the political regimes governing cities operate in an unstable context marked by weak institutions and scarce resources. There is little effective governance and urban management, let alone scope for participation.

Sub-Saharan Africa

The colonial legal inheritance has greatly influenced the nature of, and scope for, participation in urban planning in most of sub-Saharan Africa. A comprehensive master planning approach was generally enshrined in the inherited colonial legislations, which required governments to seek the opinions of interested parties through public surveys and hearings on draft plans, while maintaining the ultimate

---

Developed countries invariably have representative democratic political systems

Since 1989 ... most transitional states have introduced new legislation that includes provision for participants

decision-making authority. In the post-independence period, the expectation that governments would take responsibility for development was associated with a technocratic approach to national development planning that inhibited the direct involvement of citizens or other non-governmental stakeholders in planning and decision-making. Radical revisions to the inherited legislative base for this technocratic blueprint approach to planning have been rare, despite its failure to provide effective guidance for rapid urban growth.[18] The post-independence period has also been marred by unstable government alternating between authoritarian and democratic rule (with periodic or long-standing civil conflict in many countries), further restricting the consolidation of participatory planning processes.

During the 1970s in many cities, the need to solve urgent problems led to the adoption of an action-oriented approach linked to individual sectors or projects (e.g. upgrading of informal settlements or the provision of serviced plot areas for low-income housing). Sometimes, those affected were consulted, although their views did not necessarily have much influence on the proposals. Often, low-income households were expected to participate by contributing their labour to infrastructure installation and improvement, as well as construction of their own houses.[19]

Since the 1980s, the inability of government agencies to implement urban development plans and the irrelevance of these to the majority of residents living in informal settlements led to attempts to revise planning legislation and adopt more realistic, flexible and participatory approaches to urban planning. These have often been facilitated by external agencies, including through the Sustainable Cities Programme,[20] the Urban Management Programme,[21] the Municipal Development Partnership[22] and the CDS approach.[23] Furthermore, state withdrawal from basic service provision led some communities to more proactively seek to influence key urban decisions. For example, in West African countries such as Mali, Senegal and Burkina Faso, structural adjustment in the 1980s resulted in the formation of various types of community-based organizations (CBOs) that fought for increased participation in urban management.[24]

The scope for democratic participation has further increased since democratization and decentralization during the 1990s. In Francophone West Africa, public hearings serve as the main vehicle for participation in plan preparation. Hearings last at least two months, are widely publicized and record all observations on, and objections to, draft master or subdivision plans. Yet, in practice, organized interests rather than individuals participate in this way, unless their individual properties are affected, and all major decisions are taken by the government.[25]

Upgrading and rehabilitation projects continue to provide more meaningful opportunities for participation than urban plan preparation, although often those funded by international agencies remain pilot projects whose approaches are not replicated on a large scale (e.g. Yentala in Niger; Nylon in Cameroon; Sokoura in Aboisso, Côte d'Ivoire). An example of a recent large-scale project is Dalifort in Dakar, where three structures for participation

were established: an advisory committee comprised of area representatives, important people and religious leaders; sectoral technical committees (women, health, environment, etc.); and a local business initiative involving all plot owners. Local planning offices enabled staff to work with residents to identify problems and develop appropriate solutions, using participatory diagnosis and planning tools.[26]

On the whole, in much of sub-Saharan Africa, although some countries such as Mali, Burkina Faso and Guinea have prepared local participatory planning guides,[27] serious efforts to involve citizens in decision-making are uncommon and participation often takes the form of consultation, which may or may not result in influence. Moreover, the institutional base for effective urban management and planning is weak and often in a state of flux. Local governments mostly have a limited revenue base, inadequate technical and administrative skills, and insufficient autonomy, despite renewed attempts to decentralize in the 1990s. There are especially wide gaps in capacity and resources for effective urban management between large metropolitan areas and smaller municipalities. Even where local government has a strong mandate and is relatively well resourced, as in South Africa, lack of appropriate skills in local government and weak civil society organizations hinders effective participation.[28] In practice, therefore, decisions tend to be made by technocrats, with some input from elected representatives.

There has been considerable discussion about whether, given the weakness and limited legitimacy of local governments and methods of decision-making, a role could be played by traditional authority structures. In some African cities, customary authorities (family, lineage, chief) continue to supply affordable land for residential use through processes of informal subdivision, both for allocation to eligible members of indigenous communities and for sale. In addition, especially in countries where the colonial authorities adopted a system of indirect rule, customary authorities retain a role in the administration and management of local areas. Often, their decision-making style is deliberative and consensual. They may, therefore, demonstrate methods for participation, consultation and decision-making that could be emulated and play a role in certain governance tasks (e.g. land administration and dispute resolution). However, their potential contribution to participatory planning should not be overestimated. In many cities, direct rule eliminated traditional authority structures or substituted government appointees for traditional leaders (as in Kenya). Moreover, traditional authority structures are hierarchical and patriarchal, often disadvantaging women and young people. Authority and participation in decision-making only apply to the relevant indigenous group, which is increasingly irrelevant as in-migrants swell city populations and increase their diversity.

Asia

Democratic local government in the urban areas of Southern Asia has shallow roots. Before recent reforms, it either did not exist (e.g. in Pakistan during periods of military rule) or

In much of sub-Saharan Africa ... serious efforts to involve citizens in decision-making are uncommon

Democratic local government in the urban areas of Southern Asia has shallow roots

Box 5.1 People's campaign for decentralized planning, Kerala, India

The State of Kerala launched a participatory planning process in 1996 that aims to strengthen democratic decentralization by identifying local needs and establishing local development options and priorities through local consultation and participation. The basic nested structure of participation in the annual planning and budgeting cycle of Kerala's decentralized planning has four stages:

1   mobilization of citizens for identification of felt needs;
2   systematic appraisal of felt needs by development seminars comprised of local representatives, local political representatives, officials and experts;
3   conversion of recommendations of the development seminars into projects by task forces; and
4   prioritization of the projects by elected local self-government institutions and incorporation within a local plan for implementation.

The local participatory process is supposed to be linked into longer-term district and state planning processes.

Assessments of the campaign experience range from the adulatory to the critical. Evaluations that consider urban and rural areas separately have been limited. However, a thorough state-wide evaluation of the first stage of the campaign (1996–2001) in 2002 found that:

•   There has been substantial fiscal devolution: 35 to 40 per cent of the state development budget is allocated to local governments, mostly grants in aid that are directly under the control of the municipalities.
•   Local governments have power to plan, fund and implement a full range of development policies and projects, subject to compliance with state policy and advice. So far, about 1200 plans and more than 100,000 projects have been prepared.
•   The participatory process, which is repeated annually in all local government areas, has been institutionalized. There are high levels of socially inclusive participation, although levels have declined over the years.
•   The process was perceived by all types of actors involved (including opposition party politicians) to have had positive developmental impacts, the primary beneficiaries of which were the poor.
•   The campaign is judged to have reduced corruption and increased transparency and accountability of both representatives and officials.
•   The campaign has resulted in increased citizen voice. Measures to encourage the establishment of women's neighbourhood groups and women's participation in the planning process have resulted in a dramatic increase in women's representation and voice. While traditionally, strong organizations (trade unions and parties) have continued to be active, disadvantaged groups have been able to participate.
•   The positive achievements 'have significantly increased the legitimacy of democratic local government and widened the political space for local politicians and civil society. Citizens now expect more of local government, and such expectations are what sustain democratic practice.'

A number of factors were important for the success of the campaign from 1996 to 2001, and the institutionalization that has subsequently occurred. These must be taken into account in any assessment of whether the Kerala experience is transferable. They include political commitment, clear procedures and guidance by the state government, capacity-building through a massive training programme at the local and district level, and the ability to build on the experience and draw on the volunteers of civil society organizations.

Source: Chettiparamb, 2007; Heller et al, 2007

Although there is a trend towards decentralization, capacity is often restricted, particularly at the local level

was frequently suspended by central government, with officials being nominated to run municipalities. Conceptions of urban planning in countries of the region and the legislative basis for it have changed little, despite the patchy trend towards more democratic local government since the 1990s. Despite the shortcomings of conventional master planning, there is limited evidence of alternatives being seriously entertained among planners.[29] There is not much provision for participation in plan preparation, by elected representatives, private-sector interests or urban residents, in general. Government is often highly fragmented. Although there is a trend towards greater decentralization, capacity is often restricted, particularly at the local level.

Nonetheless, some countries in the region have made significant progress with regards to participatory urban planning. In India, for example, the federal and state governments have adopted a variety of measures to increase citizen participation and the responsiveness and accountability of government at all levels. Since a constitutional amendment in 1992, municipalities have become the principal representa-

tive platforms for the urban population, with the electoral representation of women and weaker sections of society assured. The Ministry of Urban Affairs has produced guidelines for preparing citizens' charters for municipal services, and charters have been prepared by some cities, such as Delhi and Mumbai. Some widely known attempts to develop a participatory approach to planning have also emerged in India, including the preparation of city development plans under the Jawaharlal Nehru National Urban Renewal Mission and the Kerala People's Campaign for Decentralized Planning (see Box 5.1). However, in practice, the autonomy of local government in India is limited by continued state government control over the decentralization of decision-making and limited resources, as well as external appointment of the chief executive.[30] Progress with democratic decentralization has been even more limited in other countries, including Pakistan,[31] Bangladesh and Nepal.

The ability of both local communities and disadvantaged groups to hold government to account depends upon their ability to organize. Advocacy and lobbying, as well as the use of public interest litigation, are, however, often dominated by elite interests (e.g. in Delhi).[32] Most commonly, residents in low-income areas have to access local power holders through clientelist links with local parties, politicians and bureaucrats, often mediated through informal community leaders or brokers. Studies show that political access in India is less amongst people living in the poorest slums than amongst those who are better established, but that even the poorest communities can gain access to sources of authority if they are well organized.[33] Furthermore, in some cities strongly organized civil society, including high-profile NGOs, work on behalf of poor residents. They have developed tools such as citizen report cards to assess the performance of government agencies and to hold them to account. In addition, they support the organization and networking of CBOs.

In East and South-East Asia, many countries, particularly the transitional economies, have a weak democratic tradition, with limited civil liberties and political rights. Although this is changing in most countries, the pace of change varies greatly. Formal strategic and spatial planning for urban development and growth in this region is frequently not well provided for at either central or local government levels, with outdated legislation still in place in many countries. Stakeholders therefore play a minimal part in the planning process.[34]

In several countries of East and South-East Asia, government is highly centralized and top down, although economic reforms and globalization have induced changes, especially in the transition economies. In China and Viet Nam, for instance, a master planning approach, in which plans were production-oriented technical documents intended to determine land allocation and infrastructure development, has gradually evolved from project-based detailed control planning to more strategic spatial planning. The latter combines elements of both socialist and market-oriented approaches to planning (see Box 5.2). Government institutions are beginning to acknowledge their role as enablers of development as opposed to mere service providers, and both inter-agency cooperation and public consultation are becoming more widespread.

At a local level, community-driven development approaches to basic service provision are being pursued in a number of countries. These involve participatory demand-driven support to defined communities, in which poor people and their organizations are treated as active partners and are often solely responsible for the project planning, implementation, monitoring and management. For example, community-driven approaches have been used in post-disaster areas in Indonesia, such as the North Java Flood Control Sector Project, reconstruction after the 2006 earthquake in Yogyakarta, and rehabilitation and reconstruction after the 2004 tsunami in Aceh and Nias. Facilitated and coordinated by government agencies, communities have been able to contribute information, voice their opinions and make decisions pertaining to such projects.[35] In Cambodia, Thailand and the Philippines, federations of the urban poor made up of community-managed savings and credit groups have worked with national and local governments to design

---

Box 5.2 Urban planning and participation in China

In China the urban administrative system is a nested hierarchy of spatial units. Conceptually, public opinion can be assembled at the lowest (*xiazhu*) level (units of as few as 15 to 20 households) and channelled up the pyramid. While sometimes claimed to be a system of direct or delegative democracy, the emphasis is on consensus and a unitary conception of the public good. It has been observed that, in practice, the hierarchy of spatial units functions as a mechanism for downward control and the centralized delivery of societal goods. This hierarchy is overlain by a system of *danwei* (urban production or work units, through which jobs are provided). Marketization has shifted the locus of power down the hierarchy because the control of local units over property has enabled the rise of town and village enterprises and diversification of their functions. The local administrative units have considerable autonomy. Urban spatial planning was reinvigorated in the 1980s as a statist top-down administrative exercise motivated by the desire to direct and regulate investment in the market economy. The 1983 and 1989 planning acts provided for master plans, a strong role for planners and a stronger role for the *jiedao* (sub-district or street committee) and *danwei* units through their control over land. The acts have emphasized an essentially technical approach to urban spatial planning with regulatory structures that perpetuate a depoliticized decision-making environment.

Thus, the state's priority and the function of the planning system are to achieve economic development while maintaining social and spatial control. Most influence is exercised by centrally appointed local leaders, whose primary allegiance is to central government, which determines their career progress. They are judged by their ability to use local units' fiscal autonomy to deliver local development, in compliance with centrally set goals and regulations. There are new urban actors, which include consumers' and citizens' groups, although investors are the most important. However, there is limited scope for citizens, especially the floating population, to have a say in decision-making. Instead of being accountable to local residents, leaders are answerable to the upper levels of government and new developments are more about checking corruption and limiting the clientelist practices and actions of local officials through elite scrutiny than about democracy and participation.

Source: Leaf, 2005a; Leaf and Hou, 2006, p574

---

and implement programmes to provide housing and sanitation to slum dwellers.[36]

The presence of organized civil society varies greatly between countries within the region of East and South-East Asia, from the most developed in the Philippines to countries such as China, Viet Nam and Cambodia, which do not emphasize civic participation and do not yet have a vibrant civil society. Even in countries that have attempted to deepen democracy in recent years, civil society organizations are not necessarily well developed (e.g. Indonesia, especially outside Jakarta). Lack of awareness and understanding of the aims of, and arrangements for, decentralization and participation amongst the urban population can hinder both. Interest in participation and the capacity to become involved is lacking for various reasons, including a preoccupation with meeting basic needs, and fear and distrust of government institutions.[37] Other barriers to participation include high levels of diversity in urban areas and limited capacity of government agencies and CBOs. Despite the existence of promising examples of participation at the city and local levels, in most countries in the region urban planning remains a top-down process.[38]

Latin America and the Caribbean

In Latin America and the Caribbean, there were limited attempts to introduce participation before the 1980s,

In East and South-East Asia, many countries ... have a weak democratic tradition usually on a project-specific basis and limited to consultative or instrumental forms of participation – for example, in projects to build self-help housing or regularize informal settlements. Critics noted that these token efforts failed to ensure that disadvantaged groups gained access to adequate housing, work and political rights.

During the 1980s, economic crises increased poverty, eroded the resource base for clientelist politics and fuelled pressures for political change. Mobilization of civil society organizations contributed to widespread democratization at both the national and local levels. More recently, social revolts against neo-liberal policies and their impacts have led to the establishment of a number of leftist governments. The impacts of this more recent transformation are still unfolding.[39]

Throughout the region, the need for the newly elected democratic governments to establish their political credibility and the growing importance of municipal government led to experiments with participatory governance to complement representative democracy. Many of the best-known cases have emerged in cities governed by political parties of the left. However, governments run by political parties with widely different political ideologies are now experimenting with deliberative forms of governance, in part to increase their legitimacy in the face of a citizenry that is increasingly mobilized and sceptical about progress with democratic consolidation. They engage citizens in decision-making between elections through collective dialogue and decision-making on policy and resource allocation, both directly and through neighbourhood councils, in coordination with elected bodies.

The extent to which participatory approaches have been institutionalized in national or local legislation varies across the region, with countries such as Brazil and Bolivia having made the most progress.[40] The best-known and most widely emulated of these is probably participatory budgeting, which will be considered in more detail later in this chapter. In addition, building on a longer tradition and influenced by government practices in the US, elected government may be complemented by various consultative and advisory councils, which make the views and expertise of important urban stakeholders available to elected governments.

Other arenas for the exercise of political voice in the region include the media and public spaces. Different types of media are widely used to convey information and there is increasing use of participatory media, and information and communication technologies. For example, in the Ajusco foothills of Mexico City, newspapers have been used to inform residents how to obtain land titles and services.[41] Television and radio stations and internet websites (including some government websites) may conduct public polls to gauge opinions regarding planning matters with a view to setting priorities or resolving conflicts. These allow people to appreciate the complexity of issues and the pros and cons of alternative solutions, and can potentially involve more people than could possibly participate in face-to-face consultations.

Street politics, meaning the enactment of demonstrations in public spaces to make claims and call the attention of decision-makers, the media and the public at large to broad issues or particular grievances, are also a long-standing way of exercising political voice in Latin American cities. The design and creation of such spaces and regulations about their use are both symbolically and practically significant, an important focus of planning attention.[42]

Despite the significant political changes and participatory initiatives outlined above, approaches to planning in the region have not changed commensurately or kept pace with new ideas about governance.[43] Technocratic planning persists. It may in certain circumstances achieve positive results (e.g. Curitiba; see Box 5.3), although it is often ineffective, hindered by a lack of political will, technical expertise and adequate data. Physical planning has been used to improve or beautify formal parts of cities, and in some cases to upgrade informal settlements. Although some of these plans balance physical and social aspects, many are criticized for their neglect of social dimensions.

At the same time, planning is often heavily politicized, with party-based issues frequently trumping technical expertise or community inputs. Participatory approaches are hindered by short political time horizons and clientelism. Implementation problems are particularly severe during periods of political transition and uncertainty, where distrust between those loyal to different political factions in the past hinders planning initiatives by new governments. For example, in countries with newly elected left-leaning governments, old oligarchies and bureaucracies continue to resist change.[44]

Differential openness to more participatory planning in the region is explained largely by the political orientation of governments. Where deliberative arrangements such as those referred to above have been introduced, they have increased citizens' agency, altered top-down relationships, opened communication channels between governing agencies and citizens, tilted resource allocation towards poorer people, and responded directly to the expressed needs of participants.[45] However, they may also pit communities against each other in a competition for resources, have limited leverage over total municipal resources, fail to deal with city-wide issues, enable more organized groups to gain at the expense of poorly organized groups, and be manipulated by political or economic elites.

To be effective, therefore, neighbourhood-level community organizations need to be linked to both wider networks and the representative political system. They are also likely to need support, including measures to build the capacity of under-represented groups such as women or minorities to participate. They seem to have been most successful when they complement rather than replace vibrant representative democracy.[46]

Factors shaping the processes and outcomes of participatory urban planning

Some of the factors that determine the opportunities for participatory planning, as well as its form and outcomes, can be identified from the above regional overviews:

Marginal notes:

Mobilization of civil society organizations contributed to widespread democratization at both the national and local levels

Planning is often heavily politicised with party-based issues frequently trumping technical expertise or community inputs

To be effective ... community organizations need to be linked to both wider networks and the representative political system

- the formal and informal characteristics of the political system, which influence the motives of those who are politically active at the city level; the scope for involvement in policy formulation and resource allocation by elected representatives, residents and other interests as well as appointed officials; and who may initiate participation, including government, external actors such as NGOs or donors, and citizens' organizations;
- the legal basis for local governance and planning, which determines whether local political arrangements include provision for representative bodies (elected local government, advisory bodies, etc.) and participatory processes (including specification of whether the outcomes of participation must be taken into account in plan-making), as well as the types of plans that governments are required to prepare and their ability to regulate land use and development;
- the historical evolution of planning, which reflects both ideas about its nature and purpose and its relationship to the state;
- the allocation of responsibilities for planning, implementation and development regulation between levels of government, local government and other agencies, which influences the scope for cooperation and partnership, the level at which planning and decision-making occurs, and the accessibility of political forums;
- government capacity, especially at the local level, which influences awareness of approaches to participation, as well as its potential benefits and pitfalls; the availability of appropriate skills to prepare and implement plans; and the availability of resources to respond to locally articulated needs and priorities;
- citizens' awareness of their entitlements to political representation and participation, as well as their capacity to organize, identify their needs and articulate their priorities; and
- the scale and scope of planning, which influences the opportunities for meaningful participation – the incentives for participation and the likelihood of practical benefits are greater at the community level, especially when adequate resources are made available to tackle the issues identified, than they are at the wider metropolitan or city level, which is harder for citizens to comprehend, is more remote from their everyday lives, and produces results only in the longer term.

INNOVATIVE APPROACHES TO PARTICIPATORY URBAN PLANNING

Increasingly, the need for direct participation in planning is recognized, and in some countries and cities, determined efforts have been made to develop innovative ways of involving a wide range of stakeholders in decision-making. Some of these approaches will be reviewed in this section. The analysis will start at the community level and then examine participation in strategic planning at the city level. In order

---

Box 5.3 Modes of decision-making for planning, Curitiba, Brazil

During a period of authoritarian government in Brazil, the appointment of a particularly well-qualified and forward-looking mayor in Curitiba (who was later re-elected several times) led to the development of new approaches to urban planning and implementation that have been internationally recognized. To guide discussions on the municipal master plan (*Plano Diretor*), first an advisory commission and then an independent public institution, the Institute of Urban Planning and Research of Curitiba (*Instituto de Pesquisa e Planejamento Urbano de Curitiba*), was created. This entity, set up in 1965, was able to overcome bureaucratic inertia by including representatives of all relevant government departments on its council. Although initial plan preparation did not provide opportunities for wide citizen participation, members of the economic elite were consulted and benefited from the plan. The continuing existence of this planning agency, backed by successive mayors and governors, ensured effective plan implementation.

However, it has not been possible to institute effective government and planning for the Curitiba Metropolitan Region, in which rival municipalities continue to resist any loss of their decision-making power to the metropolitan body composed of their mayors. The municipality has, over the years, devised innovative ways of involving citizens in managing and improving the city. Nevertheless, relatively weak civil society organization and limited accountability have resulted in failure to acknowledge many persistent problems, particularly those facing lower-income residents.

Source: Irazábal, 2006

---

for other countries and cities to learn from these approaches, it is important to not only describe the positive experiences but also identify the constraints and obstacles faced. Analyses of whether participatory approaches to planning have improved implementation are few and far between, not least because of the relatively recent adoption of many of the approaches discussed, the timescale required for implementing urban plans, and the general paucity of *ex post* evaluations of urban plans (see Chapter 9).

Participation in local planning

Participatory planning at the community level has, in recent years, taken many different forms, with varying outcomes. A variety of terms are used for these approaches, although in practice they have common characteristics, especially a focus on identifying needs and priorities, devising solutions, and agreeing on arrangements for implementation, operation and maintenance. The process of identifying needs and priorities is often called participatory urban appraisal, while arriving at proposals and implementation arrangements is frequently called community action planning. Typically, the primary motivation has been upgrading or regeneration to improve housing and infrastructure, rather than land-use planning.

Participatory urban appraisal has its roots in participatory rural appraisal methods.[47] It has been demonstrated that such methods can be used, with appropriate adjustments, in urban areas, where communities are larger, populations more transient and pressures on residents' time greater. Participatory urban appraisal methods are, however, primarily for collecting community-level information and undertaking preliminary needs assessment. They need to be complemented by systematic city-wide data that is capable of small area disaggregation with respect to critical service provision and well-being indicators, as well as by social group

Participatory urban appraisal methods are ... primarily for collecting community-level information (gender, age, etc.). In addition, participatory urban appraisal provides information inputs into decision-making rather than itself being a decision-making tool and therefore needs to be taken further in a process of participatory action research or community action planning.[48]

Various actors may initiate a participatory process at the local level, including governments, external agencies, communities, CBO federations and NGOs (see Box 5.4). The appropriate organizational arrangements for participation and planning at the local level vary depending upon the size and social characteristics of an area and the nature of the political system. The nature and outcome of participation at the 'community' level depends, amongst other things, upon the source of the initiative and the nature of relationships between communities, NGOs and the urban administrative and political system.[49] Sometimes these are collaborative. In the Philippines, for example, CBOs are more likely to emerge in municipalities where politicians are open to collaboration than those where they are hostile. The former are likely to be municipalities where the votes of *barangay* (neighbourhood) residents are important to those holding political control. The attitudes of elected politicians also affect CBOs' sense of agency, with those experiencing hostility finding it harder to sustain collective action.

Just as frequently, however, relationships between communities and the broader political systems are characterized by clientelism or confrontation. In the former circumstances, claims and demands are traded for votes and neighbourhoods are in competition; the latter occurs especially where informal settlements are illegal and threatened by eviction. There is a potential intermediary role for suitable NGOs in facilitating a process of participatory urban appraisal and community action planning, especially if local government is associated with unsuccessful past interventions, municipal staff or residents have a limited understanding of participatory methods, or political control at the city level is not pro-poor. In some circumstances, community organizations are susceptible to elite capture; but participation may also create local democratic spaces in which new local leaders can emerge and citizens' expectations of their interactions with government shift, contributing to democratic consolidation.[50] In addition, poor communities do not exist independently of the external

There is a potential intermediary role for ... NGOs in facilitating a process of participatory urban appraisal and community action planning

economic, organizational and political context, nor can they be self-sufficient with regard to resources. Even where community-level participation and activity are appropriate, therefore, neighbourhood planning needs to be linked to wider political and administrative systems.

Participation in city-level and strategic decision-making

Even if some community action planning is desirable and some community initiatives are feasible, city-level planning and support is essential. In addition, many policies and decisions are strategic in the sense that they refer to a wider geographical area and longer timescale than those typically dealt with in community action planning. Depending upon the size of the urban centre, intermediate, city and metropolitan arrangements are needed for the aggregation of local plans, setting broader objectives, allocating resources and resolving conflicts over priorities. Experience of participation at the city level is illustrated below through a review of participatory budgeting and the CDS.

■ Participatory budgeting

Participatory budgeting originated in Brazil and is now being emulated more widely in Latin America and beyond. In addition to democratization and decentralization, the 1988 constitution in Brazil provided several mechanisms for deliberative democracy and public oversight, especially at the local level. Building on earlier experiments in several municipalities and increased volumes of municipal finance, participatory budgeting was adopted in an increasing number of cities during the 1990s, following the landmark experience of Porto Alegre. In Porto Alegre and many other cities, the arrangements have four elements:

> *The first is the delegation of sovereignty by elected mayors in a set of regional and thematic assemblies which operate through universal criteria of participation. Every citizen can participate and vote on budget issues in [these] ... assemblies. The second characteristic is the combination of different elements of participation rooted in alternative participatory traditions, such as direct participation and the election of local councillors. The third element is the principle of self-regulation. The rules for participation and deliberation are defined by the participants themselves and are adapted or changed every year ... The fourth element is the attempt to invert the distribution of public goods through a combination of participation and technical decisions.*[51]

Since 1989 in Porto Alegre, 16 regional and 5 thematic plenary assemblies participate in the budget preparation process. In the first round of assemblies each year, city officials present audiences with general information about the city budget and participants elect their representatives to year-round forums. Following neighbourhood meetings during which residents identify their priorities for infrastructure investment, a second round of assemblies is held. At these, delegates are elected for each district and negotiate district-wide priorities in district budget forums. Finally, district delegates to the Municipal Budget Council decide how to distribute available funds between districts. The council and district forums monitor investment and engage in a broader dialogue with service-providing agencies. Evaluations show that participatory budgeting in Porto Alegre has:[52]

- strengthened civil society by encouraging the development of open and democratic civic associations and triggering wider participatory processes;
- given previously excluded groups influence over decision-making (although the poorest are generally not involved in the participatory process);
- brought investment to neglected communities;
- provided a partial alternative to clientelist political practices by enabling the Workers Party (*Partido does Trabalhadores*) mayor to circumvent the legislative body on which the party was in a minority; and
- probably helped to re-elect the Workers Party mayor who introduced it.

In order to ensure that women and men participated more equally in budgeting meetings, the Women's Coordination Group of Brazil introduced three initiatives in 2002 aimed at increasing women's participation. First, mobile play areas were installed at meeting locations to allow women with childcare responsibilities to bring children and attend meetings. Second, information about the process was distributed in areas where meetings were to take place in order to encourage women to participate. Third, meetings between government officials and women's groups were held to discuss how to encourage women to participate. One of the outcomes of this was to create a thematic forum on women, specifically looking at issues for women in communities.[53]

Participatory budgeting spread to a large number of Brazilian cities (170 by 2005) and has been emulated around the world, with support from the World Bank and the Urban Management Programme. The arrangements and outcomes have varied, both within Brazil and elsewhere. An analysis of the Brazilian experience, for example, argues that the conditions that account for participatory budgeting's success in Porto Alegre are not necessarily present in all Brazilian cities.[54] Cities that have developed successful and long-lasting participatory budgeting systems tend to have strongly developed civic associations, especially in lower-income neighbourhoods; a previous tradition of participation; a reasonable level of prosperity so that there are meaningful resources for redistributive investment; and a unified (generally left-wing) governing coalition committed to fostering participation.

Evaluations further indicate that participatory budgeting processes in Brazil are not technical processes that can be detached from local political structures and relationships and power dynamics, all of which affect both the design of the process and its outcomes. For positive results, the process must be based on three basic principles:[55] grassroots democracy through open local assemblies; social justice through the allocation of a larger share of resources to the most disadvantaged districts; and citizen control through an ongoing participatory budgeting council that monitors implementation. Enshrining the requirements for, and basic parameters of, participatory budgeting in law, as some municipalities have done, may be useful, although this can also reduce a municipality's ability to adapt the process in the light of experience.[56] In addition to the conditions in which participatory budgeting flourishes, transparency is critical for a successful process: revealing the resources available, clear and uniform criteria to guide priority-setting and redistribution between districts, and monitoring actual investment. Where there is opposition from the elected councillors (because of ideological differences or resentment that budget forums are usurping their role) or too many key expenditure decisions are made by the executive, participatory budgeting is less successful.

The context must be also characterized by a culture of participation. Participatory budgeting is not a substitute for healthy local politics, based on a representative political system and effective political parties. It cannot by itself produce 'more democracy, social justice and transparent administration'.[57] Nowhere is this illustrated more graphically than in Buenos Aires (see Box 5.5), where the lack of political commitment, dearth of developed civic associations, and political and institutional features that favoured middle- over low-income participation hindered the introduction and implementation of effective participatory budgeting processes.

In addition, although participatory budgeting can grow out of participatory plan-making at the city level (or vice versa), a major challenge is the relationship between participatory budgeting and a city's long-term strategic and development plans.[58] For this reason, in the health sector, parallel deliberative councils have been established in some Brazilian cities for city-wide decision-making.[59]

By 2006, it was estimated that participatory budgeting had been introduced in more than 1000 of the 16,000 municipalities in Latin America, and by 2007, it had been tried in seven (mainly west) European countries (over 100 cities).[60] Evaluations of these participatory budgeting experiences show an even greater variety of arrangements and outcomes than in Brazil.[61] A review of the experience of 25 municipalities in Latin America (including Brazil) and Europe finds that the resources allocated for participatory budgeting range from 1 to nearly 100 per cent of the municipal budget, with the proportion being non-transparent and/or politically contested in some cities.[62] Another study in more than 20 European cities concludes that many of the consultative processes not only fall short of true participatory budgeting, but also that only what they term 'Porto Alegre adapted for Europe' results in 'empowered participatory governance'.[63]

■ City Development Strategies (CDSs)

In developing countries, especially outside Latin America, many of the attempts to encourage and support greater participation in city-wide planning have come from outside,

Participatory budgeting … has … given previously excluded groups influence over decision-making

Cities that have developed successful … participatory budgeting systems tend to have strongly developed civic associations

---

Box 5.5 The characteristics and outcomes of participatory budgeting, Buenos Aires, Argentina

In Buenos Aires, participatory budgeting was required by the city's new constitution, adopted in 1996. However, between 1996 and 2002, its implementation was hindered by a conspicuous lack of political will to open up decision-making spaces to civil society. It was only in June 2002 that the Buenos Aires participatory budget was inaugurated.

Out of a population of 3 million, 4500 participants joined the pilot experience, and about 9000 and 14,000 participants registered at the beginning of the process in 2003 and 2004, respectively. In 2005 and 2006, however, participation dropped significantly by nearly 50 per cent. Participants and observers agree that attendance at meetings tends to decrease over the course of each annual cycle. The decline in interest and participation since 2004 may be explained by the inappropriate handling of the participatory budget by local state officers, and the weak level of state compliance with the budgetary expenditures voted on by participants.

Between 2002 and 2007, the methodological and operational supervision of the participatory budgeting process was left to the city's decentralized politico-administrative entities, the management and participation centres (*Centros de Gestión y Participación*). However, because of incomplete decentralization, these units did not have the necessary political and economic resources to fulfil their role. In 2007, however, the process of decentralization was completed, with the establishment of new local political entities with extended powers, the communes (*communas*), the creation of which, it is hoped, will give the participatory budgeting a fresh start and renew confidence in it.

Implementation of participatory budgeting priorities was also limited. Less than 2 per cent of Buenos Aires's total annual budget has been typically dedicated to participatory budgeting, a predictable consequence of the non-statutory character of the priorities identified and the lack of political will to comply with these priorities. Such a disregard of the investment agenda of participatory budgeting has detrimental consequences for participation rates. However, the municipal administration which took office in 2007 announced that it would progressively implement a number of unaddressed past priorities.

There are deep socio-territorial disparities between the privileged and highly developed northern neighbourhoods of the City of Buenos Aires and its deprived southern area, which contains 650,000 inhabitants and where 95 per cent of the city's slum settlements are concentrated. Participatory budgeting is expected to address such socio-spatial inequalities. Unfortunately, in Buenos Aires, performance has been disappointing. This seems to be related to the characteristics of those who participate, who are mainly middle-class citizens aged between 40 and 60. In the absence of measures to promote the involvement of deprived citizens, poor unorganized groups have remained under-represented; consequently, their needs have not been reflected in the resulting investments.

In spite of these difficulties, prospects for the future of the Buenos Aires participatory budgeting are not necessarily bleak. The scheme has been able to survive changes of political administration, demonstrating that it has attained a certain level of institutionalization. With greater political and administrative support on the part of the local state, participatory budgeting can contribute to reducing socio-spatial inequalities and help to build more participatory democracy in Buenos Aires. The municipal administration that took office in 2007 announced a revamping of the participatory budget, together with the creation of a School of Citizen Participation, designed to promote and develop more meaningful popular participation. Whether these have positive results will determine the outcome of participatory budgeting in Buenos Aires.

Source: Crot, 2008

---

especially from the international agencies, including the World Bank and UN-Habitat, under the auspices of the Urban Management Programme, the Sustainable Cities Programme and, more recently, the Cities Alliance. The approach currently being promoted by the Cities Alliance focuses on CDSs. These are approaches to city-based strategic planning that use similar participatory processes to develop an action plan for equitable growth in cities, although their format, scale and priorities vary. To date, over 150 cities worldwide have been involved in developing City Development Strategies.[64] Current approaches to the production of CDSs draw on earlier experiences in developed countries.[65] Although the importance of consultation is accepted, the intention is that stakeholders participate in problem identification, prioritization, visioning and development planning, rather than merely commenting on draft plans. The participatory process is intended to lead to an agreed vision, goals and priorities for a city, a set of strategies and action plans, and the establishment of institutional mechanisms to secure implementation, monitoring and evaluation.

It is, however, recognized that resources may constrain the scope of participation. Moreover, it may not be possible to consult all the stakeholders at the same time; stakeholders' capacity to advance their views varies, and greater weight is likely to be attached to the views of those who provide political or financial support to the government in question. The final product may also vary depending upon the:

- stage of development of a city and the opportunities and threats it faces;
- stage of development of the CDS, many of which start by addressing a specific sector or issue, only adopting a multi-sectoral approach later; and
- scale of the problem or size of the city, although the general approach is usable in both large and small towns and cities.[66]

There are few independent evaluations of the CDS approach, let alone of the outcomes of CDSs. There is limited evidence on whether this approach is producing better results in terms of wide stakeholder involvement, more effective implementation and more satisfactory outcomes than conventional plan preparation processes. However, it has generated considerable support amongst

City Development Strategies ... use ... participatory processes to develop an action plan for equitable growth in cities

local governments, professionals and international agencies. Focusing on the participatory element and drawing on comparative evaluations of CDS experience[67] and detailed studies of Bagamoyo and Dar es Salaam (Tanzania) and Johannesburg (South Africa),[68] the positive outcomes of the participatory approach adopted during the preparation of CDSs include the following:

- Joint identification of needs and priorities in key sectors leads to improved coordination and greater coherence of the efforts of local and international partners, as well as acceptance amongst stakeholders that not all problems can be addressed simultaneously because of resource limitations.
- Consultative and participatory mechanisms are developed, strengthened and consolidated, and they are regarded by those involved as important, although the extent to which they become part of the established planning process varies.
- Processes of wide stakeholder consultation help to identify local needs and priorities, especially those of groups that are poorly understood by planners and do not have an effective voice in the political system.
- A broader range of solutions is considered than in conventional master planning.[69]

However, the evaluations note a number of common challenges:

- Building participatory approaches and consensus requires time.
- Few cities have established any means for assessing how effective or systematic their participatory processes are, and they are not always institutionalized as part of the ongoing planning process.
- There may be resistance to wide and lengthy participatory processes from both planners and other officials (because they are time consuming and may not produce consensus or clear pointers on priorities), and elected representatives (who consider it their job to make decisions) (as seen in Johannesburg; see Box 5.6).
- Concentration on participatory planning at the expense of broader political processes may threaten the process and content of planning, while participation may not tackle entrenched power inequalities.
- Achieving a balance between economic development, service provision and environmental sustainability is a major challenge for any city, and participatory planning may not be able to resolve the conflicts between priorities.

ENHANCING PARTICIPATION IN URBAN PLANNING

Lessons from the experience reviewed above suggest a number of ways in which participation in urban planning can be enhanced and also point to a number of pitfalls to be

The Johannesburg City Development Strategy (CDS) emerged (with limited external assistance) out of the local demand for a post-apartheid vision for the city. By 1997 the four municipalities into which the city was divided had spent their way into a serious financial crisis, partly as a result of poor revenue collection, a huge backlog in services in poor black areas and a rates boycott by wealthy residents. By 2000 the transitional arrangements had been phased out and the first integrated metropolitan government was established. Institutional changes included the production of an interim management plan (iGoli, 2002). A long-term city visioning process (iGoli, 2010) was initiated, driven by research and data collection by external consultants and managed by a project team advised by a steering committee comprised of key stakeholders from the business sector, communities, labour unions and government.

Building on established local practices of negotiation and consensus-building, an extensive process of consultation was undertaken in 2000 through a stakeholders' forum, focus groups and a city summit. However, following elections at the end of 2000, the commissioned research was drawn into a separate process of internal policy formulation, which resulted in the adoption in 2002 of a long-term strategy (Johannesburg 2030), with a strong focus on the economy. Between 2003 and 2005, this was integrated with a newly formulated human development agenda and the existing environmental management plan to produce a revised strategy (2030 City Development Strategy). Opposition to the restructuring of municipal services associated with iGoli 2002 (including limited privatization) crystallized around the New Privatization Forum, which linked trade unions, leftist intellectuals and emerging popular movements, and led to a breakdown of relations between the council and the trade unions. The production of Johannesburg 2030, therefore, did not involve the wider public. Backed by councillors and the African National Congress, it focused on positioning Johannesburg as a competitive emergent global city. However, formal processes of participation, including electoral representation, ensured the consideration of pro-poor concerns in the CDS. In response to both external and internal critiques of CDS proposals, more attention is being paid to improving services and living conditions and reducing poverty in ongoing planning processes.

Sources: Parnell and Robinson, 2006, p345; Lipietz, 2008, p135

avoided. It is clear that no one model of participation can be adopted in all situations, as emphasized in Chapters 3 and 4. Participation can be enhanced by matching its form to the conditions in a particular city; but it is also possible to encourage wider and more meaningful participation by addressing the factors outlined below, to create a favourable environment and adequate support system.

An enabling political context and system

Participation implies a more active concept of citizenship than electoral democracy usually assumes. However, participatory processes that involve a wide range of stakeholders do not occur in isolation from the political system, the nature of which influences the likelihood that participation in plan-making will occur and be welcomed. Table 5.2 identifies types of urban political systems and the forms of participation that are likely to be possible in each identified.

The importance of the political context in determining the scope for, and likely outcomes of, participation does not mean that supporters should not advocate stronger forms of participation even in unpromising political contexts. But it does sound a note of caution and provide guidance on selecting forms of participation that are likely to produce results, at least while support is developed for more ambitious approaches.

Participatory processes ... do not occur in isolation from the political system

Table 5.2

Political systems and the scope for participation

Modes of urban politics and governance	Forms of participation				
	Nominal	Consultative	Instrumental	Representative	Transformative
Inclusive democratic: politicians are elected on the basis of a strong social contract and a rights-based programme that addresses both the priorities of the majority and the needs of minority and marginalized groups, to whom they are accountable.		✔	✔	✔	✔
Corporatist: politicians and powerful civic leaders are the key decision-makers. They negotiate only with the most important interests, usually elite business interests or trade unions, whose support they need to realize their political objectives.	✔	✔	✔	✔	
Managerialist: politicians and appointed officials are the key decision-makers. Their goals are practical, often placing considerable emphasis on strong government, effectiveness and efficiency.	✔	✔	✔	✔	
Pluralist: competing interests are assumed to be sufficiently well organized to exercise influence over the political process, the role of which is to mediate between competing interests while achieving public objectives. Politics is conceived of as a bargaining process.	✔	✔	✔	✔	
Populist: these emerge where politicians (often a single politician such as an elected mayor) mobilize popular support as a way of setting and implementing their political agenda and maintaining themselves in power. Municipal goals appear to address the priorities of the majority, but are, in practice, symbolic: resource allocation does not match them.	✔	✔	✔		
Oligarchical: in this variety of populist governance, members of the elite hold political power. They mobilize popular support to legitimize their dominance and maintain themselves in power.	✔	✔	✔		
Clientelist: relations between politicians, bureaucrats and citizens are particularistic and personalized. Pragmatic exchange relations guarantee decisions that advance the interests of constituents in return for electoral support.	✔		✔		
Authoritarian: in these non-democratic political systems, rule at the city level is by an appointee of the national leader (or single political party) backed by a subordinate bureaucracy. Government is by command, concessions are obtained as personal favours, only welfare-providing NGOs are tolerated, and community-level organization tends to be a mechanism for control over the population rather than a means for residents to exercise their political rights.	✔		✔		

Source: based on DiGaetano and Strom, 2003, p366; Rakodi, 2004, p92

Civil society and private actors have important roles in the practice of participation

Recent governance thinking stresses that government agencies cannot and should not take sole responsibility for urban planning and management, but rather work in partnership with other actors. Civil society and private actors have important roles in the practice of participation and can contribute to developing political support for participatory approaches. Their involvement in direct democracy and transformative participation can consolidate democratic practice and lead to reform of the formal political system.[70] However, many of the serious problems faced by cities cannot be tackled effectively by non-governmental actors. Responsive and accountable formal political institutions are needed for effective urban governance.

A strong legal basis for planning and participation

For participation in plan-making to be … influential, a strong legislative basis is needed

Conventional planning legislation typically allows for draft plans (prepared by technical planning organizations within or outside government) to be made available for a limited period for residents and others to comment upon. The specification of those who are permitted to comment may be narrow or wide. They may include only those directly affected or wider groups and interests. The planning agency may or may not be required to take into account the suggestions or objections in the production of the final plan, which

is typically approved by a government agency or political executive. Provisions for ensuring that all of those interested know that the plan is available vary from minimal to extensive. Procedures for recording the results of consultation also vary, with some countries specifying public hearings by independent officials to ensure that all those with an interest get a fair hearing. Initiatives to extend participation beyond the minimum specified by the legislation may be taken within the urban planning system, but are also often associated with interventionist policies (such as regeneration and renewal), rather than the plan-making process *per se*. For participation in plan-making to be both substantive and influential, a strong legislative basis is needed, although the arrangements may vary between countries and between national and city levels. Brazil's Cities Statute is an excellent example of such legislation (see Box 5.7).

In addition to the plan preparation process, there may also be provisions for 'participation' in the legislation governing development regulation. Typically, those who have the right to comment upon or object to an application for development permission are those directly affected, although often this also depends upon the scale and significance of the proposed development, with major infrastructure or urban development proposals being subject to wider consultation than minor applications. However, there is more scope to express opinions on applications for development permission in 'discretionary' planning systems than in 'zoning' systems, in which decisions on development applications are purely administrative and based on legal frameworks.

In countries with well-developed local government and planning systems, the legislative frameworks for local government and planning have periodically been revised. During the 1990s, changes to the legislation governing local government often aimed at democratic decentralization, although the extent to which national governments have been willing to give local governments significant roles, resources and autonomy varies. Planning legislation has been revised in the light of changing conceptions of the role and nature of planning, changing circumstances and challenges, and in a quest to make planning more effective. However, often revisions to planning legislation are overdue. When they occur, the provisions regarding participation should be strengthened, made applicable to multi-sectoral urban development planning, and not restricted to the urban land-use plan preparation process. While inserting requirements for consultation and collaborative approaches in legislation is insufficient to ensure real and equal commitment by all local governments, without a mandatory requirement, opposition from vested interests, including political actors, or changes in political control can reduce citizens' rights to participate.

Understanding the pitfalls of participatory approaches

Experience has shown that participatory approaches to planning have considerable potential for producing more appropriate pro-poor and redistributive plans and proposals and enhancing the likelihood of implementation. However, methods and tools appropriate for the context, form and purpose of participation, resources available and stakeholders involved are all important factors.[71]

If participation by low-income groups in the design of projects is not accompanied by a wider redistributive programme, they may see few improvements in their living conditions. Giving people a say in inconsequential decisions is unlikely to generate lasting enthusiasm for the participatory process or to empower them. Local participation in projects with immediate practical outcomes should therefore be accompanied by opportunities to participate directly or indirectly in decisions related to the allocation of resources at the city level, lest poor residents become disillusioned with its outcomes.

Decisions about who will be consulted or invited to participate are sometimes taken by politicians or officials rather than stakeholders themselves, biasing the outcomes of participation. In addition, different categories of stakeholders may not take advantage of opportunities provided by consultative and participatory processes. These may be well-organized powerful stakeholders who feel that they can exert influence more effectively through other channels (e.g. lobbying and political representation). There may also be disadvantaged social groups who have little political voice, are fragmented and poorly organized, lack confidence or time, lack knowledge of municipal functions and processes, or fear reprisals. In addition to measures to improve their

> **Box 5.7 The City Statute, Brazil**
>
> The enactment of the City Statute of Brazil in 2001 represented a groundbreaking development with regards to the creation of an inclusive local decision-making framework for cities. The statute consolidates the role of municipalities in the development of policies and responses to address multiple challenges of urbanization in Brazil. Mandated by the national constitution and the Cities Statute, municipalities in Brazil with a population of more than 20,000 are expected to adopt a master or comprehensive planning approach.
>
> The City Statute in Brazil has been further promoted with the formation of the Ministry of Cities in 2003. This institution works with states, municipalities, civil society organizations (CSOs) and the private sector in the areas of housing, environmental sanitation, transport and mobility and other related urban programmes.
>
> In 2004, a Cities' Council was created to add a further instrument for democratic management of the National Urban Development Policy. This is a collegiate body of a deliberative and advisory nature, which guides the formulation and implementation of the National Urban Development Policy and other policies and planning processes. Currently, the council is comprised of 86 members (49 civil society and 37 government representatives), with 9 observers representing state governments, each of which has also been mandated to establish Cities Councils.
>
> *Source:* Irazábal, 2008a

representation and effectiveness in the formal political representative system, specific actions are needed to ensure that such groups can and do participate, including building their knowledge and organizational capacity, and designing events and activities tailored to their needs.

Gender equality in planning, for instance, seeks to enhance the involvement of women who are often marginalized from decision-making. It does so in two key areas: within the political, administrative structures and mechanisms of a city, and within the consultative and participatory structures of a city. As theories and practices about community participation in planning have evolved, so too has the understanding of the importance of gender in participation.[72] A plethora of tools and practices now exist to aid gendered participation in decision-making processes, including:

- gender disaggregation of data (as part of general data disaggregation);
- gender budgeting (as part of participatory budgeting);
- women's hearings (as part of city consultations);
- women's audits (especially of safety);
- training programmes for women community leaders and councillors; and
- facilitating the formation of networks of women's groups, leaders and representatives.

It is also important to recognize that the outcomes of participation are unpredictable. Participation may yield limited benefits if intended beneficiaries choose not to take part or the outcomes are ignored by decision-makers. However, even limited participation (e.g. consultation) can bring hidden issues and voices into the open in a way that they cannot be ignored by the state. Instrumental participation, for instance, can supplement genuinely limited public resources, enable users to influence project design, encourage ownership of services provided and commitment to their maintenance, and provide a springboard for increasing the

Gender equality in planning ... seeks to enhance the involvement of women who are often marginalized from decision-making

Participation may yield limited benefits if ... the outcomes are ignored by decision-makers

accountability of public agencies. While strong forms of participation that provide stakeholders with influence or control over decisions are desirable, where these are not (yet) feasible, 'weaker' forms should not be neglected. In all cases, not least because the outcomes of participation cannot be guaranteed, it is important to ensure that participatory procedures themselves are fair and inclusive.

Sufficient resources to support participatory processes

Participatory approaches to urban planning demand resources and time. In addition to political and official commitment, they need adequate financial resources and appropriately trained facilitators and planners, with a good knowledge of a range of appropriate tools.

Commitment to participation by both politicians and planning agencies is essential. For the former, the benefits of participation (responsiveness to voter needs, wide ownership of decisions and commitment to implementation) must be seen to outweigh any potential threats to their role and decision-making responsibilities. Planning agencies vary in their openness, organizational objectives and needs, geographical scope, substantive influence on decision-making and responsibilities. Their commitment will depend upon an appreciation of the benefits of participation: improved information, better and more acceptable policies and proposals, political backing for implementation, and partner commitment to resource allocation and implementation. To achieve these beneficial results, municipal councils and planning agencies must allocate adequate human and financial resources to initiating and sustaining participatory processes.

Facilitators, who may or may not be urban planners themselves, need a good knowledge of the potentials and pitfalls of participation. As well as a technical knowledge of planning issues, they need respectful attitudes to all social groups, political awareness, the ability to select and use appropriate participatory methods, and negotiating and consensus-building skills. Commonly, planning courses do not include these skills. Even if planners themselves are not the most appropriate facilitators of participatory processes, their training needs to incorporate a good grounding in social analysis, the participatory methods available and ways of taking the outputs into account in plan preparation. When it is not possible to reach consensus during the participatory processes, decisions should balance conflicting views and interests. Often, planners themselves do not take such decisions. However, they can have a significant influence on those who do by the way in which they (selectively) use the outputs from participation and draft policies and plans.

Participation thus poses a number of ethical issues for planners. As noted above, when facilitating participation in plan-making, they have considerable influence over the selection of participants, choice of methods, and what happens to the results. Facilitators' and planners' own social attitudes and political allegiances may be obstacles to wide and inclusive participation. They may also be faced with dilemmas if politicians or bureaucrats in other departments are less committed to inclusive and pro-poor processes. The

Participatory approaches need adequate financial resources and appropriately trained facilitators

Participation is more likely to occur if the outcomes affect people's everyday lives

laws and regulations that specify requirements for participation in planning, professional bodies and planner's training can all play an important role in providing them with ethical guidance and protecting them if they come under pressure not to adhere to the specified practices.

Participatory mechanisms relevant to the scale and purpose of planning

The need and opportunities for participation may differ depending upon the scale of planning. Experience shows that participation is more likely to occur if the outcomes affect people's everyday lives. In this case, those interested generally participate to protect their own interests. This can be positive if planning proposals can be improved to better reflect stakeholders' needs and priorities, as in many upgrading and regeneration projects. However, it can also be negative if proposals that are important to the achievement of higher-level objectives or that have wide social benefits are opposed because of their anticipated adverse effects on a few.

Issue-based participation can help to broaden coalitions among different communities to influence decision-making and higher levels of government.[73] It is harder to ensure political interest and wide participation in strategic and long-term policy-making and planning, which seems remote to many citizens, and which has time horizons longer than typical political terms of office. As a result, city-wide participatory processes may be dominated by business and property interests. By building on local participation in practical projects, however, local actors can be interested in wider issues and enabled to make constructive inputs into city-wide planning.

In every city, at least two levels of participatory political representation and planning are needed (i.e. the neighbourhood/community and city levels). In the largest cities and metropolitan areas, three are more likely to be desirable (i.e. the neighbourhood, sub-metropolitan and metropolitan levels). This will ensure that local politicians are accessible to residents, that local plans and service delivery are responsive to local needs, that administrative efficiency and cost effectiveness in service delivery are achieved, and, where appropriate, that metro-wide strategic issues are addressed. To ensure that there are opportunities for a variety of stakeholders to participate at these levels, delegative and advisory arrangements are needed, as well as a means of aggregating the diverse outcomes of bottom-up processes.

Participatory approaches to planning may be more feasible at the city scale in small cities than in large metropolitan areas. Wide participation is likely to be most practical at the local or neighbourhood level. Direct democracy is more appropriate at the sub-metropolitan than the metropolitan level. Thus, as the scale at which decisions need to be taken increases, it is inevitable that only a small subset of those affected can participate.

There is a difference between periodic intensive participatory exercises when plans are prepared or revised and continuing engagement in agenda-setting, monitoring, policy review and decision-making. What may be feasible on a periodic basis (e.g. opinion surveys, large city-level meetings, wide consultations, referendums) is not necessarily feasible or appropriate on an ongoing basis. Therefore, in order to sustain direct democracy alongside representative democracy, it is necessary to institutionalize participatory channels and strengthen the organizational capacity of disadvantaged sections of the city population, as well as secure ongoing support from elected representatives.

The ineffectiveness of conventional land-use planning has led to the emergence of multi-sectoral approaches to urban development planning and management. In many cities, the links between the two are weak. Greater attention needs to be given to linking land-use planning with multi-sectoral planning and management, including harmonizing the arrangements for direct and indirect participation in decision-making.

Successful participation: Conditions and characteristics

Conditions for meaningful and inclusive participation can be identified from the experiences reviewed in this chapter, although, as noted above, participation may yield useful and unexpected results even when not all these conditions apply. These conditions can, in turn, be linked to the following features of successful participation:[74]

- committed city leadership, both political and bureaucratic;
- a conducive national policy and legislative framework, with support from higher levels of government;
- suitable political arrangements at the city or metropolitan level to ensure coordination and accountability, complemented by provision for direct and indirect participation;
- participation that is broad and inclusive involving all relevant stakeholders, especially disadvantaged groups with multiple channels for participation to involve all social groups at various levels of government;
- timeliness – opportunities for participation that can influence decision-making;
- a high likelihood of outputs being adopted through prioritization and sequencing of action;
- open, fair and accountable processes, which are comprehensible, transparent and based on clear ground rules;
- skilled, independent and flexible facilitation by planners to be built through professional education, continuing professional development and peer exchanges;
- a distinction between short- and long-term objectives, with rapid progress on selected short-term actions to build legitimacy and sustain commitment, and proposals linked to investment plans and a financing strategy;
- a willingness to strive for consensus, backed up by conflict resolution techniques and sound political decision-making;
- support for and collaboration with civil society and community organizations and learning from their proven methods for organizing and empowering the poor;
- tools appropriate to the form and purpose of the participatory process;

- monitoring and evaluation processes to track progress and outcomes and learn from experience, including mechanisms for citizen involvement in supervising implementation;
- provision of long-term support to cities by their associations, national governments, bilateral donors or international agencies, and promotion of knowledge-sharing between them; and
- closer links in legislation and practice between multi-sectoral urban planning and management and land-use planning so that promising participatory approaches can benefit land-use plan preparation and planning decisions.

CONCLUDING REMARKS

A number of factors have led to consultation and mobilization increasingly forming part of the urban planning process, although participatory influence on decision-making has often been limited. First, it was recognized that consultation could improve the information available to planners and result in more appropriate policies and plan proposals. Second, it became clear that mobilization of citizens' contributions of labour and money could lead to a greater sense of ownership of local infrastructure and facilities (including commitment to maintenance), as well as supplementing scarce government resources. Finally, there was increasing recognition that conventional approaches to planning were ineffective in dealing with either rapid growth or urban regeneration. Increasing numbers of cities have therefore adopted more collaborative processes of strategic development planning linked to action programmes and investment plans. In this, they were often assisted by international programmes, such as the Urban Management Programme, the Sustainable Cities Programme and the Cities Alliance and its predecessors.

At the same time, it has been observed that much participation is consultative or instrumental and provides participants with little real influence over plans or public expenditure. Even more recently, methods for empowering poor urban people through the establishment of savings groups, detailed community surveys undertaken by residents themselves, and networking of savings and community groups have demonstrated that people are willing and able to participate effectively if they are supported to do so and receive practical benefits as a result. Moreover, experiences have shown that small-scale neighbourhood participation can be scaled up into meaningful city-level processes of budgeting or informal settlement upgrading.

The main positive lessons from the review of participation in urban planning in recent decades are that:

- Approaches to urban development planning and management can be improved by the adoption of collaborative approaches in the preparation of CDSs that involve all the main stakeholders, and result in agreement on priorities, actions and the allocation of responsibilities between relevant agencies.

Increasing numbers of cities have therefore adopted more collaborative processes of ... planning

- Participation in project planning can result in more appropriate design and significant resident contributions, leading to improved living conditions in low-income settlements.
- Participation by residents in planning and implementing practical improvements in the areas where they live and work, municipal budgeting and local plan preparation has positive outcomes. Participation at the local level can also be aggregated and scaled up to play a role in city-level planning and resource allocation.

However, for participatory approaches to be adopted and have these favourable outcomes, certain conditions need to be satisfied. These particularly apply to stronger forms of participation that involve empowerment leading to citizen influence or control over decision-making. A number of challenges also need to be addressed to ensure that participation is meaningful, socially inclusive and contributes to improving spatial planning.

NOTES

1   Pretty, 1995; White, 1996.
2   Cornwall, 2008, p270.
3   Cornwall, 2008, p271 see also Cooke and Kothari, 2001.
4   Greed and Reeves, 2005.
5   Notable contributions include Jane Jacobs (1963) *The Death and Life of Great American Cities* and Dolores Hayden (1980) *What Would a Non-Sexist City Look Like? Speculations on Housing, Urban Design and Human Work.*
6   See Moser, 1993.
7   UNIFEM, cited in Todes et al, 2008.
8   Garau, 2008, p29.
9   Booth, 2005.
10   Day, 1997.
11   Garau, 2008, p30.
12   Golobic and Marusic, 2007.
13   Carmin, 2003.
14   Hirt and Stanilov, 2008.
15   Hirt and Stanilov, 2008.
16   Pagonis and Thornley, 2000.
17   Farmer and Farmer, 2001; Babjanian, 2005.
18   Attahi et al, 2008; Okpala, 2008.
19   Attahi et al, 2008.

20   See www.unhabitat.org/content.asp?cid=5025&catid=540&typeid=19&subMenuId=0.
21   See www.unhabitat.org/categories.asp?catid=374.
22   See www.mdpafrica.org.zw/.
23   See www.citiesalliance.org/index.html.
24   Attahi et al, 2008.
25   Attahi et al, 2008.
26   Attahi et al, 2008.
27   Attahi et al, 2008.
28   Buccus et al, 2008.
29   Ansari, 2008.
30   Ansari, 2008.
31   Siddiqui and Siddiqui, 2004.
32   Ansari, 2008.
33   Benjamin, 2000; Jha et al, 2007.
34   Yuen, 2008.
35   Yuen, 2008; http://web.worldbank.org/WBSITE/EXTERNAL/TOPICS/EXTSOCIAL DEVELOPMENT/EXTCDD/0,,menuPK:430167~pagePK:149018~piPK:149093~theSitePK:430161,00.html.
36   Garau et al, 2005.
37   Yuen, 2008.
38   Yuen, 2008.
39   Irazábal, 2008a.
40   Irazábal, 2008a.

41   Diaz Barriga, 1996.
42   Irazábal, 2008b.
43   Irazábal, 2008a.
44   Irazábal, 2008a.
45   Irazábal, 2008a.
46   Selee, 2003; Souza, 2007; Irazábal and Foley, 2008.
47   Chambers, 1994a, 1994b, 1994c, 2004.
48   See, for example, Hamdi and Goethert, 1996.
49   Ward and Chant, 1987; Mitlin, 2004.
50   Mitlin, 2004.
51   Avritzer, 2006, pp623–624.
52   Abers, 1998; Jacobi, 1999; Souza, 2001; Houtzager, 2003; Avritzer, 2006.
53   Women's International News, 2003.
54   Avritzer, 2006; see also UN, 2009.
55   Sintomer et al, 2008.
56   Schönleitner, 2004.
57   Sintomer et al, 2008, p176.
58   Cabannes, 2004a, p41.
59   Schönleitner, 2004.
60   Cabannes, 2006; Sintomer et al, 2008.
61   See Cabannes, 2004b.
62   Cabannes, 2004a.

63   Sintomer et al, 2008.
64   Cities Alliance, www.citiesalliance.org/activities-output/topics/cds/cds-work-with-ca.html.
65   For example, Wellington (New Zealand), Toronto (Canada), Chattanooga (US), Barcelona (Spain), Glasgow (UK), Brisbane (Australia) (GHK, 2000).
66   For example, see Halla (2005) on the small town of Bagamoyo, Tanzania.
67   In 11 cities: ECON Analysis and Centre for Local Government (2005), and 4 cities: Universalia (2006).
68   Kombe, 2001; Halla, 2005; Parnell and Robinson, 2006; Sheikh and Rao, 2007.
69   For example, Haiphong, Viet Nam (GHK, 2000).
70   Houtzager, 2003.
71   A number of guides and toolkits are available (see Plummer, 2000; UNCHS, 2001b).
72   Seaforth, 2002.
73   Irazábal, 2008a.
74   See also Newman and Jennings, 2008.

PART III

GLOBAL TRENDS: THE CONTENT OF URBAN PLANS (SUBSTANTIVE)

CHAPTER 6

BRIDGING THE GREEN AND BROWN AGENDAS

One of the most significant contributions of the United Nations to global thinking about the future in recent decades has been the concept of sustainable development. Its application to cities, as discussed in this chapter, has helped to catalyse the rediscovery and renaissance of urban planning. Sustainable development, or sustainability, was defined by the Brundtland Commission[1] as development that meets the needs of people without compromising the ability of future generations to meet their own needs. In urban planning, as in other professions, this has meant a new recognition of how environmental and social aspects of development need to be integrated with economic development, as well as meeting basic human needs for the poorest parts of the world.

Because of the dominance of cities and towns in developed countries and rapid urbanization in developing countries, it is inevitable that urban areas currently use resources in very concentrated ways, with a major proportion of pollutants affecting the air, lakes, rivers, the ocean and the soil being generated there. On the positive side, however, it is in urban areas that most economic development is located, technological and social advances are made, and the wealth upon which national development depends is created.

As indicated in Chapter 1, sustainable cities should be environmentally safe, socially inclusive and economically productive. Simultaneously achieving these goals entails careful balancing of environmental management objectives against built (or human) environment objectives, as it is through the latter that basic human needs are met. Since the early 1990s, it has been recognized that the concept of sustainable cities has to include a number of fundamental objectives – that is, minimization of the use of non-renewable resources; achievement of the sustainable use of renewable resources; and staying within the absorptive capacity of local and global waste absorption limits. Action to attain these objectives provides the link between the natural and the built environment, or between the green and brown agendas. How these objectives have been and are being addressed in urban planning is the focus of this chapter.

SUSTAINABLE URBAN DEVELOPMENT: THE GREEN AND BROWN AGENDAS

Thinking on the application of the concept of sustainable development to cities started in the early 1990s, following the United Nations Conference on Environment and Development (UNCED) in 1992, and the United Nations Commission on Human Settlements at its 15th session in 1995, which identified the key measures needed to make sustainable development applicable to human settlements.[2] The commission showed that sustainable development was not simply a new way to describe environmental protection, but was a 'new concept of economic growth which provides for fairness and opportunity for all people in the world without destroying the world's natural resources and without further compromising the carrying capacity of the globe'. In 1996, the United Nations Centre for Human Settlements (UNCHS) (now the United Nations Human Settlements Programme, or UN-Habitat) extended the concept of sustainable development to urban planning, stating that 'Settlement planning is central to ensuring that urban development and management meets sustainable development goals.'[3]

The application of sustainable development to cities has challenged urban planning to find new ways of addressing the pressing issues of urban poverty and wealth creation while simultaneously addressing urban environmental issues, both natural and built, and the social and cultural issues of urban communities. Urban planning is one of the few professions with a specific remit that encompasses these three areas of need – economic, environmental and social – and should therefore be at the centre of attempts to define new approaches that integrate solutions seamlessly. It is also very specifically oriented towards long-term issues, as city-building is a continuous process. Thus, urban planners should embrace the sustainable development approach if they are to leave a positive legacy for future generations.

Urban planning was probably not ready for the challenge of sustainable development, although it is not the only profession to fall behind in this respect. Many professions have been caught up in a kind of scientific modernism

The application of sustainable development to cities has challenged urban planning to find new ways of ... addressing urban environmental issues, both natural and built

The green agenda	The brown agenda
Natural systems, global, regional and local, used as services by cities	**Human systems required to make cities healthy and liveable and which are part of the metabolism of the city**
Ecosystems that provide green open space used by the city for biodiversity protection and recreation.	Waste systems to recycle and remove wastes from cities, including solid, liquid and air waste.
Water systems that cities use to tap the natural flow for water supply and waste disposal.	Energy systems to provide power, heating, cooling and lighting for all city functions.
Climate and air systems that provide cities with the requirements for healthy life.	Transport systems to enable mobility in the city, including the fuel.
Other ecological services, including agricultural and forestry systems providing food and fibre for cities.	Building and materials systems that provide the physical basis of life in cities.

Table 6.1

Characteristics of the green and brown agendas in the urban environment

A significant ... dilemma for planners ... is how to integrate the ... 'green agenda' and the 'brown agenda'

that has reduced issues of development down to manuals and formulas inherently incapable of including all facets of need in cities. As stated in Chapter 3 of this Global Report, urban planning was, in many countries, caught up in a paradigm of master planning that sought to impose one best way of shaping urban development. This led to the New Towns of England and North America as well as the 'ideal cities' of Brazilia, New Delhi and Canberra. It led to the large-scale 'urban renewal' programmes that tore down generations of organic urban building and replaced them with high-rise uniformity. It led to the formulas of traffic engineering that imposed intrusive road structures and car dependence upon a generation of urban dwellers in wealthy cities, leaving them vulnerable to the vagaries of oil prices and climate change. Fixed notions of 'what should be' led to a paralysis over what to do about the rapidly growing informal settlements in the developing world, which exploded across cities, leaving millions without basic urban services.[4]

Box 6.1 The green agenda as set out by the Millennium Ecosystem Assessment

- Species extinction rates are now 100 to 1000 times above the background rate. During the last several decades, 20 per cent of the world's coral reefs have been lost and 20 per cent degraded, whilst 35 per cent of mangrove area has been lost.
- 60 per cent of the increase in the atmospheric concentration of carbon dioxide (CO_2) since 1750 has taken place since 1959. Climate change now threatens biodiversity and ecosystem services across the planet.
- Human beings produce as much biologically available nitrogen as all natural pathways and this may increase by a further 65 per cent by 2050.
- Approximately 60 per cent (15 out of 24) of the ecosystem services evaluated in the Millennium Ecosystem Assessment are being degraded or used unsustainably.
- 5 to possibly 25 per cent of global freshwater use exceeds long-term accessible supplies and 15 to 35 per cent of irrigation withdrawals exceed supply rates and are therefore unsustainable. People now use between 40 and 50 per cent of all available fresh water running off the land. Water withdrawal has doubled over the past 40 years.
- A number of countries that appeared to have positive growth in net savings (wealth) in 2001 actually experienced a loss in wealth when degradation of natural resources was factored into the accounts.
- There is evidence that changes being made in ecosystems are increasing the likelihood of non-linear changes in ecosystems (including accelerating, abrupt and potentially irreversible changes), with important consequences for human well-being.
- One of the targets of the Millennium Development Goals is that, by 2010, there should be a significant reduction in the rate of loss of biodiversity and a reversal in the loss of environmental resources.

Source: Millennium Ecosystem Assessment, 2005

'Sustainability could be called the post-modern equivalent of a grand narrative.'[5] In terms of urban planning, the grand narrative calls into question the modernist formulas of urban planning from the past century and challenges it to find new ways of integrating land development with sustainability. This is not a simple task, however, and practical guidelines on planning for sustainable urban development are still being developed. This chapter seeks to outline some of these new approaches. In the remaining part of the current section, the green and brown agendas are defined, showing how they need to be integrated at the city level. This is followed by a presentation of eight global trends in planning for sustainable urban development, highlighting recent innovations in bridging the green and brown agendas in cities all over the world. Finally, the chapter highlights some of the approaches that are necessary for integrating these innovations within urban planning and governance, drawing from recent practices that appear to be working.

The green and brown agendas

A significant practical dilemma that faces planners – as well as other urban professionals and politicians – when they try to implement sustainable urban development is how to integrate the two different sets of concerns of the 'green agenda' and the 'brown agenda' (i.e. the natural environment and the human environment; see Table 6.1).

The green agenda is about the natural systems of the local, bioregional and global ecosystem, which are used by cities and other settlements as services for open space, biodiversity, water provision, waste dispersion, healthy air, and reliable climate, food and fibre. These services were outlined in detail in the global Millennium Ecosystem Assessment and were shown to be in decline in most parts of the world (see Box 6.1).

One of the aims of urban planning is to ensure that the green agenda is managed effectively, as green functions in a city are not always provided through the market mechanism. However, they are often seen as non-essential – even water, food and fibre can be brought in from long distances, rather than from the local bioregion, and the green spaces and waste absorption systems are often traded off for other urban functions. The changes that have been made to ecosystems have contributed to substantial net gains in human well-being and economic development. Since 1960, while the world's population has doubled and economic activity increased sixfold, food production has increased 2.5 times, food prices have declined, water use doubled, wood harvest for pulp tripled, and hydropower doubled.[6] But these gains have been achieved at growing ecological costs which, unless addressed, will substantially diminish the benefits that future generations obtain from ecosystems.

The rapid growth of cities in the past 50 years has meant that managing the built (or human environment) while coping with environmental pollution and degradation has overwhelmed many cities, especially in the developing world. Box 6.2 sets out some facts about the brown agenda in cities.

The brown agenda is essential for making a city work, for a healthy and liveable environment, and for creating the human and economic opportunities that have driven cities throughout their history. All cities consume land and resources such as energy, water and materials, which they use for buildings and transport. In the process of making a city functional, these resources are turned into wastes. It is now possible to quantify this impact in one parameter called *ecological footprint*.[7] The brown functions of a city generally consume and degrade its green resources and processes, respectively, unless the city intervenes through processes such as urban planning and environmental management.

The brown agenda depends upon how the metabolism of the city is managed (i.e. how the throughput of resources into wastes is managed). Thus, the brown agenda is about the optimization of land use, engineering of waste systems, the minimizing of energy consumption and transport, the reduction in use of materials, and the creation of an efficient built environment. These systems have always been provided in cities using an increasing ecological footprint. In other words, the brown agenda has always tended to assume the green agenda, to consume it and to dominate it. Since this is no longer feasible, cities need to reduce their impact upon the natural environment locally, ensure that bioregional ecosystems are not degraded and that the global ecosystem is not damaged by climate change.

The green natural systems of a city have real limits and capacity issues associated with their use. The challenge for urban planning is to find ways that cities can integrate these two agendas – to respect the natural environment and to improve the human environment, at the same time.

The goal of sustainable urban development is to reduce the impact of consumption of natural systems (global, regional and local) by the city, thus keeping within natural limits, while simultaneously enabling human systems to be optimized for improving the quality of urban life. Thus, sustainable urban development must integrate the green and brown agendas – improving the human environment while reducing the impact of natural resource use and improving the natural environment of the city.

Ensuring that natural systems are part of the way in which cities function and are not engulfed by the city has been a part of the challenge of cities from their very beginning.[8] Separating clean water for drinking and recreation from wastewater was a very early insight and most ancient cities had systems in place to do this. However, it was the rise of industrial cities that brought the green and brown conflict to a head, as industrial metabolism consumed land and water, and spewed much larger amounts of waste into the environment. Cities rapidly grew and their ecological footprint grew faster. Limits to the capacity of air and water to absorb these wastes were quickly reached. Two professions emerged in response: first, *sanitary engineering* (now called environmental engineering), which was able to develop sewerage systems, storm water systems, air pollution control systems and solid waste disposal systems; and, second, *town planning*, which was able to show how land-use planning could help to site industry away from housing

---

Box 6.2 The brown agenda in cities: Some facts

- In cities of the developing world, one out of four households lives in poverty; 40 per cent in African cities.
- 25 to 50 per cent of people in developing cities live in informal settlements.
- Fewer than 35 per cent of cities in the developing world have their wastewater treated; 2.5 billion people have no sanitation and 1.2 billion do not have access to clean water.
- Half of the urban population in Africa, Asia, Latin America and the Caribbean suffer from one or more diseases associated with inadequate water and sanitation.
- Between one third and one half of the solid waste generated within most cities in low- and middle-income countries is not collected.
- Less than half of the cities of the world have urban environmental plans.
- Millennium Development Goals aim to halve the proportion of people without sanitation and clean water by 2015 and significantly improve the lives of at least 100 million slum dwellers by 2020.

Sources: UNEP, 2002; UN-Habitat, 2008b

---

and which could set aside clear areas of natural systems to be part of city life.

Today, the green agenda has developed in several ways. First, it has become a global and regional agenda and not just a local one, as it was with the emergence of the first industrial cities. The metabolism of cities is such that global systems of climate and air are being adversely affected and global governance has now set limits to how much carbon can be expelled into it.[9] Global biodiversity limits are also now being addressed through mechanisms such as the Millennium Ecosystem Assessment. Similarly, limits are being set on a regional basis for issues such as open space, quality of water from rivers that feed cities along their water sheds, and for air quality in the air sheds of city-regions that are reaching limits from smog and particulates.

Second, the green agenda for ecological health – in terms of biodiversity and management of natural ecosystems – has shifted from addressing the means through which cities can reduce their impact to addressing the issue of how cities can enhance their natural environments and be part of the solution to biodiversity. This is difficult in many developing cities, but is now becoming feasible in the developed world.

The following section examines the interaction between the green and brown agendas by identifying and discussing the main innovations that are occurring all over the world in order to synergise the green and brown agendas.

INNOVATIONS IN ACHIEVING GREEN AND BROWN SYNERGIES: GLOBAL TRENDS

Globally, eight major trends in the integration of the green and brown agendas in cities are identifiable. These focus on:

1. developing renewable energy;
2. striving for carbon-neutral cities;

The brown functions of a city generally consume and degrade its green resources

Box 6.3 Renewable city models for the future

Dongtan is a new Chinese city near Shanghai which is designed to use 100 per cent renewable energy in its buildings. It will also be self-sufficient in water and food sourced from the surrounding farmland, and will feature a zero-carbon public transport system powered entirely by renewable energy. What happens to cars in the city is not yet clear. Energy plants will burn rice husks, normally just waste, near the city centre and the energy will be generated on a decentralized model, using combined heat and power.

Masdar City in the United Arab Emirates is an important first example of a city built from scratch with 100 per cent renewable energy and zero car use (in theory). It is being built with a 60MW solar photovoltaic plant to power all construction, and eventually a 130MW solar photovoltaic plant for ongoing power, as well as a 20MW wind farm and geothermal heat pumps for cooling buildings. Electric automatic pod cars on an elevated structure will be the basis of the transport.

North Port Quay in Western Australia will be home to 10,000 households and is designed to be 100 per cent renewable through solar photovoltaic small wind turbines called wind pods and a nearby wave power system. The development will be dense and walkable, with an all-electric transport system featuring electric public and private transport, linked to renewable power through battery storage in vehicles.

Source: Went et al, 2008; Newman et al, 2009

3   developing distributed power and water systems;
4   increasing photosynthetic spaces as part of green infrastructure;
5   improving eco-efficiency;
6   increasing a sense of place;
7   developing sustainable transport; and
8   developing 'cities without slums'.

These trends, some of which are quite innovative, are obviously overlapping in their approaches and outcomes; but each provides a perspective on how attempts to simultaneously improve the natural ecological base of cities and the human or built environment have been made.

While no one city has shown innovation in all eight areas, some are quite advanced in one or two. The challenge for urban planners is to apply all of these approaches together in order to generate a sense of purpose through a combination of new technology, city design and community-based innovation.

Development of renewable energy

There are now a number of urban areas that are partly powered by renewable energy techniques and technologies, from the region to the building level. Renewable energy enables a city to reduce its ecological footprint and, if using biological fuels, can be part of a city's enhanced ecological functions.

Renewable energy production can and should occur within cities, integrated within their land use and built form, and comprising a significant and important element of the urban economy. Cities are not simply consumers of energy, but catalysts for more sustainable energy paths, and can increasingly become a part of the Earth's solar cycle.

While some solar city projects, such as those in Box 6.3, are under way (including Treasure Island in San Francisco), there are currently no major cities in the world

that are powered entirely by renewable energy. Movement towards a renewable energy future will require much greater commitment from cities themselves at all levels, including at the local and the metropolitan levels.

Urban planning is necessary to create the infrastructure needed to support solar and wind power at the scale required to help power a city. While finding locations for large wind farms near urban areas has been controversial (such as the wind farm proposal that was defeated off the coast of Cape Cod, Massachusetts, US), there are significant opportunities to harness solar and wind power. Studies are now also showing that wind (like photovoltaic solar) power can be integrated within cities and their buildings. A study at Stanford University examined the potential for wind power in regions and in cities globally. The study concluded that 'wind, for low-cost wind energy, is more widely available than was previously recognized'.[10]

Hydropower has also been used in cities such as Vancouver (Canada) and Christchurch (New Zealand) for decades. Hydropower is growing slowly due to the impact of large dams, but geothermal power appears to be offering a similar level of base-load renewable power.

New model cities that are 100 per cent renewable are needed, but retrofitting existing cities is just as important. For example, Cape Town (South Africa) has an Integrated Metropolitan Environmental Policy, which has an energy strategy designed to put the city in the lead 'in meeting energy needs in a sustainable way, where everyone has access to affordable and healthy energy services, where energy is used efficiently, and where transport is efficient, equitable and emphasizes public transport and compact planning'. This integration of the green and brown agendas includes 10 per cent of the energy supply coming from renewable sources by 2020. Another example is Adelaide, which has gone from 0 to 20 per cent renewable energy in ten years by building four large wind farms.[11]

The shift in the direction to the renewable city can occur through many actions: demonstration solar or low-energy homes created to show architects, developers and citizens that green can be appealing; procurement actions that source regionally produced wind and other renewable energy to power municipal lights and buildings; and green building standards and requirements for all new public as well as private buildings.

Few cities have been as active in seeking and nurturing a reputation as a solar city as Freiburg (Germany). Known to many as the 'ecological capital of Europe', Freiburg has adopted an impressive and wide-ranging set of environmental planning and sustainability initiatives, many focused on renewable energy, as shown in Box 6.4.

The City of Adelaide, in the State of South Australia, also envisions itself as a renewable city as part of its larger green city initiative. It has designated solar precincts for the installation of photovoltaic panels on the rooftops of buildings, including the Parliament House. There is a solar schools initiative, with a target of 250 solar schools with solar rooftop installations and educational curricula that incorporate solar and renewable energy issues. This idea has since been taken up by the Australian federal government to be

Movement towards a renewable energy future will require much greater commitment from cities

applied to every school in the country. Most creatively, the city has been installing grid-connected photovoltaic street lamps that produce some six times the energy needed for the lighting. These new lights are designed in a distinctive shape of a local mallee tree. This is one of the few examples of solar art or solar 'place' projects.

Along with incentives (financial and otherwise), solar cities recognize the need to set minimum regulatory standards. Barcelona has a solar ordinance, which requires new buildings, and substantial retrofits of existing buildings to obtain a minimum of 60 per cent of hot water needs from solar. This has already led to a significant growth of solar thermal installations in that city.

Transport can also be a major part of the renewables challenge. For example, the more public transport moves to electric power, the more it can be part of a renewable city. Calgary Transit's creative initiative called Ride the Wind provides all the power needed for its light rail system from wind turbines in the south of Alberta (Canada). Private transport can now also be part of this transition through a combination of electric vehicles and new battery storage technology, together called Renewable Transport.[12] Not only can electric vehicles use renewable electricity to power their propulsion, they can also be plugged in during the day and run on their batteries, as their power systems store four times their consumption. They can thus play a critical role in enabling renewables to build up as a much higher proportion of the urban energy grid. However, this breakthrough in technology will need to be carefully examined to ensure that cities use it to be fully sustainable and not justify further urban sprawl.

Renewable power enables cities to create healthy and liveable environments while minimizing the use and impact of fossil fuels. But, by itself, this will not be enough to ensure sustainable urban development.

Striving for carbon-neutral cities

The key objective of the trend towards 'carbon-neutral' cities is to ensure that every home, neighbourhood and business is carbon neutral. Carbon-neutral cities are able to reduce their ecological footprint through energy efficiency and by replacing fossil fuels, thus providing a basis for ecological regeneration by creating offsets in the bioregion.

In 2007, the head of News Corporation, one of the biggest media empires in the world, announced that his company would be going carbon neutral. This led to some remarkable innovations within the company as it confronted the totally new territory of becoming a global leader in energy efficiency, renewable energy and carbon offsets.[13] Many more businesses, universities and households are now committing to minimizing their carbon footprint and even becoming carbon neutral. But can it become a feature of whole neighbourhoods and even complete cities? There are those who suggest it is essential if the world is to move to 'post-carbon cities'.[14] Carbon neutrality can become the goal for all urban development but will require a three-step process:

1 reducing energy use wherever possible – especially in the building and transportation sectors;
2 adding as much renewable energy as possible, while being careful that the production of the renewable energy is not contributing significantly to greenhouse gases; and
3 offsetting any CO_2 emitted through purchasing carbon credits, particularly through tree planting.

There are a number of initiatives that focus on helping cities to reach these goals, including the International Council for Local Environmental Initiatives (ICLEI)-Local Governments for Sustainability's Cities for Climate Change, Architecture 2030, The Clinton Foundation's C-40 Climate Change Initiative, and UN-Habitat's Cities for Climate Change Initiative (CCCI). And as mentioned in the previous section, many municipalities have started to offer incentives and/or require that new buildings meet certain green building standards. Minimizing carbon at the building level has momentum as it is easier to integrate the technology within new buildings, and the benefits have been proven – not just in energy savings, but in increased productivity and fewer sick days in green office buildings.

In Sydney (Australia), the State of New South Wales, through its Building and Sustainability Index programme, has mandated that new homes must now be designed to produce 40 per cent fewer greenhouse gas emissions, compared with an existing house (after initially requiring 20 per cent and finding it was relatively easy to achieve), as well as 40 per cent less water use. The programme aims at reducing CO_2 emissions by 8 million tonnes and water use by 287 billion litres in ten years.[15]

Zero-energy buildings and homes go well beyond what is required by any green building rating system. These have been built in The Netherlands, Denmark and Germany for at least ten years, and there are now increasingly positive examples in every region of the world. The UK government has decided that all urban development will be carbon

Carbon neutral cities are able to reduce their ecological footprint neutral by 2016, with phasing in from 2009. The Beddington Zero Energy Development initiative is the first carbon-neutral community in the UK. It has extended the concept to include building materials and, as it is a social housing development, it has shown how to integrate the green and brown agendas. In Sweden, the city of Malmö has stated that it has already become a carbon-neutral city, and Växjä has declared its intention to become a fossil fuel-free city. Other cities that also aspire to be carbon neutral include Newcastle in the UK and Adelaide in Australia. Each has taken important steps in the direction of renewable energy.

By committing to be carbon neutral, cities can focus their offsets into bioregional tree planting as part of the agenda for biodiversity as well as climate change. Preserving and planting trees helps to sequester carbon that is emitted. In all Australian cities, for instance, the carbon and green-house gas emissions associated with many municipal motor pools are being offset through innovative tree-planting initiatives and through organizations such as Green Fleet, which has recently planted its 2 millionth tree. The carbon offsetting is accredited through a federal government scheme called Greenhouse Friendly and provides a strong legal backing to ensure that tree planting is real, related to the money committed and guaranteed for at least 70 years, as required by the Kyoto Convention. Many of the carbon-offsetting programmes are going towards biodiversity plantations that are regenerating a bioregional ecology around cities.

Tree cover also helps to naturally cool buildings and homes and can reduce the use of energy for artificial cooling. An example of an urban initiative to provide greater tree coverage is the tree planting programme at the Sacramento Municipal Utility District in the US State of California. The programme has been actively promoting tree planting as a way of reducing energy consumption, and effectively addressing the urban heat island problem. Since 1990, the programme, which provides residents with free shade trees, has resulted in the planting of some 350,000 trees.[16]

All of these are good programmes; but none are committed yet to a comprehensive city-wide carbon-neutral approach that can link tree planting to a broader biodiversity cause. If this is done, cities can raise urban and bioregional reforestation to a new level and contribute to reducing the impact of climate change, simultaneously addressing local and regional green agenda issues.

Distributed power and water systems

The development of distributed power and water systems aims to achieve a shift from large centralized power and water systems to small-scale and neighbourhood-based systems within cities, including expansion of the notion of 'green infrastructure'. The distributed use of power and water can enable a city to reduce its ecological footprint, as power and water can be more efficiently provided using the benefits of electronic control systems; particularly through water-sensitive urban design, a city can improve its green character.

In large cities, the traditional engineering approach to providing energy has been through large centralized produc-

tion facilities and extensive distribution systems that transport power relatively long distances. This is wasteful because of line losses, but also because large base-load power systems cannot be turned on and off easily, so there is considerable power shedding when the load does not meet the need.

Most power and water systems for cities over the past 100 years have continued to become bigger and more centralized. While newer forms of power and water are increasingly smaller scale, they are often still fitted into cities as though they were large. The movement that tries to see how these new technologies can be fitted into cities and decentralized across grids is called 'distributed power and distributed water systems'.[17]

The distributed water system approach is called 'water sensitive urban design'. It includes using the complete water cycle (i.e. using rain and local water sources such as groundwater to feed into the system and then to recycle 'grey' water locally and 'black' water regionally, thus ensuring that there are significant reductions in water used). This system can enable the green agenda to become central to the infrastructure management of a city, as storm water recycling can involve swales and artificial wetlands that can become important habitats in the city. Grey water recycling can similarly be used to irrigate green parks and gardens, and regional black water recycling can be tied into regional ecosystems. All of these initiatives require 'smart' control systems to fit them into a city grid and also require new skills among town planners and engineers, who are so far used to water management being a centralized function rather than being a local planning issue.[18]

Decentralized energy production systems offer a number of benefits, including energy savings, given the ability to better control power production, lessen vulnerability and achieve greater resilience in the face of natural and human-made disaster (including terrorist attacks). Clever integration of these small systems within a grid can be achieved with new technology control systems that balance the whole system as demand and supply fluctuates. A number of such small-scale energy systems are being developed to make cities more resilient in the future.[19]

There are now numerous cities that are able to demonstrate small-scale local water systems that are very effective.[20] The many developing country cities that already have distributed water supplies from community boreholes and small-scale sewage treatment can look to a number of cases where these have been made safe and effective without being turned into expensive centralized systems. For instance, Hanoi, the capital of Viet Nam, has a major system of wastewater reuse involving agriculture and aquaculture in the low-lying Tranh Tri district to the south of the city. Produce from the reuse system provides a significant part of the diet of the city's residents.[21]

The use of waste in a food production system must always be sensitive to public health requirements. Traditionally, wastewater has been gathered around cities and reused only after sufficient time has elapsed for human contaminants to be naturally removed. The use of the bioregion for waste treatment was feasible as its capacity to

Preserving and planting trees helps to sequester carbon that is emitted

Providing energy ... through large centralized production facilities ... is wasteful

---

Box 6.5 Urban sewage recycling in Calcutta, India

The largest single wastewater-fed aquaculture system in the world lies to the east of Calcutta, in West Bengal, India, in an area locally called the East Calcutta Wetlands. The wastewater-fed fish ponds currently occupy an area of about 2500ha, although they extended over an area of 8000ha up to the late 1950s. They are located in a 12,000ha waste recycling region for Calcutta City, which also includes cultivation of vegetables on wastewater and garbage, and paddy fields irrigated with fish pond effluent (see Figure 6.1). The wastewater-fed fish ponds have been developed by farmers who have, over the past 60 years, learned by experience how to regulate the intake of raw sewage into ponds to culture fish.

The area of wastewater-fed ponds has declined over the past 30 years, mainly due to urban expansion. Currently they provide employment for 17,000 poor fishermen and produce 20 tonnes of fish daily. Much of the harvest comprises fish less than 250g, which are purchased by poor urban consumers. The ponds provide a low-cost, natural wastewater treatment and reuse system for a city that lacks conventional wastewater treatment plants as well as providing fish food. The area of low-lying fish ponds also provides storm water drainage and a green area or lung for the city.

An important feature of the integrated wetland system is the participation of stakeholders: the Calcutta Metropolitan Water and Sanitation Authority, the local village authority, the fish farmers who lease the ponds, and the rice-farming households are all involved in the project. Agenda 21, the international plan of action which guides global, national and local action on human impacts upon the environment, emphasizes the need to institutionalize the participation of stakeholders in environmental improvement projects to achieve decentralized decision-making and management, in this case empowering a rural community for wastewater treatment and reuse. Another crucial feature is the successful implementation of a revenue-generating procedure that should ensure adequate management of the system.

Source: Newman and Jennings, 2008

Figure 6.1

The waste reuse agro-ecosystem of the East Calcutta Wetlands, India

Source: Newman and Jennings, 2008

---

treat was not exceeded. As cities have grown, the increase in waste has far outstripped natural treatment capacities. Thus, cities everywhere have to find ways of treating waste as well as reusing it. Approaches that can use new technology to totally remove waste are now feasible; but a distributed approach would try to use waste as much as possible in the bioregion for agricultural production, as in the East Calcutta Wetlands Project (see Box 6.5). Such approaches to water and waste require new technologies and management systems that integrate public health and environmental engineering with ecologically sound planning.[22]

Distributed power and water provision in cities needs community support. In Toronto a possible model similar to those outlined above in developing cities has been developed. Communities began forming 'buying-cooperatives' in which they pooled their buying power to negotiate special reduced prices from local photovoltaic companies that had offered an incentive to buy solar photovoltaic panels. This suggests the merits of combining bottom-up neighbourhood approaches with top-down incentives and encouragement. This support for small-scale distributed production – offered through what are commonly referred to as standard offer contracts (often referred to as 'feed-in tariffs' in Europe) – has been extremely successful in Europe, where they are now common. The same can be done with new technologies for water and waste, such as rainwater tanks and grey water recycling.

One other model example is the redevelopment of the Western Harbour in Malmö, Sweden. Here the goal was

to achieve distributed power and water systems from local sources. This urban district now has 100 per cent renewable power from rooftop solar panels and an innovative storm water management system that recycles water into green courtyards and green rooftops.[23] The project involves local government in the management and demonstrates that a clear plan helps to drive innovations in distributed systems.

Distributed infrastructure is beginning to be demonstrated in cities across the globe. Utilities will need to develop models with city planners of how they can carry out local energy and water planning through community-based approaches and local management.

Increasing photosynthetic spaces as part of green infrastructure

Growing energy and providing food and materials locally is becoming part of urban infrastructure development. The use of photosynthetic processes in cities reduces their ecological impact by replacing fossil fuels and can bring substantial ecological benefits through emphasis on natural systems.

There has been a positive trend in planning in the direction of an expanded notion of urban infrastructure that includes the idea of 'green infrastructure' based on photosynthetic processes. Green infrastructure refers to the many green and ecological features and systems, from wetlands to urban forests, which provide a host of benefits to cities and urban residents – clean water, storm water collection and management, climate moderation and cleansing of urban air,

Growing energy and providing food and materials locally ... can bring substantial ecological benefits

Box 6.6 Energy costs of food production in the US

The high energy costs of food production are vividly illustrated in the case of the US. It takes around 10 fossil fuel calories to produce each food calorie in the average American diet. So if an individual's daily food intake is 2000 calories, it takes around 20,000 calories to grow the food and get it to the person. This means that growing, processing and delivering food consumed by a family of four each year requires the equivalent of almost 34,000 kilowatt hours (kWh) of energy, or more than 3520 litres of gasoline. For comparison, the average US household annually consumes about 10,800kWh of electricity, or about 4050 litres of gasoline. Thus, as much energy is used in the US to grow food as to power homes or fuel cars.

Source: Starrs, 2005

among others. This understanding of green infrastructure as part of the working landscape of cities and metropolitan areas has been extended to include the photosynthetic sources of renewable energy, local food and fibre.

Renewable energy can be tapped from the sun and wind and geothermal sources using small-scale decentralized technology, as described in the previous section. However, renewable energy can also be grown through biofuels. The transition to growing fuels draws on crops and forests that can feed into new ways of fuelling buildings and vehicles. Farms and open areas around cities are being developed as sources of renewable energy, especially the production of biofuels. However, biofuels are also being produced as part of improving the urban environment. This means more intensive greening of the lower density parts of cities and their peri-urban regions with intensive food growing, renewable energy crops and forests, but greening the high-density parts of cities as well.

The city of Växjä in Sweden provides an example of a locally based renewable energy strategy that takes full advantage of its working landscapes, in this case the abundant forests that exist within close proximity of the city. Växjä's main power plant, formerly fuelled by oil, now depends upon biomass almost entirely from wood chips, most of which are a by-product of the commercial logging in the region. The wood, more specifically, comes from the branches, bark and tops of trees, and is derived from within a 100km radius of the power plant. The power plant provides the entire town's heating needs and much of its electricity needs. Its conversion to using biomass as a fuel has been a key element in the city's aspiration to become an oil-free city. Clearly, each city can develop its own mix of local renewable sources; but Växjä has demonstrated that it can transition from an oil-based power system to a completely renewable system without losing its economic edge. Indeed, cities that develop such resilience early are likely to have an edge as oil resources decline.

One of the most important potential biofuel sources of the future will be blue-green algae that can be grown intensively on rooftops. Blue-green algae can photosynthesize so all that it requires is sunlight, water and nutrients. The output from blue-green algae is ten times faster than most other biomass sources, so it can be continuously cropped and fed into a process for producing biofuels or small-scale electricity. Most importantly, city buildings can all utilize their roofs to tap solar energy and use it for local

Renewable energy can be tapped from the sun and wind and geothermal sources using small-scale decentralized technology

purposes without the distribution or transport losses so apparent in most cities today. A green roof for biodiversity purposes, water collection, photovoltaic collectors or biofuel algal collectors can possibly become a solar ordinance set by town planners as part of local government policy.

Few cities have done much to take stock of their photosynthetic energy potential. Municipal comprehensive plans typically document and describe a host of natural and economic resources found within the boundaries of a city – from mineral sites, through historic buildings, to biodiversity; but estimating incoming renewable energy (sun, wind, wave, biomass or geothermal) is usually not included. In advancing the renewable energy agenda in Barcelona, the city took the interesting step of calculating incoming solar gain. As a former sustainable city counsellor noted, this amounted to '10 times more than the energy the city consumes or 28 times more than the electricity the city is consuming'.[24] The issue is how to tap into this across the city.

As well as renewable fuel, cities can incorporate food in this more holistic solar and post-oil view of the future. Food, in the globalized marketplace, increasingly travels great distances – apples from New Zealand, grapes from Chile, wine from South Australia, vegetables from China. 'Food miles' are rising everywhere and already food in the US travels a distance of between 2400km and 4000km from where it is grown to where it is consumed. Any exotic sources of food come at a high energy cost. The growing, processing and delivering of food in the US consumes vast amounts of energy on par with the energy required to power homes or fuel cars, as shown in Box 6.6.

There are now good examples of new neighbourhoods and development projects that design in, from the beginning, spaces for community gardens that attempt to satisfy a considerable portion of food needs on site or nearby. Growing food within cities and urban (and suburban) environments can take any number of forms. Community gardens, urban farms and edible landscaping are all promising urban options.[25] Prominent and compelling examples of edible urban landscaping have shown that it is possible to trade hard-scape environments for fruit trees and edible perennials. In the downtown Vancouver neighbourhood of Mole Hill, for instance, a conventional alleyway has been converted to a green and luxurious network of edible plants and raised-bed gardens, in a pedestrianized community space, where the occasional automobile now seems out of place. New urban development can include places (rooftops, side yards and backyards) where residents can directly grow food. This has been a trend in developed cities as new urban ecological neighbourhoods have included community gardens as a central design element (e.g. Viikki in Helsinki, Finland; South False Creek in Vancouver, Canada; Troy Gardens in Madison, US), but is perhaps most famous in Cuban cities over the past few decades in response to being cut off from oil imports (see Box 6.7). Urban agriculture is also widespread in other developing country cities, where it provides food and incomes for many poor households.

Cities need to find creative ways to promote urban farming where it is feasible, without creating tension with redevelopment for reduced car dependence through increased density. This may mean that a city can utilize the many vacant lots for commercial and community farms in areas that have been blighted (e.g. the estimated 70,000 vacant lots in Chicago, US). However, if these areas are well served with good transit and other infrastructure, then such uses should be seen as temporary and, indeed, can be part of the rehabilitation of an area, leading to the development of eco-villages that are car free and models of solar building. Many cities have embarked on some form of effort to examine community food security and to promote more sustainable local and regional food production. These can be integrated within ecologically sustainable urban and regional rehabilitation projects[26] and can utilize the intensive possibilities of urban spaces, as in urban permaculture.

Progress in moving away from fossil fuels also requires serious localizing and local sourcing of building materials. This, in turn, provides new opportunities to build more photosynthetic economies. The value of emphasizing the local is many-fold and the essential benefits are usually clear. Dramatic reductions in the energy consumed as part of making these materials is, of course, the primary benefit. It is also about strengthening local economies and helping them to become more resilient in the face of global economic forces, and it is also about reforming lost connections to place.

Improving eco-efficiency

In an effort to improve eco-efficiency, cities and regions are moving from linear to circular or closed-loop systems, where substantial amounts of their energy and material needs are provided from waste streams. Eco-efficient cities reduce their ecological footprint by reducing wastes and resource requirements, and can also incorporate green agenda issues within the process.

A more integrated notion of energy and water entails seeing cities as complex metabolic systems (not unlike a human body) with flows and cycles and where, ideally, outputs traditionally viewed as negative (e.g. solid waste and wastewater) are re-envisioned as productive inputs to satisfy other urban needs, including energy. The sustainability movement has been advocating for some time for this shift away from the current view of cities as linear resource-extracting machines. This is often described as the eco-efficiency agenda.[27]

The urban eco-efficiency agenda includes the 'cradle to cradle' concept for the design of all new products and new systems such as industrial ecology, where industries share resources and wastes like an ecosystem.[28] Innovative examples exist in Kalundborg (Germany) and Kwinana (Australia).[29]

The agenda has been taken up by the United Nations and the World Business Council on Sustainable Development, with a high target for industrialized countries of a tenfold reduction in consumption of resources by 2040, along with rapid transfers of knowledge and technology to developing countries. While this eco-efficiency agenda is a huge challenge, it is important to remember that throughout

Box 6.7 Urban food production in Havana, Cuba

After the collapse of the USSR during the late 1980s, Cuba lost Soviet aid, which had provided the country with modern agricultural chemicals. Thus 1.3 million tonnes of chemical fertilizers, 17,000 tonnes of herbicides and 10,000 tonnes of pesticides could no longer be imported. Urban agriculture was one of Cuba's responses to the shock, intensifying the previously established National Food Programme, which aimed at taking thousands of poorly utilized areas – mainly around Havana – and converting them into intensive vegetable gardens. Planting in the city instead of only in the countryside decreased the need for transportation, refrigeration and other scarce resources.

By 1998, over 8000 urban farms and community gardens had been established, run by over 30,000 people in and around Havana.

Today, food from the urban farms is grown almost completely with active organic methods. Havana has banned the use of chemical pesticides in agriculture within city boundaries.

Urban agriculture now taps into a significant part of the photosynthetic resource of the city; thus, the green agenda is advanced through the brown agenda of the city synergistically.

Source: Murphy, 1999

the Industrial Revolution of the past 200 years, human productivity has increased by 20,000 per cent. The next wave of innovation has a lot of potential to create the kind of eco-efficiency gains that are required.[30]

The view of cities as a complex set of metabolic flows might also help to guide cities that rely to a large extent on resources and energy from other regions and parts of the world. Relevant policies can include sustainable sourcing agreements, region-to-region trade agreements, and urban procurement systems based on green certification systems, among others. Embracing a metabolic view of cities and metropolitan areas takes global governance in some interesting and potentially very useful directions.

This new paradigm of sustainable urban metabolism requires profound changes in the way in which cities and metropolitan regions are conceptualized, as well as in the ways they are planned and managed. New forms of cooperation and collaboration between municipal agencies and various urban actors and stakeholder groups will be required. Municipal departments will need to formulate and implement integrated resource flow strategies. New organizational and governance structures will be necessary, as well as new planning tools and methods. For example, municipal authorities that map the resource flows of their city and region will need to see how this new data can be part of a comprehensive plan for integrating the green and brown agendas.

Toronto, for instance, has a trash-to-can programme, which allows the city to capture methane from waste to generate electricity. This not only reuses waste and provides an inexpensive energy source, but captures a significant amount of methane that would otherwise be released into the air. Before it reached capacity in its operation, it is estimated that Toronto's Keele Valley Landfill generated Cdn$3 million to Cdn$4 million annually, and provided enough power for approximately 24,000 homes.[31]

One extremely powerful example of how this eco-efficiency is able to shape urban design and building can be seen in the new dense urban neighbourhood of Hammarby

Cities and regions are moving from linear to circular systems ... where ... their energy and material needs are provided from waste streams

---

Box 6.8 Informal solid waste recycling in Cairo, Egypt

The problems surrounding solid waste management are common to all cities; but some of the solutions in Cairo are quite particular. For over half a century, Cairo has hosted traditional garbage-collecting communities called the Zabaleen. These communities collect trash throughout the city and have created what could arguably be one of the world's most efficient resource recovery and waste recycling systems. With their roots based in agriculture, the Zabaleen use the collected waste to generate income by selling sorted secondary material (paper, plastic, rags, glass, etc.) and using organic waste as pig fodder. It was estimated in 1997 that the Zabaleen collected 3000 tonnes of garbage every day, which is about one third of the total rubbish produced by Cairo's 14 million inhabitants. Almost 85 per cent of this waste was successfully recycled and used by artisans or for agricultural purposes, which is significantly higher than any industrialized waste collecting system. Yet, despite the incredible efficiency, many of the practices of the Zabaleen are considered environmentally unsound and the mixed use of the spaces in the communities is thought to be a threat to the health of their inhabitants.

In recent years, the city of Cairo has begun contracting large international waste management companies in an effort to upgrade its organization and technical standards and meet the needs of its ever-increasing population. Indeed, the need for regulation is felt when the municipal solid waste collection efficiency ranges anywhere from 10 per cent to 90 per cent. The aim of this system was to provide a uniform collecting system that would dispose of the garbage into designated landfills according to standardized procedures that would limit health and environmental hazards. Because these systems are technology based, however, effective processing, recycling and disposing of waste depend upon efficient management and training programmes, which often do not meet required performance standards. This privatization of waste collection has also caused a series of negative repercussions, manifested through public resistance to the new system and measures taken to implement it. Many prefer the informal methods used by the Zabaleen, and the linkage of the rubbish-collecting fees to the electricity bill has been the source of much complaint and resistance. The rubbish-collecting communities are threatened by the competition in a variety of ways. Instead of replacing the traditional methods, a complementary approach could prove to be more adequate.

Collection methods aside, much progress has been made with respect to the cleaning-up of informal city dump sites and the construction of several sanitary dump sites for Cairo to replace existing public landfills and open informal landfills. In 2004 the Ministry of State for Environmental Affairs launched a plan for the removal of historic dump sites in the city; in 2005, 7.75 million cubic metres of rubbish were moved to designated landfills. The removal of the waste aims to prevent fire hazards, improve health standards, and alleviate visual and olfactory blight, while providing public open spaces, thus integrating the green and brown agendas.

Source: Duquennois and Newman, 2008

Eco-efficiency does not have to involve just new technology, but can also be introduced into cities through intensive use of human resources, as in Cairo's famous Zabaleen recycling system (see Box 6.8). There are many other examples of how cities across the developing world have integrated waste management within local industries, buildings and food production.[32]

Increasing sense of place

Cities and regions increasingly understand sustainability more generally as a way of developing their local economies, building onto a unique sense of place, and as a way of nurturing a high quality of life and a strong commitment to community. The more place oriented and locally self-sufficient a city's economy is, the more it will reduce its ecological footprint and ensure that its valuable ecological features are enhanced.

Local economic development has many advantages in the context of sustainable development, including the ability of people to travel less as their work becomes local. Finding ways to help facilitate local enterprises becomes a major achievement for cities in moving towards a reduced ecological footprint. For instance, initiatives designed to help small towns in the US to grow their own jobs have been developed.[33] An approach for creating local enterprises that builds on the passions and resources of the local community and supports local businesses in their early vulnerable steps has also been developed.[34] The inaugural Enterprise Facilitation project, which is designed to create local jobs, was pioneered in the small rural town of Esperance, Western Australia, in 1985, but has since spread across three continents. The success of this initiative is reflected in the words of its chair:

> *We are proud to say almost 800 businesses – or 60 per cent of the entrepreneurs – we met are still running successful, sustainable operations and have contributed more than AU$190 million in revenue to the local economy ... We have averaged almost 40 new business start-ups a year consistently in the last 20 years, which is quite a track record given Esperance has a population of just 13,500 people.[35]*

Pioneers of these initiatives have found, time and time again, that place really matters. When people have a sense of belonging and an identity in their town or city, they are keen to create local enterprises.

When communities relate strongly to the local environment, the city's heritage and its unique culture, they develop a strong social capital of networks and trust that forms the basis of a robust urban economy. As part of their local economic development priorities, many cities are placing increasing emphasis on local place identity, as social capital has been found to be one of the best ways to predict wealth in a community.[36] This approach to economic development, which emphasizes place-based social capital, has many supporters, but very few relate this to the sustainabil-

Sjöstad in Stockholm. From the beginning of the planning of this new district, an effort has been made to holistically understand the inputs, outputs and resources that would be required and that would result. For instance, about 1000 flats in Hammarby Sjöstad are equipped with stoves that utilize biogas extracted from wastewater generated in the community. Biogas also provides fuel for buses that serve the area. Organic waste from the community is returned to the neighbourhood in the form of district heating and cooling. There are many other important energy features in the design as well. The neighbourhood's close proximity to central Stockholm and the installation of a high-frequency light rail system have made it truly possible to live without a private automobile (there are also 30 car-sharing vehicles in the neighbourhood). While not a perfect example, it represents a new and valuable way of seeing cities, and requires a degree of interdisciplinary and inter-sectoral collaboration in planning systems that is unusual in most cities.

Local economic development has many advantages in the context of sustainable development

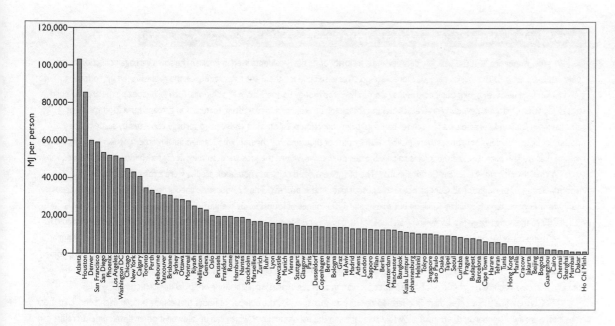

Figure 6.2

**Private passenger
transport energy use
per person in selected
cities, 1995**

Source: Kenworthy and Laube,
2001

ity agenda in cities. For example, energy expenditures – by municipalities, companies and individuals – represent a significant economic drain as they often leave the community and region. Producing power from solar, wind or biomass in the locality or region is very much an economic development strategy that can generate local jobs and economic revenue from land (farmland) that might otherwise be economically marginal, in the process recirculating money, with an important economic multiplier effect. Energy efficiency can also be an economic development strategy. For example, as noted above, research on renewable energy and the creation of related products have developed into a strong part of the economy in Freiburg (Germany).

Efforts at localizing energy, food, materials and economic development remain dependent upon the strength of the local community. A study that examined a range of European urban ecology innovations concluded that when the innovations came from a close and committed community, they became ingrained in people's lifestyles, giving the next generation a real opportunity to gain from them. However, many architect-designed innovations that were imposed on residents without their involvement tended to fall into neglect or were actively removed.[37]

Sense of place is about generating pride in the city about all aspects of the economy, the environment and the culture. It requires paying attention to people and community development in the process of change – a major part of the urban planning agenda for many decades. This localized approach will be critical to integrating the green and brown agendas. It creates the necessary innovations as people dialogue through options to reduce their ecological footprint, which in turn creates social capital that is the basis for ongoing community life and economic development.[38] City dwellers in many countries already increasingly want to know where their food is grown, where their wine comes from, where the materials that make up their furniture come from. This can move towards every element of the built environment. Thus, as well as a slow movement for local foods, a slow fibre and slow materials movement for local

fabric and building purposes can also help to create a sense of place and bring the green and brown agendas together.

City economies in the past had their own currencies and it has been argued that national currencies often fail to express the true value of a city and its bioregion.[39] Transforming urban economies towards a more bioregional focus has been assisted in some places by adopting complementary currencies that provide an alternative to national currencies and by establishing local financial institutions. It has been argued that a complementary local currency not only facilitates change, but also creates a community with a mutual interest in productive exchange among its members in the bioregion.[40] In this way, a community affirms its identity and creates a natural preference for its own products. Over 1000 communities around the world have issued their own local currencies to encourage local commerce. How this has been related to urban planning is set out in Box 6.9.

Many developed cities have created development bonuses similar to Curitiba's that are part of the non-monetary economy of the city. In contrast, cities in developing countries do not have much to invest in their public spaces; hence, the whole city economy suffers. Curitiba illustrates how cities could break that mould. Through the planning system, cities can create their own sustainability currencies for what they most need as determined by their local citizens – they just need to define them as 'development rights'. These new 'sustainable development rights' could be related to biodiversity credits, greenhouse reduction credits, salinity reduction credits, affordable housing credits or anything else that a community can create a 'market' for in their city and its bioregion.

Sustainable transport

Cities, neighbourhoods and regions are increasingly being designed to use energy sparingly by offering walkable transit-oriented options, often supplemented by vehicles powered by renewable energy. Cities with more sustainable transport systems have been able to reduce their ecological footprints

*Energy efficiency
can also be an
economic
development
strategy*

Box 6.9 Urban planning as 'complementary currency' in Curitiba, Brazil

Curitiba grew dramatically in the past few decades and a majority of its new residents lived in *favelas*. The town garbage collection trucks could not even get into the *favelas* because there were no streets suitable for them. As a consequence, the rubbish piled up, rodents got into it and all kinds of diseases broke out. Because they did not have the money to apply 'normal' solutions, such as bulldozing the area to build streets, Curitiba created a new currency: recyclables in garbage for bus tokens; biodegradable materials in garbage for a food parcel of seasonal fresh fruit and vegetables; and a school-based garbage collection programme also swapped garbage collected by students for notebooks. Soon the neighbourhoods were picked clean by tens of thousands of children, who learned quickly to distinguish even different types of plastic. The parents used the tokens to take the bus downtown, where the jobs were, so they were drawn into the formal economy.

What the city did was invent Curitiba money. The bus tokens, food chits and notebook credits were a form of complementary currency. Today, 70 per cent of all Curitiba households participate in this process. The 62 poorer neighbourhoods alone have exchanged 11,000 tonnes of garbage for nearly 1 million bus tokens and 1200 tonnes of food. During the past three years, more than 100 schools have traded 200 tonnes of garbage for 1.9 million notebooks. The paper recycling component alone saves the equivalent of 1200 trees each day.

Curitiba also has another complementary currency in its planning system that is commonly used by many cities, but is not thought of as a complementary currency. The system is called *sol criado* (literally, 'created surface') and it is similar to what many cities do by providing 'development or density bonuses', which are a form of money given whenever a developer does something that the local government wants but cannot always require (e.g. heritage restoration, conservation of green spaces, social housing or social infrastructure).

In Curitiba, like most cities, there is a detailed zoning plan that specifies the number of floors that can be built in each zone. Like most cities, there are two standards: the normal allowable standard and the maximum level, which can be allowed if other development credits can be given. For instance, a hotel with a ground plan of 10,000 square metres is being built in an area where the normal allowable level is 10 floors and the maximum 15. If the hotel owner wants to build 15 floors, he has to buy 50,000 square metres (five floors x 10,000 square metres) in the *sol criado* market. The city itself only plays the role of an intermediary matching demand with supply in that market. The supply for this *sol criado* currency is historical buildings based on another Curitiba currency. For instance, a beautiful historic landmark building called the Garibaldi House needed a serious restoration job. The club that owned it did not have the money to restore the building. But because it is located in an area where up to two floors of new construction could theoretically be built, it sold 50,000 square metres (two floors x 25,000 square metres) to the highest bidder for development rights. The proceeds belong to the club to administer, but have to be used to restore the property. Therefore, the hotel owner ends up paying for restoring the historic edifice in order to obtain the right to build the extra floors of the hotel, without financial intervention from the city.

Other sources of supply for such *sol criado* are green areas where trees are protected, and the construction of social housing in other parts of the town. Several of Curitiba's recent 16 extensive nature parks, open to the public, have been completely financed in this way. The owner of a large plot of land obtained the right to develop one side of the street on the condition that the other side became a public park. The new housing has an extra value because it is located at walking distance from the park; the people of Curitiba have another park for their weekend strolls; and the township does not have to go into debt or raise taxes to obtain all of that. Everybody wins when sustainability issues are made into a local currency.

Source: Newman and Jennings, 2008

To reduce a city's ecological footprint ... it is necessary to manage the growth of cars and trucks and their associated fossil fuel consumption

from their reduced use of fossil fuels, as well as through reduced urban sprawl and reduced dependence upon car-based infrastructure.

The agenda for large cities now is to have more sustainable transport options in order to reduce traffic while reducing greenhouse gases by 50 per cent by at least 2050, in line with the global agenda set through the Intergovernmental Panel on Climate Change (IPCC). For many cities, the reduction of car use is not yet on the agenda, apart from seeing it as an ideal to which they aspire. Unfortunately, for most cities, traffic growth has been continuous and appears to be unstoppable. To reduce a city's ecological footprint and enhance its liveability, it is necessary to manage the growth of cars and trucks and their associated fossil fuel consumption.

Figure 6.2, which shows the variations in private transport fuel use across 84 cities, illustrates that there is a very large difference in how cities use cars and petroleum fuels.[41] A number of studies have shown that these variations have little to do with climate, culture or politics, and even income is very poorly correlated; but they have a lot to do with the physical planning decisions that are made in those cities.[42] There is debate about the relative importance of urban planning parameters, although within the profession there is increasing awareness that sustainable transport will only happen if much greater attention is paid to urban form and density; infrastructure priorities, especially relative commitment to public transport compared to cars; and street planning, especially provision for pedestrians and cyclists as part of sustainable mobility management.

■ **Urban form and density planning**

The density of a city determines how close to urban activities most people can be. Very high-density city centres mean that most destinations can be reached with a short walk or they can have highly effective public transport opportunities due to the concentration of people near stations. If densities are generally lower, but higher along corridors, it is still feasible to have a good transit system. If, however, low densities are the dominant feature of a city, then most activity needs to be based around cars as they alone can enable people to reach their destinations in a reasonable time. Public transport finds it hard to be competitive as there are just not enough people to justify reasonable services. Most low-density cities are now trying to increase their densities in order to reduce their car dependence, as illustrated by the experience of Vancouver (Canada) described (see Box 6.10).

Density is a major tool available to planners in cities. It is best used where a city has good transit or wants to build transit, as the resulting transit-oriented developments (TODs) can reduce car use per capita among its residents by half and save households around 20 per cent of their income since they have, on average, one less car (and often none).[43] In the US, according to a 2007 study, shifting 60 per cent of new growth to compact patterns would reduce CO_2 emissions by 85 million metric tonnes annually by 2030.[44] TODs reduce ecological footprint in cities and undermine the kind of car-based sprawl that eats into the green agenda of cities. Thus, the TODs' strategy can enable a city to put in place a clear urban growth boundary and to build a green wall for agriculture, recreation, biodiversity and the other natural systems of the green agenda. Cairo's green belt is one attempt to do this.

If cities are dense, as in many developing countries, but do not have adequate public transport and allow too much traffic to develop in their streets, they can easily develop dysfunctional transport systems. However, their density will always enable them to provide viable public transport solutions if they invest in them, whereas low-density cities are always struggling to provide other options. High density means easier non-car-based access, but it can also mean much greater congestion whenever vehicles are used. If the vehicles in these confined spaces are poorly maintained diesel engines, then serious air pollution can result – so cities need to carefully manage the source of such emissions.

■ Infrastructure priorities and transit planning

The transit-to-traffic ratio measures how effective public transport is in competing with the car in terms of speed. A recent study has shown that the best European and Asian cities for transit have the highest ratio of transit-to-traffic speeds and have achieved this invariably with fast rail systems.[45] Rail systems are faster in every city in the study sample by 10 to 20 kilometres per hour over bus systems that rarely average over 20 to 25 kilometres per hour. Busways can be quicker than traffic in car-saturated cities; but in lower-density car-dependent cities, it is important to use the extra speed of rail to establish an advantage over cars in traffic. This is one of the key reasons why railways are being built in over 100 US cities, and, in many other cities, modern rail is now seen as the solution for reversing the proliferation of the private car. Rail is also important because it has a density-inducing effect around stations, which can help to provide the focused centres so critical to overcoming car dependence, and they are also electric, which reduces vulnerability to oil.

Many cities in the world are unable to make transit politics work effectively. While major US cities such as New York and Chicago are dense and walkable, and their mayors have been lauded for their green plans and for signing onto the Mayor's Climate Change Initiative, the mass transit

The population of the city of Vancouver, like many North American downtown areas, began declining in the 1970s and 1980s, but then began to turn around and has since grown by 135,000 people in the last 20 years. Strong leadership from the city council led the 'return to the city' initiative as the city established policies to help create quality urban spaces, good cycling and walking facilities, reliable transit (generally, electric rail and electric trolley buses) and, most of all, high-density residential opportunities with at least 15 per cent social housing (public and co-operative housing). So successful has this been that the transportation patterns in the city have been transformed. A survey between 1991 and 1994 showed that there was a decline in car trips in Vancouver of 31,000 vehicles per day (from 50 to 46 per cent of trips), while the amount of cycling and walking went up by a staggering 107,000 trips per day (from 15 to 22 per cent). In the central area, car trips went down from 35 to 31 per cent.

Vancouver has been creating a walking city and families are moving back into the city in droves so that schools, childcare centres and community centres are becoming crowded, while there are fewer cars owned in the city than five years ago – probably establishing this as a world first, especially in a city undergoing an economic boom. One of the critical policies that has helped to make this work is the 5 per cent social infrastructure policy, where the city requires public spaces and social facilities to be provided through each development equal to 5 per cent of the cost of the development. The walkability of the city is the main focus of this money. Vancouver has also redeveloped many of its station areas around the Sky Train with similar walking qualities and, apart from a recent mistake, has not allowed freeway development.

Source: Newman et al, 2009

systems of these cities continue to experience budget cuts. The city of Seattle, whose mayor is credited with initiating the US Mayor's Climate Change Initiative, has struggled to implement any type of rail system. While the State of California is a global leader on some state initiatives, it has not yet developed a plan for how its heavy oil-using cities will wean themselves off their cars.

Yet, across the world, cities are building modern electric rail systems at vastly increasing rates as they simultaneously address the challenges of fuel security, decarbonizing the economy in the context of addressing climate change, reducing traffic congestion sustainably and creating productive city centres. The trend towards fast electric rail in cities is now being called a 'mega trend'.[46] Chinese cities have moved from their road-building phase to building fast modern rail across the nation. China is committed to building 120,000km of new rail by 2020. Investment will rise from 155 billion yuan (US$22 billion) per year in 2006 to 1000 billion yuan per year by 2009 (US$143 billion), with around 6 million jobs involved. These projects are part of China's response to the recent global economic downturn.[47] Beijing now has the world's biggest metro. In India, Delhi is building a modern electric metro rail system, which has considerably boosted the city's pride and belief in the future. The 250km rail system is being built in various stages and will enable 60 per cent of the city to be within 15 minutes' walking distance of a station.[48]

In Perth, Australia, a 172km modern electric rail system has been built over the past 20 years, with stunning success in terms of patronage and the development of TODs; the newest section runs 80km to the south and has attracted 50,000 passengers a day, where the bus system carried just 14,000 a day – the difference is that the train has a top speed of 130 kilometres per hour and averages 90 kilometres per

Cities are building modern electric rail systems at vastly increasing rates

Box 6.11 Reclaiming public spaces through reducing car dependence in Paris, France

Paris, like many European cities, has a strong transit system and a walkable central area; but over recent decades it has lost a lot as it has given over more and more space to the car. Now, in a bid to reclaim its public spaces, it is implementing a series of policies to reduce the number of cars in the city, which include:

* creating a neighbourhood traffic calming programme to rival any city in the world;
* building 320km of dedicated bike lanes, along with the Velib Bike hire scheme in which bicycles are available every 300m throughout Paris;
* developing a new light rail transit (LRT) linking a dozen subway and express train lines as it goes around the city, providing cross-city linkages;
* setting aside 40km of dedicated bus-ways, or bus rapid transit (BRT), that enable buses to travel at twice their normal speed and with bus stops that have real time information;
* slowing down traffic on the 'red axes', which were once for one-way express traffic but will now be two-way 'slow ways', including cycle lanes and narrowed for the provision of more street trees;
* removing 55,000 on-street parking spaces every year;
* working towards a 'car free' oasis in the centre of Paris that includes all of the major iconic buildings and places; and
* planning to sink the Peripherique, the ring road freeway, and cover it with a huge park.

The mayor of Paris, who has swept Paris into the vanguard of best practice for greening urban transportation, says this makes good politics, as 80 per cent support has been found from Parisians for these innovations.

Source: Newman et al, 2009

hour, so the trip takes just 48 minutes instead of over an hour by car. London, especially with its congestion tax, which is recycled into the transit system, and Paris have both shown European leadership in managing the car (see Box 6.11).

While greening buildings, developing renewable fuel sources and creating more walkable communities are critical elements of the sustainable city, investing in viable, accessible transit systems is the most important component for them to become resilient to waning oil sources and to minimize the contribution of urban areas to climate change. Transit not just saves oil; it helps to restructure a city so that it can begin the exponential reduction in oil and car use so necessary for a sustainable future.

The opportunities for making major changes in a city if quality transit is a priority can be imagined; but their extent is often not seen to be more than a mere slowing of traffic growth. It has been shown that an exponential decline in car use in cities that could lead to 50 per cent less passenger kilometres driven in cars is possible.[49] The key mechanism is a quantitative leap in the quality of public transport, accompanied by an associated change in land-use patterns. This is due to a phenomenon called *transit leverage*, where 1 passenger kilometre of transit use replaces between 3 and 7 passenger kilometres in a car due to more direct travel (especially in trains), trip chaining (doing various other things, such as shopping or service visits associated with a commute), giving up one car in a household (a common occurrence that reduces many solo trips), and eventually changes in where people live as they prefer to live or work nearer transit.

Building freeways does not help either the brown agenda or the green agenda

■ Street planning and mobility management

If cities build freeways, car dependence quickly follows. This is because the extra speed of freeways means that the city can quickly spread outwards into lower-density land uses as the freeway rapidly becomes the preferred option. Building freeways does not help either the brown agenda or the green agenda. It will not help a city save fuel, as each lane rapidly fills, leading to similar levels of congestion that existed before the road was built.[50] Indeed, studies have shown that there is little benefit for cities when they build freeways, in terms of congestion, and as this is the main reason for building them, it does seem to be a waste. There is no overall correlation between delay per driver and the number of lanes of major roads built per head of population for the 20 biggest cities in the US.[51]

If, on the other hand, a city does not build freeways but prefers to emphasize transit, it can enable its streets to become an important part of the sustainable transport system. Streets can be designed to favour pedestrians and cyclists, and wherever this is done, cities invariably become surprised at how much more attractive and business friendly they become.[52]

Sustainable mobility management is about 'streets not roads' – the streets are used for a multiplicity of purposes, not just maximizing vehicle flow. The emphasis is on achieving efficiency by maximizing people movement, not car movement, and on achieving a high level of amenity and safety for all street users. This policy also picks up on the concept of integration of transport facilities as public space. One of the ways in which US and European cities are approaching this is through what are called 'complete streets', or, in the UK, 'naked streets'. This new movement aims to create streets where mobility is managed to favour public transport, walking and cycling, as well as lower speed traffic. The policy often includes removing all large signs for drivers, which means they automatically slow down: in Kensington High Road in London the traffic accident rate has halved because of this.

Gender needs to be considered in all stages of public transport planning, from design to implementation, in order to enable efficient mobility. In many developed countries, recognition of women as the main users of public transport and the multipurpose nature of their trips has led to some innovative design solutions. Stations and terminals in cities such as Tokyo (Japan) and Maryland (US) now contain grocery stores, childcare centres and improved public toilets. Changes to fare structures, such as discounts for women, families and elderly on off-peak services, have also allowed greater access to public transport. Designing public transport to suit the needs of users in this way encourages the substitution of less fuel-efficient forms of transportation such as private vehicles.

For urban planners, the choices for a more sustainable city are quite stark, although politically they are much more difficult, as the allure of building more road capacity remains very high. Many cities that have confronted the provision of a freeway have been global leaders in the move towards more sustainable transportation. Copenhagen, Zurich, Portland, Vancouver and Toronto all had to face the cathartic experience of a controversial freeway. After a political confrontation, the freeway options were dropped. They decided instead to provide other greener options – hence, the building of light rail lines, cycle-ways, traffic calming and associated urban villages began to emerge. All of these cities had citizen groups that pushed visions for a different, less car-oriented city, and a political process was worked through to achieve their innovations. Similar movements are active in Australia.[53]

Freeways have blighted the centres of many cities and today there are cities that are trying to remove them. San Francisco removed the Embarcadero Freeway from its water-front district in the 1990s after the Loma Prieta earthquake. The freeway has been rebuilt as a friendlier tree-lined boulevard involving pedestrian and cycle spaces. As in all cases where traffic capacity is reduced, the city has not found it difficult to ensure adequate transport, as most of the traffic just disappears. Regeneration of the land uses in the area has followed this change of transportation philosophy.[54] Seoul, in Korea, has removed a large freeway from its centre that had been built over a major river. The project has been very symbolic, as the river is a spiritual source of life for the city. Now other car-saturated Asian cities are planning to replace their central city freeways.[55]

What these projects have shown and encouraged is to 'think of transportation as public space'.[56] Freeways thus, from this perspective, become very unfriendly solutions as they are not good public spaces. However, boulevards with space for cars, cyclists, pedestrians, a bus-way or light rail transit (LRT), all packaged in good design and with associated land uses that attract many people, are the public spaces that make green cities good cities. In the UK, the Demos Institute has shown how public transport enables the creation of good public spaces that help to define a city.[57] The change of awareness amongst traffic engineers of this new paradigm for transportation planning is gathering momentum. 'Road engineers are realizing that they are in the community development business and not just in the facilities development business.'[58] This has been called the 'slow road' movement. In essence, it means that urban planners are asserting their role over traffic engineers or, at least, adopting an integrated approach rather than one that reduces city function down to vehicle movement.

With this changed approach to city planning, the small-scale systems of pedestrian movement and cycling become much more important (see Box 6.12). Pedestrian strategies enable each centre in a city to give priority to the most fundamental of human interactions: the walking-based face-to-face contact that gives human life to a city and, in the process, reduces ecological footprint.

Cycle-oriented strategies can be combined with the development of greenways that improve the green agenda and lower ecological footprint. Enough demonstrations now exist to show that pedestrian and bicycle strategies work dramatically to improve city economies and to integrate the green and brown agendas. Pedestrian and bicycle strategies in Copenhagen, most Australian cities, London, New York and San Francisco and Bogotá, as well as the dramatic changes in Paris with the Velib bicycle scheme and the

> **Box 6.12 The Association of Bicycle Riders in São Paulo, Brazil**
>
> São Paulo, in Brazil, is a megacity of 19 million people. The dense transit-based city has a traffic problem, like many cities that have allowed cars to increase despite limited space. The result is one of the worst smog records in the world, causing severe respiratory problems. Cycling is not therefore an easy option for people. However, a growing movement for cycling facilities has led to an innovative project called ASCOBIKE (Association of Bicycle Riders). Cyclists wanting to ride to the rail station in Mauá had nowhere to park, so the station manager created a space for bikes to be locked up. Seven hundred spaces filled quickly; therefore a facility was created to park bikes, repair and maintain them and to provide a changing area for ASCOBIKE members who pay US$5 a month for the service. Approximately 1800 members have signed up. According to the environmental secretary of the city of São Paulo and the head of the bicycle working group: 'the parking lot in Mauá is interesting because users pay a low fee for a good service, and jobs are created as well. There is no reason why we could not reproduce this successful and efficient service throughout São Paulo.'
>
> *Source:* Newman and Kenworthy, 2007

growing awareness that it works in developing country cities, are all testament to this new approach to cities.[59]

Developing cities without slums

'Cities without slums' is currently one of the most important goals of urban planning in developing countries. During recent years, there has been a resurgence of global concern about slums, manifested in the adoption of specific targets on slums, drinking water and sanitation in the Millennium Development Goals (MDGs). Attaining the goal of cities without slums will require innovative approaches that can enable slums to be upgraded, if not as models of sustainability, certainly in ways that address the most pressing brown and green agenda challenges of poor access to safe drinking water and sanitation, as well as degrading environmental conditions.

The United Nations Global Report on Human Settlements in 2003 entitled *The Challenge of Slums* presented the first global assessment of slums, emphasizing their problems and prospects. It showed that in many developing country cities, the numbers of slum dwellers far exceeded the numbers in formal residences. At present, slum dwellers constitute 36.5 per cent of the urban population in developing countries, with the percentage being as high as 62 in sub-Saharan Africa and 43 in Southern Asia. This section examines, briefly, the question of slums only in terms of the integration of the green and brown agendas and how this is contributing towards the realization of the goal of cities without slums.

Cities are about opportunity and, across the world, people have moved to cities in increasing numbers, especially poorer people seeking a new life, with greater employment or livelihood opportunities – real or perceived. In many cities the ability to provide housing and services for large numbers of poor people is limited. Slums develop because of a combination of rapid rural–urban migration, increasing urban poverty and inequality, marginalization of poor neighbourhoods, inability of the urban poor to access affordable land for housing, insufficient investment in new low-income housing, and poor maintenance of the existing housing stock.

Cycle-oriented strategies can be combined with the development of greenways that improve the green agenda

Most slums in developing country cities are generally built on empty public or private land on the periphery of the city, or elsewhere on physically unsafe land that is vulnerable to natural hazards. Often, such land is on steep slopes prone to landslides or in low-lying areas prone to flooding, or is so severely contaminated that no one else in the city wants it. Slums usually have dire consequences for the urban environment. They often deprive the city of foreshore land for flood control and natural bio-filtration from fringing wetland vegetation; severe erosion can result from steep slopes when they are settled upon; and, as the only source of domestic energy for slum dwellers is firewood, nearby land on the periphery of the city is often deforested.

Thus slums pose a significant threat to the green agenda. At the same time, the brown agenda for those living in the slums is seriously compromised as well. Most slum housing is built of simple and often makeshift materials that can only provide rudimentary protection against natural hazards. Invariably, levels of access to clean drinking water and safe sanitation are extremely low, resulting in basic health problems. Electricity is frequently stolen from grids and presents many risks in its use. The majority of slum dwellers can only participate in the informal economy, partly as a result of the social stigmatization of slums and of low levels of education and training.

Despite these obvious problems, there are some positive aspects of slums in terms of the green and brown agendas. Slums are a very organic form of urban development, similar to how most cities in the world were originally formed and grew. They tend to create dense and mixed land-use forms that are similar to most 'walking cities' of ancient times. The narrow streets between slum buildings are suitable only for walking and, hence, the resultant areas, if upgraded, can become 'car free' and desirable, thus fulfilling one of the goals of sustainable urban design. This highly compact urban form is the basis for the strong urban communities and high levels of social capital that characterize most slum areas. Community ties in slums are often found to be much stronger, with higher levels of trust than in affluent suburbs where people do not know each other.

Addressing the slum challenge is now a constant political issue in the cities of most developing countries. There are now some key guiding principles designed to help urban local authorities and governments in doing this, as further elaborated upon in Chapter 7 of this Global Report. The current trend is to address the phenomenon of slums through two strategies: first, large-scale upgrading of existing slums, which is the concern of the present discussion; and, second, adoption of urban and housing policies that prevent the emergence of new slums – which is the concern of the whole of this report.

Slum upgrading is largely concerned with the brown agenda. It consists of improving security of tenure (often through regularization of the rights to land and housing) and installing new or improving existing infrastructure and services, up to a satisfactory standard, especially water supply, sanitation and waste management, but also storm water drainage, electricity, access roads and footpaths. Typical upgrading projects provide improved footpaths, basic access roads, drainage, street lighting, water supply and sewerage. In most cases, upgrading does not involve home construction since the residents can do this themselves, but, instead, offers optional loans for home improvements. The poor are often willing and able to invest their own resources (labour and finance) in their housing. This has been demonstrated in many slum upgrading and site-and-service projects in many cities all over the world. This is the reason why the current best practice in slum upgrading involves communities from the outset and requires a contribution from poor households.

Further actions include the removal of environmental hazards, providing incentives for community management and maintenance, as well as the construction of facilities for basic social services, especially clinics and schools. Tenure rights are usually given to the occupants. Those who must be moved to make way for infrastructure may be given serviced plots in nearby areas. UN-Habitat has developed broad guidelines on large-scale slum upgrading, and some international initiatives, such as the joint World Bank–UN-Habitat Cities Alliance, have similar guidelines.[60]

Upgrading has significant advantages; it is not only an affordable alternative to clearance and relocation, which costs up to ten times more than upgrading, but it also minimizes the disturbance to the social and economic life of the community, including the often high levels of social capital – as illustrated in Box 6.13. The results of upgrading are highly visible, immediate and make a significant difference to the quality of life of the urban poor, especially in the area of environmental safety and human health.

With specific reference to the integration of the green and brown agendas, provision of basic infrastructure services, especially water supply, sanitation, waste management and energy, is at the core of slum upgrading. However, cities need to determine whether slum upgrading is appropriate if a slum community is occupying land that is vulnerable to natural hazards. Some river foreshore communities built into the river itself, for example, will always be highly vulnerable to floods. Engineering can be used to resolve this where feasible, as it is much better to enable a slum community to build on its foundations rather than be shifted.

Small-scale and distributed infrastructure of the kind that is outlined earlier in this chapter can be introduced into the narrow streets of slum communities. This will prevent complete destruction of the organic structure of slum areas by traditional pipes and roads that would not necessarily make it any better than new small-scale technology. However, there is also an argument that significant investment in city-wide trunk infrastructure by the public sector is necessary if housing in upgraded slums is to be affordable to the urban poor and if efforts to support the informal, often home-based, enterprises run by poor slum dwellers are to be successful.

Working with the community to enable them to participate in the development process and in the management of infrastructure can enable a slum community to thrive and develop pride in their green and brown achievements. They can become models of sustainability as they

Slums pose a significant threat to the green agenda

Slum upgrading is largely concerned with the brown agenda

create reduced levels of resource consumption while creating healthy and attractive living environments for the residents.

ADDRESSING THE GREEN AND BROWN AGENDAS THROUGH URBAN PLANNING AND GOVERNANCE

From the above trends in urban planning for sustainability and the many innovative examples cited, it is possible to see the potential integration of the green and brown agendas; the examples given throughout this chapter show many cities with solutions that work. One conclusion that can be made, however, is that those cities demonstrating these early elements of sustainability invariably have a serious commitment to urban planning. They were therefore prepared to try out some programmes or projects that could be seen as having long-term benefits for the city. It is, in fact, very hard to see how these innovations can be introduced into cities without viable and active urban planning systems. Thus, some conclusions are made below, drawing from these eight trends, about how urban planning can enhance sustainable urban development, before examining the kind of governance that is needed to make this happen.

Urban planning for sustainable urban development

The above eight sustainability trends (developing renewable energy; striving for carbon-neutral cities; developing distributed power and water systems; increasing photosynthetic spaces as part of green infrastructure; improving eco-efficiency; increasing sense of place; developing sustainable transport; and developing cities without slums) suggest that in order to integrate the green and brown agendas in cities, there will need to be:

- Renewable energy strategies showing how to progressively tap local resources. Such strategies should involve recognition of renewable resources in and around a city as part of the capital base of the city and establishing ordinances on buildings that facilitate the application of renewable energy.
- Carbon-neutral strategies that can enforce energy efficiency, integrate with the renewables strategy and direct the biodiversity offsets to the bioregion. This can be enforced through planning schemes that mandate standards for significant reductions in carbon and water in all development, that prevent the loss of arable and natural land in the bioregion, and direct planting to areas that are most in need of revegetation.
- Distributed infrastructure strategies that enable small-scale energy and water systems to flourish. This can be built into the requirements for urban development and can be facilitated by providing incentive packages with

> **Box 6.13 Impacts of resettlement of slum dwellers in high-rise apartments, Jakarta, Indonesia**
>
> A study of slum dwellers living along the Ciliwung River in Jakarta surveyed the residents and compared them to residents of a nearby high-rise apartment block who had previously been slum dwellers but had been moved out into a modern high-rise complex. The question Arief (1998) asked was whether the shifting of squatters was more sustainable in terms of their impact upon the environment, their economic opportunities and their community health. The apartment dwellers were found to use a little less energy and water (as they had to pay for it), and their waste management was considerably better since the slum dwellers put all waste directly into the river. In human terms, the apartment dwellers had improved incomes and employment (they were able to enter the formal economy) and had similar levels of accessibility and health (surprisingly); but in terms of all community parameters, the slum development was far superior because the layout of the housing encouraged people to know and trust their neighbours. Over 80 per cent of people were able to trust their neighbours and lend them things, while this was less than 20 per cent in the high-rise development. The lack of community orientation in the high-rise design questions the fundamentals of its development ethos. Arief points to alternatives such as the Kampung Improvement Scheme, which is a more organic way of rebuilding slums that uses the community structure in the area.
>
> *Source: Silas, 1993; Arief, 1998*

new buildings for technologies, such as photovoltaic cells, grey water systems and water tanks, with local plans for the governance of community-based systems, as well as region-wide strategies for recycling sewage.
- Green infrastructure strategies that include the photosynthetic resources of the city and which can enhance the green agenda across the city through food, fibre, biodiversity and recreation pursuits locally. This can be achieved through development controls that focus on how the rooftops (and walls) of buildings can be used for photosynthetic purposes, as well as zoning areas for urban photosynthetic activity, including growing biofuels, food and fibre, and biodiversity in and around the city.
- Eco-efficiency strategies linking industries to achieve fundamental changes in the metabolism of cities. This can be done by taking an audit of all the wastes of the city and seeing how they can be reused through stakeholder participation and government facilitation.
- Sense of place strategies to ensure that the human dimension is driving all of the other strategies. This can be assisted by local economic development strategies, by place-based engagement approaches to all planning and development processes, and by the innovative use of 'sustainability credits', or complementary currencies, to implement local sustainability innovations as development bonuses.
- Sustainable transport strategies incorporating:
  - quality transit down each main corridor, which is faster than traffic;
  - dense TODs built around each station;
  - pedestrian and bicycle strategies for each centre and TOD, with cycle links across the city;
  - plug-in infrastructure for electric vehicles as they emerge;
  - cycling and pedestrian infrastructure as part of all street planning; and

> Cities demonstrating ... elements of sustainability invariably have a serious commitment to urban planning

Urban governance function	Example structure/ mechanism	Skills required
Regional strategic planning that can cross local boundaries on transport, biodiversity, climate change, water, waste, housing, etc. and cover the whole metropolitan region	Regional planning authority	Big picture planning, visionary, strategic planning frameworks
Statutory development control function that can be encouraged at the regulate for common good outcomes and implement the regional plan in each local community	Town planning schemes and by-laws for building and development approvals	Appropriate regulation and recognition of how innovation can same time
Project assessment function that can enable infrastructure and land development to be controlled for common good outcomes	Planning and environment authority	Relates strategic goals to the assessment of spatial benefits and costs of infrastructure, as well as establishing conditions on major developments
Development facilitation function that can help to set up demonstrations of sustainability innovations, especially in redevelopment projects	Development authority	Relates strategic goals to innovations and demonstrations; sets up partnerships between government and private sector
Development financing function that can link sustainability programmes to innovative ways of financing change	Local authority and regional planning authority	Able to generate funds from rates, taxes, bonds, public–private partnerships, development bonuses (non-cash finance) and land value capture
Community engagement function that can enable decisions to be made that ensure sustainability outcomes	All planning bodies	Deliberative democracy skills that bring all stakeholders together with professionals and citizens to ensure visionary plans are translated into actions

Table 6.2

Planning and governance for sustainable urban development

- a green wall growth boundary around the city preventing further urban encroachment.
- Innovative approaches that can enable slums to be upgraded, if not as models of sustainability, in ways that address the most pressing brown and green agenda challenges of poor access to safe drinking water and sanitation as well as degrading environmental conditions.

Governance for sustainable urban development

Sustainable urban development planning, like all long-term planning, requires governance that goes beyond market forces and can help to create widely accessible infrastructure and community services.[61] Table 6.2 sets out the six core functions of urban governance that would be needed for sustainable urban development. Examples of the types of structures, or mechanisms, that are needed for this and the professional skills required are also listed.

A regional planning process to guide the integration of the green and brown agendas is necessary. The challenges outlined in this chapter cannot be addressed effectively without a regional plan that incorporates the whole city and its region. Cities have grown everywhere to engulf local authorities in surrounding rural areas; in many countries, there is now a need for a metropolitan-wide perspective on most of the issues raised in this chapter. However, this will mean nothing without a local planning process capable of

Sustainable urban development planning ... requires governance that ... can help create widely accessible infrastructure and community services

delivering public goods and services (see Box 6.14).

There is also need for an effective statutory process to enable key land-use decisions and regulations to be made legally enforceable. Urban planning has become enmeshed in regulations from the past and needs to revise these at the same time as it faces the new challenges of sustainable development. Bigger projects and decisions on infrastructure should be part of a development assessment process that can bring in wider economic benefits and reduce costs while setting common good conditions.

To balance this kind of regulatory approach, urban governance should also include a development facilitation function to ensure that innovations and demonstrations are set up in partnerships between government, industry and the community. The glue that will make this all work will be a development financing function that can tap old money sources, such as rates and taxes, and new money sources, such as public–private partnerships, development bonuses and capture of increased land value. A partnership process, including public–private partnerships in financial capital and public–community partnerships in social capital, are useful for demonstrating innovations in sustainable urban development. Private-sector partnerships in infrastructure can enable governments to do more, to spread risk, to improve their innovations and to lock in key links between infrastructure and land use, such as TODs and rail. Community-sector partnerships, as in the case of Vauban, can enable community values and visions to be tapped and turned into mainstream strategies.[62]

Finally, there is need for a participatory process that can help to develop and deliver sustainability visions, as already elaborated upon in Chapter 5. The social capital of the city needs to be strengthened as these new challenges are faced. This cannot happen without deliberative processes engaging communities in their future.[63] It is further important to incorporate a gendered perspective in planning for sustainable development and to engage women (who are often more directly dependent upon and involved with the urban natural environment) fully in the process. Many cities' sustainability strategies now include goals of equity and social justice, with gender included under this umbrella. Urban planning has experimented with emerging engagement processes and must now seek to make them part of day-to-day governance systems.

CONCLUDING REMARKS

Linking the green and brown agendas in a comprehensive and planned way is a relatively new challenge for cities. This will not be possible without a revived and regenerated approach to urban planning. As one writer suggests:

> *The urban planning profession needs a new generation of visionaries, people who dream of a better world, and are capable of designing the means to attain it. That, after all, is the essence of planning: to visualize the ideal future community, and to work towards its realization.*[64]

The sustainable urban development vision is a big one. It is being embraced, in part, by some cities; but none are able yet to fully demonstrate how to improve human health and liveability while simultaneously reducing their ecological footprints and improving the natural environment. It is likely that there will be many years of demonstrations and innovations before the necessary processes of sustainable urban development are fully mainstreamed. Urban planners should be at the forefront of these demonstrations and innovations, whether they are working in the government, private or non-governmental sector. They now need to find ways of creatively integrating these innovations within mainstream urban planning and governance systems.

Those cities that are hoping to compete in the global marketplace are realizing that they cannot only emphasize economic growth, but must at the same time create a good urban environment. This chapter has established that a good urban environment requires a simultaneous integration of improvements to the built and the natural environments. This integrated agenda is very difficult to implement without effective urban planning and an urban governance system that facilitates it. As a result, there is an increased need for urban planning to play a major role in the cities of the 21st century.

The biggest challenge facing cities in the near future will be how to manage the transition to a post-fossil fuel world, as the global governance system increasingly firms up its commitments. This will be compounded by the recent global financial downturn, which may slow down some of the major green and brown agenda integration programmes, such as slum upgrading. However, government-funded green infrastructure and energy programmes currently being initiated in some developed countries in order to stimulate economic activity and generate jobs may offer significant opportunities for cities to implement some of the innovations described in this chapter.

> **Box 6.14 Renewing urban governance in Indian cities**
>
> Like many cities in the emerging economies of the world, Indian cities have the combined challenges of a rapidly growing population, increasing consumption and mobility, inadequate infrastructure, and an urban governance system dating from colonial times. In December 2005, the Government of India announced the Jawaharlal Nehru National Urban Renewal Mission – a programme of US$11 billion over seven years designed to renew the infrastructure, clean the environment and reduce poverty in the 60 largest cities in India. However, for cities to access the fund, they must undergo 22 reforms in their urban governance.
>
> The reforms are essentially to enable cities to have a more devolved and local democratic form of governance, and to develop a more healthy municipal tax base. Both are critical to making urban planning work better. Cities in India have largely been the responsibility of state governments, particularly in the area of housing, transport and urban development. This means that they are mostly financed by small budgetary allocations from states, so local governments cannot create a strong urban planning function. Civic government expenditure in India is just 0.6 per cent of national gross domestic product (GDP), compared to 5 per cent in Brazil and 6 per cent in South Africa, and even higher levels in developed countries.
>
> The first of the Jawaharlal Nehru National Urban Renewal Mission projects are in solid waste management and sewerage systems. Changes in urban governance are under way. Delhi, for example, which is governed by a municipal commissioner appointed by the state government, will now appoint a Metropolitan Planning Committee to ensure that devolved and integrated urban planning occurs and to facilitate more effective financing of infrastructure through the use of bonds and public–private partnerships. Both innovations require local involvement through tapping of social capital and ensuring there is a local revenue base. It is hoped that as a result of such reforms, the capacity and legitimacy of urban planning will be further enhanced in the city.
>
> *Source: Johnson, 2008*

A good urban environment requires ... simultaneous ... improvements to the built and the natural environments

NOTES

1   World Commission on Environment and Development, 1987.
2   Mitlin and Satterthwaite, 1994.
3   UNCHS, 1996, p295.
4   UN-Habitat, 2003.
5   Myerson and Rydin, 1996.
6   Millennium Ecosystem Assessment, 2005.
7   Girouard, 1985; Kostoff, 1991.
8   See Newman et al, 2009.
9   See Newman and Jennings, 2008.
10 Environmental News Service, 2005.
11 Revkin, 2008.
12 Went et al, 2008.
13 See www.newscorporation.com.
14 Lerch, 2007.
15 Farrelly, 2005.
16 See www.smud.org.
17 Droege, 2006.
18 Benedict and McMahon, 2006.
19 Sawin and Hughes, 2007.
20 Newman and Kenworthy, 1999; Newman and Jennings, 2008.
21 Ho, 2002.
22 Ho, 2003.
23 City of Malmö, 2005.
24 Puig, 2008.
25 Halweil and Nierenberg, 2007.
26 Beatley, 2005.
27 Girardet, 2000.
28 McDonaugh and Braungart, 2002
29 See Newman and Jennings, 2008.
30 Hawkens et al, 1999; Hargrove and Smith, 2006.
31 Clinton Climate Initiative best practices, www.c40cities.org/bestpractices/waste/toronto_organic.jsp.
32 Hardoy et al, 2001.
33 Sirolli, 1999.
34 Sirolli, 1999; see also www.unhabitat.org/pmss.
35 Sirolli, 1999.
36 Putnam, 1993.
37 Scheurer, 2003.
38 Beatley and Manning, 1997; Beatley, 2005.
39 Jacobs, 1984.
40 Korten, 1999.
41 Barter et al, 2003.
42 Kenworthy et al, 1999; Newman and Kenworthy, 1999.
43 Cervero, 2008.
44 Ewing et al, 2007.
45 Kenworthy, 2008.
46 Rubin, 2008.
47 Dingding, 2008.
48 Jain, 2008.
49 Newman et al, 2009.
50 Nolan and Lem, 2001; Standing Advisory Committee on Trunk Road Assessment, 1994.
51 Urban Transportation Monitor, 1999.
52 Gehl and Gemzoe, 2000; Gehl et al, 2006.
53 Newman and Kenworthy, 1999.
54 Gordon, 2005.
55 See http://cheonggye.seoul.go.kr.
56 Burwell, 2005.
57 Mean and Timms, 2005.
58 Wiley-Schwartz, 2006.
59 Newman and Kenworthy, 2007.
60 UN-Habitat, 2003.
61 Talukder, 2004.
62 Scheurer and Newman, 2008.
63 Hartz-Karp and Newman, 2006; Curry et al, 2006.
64 Brooks, 1988.

PLANNING AND INFORMALITY

The dynamics of urban change include both expansion to accommodate growth and constant adaptation of urban built environments. Planning aims to facilitate and regulate both; but in practice they take place without reference to the planning system, especially in the cities of developing countries. The conventional assumption is that such development which does not conform to planning regulations is both undesirable and illegal. Much effort has been devoted to extending land-use planning and development regulation to incorporate all urban development, while existing informally developed areas have often been neglected or demolished. The impossibility of achieving the goal of controlling all new development and redevelopment, given the rapid pace of urban change and resource limitations, has led to some rethinking.

The aim of this chapter is to identify the trends and patterns of informal development in urban areas, discuss their implications for urban planning and review recent urban planning responses to informality. It begins with an overview of the concept of informality and then reviews this specifically within the context of urban areas. Trends in informal development and the resultant urban forms are examined next, with reference to various regions of the world. Based on this analysis, challenges and opportunities for planning are summarized in the subsequent section, followed by a review of innovative planning responses to informality and urban expansion. Ways in which planning can, within the context of wider urban governance and management systems, respond to informality are also outlined. Finally, the conclusion assesses the prospects for addressing the challenges posed by informal urban development more effectively through new and more responsive planning approaches.

INFORMALITY

The term 'informal sector' is attributed to Keith Hart in a paper on the working poor in Accra (Ghana) given at a conference in 1971[1] and immediately taken up by the International Labour Organization (ILO) in a study of the urban economy in Kenya.[2] Coined to describe small-scale economic activities and unregulated employment, the term is also applied to land and property development. The existence of practices and enterprises with the characteristics that came to be labelled 'informal' had, however, long been recognized in analyses of urban centres throughout the world.

Early definitions such as that of the ILO focused on three of the key characteristics of informal enterprises, including those involved in house construction and service delivery: first, in each enterprise there is a substantial overlap between the provider of capital and the provider of labour; second, the sector consists largely of unincorporated enterprises that operate outside employment regulations and without acquiring non-labour inputs, such as licences; third, the sector is characterized by the small scale of enterprise operations and high levels of competition.[3] Many studies and also official statistics adopt a definition that focuses on the second of these characteristics – the violation of formal state rules and regulations related to planning, building, employment, licensing, taxation, etc.

Often, the 'informal sector' is seen as a distinct sphere operating independently from the formal sector and the state. However, in practice there are many links between formal and informal operators and activities, and informal activities do not exist in isolation from state structures or bureaucratic requirements – rather than being 'outside' the state sphere, they interact with it in complex ways.[4] Not only do many informal operators interact with and depend upon state employees and service providers, informal activities are pervasive within bureaucratic structures, ostensibly formal development processes and formal enterprises (e.g. the use of political and personal connections to do business and the evasion of regulatory requirements).

Despite the lack of conceptual clarity, diversity of definitions and a tendency to categorize 'formal' and 'informal' as a dichotomy, the terms have continued to be widely used, even by their critics. Both have long been acknowledged as problematic concepts; but because there are no satisfactory alternatives, they will continue to be used in the remainder of the chapter on the understanding that they are 'constructed opposites':[5] rather than there being two distinct sectors or types of activity, there is a continuum of closely related development activities, enterprises and forms of work.

CHARACTERISTICS OF URBAN INFORMALITY

The formal–informal continuum is central to contemporary analyses of urban development. It has been applied to many aspects of urban development, especially the built environment, the urban economy and the provision of services. A state land administration system embraces tenure and its registration, regulation of land use and development, property taxation, and direct public intervention, often involving public landownership. Generally, urban development that comes within the purview of this system and complies with its legal and regulatory requirements is labelled 'formal' and all land subdivision and development that do not comply with one or another requirement are considered 'informal'.

The characterizations and definitions of informal urban land and housing development have varied greatly.[6] Generally labelled shanties, squatter settlements or slums, the existence of informal housing areas had been recognized and often condemned long before the 1970s, although the processes by which they were produced were often assumed rather than properly understood. Backed by the writings of Charles Abrahams and John Turner, calls for recognition of the role of 'self-help housing' in accommodating growing urban populations were made during the first United Nations Conference on Human Settlements in 1976 in Vancouver (Canada). It was recognized that land subdivision and transfer, construction, livelihoods strategies and the provision of services can have formal and informal characteristics.

Informal land and property development occurs in areas that are undeveloped because they are zoned for future development, are beyond the current built-up area or are unsuitable for development. Thus, informal settlements, especially those formed and occupied by the poor, are often on sites that are reserved for environmental conservation purposes or are vulnerable to floods, landslips or other hazards. However, much informal settlement occurs on land that is suitable for development, although it may be beyond the area served by mains services.

The extent to which development in such areas is consonant with official planning standards varies, depending upon how the process of subdivision and occupation is organized and how realistic the official standards are for low-cost development. Actual tenure rights depend upon who owns the land, who sanctions transfers to new owners, political connections, the attitude of the responsible authorities and the prospects for regularization. In many settlements, property owners have no security of tenure and therefore invest little in their houses or other aspects of neighbourhood development. Frequently, however, because the informal subdivision was undertaken by people with ownership rights to the land, time has elapsed without evictions, political connections have been made, and some services have been installed, property owners perceive their tenure as relatively secure and invest in building improvements. Typically, informal provision of the most crucial services (i.e. water, transport and electricity) is organized by individual households or local entrepreneurs as soon as settlement occurs. Other entrepreneurs open businesses to serve local demand, including personal services, building materials supply and privately run clinics, pharmacies and schools. Whether an area becomes permanent, receives official services and generates investment in house improvements depends upon whether or not it is recognized by the responsible authorities. In some cases, individual property owners may seek to register title to the land they have bought. More frequently, leaders and residents in an area seek tenure regularization and physical improvements for the area as a whole.

In addition to the processes of informal settlement described above, in many cities there is much informality in the development of middle- and upper-income residential neighbourhoods. Landowners often manage to obtain detailed layout and building permission for developments in areas not zoned for immediate development, either because the development permission process is ineffective or through influence or corruption. Such areas are often gated communities, built to high standards and self-sufficient in terms of services, but may not comply with broad strategic planning or environmental policies. Alternatively, development may occur in designated areas, but at a higher density or lower building standard than specified because development and building-control officers are powerless to enforce regulations or can be prevailed upon through influence or under-the-counter payments. Reports of buildings constructed in this way as collapsing are all too frequent. Formal service provision sometimes lags behind the development of such areas.

Informal development also occurs within existing built-up areas; as densities increase, owners invest in their properties and worn-out buildings are renewed. In both informally developed and formal areas, including areas of government housing, increased plot coverage or the construction of additional storeys may take the density of development beyond the permitted plot coverage and floor area ratios; building extensions and business operations may intrude into public space, including roads; and buildings may be put to uses other than those for which the area is zoned.

An additional aspect of informality in urban areas relates to economic activities. Urban enterprises that do not comply with registration, licensing or employment regulations are considered to be informal. Failure to comply with legal requirements may also mean that the goods and services produced are themselves illegal. However, this is not necessarily the case, and a distinction can be drawn between informal and criminal activities.[7] Informal service provision can refer either to services provided by organizations that are not registered, regulated or subcontracted by the relevant provider, or to the illegal use of official services.

Further to the close association between informality and illegality, a link is often made between informality and disorganization. This perception persists despite many analyses that have drawn attention to the complex economic and social networks that enable informal actors, processes and enterprises to operate, on the one hand, and constrain their independence, on the other.[8] In practice, informal activities,

The formal-informal dichotomy is central to contemporary analysis of urban development

Urban enterprises that do not comply with registration, licensing and employment regulations are considered to be informal

Regions	Procedures (number)	Time (days)	Cost (% of income per capita)
Developed countries	7.3	21	7.1
Developing countries	9.8	51.5	79.9
Africa	10.7	52.6	138.8
Asia and the Pacific	8.8	39.5	40.7
Latin America and the Caribbean	9.8	68.3	43.6

Table 7.1

The cost of regulation: Requirements to start a legal business

Note: Number of procedures, time and cost have been calculated as averages for countries in the respective region.

Source: World Bank, 2007a

Informal land subdivision and property development is a response to ineffective planning

like formal activities, comply with rules, although the sources of rules and the means through which they are specified and enforced are different from laws governing formal activities.[9] Sometimes the apparent lack of organization is considered to prevent the informal sector from fulfilling its potential as a generator of new employment, profits and economic growth. The policy prescriptions to which such perceptions give rise include variants on the theme of formalization and encouragement of residents and informal entrepreneurs to form organizations. The latter is said to enable groups (e.g. savings and credit groups, co-operatives, land development trusts and market committees) to assemble resources, access government services or reduce risk.

The view of informal activities as illegal or irregular has given rise to various debates – in particular, whether they occur because of the constraining effects on developers, individuals and enterprises of laws, regulations and bureaucratic requirements, and whether the public costs of non-compliance exceed private benefits. Generally, informal land subdivision and property development is a response to ineffective planning, inappropriate standards and unenforceable regulations. The presence of informal economic activities illustrates governments' inability to catch all enterprises in the regulatory or statistical net – they are informal because of arduous registration procedures and inappropriate standards or requirements (see Table 7.1). Employment in the informal sector is also generally considered as a survival strategy when there is insufficient formal employment for all and no social safety net, as well as responses to demand generated by wages earned in formal employment. The motivations for informal development thus vary, from a desperate need to find an affordable place to live and work, to a desire to maximize profit.

Views on whether the informal economy is potentially a source of economic growth and development vary. Depending upon the line taken, different responses to the informal sector are considered appropriate. For example, if informal activities are thought to occur because of inappropriate legal and bureaucratic requirements, and this is seen as hindering market development and economic growth, then reducing or reforming regulatory restrictions may be advocated.[10] Similarly, if formal actors and government agencies are perceived to be willing and able to extend their activities and reach poor households, they may be facilitated to do so, while informal processes and enterprises are temporarily tolerated or restricted. Alternatively, if informal actors are considered to be responding to demands that government agencies or formal enterprises are unwilling or unable to meet (e.g. for land subdivision, house construc-

tion, convenience retailing or personal services), then policy prescriptions may facilitate rather than constrain their activities – for example, by simplifying bureaucratic requirements or providing credit.[11] However, if the public costs of evasion are considered significant, then governments may attempt to ensure compliance with regulations, register property and bring informal enterprises and workers within the regulatory and tax systems.

In the cities of rich Northern countries with well-developed planning systems, development regulations are widely accepted and observed. When only occasional violations occur, it is possible to enforce laws and regulations, with the result that almost all development complies with land-use plans and associated standards and regulations. At the other end of the spectrum, in some cities very little development fully complies with planning laws and regulations; implementation of standards, often unrealistic, is limited; and enforcement when violations are widespread is impossible.

GLOBAL TRENDS IN URBAN INFORMALITY AND EXPANSION

In this section, trends with respect to informal urban development in different parts of the world are reviewed, with particular emphasis on processes of urban expansion, although informality within the urban built environment as it evolves over time is also considered. On the basis of the review, the factors that shape informality are identified and the influences of informality on urban forms summarized.

Asia

Much economic activity in Asian cities takes the form of 'informal' manufacturing and services, which, on average, accounted for an estimated 65 per cent of non-agricultural employment between 1995 and 2000.[12] The scanty time series data available indicates that informal employment as a proportion of total urban employment has increased over time in the region.[13] In Mumbai, for example, this has increased from one third during the 1960s to two-thirds during the 1990s, as formal job creation has not kept pace with growth in the urban labour force.[14]

Informality in cities of the region is also manifested in terms of housing. In 2005, an estimated 36.5, 42.9, 27.5 and 24 per cent of the urban population in Eastern Asia, Southern Asia and South-Eastern Asia and Western Asia, respectively, lived in slum settlements.[15] While the proportion of urban slum dwellers in the sub-regions is high on average, there are variations between countries ranging from as high as 78.9 per cent in Cambodia to 26 per cent in Thailand.[16]

Within the built-up area of cities, neighbourhoods that do not comply with planning and building regulations include both areas of tenement housing and informal settlements. The former, including, for example, *bustees* in Kolkata or *chawls* in Mumbai, are inner-city areas that may be zoned for housing, but in which densities have increased over time, services are overburdened, buildings are structurally dilapidated and the environment is degraded.

Wherever there are pockets of undeveloped public and, to a lesser extent, private land, they are likely to have been informally occupied under a variety of tenure arrangements, including squatting and informal rental, as poor people seek places to live that provide them with access to livelihoods and services. Even when tenure rights are negotiated with the landowner, the development does not comply with regulatory requirements due to its supposed temporary nature, the poverty of its inhabitants, or the use of locations unsuitable for residential use (e.g. areas liable to flooding, land in road and railway reserves).

In addition to the densification and redevelopment of existing towns and cities, it is estimated that much future urban growth in the region will be accommodated in peri-urban areas where informal development is widespread: three-quarters in Jakarta, over half in Bangkok and 40 per cent in China by 2025.[17] Demographic and physical growth in urban areas has led, over the last 20 to 30 years, to the emergence of sprawling metropolitan regions. The term *desakota*,[18] for example, was coined to describe the new urban forms observed in South-East Asia.[19] These emerged in areas with historically high rural population densities, typically associated with smallholder agriculture. They are the result of economic and physical development processes, including the outward migration of residents, entrepreneurs and developers from the built-up areas of cities in search of vacant lower-cost land; the de-agrarianization of rural economies in peri-urban areas; and the densification of villages by local landowners in response to growing demand for housing. Metropolitan growth was also encouraged by the weakness of regulatory controls. Local governments allowed substandard construction, failed to enforce environmental regulations and permitted lax labour practices in their efforts to secure investment.[20] Rapid economic growth and globalization have intensified the process, leading to the emergence of extended metropolitan regions that, in some cases, span the borders between countries.

Much of the development in expanded metropolitan regions is informal, as government and planning systems fail to cope with the pressures. Many of the settlements fail to comply with planning and building standards, lack the space for amenities, have inadequate services and are distant from mass transit.[21] Protests against the adverse environmental impacts of encroachment on areas not scheduled for development also pit environmentalists against residents of informal settlements, making it more difficult for the latter to obtain service improvements and even exposing them to the threat of eviction.[22] The juxtaposition of high-income residential areas with low-income informal settlements and rapidly urbanizing villages is, however, evident, reflecting the emergence of a middle class, increased inequalities and changing consumption patterns and lifestyles (see Box 7.1).[23]

Higher-cost residential and industrial development in metropolitan areas may also fail to comply with official requirements in one or more respects.[24] Developers are often able to exploit regulatory or governance capacity of governments in peripheral areas. This leads to large-scale private development in locations beyond the official development boundary (e.g. in Haryana, outside the National Capital Territory of Delhi), where there are fewer restrictions on the activities of private developers.[25] Local governments themselves may circumvent planning and environmental regulations to relocate heavy and polluting industries from cities, attract foreign investment or develop high-technology industries and services. In China, many local administrations that control peripheral land raise revenue by selling it for industrial or residential development. For example, in Guangdong Province, over half of the urban expansion has occurred on village collective land through informal processes.[26] The process may be marked by protests as the new enterprises compete with existing livelihood activities or local people are threatened by eviction with few safeguards against arbitrary expropriation and inadequate compensation.[27]

Today, the patterns of metropolitan development vary, from clusters of towns and cities (e.g. the Pearl River Delta in southern China), to regions dominated by megacities (e.g. the Bangkok Metropolitan Region), to urban corridors in which cities, towns and special economic zones are linked by railways and expressways, sometimes across national borders (e.g. Tokyo–Kyoto and Mumbai–Pune).[28] Similar urban forms have emerged in other parts of Asia, including the transition economies of Viet Nam and China. The latter are distinguished from extended metropolitan regions elsewhere in Asia mainly by the greater speed of their transformation in a situation of uncertainty over the legal basis for emerging land markets.[29] In the absence of planned investment in mass transit,[30] such metropolitan expansion is heavily reliant on vehicle transport, both public and private, exacerbating the process of unplanned sprawl and resulting in long journeys to work for many. The result is disjointed rather than integrated development, sometimes leading to the neglect of urban cores and a 'hollowing out' of cities.[31]

The planning approach typical of Asian countries is based on master plans that assume a 'command and control' approach, especially in the former planned economies in the region.[32] Plan preparation is time consuming and top down, plans are unrealistic and resources to implement plans are lacking. Furthermore, multiple and often inconsistent laws and administrative responsibilities hinder coordinated action. The land administration system is generally inefficient and based on outdated base and cadastral maps, disorganized, incomplete and discriminatory registration systems, costly, lengthy and discriminatory dispute-resolution mechanisms, multiple land transaction taxes and levies, and poor development control regulation enforcement. National planning agencies have generally not attempted to re-conceptualize the approach to planning, although there have been some innovations, which will be considered later in this chapter.[33] The result is that plan proposals are largely difficult to implement and the supply of formally subdivided and serviced land is limited, leading to price increases for formal land and property, and widespread evasion.

Moreover, local authorities have resorted to evicting inhabitants of informal settlements in several instances.

Much future urban growth ... will be accommodated in peri-urban areas where informal development is widespread

The supply of formally subdivided and serviced land is limited, leading to price increases for formal land and property, and widespread evasion

---

Box 7.1 An extended metropolitan region in Asia: Jakarta, Indonesia

Jakarta is subdivided into five cities and forms part of a wider metropolitan region called Jabotabek, which includes Jakarta and three surrounding districts: Bogor to the south, Tangerang to the west and Bekasi to the east, including the four cities of Bogor, Depol, Tangerang and Bekasi. The population of the metropolitan region increased from 17.1 million in 1990 to 21.1 million in 2000 and an estimated 25 million in 2005, although the population of the city itself increased relatively little from 8.2 million in 1990 to an estimated 8.7 million in 2005.

Much of the urban expansion of Jakarta in recent years has taken place in peri-urban areas to the west, south and east. Investment in roads has enabled members of rural households in peripheral areas to commute to urban jobs, and increased incomes have enabled investment in agricultural intensification, non-farm economic activities and house improvements. Gradually, villages have urbanized *in situ* and joined up by mixed-use infill development. Informal land and housing development on former rice fields in and around early urban settlements and peripheral villages has provided large numbers of affordable houses for low- and middle-income households. Today, approximately 60 per cent of Jakarta metropolitan region's population live in *kampungs* (urban villages), most of which have been provided with basic services and integrated within the city.

Along with ineffective planning and uncoordinated management, the expansion of Jakarta's metropolitan region has been characterized by haphazard land development. One of the main drivers of this has been the development permit system. Under this system, developers who have obtained investment clearance and a development permit have the sole right to purchase a site, in return for compensation based on improvements alone. Until ceilings were imposed in 1999, development permits were a powerful tool for speculation and land hoarding. Developers acquired even untitled land, forcing low-income residents to sell their land or occupancy rights at below market value.

In response to the rapid increase in demand for suburban sites for industry and housing in the 1980s, land designated for low- and middle-income housing was released to private developers, and affordable housing quotas were rarely enforced. Local officials eagerly facilitated the private real estate sector and convinced local communities to sell their land. The mega-projects of the ruling elite and politically connected individuals were especially exempted from planning controls and market competition.

The result was leapfrog development, large-scale construction for and by foreign investors, and a massive increase in high-cost housing in self-contained gated communities or dormitory settlements dependent largely upon private transport and toll roads, juxtaposed with unplanned, poorly serviced mixed-use low- and middle-income development.

Planning and management of the metropolitan area has been fragmented and ineffective; developer interests have been prioritized over planning policies, public priorities and the needs of low-income people; development control has been limited and inconsistent; and property rights are weakly defined. It is estimated that only one third of the land is fully titled, one quarter has no official title and the remainder is subject to intermediate forms of title – rights to build or use.

Despite attempts to decentralize responsibility for local development and land management, the metropolis still has poorly coordinated government, a lack of capacity to implement plan proposals, unsynchronized planning and land laws, inadequate land administration and a dysfunctional development permit system. The 'privatized planning' of new towns, gated communities and shopping malls linked by toll roads continues to provide middle- and upper-income households with protected lifestyles, while most low-income residents have little choice but to seek accommodation in existing or new informal settlements.

Source: Firman and Rakodi, 2008

Throughout the 20th century, low- and middle-income groups were unable to access affordable serviced land and formal housing

Despite legislation that entitles people living in informal settlements to proper notice, compensation and relocation, many evictions bypass formal provisions, including eviction by state agencies (e.g. in Delhi and Karachi).[34] While some informal development has been replaced by formal buildings, as low-rise structures are replaced by high-rise shopping, office and residential complexes, often these are located adjacent to slums and the replacement of worn-out infrastructure lags behind need. In Phnom Penh (Cambodia), for instance, much of the infrastructure is 70 to 80 years' old.[35] The proliferation of informal settlements therefore remains a key challenge for urban planning in the region.

Latin America and the Caribbean

As in most other parts of the world, the demographic growth of Latin American cities slowed during the 1980s; but rapid peripheral growth has continued and informal economic activities have expanded. About 60 per cent of all those employed in the region work in the informal sector, ranging from 37 per cent in Chile to nearly 90 per cent in Haiti, and it is estimated that four out of every five new jobs are in the informal sector.[36] In terms of housing, 27 per cent of the urban population in the region currently live in slums, although this varies between countries and cities. For example, over 60 per cent of urban residents in Jamaica live in slums, compared to only 9 per cent in Chile.[37] Furthermore, an estimated 70 per cent of new housing production in Latin America and Caribbean is informal.[38] The widespread use of informal transportation is closely associated with both residence in informal settlements and engagement in informal income-generating activities.

Throughout the 20th century, rapid urban demographic growth occurred in the face of limited resources and governance capacity, while the policies adopted were often inappropriate. These included public housing programmes and the concentration of public investment in infrastructure in limited areas, which raised land and housing prices. As a result, low- and middle-income groups were unable to access affordable serviced land and formal housing.[39] Informal settlements proliferated through organized invasion, incremental squatting and informal subdivision, depending upon landownership patterns, topography, political circumstances and official policies.[40] For example, in Venezuela squatting has been the main means of informal settlement development, whereas in Colombia and other countries, informal land developers are prominent.[41] The Roofless Workers of the Centre (*Movimento Sem Teto do Centro*) in Brazil had, by 2007, allotted accommodation to 400,000 urban families through the occupation of undeveloped land or vacant formal buildings.[42]

Within existing built-up areas of cities, as areas of tenement housing degenerate into slums, non-compliance with standards and regulations and informal modification of buildings often increases. In planned cities such as Brasilia (Brazil) and Ciudad Guayana (Venezuela), residents have transformed the formal planned environment by extending their housing units to accommodate additional generations of the original household. Such modifications of original building structures strain infrastructure, overwhelm road capacity and make the provision of services and policing more difficult. There are, in addition, pockets of informal housing in the core districts whose existence clashes with politicians', residents' and planners' modernist visions for the city.[43]

Although the proportion of housing that is irregular – measured by indicators such as insecure tenure or the lack of sewer connections – is declining in some countries, there is a vicious circle of informality in which the high incidence of urban poverty limits municipal revenue generation and, thus, public investment in servicing land. This leads to increased prices for formal land and housing, which forces low- and middle-income households to adopt informal options, even though these are not necessarily cheap and may further impoverish people (e.g. through the lack of economic opportunities or high journey-to-work costs). Residents' continued poverty reinforces the vicious circle.[44] Social inequalities, limited economic opportunities, political disenfranchisement and lack of reach by the public law enforcement agencies also result in continuing high levels of informal economic activity, some of which is criminal. In more extreme cases such as Brazil, drug lords have become the administrators and law enforcers in informal settlements.[45]

Informality is also a prominent feature of development in metropolitan areas. Polycentric urban forms, with a core region around the largest cities, and growth of subsidiary cities in the wider metropolitan region are evident in several countries. For example, this can be observed around Mexico City (see Box 7.2), Buenos Aires, Santiago and São Paulo, where peripheral towns and villages have been integrated within the daily sphere of influence of the metropolis and have undergone significant land-use transformations. Such metropolitan development is characterized by centrifugal flows of services and people between peripheral areas and the urban core, as well as in-migration directly into the peripheral areas. As in other parts of the world, much of the development is concentrated in corridors connecting major cities, with suburban centres around existing or new towns that provide cheap labour, services and dormitory locations for commuters (see Chapter 8). Foreign investment in offices, shopping malls, industry, residential development and leisure facilities is a key factor fuelling further expansion.

As such, the suburbs of Latin America and Caribbean cities are characterized by inadequate infrastructure, lack of safety and security, and wide disparities in wealth. Exclusive enclaves of industry, services and high-income housing are juxtaposed against extensive informal settlements. Those able and willing to pay for better living conditions and private security have segregated themselves in gated communities, which have proliferated in cities throughout the region, often leading to further informal settlement close by to take advantage of the low-wage service employment that they generate.

Informal processes have been occurring in countries of the region alongside processes of formalization: some older informal settlements are removed and all or some of their residents relocated to formal housing areas, while others are regularized, providing residents with formal tenure and improved utilities and services. However, often, political dynamics determine which settlements are regularized and improved and which are not. Community leaders may receive individual rewards in return for ensuring electoral support, while areas known to support opposition parties are denied improvements. In either case, residents' ability to influence decision-making is generally limited.[46]

Moreover, residents of informal settlements may also be reluctant to relocate, partly because many of the longer-established areas have secured utilities and services, and developed supportive communities, particularly important in the face of growing socio-spatial polarization and segregation. Formal business activities, formal-sector workers and residents in formal housing also generate demand for goods and services, much of which is met by informal enterprises, which often provide livelihoods for the residents in centrally located informal settlements. Hence, significant proportions of the urban population continue to live in informal areas, many of which are characterized by official neglect and poor-quality living environments.

Where informal settlements have been regularized, the results are often positive. However, because of the location of many settlements on land that is expensive to service, the unit cost of upgrading may exceed the cost of new development. Regularization also leads to increased land and house prices and increased service costs, which may result in gentrification, forcing low-income residents to move to informal settlements elsewhere in the city.[47]

As indicated in Chapter 3, planning approaches in many countries of the region are technocratic, with a strong spatial emphasis. They are based on master or comprehensive planning and zoning, and have changed little in the face of either planning failure or political change. The institutional framework for planning is fragmented, both territorially and between different levels of government. Agencies have poorly defined functions and responsibilities. Even planners who recognize the desirability of participatory planning are, in practice, often reluctant to abandon older planning approaches. Some municipalities are developing more strategic and proactive approaches to planning and implementation – for example, Bogotá in Colombia and Curitiba, Rosario and Porto Alegre in Brazil. However, the ways in which plan proposals deal with informal development processes are

There is a vicious cycle of informality in which the high incidence of urban poverty limits municipal revenue generation and, thus, public investment in servicing land

Political dynamics determine which settlements are regularized and improved and which are not

Box 7.2 Informal development in Mexico City

The metropolitan area of Mexico City can be divided into the existing built-up area in which the core is losing population; an inner peri-urban zone characterized by mixed urban and rural uses, which is functionally integrated within the city and which grew most rapidly between the 1970s and the 1990s; and an outer peri-urban area where growth has been rapid since the 1990s and which has only been integrated within the city more recently. Between 1990 and 2000, roughly half of the city's growth occurred in informal areas and about a third was due to the incorporation of rural areas into the metropolitan area. By 2005, the metropolitan region had a population of just under 20 million and 60 per cent of those employed work in the informal sector.

Growth has mainly occurred along three corridors: towards Pachuca, to the north-east and to the south-west. The cities and towns along these corridors are characterized by a declining share of agricultural employment, manufacturing growth, housing development, infra-structural improvements and, to the east, the emergence of large swathes of poorly serviced informal settlement. The supply of serviced land is insufficient to meet demand and drives up prices, with the result that people who earn less than three times the minimum wage cannot afford formal land or housing. Instead, they are forced to resort to informal alternatives, typically on the urban periphery.

Informal settlement occurs on both privately owned land and areas held under group tenure (*ejidal*), which until 1992 farmers were not permitted to sell. Some *ejidal* land has been converted to full legal ownership, and land in well-located areas where residential use is permitted has been sold to developers, mainly for large housing complexes for the middle and upper-middle classes. However, there are many obstacles to converting *ejidal* land to full legal ownership, including its location in areas that are unsuitable for residential development or diffi-cult to service. Thus, many farmers continue to subdivide and sell their land informally. Land subdividers regulate supply, with the result that prices have also risen in this market.

To the south of the city, urban development is invading a hilly rural area of ecological and water recharge value. In the absence of effective development regulation, creeping settlement led to the loss of 10,000ha or more of agricultural land and forests between 1970 and 1995, with adverse environmental impacts. Population growth has occurred in small towns on the mountain slopes, where farmers holding *ejidal* land have sold land illegally for urban uses, to accommodate both the towns' own population growth and for sale to middle-class in-migrants from the city, giving rise to a fragmented land-use pattern. In addition, poor people have illegally occupied land, often in risk-prone areas.

Nevertheless, more recently, better enforcement, more new housing provision in the core city and slower peripheral population growth have somewhat reduced the extent of illegal development and its adverse environmental impacts. In addition, many informal settlements have been regularized, although responsibility for regularization of settlements on private and *ejidal* land rests with different agencies, the selection of areas for regularization is often *ad hoc* and the process cannot keep pace with informal settlement growth. However, in some areas increased land and housing prices and service costs have led to gentrification and the displacement of low-income people, who are forced to seek accommodation in other informal settlements. In some cases, areas unsuitable for residential use have been regularized, threatening broader planning goals, resulting in high infrastructure costs and encouraging further informal settlement in the expectation of future regularization.

Because their lack of access to credit and low incomes force low-income families to seek land and housing in informal settlements, many of which are in the peripheral and only affordable locations, they are faced with long and costly journeys to work, often using informal public transport. A study found that 82 per cent of residents living in a peripheral and 69 per cent in a central informal settlement do not utilize formal transport networks to travel to work. Instead, roughly 39 per cent of residents in the former and 33 per cent in the latter rely on shared vans (*pesaros*) in which users pay for their portion of the journey to work.

Source: Aguilar et al, 2003; Iracheta, 2004; Wigle, 2006; Perry, 2007; Aguilar, 2008; Iracheta and Smolka, undated

Cities in Africa are ... dominated by informal activities and widespread informal settlements

inconsistent and ambivalent, with the result that many activi-ties and settlements are not integrated within regular planning processes and governance institutions.[48]

With regards to informal commerce, some city governments (e.g. Quito, Lima, Caracas, Bogotá and Mexico City) have tried to formalize it by imposing time and locational restrictions on vending activities. However, the sheer size and scale of the informal sector has made it hard to regulate. Thus, policies towards the informal economy often simultaneously embrace and condemn it.[49]

Africa

Cities in Africa are, with few exceptions, characterized by low densities, peripheral sprawl, economies dominated by informal activities and widespread informal settlements with limited services. The proportion of urban dwellers living in informal settlements is higher in Africa as a region than any other part of the world. A staggering 62.2 per cent of the urban population in sub-Saharan Africa live in slums, while, in contrast, 14.5 per cent of North Africa's urban population reside in such settlements.[50]

It is estimated that the informal economy labour force accounts for around 60 per cent of urban jobs, and an even larger proportion of women's economic activities.[51] During the early years after independence, informal economic activ-ities were seen as an 'inconvenient reality which would, no doubt, disappear as modernization spread through the economy'.[52] The relationship between informal entrepre-neurs and the state was ambivalent, marked by both periodic harassment and a degree of tolerance, albeit backed by bribes. The fall in formal-sector employment with structural adjustment and economic liberalization drove a large propor-tion of urban workers into the informal sector, but also increased competitive pressures from cheap imports. Home-based enterprises, street trade and informal markets proliferated. The mixture of toleration, support and repression continued, with the latter often justified on grounds of informal activities' illegality, contravention of health and safety regulations, and 'untidiness'.[53]

The web of formal investment in industry and infrastructure interspersed with formal and informal residential settlements that is typical of many Asian cities, and the linking of cities to metropolitan corridors are much less common in Africa. However, there are some similar urban corridors, such as Gauteng in South Africa, Cairo–Alexandria in Egypt and, arguably, the coast of West Africa, where city expansion combined with the urbanization of small towns and villages is leading to the emergence of some extended metropolitan areas such as Cotonou–Porto Novo in Benin.[54] The absence as yet of many significant metropolitan corridors reflects the relative absence of inter-urban transport infrastructure, limited investment in formal-sector enterprises and weak integration of peri-urban settlements within city economies. Commonly, the authorities under-provide infrastructure and overly restrict on-plot development, contributing to low-density sprawl, which increases costs for both firms and households and the providers of public transport. Investment climate surveys of formal manufacturing firms in urban locations in six African countries compared with four in South and South-East Asia, for instance, found that the main constraints on their operations were typically inadequate infrastructure and services.[55]

Colonial authorities in Africa often aimed to control in-migration to urban areas. One mechanism for ensuring that only those needed to provide the necessary labour lived in urban centres was to accommodate them in planned areas of rental housing. However, informal settlements frequently sprang up to accommodate those who had come to the end of their contracts or arrived in town to take advantage of the economic opportunities created by colonial urbanization. Depending upon patterns of landownership and the attitudes of the colonial authorities, such settlements involved incremental squatting on land belonging to the colonial administration, allocation of plots in areas still under customary tenure, 'shack farming' on European-owned land or occupation of hazardous areas. Independence in most countries was marked by the relaxation of migration controls, increased urban employment opportunities and rapid urban growth. The planning and housing policies inherited from the colonial authorities proved completely unable to cope with the scale and speed of urban growth, and the scale of informal settlement increased markedly.

As older informal settlements have been consolidated, densities have risen and open areas have been encroached upon. Some services have either been officially provided or have evolved informally, generally to address the most urgent health problems. Encouraged by international agencies such as the World Bank and UN-Habitat, many governments have attempted to upgrade and regularize selected settlements. Sometimes these attempts have been limited and tokenistic; but elsewhere they have been widespread, although it has proved difficult to control further development and densification or to maintain the services and infrastructure provided.

Limited capacity to supply formally subdivided and serviced land, operate development regulation or provide affordable public or private-sector housing mean that not only low-income, but also many middle-income urban households find that their only option is to seek building plots or houses in informal settlements. Even where considerable public investment in planned settlements occurs, there is frequently a mismatch between what is built and what people need and want, so that the results fall far short of those intended.

The shelter construction process is generally managed by owner-builders, funded from income and savings, and reflects an incremental process of investment and improvement, depending upon perceived and actual security of tenure and resource availability. The resulting houses and business premises rarely satisfy planning and building regulations and some are extremely makeshift. Services are generally either self-provided, or are provided by informal enterprises.

A prominent feature of urbanization and growing informality in Africa has been the expansion of the built environment into peri-urban areas. This is characterized by contestation over access to, control over and use of land-based resources, as well as limited governance capacity for infrastructure development, planning and development regulation.[56] Although there is some international investment in industry and services[57] and some investment in commercial agricultural production in these areas (e.g. horticulture and flowers for export around Kenyan and Zimbabwean urban areas), it is limited compared to cities elsewhere in the world. More often, economic liberalization in the 1990s was associated with a proliferation of small-scale investment in housing, agriculture and micro-enterprises. For example, around Dar es Salaam, the 'zone of survival' has given way to a 'zone of investment' as liberalization has improved access to private and public transport, with linear settlements along the roads being in-filled with housing and diversified small and micro-enterprises.[58]

The channels through which land for peri-urban development is supplied combine adapted customary practices with official and semi-official procedures.[59] The former are dominant where cities are surrounded by areas under customary tenure (see Box 7.3), but are also influential elsewhere because the customary rules for land transactions are widely understood by urban residents, many of whom are first- or second-generation migrants from rural areas. However, informal brokers and local government officials who unofficially draw up plans or authenticate written agreements of sale often mimic formal-sector procedures and practices, and may use their official connections to undertake their land market roles. Often, the planning standards and layouts do not comply with those specified in official plans and regulations. In some instances, however, subdividers and middle-income house builders will attempt, within affordability constraints, to emulate good practices (e.g. safeguarding road reserves and sites for schools, markets, etc.). They may also try to comply with official requirements in order to facilitate later regularization.

Box 7.3 Informal customary land management, Enugu, Nigeria

Public authorities in rapidly growing cities in Nigeria have failed to provide necessary services and infrastructure, including planned land for orderly development. In Enugu, indigenous customary landowners linked by communal and familial affiliations control the bulk of peripheral land where active conversion from rural to urban uses is occurring, with family landholding being the dominant form of ownership and control. Enugu is an important administrative, industrial and commercial centre in the eastern part of southern Nigeria, with a population in 2006 of 722,664 and an annual growth rate of 3 per cent. Its origin dates back to the discovery of coal in the area by the British in 1909. Public-sector land delivery is only able to meet a small proportion of demand.

There is evidence that, as far back as the 1930s, indigenous communities in Enugu had begun to formally subdivide their land and sell plots to private buyers. Thus, a close relationship has existed from a very early stage between formal and informal land delivery and management processes in the city. In recent years, purchasers have sought legal protection by attempting to obtain formal titles over land acquired from traditional sources. This has created an important interface between informal and formal land management practices. Verification of customary land status by government agencies before formal titling and submission of planning schemes prepared by indigenous communities to public authorities for approval represent other areas where functional interfaces between formal and informal customary land management practices have emerged.

Within a context of limited public-sector capacity to supply land for housing, the strength of customary land delivery in Enugu is its ability to deliver large numbers of plots to members of indigenous families by allocation and inheritance and to middle- and upper-income households by sale of leases in less complex, slow, unpredictable and opaque ways than the formal land delivery system. The main weaknesses of this dominant land delivery channel, however, are the inability of landowning communities to service land and to guarantee acceptable tenure security for land purchasers. Also, an urban land production and delivery system dominated by non-formal sub-markets, which does not operate within a framework of urban development plans, can be extremely costly for the economy because of the additional costs of retrofitting infrastructure in unplanned areas. Nevertheless, rather than continuing to try unsuccessfully to operate the current system or importing models from elsewhere, it is desirable that learning from local evolving practices is maximized to identify the improvements most likely to succeed.

Source: Ikejiofor, 2008

Planning approaches based on legislation that has, in some cases, changed little from that inherited from colonial times and master plans implemented through public-sector investment and development control have proved completely unable to guide urban development in much of Africa. Planning's reach has generally been confined to central business districts, high-income residential areas and their associated facilities. Its ineffectiveness can be attributed to financial and human resource limitations, especially at local government level; limited political and public understanding and support of urban planning; administrative fragmentation, especially in peri-urban areas; and the perceived incompatibility of informal employment and settlement with political and bureaucratic visions of the modern city (see Chapter 3).

Even where projects to regularize and upgrade informal settlements have been implemented, planners and other bureaucrats have often been reluctant partners, while attempts to supply low-cost serviced plots through sites and services schemes have frequently fallen victim to economic crisis. Other problems have included land and housing market distortions arising from their small scale; 'leakage' of plots targeted at low-income beneficiaries upwards to higher-income households; and corruption in plot allocation. Rather than limited planning resources being targeted at making a strategic difference to urban expansion and land supply for urban development, they have been used to prepare conventional city-wide and detailed urban plans that can only be implemented in limited sections of the city. Despite the moves towards more strategic action-oriented approaches to planning discussed in Chapter 3, the ability of planning systems in African cities to prevent or deal with widespread informal economic activity, land subdivision, housing construction and service delivery remains extremely limited, with the partial exception of South Africa.

Developed and transitional countries

There is little informal settlement in contemporary European and North American cities, with the exception of tiny travellers' settlements and some small-scale squatting, generally in disused buildings. Some informal occupation and modification of formal buildings occurs in inner-city areas, especially by slum landlords and poor urban residents, including recent migrants. The expansion of settlements into areas surrounding cities has also been observed. For example, in the Veneto Plain in northern Italy, agriculture and urban development have been closely related. The latter has occurred not just through the expansion of cities such as Venice and Padua, but also through the largely uncontrolled expansion of numerous villages for artisanal industry, commerce and residential uses. Such development has blurred the divide between urban and rural areas and transformed the whole metropolitan region into an urban–rural continuum.[60]

Typically, employment in developed countries is in formal enterprises, and urban planning and regulation systems are strongly developed. Compliance with labour and development regulations is widespread and enforcement effective. However, economic liberalization since the 1980s has been associated with the growth of various kinds of economic informality, including unregulated wage employment as a means of reducing costs or accommodating recent immigrants, as well as moonlighting or self-employment that evades the tax system. It is estimated that in the highly developed Organisation for Economic Co-operation and Development (OECD) countries, the informal economy accounts for about 16 per cent of value added.[61]

In Southern Europe, until the 1970s, planning and development regulation systems were relatively ineffective and prone to evasion. In Italy, for example, more than 1 million unauthorized housing units are estimated to have been built between 1982 and 2002.[62] On joining the European Union, access to funds was often conditional on the production of regional and urban plans. This provided a significant incentive to strengthen the weak planning and regulatory systems. Today, the planning systems of most Southern European countries are as strongly developed as those in Northern Europe.

In the transitional economies of Europe and the former USSR, city governments have had to cope with signif-

Planning's reach has generally been confined to central business districts, high-income residential areas and their associated facilities icant economic change, the restoration of private property markets and transformations in governance arrangements (see Chapter 2). The transition from centrally planned to market-based economies was associated with dramatic increases in poverty, inequality and unemployment, forcing many people formerly employed by state enterprises into informal-sector employment (see Box 7.4).

During 2002/2003, it was estimated that the informal economy accounted for about 40 per cent of GDP in 25 transitional countries.[63] An emerging group of real estate investors exploited weak planning and building deregulation to maximize their profits. Residential property prices escalated, reflecting inherited housing shortages, the growth of a middle class and demographic changes. Upper- and middle-class households have relocated to suburban residential parks, gated urban enclaves and upmarket inner-city neighbourhoods. Peripheral residential developments were often initiated by international investors and encouraged by peripheral municipalities keen to increase their revenue base.[64] Lower-income households have remained in or been pushed into privatized deteriorating housing estates or low-cost housing in peripheral villages and informal settlements, where they are joined by poor in-migrants and refugees, especially in the cities of parts of South-East Europe and the Caucasus states.

Cheaper land and low-cost services (e.g. the use of wood rather than electricity or gas for heating, water from wells and refuse disposal in roadside dumps) attract low-income residents to existing peripheral settlements. However, for many, polluting industry relocated from inner-city areas, as well as the poor levels of connectivity to infrastructure and services, result in unhealthy living conditions, physical isolation and social exclusion, especially for women, whose limited mobility can restrict their participation in business and civic life.[65] Suburbanization and urban sprawl have thus been driven by the location of warehouses, light industrial and retail developments near transport nodes beyond the suburban ring, and by global influences, such as the desire to attract foreign direct investment.

The inherited planning systems had difficulty in adapting to market-based urban development during the 1990s. They failed to cope with the implications of economic reform, decentralization and the entry of multiple actors into land and housing development, and were discredited and marginalized. Obsolete master plans, lack of municipal expertise and resources, and bureaucratic obstacles to obtaining development permission led to widespread illegal development. For example, occupants of apartments often enclosed balconies, or built extensions and additional floors to increase the living space available, or converted parts of residential buildings for small-scale enterprise. It was estimated that about one quarter of all new housing in Tirana (Albania) and half in Belgrade (Serbia) was illegal and substandard, much being built on road reserves and green spaces. Construction took place without building permits on both titled and untitled land, the latter being, in part, a result of delays in land restitution. In this chaotic period, the civil law-based master planning system that was supposed to

Box 7.4 Informal employment, Romania

In spite of continuous economic growth in recent years, informal employment is a key feature of the Romanian labour market, accounting for between 20 and 50 per cent of total employment, depending upon the definition used. Two main groups can be identified among those in informal employment: those who work informally because they have no real alternative and for whom informal employment constitutes a survival strategy, and those who deliberately evade taxes and social security contributions. The first group includes some forms of informal work in agriculture and contributing family workers. The second comprises non-registered firms, or firms which do not register their workers and hire them without labour contracts, firms that under-report their sales and workers who under-declare their earnings and receive so-called 'envelope payments' in cash.

Three main groups of factors can explain the persistence of informal employment in Romania. First, socio-economic developments following transition, such as economic restructuring and privatization of state-owned enterprises, low or negative economic growth, unemployment, and increased poverty and inequality are among the main reasons pushing people into informality. Moreover, emigration abroad, with its links to informal employment, is an additional determinant of informal work, as many temporary migrants return to Romania for short periods of time and engage in informal work. Second, institutional factors, such as labour market regulations and the structure of the tax and social security systems, also determine informal employment. In addition, bureaucracy, heavy public administration and the subsequent corruption are thought to be connected with informal work. Last, but not least, informal employment is also determined by a number of behavioural/societal factors, such as the culture of non-compliance, the lack of trust in public institutions, negative perceptions of the role of the state, and partial understanding or underestimation of the benefits derived from social security.

Some efforts have been made in recent years, especially with the reform of the tax and benefit system and the introduction of the new pension plan. However, until recently, most efforts focused on punishment rather than on prevention of informality or the creation of appropriate incentives for formal versus informal work. In addition, policies to help the most vulnerable groups and offer them the necessary skills and assets to participate in formal work are uncommon.

Source: Parlevliet and Xenogiani, 2008

provide a high degree of certainty and legality through ensuring compliance with detailed planning provisions was routinely sidestepped; amendments were granted at the whim of local officials; permission for new suburban industrial, retail and residential developments was given with little regard to their transport or environmental implications; and corrupt practices proliferated. Unauthorized changes in approved layouts were frequent. Much planning consisted of the *ex post facto* regularization of informal development, exacerbating further informal development in the expectation of future regularization.[66]

During the last ten years, however, governments in many countries in the region have reasserted control over their shadow economies and recognized the need for effective planning. A new generation of planning legislation has been introduced, reforms have revitalized planning systems, and urban development plans have been updated, especially in countries such as Slovenia, Slovakia and the Czech Republic. Nevertheless, progress is hindered by the lack of a strong legal basis for development regulation, coherent national urban development policies, detailed strategies, proper funding for implementation and effective arrangements for metropolitan government.[67]

The transition from centrally planned to market based economies was associated with dramatic increases in poverty ... forcing many people ... into informal sector employment

FACTORS AFFECTING INFORMALITY

It is apparent from the above review of urban informality trends in various regions of the world that a number of key factors give rise to informal economic activity, land and property development and service delivery. These are discussed below.

In developed and many transitional countries where most economic activities comply with formal regulatory requirements governing employment, registration, health and safety, informalization has been associated with competitive pressures arising from economic crisis, privatization, economic liberalization and global competition. For example, employers attempt to reduce costs by outsourcing aspects of production to unprotected workers (e.g. home workers) casualizing their own labour force, ignoring health and safety regulations, or evading the tax net.

In developing countries, the growth of formal enterprises is often restricted by limited domestic demand for the goods and services that they produce, international competition, shortages of capital for investment, and difficult operating conditions, including obstacles to accessing suitably located land, poorly developed infrastructure and unreliable services. In addition, contemporary manufacturing is often capital intensive, generating relatively little employment. Because the urban labour force has expanded more rapidly than formal wage employment, and in the absence of state-provided social safety nets, urban men and women have few options but to establish or seek wage employment in informal enterprises. More often than not, their limited education and skills and restricted access to institutional credit constrain the choice and scale of enterprise within the informal sector. Other niches for informal enterprise include some goods and services that the formal sector does not provide due to insufficient demand, and some for which small and micro-enterprises can undercut formal producers. Micro-enterprises' need for cheap premises further leads to the proliferation of home-based enterprises, the occupation of unused land and street trading.

Central and local governments are often unable to implement laws and regulations governing enterprise, land and housing development because of insufficient political backing and public support, inadequate organizational and financial resources, and mismatches between official approaches and the needs of most urban businesses and residents. As a result, plan proposals and regulatory requirements are over-ridden or disregarded, completely or partly, by large-scale developers, those catering for formal businesses and high-income households. They are also ignored by informal enterprises and low-income households, sometimes from ignorance, but more often because of desperate need. The evasion of planning requirements is often a result of government ineffectiveness, or may occur with the collusion of politicians and public officials.

Approaches to planning and regulation that fail to reflect the needs of many economic actors seeking land and accommodation, including households, service providers and businesses, force these actors to evade planning require-ments, lest they fail to establish viable businesses, obtain suitably located and affordable premises, and provide services for which there is effective demand. Both the content of plans and regulations, and the procedures for obtaining development and operating permission may be inappropriate. Even if planning proposals, standards and regulations are appropriate, the procedures for registration and obtaining approval may be time consuming and costly, especially when unofficial payments are required to expedite decisions. Inappropriate or excessively bureaucratic regula-tory requirements for formal-sector development directly increase housing costs and also increase prices by limiting supply, fuelling a vicious circle of informality.[68]

Public-sector agencies are, for a variety of reasons, often inefficient and ineffective providers of utilities and services. The favoured solution of the 1990s was large-scale private-sector participation. However, most urban service delivery is officially still the responsibility of public-sector agencies, especially local government. Improvements in efficiency, rehabilitation of existing systems and extension to reach unserved populations, especially the poor, have been limited in many urban centres, even where reform has been attempted and regardless of whether the public or large-scale private sector is responsible. In practice, much service delivery depends upon small-scale private-sector and infor-mal operators, who replace or supplement formal transport, water and sanitation, waste management and energy supply systems. Their activities are particularly important in infor-mal settlements, which are commonly neglected by the public authorities, but also extend into many formal business and residential areas.

INNOVATIVE PLANNING RESPONSES TO INFORMALITY

As discussed above, urban informality has generally been regarded as illegal and undesirable. Typical responses have been removal or neglect, sometimes accompanied by grudg-ing accommodation, underlain by a desire to extend conventional approaches to spatial planning and regulation to all urban land and property development and economic activity. However, the feasibility and desirability of respond-ing to the challenge of informality by extending conventional approaches to land administration, planning and regulation is uncertain in many countries. More useful pointers to appro-priate ways forward in these circumstances can be identified by reviewing innovative approaches and assessing their trans-ferability. Four groups of responses are discussed in this section: alternatives to eviction; regularization; strategic use of planning tools to influence development actors; and partnerships between public agencies and informal businesses to manage public space and provide services. In no case can spatial planning work in isolation from the rest of the land administration and urban management systems, particularly those concerned with the definition and regula-tion of tenure, political and participatory arrangements and processes, and revenue generation and financial planning.

In developed and many transitional countries ... most economic activities comply with formal regulatory requirements

In developing countries ... urban men and women have few options but to establish or seek wage employment in informal enterprises

Alternatives to eviction

Often, public agencies' preference is to halt and remove informal developments and economic activities that do not comply with plans, policies and regulations, as well as seeking to evict occupants of land required for public purposes. Private owners use the courts or strong-arm tactics to harass or evict squatters or unwanted tenants. Eviction has sometimes been used to achieve hidden intentions, such as settling political scores or 'ethnic cleansing'. Forced evictions disproportionately affect certain groups such as women, travellers, migrants and indigenous people.[69] Evictions are further associated with violence, especially towards women, which may include intimidation, coercion, rape and beatings.[70] Evictions also occur through market forces when the demand for well-located land increases. As some residents respond to rising prices by selling their rights to land and property, it may become increasingly difficult for others to resist pressure from purchasers to sell, sometimes at below market prices.

International law now regards forced eviction as a human rights violation and urges governments, first, to consider all feasible alternatives and, second, to adhere to good practice guidelines if eviction is necessary.[71] It essentially recognizes people's rights to decent work and security of tenure, including the right to housing, privacy and the peaceful enjoyment of their possessions. International agencies such as the World Bank and the Asian Development Bank, as well as UN-Habitat's Advisory Group on Forced Evictions, specify that the people affected should be:

- consulted before the decision to evict is taken;
- given adequate notice of when eviction will occur;
- provided with information on the purpose for which the land is required;
- provided with the legal right to appeal and legal aid where appropriate; and
- provided with fair and equitable compensation for lost assets, livelihoods and incomes.

Increasingly, international law is being incorporated into domestic law, protecting people against forced eviction and providing them with various rights if they are evicted.[72] Once governments improve domestic laws to protect informal occupiers, including landholders and entrepreneurs, their ability to ensure that private landowners adhere to the legal provisions regarding eviction and encourage dialogue between occupants and owners about alternatives is strengthened.

A growing acceptance of 'the informal city' has been detected in recent years. Sometimes this arises from recognition of the fact that informal economic activities are vital to the urban economy and the livelihoods of many urban residents, especially when governments cannot provide safety nets to sustain large numbers of households above the poverty line. At other times it arises from recognition of the fact that the supply of formal public and private plots and houses not only falls far short of demand, but is unaffordable for a large proportion of households, a gap that is filled by informal settlements.

Often the most feasible and appropriate action open to governments is to stop the most harmful ways in which they intervene, such as forced evictions.[73] For example, in Turkey, informal settlements, or *gecekondus*, are tolerated and have been subject to periodic amnesties.[74] Publicly calling a halt to harassment and eviction of informal occupants of land in public ownership immediately increases their security of tenure, encouraging them to invest in their houses and enterprises, and improving the prospects for dialogue about the future of the areas concerned.[75] However, although recognition of the status quo removes the threat of eviction, it is often politically motivated, easily overturned and rarely provides more than short-term security of tenure.

Inevitably, some settlements are in locations that are too unsafe for permanent residence, while other settlements and some informal economic activities are on land required for legitimate public purposes or compete with other users of public spaces, such as streets and squares. Announcement of a moratorium on evictions provides a window of opportunity during which a survey of all informal settlements and locations with significant concentrations of informal enterprises can be conducted. In this way, it is possible to identify those for which no alternative to eviction exists and to devise a programme for further action in those suitable for long-term use. Such a process is likely to be politically contentious because of the conflicting interests involved and the fear that tolerance of informal activities may encourage further informal development. Ultimately, political decision-makers may have to make unpopular decisions. However, consultation also provides opportunities for occupants to suggest alternatives to eviction.

In Thailand, for example, most informal occupiers have rental agreements with private owners of undeveloped sites, with the result that when an owner wishes to redevelop a site, eviction is unacceptable. In some instances, on both publicly and privately owned land, land-sharing has been successfully negotiated as an alternative. Under this arrangement, the landowner leases or sells part of it to existing occupants, who redevelop their houses at higher densities, typically multi-storey apartments, and develops the rest. The result is that their occupation is formalized and living conditions improved. It may be necessary to modify standards to permit the owner to develop more intensively than permitted by the zoning provisions and to ensure that the replacement housing is affordable by existing residents.

Land-sharing is complex to negotiate and has been possible only with non-governmental organization (NGO) support in well-organized communities. In addition, some households may have to leave to make densification feasible and some may be unable to afford the newly built accommodation. An alternative is for the landowner to pay sufficient compensation that enables occupiers to vacate the land and buy land elsewhere.[76] In the Philippines, those who have to be evicted are offered five resettlement sites from which to choose.[77] Other alternatives to eviction will be explored further below.

International law now regards forced eviction as a human rights violation and urges governments … to consider all feasible alternatives

A growing acceptance of 'the informal city' has been detected in recent years

Regularization and upgrading of informally developed areas

Regularization and upgrading of informally developed areas is preferable to neglect or demolition. Regularization implies recognition and provision of secure tenure, while upgrading generally focuses on the provision or improvement of basic services, although it may also involve replanning and redevelopment to ensure compliance with planning and building regulations. Formalization of tenure is generally taken to involve the provision of title to individual plots – the strongest legal form tenure rights can take. Titles give landowners rights and political voice, are guaranteed by the state, may enable owners to borrow using the property as collateral, and therefore are expected to encourage investment. In addition, title registration accompanied by a cadastre is expected to facilitate planning by providing decision-makers with relevant information and accurate maps.

However, the merits of titling have been widely contested for various reasons.[78] It is also the most complex and costly form of tenure to institute, requiring a formal plot survey and checks on all rival claims to the land. While some countries have succeeded in adopting a universal system of titling registration (e.g. Australia), in many the complexities of a centuries-old landownership system mean that titling is accompanied by deeds registration and provisions for resolving conflicting claims over land.[79]

In addition, titling can lead to overt conflict over overlapping forms of rights and the dispossession of the less influential, including tenants, new occupiers and women. Many countries have limited legal protection for women's property rights and, where it does exist, it is not always acted upon due to weak enforcement and an unquestioning acceptance of patriarchal power.[80] Some of the supposed benefits of titling are also not necessarily relevant to low-income households, who seldom wish to mortgage their sole asset and to whom financial institutions are reluctant to lend, in any case. This is demonstrated in regularization processes where occupants are content with intermediate forms of tenure and do not transform these into titles even when they are entitled and expected to do so (e.g. in Dakar, Senegal).[81] As a result, remarkably little progress has been made globally with large-scale titling.[82]

The main purposes, means of registration and bundles of rights allocated may all vary. Evidence shows that low-income landholders prioritize 'good enough security' that protects them from eviction, enables them to improve their houses when they can afford to do so, enables them to bequeath their property with confidence to their heirs and provides them with access to affordable and accessible channels for resolving conflicts when necessary. Public agencies may be primarily interested in providing services to enhance health and safety, knowing the identity of occupants to improve security and enable cost recovery, and bringing informal settlements into the revenue-generation net. Both occupants and public agencies are interested in safeguarding access and providing sites for public facilities, such as schools or markets, improving drainage and services, and a registration system that is relatively streamlined,

affordable and easily updated. These purposes may be achieved by recognizing and registering previous land transactions in a deeds registration system and current occupancy in a financial cadastre or street addressing system, although care must be taken to recognize the rights of both men and women, depending upon their position in the family.[83]

Where landholders in informal areas are squatters, the basis for registration can be usufruct or adverse possession. In the Philippines, for example, occupation and use can be a basis for a group tenure claim.[84] Adverse possession entitles a person or community in possession of land owned by another to acquire rights. Certain legal requirements need to be satisfied in this case – for example, that the claimant does not own any other land and that the occupier has been in possession continuously, without challenge from the legal owners, for a specified term. There are provisions for adverse possession in the laws of many, but not all, countries. For example, it has been incorporated into the 2001 City Statute in Brazil. Because of the provision for continuous occupancy and use, speculators and land hoarders are excluded.[85] Many informal settlements, however, have developed on land informally subdivided by landholders with legal ownership rights in the form of either title or customary tenure, in which case registration can be based on a combination of the written evidence of transactions (which is almost always available) and the testimony of witnesses, such as village elders or local officials.[86]

A 2001 to 2003 review of 30 years of upgrading informal settlements in African cities found that early upgrading projects were ambitious in their scale and scope, seeking to regularize tenure, invest in infrastructure and improve housing. Over time, in recognition of the complexity of tenure regularization, interventions have become more modest, focusing on infrastructure improvements as a means of enhancing tenure security and encouraging investment in housing, rather than tenure security being regarded as a necessary precursor to other improvements. Within this general pattern, programmes have varied widely, especially with respect to infrastructure standards, cost recovery and the extent to which they were demand driven and participatory.[87] Contemporary programmes that have proved capable of implementation at a large scale include those in Thailand[88] and Argentina. Even in China, increasing attention is being paid to upgrading existing housing and living environments, both in inner-city areas and in peripheral villages that have now become part of the city.[89] Brazil's legislative framework is rights based and incorporates provision for regularization and upgrading of *favelas*, alongside increased roles and responsibilities for municipal governments with respect to spatial planning and participatory budgeting.

A flexible approach to planning for regularization and upgrading is an essential tool for improving the liveability of informal settlements. Experience has demonstrated that modest and incremental approaches developed in conjunction with residents, local decision-makers and land market actors can be implemented at scale and need not result in gentrification. However, the processes are complex and it may be costly to retrofit infrastructure and to provide facili-

Regularization and upgrading of informally developed areas is preferable to neglect or demolition

Remarkably little progress has been made globally with large-scale titling ties if sites have not been set aside for this purpose. Often low-income tenants and owners are forced to move out as a result of increased costs arising from liability for user charges and/or property tax. Regularization may also conflict with other planning objectives, such as conserving ecologically important areas. Upgrading of informal settlements is not, therefore, the whole answer. A twin-track approach is needed, in which regularization is accompanied by a programme of new land development at a sufficient scale to ensure affordability and inhibit new illegal settlement.

Influencing development actors by strategic use of planning tools

During the 1970s a number of developing countries nationalized land and attempted to meet the need for urban land through administrative allocation in order to ensure that development occurred in accordance with a master plan. Experience demonstrated the limitations of this model and today promising approaches concentrate on using public planning and financial resources strategically to guide development. This implies working with private actors, including informal subdividers, developers and operators within a policy and legislative framework. It includes the use of public investment in trunk infrastructure to influence patterns of development, guided land development using strategic/outline planning, land pooling or readjustment and the gradual extension of detailed planning and development control.

■ Construction of trunk infrastructure

This can be used to attract investment to preferred locations – for example, increasing the attraction of secondary centres within extended metropolitan regions in order to reduce congestion in the core city by improving links between them (see Chapter 8). For example, New Mumbai was established in 1972 around the port of Nava Sheva, with rail and road links with the city of Mumbai. By 2001 it had a population of 1.5 million.[90] Currently, there are 24 rail-based rapid transit systems under construction and 10 more in the planning stages in Asian cities. Although such plans often reflect world city aspirations rather than being based on realistic assessments of the costs of construction, operation and maintenance, or the fares that users can pay, such investment can be used to encourage development in planned directions and to generate revenue for public investment, as in the well-known example of Curitiba in Brazil. However, without proper planning of new development and complementary policies, the outcomes may primarily benefit large-scale investors and developers and high-income households, as shown by the example of Jakarta, Indonesia (see Box 7.1).

■ Guided land development

Planning in advance of development is preferable and more efficient than regularization.[91] Where planning capacity and resources are limited, attempts have been made to ensure an adequate supply of land for expansion by guided land development. This requires an outline strategic plan that identifies the main areas for phased urban expansion, including industrial areas and the location of urban commercial centres; reserves sites for major public facilities such as universities or secondary schools; protects the areas of greatest environmental significance; and is linked to a programme of major infrastructure investment, especially main roads, drainage and water supply. For example, it has been suggested that expansion areas sufficient for 20 to 30 years ahead should be identified and defined by a grid of secondary roads 1km apart, or within a ten-minute walk of every location for access, public transport and main infrastructure provision. Adaptations to the grid can be used to accommodate topography and steer development away from unsuitable areas. Phased construction of roads and water supply will, it is further proposed, guide developers to appropriate grid superblocks, within which detailed planning regulation may not be necessary. An experiment with the approach is under way in Ecuador.[92] Provision for Urban Reference Plans has been made in a number of Francophone African countries, based on an urban grid of main roads intended to protect areas for public use, provide a basis for more detailed planning and prevent the emergence of informal settlements. Plans are based on five-year population

> **Box 7.5 Innovative responses to informality in Brazil**
>
> Since the mid 1980s, at national and subsequently at local level, based on previous experience and progressive practices, Brazil has institutionalized processes of deliberative democracy and introduced constitutional and legal innovations. First, according to Article 182 of the constitution, the objective of urban policy is 'to organize the full development of the social function of the city'. The same article established that urban property has a social function, allocating the responsibility for promoting desirable land use through expropriation, forced subdivision and progressive taxation to local governments. Second, Article 183 created a form of adverse possession available to residents of five years' standing without challenge from the landowner. Based on the principles of 'rights to the city' and the social function of property, in 2001, the City Statute defined the framework and instruments for registering and using land for social purposes. This involved recognition of the informal sector as part of the city and the subject of rights, democratic participation in urban management and empowerment of municipalities as the main agents entitled to regulate land use and occupation. It incorporated a number of innovative approaches to informality, including the use of planning as a tool for addressing social disparities, provision for local governments to recover a proportion of public investment that results in increased real estate values, and provision for regularization of informal settlements.
>
> During the 1980s, the proportion of the urban population living in *favelas* increased to about one fifth. The new legislation provided for them to be designated as special social interest zones in municipal zoning schemes as a basis for infrastructure installation, service provision and construction of social facilities, with a view to integrating them spatially and socially within the city. *Favela* residents are generally opposed to titling because they are not interested in mortgaging their homes and do not wish to be liable for property tax or enforced compliance with the building code. The *favela barrio* programme therefore concentrated on the right to adequate and affordable housing rather than absolute property rights, especially when regularizing settlements on public land. A form of leasehold, the concession of the real right to use, was adopted. It is typically 30 years, inheritable and registered in the names of both partners where appropriate. Specific planning regulations appropriate for the existing low-income population can be adopted (e.g. plot size, land use and construction standards) and annual expenditure programmes are decided through the city-wide participatory budgeting process. Although city programmes (e.g. in Rio de Janeiro, Belo Horizonte, São Paulo, Porto Alegre and Recife) were backed up in 2003 by a national regularization policy, progress on the ground lags behind innovative legislation and policies.
>
> *Source:* Fernandes, 2001; Caldeira and Holston, 2005; UN-Habitat, 2007a; Irazábal, 2008a

Today promising approaches concentrate on using public planning and financial resources strategically to guide development

Planning in advance of development is preferable and more efficient than regularization estimates for each district within a city, including extension zones and improvement options for existing areas.[93] A recent study agrees that blocking out areas for new settlement in advance and the installation of basic street layouts and sanitation is more efficient than regularization and upgrading.[94] This strategic approach to planning can be supported by tools such as geographic information systems (GIS) and satellite imaging, as in the case of the 2020 master plans for Karachi and other Pakistani cities, as well as utility mapping in Delhi.[95]

■ Land readjustment

If development is to occur within the blocks defined by a strategic plan, a series of supporting activities and instruments that provide both sticks and carrots to developers are required. The first challenge for public authorities is to assemble the land and finance for infrastructure investment and acquisition of sites for major public facilities. In many cities, there are no longer extensive areas in public ownership and public agencies must work with private or customary owners and private developers, both formal and informal, to ensure that phased development occurs.

There have been thorough reviews of experience in Japan and other countries which show that certain conditions must be present for land pooling to be successful: recognition by landowners that they cannot act independently to service, subdivide and sell their land at good prices; a large difference between rural and urban land prices, enabling owners to realize a profit that gives them sufficient incentive to participate after contributing the required share of their land; landownership that is clear or easily clarified and documented; and a responsible agency with the necessary skills and expertise. The land pooling approach has been less successful elsewhere (e.g. in India).[96] An evaluation of the progress and outcomes of a land pooling initiative in the Kathmandu Valley during the 1990s acknowledges that many problems remain to be resolved, but expresses optimism about its potential.[97]

Land readjustment is a market-led approach that provides plots for middle- and upper-income housing – it rarely provides low-income housing. A few examples of public–private partnerships for subdivision to produce low-cost plots are available, although much more experimentation is needed. For example, the Social Urbaniser is a new public initiative in Brazil that attempts to provide incentives to private developers to comply with planning regulations by adjusting standards in return for issuing development permission. The first successful case was negotiated in 2008 in São Leopoldo, where a developer was given permission to subdivide into smaller lots than specified in the regulations, in order to reduce the cost of the houses produced, in return for investment in on-site infrastructure and services.

One innovative way of financing infrastructure is through transferable development rights, in which a certificate is issued to the owner who cedes land, which can be traded for a roughly equivalent land area or floor space in the new building, or sold to a developer who may be able to use it to build additional floor area above the standard floorspace index (see Chapter 6).[98]

Group or communal arrangements may also provide a way forward. For example, in Colombia, there is provision for community land trusts involving the landowner, an association of prospective owner-occupiers that will hold intermediate tenure, and low-income families, who will eventually be issued with individual titles. Unlike private developers or individual families, such associations qualify for a subsidy, provided that they are non-profit and the units produced are cheaper than those built by private developers.[99] In Mexico, partnerships between public or private developers and agrarian communities who own between 20 and 70 per cent of land around cities are encouraged in order to generate large numbers of low-income plots. Reservations have been expressed about the prospects of informal settlements being displaced, although there is recognition that in the first tranche of projects implemented since reforms in 1991, efforts were made to tackle the problems.[100]

Partnerships with informal or low-income landowners or groups are unlikely to work if unrealistic standards and cumbersome procedures are imposed. Flexible attitudes to standards and participatory approaches to decision-making by planners and other professionals are therefore essential. Emphasis should be on 'working with' those who provide large volumes of affordable land and housing, through advice and advocacy rather than heavy-handed regulation.

■ Gradually extending effective planning in defined areas

In low-income and many middle-income countries, limited governance capacity and lack of support for planning and regulation limit what conventional planning and development regulation can achieve. Before detailed planning and development control can be successfully applied to all development, there is a need to demonstrate that the benefits outweigh the costs to landowners and developers. It can be argued that limited planning and financial resources are best used by concentrating efforts on the public realm and areas where development has major environmental and safety implications, while limiting intervention, especially detailed development regulation, in other areas, particularly middle- and low-density residential areas. Areas of concentration include city and town centres, special economic zones, industrial estates, environmentally important or hazardous areas, and major buildings used by large numbers of people such as shopping malls, cinemas, meeting halls and schools. In urban expansion areas, much subdivision and construction would not be subject to detailed regulation. Planners can, however, work with developers in these areas when opportunities arise and resources permit, either through regulation or through advocacy and advisory work, to encourage good layout planning and compliance with basic standards. Not only does this selective response mean that planning resources are available for strategic planning for the city as a whole, but it can also be used to build developer and public support for planning. In the context of China and Viet Nam, the development of such areas demonstrates that governments are reasserting their control incrementally, following a period of informal development and rapid change

Partnerships with informal or low-income landowners or groups are unlikely to work if unrealistic standards and cumbersome procedures are imposed

Limited planning and financial resources are best used by concentrating efforts ... on areas where development has major environmental and safety implications

associated with the transition to a market-oriented economy, during which governments were forced to prioritize needs other than regulating development.[101] For selective planning to succeed and comply with overall planning objectives, it needs to fit within a strategic framework.

Working with informal economic actors to manage public space and provide services

Informal economic actors include those engaged in retail trade and related services, manufacturing and repair services, as well as providers of transport, water and other services. A variety of ways in which public-sector agencies are working, and can work, with these actors to improve the management of public space and the provision of services can be identified. Innovative approaches are based on an acknowledgement of, first, the important contribution that informal activities make to the urban economy and their vital role in household livelihoods, and, second, the right of informal entrepreneurs to operate in the city. This provides a basis for understanding the economics of their operations, the positive roles that they play in providing goods and services, the constraints under which they operate and any adverse effects of their operations. This, in turn, enables the development of policies and programmes that counter adverse effects and address constraints without undermining the viability of their enterprises. City governments rarely have coherent policies with respect to informal enterprises, whether they are operating in public spaces, mixed-use neighbourhoods or designated areas. The aim should be to develop coherent policies that can guide the planning, regulation and day-to-day management of informal economic enterprises and actors.

■ Recognition of informal entrepreneurs' property rights

As with informal land and housing development, public agencies all too often harass and evict enterprises to restore physical order, enforce health and safety regulations or serve the interests of formal entrepreneurs who regard informal operators as competitors. For example, most cities assign the handling of street traders to agencies that deal with law and order, such as the police, resulting in evictions that destroy or disrupt livelihoods and involve the excessive use of force. Even if, in practice, informal enterprises are tolerated, the illegality of their operations makes them vulnerable to harassment and demands for bribes by police, municipal officials and other vested interests.[102] As noted above, harassment and forced eviction should be avoided wherever possible. The right of entrepreneurs to operate in the city should be recognized, the property rights they already have respected, and improved property rights negotiated. This may be done through managing the use of urban space and an appropriate regulatory system, as discussed below.

■ Allocation of special purpose areas

City authorities which accept that forced eviction fails to recognize the positive contribution made by informal opera-

tors often attempt to remove them from areas zoned for other uses, land unsuitable for development or public spaces to sites designated for markets or industrial estates. Relocation to planned areas is frequently associated with enforced compliance with official licensing and other regulatory requirements.[103] This rarely works well.[104] Planned markets are often less well located and are unpopular with both vendors and customers, relocation disrupts established economic networks, and the increased costs associated with relocation to planned markets or industrial areas, or licensing and regulation may threaten the viability of informal businesses.

In some cases, however, it is desirable and feasible to provide dedicated spaces for informal economic activities in markets and industrial areas. Markets are successful where their location, the facilities provided and the management arrangements are agreed by trader organizations and the public authorities. Often historic market sites or markets developed informally on undeveloped land are the most economically viable and successful. Regularization and upgrading are the most appropriate approaches in these situations.

When a site is needed for other uses or becomes too congested, relocation may be unavoidable. For example, when 2000 hawkers operating near the Red Fort in Delhi were evicted in August 2001, three associations negotiated over alternative sites, eventually agreeing on one, which opened in 2005. The businesses of those who tried to operate from the new market were, however, constantly undermined by traders operating on the streets around the Red Fort, necessitating periodic negotiations with the authorities for enforcement of the regulations.[105]

Traders are generally willing to pay licence fees or user charges if they feel that they are getting good value for money (e.g. in the form of security of tenure, access to water and sanitation facilities, and public transport access). Once markets are recognized, services may be provided by the market association independently or in collaboration with the municipal government.

■ Managing shared public spaces

Informal operators, especially vendors, commonly share public space with other users, especially vehicles, cyclists and pedestrians. Because of their dependence upon passing customer traffic, they are reluctant to relocate. Often, innovative solutions can be devised to ensure access to civic spaces by both traders and other social groups.[106] The aim should be to clarify the rights of users of public space in order to give vendors more security of operation, while safeguarding health and safety. Limited investment can reduce conflicts and produce dramatic improvements in circulation, hygiene and the operating environment for enterprises, as illustrated by the case of Warwick Junction in eThekwini, South Africa (see Box 7.6).

The absence of a regulatory environment can be as costly to informal operators as excessive regulation, so regulation is needed; but it should be streamlined to increase the likelihood of compliance. The incentives to comply must at least balance the costs of doing so – for

The right of entrepreneurs to operate in the city should be recognised, the property rights they already have respected, and improved property rights negotiated

The absence of a regulatory environment can be as costly to informal operators as excessive regulation, so regulation is needed

Box 7.6 Supporting informal street traders, Durban, South Africa

The newly established metropolitan local government for the city of Durban and its surrounding areas adopted an informal sector policy in 2001, based on the premise that informal activities are an important source of employment and contribute to poverty reduction. The policy commits the city to provide support to micro-enterprises, including business skills training and legal advice, and to improve its management of informal economic activities. The latter includes both restrictions (e.g. prohibited and restricted trading zones in the inner city) and positive measures, including the demarcation of sites for market trade. The city has also been experimenting with area-based management in selected areas, including the inner-city site of Warwick Junction, where proposals for physical improvements have been developed and implemented and day-to-day management improved by cooperation between officials from various municipal departments and informal operators.

Warwick Junction is the main public transport interchange, with as many as 460,000 commuters passing through daily and 8000 street traders. During the late 1980s, previous prohibitions were lifted to enable traders to operate legally. However, by the mid 1990s, their number had grown to nearly 4000 and the area had become known as a 'crime and grime hotspot'. In 1997, the municipality set out to examine safety, cleanliness, trading and employment opportunities and the efficiency of the public transport interchange. Teams were established to deal with a variety of issues identified by the municipality and traders, including ablution facilities, street cleaning and street sleeping, leading to a variety of negotiated improvements. For example, a Herb Traders Market was designated, with shelter, water and toilets. Today it accommodates nearly 1000 traders, supporting 14,000 other businesses – for example, people who gather medicinal herbs. More hygienic facilities have also been provided for street food processors and sellers. For relatively modest investment, significant improvements in organization and management of the area have been achieved and the value of an area-based management team that can coordinate municipal departments and work with traders' organizations demonstrated.

Sources: Skinner and Dobson, 2007; Skinner, 2008

---

example, by simplifying procedures, reducing or differentiating fees, and linking compliance to access to services or other forms of support.[107] Enforcement of location and time restrictions on street trading is difficult because of the sheer size of the informal retail sector. Nevertheless, arrangements for sharing trading locations can include space and time zoning, including demarcation and provision of dedicated trading areas in pedestrian areas and temporary closure of streets for markets. Thus, licensing can be used as an enabling rather than restrictive tool that provides traders with rights to general or location-specific trading on a daily basis or for a specified period, and the municipality with resources to invest in improved facilities. If licences are tied to a particular location, traders have an incentive to promote good management of the area, while membership of an association provides traders with a means of expressing voice and negotiating with municipal councils.[108]

Based on the work of the Sustainable Dar es Salaam Programme and its working group on micro-trade, guidelines for petty traders were produced in 1997.[109] These require traders to use markets or designated sites, form associations, adhere to regulations related to hygiene, etc. and refrain from trading outside certain buildings where heavy pedestrian traffic supposedly makes it unsafe. In the city centre, in particular, designated sites have been agreed upon and metal stands have been provided for street vendors to use. The latter facilitate sharing of space between traders and pedestrians and street cleaning. Thus, informal trade is well managed in the city centre and high-income areas and traders' associations have good relations with the city authorities.

> The provision of services to informal operators ... can support their operations ... and improve the working environment for the operators

■ Provision of basic services and support

Informal operators are both users and providers of basic services. Whether located in designated areas or shared public space, the provision of services to informal operators (e.g. electricity, water and sanitation) can support their operations, increase the likelihood of compliance with official hygiene standards, and improve the working environment for the operators themselves.

As providers, informal operators complement large-scale public or private agencies, especially in meeting the needs of households and businesses that cannot access formal services because of their absence, inadequacy or cost. Their contribution must be recognized while the weaknesses of the services they provide are addressed. For example, informal public transport operators provide a vital service in areas where official public transport is either not provided or too costly for residents, but their driving standards and safety record may be poor. Informal water vendors likewise fill gaps in the piped water supply network; but often the water they sell is costly and of inferior quality due to poor storage practices, even though it is usually sourced from the public supply. Informal pit latrine evacuators or refuse collection and recycling services assist in maintaining the environment in informal settlements, especially as densities increase; but the working conditions for operators are often unhealthy and waste disposal practices may be environmentally unsound.

An important element of a comprehensive approach to formal service provision is to work with informal operators through licensing, capacity-building, the enforcement of appropriate regulations and the development of alternatives when current livelihoods are damaged by policies. For example, when cycle rickshaws were banned in central Dhaka (Bangladesh), their continued operation in residential areas was permitted. In several Francophone West African countries, water resellers have formed associations to manage standpipes and extend the piped supply. In Côte d'Ivoire, the formal water provider, Société de Distribution d'Eau de Côte d'Ivoire, registers water resellers.[110] What is most important for planners is to be aware of the role played by informal service providers, to take their needs into account in land-use planning and development regulation, and to work with other agencies to address the constraints on their operation.

The provision of business support technical assistance also needs to be considered when developing responses to informal economic activities. Such support services are likely to include savings and credit arrangements, and technical assistance to realize productivity gains. Thus, as well as an appropriate policy and regulatory framework, and planning policies that secure informal operators access to appropriate urban space, complementary development policies differentiated for different sectors of the informal economy are needed.

■ Mixed-use zoning

Many informal economic activities, especially those of women, occur within residential areas and buildings. Often, conventional plans are based on single-use zoning and mixed uses are forbidden. In many countries with effective planning systems, the limitations of single-use zoning have long been realized, and more emphasis is now placed on mixed uses to produce vibrant and convenient living environments. Planning legislation in many poorer countries has not caught up, despite the popularity of mixed uses evident in most cities where enforcement of single-use zoning is weak. However, planners are becoming more realistic and are incorporating mixed uses into plan provisions. For example, the 2007 Delhi Master Plan has accepted mixed-use zoning as a way of accommodating non-polluting industry, informal trade, retail shops, professional activities, clinics, etc. in residential areas. The plan provides for one informal shop or unit per 1000 residents in new housing areas, five to six units for informal enterprises for every 1000 formal employees, and permits for informal traders in approved locations.[111] The positive result of such changes to law and policy is that most informal activities in homes and residential areas are no longer illegal. However, extending effective planning and building control to home-based enterprises and mixed-use areas in low-income countries is unlikely to be feasible for some considerable time.

■ Organization of informal operators

Effective organization enables informal operators to interact effectively with public agencies and strengthens their own ability to solve problems. It provides a channel through which their needs and priorities can be identified and presented to public authorities and appropriate approaches negotiated. The potential of trader organization is illustrated by the Dar es Salaam and eThekwini examples and the achievements of the Self Employed Women's Association in India, which, in 2006, had nearly 1 million members in nine states and had enabled its members to address a variety of constraints on their operations, including access to space and services.[112] Effective organization is also illustrated by the prevalence and increasing size and professionalism of associations amongst informal transport operators in Thiaroye-sur-mer in Pikine, Dakar, Senegal.

In summary, it is clear that for approaches to work well, local governments need to develop a good understanding of the economics of informal enterprise operation, adopt a flexible approach to the management of urban space and regulation of operators, and be prepared to use participatory and collaborative approaches to policy formulation and day-to-day management. The key elements of policy to facilitate and manage informal enterprises include:[113]

- supportive regulation and licensing;
- modest financial contributions by operators to pay for regulation, space allocation and management and services;
- traffic, public transport and road management;
- planning and design of civic spaces;
- provision of sites for markets and small producers in appropriate locations;
- provision of basic infrastructure and services;
- encouragement of traders' associations;
- municipal capacity-building to improve understanding of the economics and operation of informal trade; and
- participatory approaches to policy-making and management.

RESPONDING TO INFORMALITY THROUGH PLANNING AND GOVERNANCE

On the basis of the debates and trends reviewed above, a process through which urban planning and governance can gradually increase the effectiveness of its responses to informality can be identified. This involves three basic steps:

- *Step 1:* recognize the positive role played by informal land and property development and economic activities, and halt official actions that hinder their operations. Responses to informality such as harassment and eviction adversely affect livelihoods, cause inconvenience to suppliers and customers, and hinder the ability of subdividers, builders, entrepreneurs and service providers to meet the needs of urban residents and businesses.
- *Step 2:* change policies, laws and regulations. Consider the need and potential for formalization and regularization of economic activities, land supply and housing development, while being aware of the possible disadvantages of doing this, especially for the poor and marginalized social groups, including women. Formalization and regularization need not imply that informal activities must comply with existing standards and requirements, especially if these are inappropriate and impossible to enforce. Instead, adaptation of standards and procedures is likely to be necessary, including recategorizing certain informal practices as legitimate. Justifiable motives for formalization and regularization include the desire to bring occupants and enterprises within the municipal tax net in order to generate revenue to improve services; to improve construction, health and safety standards; and to safeguard environmentally sensitive areas. Appropriate tactics can include strategic enforcement of regulations in areas where risks to the public are greatest and the adoption of differentiated regulations, which are appropriate to the income levels and needs of particular areas or sub-sectors of the informal economy. Interventions should be guided by the following basic principles:
  - interventions restricted to the minimum necessary to safeguard the public;
  - incremental improvements, through step-by-step changes in standards, tenure arrangements and

The limitations of single-use zoning have long been realized, and more emphasis is now placed on mixed uses

Effective organisation enables informal operators to interact effectively with public agencies services, requiring a flexible approach on the part of official agencies;

- methods for developing policy, preparing plans, and day-to-day management based on participation, mutual learning and cooperation between public agencies, NGOs and informal actors; and
- formalization and regularization through a mixture of incentives and enforcement.

• *Step 3:* strengthen the reach and legitimacy of the planning system to reduce the extent of informality. For planning and regulation to be effective, it must gain widespread support from informal actors, politicians, residents and businesspeople. For such support to increase, each stakeholder must perceive the benefits of planning and regulation to outweigh the costs. This can be achieved through a combination of the selective use of limited planning resources to achieve impact, approaches that do not undermine the positive contribution made by informal activities, and strategies to educate citizens on the role and benefits of planning.

CONCLUDING REMARKS

This chapter has shown that the prevalence of informality in cities varies. On a global scale, there are many countries in which informality is extensive and growing, and much fewer countries where informality is either limited or becoming less prevalent. It is limited in countries where there is effective regulation of development and enterprises, but extensive in countries where large businesses account for a limited proportion of all economic and urban development activity, and planning and regulation are ineffective.

There is no single planning model for responding effectively to the challenges arising from urban informality. First, the appropriate model varies according to the principles of the national legal system, the political culture and governance arrangements – the key is that the approach is appropriate for its context. Second, approaches to policy formulation and plan preparation have continued to evolve even in countries that have had effective planning and regulatory systems for half a century or more, as the shortcomings of conventional approaches have become evident and the need for participation recognized. The problem with many ineffective approaches is that they have failed to change. In many developing countries, technocratic blueprint approaches, high standards and strict regulatory requirements persist, despite their obvious ineffectiveness in the face of widespread informality, intense conflicts of interest and limited governance capacity. The challenge is to devise an approach to planning that is capable of tackling the undesirable outcomes of informality while recognizing the contribution of informal developers, entrepreneurs and service providers to the urban development process.

Innovative approaches to informality are not confined to the planning and regulatory systems, although this chapter has focused on the spatial and development regulation aspects of the approaches identified. The first group of responses are alternatives to eviction or, where eviction in the public interest cannot be avoided, adherence to good practice guidelines to avoid further impoverishment and informal development. The second group entails the recognition, regularization and upgrading of informal land and property development wherever this is feasible, modifying tenure arrangements and regulatory requirements as appropriate in order to ensure that low-income residents and small and micro-enterprises benefit. A third group of responses focuses on the strategic use of limited planning and public-sector resources to guide and steer new development, rather than micro-plan it. Working with private-sector actors, especially informal land subdividers and builders, the aim is to ensure that the supply of affordable serviced land in suitable locations meets demand. Affordability can be enhanced by the adoption of appropriate standards, streamlining complex registration and regulation procedures and the adoption of appropriate cost-recovery policies. Rather than requiring development to comply with ideal standards or a desirable sequence of planned development from the outset, once the large-scale infrastructure and basic services are in place, subdivision, improvements to infrastructure and services, and investment in housing can proceed incrementally.

In many countries, especially in the developing regions of the world, governments have limited resources and limited legitimacy. There is a need for smart targeting of such limited resources to improve effectiveness and to build public support for planning and regulation. Only when land administration is streamlined and there is general public acceptance of the need for restrictions on property rights in the public interest will the wide enforcement of development controls be feasible. What is needed, therefore, is a differentiated and incremental approach. Once internationally recognized rights to decent work and housing and protection from harassment and eviction are realized, changes to policy, laws and practices to permit regularization and other innovative approaches to informality can be considered. Through participatory and collaborative approaches, these can both contribute to the development of more effective approaches and build wider support for planning and regulation. Conflicting interests and priorities mean that responses to informality are as much political as technical. Not until the actors involved feel that they can both influence and benefit from the planning, urban management and regulatory systems, in ways that are transparent and fair, can their effectiveness be enhanced.

On a global scale, there are many countries in which informality is extensive and growing

There is no single planning model for responding effectively to the challenges arising from urban informality

NOTES

1   Hart, 1973.
2   ILO, 1972.
3   See also Lipton, 1984; Guha-Khasnobis et al, 2006.
4   Meagher, 2005.
5   Guha-Khasnobis et al, 2006, p1.
6   UN-Habitat, 2006h.
7   Defined by Tripp as: 'Illicit activities that have no legal counterpart in the society in question ... [including] drug dealing ... extraction of rents, kickbacks and other forms of criminal activity' (Tripp, 2003, p303).
8   Bromley, 1978; Moser, 1978; Meagher, 2005; Leduka, 2006b; Rakodi, 2006.
9   Sindzingre, 2006.
10 de Soto, 2000; Guha-Khasnobis et al, 2006; UN-Habitat, 2006h.
11 Amis, 2004; UN-Habitat, 2006h.
12 UN-Habitat, 2006h, p11.
13 Ansari, 2008.
14 Ansari, 2008.
15 UN-Habitat, 2008b.
16 UN-Habitat, 2008b.
17 Webster and Muller, 2004 (see also Ansari, 2008).
18 Derived from the Bahasa words *desa* (village) and *kota* (town).
19 McGee, 1991.
20 McGee, 1991; Leaf, 2005b; Dupont, 2007; Schenk, 2002.
21 Ansari, 2008.
22 Ansari, 2008.
23 Douglass, 2008.
24 Ansari, 2008.
25 Ansari, 2008.
26 Yuen, 2008.
27 Ansari, 2008; Yuen, 2008.
28 Choe, 1998; Yeung and Lo, 1998; Laquian, 2007.
29 Leaf 1999, 2002, 2005b; Quang and Kammeier, 2002; Leaf and Hou, 2006; Liu and Wu, 2006; Waibel, 2008.
30 With a few exceptions, although the investment is often motivated by global ambitions related to economic development or mega-sports events, and concentrates on airports and limited transit routes that do not necessarily serve the poor (Yuen, 2008).

31 Ansari, 2008; Yuen, 2008.
32 Yuen, 2008.
33 Ansari, 2008.
34 Centre on Housing Rights and Evictions, 2006, pp74, 85; see also UN-Habitat, 2007a.
35 Yuen, 2008.
36 Perry, 2007, p29.
37 UN-Habitat, 2008b.
38 Magalhaes and Rojas, 2007.
39 Iracheta and Smolka, undated.
40 Gilbert, 1998.
41 Ferguson and Navarrete, 2003.
42 Phillips, 2006; Duffy, 2007.
43 Irazábal, 2008a.
44 Biderman et al, 2008; Iracheta and Smolka, undated.
45 Irazábal, 2008a.
46 Irazábal, 2008a.
47 Iracheta and Smolka, undated.
48 Irazábal, 2008a.
49 Irazábal, 2008a.
50 UN-Habitat, 2008b.
51 Kessides, 2006; UN-Habitat, 2006h, p11.
52 Potts, 2007, p10.
53 Hansen, 2004; Kamete, 2004; Kazimbaya-Senkwe, 2004; Lourenco-Lindell, 2004; Potts, 2007.
54 Kessides, 2006; Attahi et al, 2008.
55 Kessides, 2006.
56 Mbiba and Huchzermeyer, 2002.
57 Jenkins, 2000.
58 Briggs and Mwamfupe, 2000.
59 Lasserve et al, 2002; Durand-Gatabaki-Kamau and Karirah-Gitau, 2004; Ikejiofor, 2006; Jenkins, 2004; Kalabamu, 2006; Leduka, 2006a; Musyoka, 2006; Nkurunziza, 2006; Rakodi, 2006; Attahi et al, 2008.
60 Tempesta and Thiene, 1997.
61 Schneider, 2007.
62 Istituto Nazionale di Urbanistica, 2006.
63 Schneider, 2007, p19.
64 In many Eastern and Central European cities, and cities in the former Soviet Union, high-income residents have also converted existing *dacha* settlements (temporary summer houses on small plots) into exclusive villa develop-

ments – for example, on the western edges of the metropolitan areas of Moscow and Budapest (Medvekov and Medvekov, 2007; Kovàcs and Tosics, forthcoming).
65 Informal settlements accommodating Roma minority populations existed during the centrally planned era in many Eastern European towns and cities (Hirt and Stanilov, 2008).
66 Nientied, 1998; Hirt, 2005; Vujovic and Petrovic, 2007; Hirt and Stanilov, 2008.
67 However, in some countries the share of the informal sector continues to be very large (e.g. between one third and one half of total economic output in Central Asia; basic planning and environmental legislation has not yet been updated; and outdated plans continue to be used, e.g. Azerbaijan, Armenia; Hirt and Stanilov, 2008).
68 Biderman et al, 2008.
69 Scholz, 2002; UN, 2006a.
70 Scholz, 2002.
71 ADB, 1998; World Bank, 2004; UN-Habitat, 2007a.
72 UN-Habitat, 2007a.
73 Amis, 2004.
74 UN-Habitat, 2007a, p141.
75 For example, in India; see Kundu, 2002.
76 Mohit, 2002; UN-Habitat, 2003.
77 ADB, 1998.
78 See, for example, de Soto, 2000; Payne, 2001; Gilbert, 2002; Payne et al, 2007; Varley, 2007.
79 Deeds are the written agreements that signify transactions in property rights. Until relatively recently, they were the only evidence of landownership in some countries (e.g. the UK). In a deeds registration system, a purchaser of land rights registers the claim without the state guaranteeing its validity.
80 National Commission for Women, 2005; UN, 2006a.
81 Payne et al, 2007.
82 Peru is an exception (Kagawa and Turkstra, 2002).
83 See, for example, UN-Habitat,

2007b; Varley, 2007.
84 Yuen, 2008.
85 UN-Habitat, 2007a.
86 Rakodi, 2006; UN-Habitat, 2007a.
87 Gulyani and Bassett, 2007.
88 Thailand's nationwide slum upgrading programme includes land-sharing, upgrading and relocation (Boonyabancha, 2005, 2008).
89 See Liu and Wu (2006) on Naning, PRC.
90 Laquian, 2007.
91 Sivam and Evans suggest a methodology for assessing how improvements to the supply of land for development through the formal land administration system might be identified by assembling examples from a range of cities and using local experts to assess their transferability to a new location in their example, Delhi, using a range of criteria by which to assess their potential effectiveness (Sivam and Evans, 2001).
92 Angel, 2008.
93 Attahi et al, 2008.
94 Kessides, 2006.
95 Ansari, 2008.
96 UN-Habitat, 2003.
97 Karki, 2004.
98 Ansari, 2008.
99 Aristizabal and Gomez, 2002.
100 Jones and Pisa, 2000.
101 Waibel, 2008.
102 Yuen, 2008.
103 Roever, 2005.
104 See Hansen (2004) on Lusaka, Zambia.
105 UN-Habitat, 2006h.
106 Brown and Rakodi, 2006; Douglass, 2008.
107 Neto et al, 2007.
108 Brown, 2006.
109 Nnkya, 2006b.
110 Attahi et al, 2008.
111 A. K. Jain, pers comm, 2008.
112 Jhabvala, 2007.
113 Brown and Rakodi, 2006; see also Lyons and Mbiba, 2003.

CHAPTER 8

PLANNING, SPATIAL STRUCTURE OF CITIES AND PROVISION OF INFRASTRUCTURE

The spatial structure and degree of densification of the built environment ... has a major impact upon urban efficiency and sustainability

While planning potentially plays important roles in the way in which infrastructure and facilities are organized and in the spatial structuring of cities, its role has been relatively weak in many contexts

The provision of infrastructure such as transport networks, water, sewerage, electricity and telecommunications plays key roles in the development of efficient, healthy and sustainable cities. Other urban facilities and amenities such as schools, health services, social services, markets, and places for gathering, worship and recreation are also important to the development of liveable cities. Infrastructure, facilities and amenities of this sort are necessary to meet people's everyday needs and are acknowledged as critical in the Habitat Agenda.[1] Improvements in water and slum conditions are core commitments of the Millennium Development Goals.

These elements of infrastructure and facility provision are important in shaping the spatial structure of cities, at a city-wide and more local scale, and can result in certain sections of the population becoming spatially marginalized and excluded from access to urban opportunities. The spatial structure and degree of densification of the built environment also has a major impact upon urban efficiency and sustainability. Thus, the compact, mixed-use and public transport-based city is increasingly seen as more environmentally sustainable, efficient and equitable.[2] Yet, the trends in many parts of the world are towards declining densities and increasing outward expansion,[3] often across municipal boundaries. Furthermore, the relevance of these ideas to the urban poor on the urban periphery is open to debate.

Earlier chapters have shown the complex dynamics through which urban growth occurs, and its variations across contexts. It has pointed to the important roles of entrepreneurs, individuals and consumers who make location decisions; providers of infrastructure and services; those who make undeveloped land available; and property developers. Informal land development processes are also critical in most developing countries. Municipal and government agencies are among a large number of actors shaping urban spatial organization, which is always evolving. While planning potentially plays important roles in the way in which infrastructure and facilities are organized and in the spatial structuring of cities, its role has been relatively weak in many contexts. Informal urban development processes,

the growing importance of urban mega-projects and privately driven development with little relationship to urban spatial planning, institutional divides and the limitations of urban spatial planning have all been contributors. Yet, there is a need for a closer connection between spatial planning and both infrastructure provision and mega-projects, as these have significant urban impacts.

To address these issues, this chapter is divided into six sections. The first section provides a brief overview of contemporary urban spatial trends internationally, and their links to access to infrastructure and exclusion. The next section explores the way in which these trends are being shaped by the 'unbundling' of infrastructure development, disjointed from spatial planning through forms of privatization, developer-driven growth and urban mega-projects. The third section examines the links and interrelationships between forms of infrastructure provision, spatial organization and access.

The relationships between urban form, sustainability, efficiency and inclusiveness are considered in the fourth section, through a focus on the compact city debate and a discussion of the relevance of compaction ideas across contexts. There is some debate over whether planning can influence the spatial organization of cities; yet it does have important material effects. Linking spatial planning to major infrastructure development provides a potential avenue for shaping the future growth of cities, and the fifth section thus explores various contemporary initiatives to align spatial planning and infrastructure development. The chapter concludes by drawing out key findings and policy implications.

URBAN SPATIAL TRENDS, INFRASTRUCTURE AND EXCLUSION

Previous UN-Habitat reports[4] have provided extensive analysis of the changing spatial structure of cities and of levels of infrastructure and service provision in the world's cities. This section provides just a brief recapitulation of these patterns as they relate to infrastructural developments and urban planning.

As noted in Chapter 2, more than one third of all urban residents in developing countries are currently living in slums, characterized by poor and crowded housing conditions, tenure insecurity, and without access to improved drinking water and sanitation. While many urban poor live in inner-city slums, the majority of the urban poor in developing countries are living in informal settlements on the urban periphery. These settlements are likely to have better housing than inner-city slums, but often have low levels of services, which can become problematic with densification. Access is also likely to be difficult since mass transit systems are often poorly developed, and areas accessible to the poor may not be located on main routes. Hence, considerable time (as much as three to four hours per day) and cost (up to 30 per cent of income) can be spent on accessing employment, markets, schools and other public services. These long distances are especially burdensome for women who travel to work and are also responsible for housework and childcare.[5]

The growth of peri-urban areas around cities, particularly as urban growth outpaces infrastructure development, is one of the most prominent current changes to urban structure. In Asia, this is occurring on a dramatic scale: in Jakarta and Bangkok, some 77 and 53 per cent of urban growth by 2025, respectively, is expected to be in peri-urban regions, while in China, some 40 per cent of urban growth by 2025 is expected to be in peri-urban areas as far as 150km to 300km from core cities. In Asian cities, lateral spread is occurring along transport corridors, creating a form of 'regional urbanization'.[6] Some cities, nevertheless, such as Bangkok, remain relatively centralized in terms of employment and labour markets, particularly for the poor.

The growth of small- and medium-sized towns and development along transport routes within the commutable distance of metropolitan agglomerations – as well as the development of peri-urban areas – are occurring in Latin America and the Caribbean and in the transitional countries.[7] Peri-urban informal development is a key pattern in sub-Saharan Africa, particularly on customary land.

The growth of city-regions, or 'metropolitanization', is occurring mainly through formal processes in developed countries, and is underpinned by the development of polycentric cities, the expansion of highway systems and increased reliance on cars. Such patterns are most prominent in the US, where central business districts retained only 10 to 20 per cent of employment by the late 1990s, as economic activity moved to suburbs and major nodes outside the core city. The decentralization of employment within cities has not reduced levels of commuting, as jobs and housing are not generally co-located.[8] In Europe, central cities have retained their importance to a greater extent, but trends towards sprawl are nevertheless evident.

Most recent studies of cities point to rising levels of class segregation, particularly with the growth of urban enclaves in the form of gated communities. Gated residential estates for middle- and high-income groups are emerging in places where fear of crime is a major concern, such as in Latin America, South Africa and in parts of the US. Nevertheless, this phenomenon is prevalent in most regions of the world, although it is less significant in Europe. In Asia and, to some extent, in Latin America, major complexes, including a range of services, facilities (including schools) and economic activities are also being developed.[9]

In Asia, and to a lesser extent in other parts of the world, there has been a significant emphasis on infrastructural upgrading to respond to growth to produce 'world-class cities': with high-quality transport, information and communication technologies, modern industrial parks, in association with suburban or high-rise housing and shopping complexes, such as the Pudong development in Shanghai (China) and the Madinat al-Hareer development in Kuwait.[10] The rapid growth of enclave development and rising levels of socio-spatial polarization reflect processes of globalization, economic restructuring and growing income inequality; but they are also the product of a neo-liberal era in which important elements of urban development have been privatized or driven by private developers in many countries. The following section explores these issues.

The majority of the urban poor in developing countries are living in informal settlements on the urban periphery

SPATIAL PLANNING, THE PRIVATIZATION OF INFRASTRUCTURE DEVELOPMENT AND MEGA-PROJECTS

As indicated in Chapter 3, traditional approaches to planning attempted to align land-use planning with infrastructure provision through a comprehensive master planning approach, and through the public provision of infrastructure. There were, however, many deficiencies in these processes, and from the 1980s, new urban development and infrastructure provision became far less a matter of planning, and far more dominated by private-sector interests. This section explores these issues and shows how this process of 'unbundling'[11] has, in part, underpinned the spatial trends discussed in Chapter 2 and the previous section. The first two sub-sections trace the history of the links between spatial planning and infrastructure development, and the impact of 'unbundling', while the third sub-section considers the contemporary focus on mega-projects.

The growth of city regions, or 'metropolitanization', is occurring mainly through formal processes in developed countries

Master planning and infrastructure

From the 1850s to the 1960s, the supply of infrastructure and services in cities shifted from fragmented and privately organized goods to centralized and standardized services provided by the public sector.[12] These large-scale systems underpinned much of the growth of cities after World War II and significantly shaped their spatial form.

One of the core functions of traditional master planning was to provide the basis for the integrated provision of transport, energy, water and communication with urban development. Master plans provided projections and guidance for the location, extent and intensity of particular land uses in the city. Planners thus targeted densities and land uses in particular areas. In theory, this kind of planning enabled authorities responsible for transport, water, sewerage, energy and other public facilities to develop infrastructure and services on a 'predict and provide' basis. Thus, infrastructure provision was intended to follow spatial planning.

While this kind of planning might have been effective in some developed countries, there were problems in many others. Under communism in Eastern Europe and Central and Eastern Asia, master plans were driven by economic targets developed at the national level, without consideration of local needs.[13] In most colonial contexts, planning and infrastructure provided by the public sector was only for an elite, and projections anticipated a small population that was soon outstripped by growth in the post-colonial period.[14] For example, infrastructure developed in Lagos (Nigeria) provided for only 10 per cent of the eventual population.[15] Nor did patterns of development necessarily follow those anticipated, particularly with the rapid growth of high-density informal settlements. Even in developed countries, shifting social and economic patterns, such as declining household sizes, new patterns of economic activity and the like, meant that plans proved to be out of synchrony with actual needs for infrastructure. The accuracy of the 'predict and provide' approach was called into question.

In several countries, spatial planning occupied a marginal institutional position in relation to far more powerful departments responsible for various kinds of infrastructure planning and development.[16] Departments 'working in silos' developed their own plans, which did not necessarily link to one another or to the master plan. In these contexts, the provision of infrastructure has been far more powerful in shaping the spatial form of cities than planning.

Private-sector led infrastructure development

From the late 1970s, the 'unbundling' of infrastructural development through forms of corporatization or privatization of urban infrastructure development and provision, and developer-driven urban development, has tended to drive patterns of fragmentation and spatial inequality in many countries. In several post-colonial contexts, such as Jakarta (Indonesia) and Mumbai (India), these processes overlaid an already fragmented and unequal system of infrastructure and service provision.[17] In many countries, a local government fiscal crisis underpinned a shift towards the privatization of service provision. These changes occurred in the context of the decline of the welfare state or the collapse of communism and a movement towards neo-liberal economic and institutional policies, which have tended to promote the market and market principles. Some large, influential international agencies, have also promoted the idea of privatization of infrastructure and services.[18] Large multinational firms have emerged in the field of infra-

structure provision, with a focus on project-by-project investment.[19]

In both transitional and developing countries, there seems to be a shift towards privatized provision of infrastructure in the context of local fiscal crises, which has underpinned new forms of sprawling and unequal development. By the 1990s, many cities in transitional countries had ageing infrastructures, which were not refurbished as a consequence of the economic crisis and the withdrawal of state subsidies. Instead, new development occurred on a privatized or non-legal basis. Particularly in Central and Eastern Europe, there has been extensive privatization and outsourcing of utilities. Similarly, in Latin America and the Caribbean, fiscal constraints have meant a reliance on privatized provision of services in many countries. In Eastern Asia, South-Eastern Asia and the Pacific, however, the bulk of infrastructure is still provided by the public sector, with only 20 to 25 per cent being developed by private finance institutions and through various arrangements with the private sector. Privatized, or even individualized, provision of infrastructure is also occurring in contexts where large-scale systems of infrastructure provision are inoperable or only serve a small part of cities, such as in some African cities.[20]

'Unbundling' has taken various forms and has occurred in both the provision of infrastructure and services, and in urban development projects. It includes leases and concessions; public–private partnerships of various kinds,[21] but also in major urban development projects; involvement of the private sector in building, financing and managing infrastructure;[22] and private concessions to build and run toll roads, for example. Small local entrepreneurs and systems of community management are also being used in solid waste collection, water, housing and sanitation in countries such as Cambodia, Thailand and the Philippines, and in parts of Latin America and Africa, amongst others.[23]

The private sector has tended to focus on more profitable aspects of infrastructure development: shopping centres, middle- and high-income residential enclaves, mega-projects and the like. Nevertheless, privatized provision of services has also occurred through contractor models in poorer communities. These processes have been controversial: while they sometimes extend services to areas that would not otherwise have them, they also impose considerable costs on the poor, and limit the use of resources that are necessary for healthy cities.[24] The privatization of public services has in some cases been resisted by communities – for example, in Latin America[25] and parts of South Africa.[26]

In the context of increasing global competitiveness, local governments in many parts of the world are also being driven to become more entrepreneurial, focusing on enabling and attracting private-sector development. This approach has sometimes led to a relatively *laissez faire* approach to development, where proposals by developers are accepted even when they are contrary to plans, such as in some Latin American countries.[27] In Durban, South Africa, a developer-driven approach has resulted in urban sprawl, contrary to the compaction principles of the city's spatial framework (see Box 8.5).

From the late 1970s, the 'unbundling' of infrastructural development ... has tended to drive patterns of fragmentation and spatial inequality in many countries

Privatized provision of services ... imposes considerable costs on the poor

Mega-projects

The period since the 1980s has also seen a major growth of urban mega-projects linked to the new emphasis on urban competitiveness and urban entrepreneurialism. In many cases, particularly in Europe, mega-projects are linked to urban regeneration initiatives designed to reposition declining economies to capture new or growing economic niches. In several Asian cities, mega-projects are being developed *de novo*, not only as prestige projects, but also to lay the basis for new forms of economic development. Box 8.1 summarizes six common forms of mega-projects.

Projects of this type have varying relationships to the public sector. While some are completely privately driven and provided, in other cases, they are initiated and funded by the public sector in the hope of attracting private development, and are driven by special agencies. Private–public partnerships, or arrangements in which the public sector provides bulk infrastructure and connections while the private sector undertakes development within these parameters, are also common.

Although there are some examples where such projects work with spatial planning processes and inclusive visions of urban redevelopment – such as in Plaine Saint-Denis, Paris (see Box 8.6) – in many cases, mega-projects are in contradiction to spatial plans, and enable unequal development out of synchrony with the needs and aspirations of ordinary residents. In Europe where such projects are generally state led and often funded by government, they are frequently run by special agencies which compete with and supersede local and regional governments.[28] Frequently, existing plans and associated regulatory processes are bypassed, and the usual participatory processes are replaced by stakeholder participation. Methods of assessing impacts are changed, and research indicates that there tends to be pervasive misinformation on costs, benefits and risks.[29]

In Indonesia, mega-projects in the greater Jabotabek mega-urban region (centred on Jakarta), have involved public development of large-scale infrastructure, including a new airport, toll highways linking key axes of development, as well as major private housing, shopping malls, industrial areas, tall buildings and gated residential developments. While aspects of the development were consistent with the Jakarta master plan, which included an industrial corridor, various controls have been reduced, and development has occurred on land which was intended to be protected from urban development for environmental reasons. Development is taking place on prime agricultural land and green spaces in the region's principal area of water supply and its main aquifer, thus undermining the region's water supplies.[30]

THE INFLUENCE OF INFRASTRUCTURE ON URBAN SPATIAL STRUCTURE AND ACCESS

Previous sections of this chapter have provided an overview of key spatial trends and contemporary drivers of urban form. This section shifts the focus towards considering the way in which urban infrastructure shapes the spatial organization of cities, and how this, in turn, affects access and liveability from the perspective of different groups of people. The focus is particularly on transport networks and systems since these are generally acknowledged to be the most powerful in shaping urban spatial structure;[31] but other elements of infrastructure provision and inclusive spatial and infrastructure planning at a local level are also considered.

Transport systems and networks

At the heart of the transport/land-use relationship is the importance of accessibility for both the development of housing and for economic activity. As recognized in classical urban economic models, the significance of access translates into higher land values around nodes and routes offering high access. Thus, economic activities requiring high levels of accessibility cluster around rail stations and tram routes, along main roads or in nodes close to major intersections of

In many cases, mega-projects are in contradiction to spatial plans

Transport networks and systems ... are generally acknowledged to be the most powerful in shaping urban spatial structure

---

Box 8.1 Common forms of mega-projects

The six common forms of mega-projects are as follows:

1   Developments linked to event tourism, such as conference centres, exhibition sites and sports stadia.
2   Redevelopment of old industrial areas and ports towards a new service, leisure and tourist economy.
3   Development of new areas linked to high-tech industries and economic activities, such as Malaysia's super-corridor between the capital and the airport (Yuen, 2008). These developments can include residential, commercial and industrial space and may be linked by premium transport infrastructure, both road and rail. In Uttar Pradesh (India), the provincial government has instituted a policy to enable 'high-tech cities' as new enclaves within cities (Ansari, 2008).
4   Major new satellite cities with international standard facilities, such as Muang Thong Thani, which is planned for a population of a million, 40km from Bangkok (Thailand) (Yuen, 2008). Significant new towns of this sort are also being planned and built in Western Asia. For example, Saudi Arabia is planning to complete some five megacities by 2020 (Nassar, 2008).
5   Major enclave developments taking the form of gated communities containing a variety of retail, school, entertainment and other facilities for the wealthy, linked by privatized transport routes.
6   Enterprise zones or special economic zones set up by national or local governments to attract new investment, sometimes linked to major airports and other developments. In transitional countries, these are occurring on municipal peripheries. Such zones are often duty-free enclaves where local laws and revenue regulations do not apply.

Figure 8.1

Designing for accessibility

Source: Behrens and Watson, 1996

highway systems. Firms that favour a particular transport mode will cluster near points of high access for that mode.[32] Residential developments similarly seek accessibility; thus the development of new routes and transport systems provides important ways of structuring cities over the long term. The accessibility–value relationship, however, means that high-income groups are more able to pay for access and, thus, to locate close to good transport routes that suit the transport mode which they use, although they may also choose more distant locations and longer travel times.

Much has been made of the role of highways in facilitating the suburban form of development, and in

encouraging urban sprawl.[33] Detractors in the US – where much of the debate has occurred – point to the role of other factors, such as rising car ownership and incomes, cheap credit, mortgage loans, family formation, taxation, a desire to escape congested inner cities, an attraction for suburban life, and the suburbanization of employment. The growth of car-oriented suburban development has also been dependent upon an era of cheap oil, which may be drawing to a close. Clearly, the spatial form of cities is not a simple effect of transport routes, and will be the outcome of a range of social, political, institutional and regulatory conditions in various contexts. Nevertheless, studies suggest that highways play powerful roles as conduits for development in particular parts of cities.[34]

Accommodating the motor car has been an important theme of 'modern' planning in many parts of the world. High levels of dependence upon the motor car, and the low densities associated with car-dominated cities, however, make access difficult for those without this form of transport: the elderly, disabled, youth, women in families with single cars, and low-income workers in suburban office locations and homes, such as cleaners, domestic workers, and clerks.[35] Furthermore, the emphasis on planning for mobility in cities neglects the significance of pedestrian and non-motorized forms of transport in cities in developing countries.[36] In most cities, little attention is paid to the needs of pedestrians, cyclists and other users of non-motorized transport for road space, crossings and other amenities, resulting in high levels of accidents.

Several influential design approaches treated residential areas as introverted cells linked to highway systems,[37] and focused on central facilities, with the expectation that pedestrian movement is internal to the cell. These forms of local design can result in very inconvenient conditions for those without cars who need to access facilities and employment outside the area, such as the aged, disabled and women. In low-income areas, car ownership is low and planned central areas are likely to be poorly developed, requiring movement outside of the area, often on foot. For working women who have to travel to work as well, these types of design may compound the difficulties of negotiating everyday life.[38]

The emphasis on accommodating the motor car in the design of local areas has also been criticized. Much greater attention is now being paid to 'traffic calming' (i.e. slowing traffic through various devices, and the accommodation of pedestrians and cyclists in local planning).[39] UN-Habitat's Bicycle Transport Project in Kibera (Kenya), for example, combines the introduction of modified bicycle transport with improved road access for their use.[40] Arguments for moving away from introverted neighbourhoods to areas with permeable boundaries, joined by centres and strips containing commercial activities and public facilities, linked to public transport, are also made by those advocating a greater focus on planning for accessibility rather than purely for mobility (see Figure 8.1).[41] Amsterdam provides an example of where sustainable accessibility has been created through a combination of appropriate land-use and transport policies, as indicated in Box 8.2.

Box 8.2 Sustainable accessibility in Amsterdam, The Netherlands

In Amsterdam, a combination of evolving policies, shaped at times by contestation, has helped to create a city which is highly accessible to those without cars. Some 35 per cent of commuting is by non-motorized transport – a world high – as a consequence of the importance of the bicycle. During the 1960s, a policy of 'concentrated decentralization' of population and employment in growth centres, which were well linked by both public transport and car, enabled the development of an accessible polycentric city. The compact city policy of the 1980s promoted transport modes other than the car, particularly walking and cycling, and encouraged concentrated mixed-use developments, providing services close to homes. The city centre has been preserved and is mainly accessible by public transport, while the edge of the city with its sub-centres offers good access to both the inner city and to places elsewhere. These policies have been reinforced by transport policies: rail, motorways and good linkages between modes, particularly rail and bicycle. Policies did not always work as intended – for example, people do not live and work locally as expected, and there are still problem areas (e.g. the city still lacks a comprehensive integrated urban-regional public transport system), but a form of sustainable accessibility has been created.

Sources: Le Clercq and Bertolini, 2003; Bertolini, 2007; Bertolini et al, undated

The structure of public transport systems can also shape the spatial organization of cities in important ways, and has been a crucial element of attempts to restructure cities spatially – for example, in Curitiba (Brazil) and Portland (US).[42] Heavy rail systems in large, dense cities (often taking the form of underground systems in central areas) are critical in supporting both good interconnections in central areas, as well as links between central and outlying areas. Commuter rail systems mainly link outer areas to the centre, while light rail and tram systems provide good connections within central areas, and between these and secondary nodes and suburban corridors. Rail and train stations provide potential points for the growth of nodes and more intensive development; but potentials are contingent upon the way in which these services are used, as well as how stations are regulated and developed.[43]

Buses are more adaptive, and require lower densities to operate, but are also slower and less efficient, and are likely to have less impact upon spatial organization. The use of dedicated bus-ways, however, increases speed and capacity and, thus, usage, and creates more structured routes around which more intense development can occur.[44] In many developing countries, the provision of public transport is poor; thus, private forms of public transport – such as minibus taxis, *jeepneys*, *jitneys*, *matatus* and the like – have emerged. These forms of transport, termed 'paratransit' by some authors,[45] can operate in highly congested conditions, but also emerge in sprawling low-density cities. These systems are reactive to an existing spatial context; but in developing countries, important paratransit collection points can become significant places for informal trade, markets and the like as a consequence of high passenger volumes.

Water, sewerage, electricity and telecommunications

Major infrastructural systems for water, sewerage, electricity and telecommunications have also structured cities spatially in important ways, although their direct impact is less obvious than is the case for transport systems. All of these systems involve the establishment of major bulk elements which require large fixed investments and, thus, provide capacity for growth in particular areas. Such bulk elements include dams and water treatment works, reservoirs, pump stations, sewerage treatment facilities, power sub-stations, mobile phone masts and fibre-optic cables. Water and sewerage pipelines and electricity transmission lines distribute services to local areas and within them. Water and electricity can easily be led to different parts of the city and the bulk infrastructure required to open up new areas is not especially costly; but investment in these facilities enables new development there, and reduces its cost, until a particular threshold is reached. It thus influences the spatial direction of development. The impact of sewerage treatment plants is more significant since they are much more costly and serve much larger areas.[46]

The availability of trunk lines for water, sewerage and transmission lines for electricity in particular areas reduces development costs and thus influences future patterns of growth. While bulk infrastructure does not usually feature high on planners' agendas, it can be crucial in shaping patterns of spatial development. The discussion later in this chapter shows how planning is attempting to link with infrastructure development in various contexts.

As stated in Chapter 6, stand-alone or small-scale distributed systems of water, sewerage and energy provision reduce dependence upon these major systems, improve efficiency and can have diverse spatial outcomes and affect access. Thus, sewerage package plants, the bucket system, the use of septic tanks and French drains, and various forms of ventilated pit latrines do not depend upon broader sewerage systems, but are generally more suitable for lower-density development. Water kiosks and water tankers can be used outside of areas connected to water pipelines, but are usually much more costly per unit than water received through reticulated systems. The use of solar energy at the household level also offers alternatives to connection to electricity grids; but installation charges are still high, although overall costs could be reduced, partly through the development of 'smart' grids. The alternative, especially in low-income communities, is more often the use of energy sources such as wood, coal, paraffin and candles, which may be both costly per unit, and can generate greater pollution. However, proximity to networks for water, energy and sewerage does not mean that households can afford access to them.

Studies during the early 1990s predicted that information and communication technologies, such as mobile phones and the internet, would lead to the 'death', or 'abolition', of distance and the declining importance of both cities and central places within them as people increasingly worked from home and communicated using information and communication technologies. Although the practice of working from home has increased, as has the use of information and communication technologies, both cities and central places within them remain important due to the significance of agglomeration economies, diverse labour markets, face-to-face contact and interpersonal relationships. While some substitution of electronic communication for physical movement may occur, the two work in complementary ways and the overall expansion of both forms of communication makes it difficult to detect. Instead of the death of distance, new forms of 'information districts' and high-tech centres are emerging within cities.[47] Nevertheless, other shifts may occur over the long term, particularly with rising energy costs.

Physical infrastructure to support information and communication technologies generally follows the lines of other forms of infrastructure, particularly roads, electricity transmission lines, sewerage and water pipelines. Combined with road infrastructure, 'smart corridors' have been important in structuring the development of new economic centres focused on high technology in some Asian cities.[48] For the most part, infrastructure to support new technologies is provided by the private sector and follows customers, privileging both business and higher-income consumers. Thus, studies show that a digital divide tends to overlay patterns of wealth and poverty in cities.[49] Unequal access, however, may

Major infrastructural systems for water, sewerage, electricity and telecommunications have also structured cities spatially in important ways

Proximity to networks for water, energy and sewerage does not mean that households can afford access to them

be more a matter of affordability than physical access to infrastructure. To some extent, 'smart city' approaches, extending networks through municipal connections and providing affordable internet access points in low-income areas can help in addressing this form of exclusion.[50]

Infrastructure and inclusive local planning

The spatial form of cities – their liveability and inclusiveness – is also shaped by access to a broader range of infrastructural facilities and amenities, such as schools; clinics; crèches; community halls; libraries and learning facilities; safe spaces for recreation, ranging from playgrounds to gathering places for the elderly; spaces for religious and cultural practices; fresh food and other local markets and retail outlets; and appropriate spaces for economic activity.

Ideally, local planning should create places that meet the everyday requirements of diverse groups of people: men and women; old and young; the disabled; different cultural groups; and so on. Understanding and responding to these diverse needs is an important part of planning.[51] The tradition of gender analysis and gender mainstreaming within planning is increasingly providing useful methodological tools and frameworks for assessing needs and potential responses, as does the more recent emphasis on planning for diversity.[52] Box 8.3 provides the example of the safer city audits used in UN-Habitat's Safer Cities Programme approaches.

The Safer Cities Programme represents a form of local inclusive urban regeneration. This kind of planning for local infrastructure improvement is likely to be important in many parts of the world, and particularly in slums. There are also many examples of participatory approaches to slum upgrading, including improvements in social services and facilities, as shown in Chapter 5.

UN-Habitat's planning initiatives in post-conflict and post-disaster situations provide examples of inclusive local planning that addresses a range of infrastructure and facilities according to diverse local needs. For example, in post-tsunami reconstruction in Xaafun (Somalia), UN-Habitat designed housing that enabled home-based economic activities, developed a women's centre close to the market, and created safe public spaces with playgrounds and water points.[53]

The creation of appropriate spaces and infrastructure for economic activities is also critical as it influences viability and, hence, livelihoods. Informal trading activities are highly sensitive to pedestrian movement and need to be accommodated in places of high access (such as major commuter stations, transport interchanges and main roads). Strategies to displace these activities to less intense spaces are rarely effective. The complex interests involved in planning for appropriate infrastructure for markets requires a participatory approach, as demonstrated in planning for the reconstruction of markets in post-conflict Galkaio (Somalia)[54] and the Warwick Triangle in Durban (South Africa).[55]

From these experiences, it is clear that spatial planning needs to work much more closely with the planning of infrastructure at both a city-wide and more local level if it is to have an impact upon the way in which cities develop, and their sustainability, efficiency and inclusiveness.

THE COMPACT CITY DEBATE: SUSTAINABILITY, EFFICIENCY AND INCLUSIVENESS

While previous sections have shown that the predominant spatial trend in most cities is towards sprawl, many analysts argue for promoting more compact cities.[56] These arguments have been adopted as policy in various contexts. The 1992 United Nations Conference on Environment and Development (UNCED), held in Rio de Janeiro (Brazil), accepted arguments that low-density cities promote excessive use of energy, while the 1990 European Green Paper had earlier promoted the idea of compact cities.[57] Some countries, such as South Africa, and cities such as Curitiba (Brazil), and those linked to the 'smart growth' movement in the US, have adopted these ideas as policy, although implementation often falls short of intentions. This section explores the compact city debate in various contexts, and considers the implications of this debate for planning and managing urban change.

The compact city debate

Arguments in favour of compact cities revolve around claims that they are more efficient, inclusive and sustainable. The costs of providing infrastructure are lower, there is better access to services and facilities since thresholds are higher, the livelihoods of the urban poor are promoted and social segregation is reduced.[58] The time and cost spent travelling is also lower. Compact cities are less reliant on cars and minimize distances travelled and, hence, fuel use, and have less impact upon farmlands and environmental resources. As a consequence, they are theoretically more resilient in the

Gender analysis and gender mainstreaming within planning is increasingly providing useful methodological tools and frameworks for assessing needs and potential responses

Spatial planning needs to work much more closely with the planning of infrastructure ... if it is to have an impact upon the way in which cities develop

---

Manzese is a densely populated middle- and low-income area containing some informal settlements. It accounts for about one quarter of recorded crime within Dar es Salaam, and levels of violence against women are high. The safety audit was intended to help find ways to enhance safety through planning and design and to increase community awareness of the environment. The audit included a walk through the area with local women and officials and a discussion of findings and possible solutions. The following suggestions emerged, amongst others:

*   widening streets to ease vehicular circulation;
*   refurbishing abandoned buildings that have become criminal hideouts;
*   improving street lighting;
*   using the spaces between houses for allotments, playgrounds and other community activities;
*   improving drainage channels, sewer systems and pit latrines;
*   addressing the lack of well-designed secure public open space; and
*   improving the accessibility and visibility of certain areas, such as narrow, blocked-off and unlit streets.

Source: UNCHS, 2001b; Mtani, 2002; Todes et al, 2008; see also UN-Habitat, 2009 context of climate change and have, generally, fewer harmful impacts.[59] Critics, however, question several of these claimed benefits, and argue that compaction is contrary to market forces towards sprawl, the decentralization of work and residents' desires, and, hence, is not politically feasible – or even desirable. Higher density, they argue, is associated with congestion and pollution, higher crime rates, and puts greater pressure on natural resources.[60] Containment policies push up land costs and also encourage development beyond restricted zones.

Much of the debate has focused on cities in developed countries, where high car ownership rates in an era of low fuel costs have propelled low-density sprawl. Although research showing that higher-density cities use less fuel[61] has had its detractors,[62] the relationships established are remarkably robust,[63] and there seems to be a clear association between higher densities and public transport, and between low density and reliance on cars.[64] Nevertheless, higher densities only provide the conditions for public transport; they do not guarantee it. Nor do they prevent rising car ownership and use, even where public transport systems are relatively good, as, for example, in Japan.[65] Some research has found that higher densities are associated with less usage of the motor car for some trips, but not for all,[66] and that households in places designed along new urbanist lines may nevertheless drive elsewhere to work, shop and use facilities.[67] The complexity of these relationships (and of urban forms) means that many attempts to prove the benefits of compaction statistically are weaker and more equivocal than expected. Nevertheless, if oil prices rise over the long term, as they did so dramatically in 2007/2008, these relationships may change. One of the greatest critics of compaction during the late 1990s, for example, spoke of the irrelevance of compaction ideas given the energy glut at the time and the availability of surplus farmland.[68] These conditions have changed significantly since then.

Cities built on low-density lines may, however, find adaptation or change towards greater compaction difficult to achieve. Cities are 'path dependent' in that their spatial structures are largely set in place and change slowly. Research indicates that it is difficult to provide efficient public transport in cities with lower densities than 30 people per hectare; but the actual threshold varies by transport type[69] as well as in terms of contextual factors such as spatial organization and topography. Table 8.1 shows the effect of densities on access to public transport in the case of sprawling Atlanta (US) and denser Barcelona (Spain).

Movements towards smart growth and transit-oriented development are seen as ways of shifting cities in these directions; but critics argue that without very significant redevelopment, changes are likely to be marginal.[70] Major changes require well-coordinated and consistent policy and implementation over a long period of time on infrastructure development, taxation and land-use regulation, and there are few cases where this has been possible – Curitiba (Brazil) being a notable exception.[71] The regeneration of Plaine Saint-Denis on the periphery of Paris (France), however, provides an example of development along lines favoured by compact city advocates (see Box 8.6).

	Atlanta	Barcelona
Area (km²)	137	37
Population (millions, 1990)	2.5	2.8
Density (people per hectare)	6	171
Population close to metro	4% within 800m	60% within 600m
Trips undertaken by public transport	4.5%	30%

The relevance of compaction ideas to developing countries

Pre-existing conditions for compaction vary between contexts. On the whole, urban densities are much higher in developing than developed countries, but there are also variations within these categories, with the highest densities in Asian cities, somewhat lower densities in Latin American, African and European cities, and lowest in North American and Australian cities. Critics question whether the concept has relevance in the cities of developing countries, which already contain many elements of urban compaction: mixed use largely as a consequence of the lack of regulation, very high densities (at least at the centre) and a reliance on public transport, largely as a consequence of low incomes.[72] Densification processes are often occurring in informal settlements through processes of autonomous consolidation. The role of public policy or planning in this context is thus questioned.[73]

Yet, the benefits of urban densification, at least for the inner-city poor, are apparent: while housing costs are high and they have less space, they have greater livelihood opportunities (particularly in the informal sector) and access to employment. Transport costs are low and they are able to rely to a greater extent on non-motorized transport.[74] In many respects, dense areas in cities of developing countries, including informal settlements, are living versions of compact city ideas – and they arguably have greater relevance in this context. Planning and public policy might most appropriately work with these processes of change to consolidate the position of the inner-city poor and to support existing processes of informal upgrading, and improvement of infrastructure and services. Avoiding displacement or forced relocation of slums, as has often occurred through modernist planning in the past, is also important. In Mumbai (India), for example, floor space bonuses were rewarded to developers who made provision for low-income housing in commercial developments.[75] In Brazil, participatory informal settlement upgrading – including the provision of a range of social services and facilities – has helped to improve living conditions in Rio de Janeiro's *favelas*.[76]

Nevertheless, dense inner-city areas in developing countries are often very congested and polluted.[77] Some cities combine high densities with poor public transport and a reliance on paratransit, thus increasing levels of congestion and air pollution. Rising levels of car ownership as incomes increase are placing considerable pressure on these cities. Wealthy dense Asian cities, such as Singapore, Hong Kong and Tokyo, however, have been able to constrain the use of motor cars, provide good public transport and manage environmental conditions; but they are also places with

Table 8.1

Density and public transport access: Comparing Atlanta (US) and Barcelona (Spain)

Source: Bertaud, 2004

Cities are 'path dependent' in that their spatial structures are largely set in place and change slowly

In many respects, dense areas in cities of developing countries, including informal settlements, are living versions of compact city ideas considerable capacity and few alternatives to accepting compact development.[78]

Do compaction ideas have value for development on the periphery of cities in developing countries or for managing urban growth? The urban periphery has, in some cases, provided space for households willing to trade lower housing costs and more space for longer travel distances to economic activities. Where there are local economic opportunities or few commuters in a household, peripheral location is likely to be attractive. The opportunity to rent housing or to combine incomes from rural and urban economic activities are some of the livelihood opportunities for households located on the periphery in many developing countries, suggesting that the needs and livelihood strategies of poor households are diverse and generally logical.[79] The increasingly polycentric form of cities has meant that accessibility is more complex than simply distance to urban centres.[80] But in other contexts, as previous sections showed, distance from work and transport costs are major concerns. Improving infrastructure, services and facilities in sprawling developments on the periphery, and promoting employment and economic development there is critical.

It is clear that satellite city policies have had little value in either developed or developing countries: there is no necessary match between those employed and those living in these areas. Cities are major labour markets and people move in multiple ways across the city.[81] In several instances, satellites have not proved particularly attractive to economic activities, resulting in large concentrations of poorly located housing and long commuting distances.[82] The notion of concentrating and intensifying development along major transport routes, and of promoting nodal development of economic activities and public services[83] in peripheral areas has greater merit; but obviously potentials and possibilities are contextually defined. While it is unlikely that the public sector is in a position to provide urban services to all in most developing countries, planning can seek to shape the infrastructural framework of major roads, rail lines and bulk services, as the following section argues.

Cost efficiency and compaction

The cost efficiency of providing infrastructure and services to higher-density developments, and to existing areas – and, thus, of 'compact' rather than 'sprawling' development – is perhaps the least contested of the compact city claims. However, research shows that relationships are far more complex.[84] The study which originally made these claims[85] based its arguments on conceptual models rather than on actual development. In reality, however, unit costs vary considerably between types of infrastructure, topography and geotechnical conditions, and on the basis of available capacity and service thresholds.[86] Hence, there is no necessary relationship between compaction, cost and efficiency: rather, such relationships are highly contextual.

CONTEMPORARY APPROACHES TO LINKING SPATIAL PLANNING TO URBAN INFRASTRUCTURE

Previous sections of this chapter have shown that urban infrastructure developments have shaped the spatial form of cities, but in ways that intersect with social, economic, political and institutional dynamics. While the detailed and static land-use planning associated with traditional master planning has generally been discredited, and there are questions as to the relevance, feasibility and possible influence of large-scale city-wide spatial planning, strategic spatial planning that is able to give direction to major infrastructure development is an important part of the new approach to planning. Conversely, it is also important to link and tie the development of mega-projects to strategic spatial plans for cities.[87] This section explores various contemporary initiatives to link spatial planning to urban infrastructure development, and to use major elements of urban infrastructure, such as transport routes and systems, to influence spatial form. Table 8.2 provides a simplified summary of the discussion below.

Smart growth and transit-oriented development

As discussed in the previous section, the 'smart growth' movement has gained support in North America and has promoted the creation of more compact and integrated urban development. Smart growth supports the intensification of urban development and attempts to limit growth beyond the urban edge. It encourages increases in density; mixed-use and cluster developments; a variety of housing types beyond detached units; protection of open space, agricultural lands and ecologically sensitive areas; the reduction in use of private and motorized forms of transport; the promotion of public transport systems; and the design and redesign of areas to support such use.[88] Mechanisms to promote such growth include both regulations and tax incentives, but also rely on urban plans linking land use, transport and other aspects of infrastructure development. In Maryland (US), where smart growth legislation was adopted in 1997, subsidies for new roads, sewers, schools and other elements of infrastructure are limited outside of areas designated for growth, and funding is instead channelled to priority growth areas and in ways that do not encourage sprawl. Several states which have adopted smart growth ideas require consistency between local plans and the planning and programming of capital facilities.[89]

Transit-oriented development occupies an important place within the smart growth movement.[90] It posits the restructuring of regions towards greater use of public transport by improving or creating light rail or rapid bus transport systems, and generating dense mixed-use nodes around transit stations. Retail, public facilities and office and other work spaces are created around these stations, along with relatively high-density residential development, within a radius of 400m to 800m. The intention is to create human-

Approaches linking spatial planning to urban infrastructure

Broad approach	Important terms and approaches	Strengths	Weaknesses and contingencies
Smart growth and transit-oriented development	Smart growth Compact development Integrated development Mixed-use development Intensification Coordination Transit-oriented development	Encourages inter-sectoral and inter-agency links Encourages links between planning and implementation Improves sustainability Improves public transport Strong transport–land-use links Can slow urban sprawl	These good links are difficult to achieve Assumes significant capacity and organization Poor or narrow implementation undermines prospects Popular support difficult to achieve due to conflicting views and lifestyles Claimed benefits contested
Integrating land use and transport	Bus rapid transit (BRT) Corridors and axes Integrated rail redevelopment Linking economic activities to transport type New transport/land-use models	Improves public transport Improved usage of public transport Reduces energy and improves efficiency Better transport–land-use links New models enable better understanding of patterns	Heightened property prices on transport axes can marginalize the poor Required integration can be difficult to achieve Needs good understanding of social and economic dynamics and space – difficult to achieve Land use–transport links undermined by different logics, institutional divides New models still data hungry, aggregated, distant
Strategic spatial planning and infrastructure planning	Strategic plans Infrastructure plans Transport–land use links	Can give long-term direction to development Can avoid inequitable and unsustainable development Avoids fragmented development	Conditions required to work are demanding/difficult to achieve Credible analysis Inter-sectoral coordination Stakeholder involvement and buy-in Regular review Internal champions Special agencies
Integrated urban development and management plans	Multi-sectoral investment plans (MSIPs) plans (PEDPs) Physical and environmental development	More flexible, less data demanding, and easier to prepare than master plans Participatory Helps to manage urban growth in context of scarce resources/capacity Can be used iteratively in decision-making process	Problematic if seen in static or narrow way Required inter-sectoral cooperation hard to achieve Can be countered by political decision-making
Strategic structure planning	Integrative framework Long-term vision	More flexible, less data demanding and easier to prepare than master plans Participatory Multifaceted approach Combines short-term actions with long-term planning	Required political and stakeholder buy-in may be difficult to achieve May still be relatively technocratic May not provide detail necessary for some decisions
Linking spatial planning to infrastructure planning	Integrated development plans Spatial frameworks	More flexible, less data demanding and easier to prepare than master plans Participatory Gives direction to infrastructure planning GIS-based models can be used as an input	Required consistency in policy and coordination between agencies difficult to achieve Can be too broad to be useful May be contradicted by the market
Linking mega-projects to infrastructure development	Urban regeneration Multifunctional	Powerful driver in urban form Evolving approaches allow linking to planning over the long term Building cooperation between various sectors and agencies	Mega-projects often politically driven and one-off: approach is hard to achieve Level of integration and cooperation difficult to achieve

Smart growth and transit-oriented development ... need to be carefully adapted to local contexts

scaled, walkable spaces, encouraging the use of public transport (see Figure 8.2). In Portland (US), where the transit-oriented development idea has been adopted, light rail is combined with a feeder system of bus networks and three types of centres of different sizes and intensities. Proponents argue that smart growth and the transit-oriented development system is enabling Portland to become more compact, is encouraging greater use of public transport, and is reducing traffic congestion.[91]

There are considerable debates over the impact of these ideas and their requirements for success. Research shows that smart growth has slowed urban sprawl and declining densities in Maryland (US), although, overall, the dominant trend is still towards sprawl and car usage.[92] While proponents claim that Portland's urban growth boundaries have contained growth, others argue that growth has spilled over into adjacent areas.[93] Successful implementation therefore requires consistent policies between plans at various

levels, and the coordination of various methods and agencies.[94] Critics argue that while many cities have adopted forms of transit-oriented development, it is often implemented in narrow and partial ways.[95] In Vancouver (Canada), metropolitan planning was based on compaction ideas; but they were not shared by suburban communities and municipalities, whose ideas of liveability were very different – thus, development there did not follow the plan.[96] Whether these concepts have purchase in developing country contexts is open to debate: both smart growth and transit-oriented development depend upon high levels of coordination and integration, as well as consistent programmes and policies. These conditions may be difficult to achieve in contexts where administrative capacity and finances are scarce, and there is a dominance of political decision-making. Concepts of smart growth and transit-oriented development also need to be carefully adapted to local contexts and to be based on an understanding of conditions there.[97]

Transit-oriented development: Development around a transit stop

Source: Calthorpe, 1993

Core to the transit-oriented development idea is the integration of transportation and land use

Sectoral and segmented planning and urban management practices result in haphazard and unplanned development

Integrating land use and transportation

Core to the transit-oriented development idea is the integration of transportation and land use; but there are several ways in which this has occurred internationally. The case of Curitiba (Brazil) represents a well-known example where ideas of this sort have had a real impact (see Box 8.4). Curitiba's model of rapid bus transport has been emulated and elements have been adopted (and adapted) by other Brazilian and Latin American cities (most famously the *Transmilenio* system in Bogotá, Colombia), as well as by cities elsewhere in the world.[98] The *Transantiago* system in Santiago (Chile), however, provides an example of 'failed implementation'[99] of this approach, partly as a consequence of the lack of integrated transport planning, poor links to urban planning, and the failure to understand the complex ways in which people use space and transport in the city.[100]

There are many other examples of linking transport and spatial planning in urban development. The redevelopment of rail stations in Naples (Italy), involved integrated consideration of timetables, service lines, stations, modal interchange facilities, urban renewal around rail stations, and the design of stations. These improved the quality and acceptability of services to the extent that usage increased by some 43 per cent over the 2001 to 2004 period.[101]

While transport is generally acknowledged to be the key element of infrastructure shaping urban form, and the importance of linking land-use and transportation planning is widely accepted,[102] the links between the two are often poor. In part, there are varying discourses and logics of these forms of planning[103] and institutional divides, and the traditional modelling approaches often used by transport planners were subject to many of the criticisms of large

urban models: overly comprehensive and data hungry, too aggregated to be useful and too distant from actual behaviour.[104] More recent models, using more sophisticated technology, geographic information systems (GIS), and new theoretical approaches enable a better understanding of transport–land-use relationships, but remain very data intensive, and are still moving towards usefulness in policy terms.[105]

Strategic spatial planning and infrastructure planning

In response to the problems associated with master planning, there has been experimentation with new forms of strategic spatial planning. In Europe and North America, strategic planning based on developing a consensus on the main directions for development has been important and may include infrastructure development.

Several Australian cities are now including an infrastructure plan as a core element of strategic spatial planning since the previous focus on flexible market-driven approaches made it difficult to manage important outcomes and resulted in a lack of coordination. Integrated approaches linking land-use and infrastructure planning, funding and delivery are relatively recent; but early findings from these initiatives suggest the importance of a well-supported long-term strategic plan leading the process. The involvement of a wide range of stakeholders is key to the development of a shared and consistent approach; but the plan itself also needs to be based on credible analysis and understanding of trends and forces. The strategic plan identifies the expected economic base, drivers for change and major factors affecting the spatial distribution of population, employment and services. It considers the influence of technology and social change on patterns of development, and on the demand for services and infrastructure. Plans, however, cannot be old-fashioned master plans. They require regular review, consideration of sequencing, reinforcing funding and pricing, and institutional coordination. The importance of internal champions and special agencies for coordination are stressed. Although several plans attempt to coordinate across a range of sectors, it is argued that transport/land-use links are crucial, and that other forms of infrastructure can follow.[106]

Integrated urban management and development plans

While the approach adopted in Australian cities may, like master plans, require far more data and analysis than is generally available in many developing countries, there have similarly been initiatives to link strategic plans with infrastructure planning. A movement towards integrated urban management and development plans was based on the argument that 'unless an integrated and holistic approach to urban development and infrastructure development planning is applied, the current sectoral and segmented planning and urban management practices will continue to result in haphazard and unplanned development'.[107] Proponents argue that while the logical route is for government to plan for future development, acquire land and provide bulk/mainline infrastructure, which then provides the framework for the private sector to subdivide and connect to services, this frequently does not occur in Asian countries.[108] Instead, fragmented private development occurs on fringe land in the absence of distributor/collector roads and utility lines, with government (sometimes) later 'catching up' and providing these services.

One influential approach arose from action planning and proposed the development of strategic structure plans focused on guiding urban infrastructure development in combination with multi-sectoral investment planning. This approach departs from master planning, both in the methodology used for spatial planning and in the strong link to planning for infrastructure investment. In contrast to master planning, which did not focus on financial and institutional aspects, and did not have an emphasis on implementation, the intention here is to move towards integrated investment packages for infrastructure linked to broader planning processes.[109] Considerable attention is also paid to institutional and capacity issues, and community consultation is included in the process. Multi-sectoral investment planning is preceded by a 'physical and environmental development plan', which includes a rapid analysis of key spatial and environmental profiles, problems and trends, and then develops scenarios and strategy, and a broad spatial framework for urban development. A long-term view is developed, coupled with a shorter five-year action plan, which links to the multi-sectoral investment planning. The physical and environmental development plan provides a phased programme for expansion of the city. This approach excludes detailed land use and zoning, and operates at a broad level associated with structure planning, but with a focus on infrastructure development.[110] Planning for infrastructure needs is linked to the spatial plan so that the multi-sectoral plan includes the location, timing and type of infrastructure development. The intention of spatial planning in this context is to help manage urban growth, particularly through improving the coordination of the supply of infrastructure and facilities in time and space.

The approach was supported by several international agencies, including UN-Habitat and the German aid agency Deutsche Gesellschaft für Technische Zusammenarbeit (GTZ), and was applied in Indonesia ('integrated urban infrastructure development planning'), Nepal and India during the 1990s. In Indonesia and Nepal, where evaluations were conducted in the late 1990s,[111] the impact of spatial planning was far less than anticipated. While the spatial plans produced were for the most part consistent with intentions (or overlaid other plans), there were limits to the way in which these were used and how they intersected with infrastructure planning. In Nepal, investment plans tended to be seen in a static way, rather than requiring annual revision as intended. In Indonesia, plans were seen as the responsibility of central government and were not integrated within municipal planning. At the same time, central government agencies did not properly participate in planning, nor follow its recommendations. Projects were often assessed on the basis of financial issues, and locational questions and

Box 8.4 Integrated land-use and transport system, Curitiba, Brazil

Curitiba's 1965 master plan structured its development around a set of transport axes with dedicated bus lanes, carrying express high-capacity articulated buses, flanked by high-density residential development, as well as offices, commerce and services, in areas adjacent to the route. Large bus terminals at the ends of these express bus routes permit transport between routes, as do medium-sized terminals along the routes. Passengers may transfer to inter-district and local buses using a single ticket. Proponents claim that residents spend a comparatively low 10 per cent of their income on transport, and that fuel consumption is 25 per cent lower than in comparable Brazilian cities. And while there is a high rate of car ownership, more than 1.3 million passengers a day take the bus, with 85 per cent of residents using it. The success of this model has been attributed to a planning process that strongly integrated land-use and transport planning, and to persistent long-term implementation of the plan. While a master plan was used, its focus was on a strategic vision and principles to guide development, and on the use of appropriate systems and incentives.

Despite the many benefits of the Curitiba planning and development approach, it has not escaped the realities of urban spatial inequalities. Curitiba sits within a broader metropolitan context in which the poor live on the periphery with limited services, amenities and an absence of public transport. In addition, although the transport axes within Curitiba were meant to house middle- and low-income people, the supply of good infrastructure has pushed up property prices to the extent that this is no longer possible, and the poor are forced to live on the periphery.

Source: Rabinovitch and Leitman, 2004; Irazábal, 2008a

broader impacts were ignored. Difficulties with land acquisition also impeded planned projects. Despite the participatory process, priorities did not necessarily follow the plan: projects favoured by the elite were supported, whether or not they were part of the plan, and decisions on priorities were made on a political basis. As a consequence of extensive service backlogs, there was a tendency to focus spending in addressing backlogs, rather than anticipating future development,[112] negating the significance of the plan.[113]

Despite these difficulties, the approach is still seen as valuable by its proponents. The methodology for developing a spatial plan has proved to be robust, and is now the basis for more widespread training on developing alternatives to master planning.[114] The spatial plan itself and its value is also seen in a different way. Recognizing that it is unrealistic to expect spatial plans to replace political decision-making, or to expect a simple movement from plan to implementation, it is argued that the plan nevertheless can be brought into decision-making at various stages. It is not therefore conceived as a single driver or a static plan, but rather provides information and approaches that can be used throughout the development process.[115] Similar conclusions arise from initiatives linking spatial planning to infrastructure planning in Durban (South Africa) (see Box 8.5).

Strategic structure planning

The idea of strategic structure planning has been used in several projects undertaken by UN-Habitat in post-disaster, post-conflict and other areas.[116] These plans provide an integrative framework and a long-term vision of development, based on analysis and engagement with stakeholders and communities, but also a focus on key strategic projects

> The development of strategic structure plans focused on guiding urban infrastructure development in combination with multi-sectoral investment planning

> Despite the participatory process, priorities did not necessarily follow the plan: projects favoured by the elite were supported ... and decisions on priorities were made on a political basis

Under apartheid, the Greater Durban metropolitan area was run by fragmented and racially based local government. The city was divided on racial lines, and low-income African people were forced to commute long distances from peripheral locations to more centrally located areas of employment. In the post-apartheid period after 1994, the region was consolidated under a single municipality, eThekwini, through two phases of local government reorganization, and a spatial framework intended to achieve 'compact' 'integrated' development was put in place.

However, development trends did not follow the spatial framework and patterns of relatively low-density urban sprawl and the peripheral location of the urban poor continued. Significant growth has occurred in the northern area of the city, driven, in part, by large landowners in the area and by the provincial government, which is developing a new airport there. This growth is largely taking the form of upmarket development of gated communities, shopping and office development, with little provision for the urban poor. Some of this development is the consequence of earlier divided local government, but is also the result of a concern to support economic growth. In addition, the way in which the South African housing subsidy system is designed makes it difficult to support the development of low-cost housing in areas where land costs are high. The spatial framework was largely ignored in decision-making on land development applications, and was too broad to provide a basis for infrastructure planning. Instead, a developer-led approach predominated.

In recent years, however, the limits of earlier spatial planning have been recognized, and there are initiatives to link infrastructure planning and spatial planning more closely. Geographic information systems (GIS) and urban modelling have been used to highlight key interrelationships between forms of urban development and infrastructure costs, and to feed into decision-making. A set of scenarios was developed to model the impacts of various spatial development patterns on the requirements for infrastructure and its cost, as well as to identify key patterns. This assisted in choices over long-term development directions. A cost surface model was developed to predict the cost of providing bulk services to new housing developments, highlighting the costs of peripheral location and enabling arguments for greater expenditure on development in better located areas. An accessibility model was used to assess the need for facilities in new housing developments. These models have not determined development directions. Rather, they are an input into development decision-making, and by presenting information and choices in a clear way, they allow more informed discussion between various groups of officials, and between councillors and communities. These approaches have suggested the value of the use of harder data and GIS-based models; but they also point to the need for a clear long-term spatial development vision, based on engagement and agreement between various stakeholders, councillors and officials, and amongst municipal departments.

Source: Breetzke, 2008

Linking spatial planning to infrastructure planning

The idea of integrated urban infrastructure development was influential in the formulation of South Africa's 'integrated development plans',[118] strategic municipal plans intended to provide a five-year development plan and programme of action for both the municipality and other agencies operating in the area, as explained in Chapter 3. Spatial development frameworks, which provide the spatial component of integrated development plans, are also cast as broad-ranging strategic spatial visions. In reaction to critiques of master planning and blueprint planning, they have tended to focus on indicating the main areas for growth and development, the major 'corridors and nodes' that are intended to structure the city, major areas for intervention, and spaces for conservation. Compact city ideas have been influential, with the intention of concentrating development around nodes and corridors, and containing growth, often through the use of an urban edge.

While the expectation was that these spatial frameworks should give direction to infrastructure planning and to low-cost housing development sponsored by government (with the intention of integrating it within the city), spatial frameworks have not been effective in doing so. In part, housing policy has tended to encourage detached units in peripheral locations, in contradiction to plans, and transport policy has not been able to give effect to public transport systems supporting corridors. Although spatial frameworks avoided the detailed land-use zoning associated with master planning, this nevertheless exists – in many cases untransformed since the apartheid era. Decisions on site-level developments – often dominated by the demands of the market, and in many cases in contradiction to spatial plans – exert a powerful influence on spatial form. Housing and private developments have tended to lead, while infrastructure development and spatial planning have followed. Spatial planning has also been too broad and conceptual to give direction to infrastructure planning, which has taken its cues from elsewhere. Box 8.5 presents the example of Durban (South Africa), which demonstrates these points, but also points to new initiatives to link spatial and infrastructure planning.

Linking mega-projects and major infrastructural developments to spatial planning

Finally, it is critical to link mega-projects and major infrastructural developments to spatial planning. Previous sections have shown how these are often contrary to spatial plans and are frequently contributing to fragmented and sprawling developments. Yet, in many instances, mega-projects provide support for long-term planning, and they have proved a powerful driver of urban form in many cities. Such success is often linked with their ability to build cooperation between various sectors and agencies. Plaine Saint-Denis in Paris, discussed in Box 8.6, provides a positive example where a major regeneration initiative worked with spatial planning and was consistent with its ideas.

One major problem with mega-projects is that they are often politically driven and one-off. If political interests

to address immediate problems. Enabling conditions to facilitate long-term success are addressed. This kind of planning does not only focus on infrastructure – rather, it deals with problems in a multifaceted way, but will generally also include infrastructure development and service delivery within localized projects.

Similarly, the Dar es Salaam Strategic Urban Development Planning Framework combined stakeholder participation with spatial analysis, issue assessment and development of a framework for urban expansion, an identification of prioritized areas for redevelopment, densification and investment, as well as a set of environmental concerns to be addressed. Action plans focused on immediate strategic issues to be addressed.[117]

> One major problem with mega-projects is that they are often politically driven and one-off

take centre stage, these may obstruct cooperation between the various stakeholders. The case of the Rotterdam Central Station project in The Netherlands is a case at hand. During the 1990s, this project was identified as one of six 'strategic' projects that would enhance the city's international profile. The project involved the redevelopment of the central railway station and the surrounding area. A foreign company was selected to redesign the area and two private developers played a central role in the plans, which were projected to be implemented over an 18-year period. However, during municipal elections in 2002, a new political party – calling itself Liveable Rotterdam – garnered 30 per cent of the vote and thus fundamentally changed power relations in the city. The majority of the reconstituted city council represented the interests of small (and local) businesspeople, and were opposed to the 'corporate' approach of the Rotterdam Central Station mega-project, which had been spearheaded by the social democratic party. The new council placed a higher emphasis on safety in the streets, and the mega-project was downsized, to be redesigned by a 'home-grown' architect.[119]

CONCLUDING REMARKS

This chapter has shown the role of infrastructure and the way in which it intersects with a range of social, political and economic dynamics to shape the spatial structure of cities, and their impact upon access and inclusion. The 'unbundling' of urban development, and a weakened role for the public sector and for planning, has, in part, underpinned strong trends towards socio-spatial polarization and growing urban sprawl. Yet, there is a growing recognition of the problems associated with these patterns, and a search for new approaches to spatial planning that link more closely with infrastructure development in this context.

Planning has important roles to play in managing urban growth and in creating more inclusive cities and spaces. At a local scale, planning should recognize the diversity of needs in an area and create environments offering a range of services, facilities and amenities which meet these needs, and which support the livelihoods of the urban poor. The significance of pedestrian movement, particularly for lower-income groups, also requires recognition. Understanding these needs requires analysis of diversity, including, *inter alia*, gender, disability and age, and a strong participatory approach.

International studies of urban growth show a massive expansion in the spatial footprint of cities over the past decades, and suggest that these trends can be expected to continue. Attempts to develop more compact urban forms play a role in managing this growth: the importance of inner-city development, the usefulness of some smart growth principles and the role of transit-oriented development and related systems have been noted. Planning should seek to promote compaction in ways that are appropriate to the local context. Yet, most future development is likely to continue to involve further expansion on the periphery. If planning is to be effective, it must seek ways to direct, support and structure this growth, and to reinforce informal processes of

Box 8.6 Linking mega-project development to spatial planning: Plaine Saint-Denis, France

Plaine Saint-Denis is an area north of Paris, located on the axis linking the metropolitan centre to the Roissy-Charles de Gaulle International Airport. Between 1840 and 1960 it had been one of Europe's largest industrial zones, and provided some 50,000 jobs in 1940. However, industrial restructuring in the 1970s affected the area badly, and by 1990, the number of jobs had fallen to 27,000.

Urban regeneration began as a partnership between the three local authorities in the area, which set up an urban project to regenerate the area. The project envisaged the development of a multifunctional and diverse area, housing a range of groups of people, consistent with broader ideas about sustainable development in Paris. Some 23,000 jobs and 10,000 dwelling units were to be established. This vision of a 'city for all' – an intense mixed-use, pedestrian-oriented city – focused on maintaining industrial activities and low-income households in the heart of the Paris region, while creating new development around a network of transport and social infrastructure in the broader region.

The project developed slowly at first, but picked up momentum with several rounds of development. During the early 1990s, the Regional Structure Plan designated the area as an 'urban redevelopment centre', giving it priority for investment in infrastructure. The location of the 1998 Soccer World Cup gave the area a further boost, and drew private developers into the area. In contrast to many other examples of urban redevelopment associated with event tourism, the developments associated with the World Cup were consistent with the planning and vision for the area. Private-sector development has accelerated in what was once a depressed area, but has not displaced business and local residents. The area has become an important location for a range of new economic activities, and is seen as a strategic area for development within the region. Nevertheless, there are some mismatches between local skills and jobs, and old and new residents. Housing renovation and environmental improvement in some areas is still wanting.

On the whole, however, Plaine Saint-Denis represents a successful regeneration initiative. Rather than a single large flagship project, the development of the area evolved over time, using various instruments, and linked to both broader strategic planning processes and to opportunities created by event-led development, but always with the idea of supporting the planning intentions for the area. Importantly, the success of the development is linked to the building of cooperation between levels of government, different parts of the public sector, various private-sector interests and local communities.

Source: Lecroart, 2008

upgrading and consolidation. Enabling the expansion of economic activity and of the livelihoods of the poor, and improving infrastructure, services and facilities on the periphery is also important.

Linking spatial planning to infrastructure development is critical in this context. The public sector should provide the main routes and infrastructure trunk lines in advance of development, allowing the private sector, NGOs, other agencies and communities to connect to these main lines as they are able.[120] One study suggests that if the public sector cannot afford to pay for infrastructure, they should purchase rights of way to enable later infrastructure improvements.[121] Yet, there is also a growing movement that supports small-scale, neighbourhood-based distributed infrastructure systems, especially for water and power supply. Clearly, what is possible varies across contexts: in many countries, much more ambitious planning is feasible, and strategic spatial plans linking to infrastructure development might, for example, promote more compact forms of urban expansion focused around public transport, and attempt to improve urban services, environmental conditions, economic opportunities and livelihoods on the existing

The public sector should provide the main routes and infrastructure trunk lines in advance of development urban periphery, as well as in relation to new development. Linking major infrastructure investment projects and mega-projects to strategic planning is also critical; but the real prospects for doing so are likely to vary considerably.

Planning of this sort will require a good understanding of trends, development directions and market forces; but it will also need to be based on collaborative processes that draw together various public-sector agencies and departments with a range of other stakeholders from civil society and business. Building a common spatial vision of urban development, and a common discourse or storyline, is important to these processes; but it is unlikely that planning of this sort will be a single event. Rather, the examples of Durban (Box 8.5) and Plaine Saint-Denis (Box 8.6) point to iterative processes building on agreements, past developments or bringing to bear new information and approaches. Harder analytical, modelling and GIS-based approaches may be useful in this context, as an input into discussion and decision-making, but are unlikely on their own to determine outcomes.

NOTES

1   UNCHS, 1997 (see, for example, paragraph 90).
2   See Chapter 6.
3   Angel et al, 2005.
4   UNCHS, 2001a; UN-Habitat, 2003, 2004a, 2006f, 2008b.
5   UN-Habitat, 2003.
6   UN-Habitat, 2004a, p63.
7   Irazábal, 2008a; Hirt and Stanilov, 2008.
8   UNCHS, 2001a; UN-Habitat, 2004a; Bertaud, 2004.
9   Irazábal, 2008a; Yuen, 2008; Ansari, 2008.
10 Yuen, 2008; Nassar, 2008.
11 Graham and Marvin, 2001.
12 Graham and Marvin, 2001.
13 Hirt and Stanilov, 2008; Yuen, 2008.
14 Harris, 1983.
15 Gandy, 2006.
16 See Sivaramakrishan and Green (1986) on Asian countries.
17 Kooy and Bakker, 2008; Zérah, 2008.
18 Such as the World Bank and the Asian Development Bank; Yuen, 2008.
19 Graham and Marvin, 2001.
20 Hirt and Stanilov, 2008; Irazábal, 2008a; Yuen, 2008, p98.
21 For example, in water and sanitation projects.
22 For example, the build–operate–transfer (BOT) projects for major transport works, such as the rapid bus transport systems in Latin America.
23 Irazábal, 2008a; Yuen, 2008.
24 Batley, 1996.
25 Irazábal, 2008a.
26 McDonald and Pape, 2002.
27 Irazábal, 2008a.
28 Swyngedouw et al, 2002.
29 Flyvberg, 2007.
30 Goldblum and Wong, 2000; Douglass, 2005.
31 Thomson, 1977; Newman and Kenworthy, 1996; Bertaud, 2002.
32 Boarnet and Haughwout, 2000.
33 See Boarnet and Haughwout (2000) for a summary.
34 Boarnet and Haughwout, 2000.

35 Newman and Kenworthy, 1996; Gounden, 1999.
36 Rao and Sharma, 1990; Behrens, 2005.
37 Such as the neighbourhood principle, Radburn; see Behrens and Watson, 1996; Behrens, 2005.
38 See, for example, Posselthwyte (1986) on Mitchell's Plain in Cape Town.
39 See Chapter 6.
40 Candiracci, undated.
41 Behrens and Watson, 1996; Behrens, 2005; Curtis, 2005. There are obvious links here to new urbanism and neo-traditional design.
42 See section on 'Contemporary approaches to linking spatial planning to urban infrastructure'.
43 Cervero, 2004. For instance in the US, commuter rail is only used at peak hours and land around stations is used to accommodate parking.
44 Cervero, 2004. See also Chapter 6.
45 Cervero, 2004.
46 For instance, in Durban (South Africa), a major strategic decision concerned whether a further sewerage treatment plant should be developed in the west, where large numbers of informal settlements and low-income housing developments had developed, or the north, where major economic projects and upmarket housing developments were being promoted by private developers and provincial authorities. The decision to provide bulk infrastructure in the north will shape the future spatial direction of growth. See Breetzke, 2008.
47 Graham and Marvin, 1999. See also the section on 'Urban spatial trends, infrastructure and exclusion'.
48 Rutherford, 2005; Odendaal and Duminy, 2008. See also section on 'Urban spatial trends, infrastructure and exclusion'.
49 Graham, 2002; Baum et al,

2004; Odendaal and Duminy, 2008.
50 See Odendaal and Duminy, 2008.
51 See the discussion of various forms of participatory planning approaches in Chapter 5 for more details.
52 See, for example, Moser, 1993; Reeves, 2003; Office of the Deputy Prime Minister, 2005.
53 UN-Habitat, 2006e.
54 See UN-Habitat, 2006c.
55 See Skinner and Dobson, 2007.
56 See, for example, texts by Jenks et al (1996), Jenks and Burgess (2000) and Williams et al (2000), which bring together much of the literature assessing the compact city idea. See also Chapter 6.
57 Mindali et al, 2004.
58 Feminists have also been critical of cities built around land-use separations since they isolate women at home, and make it difficult for working women to negotiate various spatial demands. See, for example, Mackenzie and Rose, 1983.
59 See Chen et al (2008) for a summary of arguments; Ewing, 1997; Newman and Kenworthy, 2000. See also Chapter 6.
60 See Chen et al (2008) for a summary; Breheny, 1995; Gordon and Richardson, 1997.
61 Newman and Kenworthy, 2000.
62 See, for example, Gordon and Richardson, 1997; Simmonds and Coombe, 2000; Mindali et al, 2004.
63 Breheny (1995), generally a critic of compaction arguments, confirms it.
64 Bertaud, 2004.
65 Taniguchi and Ikeda, 2005.
66 Simmonds and Coombe, 2000.
67 Handy, 2005.
68 Gordon and Richardson, 1997.
69 See Bertaud, 2004, Table 1. Drawing from the US Institute for Transport Engineers, Bertaud cities the following minimum residential densities for different forms of transport: 1 bus per hour (30

people per hectare); 1 bus per half hour (44 people per hectare); light rail and feeder traffic (53 people per hectare).
70 Bertaud, 2004.
71 Irazábal, 2008a. See also Box 8.4.
72 Richardson et al, 2000.
73 Zillman, 2000.
74 Brown and Lloyd-Jones, 2002.
75 Richardson et al, 2000.
76 UN-Habitat, 2003.
77 Barter, 2000.
78 Zhang, 2000.
79 Todes, 2003; Schoonraad, 2000; Cross et al, 1996.
80 See Biermann et al (2004) on Diepsloot in Johannesburg, which is relatively close to emerging new nodes in the city.
81 Bertaud, 2004.
82 See the case of Atlantis, in Cape Town (South Africa). See also Lloyd Jones, 2000; and Brown and Lloyd-Jones, 2002.
83 Jenks, 2000.
84 Biermann, 2000.
85 RERC, 1974.
86 See also Breetzke (2008) on Durban.
87 See also the earlier sub-section on 'Mega-projects'.
88 Burchell et al, 2000.
89 Burchell et al, 2000.
90 See Chapter 6.
91 Dieleman and Wegener, 2004.
92 Burchell et al, 2000; Shen et al, 2007.
93 Jun, 2004.
94 Godschalk, 2000.
95 Belzer and Autler, 2002.
96 Owens, 2008.
97 Wilkinson, 2006.
98 These systems generally involve public–private partnerships, with the public sector developing infrastructure and regulating system, while the private sector runs the vehicles.
99 Jiron, 2008.
100 A system of trunks and feeders with poor cross-routes replaced the previous more chaotic bus system, but in the

process made it difficult to move across the city outside of these parameters. Nor did planners understand the way in which various modes of transport were used by people and how patterns of movement were socially constructed. In addition, the number of buses and, hence, frequency was cut, reducing convenience. See Jiron, 2008.

101 Cascetta and Pagliara, 2008.

102 See, for example, Auckland Regional Council, 2006.

103 Wilkinson, 2002. The links between other forms of infra-

structure planning and spatial planning are also not automatically made as a consequence of differences in methodology, scale and time, although there are potentials to link them. See Ramnath, 2007.

104 Lee, 1973; Kane and Behrens, 2002.

105 Iacono et al, 2007.

106 Auckland Regional Council, 2006.

107 Singh and Steinberg, 1996, p17.

108 Archer, 1996.

109 See Chapter 3.

110 Singh and Steinberg, 1996.

111 Mattingly and Winarso, 2000; Mattingly, 2001.

112 Mattingly and Winarso, 2000.

113 Ansari, 2008. Similar problems occurred in Nepal.

114 Mattingly, 2001.

115 Mattingly, 2001.

116 UN-Habitat, 2006d. See also UN-Habitat, 2006a, 2006c.

117 UN-Habitat, 2006g.

118 Harrison, 2001.

119 For more details, see UN-Habitat, 2004a, pp167–168.

120 Archer, 1996; Angel et al, 2005. Where project finance is available for communities to

undertake development projects, support around project preparation (such as feasibility studies, basic planning, land availability, business plan) can help to bridge the gap between planning and implementation. The Project Preparation Trust, a South African NGO, has developed successful methodologies for a range of development projects.

121 Angel et al, 2005.

PART IV

GLOBAL TRENDS: MONITORING, EVALUATION AND EDUCATION

CHAPTER 9

THE MONITORING AND EVALUATION OF URBAN PLANS

Planning and managing cities is an increasingly complicated proposition in both developed and developing countries. Challenges such as the provision of safe and affordable housing, a safe and liveable physical environment, improved incomes, potable water and safe sanitation, a decent level of healthcare and education, employment and livelihood opportunities, and social stability, among many other issues – all of which have been addressed by the international community during the last two decades – have already been discussed in some detail in earlier chapters.

Regardless of the context – growth or decline, developed or developing countries – urban planners and decision-makers need to know how best to use limited resources to address the complex urban challenges (and opportunities) that are presented. Urban planning seeks to be *efficient* (make optimal use of resources), *effective* (create desired and meaningful impacts and outcomes), and also seeks to enhance *equity* (of opportunity, rights and power, especially with regard to gender).[1] To achieve these '3Es' of good planning practice, decision-makers need a solid foundation of information and direction that can be provided by urban planning – specifically, the monitoring and evaluation of urban plans.

Urban plan monitoring and evaluation generates many benefits. Continuous monitoring and evaluation of plan relevance, integrity and coherence helps decision-makers to make informed decisions about resource allocations. Monitoring and evaluation can demonstrate whether urban planning has made a difference, whether it has improved (or undermined) the quality of life and well-being of the city's residents, enhanced sustainability, or achieved related goals and objectives.

The objective of this chapter is to review how monitoring and evaluation of urban plans is currently being practised in different regions of the world. The following section provides a brief overview of various types of monitoring and evaluation, and introduces key terms and concepts. The second section examines monitoring and evaluation in the context of current urban planning practice, while the third section considers some caveats and considerations based on this practice. The final section offers concluding remarks and lessons for policy.

TYPES OF MONITORING AND EVALUATION

As noted above, all organizations – public, private and not-for-profit – must contend with considerable challenges in their operating and decision-making environments. For many organizations, especially in the public sector, decision-makers must somehow plan for and manage increasing demands for services, or provide basic services, while levels of resources are decreasing.

Given the rapid pace and extent of change in local government decision-making environments, there is a need for constant assessment of trends, activities and performance. This has led to increased interest in programme monitoring and evaluation. There are many definitions of the key components of this process (i.e. monitoring, evaluation and related indicators).[2] In operation, evaluation is an episodic exercise. Monitoring is a continuous process that feeds the evaluation process and signals issues (or opportunities) that must be addressed. Indicators provide the foundation of data and information that directly support monitoring and, ultimately, evaluation (see Box 9.1).

Evaluation and performance measurement are similar but distinctive analytical processes. Performance measurement focuses on programme delivery issues (*efficiency*), whereas evaluation challenges the validity, relevance, outcomes and impacts of a programme, plan or project (*effectiveness*).

Evaluations take many forms. Many international agencies[3] require programme evaluation and project evaluations that are associated with development initiatives – for example, the evaluation of urban development, health, economic, social and/or environmental programmes. Project evaluations tend to be narrow in scope, focusing on specific project activities. Programme evaluations are more comprehensive in nature, reflecting the diverse elements (e.g. projects, processes and plans) that can comprise a programme. In each case, the starting point is an existing programme or project. There is general agreement that generic programme evaluation has two main streams: formative evaluation and summative evaluation. These evaluation processes play different yet complementary roles. It is possi-

> Continuous monitoring and evaluation of plan relevance, integrity and coherence helps decision-makers to make informed decisions about resource allocations

> Performance measurement focuses on programme delivery issues (efficiency), whereas evaluation challenges the validity, relevance, outcomes and impacts of a programme, plan or project (effectiveness)

Box 9.1 Defining 'monitoring', 'evaluation' and 'indicators' in urban planning

Monitoring refers to the ongoing collection and analysis of information about trends, activities and events that could affect the plan's performance. Monitoring can also address whether the plan has been efficiently managed through plan administration processes.

Evaluation tells decision-makers whether, and how effectively, the plan has achieved its intended goals and objectives. It is the measurement of plan performance in terms of the outcomes and impacts compared with intended goals and objectives, and the efficiency with which related resources have been used and the programme has been administered. Three main forms of evaluating urban plans exist:

1   *ex ante evaluation* (undertaken during plan formulation – i.e. before implementation starts);
2   *formative evaluation* (undertaken as part of plan administration – i.e. during plan implementation); and
3   *summative (ex post) evaluation* (undertaken normally after implementation of plans).

Indicators provide the quantitative data and/or qualitative information that demonstrate trends and patterns. This information tells us something about phenomena in the decision-making environment. In the process of monitoring, the information and data generated by indicators are checked and updated regularly. When monitored properly, these data and information provide the evidence that is required to support evaluation. The results of plan monitoring and evaluation processes directly affect local government strategic planning and management decisions.

---

ble to have a highly effective programme that does not make efficient use of resources (and *vice versa*) – hence the need to use both types of evaluation:

- *Formative evaluation* is conducted early in the plan, project or programme implementation process as a way of assessing and modifying programme delivery. This is largely an efficiency form of evaluation. It is a process refinement tool, typically internal and reflexive in nature, designed to give feedback to decision-makers. This exercise allows adjustments to be made to the direction or performance early on in the life of the policy or programme. Formative evaluations are used to change aspects such as programme administration and programme design. This is usually an internally driven exercise (e.g. by department or agency).
- *Summative evaluation (ex post)* occurs once a plan, project or programme has been completed and/or it has achieved sufficient maturity to permit an assessment of performance. This type of evaluation examines effectiveness (impacts and outcomes) of programmes. It is often externally driven (e.g. by donor agencies or national government) and it is considered objective. It can be used to make decisions about the future of the intervention or to make improvements in its components and strategies. Summative evaluations demonstrate whether programme goals and objectives have been met as intended; they can also identify unintended as well as intended results.[4]

Monitoring can also take many forms and have diverse applications:

- *Context monitoring* is used by organizations to track trends and forces of change in their operating environ-

ment. Depending upon organizational mandate, this could include monitoring changes to the economy, demography, technology, the environment, socio-cultural patterns and political-institutional activities (e.g. policy changes). This is a continuous process that occurs throughout the life of the programme.
- *Process monitoring* is used to determine whether and how the programme is being delivered as proposed. This monitoring approach is used to fine-tune programme administration. Process monitoring supports formative evaluations. Monitoring systems can also be designed to track outputs from programmes to determine whether the programme has generated the desired products; these forms of monitoring support summative evaluations.
- *Outcome monitoring* is a related and important use of monitoring methods. Here, monitoring is used to help determine whether the desired effects of the programme have been realized as intended and framed by the programme's goals and objectives.
- Finally, *impact monitoring* helps programme designers and managers to understand whether the programme and its deliverables have made a difference to the programme's end-users.

The monitoring and evaluation process has been described in many ways, often depending upon the application and sponsoring agency. However, it is possible to identify several core and common stages in monitoring and evaluation design:

- Formulate goals and outcomes.
- Select outcome indicators to monitor.
- Gather baseline information on the current condition.
- Set specific targets to reach and dates.
- Regularly collect data to determine progress.
- Analyse and report the results.[5]

The organization conducting the evaluation must have a supportive culture. In this context, culture refers to the attitudes of staff, as well as demonstrable support from senior management and politicians. However, many organizations are change and risk averse, avoid criticism, and are content with the status quo. In that context, monitoring and evaluation activities would be seen as threatening and would be regarded with suspicion. Organizational culture is thus a very important determinant of success or failure with monitoring and evaluation processes. The situation can be even more complicated when governments struggle with severe resource constraints. In either case, it can be difficult to garner sufficient resources and commitment to support evaluation.

Accordingly, considerable restraint and discipline is required when designing an evaluation. The temptation to overly complicate the evaluation must be resisted. Monitoring and evaluation is a means to an end, which is improvement in programme design and delivery; it should not be treated as simply an abstract intellectual exercise. Expensive and time-consuming evaluations can drain resources and try patience in organizations, especially if the

The organization conducting the evaluation must have a supportive culture

Expensive and time-consuming evaluations can drain resources and try patience in organizations

results are negative. Advocates of monitoring and evaluation must be skilled analysts and methodologists; they must also be politically astute and highly strategic communicators. The monitoring and evaluation process must be seen to add value to the organization. It has to be perceived as relevant, credible and important.

Finally, and perhaps most importantly, the monitoring and evaluation approach *must* reflect organizational realities – the constraints and opportunities that are presented. Box 9.2 describes some of the challenges that can be encountered when designing and administering monitoring and evaluation in organizations. The next section explores how these generic evaluation models and methods are used in urban-oriented monitoring and evaluation practice.

CURRENT PRACTICE IN URBAN PROGRAMME AND PLAN EVALUATION

There are lessons to be learned from recent experiences with urban-based applications of monitoring and evaluation models and methods. The use of various types of indicators is well established in many urban planning exercises in both developed and developing countries. However, it is apparent that monitoring and evaluation in the context of urban governance, and as specifically applied to urban plans, is a recent phenomenon. This section describes recent trends and current practice in monitoring and evaluation of urban plans and programmes.

Urban monitoring and evaluation has become part of practice in the more progressive planning departments of cities and regions in developed countries. In many cases, monitoring and evaluation of urban plans reflects an interest in evaluating progress made towards achieving urban sustainability or healthy community goals and objectives. Some of these initiatives have been bottom up, driven by communities and enacted by city planning departments, as in Seattle (US)[6] and Hamilton (Canada),[7] while others have been the product of state legislation and policy, as in New Zealand[8] and the UK.[9]

In the formerly communist countries of Central and Eastern Europe, however, very little progress has been made so far in embracing monitoring and evaluation as integral parts of the urban planning process. Among the reasons for this is the lack of traditions in monitoring and evaluation. Objective assessments of stated goals were not an important element of communist planning, which was dominated by strict ideological imperatives. This legacy is hard to overcome, especially since the political structure in most such countries is still entrenched in centralized approaches to government and is not conducive to independent reviews of plans and plan implementation.[10]

Interest in urban planning applications of monitoring and evaluation – specifically plan evaluation – emerged during the mid 1990s in developed countries, reflecting increasing concerns for efficiency, effectiveness and accessibility, as well as performance and productivity in municipal government. However, the first phase of urban plan monitor-

---

Box 9.2 Common monitoring and evaluation challenges

- Inadequate understanding of and attention to monitoring and evaluation in project design and subsequently inadequate resource allocation and hierarchical organization of decision-making and analysis.
- Lack of commitment to monitoring by project staff and implementing partners. This leads to delays in implementing monitoring systems and to lack of information use by project management.
- Monitoring is seen as an obligation imposed from outside, with project staff mechanically filling in forms for managers and the project managers seeing monitoring only as a form of data collection in the process of writing reports for donors.
- Irrelevant and poor-quality information produced through monitoring that focused on physical and financial aspects and ignores project outreach, effect and impact.
- Almost no attention to the monitoring and evaluation needs and potentials of other stakeholders, such as beneficiaries and community-based and other local cooperating institutions.
- Very few internal project reviews or ongoing evaluations, with adjustments triggered mainly by external evaluations or supervisions.
- Widespread lack of integration and cooperation between project monitoring and evaluation and project management, with no clear, mutually agreed-upon guidelines.
- Monitoring and evaluation documentation that does not address or resolve identified problems.
- Overambitious monitoring systems, with too much being asked in terms of information and methods.
- Poor use of participatory and qualitative monitoring and evaluation methods due to limited capacity and inability to see the need for such information.
- Monitoring and evaluation staff with insufficient relevant skills and experiences, and few efforts made to fill the capacity gap.
- Differentiation of monitoring from evaluation activities, with evaluation being contracted out. This leads to monitoring and evaluation not being an integrated system for improvement-oriented critical reflection.

Source: IFAD, 2002

---

ing and evaluation occurred during the 1960s and early 1970s, coincident with the emergence and early rise of generic programme evaluation theory development. These early approaches – referred to as *ex ante* evaluation – advocated highly rational and technical analyses of urban planning goals and project proposals, including impact analysis, as the urban plan evolved.[11] This application of *ex ante* tools distinguishes urban planning applications of monitoring and evaluation from generic programme or project evaluation, which takes an *ex post* or retrospective (summative) and in-process (formative) view of programme performance and impact.

Evaluation of project, policy or programme suitability in plan-making

Ex ante forms of evaluation are commonplace in urban planning practice. Planning organizations dedicate considerable resources to the developing and testing of policy, programme and project alternatives as part of the plan-making cycle. This is in keeping with one of the basic tenets of the traditional (and ubiquitous) rational comprehensive model of urban planning, which provides the decision-making framework for much of urban planning practice.

Most long-range plans have policies, programmes and projects that are derived from an evaluation of their fit with

> The monitoring and evaluation approach must reflect organizational realities

> Monitoring and evaluation in the context of urban governance, and as specifically applied to urban plans, is a recent phenomenon

plan or project goals and objectives. Certainly, modern planning practice in most developed countries requires the completion of an array of impact analyses – social, fiscal and environmental – to guide plan decision-making about alternative courses of action. Cost–benefit analysis and cost-effectiveness tools remain the mainstay of evaluation practice in urban planning.[12] Various modelling, forecasting and projection tools (e.g. demographic, economic and environmental) are used to determine likely consequences for housing, infrastructure, recreation, economic development, and health and education, among many other policy realms.

This rigour is a response to the expectations of an increasingly critical public, who demands accountability for plan-making decisions, and an improved understanding of the range of impacts and externalities produced by plans and projects. These tools are often part of elaborate and multi-faceted multi-stakeholder plan-making exercises that have become the norm in many developed countries over the past 30 to 40 years. This is especially the case in larger metropolitan regions, such as Paris, Chicago, London and Los Angeles, which have applied sophisticated modelling exercises. In these city-regions, the full range of *ex ante* analytical tools has been employed, particularly to transportation and transit-system planning, and to population forecasts.

These are complicated, highly technical and expert-driven evaluation exercises that very much follow the tradition of rational comprehensive planning, tempered by the inclusion of public outreach and consultation. The use of environmental impact assessments and similar impact analysis techniques in developing countries reflects growing concern with the externalities generated by rapid industrialization and urbanization, and the dictates of international aid-agency funding criteria. However, the dominance of these highly technical and expert-driven approaches is currently being challenged by the increasing importance of strategic planning and inclusive participatory approaches, as shown in Chapters 3 and 5.

The evaluation of plan and programme performance

More recently, there has been greater acceptance of the need to monitor and evaluate the impacts and outcomes generated by urban plans, especially in developed countries. This shift in emphasis can be attributed to the emergence and evolution of sustainable development and the healthy community models over the past 20 years. It also reflects an understanding that the tangible impacts of sustainable development and healthy community programmes, projects and plans are felt at the urban level.

A second group of evaluation methods (formative or *process* evaluation) has been used since the 1990s to assess the efficiency of the planning process and programme administration and delivery. Performance measurement is an integral part of urban planning practice in many jurisdictions in developed countries.[13] This form of evaluation examines the extent to which outputs comply with the plan's guidelines – for example, whether subsidiary and associated plans

align with the urban plan – and whether plan administration processes and tools (e.g. development control and zoning) support plan implementation.

A third group of methods falls within the *ex post* (summative or *impact*) evaluation cluster. Here, decision-makers seek to determine whether, and to what extent, urban plans have achieved their intended goals and objectives (e.g. sustainable forms of development, the public good and equity), and the types of impacts and outcomes that these plans have generated. The summative evaluation process examines the effectiveness of the urban plan, and generates findings that could guide plan revisions and future plan-making processes.

Sophisticated and numerically oriented summative evaluation takes place typically at the national level, less so at the urban scale. This is especially the case in developing countries. Evaluations tend to focus on national economic, education or health issues. These evaluation exercises are *ex post* in nature; they examine the impacts of programmes that often receive international financial support (e.g. from the World Bank, Asia Development Bank, International Fund for Agricultural Development, etc.). Indeed, there is considerable emphasis in developing countries on the selection of relevant indicators that are used to support national-level programme evaluation and performance measurement.

Performance measurement in cities is of interest to agencies such as the World Bank, which recognizes the pivotal role that indicators serve in the effort to achieve economic development, sustainability and healthy communities. UN-Habitat's Urban Indicators Programme and Global Urban Observatory represent the serious efforts that the agency has made to create and institutionalize indicators as a key contributor to enhanced decision-making and, thus, more efficient and effective use of resources.

In developing countries, the most extensive application of monitoring and evaluation has occurred with development programmes that are funded by international agencies, managed by state organizations, and implemented by local authorities. Most of these programmes and projects have an impact at the urban or regional level and represent urban-oriented applications of monitoring and evaluation practice. Programmes cover a wide range of social, economic, environmental and institutional topics that include poverty eradication,[14] urban infrastructure (including water and sanitation), slum upgrading, low-income housing, HIV-AIDS, etc. Examples of monitoring and evaluation practice include the World Bank's *Global Monitoring Report*, World Development Indicators, and Development Impact Evaluation (DIME) initiatives.[15]

UN-Habitat's Global Urban Observatory supports city-based monitoring and evaluation capacity-building through its country and city projects on local and national urban observatories. These projects are designed to assist city governments and national authorities, non-governmental organizations (NGOs) and academic institutions to:

- develop their own performance monitoring frameworks for municipal services, local development plans or programmes;

Formative or process evaluation ... has been used since the 1990s to assess the efficiency of the planning process and programme administration and delivery

Summative or impact ... evaluation ... seeks to determine whether, and to what extent, urban plans have achieved their intended goals and objectives ... and the types of impacts and outcomes that these plans have generated

- collect, analyse and report indicators data – with a focus on data disaggregation at the sub-city level;
- use performance results for improving urban management and public accountability; and
- establish regular, sustainable data collection processes through local and national urban observatories and personnel training.[16]

Most cities want to establish whether and to what extent the end result of policy planning – projects on the ground – reflect the intent of comprehensive plan goals, objectives and policies. The premise is that there should be a high degree of conformity within a planning hierarchy; the high-level comprehensive plan's intent should be reflected in and guide suburban, subdivision and site planning decisions.

Where lack of conformity of results with plan intentions is an issue, several reasons for this conflict are possible, including lack of clarity in policy design; unrealistic goals and objectives; or inconsistent interpretation of policies. These indicate faults in design or execution. This evaluation of the planning process enables cities to revisit and correct plan content and administrative processes. In most cases, urban plans in developed countries include sections with monitoring and evaluation protocols. There are directions for the use and interpretation of specific indicators. Furthermore, the intent of these indicators is usually clearly expressed. This clarity serves to inform and reassure stakeholders who need to understand what is being evaluated, and how. Regular plan monitoring reports are produced for that purpose. A tangible and applied example of urban plan monitoring – in this case, on land development activity – is provided in Box 9.3.

In developed countries, there is considerable experience with monitoring and summative evaluation of urban-related programmes, especially in transportation, regional economic development, the environment, and many other policy portfolios and programme interventions. National governments and the more progressive sub-national state or provincial governments have typically required evaluation of programme performance. There are also examples of international monitoring and evaluation initiatives – for example, of transnational spatial planning exercises in the European Union.[17] Summative evaluation of high-level urban plans is often mandated by the state. In many jurisdictions, there are national, state or provincial planning laws and policies that require regular evaluation of community plans (also known as development plans, official community plans, official plans, etc.). These evaluations involve a critical and regular assessment of the extent to which an urban plan's goals, objectives and policies have been met.

The intent is to ensure that plans are relevant, strategic, and action oriented. There is also an expectation that regular evaluations will lead to outcomes and impacts that reflect good planning, and ensure compliance with state rules and policies. These evaluation processes are supported by an active monitoring process in which key indicators are tracked and information is assessed.

In New Zealand, the 1991 Resources Management Act mandates regular monitoring and evaluation of urban

> **Box 9.3 Development permit system: Protecting the natural environment through monitoring**
>
> Since 2007, municipal governments in the Province of Ontario, Canada, have used the development permit system to support environmental planning efforts. The development permit system has been designed to allow the imposition of development conditions, such as the monitoring of groundwater quality, the integrity of natural features, and health and safety issues. The system obligates developers to monitor project impacts on an ongoing basis post-development. This anticipated use of monitoring is expected to be an effective means of ensuring proper mitigation interventions.
>
> *Source: Ontario, 2008*

plans, policy statements and/or planning conditions (e.g. development approvals). New Zealand's extensive experience with monitoring, evaluation and indicators has led to the conclusion that plan monitoring and evaluation can result in more robust and defensible decisions that are supported by better information. Furthermore, monitoring and evaluation can clarify roles and responsibilities, and make expectations of plan performance more realistic. Finally, monitoring and evaluation can enhance mutual understanding of urban planning processes and context among stakeholders, contribute to decision-making transparency and foster collaborative planning.[18]

Many types of plans are evaluated with summative methods, such as economic development plans (e.g. Ministry of Economic Development, New Zealand[19]), recreation and resource management master plans (e.g. City of Los Angeles, US;[20] National River Administration, Israel;[21] Mekong River Commission for Sustainable Development[22]), water and waste management plans (e.g. Region of Waterloo, Ontario, Canada;[23] New York City Department of Environmental Protection, US[24]), and downtown plans (e.g. the City of San Francisco, US;[25] City of Victoria, British Columbia, Canada;[26] City of Kitchener, Ontario, Canada[27]). There are many more examples of urban planning monitoring and evaluation in practice in developed countries. The same principles of monitoring and evaluation apply, but at a different scale of enquiry. In downtown plan monitoring and evaluation, for example, the issues are more immediate and tangible; this can make monitoring and evaluation a comparatively straightforward exercise because many of the issues are geographically contained.

There is less evidence of community/official plan-level monitoring and evaluation in developing countries. There are typically few resources for planning generally, and especially for plan enforcement or monitoring. In countries with reasonable planning capacity, the emphasis is typically on the production of comprehensive land-use plans, master plans and urban design plans, as indicated in Chapter 3. The emphasis is on problem-solving and implementation to meet short-term needs for housing, potable water, waste management, economic development and infrastructure. Urban planning in this context is often adversely affected by serious governance problems caused by political instability, and a sheer lack of social and fiscal capital, technical capacity and institutional instability, among other complex and interconnected challenges.

In developed countries, there is considerable experience with monitoring and summative evaluation of urban-related programmes

There is less evidence of community/official plan-level monitoring and evaluation in developing countries

Function	Description	Answers the question...
Description	Describe conditions or problems Increase general understanding	'What are things like?'
Simplification	Simplify complexity; provide a representative picture with significance extending to a larger phenomena of interest	'What's the big picture?'
Measurement	Measure characteristics of quality of life; measure performance activities or services	'How much?'
Trend identification	Establish baseline data; identify trends or patterns; show direction, improvement, disintegration, no change Two types: 1 Past orientation. Indicators are chosen in light of their 'historical trend-identification properties' (i.e. showing how dimensions of an identified phenomenon have been changing). 2 Future-orientation. The indicator is a 'forward-looking instrument' used as a predictive forecasting device.	'How did we do?' 'Where are we headed?'
Clarification	Clarify analytical issues or long-term goals; highlights areas of concern or improvement	'What is most important?'
Communication	Translate data into terms understandable by wide range of users	'How do we explain ... ?'
Catalyst for action	Stimulate public, stakeholder and political awareness, as well as interest, and will to work towards change	'What next?'

Table 9.1

Key functions of urban planning indicators

Source: Hoernig and Seasons, 2005

Increased transparency, increased sense of ownership ... and increased flexibility to adapt ... are among the main positive outcomes of participatory monitoring and evaluation

There is, however, considerable evidence indicating the usefulness of participatory monitoring and evaluation approaches. As discussed in Chapter 5, community participation has proved to be an important element in all parts of the urban planning process, including monitoring and evaluation. Participatory urban appraisal and participatory budgeting,[28] in particular, have proved very useful to achieve the '3Es' of good planning practice – *efficiency*, *effectiveness* and *equity*. As evidenced in Chapter 5, increased transparency, increased sense of ownership of the development process itself among the intended beneficiaries/clients, and increased flexibility to adapt by learning from experiences during plan implementation are among the main positive outcomes of participatory monitoring and evaluation. The experience with the use of citizen report cards in Bangalore (India) (see Box 9.4) also shows the effectiveness of involving the users themselves directly in monitoring and evaluation of urban activities.

Although, as noted above, there has been very little progress in embracing monitoring and evaluation as integral parts of the urban planning process in the formerly communist countries of Central and Eastern Europe, there are some indications that this may change in the future. The participation of such transitional countries and city governments in internationally funded programmes and projects has made public institutions in participating countries aware of the need to enforce transparency and accountability in all their actions related to the use of public resources. The active involvement of many Eastern and Central European countries in the European Spatial Planning Observation Network (ESPON) is a clear testimony to the value of such broad initiatives which cut across national boundaries and provide valuable experience for the participating parties.[29]

Indicators and urban plan evaluation

There is no single unitary set of indicators for urban plan monitoring and evaluation.[30] Table 9.1 summarizes key functions of urban planning indicators. Common planning-related measures could include economic indicators (rates of employment or unemployment; vacancy rates; income per capita; productivity rates); social indicators (e.g. highest level of education; literacy rates; language; age and sex); environmental indicators (e.g. air and water quality; water consumption rates; levels of pollution; amount of recreational land per capita); sustainability indicators and, most recently, indicators of urban creativity. In most cases, numerous potential indicators can be identified for each key issue. There is also the possibility of information overload, and the considerable effort involved in the collection and maintenance of data for indicators; this means that it is essential to be highly strategic in the choice of indicators that support urban plan monitoring and evaluation efforts.

As in the case of programme evaluation, there are many types of urban indicators that could be applied. More recently, equity and gender mainstreaming, in particular have become integral parts of monitoring and evaluation,

There is no single unitary set of indicators for urban plan monitoring and evaluation

---

Box 9.4 Using citizen report cards as a strategic tool to improve service delivery, Bangalore, India

Bangalore is India's third largest city and is located in the southern part of the country. The city's municipal government was aware of the need to provide and deliver urban services in a more efficient and effective manner. Accordingly, in 1994, a civil society organization – the Public Affairs Centre – prepared 'citizen report cards', which were used to communicate the citizens' perspectives on what they considered dreadful levels of service delivery (e.g. water supply, transport, power, healthcare and transportation).

The report cards were based on random sample surveys, using structured questionnaires, reflecting actual experiences of people with a wide range of public services. Agencies were rated and compared in terms of public satisfaction, corruption and responsiveness. The results of the survey were striking. Almost all public service providers received poor ratings. These Bangalore 'report cards' were sent to the appropriate government agency for action, and the media were alerted.

The public discussion that followed brought the issue of public services out in the open. Civil society organizations demanded action, and, as a result, many public service providers took steps to improve their services. The release of new 'citizen report cards' in 1999 and in 2003 revealed that remarkable improvements had been achieved in the city's public services. Intense public scrutiny had, in fact, been translated into improved levels of service and less corruption.

After more than a decade of monitoring by civil society organizations, the city of Bangalore 'has achieved real progress in improving the quality and cost-effectiveness of its public services'. The Bangalore experience is considered an excellent example of civil society engagement with government authorities. This model has since been used with considerable success elsewhere in India and in other developing nations.

Source: www.capacity.org/en/journal/tools_and_methods/citizen_report_cards_score_in_india

---

Box 9.5 The Local Urban Observatory for Jinja Municipality, Uganda

Urban-based indicators have considerable potential in the developing world. The city of Jinja (the second largest city in Uganda) is a case in point. The city must contend with complex and interconnected issues, such as poverty, malnutrition, lack of affordable or good-quality housing, and poor health and educational facilities. Since 2000, indicators have been developed to support the city's efforts to understand the nature and extent of these challenges, and to provide the basis for monitoring, evaluation and development of appropriate policy responses.

The indicators were selected to monitor social, economic and environmental issues of importance to the community (e.g. solid waste management, sewage and sanitation). The indicators are based on UN-Habitat's Minimum Urban Data Set (MUDS) with the support of the International Council for Local Environmental Initiatives (ICLEI). It is also important to note that these indicators are the result of a consultative process with local stakeholders; community-based knowledge was an important factor in selecting indicators. The results include consensus about the selected indicators, the engagement of citizens in the assessment of urban issues, and planning exercises that are carried out in partnership with stakeholder groups.

Source: http://ww2.unhabitat.org/programmes/guo/country_and_city_projects.asp

---

and this has been reflected in the selection and use of indicators. As indicated earlier in this chapter, UN-Habitat, for example, carried out pioneering work at the global level in indicators development through its Urban Indicators Programme.[31] More recently, UN-Habitat has also launched the Monitoring Urban Inequities Programme, which focuses on access to basic urban services.[32] The World Bank has initiated the Global City Indicators project that provides a framework and information clearinghouse on urban indicators.

In many developed countries, more gendered statistics are being produced at the level of central government.[33] However, such statistics tend to be based on existing data sources which historically may not have taken full account of gender or issues of particular concern to women and men. Gender statistics need to relate to policy goals and indicators of success. Gendered indicators are important in that they can help to drive and focus implementation. Unfortunately, gender is often not considered relevant to high-level indicators. The result is that there are no criteria to assess whether policies and projects are going to promote gender equality.[34]

Performance measurement in urban service delivery is a key policy issue for international development agencies, and for progressive developing countries. Users of public services can tell governments a lot about the quality and value of the public services provided. Although user feedback is a cost-effective way for public authorities to assess whether its services are reaching all segments of the population, this is not a method that is known, or used, in many developing countries. The continuing poor quality of services is, in part, a consequence of this fact. The city of Bangalore (India) uses the 'report card system' to demonstrate whether and to what extent its services have been delivered (see Box 9.4). In Jinja (Uganda), indicators are used to monitor urban trends and conditions and to evaluate the impact of programme interventions (see Box 9.5).

Urban-oriented indicators support programme and development plan monitoring and evaluation exercises in developing countries – for example, the CDS for Addis Ababa (Ethiopia), which addresses poverty alleviation by integrating this issue within a policy and urban management framework. The goal is to reduce and prevent urban poverty. The objectives are to promote more equitable forms of economic growth, manage the city's resources to enhance sustainability, and empower stakeholders to address key urban development issues.[35] Santiago (Chile) has developed

> Users of public services can tell governments a lot about the quality and value of the public services provided

---

Box 9.6 Santiago 2010 Strategic Plan, Chile

Santiago 2010 Strategic Plan was designed to guide urban development in the city. However, the municipality of Santiago realized that ongoing monitoring of plan implementation was essential to the success of the plan. The key components for effective monitoring were identified as:

- the establishment of a system whereby all stakeholders can easily access and exchange information on plan implementation;
- development of methodologies and instruments, such as indicators, for measuring compliance with goals and objectives;
- periodic analysis of local, regional and global conditions; and
- the establishment of mechanisms for engaging local community stakeholders in assessing progress and performance of development planning.

The monitoring and evaluation process that was established as part of the Santiago 2010 Strategic Plan was the first of its kind in Santiago, and it was designed to track progress towards achieving the plan's goals, objectives and development targets.

Since 2000, the city has prepared 73 locally relevant indicators that facilitate the monitoring of the impacts of urban development policy upon urban conditions. These indicators help the city to establish its position relative to other cities, based on the Global Urban Observatory (GUO) network of indicators.

This monitoring and evaluation process design, and indicators development, has strengthened the city's information collection and analysis capacity, and its ability to make informed decisions on urban development. The process has also produced an important side benefit: greater trust among key stakeholders in the community and local government.

Source: http://ww2.unhabitat.org/programmes/guo/country_and_city_projects.asp

Box 9.7 Master Plan for Delhi 2021, India

The Delhi Master Plan has a section that provides considerable detail on the purpose of plan monitoring and evaluation. A monitoring framework has been prepared to:

- evaluate effective implementation of the plan within the planning period (2007–2021);
- ensure that the plan is responsive to changes (e.g. socio-economic);
- help to manage unintended urban development and growth; and
- monitor the relevance and suitability of plan policies.

The city has identified key indicators (environmental, socio-economic, land use and infrastructure) and it advocates community participation in the planning process. The plan also recommends the establishment of a dedicated plan monitoring group with responsibilities shared among several 'management action groups'.

Source: Puri, 2007

CAVEATS AND CONSIDERATIONS IN THE MONITORING AND EVALUATION OF URBAN PLANS

Typically (and quite understandably), the proponents of monitoring and evaluation emphasize its many successes. There is certainly tremendous potential to be realized through the design and implementation of a monitoring and evaluation process, supported by appropriate indicators. However, it is important to note that most urban plan-based monitoring and evaluation has occurred in the cities of developed countries, and this has been a relatively recent phenomenon. These are places that have a reasonable base of finances and technical planning expertise, political stability, sophisticated governance structures, and comparatively manageable rates of urbanization. The scale and type of challenges is significantly different from their counterparts in developing countries.

Furthermore, there has been little critical analysis of these urban plan monitoring and evaluation experiences.

a monitoring and evaluation system, supported by indicators that assess progress towards achieving the city's urban development goals (see Box 9.6). The city of Delhi (India) has produced a master plan that includes clear directions for plan monitoring and evaluation (see Box 9.7).

There has been little critical analysis of these urban plan monitoring and evaluation experiences

Box 9.8 Challenges in evaluating liveability in Vancouver, Canada

Vancouver is widely regarded as one of the world's most liveable urban areas. It is noted for rejecting freeways and for developing a bustling, 'living first' downtown and an extensive public waterfront. Its collaborative approach to urban development, which features extensive public and stakeholder engagement, has been recognized through a variety of awards and distinctions. While the city of Vancouver has been presented as a leader in urban development, much of the Vancouver region resembles the sprawling, automobile-focused development familiar to most North Americans. Even in the city of Vancouver, major concerns, such as growing income inequality, lack of affordable housing, uncertain economic prospects and a large ecological footprint, have raised questions about whether the Vancouver achievement is sustainable and, indeed, whether all of its citizens find it equally liveable.

While growth was producing great material abundance, many citizens in Vancouver perceived a diminishing quality of life by the 1960s. In 1971, the Greater Vancouver Regional District responded by declaring a new planning purpose. 'Liveability' would become the overarching philosophy for regional planning. Outcomes of the 1970s Liveable Region Plan were to be evaluated by monitoring specific targets of population and job growth, transit expansion and green space protection. However, what liveability meant and, specifically, how to view the relationship between growth and liveability was complicated. How to evaluate liveability emerged as a perplexing question. Various computer models, social indicators and liveability indices were explored but were found, by themselves, to be unsatisfactory. Ultimately, the planners, politicians and citizens had to grapple with the question of what liveability actually meant and how it could be measured. As a result of a lengthy public consultation process, it became clear that liveability was a more or less universal aspiration. Furthermore, the planners rejected the rational planning model where monitoring and evaluating were merely one step in a linear process. Rather, they advanced the view that monitoring and evaluating would be an ongoing deliberative process – a continuous adaptive learning exercise. In this systems approach, complexity and uncertainty were best respected through involving more individuals.

In 2001, the Greater Vancouver Regional District advanced a new framework within which to consider growth management called the Sustainable Region Initiative. With the implementation of this initiative, the focus shifted from liveability to sustainability. A major component of the initiative is the development of a set of indicators that can evaluate progress within the context of the sustainability framework. This process has been informed and guided by work on sustainability indicators, which has been produced by a number of Vancouver-area research organizations that are trying to gain a more comprehensive understanding of the economic, ecological, social and cultural state of the region.

There are important lessons to be learned from the Vancouver experience with the monitoring and evaluation of regional plans. Clarity of terminology, concepts and intents is essential – for example, the meaning of 'liveability' and 'sustainability'. Indicators cannot be selected until there is consensus on the concepts. Plan monitoring and evaluation efforts can be enhanced through extensive and meaningful consultation with diverse publics and stakeholders. Extensive discussion of concepts and indicator validity can enrich and guard against 'groupthink'. However, one group's views on plan performance success could be interpreted by another group as failure. It can be difficult to reach consensus about goals, objectives, policies and their realization 'on the ground'. Monitoring and evaluation can be an important part of an evidence-based decision-making system. It is also an inherently and highly political act in a complex multi-stakeholder planning environment.

Source: Owens, 2008

This presents an opportunity for comparative primary research on this topic. It also means that there is not yet a good sense of the range of experiences, positive and negative, with urban plan monitoring and evaluation. However, it is possible to learn from the existing body of knowledge and limited experience to identify some common lessons for practice.

A key challenge, and a common argument against introducing plan monitoring and evaluation, is the lack of adequate resources – money, technical services and trained professional staff. This is a real issue in most developing countries and in some developed countries, as well. Many local governments struggle to deliver basic services. In that context, a comprehensive urban planning function is not possible, let alone a sophisticated system of plan monitoring, evaluation and indicators. There can be a temptation to overly complicate plan monitoring and evaluation processes, thus making them too resource and information intensive.

The concept of monitoring and evaluation can be difficult to understand in local governments that face complex energy-sapping urban challenges. There may be no time (or will) to learn about and embrace monitoring and evaluation. Monitoring and evaluation could be regarded (and resented) as an obligation imposed by external sources (e.g. funding agencies or national government) without consideration for local capacity to design and deliver these systems. It may be that monitoring and evaluation is not the highest priority

need for a local government, or there is no apparent application for monitoring and evaluation.

Monitoring and evaluation can produce negative as well as positive results. The latter situation is often embraced by local decision-makers, while the former may be ignored, downplayed or even rejected. In the worst case, negative results could present a direct challenge to organizational leadership and its decision-making. Thus, monitoring and evaluation are often looked upon less favourably in such situations. The lack of commitment by decision-makers and staff often jeopardizes the introduction, and constrains the application, of monitoring and evaluation processes. Indeed, lack of political will and bureaucratic inertia explain the slow take-up and application of monitoring and evaluation in many countries (as illustrated in Boxes 9.8 and 9.9).

It is important to ensure that monitoring and evaluation is integrated with other local government corporate planning and decision-making processes and reporting systems. Monitoring and evaluation should operate in conjunction with well-established local government processes, providing the opportunity to inform decision-making in a comprehensive, integrated and meaningful manner. Table 9.2 expresses many of the challenges faced when introducing and maintaining plan monitoring and evaluation processes, while Box 9.10 describes key considerations when selecting indicators to support plan monitoring and evaluation.

> Monitoring and evaluation can produce negative as well as positive results. The latter situation is often embraced by local decision-makers, while the former may be ignored, downplayed or even rejected

> It is important to ensure that monitoring and evaluation is integrated with other local government corporate planning and decision-making processes and reporting systems

Box 9.9 Monitoring and evaluation in China's urban planning system

China is undergoing rapid urbanization, which has increased demands for urban plans to guide city development. Evaluation in urban planning practice, especially in plan implementation, is normally of secondary consideration. In China, plan monitoring and evaluation plays only a minor role in the large number of plans prepared every year. The governments and planners keep preparing plans to catch up with rapid urbanization; normally, they simply repeat what they did before and have no time to improve flawed or outdated practices. The situation is that no matter the results of plan implementation, new plans will be prepared soon.

The types of evaluation are limited; most planning evaluations in China are formative or *ex ante* in nature. The focus is on evaluation of alternative plans, and there have been few attempts to use summative evaluation. However, with the social, economic and public reforms, and the improvement of information systems, increasing attention has been paid to evaluation and monitoring in planning policy-making, in academic research and in practice during the last ten years. It is expected that plan monitoring and evaluation will play more important roles in the future and lead to improvement in planning procedures and management.

The subjects of plan evaluation are broad and include urban transit planning, water resources, environmental impact, land-use development near high-speed railway stations, green space, etc. In China, it is generally the government and developers who carry out planning evaluations. Monitoring focuses on city master plans, scenic reserve plans, historic city plans and detailed plans. Generally speaking, plan monitoring plays only a small role in planning management in China; however, a system of individual 'monitors' now helps to enforce planning monitoring. This monitor programme was first introduced by the Ministry of Housing and Urban–Rural Development in 2006. In the same year, 27 planning monitors were sent to 18 cities for a one-year programme. Monitors are usually experienced retired planners or planning officials. They are familiar with planning regulations, standards and management processes and are good at communicating with different departments. Hence, they can identify most problems in plan implementation and provide measures to solve these in a timely manner. This monitoring system is an innovation used to reinforce the current system. Its implementation has had remarkable effects: planning departments have improved their performance, and many illegal construction sites have been found at an early stage.

Although some progress has been made in planning monitoring, many aspects need to be improved, especially those that involve the public, who remain largely excluded from the planning process. There is an absence of discussion and dialogue about planning performance among both local authorities and professional planners. Most plan evaluation is carried out internally (i.e. within the planning organization, municipality and higher levels of planning departments). In-house staff usually only assess a plan's adherence to its own stated goals and objectives (e.g. plan conformance). There is seldom any involvement of external evaluators, such as community groups. Internal staff, composed of academic experts, officials and professional planners, often have a comprehensive and sound understanding of the Planning Act, regulations, policies, resources and project context. However, the Chinese experience has been that personal bias, as well as organizational politics and culture, can adversely affect the monitoring and evaluation process.

Source: Chen, 2008

Category	Elements
Theoretical issues	What is the role of plans?
	What ability do plans have to effect change?
	What is the function of the evaluation?
	What is the role of values?
	Who are the clients?
	What are the criteria of success – effectiveness, efficiency, equity?
Strategic issues	Timing (frequency, point in time)
	Level (street, neighbourhood, city, region) of measurement/analysis
	Establishing baseline community conditions
Definition and measurement issues	Defining targets, operationalizing problems
	Capturing plurality of impact, both perception and experience
	Tracking unintended impacts or invisible impacts (what has been protected, what has not been built)
	Translating policy objectives into measurable indicators (i.e. accessibility, interaction indicators)
	How to measure people's perception of impact versus the actual impact on their behaviour, as well as benefits and costs to people, thus establishing cause-and-effect relationships of plan policy on people and their behaviour
	Sphere (social, economic, environmental, spatial) of measurement and analysis
Data management	Data manageability and feasibility of monitoring
	Data availability, quality and access
	Data analysis and synthesis
Process issues	Understanding linkages and synergies
	Establishing a supportive environment for monitoring and evaluation
	Capturing the impact of policy upon community capacity through participation of a cross-section of community members
	Ensuring that monitoring and evaluation becomes the basis of critical self-reflection and learning

Table 9.2

Challenges in monitoring and evaluating urban plans

Source: Hoernig and Seasons, 2005

Central to the discussion in this chapter is the choice of evaluation strategies and their application in urban planning practice. There are many perspectives on this, but also considerable convergence of opinion. The intent is to improve planning practice by examining how planning decisions are made, how the planning and plan-making processes are carried out, and the impacts and outcomes associated with planning interventions. In the urban planning context, evaluations address these key questions:

- *Plan formulation (ex ante):*
  - How well does the plan evaluate alternatives prior to plan implementation?
  - Does the preferred alternative represent the best fit with the plan's goals and objectives?
- *Plan administration (formative):*
  - How efficiently is the plan being administered?
  - Is there a need to revise plan review and approval procedures?
  - Are implementation tools aligned with and supportive of the plan?
- *Plan impacts (summative, ex post):*
  - How well do plan outcomes, results and impacts meet plan objectives?
  - Is the plan implementation process efficient and effective?
  - Have outputs and outcomes justified inputs, and has the plan met policy requirements?[36]

It is essential that decision-makers have a very clear understanding of what they need to know to make sound evidence-based decisions. This requires a solid rationale for introducing and maintaining a monitoring and evaluation model, clarity about the required information, how the information should be collected and by whom, and the uses of the products of monitoring and evaluation. Box 9.11 provides guidelines to consider when designing an urban plan monitoring and evaluation model.

If poorly designed – for example, if the monitoring and evaluation system is made too complicated – urban planning evaluation can become an administrative burden. Planners and planning departments are usually too busy with conducting applied research, managing stakeholder consultation programmes, and crafting and implementing plans; they often simply do not have the time, energy, training, administrative or political support to monitor and evaluate in a regular and consistent manner. The opposite is generally

Box 9.10 Indicators: Potential and constraints

- *Indicators do not drive policy.* They play a key role in identifying issues that require attention. Indicators are one of many contributors to decision-makers' analytical processes.
- *Indicators can be influential under certain conditions.* They can indicate the nature and extent of a planning issue. However, their role and message must be considered in the context of the evaluation challenge and integrity of the information. They must be linked to action.
- *Indicators' main influence is not primarily after they are developed and published, but rather during the course of their development.* The process of indicator development and selection, which involves time, trial and error, is an important investment to ensure accuracy, relevance and applicability of the indicators. The process of indicator development forces those involved to carefully consider their positions.
- *If an indicator is to be useful, it must be clearly associated with a policy or set of possible actions.* The application of this knowledge must be clear; the test of relevance is important. Ideally, policies should be developed in unison with supportive indicators.
- *Indicators influence most through a collaborative learning process.* Planners might facilitate indicator development. Ideally, indicators should be selected through a process of collaboration among planners, decision-makers and stakeholders. Indicators have real power when they are used and referred to in decision-making processes.
- *It matters how the indicators are produced.* Expert opinion is a necessary but not sufficient condition for success with indicators. The perspectives of stakeholders must be reflected in the indicator development process.
- *For indicators to be used there must be not just opportunity, but also a requirement to report and publicly discuss the indicators in conjunction with policy decisions that must be made.* There is a need to be sensitive to political currents when developing and using indicators.
- *The development of an influential indicator takes time.* It could take five to ten years for an indicator to be properly tested, refined and made an integral part of the policy-making process.

Source: Innes and Booher, 2000, p178

true of *ex ante* evaluation methods, which are often required practice elements under state planning legislation (e.g. strategic environmental assessments) and by funding agreements. The objective is to ground monitoring and evaluation in urban planning practice, and to integrate it as part of daily decision-making.

The key is to establish the goals and objectives of the urban plan evaluation exercise – what do decision-makers need to know? This will frame the choice of indicators and the evaluation strategy overall. Since urban planning occurs in a multi-stakeholder environment that is characterized by different values and perceptions about planning issues, there is a need to clarify the meaning and intent of planning terms and basic concepts. There is also an obligation to involve stakeholders in the indicator selection and monitoring process; this can become a mutual learning process that will enhance the potential for buy-in to the urban plan evaluation process and its results. Participatory evaluations are very much the norm in the developing countries' urban programme evaluation exercises.[37]

In cities that are contemplating the introduction of an urban plan monitoring and evaluation system, it makes sense to select a small, manageable set of urban planning-oriented indicators. Ideally, it would be wise to start with indicators that relate to high-profile and well-established urban planning issues in the community. The point is that the quality and meaning of indicators matters more than the number of indicators. The indicators must explain something in clear, unambiguous terms. They must have significance to and resonate with urban planning stakeholders. They should be relatively straightforward to use and analyse.

Indicators should make optimal use of existing information, with the caveat that ease of access to the usual sources of data may not coincide with the evaluation's information needs. This also means that urban planning organizations need to collect and monitor information that supports evaluation, and that urban plan goals, objectives and policies need to be designed with monitoring and evaluation in mind. Finally, indicators evolve through testing and verification over time.

CONCLUDING REMARKS

Monitoring and evaluation of urban plans has a great deal of potential to improve decision-making capacity, inform planning practice and educate community residents. Local governments need enhanced analytical capacity to anticipate and manage increasingly complex urban challenges, and decision-makers are under pressure to make evidence-based, defensible decisions. Urban planners are therefore expected to create plans and manage urban development that achieves goals of effectiveness, efficiency and equity. Community residents want to know whether urban life is improving or deteriorating. However, there is a need to explore whether and to what extent this potential could be realized. The body of knowledge on monitoring and evaluation practice in urban planning in both developed and developing countries is limited. This calls for primary research that investigates the nature of urban planning practice, generally, and the role of

Box 9.11 Monitoring and evaluation design strategy
• Think about evaluation from an early stage. You cannot evaluate how things have changed and why if you don't have a clear picture of the starting point (the baseline) and of what you are trying to do.
• Build a 'culture' of evaluation – get the commitment of everyone involved – from projects to partnership board, to gathering information and using it.
• Decide what local work is needed to manage a scheme effectively and to understand its impact. How and when will individual projects be evaluated? What about the scheme as a whole?
• Ensure that evaluation covers the key themes a scheme or project is targeting – and that it also looks at how things are being done, overall effectiveness and sustainability.
• Make links between monitoring and evaluation. Competing demands for information can create difficulties, so it is helpful to think about evaluation, as well as more routine monitoring, when you are setting targets and agreeing outputs and indicators.
• Involve the local community. Properly done, evaluation can be an important part of accountability to local people, ensuring local voices are heard and providing vital information to feed back to local people. Use evaluation to shape work in progress and to inform forward strategies and other local developments.

Source: www.eukn.org/unitedkingdom/themes/Urban_Policy/Economy_knowledge_and_employment/Research_and_innovation/how-to-evaluate-a-project_1149.html

monitoring and evaluation in that context; assesses the extent to which monitoring and evaluation of urban plans takes place; and evaluates the models and processes that are used in practice. The results of such research would provide the information needed to support interventions by national (or regional) governments, funding agencies, local governments and urban planners. A number of strategies can be identified as decision-makers move to implement urban plan monitoring and evaluation:[38]

* *Ensure that monitoring and evaluation of urban plans is mandated under national and/or state planning legislation.* Plan monitoring and evaluation should be considered an essential part of urban planning practice and local government administration. Monitoring and evaluation should be made a legal requirement, supported by relevant legislation (e.g. a planning and development act).
* *Support local government urban plan monitoring and evaluation.* Legislation is a necessary but insufficient condition for successful urban plan monitoring and evaluation. The state is often in a position to build local government monitoring and evaluation capacity. This could occur by providing financial resources, training programmes, information on best practices, data-sharing and access to technical resources (e.g. GIS).
* *Design urban plans that integrate monitoring, evaluation and indicators with goals, objectives and policies.* The local government's urban plan should explain the monitoring and evaluation philosophy, strategy and process. A separate chapter on the management of evaluation should be incorporated within urban plans. Ideally, indicators should be attached to each chapter of a plan's narrative content. It should be possible to trace the path from goals and objectives to policies and strategies, and then to related indicators.

Monitoring and evaluation of urban plans has a great deal of potential to improve decision-making capacity, inform planning practice and educate community residents

Box 9.12 Guidelines for designing results-based evaluation systems

Step 1: Readiness assessment

Roles and responsibilities for evaluation must be clearly articulated. The urban plan should explain the monitoring and evaluation philosophy, strategy and process. Accordingly, a separate chapter on the management of monitoring and evaluation should be incorporated in municipal plans. Ideally, indicators should be attached to each chapter of a plan's narrative content. Decision-makers should be able to trace the path from goals and objectives to policies and strategies, and then to supportive indicators.

Monitoring and evaluation exercises should involve extensive consultation with, and contributions by, all plan stakeholders, including members of the community at large, neighbourhood residents and special interest groups. There should be opportunities for stakeholders to advise on the design of the plan monitoring and evaluation process, contribute information and insights, and help to maintain the monitoring and evaluation system once implemented.

To be successful, the urban plan needs a champion. At the local government level, this could be the director of the planning department and/or the chief administrative officer, as well as members of council. Monitoring and evaluation of the urban plan will usually be the responsibility of the planning department. Planning staff will need to have the capacity – the skills and knowledge, and resources – to effectively and efficiently carry out the monitoring and evaluation function.

Most important, monitoring and evaluation has to be (and be seen as) an integral part of urban plan decision-making. The corporate and departmental approval process should include consideration of the findings of the monitoring process; the evaluation of plan performance will guide future revisions to the plan. The monitoring and evaluation process must be reasonably straightforward. Local governments must find a way to evaluate plans and planning processes in a manner that meets obligations for reporting and analysis, yet does not overtax planning staff.

Step 2: Select outcomes

Plan outcomes reflect organizational priorities and preferences and stakeholder perspectives. Often, the outcome will correspond to a plan goal statement – for example, a diversified local economy. In this example, the impact of such an outcome could be a workforce that has more choice in employment, more meaningful employment, etc. The ultimate impact of such an outcome could be a healthier individual and, by extension, a healthy community. Urban plan goals and outcomes may be established by the state or local government, preferably through extensive participatory plan-making processes. Some outcomes are unanticipated; these can be positive or negative.

Step 3: Select indicators

Indicators will evolve through application and experience. Indicator selection should reflect stakeholders' interests and concerns. Data collection and analysis issues pervade urban planning practice in many countries. There are often problems with lack of data, the cost of retrieving and analysing data, inconsistent collection or presentation of data, and simply incorrect information. The focus should be on reliability, credibility, accuracy and relevance of information.

It is essential to be very clear about the purpose of the evaluation, the knowledge sought and the role of indicators in that context. Different types of evaluation will call for different monitoring strategies and supportive indicators.

Step 4: Establish baseline data

The baseline serves as a point of reference against which subsequent activities could be assessed. The focus here is on historic trends and current activities. Examples of policy-based baseline indicators could include population statistics, demographic profiles, environmental quality, economic performance, etc.

Step 5: Set targets

Simply put, the urban plan should have fixed targets. These could be outputs, impacts and/or outcomes. Targets can be derived from quantitative and/or qualitative analysis, involving the introduction of political considerations and stakeholder perceptions of reasonable target characteristics.

Step 6: Monitoring

Monitoring has to occur on a regular basis for monitoring to be effective. The monitoring findings must feed directly into the plan evaluation process. Therefore, the needs of the plan evaluation function will drive the type and timing of the monitoring activity.

Urban plan monitoring is typically the responsibility of the planning department. Information collection and analysis could be led by urban planning staff, with contributions from professional staff in other departments. Secondary research can be used for monitoring (e.g. related studies and research), although primary research (such as surveys and censuses) is also commonly used. Qualitative methods can provide insights and context for quantitative analysis. Geo-referenced data provided by geographic information systems (GIS) can be used to track changes in land-use and consumption patterns, and the impacts of urban development on the natural environment.

Step 7: Evaluation

Urban plan evaluation proceeds on the basis of a shared understanding of several elements: plan goals and objectives; outputs, outcomes and impacts; the foundation of indicators; baseline information; and monitoring protocols. Individual project impacts and outcomes could be evaluated (summative evaluation). The efficiency with which plan administration processes are performing could be evaluated (formative evaluation). While plan monitoring is a continuous process, plan evaluation would occur less frequently. Urban plan evaluation is often required every five years, with the intention that the plan's goals, objectives and policies could be fine-tuned to reflect changes in the community's decision-making environment. It would still be advisable to complete an annual evaluation of plan performance and impact, especially in communities affected by considerable change and turbulence (e.g. rapid growth or decline in population and/or economy; shifting national policy foci; updates to national or local government laws).

Step 8: Reporting findings

Communication of urban plan evaluation findings may be required by law, expected by the local government council, and/or requested by external stakeholders. The findings of the monitoring process should be reported to end-users (decision-makers) and plan stakeholders in a structured and accessible manner. Communications strategies could include monthly reports, annual report cards on urban plan progress, regular briefings of council and staff, year-end town hall meetings, etc.

Stage 9: Applications of evaluation

Plan evaluations may be required as a condition of aid funding (e.g. by the World Bank). Evaluations may be mandated by state law and by policy (e.g. by the Planning Act). Evaluations can also be a powerful learning tool and an effective communication mechanism. Planning department staff can use plan and planning process evaluations to improve practice. Decision-makers can use plan evaluations to better understand the impacts and outcomes generated by government investment in urban planning. Stakeholders could use plan evaluations to learn about the planning process, and to determine whether and to what extent their advice was incorporated in the plan and their needs met.

Some types of planning instruments are more amenable to monitoring and evaluation than others. For example, the outcomes and impacts of long-range plans are difficult to evaluate because of the myriad influences and factors that are at play in communities over time. However, site plans, subdivision plans and neighbourhood plans may be more conducive to monitoring and evaluation because these tend to be more tangible types of plans. Similarly, it should be easier to design and manage monitoring and evaluation processes, and indicators, in smaller places and in municipalities where little change occurs over time.

Step 10: Sustaining monitoring and evaluation

Urban plan monitoring and evaluation requires continuous support – political, financial and technical. The local government's culture – the way of doing business and making decisions – has to be supportive. Stakeholders should be consulted. Local government should be comfortable with, and responsive to, demands for accountability and transparency. Monitoring and evaluation has to be respected for it to be carried out effectively. Decision-makers have to see value and a good return on investment when designing monitoring and evaluation systems; they have to understand the consequences of not monitoring and evaluating urban plans. Monitoring and evaluation needs to be a regular, sustained process carried out in the interests of improving plan performance, justifying the planning activity, and addressing the expectations of stakeholders in planning exercises.

Urban plan monitoring and evaluation can be undermined by political opportunism or corruption (which are forces beyond the control of urban planning alone), resource cuts, absence of meaningful links between monitoring and evaluation and plan updates, and indifference or hostility from senior administration. The results of plan evaluations can be negative; they will not always produce positive findings. This could threaten an insecure leadership and certainly challenge those with a vested interest in the status quo. Organizational culture, leadership and patience are virtues; they are also essential when introducing and sustaining urban plan monitoring and evaluation.

- *The monitoring and evaluation process must be reasonably straightforward*, given the lack of capacity, resources or time that is typical in many urban planning departments. Local governments must find a way to monitor and evaluate plans and planning processes in a manner that meets obligations for reporting and analysis, yet does not overtax planning staff. Specific staff should be assigned responsibility for plan monitoring and evaluation. Roles and responsibilities must be clearly established and reinforced. The purpose and applications of monitoring and evaluation need to be clarified and communicated. The applications and value added of plan monitoring and evaluation must be clearly understood and accepted by stakeholders in the plan-making and implementation processes. This would help to build and maintain an evaluation-supportive culture.
- *Allocate resources to policy planning and research functions.* It is also important to note that many (urban) local government planning departments focus on plan delivery and land development planning (plan administration). There is often greater emphasis placed on development planning than on policy planning; a more balanced allocation of resources (e.g. training, technical support and staff positions) is required to support monitoring and evaluation activities.
- *Indicators and the monitoring and evaluation system must be simple, easy to understand and workable within existing resource limits.* Indicators require validation through testing. The quality of indicators is more important than the number of indicators. There is generally no need to collect and analyse excessive amounts of information. It is essential, however, to be very clear about the purpose of the evaluation, the knowledge sought and the role of indicators in that context. Plan evaluators need to ensure that the data and information collected and analysed have value and relevance.

- *Monitoring and evaluation exercises should involve extensive consultation with, and meaningful participation by, plan stakeholders.* The technical analysis aspect is a necessary but insufficient condition for plan monitoring and evaluation. Evaluations can play an important educational role for decision-makers and planning staff, as well as community stakeholders. Participation by stakeholders can enhance plan quality and effectiveness through the contribution of insights, intelligence and perspectives that might otherwise not have been captured by the formal plan-making process. Stakeholders can help to evaluate the effectiveness (impacts and outcomes) of a plan, and help to position successive plans by offering critiques of plan performance. Collaborative and participatory approaches to urban plan-making and evaluation are appropriate and encouraged.

- *Continue to evaluate proposed policies, programmes and plans.* Tools such as cost–benefit analysis, cost-effectiveness analysis and fiscal impact assessment will be especially relevant given the realities of local government resource constraints. In addition, greater interest in performance measurement, return on investment and results-based management principles means that these tools have a strong role in planning practice.

- *Use appropriate research methods.* Qualitative and quantitative research tools can be used in evaluation practice. Qualitative methods can provide insights and context for quantitative analysis. The methods, including triangulation, must support an evidence-based monitoring and evaluation process.

- *Integrate monitoring and evaluation of plan impacts and outcomes in local government urban planning processes.* This has to be a regular, sustained process carried out to improve plan performance, to achieve the plan's goals and objectives, and to address the expectations of stakeholders in planning exercises. Ensure that monitoring and evaluation considerations are incorporated within plans from the outset; design plans to be monitored and evaluated. Finally, ensure that plan monitoring processes are clearly and closely linked to, and supportive of, plan evaluation.

Box 9.12 – which is based on the World Bank's results-based evaluation model,[39] but has been adapted here for application in urban planning – provides useful guidelines for the design of urban planning monitoring and evaluation systems.

NOTES

1   See Moser, 1993; Hunt and Brouwers, 2003.
2   See OECD (2002) for a comprehensive glossary of evaluation terms. See also Scriven, 1991; Weiss, 1998; Rossi et al, 1999; Pal, 2006.
3   Such as UN-Habitat, the World Bank, the African Development Bank and the Organisation for Economic Co-operation and Development (OECD).
4   Some evaluators consider process evaluation a subset of summative evaluation. Process evaluation traditionally examines how well the services delivered match those that were planned.
5   Kusek and Rist, 2003, p23. The World Bank's *results-based* monitoring and evaluation system offers an excellent example of process design (see Box 9.12).
6   See www.sustainableseattle.org/Programs/IndicatorsIntoAction/.
7   See www.myhamilton.ca/myhamilton/Cityand Government/Projects Initiatives/V2020.

8   See www.ccc.govt.nz/LTCCP/CommunityOutcomes/Monitoring/AboutMonitoring Programme.asp.
9   See www.rtpi.org.uk/item/1803.
10 Hirt and Stanilov, 2008.
11 See Hill, 1968; Teitz, 1968; Boyce, 1970; McLoughlin, 1970; Lichfield et al, 1975; .
12 See, for example, Bracken, 1981.
13 See, for example, the government of Ontario's Municipal Performance Measurement Program, www.mah.gov.on.ca/Page297.aspx.
14 For a discussion of Lima Peru's poverty strategy, see www.citiesalliance.org/cdsdb.nsf/9ced09a1ac86c4cc85 25683b006abf1a/cd4bf7c94991 d9ea86256cec0078e56e! OpenDocument.
15 http://go.worldbank.org/1FIW42VYV0.
16 See http://ww2.unhabitat.org/programmes/guo/urban_indicators.asp.
17 See www.espon.eu/mmp/online/website/content/projects/947/1296/index_EN.html.

18 New Zealand, 2009.
19 See www.med.govt.nz/templates/StandardSummary___13875.aspx
20 See www.laparks.org/environmental/pdf/bellevue/bell evueMMRP.pdf.
21 See www.mfa.gov.il/MFA/MFAArchive/2000_2009/2002/1/Restoring%20Israel-s%20 Rivers.
22 See www.mrcmekong.org/programmes/bdp.htm.
23 See www.region.waterloo.on.ca/web/Region.nsf/97dfc347666 efede85256e590071a3d4/a 54425a423ced1b18525741000 4d2997!OpenDocument.
24 See www.nyc.gov/html/dep/html/harbor_water/index.shtml.
25 See www.municode.com/content/4201/14131/HTML/ch010e.html.
26 See www.victoria.ca/cityhall/departments_plnpln_downtown.shtml.
27 See www.kitchener.ca/city_hall/departments/downtown/downtown_monitoring_report.html.

28 See the experience with such processes in Brazil, particularly in the sub-section on 'Participatory budgeting' in Chapter 5.
29 Hirt and Stanilov, 2008. See also Box 10.2.
30 Wong, 1995, p114.
31 See http://ww2.unhabitat.org/programmes/guo/urban_indicators.as.
32 See http://ww2.unhabitat.org/programmes/guo/muip.as.
33 Breitenbach, 2006.
34 Reeves et al, 2009.
35 See www.citiesalliance.org/cdsdb.nsf/47b563a0f7b2695485 25683b006ae379/03d008f4625 7601f86256cec007691d7! OpenDocument.
36 See Hill, 1985; Talen, 1996, 1997; Baer, 1997.
37 See Chapter 5.
38 See, for example, www.eukn.org/unitedkingdom/themes/Urban_Policy/Economy_knowledge_and_employment/Research_and_innovation/how-to-evaluate-a-project_1149.html; New Zealand, 2009.
39 See Kusek and Rist, 2003.

CHAPTER 10

PLANNING EDUCATION

As noted in previous chapters, urban planning is essential to crafting solutions to the pressing urban problems of the 21st century, yet the professional planning practices in place have not always been able to keep pace with the challenges faced by urban areas. This is particularly the case in developing countries. Rapid urbanization in most developing countries has forced planners to respond to escalating demand for housing, infrastructure and services – from both formal and informal sectors. In a globalizing world, cities are increasingly becoming linked to international economic and social networks. At the same time, climate change is posing a whole range of new challenges for cities all around the world. In this situation, it is clear that greater breadth of knowledge among planners is required to plan effectively.[1]

Furthermore, while planning in the past was the domain of public-sector authorities in most countries, it is increasingly becoming the focus of action by a wide variety of private, civil society and even informal-sector organizations as well.[2] Even within government, expansion of the number of authorities involved in specific decisions, coupled with changes in levels of decentralization, have the result that planners work in the midst of conflict and coordination demands that were much less frequent in the past.

In addition to rural–urban migration, cities are also increasingly experiencing the arrival of international migrants. The multicultural nature of many cities requires multicultural planning skills. So, together with changes in technical knowledge essential to successful urban planning, there have been changes in the softer 'people' skills needed to manage the processes of change.[3]

This chapter examines how urban planning education is addressing these challenges. It also reviews the extent to which planning schools worldwide have the capabilities needed to lead the next generation of urban planning practice in light of the challenges identified above. The first section contains a summary of the historical development of urban planning education at the university level, and identifies the key philosophical and practical debates that framed planning education during the 20th century. The second section presents an initial global inventory of university-level urban planning programmes, reviewing the number and regional distribution of planning schools, characteristics of academic staff, curricular orientations on certain dimensions linked to the development challenges outlined above, as well as linkages to scholarly and professional networks. The third section assesses the capacities of planning schools and suggests directions for positive change. The chapter ends with recommendations aimed at more closely aligning the curricula of planning schools with the needs of practice.

HISTORICAL DEVELOPMENT OF PLANNING EDUCATION

While urban planning practice has ancient roots, it appears that planning education at the university level did not begin until the early 20th century (see Table 10.1). The first such urban planning courses were taught for the benefit of architects, landscape architects and engineers who wished to expand their practices into the city planning domain.

The sub-sections below review the key debates that have framed the development of planning education during the 20th century – namely, design versus policy, rationality versus deliberation, master planning versus development management, and 'one-world' versus context-specific planning education.

Design versus policy

The first university-level urban planning course is widely cited to be the 'civic design' programme at the University of Liverpool. As the name suggests, these early years of planning education were firmly set in the design profession tradition, while drawing on the growing sentiment for scientific applications in government and industry.[4]

Greater breadth of knowledge among planners is required to plan effectively

Table 10.1

A selection of early university-level courses in urban planning

Note: * In 1930, known as the Leningrad Institute for Civil Engineers (Soviet Union).

Source: Adams and Hodge, 1965; Pawtowski, 1973; Batey, 1985; Frank and Mironowicz, 2008; Hirt and Stanilov, 2008

School	Planning course offered
University of Liverpool (UK)	Offered course in 'civic design' from 1907
Lvov Technical University (Poland)	Department of Town Planning established in 1913
University of Karlsruhe (Germany)	Granted town planning degrees by 1915
Harvard University (US)	The first North American degree course in 1928
Saint-Petersburg State University of Architecture and Civil Engineering* (Russia)*	Offered planning courses in its architecture and civil engineering programmes by 1930 and offered a city building degree by 1949

The growth of urban planning education during the early decades was modest, with only nine programmes established in the US by 1941.[5] By the end of that decade, however, design was no longer the sole orientation of planning schools, with new schools formed in social science settings, and other schools in design college settings admitting students whose prior work had been other than in a design profession.[6] The UK was quick to join the adoption of a social science orientation. While some European countries clung to the design paradigm, economic planning flourished as a distinct enterprise in the Soviet Union and Eastern European universities throughout the communist era.[7]

With the decline in dominance of the design orientation and the adoption of applied social science tools, planning schools were free to branch into wider ranges of policy concerns, building regional coverage and adding transportation, housing, social welfare, environmental resource issues and economic development. By the late 1970s, many planning schools covered much of the range of domestic policy matters affecting human settlements.

The broadening of scope was a challenge for urban planning schools. By the mid 1950s, a 'generalist with a specialty' framework[8] had been articulated for University of Chicago planning students. This framework spread widely and became a key component of US accreditation criteria when those began in 1984. Today, the phrase may be found on the websites and in student manuals of many planning schools worldwide. At the same time, the breadth led inevitably to weakened focus, and there were challenges from practitioners and from scholars in other fields that the boundaries of planning had become too diffuse. Policy scientist Aaron Wildavsky famously asked: 'If planning is everything, maybe it's nothing?'[9] UK schools moved away from the 'generalist with a specialty' model beginning in the 1970s.[10]

The numbers of schools and numbers of students skyrocketed during the 1960s and early 1970s, coinciding with the broadening of scope. This may have been a function of the lower-cost models in social science colleges compared with design colleges, and it may have been driven by workplace demands tied to government planning initiatives in the US, UK and other European countries. In 1975, almost 1500 Master's degrees were awarded by nearly 65 US planning schools, and planning-related instruction became commonplace in departments of geography, urban studies and other social sciences.[11] By the late 1970s, there were 211 diploma or specialization programmes in the UK.[12]

The growth was not without problems. Criticism of loss of technical content from the profession was being heard. Commentators tied the skill deficit to the adoption of the social science paradigm and the emphasis on doctoral degree requirements, in contrast to professional practice degrees and experience, for academic staff,[13] one notably asking: 'Why can't Johnny plan?'[14] Others saw the skill changes as following planning job definition changes, from design consultant to staff policy analyst in government responsible for 'generating information for decision-makers'.[15]

The spread of planning education beyond Europe and North America dates from the late 1940s, with the establishment of two programmes at the South Australian School of Mines and Industries, and the University of Sydney in 1949. Developing country-based planning programmes date from at least the mid 1950s with the establishment of the School of Planning and Architecture in New Delhi (India) in 1955[16] and the planning programme at Ghana's Kumasi College of Arts, Science and Technology in 1958 (see Box 10.5). Initial growth was slow, however, and few developing countries had planning programmes until the 1970s.[17] Many countries, including some in the European periphery, did not have any planning degree programmes until the 1990s.[18]

Most often, programmes in developing countries reflect colonial ties,[19] and it is quite common for developing country planning programmes to be housed in departments of geography, architecture or other related fields.[20] In the early years, the challenges of developing country schools were widely discussed as tied to technology transfer and inadequate resources.[21] The flow of information and technology was largely from North to South.[22] More recently, the debate has widened (see below); but it still remains true that information and technology flows are largely unidirectional.[23]

There has been a resurgence of design in planning schools in the past decade, driven by the wide interest in new urbanism, walkable communities, urban design, more broadly, and the emphasis in European policy on spatial planning. However, in countries of the Anglo-American and Northern European spheres of influence, this has supplemented, rather than diminished, the social science orientation.[24] Ironically, physical design has become the basis of much communication between planners of developed countries and those in countries such as China, where Western policy perspectives may be seen as politically volatile.[25]

Rationality versus deliberation

The policy analytic framework for planning is probably best understood under the terms of the *'rational planning model'*, which originated during the 1930s, but gained widespread use in the mid 1950s. Franklin Roosevelt's 1930s New Deal brain trust included Rexford Tugwell, who was influenced by Keynesian economics, and Frederick Taylor's notions of scientific management. Tugwell championed the notion of planning as a 'fourth power of government'[26] and was influential in adopting powerful experiments with planning in city development, housing, water resources and other contexts by the US government.

After World War II, Tugwell joined the University of Chicago's newly created Program in Education and Research in Planning, where his colleagues included Harvey Perloff and Edward Banfield. Perloff, also a Keynesian economist, pushed the faculty to define and systematize core areas of knowledge in planning, perceived as essential to practice. It was the search for this core for the profession that led to the development of a generic model for planning in capitalist democratic countries and incorporation of ideas from various

[margin notes:]

The numbers of schools and numbers of students skyrocketed during the 1960s and early 1970s

The flow of information and technology was largely from North to South social scientific disciplines, including economics and political science. Banfield's[27] new generic model, the 'rational planning model', outlined in Box 10.1, became a guide in the profession and beyond as an approach to problem-solving in the public sphere.[28]

Reproduced in countless presentations since, these five steps describe a problem-solving framework for complex human enterprises. The model is both self-evident, due to its simplicity, and unachievable, due to its demands on resources and expertise. Banfield recognized complexities, including the elusiveness of the aim of serving the public interest, as well as politics' resistance to scientific analysis.[29]

For about 20 years, the 'rational planning model' remained the most widely subscribed planning theory. To this day, its logic can be found in the justifications and methodological outlines given in the introductions to most plans. It remains a major underpinning of planning school curricula. Furthermore, it spawned the principal language that urban planners use in methodological discourse.[30] Moreover, theoretical and methodological work detailing and extending the model continues. This includes efforts to compare alternative rules for aggregating individual preferences, examination of the implications of risk and uncertainty, and consideration of the impact of new and faster computers on our abilities to ascertain public preferences and completion of the necessary calculations.[31]

By drawing on Keynesian economics and policy studies in political science, the 'rational planning model' led to the incorporation of numerous social scientific concepts within planning offices. It highlighted planning's role in correcting market failures related to externalities, public goods, inequity, transaction costs, market power and the non-existence of markets. Planning borrowed the tools and language of cost–benefit analysis and operations research, including notions of decision criteria, multiple objectives, constraints, shadow pricing, willingness to pay, optimization and minimization.[32] Data analysis became more central and with it the growth of computer-based analytic skills.[33]

The social unrest of the 1960s in many countries subjected the 'rational planning model' to intense criticism. Radical planners saw the model as a tool used by elites to disenfranchise poor inner-city residents who often lacked education and access to professional consultants and could not argue effectively with the scientific analyses presented as objective by city planning staff, but seen as highly subjective by the residents.[34] As shown in Chapters 3 and 5, the legacy of this criticism and the planning profession's responses have been a series of models for greater *deliberation* in planning, including greater involvement of community residents and other stakeholders in planning processes, such as advocacy planning, citizen participation, empowerment and civic engagement. Each has held sway in planning school curricula for its time, and movement internationally has been uneven. This 'communicative turn' in planning research and practice remains a major force today.[35] Yet, at the same time, distrust of indigenous knowledge and fear of decentralized power remains a concern in many countries.[36]

Advocacy planning calls for the distribution of planning services into low-income minority neighbourhoods

---

Box 10.1 The five steps of the 'rational planning model'

The five steps comprise the following:

1   ends reduction and elaboration ('Desires');
2   designs courses of action ('Design');
3   comparative evaluation of consequences ('Deduction');
4   choice among alternatives ('Decision'); and
5   implementation of the chosen alternative ('Deeds').

Source: Stiftel, 2000, pp5–6, citing Banfield, 1955; and Harris, 1967

---

through a cadre of advocate planners working in the neighbourhoods and representing the interests of the residents in city-level planning processes. Advocacy planning led to significant equity accomplishments, but was criticized for not going far enough, even for taking political wind out of the sails of the poor.[37] Critics said planners should help the poor to plan for themselves, rather than try to represent the poor to the city.[38]

Citizen participation practice enjoyed popularity during the 1960s and 1970s. Planning schools incorporated courses within public participation in an effort to meet the demand, drawing from social psychology and small group processes. Practice results were often mixed, with citizen knowledge helping to make better plans, but real control of planning outcomes retained by traditional interests.[39]

The problems of advocacy and citizen participation led to various efforts to support stronger planning by the poor, ethnic and other minorities, and other historically disenfranchised stakeholders. By the mid 1990s, the *empowerment* movement was widely practised with the guiding principle that planners have a responsibility to assist those who are affected by plans to develop the skills to actively participate in the creation of the plans.[40] Thus, planners and planning schools have turned their attention to identifying invisible populations – supporting the factual and analytic needs of ethnic and other minorities and poor people's movements, and skill building among community constituencies more broadly.

During recent years, sociologists and political scientists have recognized declines in social capital and *civic engagement* and have documented the negative consequences of these trends on democratic realities in many countries.[41] Planning schools have embraced these concerns and have actively sought to promote higher levels of civic engagement through planning processes in the hope of also developing plans that better reflect the needs of the full range of affected stakeholders, and are thus also more likely to be implemented.[42] Training in group process skills, including facilitation, mediation and conflict resolution, have been widely embraced in planning schools in some countries. More bottom-up community organizing skills have been addressed in many schools. Planning schools in some countries anticipated these challenges, teaching practices tied to so-called *social learning* approaches as early as the 1970s; but widespread concern with civic engagement did not take place until the 1990s.

> The social unrest of the 1960s in many countries subjected the 'rational planning model' to intense criticism

> Training in ... facilitation, mediation and conflict resolution ... have been widely embraced in planning schools in some countries

Master planning versus development management

As outlined in Chapter 3, the planning profession's origins were, of course, steeped in the preparation of plans. In the earliest days, these tended to be land-use plans; but by the 1950s the scope had broadened to include related issues, and the practice was often labelled comprehensive, general or master planning. Plan implementation through zoning and other means was important, but was usually seen professionally as subsidiary to the production of the plan itself.[43] At the same time, implementation often failed, and so could not be taken for granted.[44]

Evocatively referred to as 'the child that grew up in the cold',[45] development management in the UK reflects increasing attention to implementation by planners in the latter half of the 20th century. Planning scholars debated the relative merits of long-range plan-making and immediate-range permit review during the 1950s and 1960s, leading to proposals for a *middle-range bridge*[46] and *mixed scanning*.[47]

By the 1980s, much government planning legislation in developed countries contained detailed provisions for managing development, and *growth management* and *development control* were mainstream parts of planning school curricula, including coursework in zoning and subdivision regulation, impact assessment, site plan review and, later, negotiation.

Today, as shown in Chapter 3, master planning remains problematic in developing countries as a result of high rates of population growth, coupled with limited regulatory/implementation capacity in local governments. Various practice programmes are intended to move planning in developing countries towards greater attentiveness to implementation, including strategic spatial planning, 'new' master plans, integrated development planning and key elements of United Nations-supported programmes such as the Urban Management Programme, the Sustainable Cities Programme, the Localizing Agenda 21 Programme, the Safer Cities Programme and the Disaster and Risk Management Programme.[48] Beyond the movement towards implementation, some of these innovative programmes have embraced a less comprehensive and therefore more focused vision of good planning, often referred to as strategic planning.[49]

'One-world' versus context-specific planning education

Planning schools traditionally focused on local-scale issues, broadening to metropolitan regional issues in the mid 20th century. The result is that planning education has been tied to the institutional, legal and cultural context of specific countries. When planning schools in the major developed countries found that they were enrolling students from developing countries in significant numbers, they initiated specializations oriented towards practice in the developing country setting. This transition faced several key challenges.

The generalist with a specialty framework of planning education follows the tenet of focus on general theory and method, supplemented with contextual knowledge needed to understand the problems and institutions of specific areas of practice. This contextual knowledge is comparatively easy to relay in a one nation-focused classroom; but when students come from many countries, teaching of context becomes much more difficult. Much planning scholarship assumes the context of democratic governance and market-based economics.[50] While other work is focused in other contexts, it is highly unusual to find theoretical or methodological work that systematically addresses implications across all major political and economic systems.[51]

In addition, the treatment of international development planning as a specialization, as has been the case in most planning schools located in developed countries, assumes the appropriateness of ideas and tools drawn from developed countries for practice in developing countries. This assumption is often not justified.[52]

The '*one-world*' approach to planning education seeks to bypass these challenges by fundamentally altering planning school curricula to provide internationally relevant training regardless of the anticipated future location of the student's practice. This universalist orientation seeks to broaden the focus of general planning theory and method so that it is relevant and useful everywhere,[53] and is expressed in the justification of the Network for European–US Regional and Urban Studies:

> *... the experience and imagination of graduate students preparing for domestic professional practice will be enhanced substantially by studying how planning or policy problems are addressed in other countries under different sets of governmental and planning institutions, norms of professional practice, and ideologies.*[54]

The European Union has advanced a multinational orientation in professional education, first through the European Region Action Scheme for the Mobility of University Students (ERASMUS) programme[55] and, more recently, through action under the Bologna Declaration,[56] which aims to facilitate cross-border movement of professionals regardless of the country of education.[57]

One-world planning education faces its own challenges, not the least of which is the difficulty of defining meta-frames of reference across a wide range of planning systems that involve divergent socio-cultural and historical backgrounds and value systems.[58] As planning practice has increasingly emphasized the importance of place and identity, singular models are less convincing.[59] There is a concern that one-world approaches may overemphasize ideas from developed, particularly Anglo-American countries.[60] There is also the problem of limited access to scholarship and practice documents produced in many countries in various languages primarily for local or national consumption.[61]

The tensions between context-specific and one-world planning education approaches may not be as significant as some believe in that planning education is, in fact, generalizable across many national contexts.[62] In particular, the cross-national challenge may not be as powerful as the more basic problem of including real-world practical experiences

When planning schools in ... developed countries found that they were enrolling students from developing countries ... they initiated specializations oriented towards practice in the developing country setting

The 'one-world' approach to planning education seeks to ... provide internationally relevant training regardless of the anticipated future location of the student's practice

in planning education.[63] Indeed, the movement towards internationalization may pull planning academics away from practice in their own countries and further divorce the educational enterprise from practice.[64]

PLANNING SCHOOLS WORLDWIDE[65]

A core of university programmes teach urban and regional planning under the sanction of national or international accreditation agencies to students who intend to formally practice the profession. This group, however, is only the tip of an iceberg of urban and regional planning education, which includes urban and regional planning degree programmes in countries where there is no accreditation system, as well as modules of study focused on planning that are delivered within degree programmes in architecture, economics, engineering, geography, landscape architecture, law, urban studies and other fields. Finally, there are non-degree-granting units within universities and elsewhere that teach urban and regional planning skills to working professionals and/or lay people.

This section attempts to provide an overview of formal urban planning education at the university level worldwide. Thus, it does not present a complete picture of urban planning schools worldwide. Furthermore, due to methodological issues, it may not necessarily be exact. Yet, the survey results provide a unique overview of the regional distribution of planning schools, school characteristics, curricular emphasis, international collaboration between planning schools and accreditation systems.

Regional distribution of planning schools

The inventory produced for this Global Report indicates that there are 550 universities worldwide that offer urban planning degrees.[66] As can be seen from Table 10.2, more than half of these (320 schools) are located in ten countries, all of which have more than 15 planning schools each. The remaining 220 schools are located in 72 different countries. More than half of the world's countries have no planning schools at all.

Furthermore, the survey reveals that more than half of the world's planning schools (53 per cent) are located in developed countries. When comparing the number of schools with regional populations, it becomes clear that there are major regional imbalances. While the developing countries have less than half of the world's planning schools, they contain more than 80 per cent of the world's population.[67]

While university degrees in planning are relatively less common in Latin America than in developed countries, short-term online and certificate programmes in specialized planning topics are increasingly available. There has been much growth in courses covering geographic information systems, computer-aided design and modelling in the real estate and transportation contexts.[68]

Region/country	Number of schools	Region/country	Number of schools
Developed countries	**290**	Kenya	3
Albania	2	Lesotho	1
Australia	19	Morocco	1
Austria	3	Mozambique	1
Belgium	3	Nigeria	39
Bulgaria	1	Rwanda	1
Canada	21	South Africa	11
Czech Republic	3	Tanzania	1
Denmark	2	Togo	1
Estonia	1	Tunisia	1
Finland	3	Uganda	1
France	17	Zambia	1
Germany	8	Zimbabwe	1
Greece	3	*Asia and the Pacific*	164
Hungary	1	Bangladesh	1
Ireland	3	China	97
Italy	13	China, Hong Kong	1
Japan	2	China, Taiwan	3
Latvia	1	India	15
Lithuania	1	Indonesia	16
Malta	1	Iran	1
Netherlands	12	Israel	1
New Zealand	5	Lebanon	1
Norway	7	Malaysia	4
Poland	12	Pakistan	1
Portugal	7	Philippines	1
Romania	2	Republic of Korea	7
Russian Federation	8	Saudi Arabia	1
Serbia*	2	Sri Lanka	1
Slovakia	1	Thailand	6
Slovenia	1	Turkey	5
Spain	3	United Arab Emirates	1
Sweden	6	Viet Nam	1
Switzerland	2	*Latin America and the Caribbean*	27
TFYR Macedonia	1	Argentina	3
United Kingdom	25	Brazil	6
United States of America	88	Chile	2
Developing countries	**260**	Colombia	2
Africa	69	Guatemala	1
Algeria	1	Jamaica	1
Botswana	1	Mexico	9
Egypt	3	Peru	1
Ghana	1	Venezuela	2

Table 10.2

Urban planning schools inventory (university level), by country

Note: * Includes one planning school in Kosovo.

Source: unpublished Global Planning Education Association Network (GPEAN) survey

There are 550 universities worldwide that offer urban planning degrees

Characteristics of planning schools

About two-thirds of the schools award undergraduate degrees in planning; three-quarters award postgraduate professional degrees; and one third award doctoral degrees. The patterns vary considerably by region: while undergraduate degree offerings far outpace postgraduate degrees in Asia, postgraduate degrees are offered by substantially more institutions than undergraduate degrees in the Americas. In Latin America there are very few undergraduate planning programmes as planning education is traditionally linked to schools of architecture. Much of the urban planning undertaken in Latin America is, in fact, undertaken by architects, without formal training as urban planners or urban designers.[69]

In countries where urban planning is primarily taught at the undergraduate level (such as in many countries in

Box 10.2 Planning education in Poland

The development of planning education programmes in Poland is both indicative of the struggles of adjusting planning education and practice from communism to the demands of a market-driven economy, and exceptional in the level of progress achieved over a relative short timespan.

Throughout the communist era, planning was merely a professional specialization of architecture or engineering, emphasizing physical and technical aspects of plan preparation or economics. The first free-standing programme in spatial planning and land economy was established only in 1991. Since then, a range of independent interdisciplinary planning programmes have been established across 17 higher education institutions. During the period of 1991–2008, these institutions have conferred over 3000 planning degrees.

Establishing higher education programmes afresh is a complicated matter, and, in transition countries, rapidly changing policy and legal frameworks can present additional barriers. The planning field faced further adversity in that planning carried (and still carries) negative connotations linked to past experiences with central state management. Hence, the speed and efficiency with which Polish academics established these planning education programmes is all the more remarkable. Key success factors are believed to be academics' ability to draw on a well-developed research culture in economic and spatial planning and their fruitful efforts to link with and garner support from established planning schools networks (e.g. AESOP, the Association of European Schools of Planning) and organizations. In addition, with Poland's application for European Union membership, planning became a political and economic factor associated with progress. Knowledge of spatial planning, policy and economy became vital to the successful implementation of pre-accession instruments supporting the transformation of new European Union member countries. This prompted the state to actively encourage universities to develop planning programmes to build capacity.

Tight regulation governing programme provision through Poland's Higher Education Act and extensive state-level guidelines had to be adhered to in order to get programmes established. The guidelines detail everything, from the programme category to the length of programmes. Core subjects, key competencies and teaching methods, as well as basic levels of staffing and academic expertise required to offer programmes are also prescribed.

Planning programmes established after 2002 have all adopted the new three-cycle structure (Bachelor–Masters–Doctorate) mandated by the Bologna Declaration, which seeks to foster comparable degree structures and professional mobility across Europe. Degree lengths vary slightly, based on the type of conferring institutions. This means a Bachelor's degree in planning at non-technical universities requires a minimum of six semesters (three years of study), leading to a professional title of 'licentiate' (*licencjat*); at technical universities, a Bachelor's in planning requires a minimum of seven semesters, leading to the title of 'engineer' (*inżynier*). Planning curricula must offer tuition for a mix of fundamental science subjects, knowledge and skills such as mathematics, statistics, economics, sociology, technical and planning drawing, urban history, introduction to law and a wide range of specialized courses.

Master programmes require a minimum of four semesters for those who hold a Bachelor's degree from a non-technical university, and three semesters for students with a professional title of 'engineer'. Entry to Master's degree studies is open to all students who have completed 60 per cent of all compulsory courses of an undergraduate planning degree. This is relatively easy to achieve for students in environmental studies, geography or architecture.

Since only about half of the curricula at both levels are compulsory, universities have considerable freedom to develop their own specialization. Interestingly, planning programmes were established not only in design and engineering-oriented schools, but were also built up from specializations in economics and environmental sciences. Thus, 4 of 17 universities offer a planning curriculum with a heavy emphasis on economic aspects of planning, 2 institutions offer a strong design focus, while another 2 place a strong emphasis on environmental issues and planning. The remainder of the planning schools offer rather more balanced programmes. Several programmes also offer specializations in European spatial policy and instruments, and rural, heritage and tourism planning.

While the current education provision is comparatively well developed, further improvements are needed. With considerable construction activity, there is a shortage of planners certified to process building permissions. In 2008, the 1200 members of the Chamber of Town Planners – the state-supported body that certifies planners – faced a caseload of over 200,000 applications for residential and commercial buildings projects. Fee levels have, however, stratified chamber membership towards architects, which strains the body's relationship with planning schools and exacerbates the paucity of qualified practitioners.

Planning programmes face issues with marketing as there is no clear profile of planners as an independent profession. Planning is still regarded by many as an obstacle rather than as a means of retaining and improving quality of life and environment. There is no mandatory continued professional development for practitioners, although members of the Chamber of Town Planners are offered seminars and training on legal changes in the Polish planning system and some schools offer postgraduate certificates to help address skills gaps.

Source: Frank and Mironowicz, 2008

Asia), planning schools generally have a close affiliation with other disciplines, most often architecture, engineering or geography. In other countries (such as Australia), there are signs of a shift from undergraduate to graduate focus for planning education, with Melbourne University, a leading institution, dropping its undergraduate degree and starting a two-year Master's degree programme.

Worldwide, the mean number of academic staff per school is 23, including full- and part-time academic staff, although caution is necessary in interpreting this statistic since definitions of staff status and even of full- and part-time status vary across institutions and countries. The staffing varies, from the very small in New Zealand – where one planning school has a staff of three – to a school in China with a staff of 132. The latter school graduates about 60 undergraduates and 30 Master's degree students of planning per year.

In terms of the academic credentials of staff, there are

major regional differences. Planning schools in developed countries generally require a doctoral degree of all full-time academic staff members. In contrast, most planning schools in developing countries require a Master's degree only, and some of these schools require only an undergraduate degree for their full-time academic staff. Obviously, this has impacts for the quality of education provided.

There are wide differences in the relative emphases on teaching, research, professional outreach and public service among the universities offering urban and regional planning degrees. Indeed, the debates among these objectives are a cause of tension in many schools.[70] There are regional differences; but differences among countries within regions and among institutions within countries, as well. Schools in countries that are keen to promote international standing of their universities often find that their universities or governments push them to emphasize research.[71] Schools in countries that are eager to promote development, but do not have adequate planning labour forces (such as in much of Africa and Asia), often attempt to respond to these labour market pressures by emphasizing teaching and outreach. Schools where university budgets are highly limited (such as in Latin America and some smaller European countries) may undertake professional planning project work as a source of supplementary revenue. Moreover, schools differ widely in the relative percentage of full-time and part-time academic staff, with part-time staff often maintaining planning practices as additional work activities outside the university. The resulting diversity among schools with respect to faculty work is substantial.

Curriculum emphasis

As noted above,[72] urban planning education has moved from a focus on physical design towards an increased focus on policy and social science research. During the last decade, however, there has been a resurgence of design in some schools. While the curricula of a majority of planning schools worldwide combine design and policy approaches to planning, there are some regional variations. Planning schools in China and Mediterranean countries,[73] for example, tend to focus on physical design, while those in the UK and US tend to emphasize policy/social science approaches. Box 10.2 illustrates the mix of these two approaches in Poland following the transition towards a market economy.

Curriculum content in the areas of sustainable development, social equity, participatory and deliberative planning and climate change is quite prevalent among planning schools. Quite naturally, its prevalence is tied to the prevalence of policy/social science approaches. In the transitional countries of Eastern Europe (and Greece[74]), however, the lack of integration of design and social science in planning curricula is an impediment to effectively incorporating sustainability in planning in these schools. Despite this, sustainable development enjoys growing prominence in higher education curricula in these countries as well.[75] In contrast, in many schools in North America, sustainability is a unifying theme to the curriculum. Box 10.3 describes such

> **Box 10.3 Pioneering of sustainability education: University of British Columbia, Canada**
>
> The School of Community and Regional Planning at the University of British Columbia defines its mission as advancing the transition to sustainability through excellence in integrated policy and planning research, professional education and community service. It sees its primary challenge as the need to give practical meaning to the concept of ecologically sustainable social and economic development and to explore local and global paths towards achieving it. It approaches this task through practised interdisciplinarity. The integration of teaching, research, capacity-building and practice is oriented towards providing the knowledge and skills required to ensure the viability of communities and regions in a rapidly evolving world. From the university's perspective, adapting to global ecological change and economic rationalization requires a new generation of planners who are dedicated both to understanding the issues and acting to resolve them in a wide variety of public and private settings.
>
> The university began pioneering work on sustainability before the concept was widely used, as early as the mid 1970s, championing notions of adaptive environmental management. By the time of the 1992 United Nations Conference on Environment and Development (UNCED), held in Rio de Janeiro, Brazil, the university's planning school had established a Centre for Human Settlements and had developed a well-known research programme focused on sustainability ideas and issues. The centre now partners with the university's Institute for Resources, Environment and Sustainability. Current projects include investigations of ecological footprints of countries, and sustainability impact assessments of land development projects. The school is moving towards objectives of addressing sustainability implications for urban governance, potential for using new media to increase public awareness of sustainability issues, and deepening research by examining intrinsic sustainability issues of resilience, infrastructure and public service systems and ecological stocks.
>
> The university's planning school prides itself on the fact that its commitment to sustainability has fostered a climate of productive disagreement and greater intellectual interaction among faculty, as they struggle to resolve the tensions inherent in operationalizing cultural, economic and environmental sustainability.
>
> *Source:* based on correspondence with Thomas Hutton (Vancouver, Canada), 2009

a circumstance at the University of British Columbia, which holds out sustainability as the key focus of its planning curriculum. On a global level, three-quarters of planning schools teach sustainable development, more than half teach participatory and deliberative planning, a similar number teach social equity, while one third of planning schools teach climate change.

Despite awareness of the importance of gender in planning practice, gender is not a common core part of the syllabus in many urban planning schools.[76] While, as noted above, about half of the planning schools are teaching social equity issues in their curricula, only a minority of these are specifically teaching gender-related issues. Table 10.3 provides a list of only four programmes worldwide that currently address gender and urban planning.[77] The absence of gender-specific modules has impacts upon the type of courses delivered and how gender and diversity is discussed in the wider framework of urban planning education.

There are significant regional variations in terms of the relative importance given to technical skills, communicative skills and analytic skills in planning curricula.[78] Again, the variations are linked to the prevalence of policy/social science approaches, as opposed to design. While planning schools in Asia rate analytical skills as the most important, followed by technical skills and communication skills, the focus varies substantially in Latin America. Overall, in Latin

Curriculum content in the areas of sustainable development, social equity, participatory and deliberative planning and climate change is quite prevalent among planning schools

In many schools in North America, sustainability is a unifying theme to the curriculum

Title of course	School	Modules taught
Gender and Equity (compulsory course)	University of Auckland, New Zealand	• Social inclusion/exclusion • Gender analysis • Planning and spatial equity • Gendered space • Crime and safer design • Social infrastructure assessment tools
Gender and the City	Florida State University, US	• Gender perspectives on the city • Globalization • Gender and development • Gender housing and transport • Violence urban space and gender • Race and class and sexuality • Queer theory implications for gender
Planning and Diversity (taught in 2007)	Virginia Polytechnic and State University, US	• Gender • Sexual preferences • Culture • Participation
International Development and Gender (elective course)	University of Wisconsin, US	• History of gender in development processes • Role of international agencies • Access to resources • Empowerment

Table 10.3

Currently existing university courses on gender and urban planning

Source: Reeves et al, 2009

America, technical rationalist perspectives are the norm, with skills such as master planning, urban design and econometric modelling more common than those of participation or negotiation.[79]

Concerns have been raised about the fact than students from many developing countries travel to developed countries to obtain their planning degrees. In the US, for example – which is a leading country in the award of planning doctoral degrees – 44 of the approximately 90 doctorates awarded in 2005 went to foreign students. It is suggested that when these planners return home they may be ill prepared to address the planning concerns in their own countries. It appears that many planning schools in developed countries have taken note of such concerns, as many have responded to their significant enrolment of international students by offering specializations in international development planning, or by including various international curriculum components.

European countries show a wide diversity of urban planning approaches. Many disparate approaches have had their origin here and planning education in the region is characterized by a diversity of focus and curriculum contents. Much of this diversity will persist in the foresee-

---

Box 10.4 Planning education in Europe: Diversity and convergence

Diversity in national approaches is a main characteristic of planning education in Europe. Programme foci and structures, programme size, accreditation requirements, costs and curriculum content all vary across the continent. The types of planning education provided through European universities and institutions may be categorized as follows:

- an independent degree programme;
- a specialization within a cognate discipline such as architecture, landscape architecture, geography, or economics; and/or
- a second postgraduate degree and certificates of continued professional development for individuals who seek to change careers or specialize further.

This diversity of planning education provision reflects the very different planning traditions and cultures (Newman and Thornley, 1996) that have developed historically and that exist across Europe. Despite the Bologna Declaration, much of this diversity will persist in the foreseeable future as programmes need to offer avenues into the profession that suits the national context. As part of the structural programme changes from long continuous engineering degrees to the two-staged Bachelor/Masters structure, curricula have been reviewed and updated. Furthermore, quality assurance measures are being introduced. These include the establishment of accreditation criteria in national contexts where they did not exist before. Accreditation in Europe is conducted through the Royal Town Planning Institute (UK), the Association for the Promotion of Education and Research in Management and Urbanism (APERAU) (for the French language region), the state (as in Poland), or a number of newly established accreditation associations.

As a very general rule of thumb, planning education in Western and Southern continental European countries is based on an urbanism and urban design tradition, while in the Anglo-Saxon countries there is a distinct social science/economic development orientation of planning. In Eastern Europe, planning existed as a specialism of architecture or economics and only a few countries have so far successfully managed to establish interdisciplinary planning programmes able to teach planning practices and approaches suitable for democratic market economies (Maier, 1994).

With the strengthening of the European Union and the increasing influence of European policy, planning schools have integrated teaching on European Union spatial policy, territorial governance, cohesion, etc. within their curricula. Another key topic is urban renewal and regeneration and dealing with urban shrinkage. Sustainability, urban food and the implications of climate change on rural and urban areas are other emerging themes. The opening of Eastern Europe led to new discourses on the purpose of planning, ranging from ecological, to place-based, market-oriented, communicative, pragmatic, socially responsive or ethical planning, etc. (Gospodini and Skayannis, 2005).

Higher education in European countries is also becoming more competitive, seeking to attract foreign nationals from other European countries and elsewhere. This can have problematic consequences for the curriculum and teaching staff (Peel and Frank, 2008). Especially when catering to students from the least developed countries, it is questionable whether current curricula focused on planning in the European context will provide suitable planning knowledge for these students. Some of the specialist programmes that have been developed, particularly for individuals interested in working in developing countries, may be a better choice for these students.

Source: Maier, 1994; Newman and Thornley, 1996; Pezzoli and Howe, 2001; Gospodini and Skayannis, 2005; Frank, 2006; Frank and Mironowicz, 2008; Peel and Frank, 2008

> **Box 10.5 Planning education in Ghana: The Nkrumah University of Science and Technology**
>
> Planning education in Ghana started in 1958 with the establishment of a planning programme in the School of Architecture, Planning and Building at the Kumasi College of Arts, Science and Technology, now the Kwame Nkrumah University of Science and Technology. The programme entered students for the intermediate examinations of the Royal Town Planning Institute (UK). After passing the examination, students were sent to universities in the UK to obtain full professional qualifications. Even though this practice no longer prevails, staff are still enrolled in PhD programmes abroad. The department is currently the only university department officially recognized to run planning programmes in the country.
>
> The undergraduate planning curriculum combines instruction in physical design with instruction in policy development, while the postgraduate programmes focus on policy development at the macro-level, as well as development planning and management at the grassroots level. At various points in the history of planning education in the country, emphasis has been placed on physical design or policy development, according to prevailing concerns. In the current curriculum, there is an attempt to respond to the issues related to decentralization, the reduction of poverty, and the social, economic and spatial development needs of human settlements within the context of urbanization and the challenges associated with it.
>
> The department currently runs the following academic programmes:
>
> * BSc in Development Planning and in Human Settlement Planning;
> * MSc in Development Planning and Management and in Development Policy and Planning;
> * MPhil in Planning and Development Studies; and
> * PhD in Planning and Development Studies.
>
> With a total student strength of about 700 and 21 staff during the 2007/2008 academic year, the staff–students ratio stands at 1:30 and 1:3 at the undergraduate and postgraduate levels, respectively. With the assistance of partner institutions, the school has been able to undertake successful staff development and student programmes. Although there is no official accreditation programme in place, the Ghana Institute of Planners plays a vital role in curriculum design and the provision of external examiners to moderate the planning programmes offered by the university.
>
> To a large extent, the Department of Planning has been able to respond to the needs of the planning profession in Ghana by producing graduates to meet national development needs. There is, however, an urgent need for urban planners to address the physical development and management of towns and cities. In order to do this effectively, there is a need for adequate resources in terms of teaching and learning materials and space, resources for exchange with other professionals for experience sharing, and practical training of students with professional planning institutions and firms.
>
> The experience from Ghana illustrates that it is possible for planning curricula in developing countries to respond to the contextual issues and paradigm shifts. However, limited resources are seriously influencing the quality of facilities to promote teaching and learning, the orientation of planning to the development context of the country, and the relevance of planning curricula to the developmental needs of the country. The Ghana experience suggests that, for planning education to be effective, there is a need to develop the capacity of planning educators and involve professional associations and bodies in the reshaping of planning curricula. Also important is the need to network with other planning schools in developing countries in order to increase the potential for planning education to respond to the needs of the 21st century.
>
> *Source:* Inkoom, 2008

There are many calls for reform of urban planning education in Africa in order to make planning more responsive to the needs of African peoples

able future (see Box 10.4), despite certain factors that, at present, foster a convergence in European higher education, such as the Bologna Declaration, which, by seeking to establish a common European Higher Education Area, stipulates a harmonization of educational structures.[80]

Planning education in Africa is often closely tied to the educational systems of former colonial powers, often with emphasis on master planning, following the British tradition. While technical and physical planning education approaches dominated for many years, this has changed in recent decades, with greater attention being paid to expanded definitions of planners' roles to include economic development and environmental planning, as well as newer participatory and collaborative ideas.[81] At the same time, there are many calls for reform of urban planning education in Africa in order to make planning more responsive to the needs of African peoples, to better prepare planners for work in the private and non-profit sectors, to better confront issues of state power and implementation, to better understand decision processes and capital investment issues, and to be more able to retain academic staff.[82] Box 10.5 illustrates the efforts of a leading African school to meet national needs while struggling with resource limitations.

School connections with other schools and professional networks

Among the 550 universities worldwide that, according to the GPEAN survey, offer urban planning degrees, 342 are members of at least one or more of the planning school associations that are GPEAN members (see Box 10.6). This leaves 208 schools, or 38 per cent, that are not members of any such planning school association. Regional association coverage is particularly thin in Asia, where only 19 of the 161 planning schools there are members of a regional association. Of the 97 Chinese planning schools, only 1 is a

Many planning schools do not participate in national planning school accreditation systems. Strong accreditation systems exist in major Anglophone countries such as Australia, Canada, New Zealand, the UK and the US, and in countries such as China, Ghana, Hong Kong, Indonesia, Kenya, Malaysia, Nigeria, Pakistan, Rwanda, South Africa, Tanzania and Zimbabwe. But in most countries the planning profession is not well organized and no planning school accreditation system has developed. Among African schools there is considerable interest in better international ties in order to obtain collegial feedback on programmes, but also to obtain evidence of quality, which will be persuasive to university leadership. Several schools in Africa have initiated discussions that are intended to lead to international accreditation through the Royal Town Planning Institute (UK).

Accreditation for planning schools is a contentious issue in some regions, such as Latin America. Efforts to create accreditation are under way in Brazil and Mexico, and various claims are made about the desirability of international accreditation. At the same time, many are reluctant to turn curriculum influence over to external authorities that may have little understanding of national circumstances.[83]

In many developing countries (such as Brazil[84]), the fact that a large proportion of academic staff have obtained their doctoral degrees at foreign universities in various countries has led to a wide and diverse curriculum orientation. This has also led to the establishment of academic linkages with scholars and institutions abroad. On a more negative note, there is some concern that scholars sent abroad to study may not return.

CAPACITY FOR EDUCATIONAL SUPPORT OF PLANNING PRACTICE

Building on the discussion earlier in this chapter, it is important to consider how the current organization and networking of planning schools assists the revitalization of planning education worldwide, which systems can be put in place to help planning schools and their associations respond to the new challenges, and what the roles of professional associations and other organizations might be in increasing the quality and availability of planning skills.

As noted above, planning schools now exist in at least 82 countries, including at least 45 developing countries. Average staff sizes at these schools are considerable, with every continent having average staff numbers of 8 or higher and most continents enjoying average staff sizes in excess of 20. This is a substantial system of planning education reflecting a total academic staff of more than 13,000. The magnitude of the planning educational system is a recent phenomenon: only 40 years ago the size of the system was a small fraction of what it is today, and even 20 years ago the numbers were much less than they are today.

A planning education system of this size should be capable of meeting the demand for professional planners; but the system is not evenly distributed, curriculum emphases often fall short of the real demands of planning

The results of the low incidence of regional network membership of planning schools ... is that academic staff work in relative isolation

member of the regional association; and of the 16 Indonesian planning schools, only 2 are members. Similarly, in Africa less than half of the planning schools are members of a regional association. Membership rates are also low in countries with economies in transition in Europe. Notable is the absence of any regional association serving the non-French-speaking Middle East.

Cost, language, distance and even political reasons are all contributing factors to non-membership in regional planning school associations. Among the advantages of such membership is that most of these associations convene annual conferences and publish or are affiliated with professional urban planning journals. The results of the low incidence of regional network membership of planning schools in many countries, coupled with the substantial number of schools that do not operate under an accreditation system (see below), is that academic staff work in relative isolation, with limited ability to share curriculum and pedagogic practices, or to move towards consensus about best practices.

While many planning schools in developing countries (and Asian schools, in particular) are not members of regional associations, they may still have other avenues of international contacts. For example, while most planning schools in China are not connected to any other national, regional or international bodies for either their degree programmes or in terms of professional associations, many have established individual ties with schools, programmes and associations within China or in the US, UK or France. Similarly, schools in Indonesia have established ties with Australia; schools in the Republic of Korea have ties with Japan; the planning school in Hong Kong has an established relationship with a UK school; Malaysian planning schools have links with The Netherlands; and schools in Thailand have ties with France, US, Korea and other South-East Asia countries.

Planning schools now exist in at least 82 countries .... a substantial system of planning education reflecting a total academic staff of more than 13,000 practice in the 21st century, resources are frequently inadequate, staff work assignments do not sufficiently support renewal of staff or the profession, and academic labour market concerns have troubling consequences. Beyond this, the very significant needs for planning training among persons other than professional planners are not being met. Box 10.7 sets out some of the challenges facing planning education in Latin America and the Caribbean. Most, if not all, the challenges identified apply to all other developing countries and many developed countries as well.

Developing countries are generally underserved by planning schools; only one quarter of all developing countries have such educational facilities. Moreover, the bulk of the planning schools in developing countries are located in a handful of countries. Given the unique circumstances of each country's planning system and the high costs of sending students abroad for higher education, the absence of planning education from so many countries is a compelling problem.

Some countries, primarily developed countries, are increasingly treating higher education as a source of foreign exchange, and in a globalizing world, universities themselves are setting up offshore operations. Liverpool University's civic design programme in China and Carnegie Mellon University's business and computer science programmes in Qatar are two examples of this trend. The flow of human capital resulting from this system can be beneficial to countries lacking strong university resources. But, it can also be damaging, as when individuals in whom a national economy has invested extensively choose to not return to their home countries.

Leading planning schools have recognized the nature of 21st-century urbanization problems and are familiarizing their students with theory and tools related to sustainability, globalization, social equity, climate change and the full range of specializations that are involved in effective plan-making. They view planning as an integrated practice that requires technical, analytic and communicative skills, including participation and conflict resolution in a multicultural context. Unfortunately, not all schools approach these needed perspectives. Many schools treat planning as either a design or a policy practice, rather than both – as is needed. Many are focused on a narrow range of issues tied to legislative planning mandates and forgo consideration of key specializations. Many give short coverage to the softer, people-skill, side of planning, including participation with the full range of stakeholders involved in planning, such as low-income residents, but also understanding and communication with professionals in other fields. Box 10.8 illustrates some of the current professional challenges facing urban planners in Southern Asia. Many of the issues outlined in this box are undoubtedly familiar in other regions where master planning takes precedence over development management in planning education as well.

Furthermore, all too often planning schools lack the academic staff, computers, library materials and studio space to carry out their work effectively. In some developing countries, it is not uncommon for academic staff to be expected to hold second jobs in order to survive on the

salaries paid. Often universities cannot retain academic staff because of competition from industry or overseas institutions. In some countries, the most basic library materials are unavailable and staff resort to reading aloud from key sources so that students may learn from them.

In many institutions, teaching assignments are such that academic staff cannot devote energy to the professional development that is essential if they are to stay current with new developments. Fewer still are afforded the time and support resources necessary to make contributions to advancing the practice of planning, as is necessary if

> All too often planning schools lack the academic staff, computers, library materials and studio space to carry out their work effectively

---

Box 10.7 Challenges for planning education in Latin America and the Caribbean

Challenges include:

- keeping pace with the development of new technical expertise (such as geographic information systems, computer-aided design, transportation or real estate modelling, etc.) and with the equipments (hardware, software) required to perform relevant planning analyses;
- expanding negotiation, mediation, conflict resolution and consensus-building skills;
- complementing the rational planning model with participatory, advocate, democratic and collaborative planning models, as needed;
- coordinating multidisciplinary teams effectively with various forms of knowledge and knowledge production;
- addressing metropolitan and regional planning and governance;
- more effective responses to the growing environmental challenges in the region and the world;
- more effective responses to the growing socio-spatial justice challenges in the region;
- forging more collaborative relations with community and governmental organizations involved in planning so that knowledge produced in higher education can improve practice and vice versa; and
- greater emphasis on ethics education so that planning professionals can become more effective agents in combating corruption and other professional and governmental vices.

Source: Irazábal, 2008a

Box 10.8 Urban planners being sidelined from urban planning: The case of Southern Asia

Urban planning education in Southern Asia is still based in a tradition dominated by architecture and civic design rather than the multidisciplinary approach adopted in many other countries. The planning education curricula in the region thus continue to lay emphasis on physical design solutions without much consideration of the financial, fiscal and administrative dimensions of urban planning.

Having been moulded through such a limited module, planning graduates are ill equipped in skills that are needed to comprehend and resolve problems rooted in the socio-economic and cultural milieu of the region. This leads to the isolation of the physical planners from mainstream planning and development processes.

For example, planning in India at the national and sub-national levels is geared to sectoral economic planning where physical planners have very little to contribute. At the settlement level, the concerned sectoral departments and development authorities or special-purpose agencies mostly implement development works. These agencies generally prefer to involve architects and engineers rather than urban planners since the former are more useful for the kind of work that they carry out. The planners' main contribution is thus limited to preparing master plans for towns and cities. But almost all of the few hundred master plans that they have prepared remain largely unimplemented. This further diminishes the creditability of physical planners in the eyes of the decision-makers and the people at large.

Source: Ansari, 2008

Advantages include:

- opportunity for international exchange of ideas, negotiation of standards of excellence, and building of consensus about basic values and criteria;
- raising standards and accountability;
- incentives for programme improvements;
- opportunity for assistance to weaker and poorer institutions and programmes;
- tools (criteria and indicators) for individual institutions to assess themselves and determine the resources needed to achieve excellence; and
- tools for designing quality enhancement programmes.

Potential risks involve:

- unequal dialogue: prevalence of perspectives, values and judgement of more powerful countries, institutions and programmes;
- loss of programme diversity; and
- increased difficulty of contextualizing the programmes to better address local needs.

Potential challenges include:

- lack of tradition for monitoring and evaluating planning programmes – hence, resistance to incorporate those practices on an ongoing basis;
- lack of resources and/or commitment through time (sustainability) for quality enhancement programmes; and
- other competing priorities and opportunity costs.

Ethical concerns are:

- equitable participation of international and national accreditation agents (one suggestion may be to have accreditation boards of 50 per cent each of international advisory members and national judging members);
- accreditation criteria and indicators should be assessed in relation to the mission and resources of the institution evaluated and to the planning context that it should serve;
- assessment should aim at the design of a tailored, realistic quality enhancement programme;
- resources and incentives for promoting enhancement should be facilitated; and
- rewards for accomplished enhancements should be offered.

Source: Irazábal, 2008a

Between 2003 and 2006, Partners for Urban Knowledge Action and Research (PUKAR) implemented the Gender and Space Project in Mumbai (India). The project was funded by the Indo-Dutch Programme of Alternatives in Development. The research project focused on examining the use and experiences of city space, particularly public space, from a gender perspective. The project also had a 'strong pedagogic component' consisting of short elective courses and workshops.

The courses were available for students at universities and colleges in Mumbai. Workshops and one-off lectures were generally open to the public or held for specific groups working with women in the city. Topics of the courses run included:

- unveiling the city: gender, space and the built environment;
- interrogating the city: gender, space and power;
- gender consciousness and the practice of urban planning; and
- gender, space, youth and urban identity.

Source: Reeves et al, 2009, citing PUKAR, 2005

solutions to today's planning problems are to be found. It is not uncommon for highly trained academic staff to seek posts abroad in order to gain access to facilities and resources that will facilitate such work.

Many schools are not effectively networked within the broader discipline as they are not members of an international planning school association and they do not benefit from the input and questioning of a specialized accreditation system. Conferences and the debates which take place in the publication process are vital to testing the correctness of ideas. In the absence of networks and other forms of peer review, it is difficult to build quality.

Calls for international accreditation are highly problematic. To academic staff labouring in countries where there is no accreditation, the absence of such peer review and quality control can be debilitating. Certainly, where accreditation exists, it can be a powerful force leading to adequate resourcing and thoughtful design of curricula. While the purpose of international accreditation should be the promotion of standards of excellence in planning education and training, many insist that the ability of planning scholars in one country to properly evaluate the actions of planning scholars in another country is often limited. However, a number of the challenges imposed on urban planning through increased globalization – such as global warming, urbanization, ageing, migration, environmental protection and justice, etc. – are increasingly becoming shared rather than unique. Furthermore, new information and communication technologies increasingly facilitate the international exchange of planning information, making planning ideas and practices disseminate more broadly and rapidly. Likewise, transportation technologies facilitate travelling and international consulting for a planning elite, also contributing to knowledge creation and dissemination at a global scale.[85]

The case for international accreditation of urban planners should thus be further investigated. Perhaps there is a case for the international planning associations organized in GPEAN to partner with the United Nations to develop standards of excellence and ethical procedures for international planning accreditation. There is a valuable precedent for such an effort. The United Nations Department of Economic and Social Affairs (UNDESA) already partnered with the International Association of Schools and Institutes of Administration to produce the *Standards of Excellence for Public Administration Education and Training*.[86] These standards and the process that led to their creation can offer valuable insights to planning.[87] Box 10.9 outlines some of the pros and cons relating to introducing an international accreditation system for the urban planning profession.

Perhaps the greater educational challenge facing planning is the need for planning objectives and tools to be understood by architects, engineers, lawyers, administrators and the myriad of citizens and elected officials who must endorse planning interventions and support plans if they are to be adopted and implemented. University incentives in many countries do not support the education of non-degree-seeking students, with the result that planning schools are seldom major contributors to the planning education of allied professionals and lay people. Instead, this challenge is left to planning agencies and other civil society organizations. Frequently, they are not well prepared for the challenge.

As noted above,[88] there is a glaring absence of gender-related subjects in the urban planning courses taught worldwide. It has been noted that planners who have graduated from a planning course where gender was not in the syllabus, regardless of their gender, often fail to consider gender in planning. This reinforces the need for continuing professional development.[89] The Royal Town Planning Institute in the UK has worked to advance gender awareness in planning practice during recent years, and has produced tools intended to help planners address gender-related issues in a practical manner.[90] Similarly, Box 10.10 provides an example from Mumbai (India) of how the failure of formal planning schools to address gender concerns within their syllabus have been addressed in a more informal manner.[91]

CONCLUDING REMARKS

Planning education has grown exponentially and diversified broadly during the last 100 years. Most planning schools have expanded their initial architectural design focus to embrace applied social scientific approaches. Most schools have reconceptualized planning from a rational modernist perspective and have come to emphasize deliberative and participatory processes that advance civic engagement and promote citizen participation. Most have built capacity on issues of plan implementation. Many have moved from geographically specific approaches to integrated one-world approaches. Sustainability and social equity are now fundamental to planning curricula in many schools.

Planning education is conducted at both undergraduate and postgraduate levels, with different countries emphasizing one or the other, but seldom both. Expectations for faculty credentials and faculty work accomplishments vary widely by country and in some instances by institution within a country. Planning schools frequently collaborate with educational units in related fields, often architecture, engineering or geography. There is widespread cross-border movement of planning students, with both positive and negative consequences.

There is considerable need to increase the capacity of planning education in developing and transitional economies. Especially in Asia and Latin America, but also in Africa, new planning schools are needed in countries that have no school or larger countries that have only one. Beyond this, leading universities outside developing countries must increase their capacity to examine and educate for those countries. The one-world approach to planning education holds some promise in helping them to do so. The latter is particularly the case with respect to the worldwide inclusion of gender-related issues in urban planning curricula.[92]

As a system, planning education has moved vigorously towards theories and tools that respond effectively to the new challenges of 21st-century planning. Diffusion of these innovations has not been complete enough, however. Curriculum reform is needed in many planning schools. Schools which still treat planning only as a design exercise or only as a policy practice need to broaden their approaches. This is most often true among schools in Asia and Eastern Europe; but examples can be found in every region. Schools which teach planning as technical and analytic without incorporating the political and participatory facets of the profession must expand their curricula. Schools which do not yet effectively discuss questions of sustainability, social equity or climate change must do so.

Accreditation systems may be the drivers of such curriculum reform. Countries that do not now have specialized accreditation systems for urban planning may consider putting such systems in place.

Creativity will also be needed to find additional sources of revenue that can help resource-starved institutions in developing countries. Partnerships between universities and planning practice organizations may advance the goals of both, allowing universities to perform useful planning studies for which the practice community may not have capability, while funding students or permitting the purchase of needed equipment. Exchange programmes may be used to give students in one country access to resources not available in their home country. Foundations, learned societies and professional planning organizations should be engaged in the search for funds.

Planning schools need to interact with professional and scholarly networks. Planning school associations in Africa, Asia and Latin America do not effectively sustain communication and growth among their members because school staff cannot travel in sufficient numbers, and because schools cannot afford association membership fees. International development agencies would do well to consider the needs for adequate communication among university urban planning schools. There may be ways to utilize technology for improved communication; the associations themselves should be encouraged to develop these.

Education of allied professionals, elected officials and members of the lay public is a great unfilled need. This need cannot be filled by universities alone, although universities should expand their efforts in these areas. Beyond this, training programmes aimed at specific segments should be undertaken by planning professional associations and by international development agencies. Systems for sharing materials used in such training programmes would be valuable, so that similar organizations in other countries do not have to reinvent content and delivery tools.

There is a glaring absence of gender-related subjects in the urban planning courses taught worldwide

Planning schools need to interact with professional and scholarly networks

NOTES

1 Friedmann, 2005a; Irazábal, 2008a.

2 See Chapters 3 and 5.

3 Hague et al, 2006; Graham and Marvin, 2001.

4 Krueckeberg, 1985.

5 American Society of Planning Officials, 1941, pp263ff.

6 Nocks, 1974; Birch, 1980; Sarbib, 1983; Krueckeberg, 1985.

7 Hirt and Stanilov, 2008, p83.

8 Perloff, 1957.

9 Wildavsky, 1973; Alterman and Macrae, 1983.

10 Healey, 1980.

11 Krueckeberg, 1985, pp427–429.

12 Healey and Samuels, 1981.

13 Alonso, 1986.

14 Levin, 1976.

15 Hemmens, 1988, p87.

16 Ansari, 2008.

17 Bell and Packard, 1976; Stiftel and Watson, 2005.

18 Gospodini and Skayannis, 2005.

19 Mohammed, 2001; Diaw et al, 2002; Yuen, 2008.

20 Yuen, 2008; Irazábal, 2008a.

21 Rodwin, 1980.

22 Irazábal, 2008a.

23 Stiftel et al, 2006a; Stiftel and Mukhopadhyay, 2007.

24 Grant, 2005.

25 Abramson, 2005, p92.

26 Tugwell, 1939.

27 Banfield, 1955, 1959.

28 Sarbib, 1983; Garcia, 1993.

29 Stiftel, 2000.

30 Dalton, 1986; Baum, 1996.

31 Klosterman, 1994; Fischoff, 1996; Sager, 1997.

32 Klosterman, 1985.

33 Batty, 1984.

34 Goodman, 1971; Grabow and Heskin, 1973.

35 Allmendinger and Tewdwr-Jones, 2002.

36 Irazábal, 2008a.

37 Davidoff, 1965.

38 Mazziotti, 1974; Needleman and Needleman, 1974.

39 Arnstein, 1969; Mazmanian and Nienaber, 1979.

40 Friedmann, 1992; Khosa, 2001; Lyons, 2001.

41 Putnam, 2000.

42 Vidal et al, 2004.

43 UNCHS, 1995.

44 Meyerson and Banfield, 1955; Rabinovitz, 1969; Altshuler, 1966.

45 Crow, 1996.

46 Meyerson, 1956.

47 Etzioni, 1967.

48 Arimah and Adeagbo, 2000; Watson, 2007.

49 Albrechts et al, 2003.

50 Gunder and Fookes, 1997.

51 Frank, 2006, pp19–20.

52 Qadeer, 1988; Sanyal, 1989.

53 Frank, 2006; Sanyal, 1989.

54 Goldstein et al, 2006, p2.

55 Williams, 1989.

56 Bologna Declaration, http://ec.europa.eu/education/policies/educ/bologna/bologna.pdf.

57 Davoudi and Ellison, 2006; Confederation of EU Rectors' Conferences and the Association of European Universities, 1999.

58 Qadeer, 1986; Burayidi, 1993.

59 Yuen, 2008, p97.

60 Kunzmann, 2004.

61 Stiftel et al, 2006b; Stiftel and Mukhopadhyay, 2007.

62 Hinojosa et al, 1992.

63 Afshar, 2001.

64 Kunzmann, 2004.

65 Major parts of this section are based on a survey undertaken for this report by the Global Planning Education Association Network (GPEAN), an affiliation of nine planning school associations worldwide (see Box 10.6). The objective was to develop an inventory of university-based programmes that have the word 'planning', or its equivalent, in the title. However, this was not straightforward, especially in Francophone and Latin American countries where the usual title of 'urbanism' or an equivalent reflects a cross between the Anglophone usages of urban planning and of urban studies. As planning in many countries often takes place in schools of architecture, economics, geography or law, the current survey underestimates the number of planning schools. For example, while the survey indicates that there are only six planning schools in Brazil, the membership of Brazil's National Association of Postgraduate and Research Programmes in Urban and Regional Planning (ANPUR) includes 36 schools. Likewise, the GPEAN survey identified only 12 planning schools in Poland, while a case study prepared for this report identified 17 such schools (see Box 10.5).

66 See also Stiftel, 2009.

67 Although Africa seems to do relatively well in this comparison with a similar proportion of planning schools and population, the bulk of planning schools are located in Nigeria (39 schools) and South Africa (11 schools). The remainder of Africa have only 3.4 per cent of the planning schools, compared to 11.8 per cent of the world's population.

68 See also note 65 above.

69 Irazábal, 2008a.

70 Stiftel et al, 2009.

71 This is frequently the case for many larger European countries, as well as for Australia, Canada, New Zealand and the US. The Research Assessment Exercise, an effort to rank university programmes based on research impact, has been a major tool for the UK government to push its universities to greater research emphasis and has more recently been copied elsewhere, such as in The Netherlands and Hong Kong.

72 See earlier sub-section on 'Design versus policy'.

73 Including Italy, Greece, Spain and North African countries.

74 Gospodini and Skayannis, 2005.

75 Hirt and Stanilov, 2008.

76 Reeves et al, 2009.

77 According to Reeves et al (2009), these are the only currently existing programmes of this nature worldwide.

78 For the purposes of the GPEAN survey, statistics and geographic information systems (GIS) were given as illustrations of technical skills; working with the public and with elected officials and organizing workshops as examples of communicative skills, and policy analysis, cost–benefit analysis, population projections and project prioritization methods as examples of analytic skills.

79 Irazábal, 2008a.

80 See Box 10.2.

81 Diaw et al, 2002.

82 Oranje, 2008; Mabin and Todes, 2008; Kusiima, 2008; Nnkya and Lupala, 2008.

83 Irazábal, 2008a.

84 Irazábal, 2008a.

85 Irazábal, 2008a.

86 UNDESA and IASIA, 2008.

87 Irazábal, 2008a.

88 See earlier sub-section on 'Curriculum emphasis'.

89 Reeves et al, 2009.

90 RTPI, 2003, 2007.

91 Reeves et al, 2009.

92 Reeves et al, 2009.

PART V

FUTURE POLICY DIRECTIONS

CHAPTER 11

TOWARDS A NEW ROLE FOR URBAN PLANNING

This Global Report has sought to review recent and innovative trends in urban planning which appear to have the potential to address the urban challenges facing cities and towns in the 21st century. While such innovative planning approaches and their successes must always be seen as shaped by the very particular contexts from which they have emerged, there are, nonetheless, principles and concepts that may be shared across the globe. One important conclusion of this report is that there are no models or standard recipes for urban planning that can be applied everywhere. In fact, a review of current planning practice shows how the poor track record of planning in many parts of the world is partly due to the belief that master planning and modernist planning were such models that could be used everywhere, regardless of context.

A central argument in this report is that, while in some parts of the world, governments are using planning in positive ways to manage change in cities and towns, in other parts, little attention has been paid to the functioning of the planning system, and as such, legislation, regulations and processes are out of date, or are insufficiently reformed to be able to deal with the major challenges of the 21st century. Urban planning approaches in some parts of the world are directly constraining the ability of governments and civil society to deal with urban challenges and, indeed, may be contributing to urban problems. Nonetheless, it is also possible to argue that the challenges currently facing urban settlements are of such a magnitude that governments, in partnership with other sectors of society, will have to play a stronger role in managing urban change in the decades to come.

The purpose of this concluding chapter is to suggest a new role for urban planning. In many parts of the world, a 'paradigm' shift in urban planning is required to ensure tolerable urban living through the next century. This chapter first summarizes the main urban issues in various parts of the world to which planning will have to respond. There are certain issues that are important in all parts of the world and some that differ depending upon whether countries are categorized as developed, developing or transitional. The second section reviews the main findings of the Global Report, as well as the recent and innovative planning

practices which they highlight. Although the 'success cases' in planning are not many, they nonetheless serve to indicate that it is possible to use planning as an institutional instrument to shift urban environments in a positive direction. The fourth section, following on from the third, draws out the main elements of more positive urban planning. What is identified here are the main principles or concepts of innovative planning which might stimulate ideas elsewhere, although the actual form they would take will be influenced by context. The fifth section identifies the changes which would need to be in place, or the initiatives which might be supportive in promoting new approaches to planning. The last section provides a conclusion to the chapter.

THE MAIN ISSUES FOR URBAN PLANNING IN DIFFERENT PARTS OF THE WORLD

Some of the most important issues that urban planning has to respond to are relevant in all parts of the world, while others vary according to the nature of regional political economies. Common global issues include climate change, economic crises, income inequality and cultural diversity, among others. Context-specific issues range from urban informality, poverty and peri-urbanization in developing countries, through environmental pollution and urban shrinkage in transitional countries, to large ecological footprints and an ageing population in developed countries.

Global urban planning issues

The various regions of the world are now highly interlinked in terms of economic activity, information flow and population movement, giving rise to a common set of urban issues. At the same time, all parts of the world are also affected by global environmental change. While the nature of the impact of global environmental change varies across regions, it also presents a common issue to which planning needs to respond.

One important conclusion of this report is that there are no models or standard recipes for urban planning that can be applied everywhere

Common global issues include climate change, economic crises, income inequality and cultural diversity, among others

■ Climate change

In responding to the impacts of climate change, urban areas need to take action of two kinds. These are mitigation and adaptation. Mitigation consists of measures and policies designed to reduce the emission of greenhouse gases. Adaptation pertains to activities aimed at reducing the vulnerability or strengthening the resilience of cities to the effects of climate change. Both kinds of action require urban planning. Mitigation requires reducing the ecological footprint of urban areas, which includes a shift to public transport-based movement and planning for more efficient, compact and mixed-use city forms. Adaptive measures include relocating vulnerable settlements, improving drainage, hardening-up of infrastructure systems, and preventing new developments in areas likely to be affected by sea-level rise or floods.

■ Global economic crisis

In 2008, the global economic crisis occasioned by the instability of unregulated markets and banking systems caused by neo-liberal economic policies was revealed. Consequently, many countries have moved into recession. This will adversely affect economic growth, employment, foreign direct investment (FDI), international aid and development programmes in countries across the world. Less funding will be available for state-initiated urban and infrastructural projects. This, in turn, reinforces the need for governments to act in partnership with civil society and private-sector actors on urban development. It also reinforces the need for a developmental role for governments, as opposed to neo-liberal approaches which assumed that the 'market' on its own could solve most urban problems.

■ Energy supply and impacts

While the price of petroleum is relatively low (mid 2009), the volatility of oil prices in 2008 showed that price is no longer a predictable factor and that, in the long term, global oil supplies will begin to decline. The impact of carbon dioxide (CO_2) emissions from petroleum-driven vehicles on climate change is becoming better understood and this will also encourage a switch away from oil-dependent cities. The many towns and cities across the world which were planned on the assumption of high levels of individual car ownership will, at some stage, require retrofitting. Such urban settlements will have to introduce forms of public transport and plan bicycle and pedestrian movement networks. The growing costs of transporting food will increase the demand for urban agriculture spaces in cities. Low-density, car-dependent suburbs could be abandoned or turned to other uses. Energy-efficient buildings (low-rise, high plot coverage) will need to be accommodated in different open space and movement systems.

■ Food security

The rising cost of food in all parts of the world is a response to both fuel costs and the degradation of agricultural land, and is also likely to persist into the future. This has several implications, with the poor being most affected. Urban environments need to be planned so that they allow for urban agriculture to become an accepted element of the urban open space system and local fresh food markets a standard part of urban infrastructure.

■ Changing population size of towns and cities

Urban population growth and decline are to be found in all parts of the world, although the latter is more common in the developed and transitional regions. In the developing regions, population growth through urbanization and natural increase is the dominant pattern, and it has been recognized that in Africa and Asia urban growth rates will remain high for some time to come. In these parts of the world, much of this settlement is, and will be, informal and incomes will be generated largely through the informal economy. If the issue of rapid growth of poor urban households is considered in combination with the above environmental and resource issues, then it is clear that those cities and towns which are able to plan where and how this new settlement takes place will be in a far better position in decades to come. Urban shrinkage also requires planning. Properly managed decline can open up important opportunities, such as releasing land for urban agriculture.

■ Income inequality

The changing nature of urban labour markets, which shows a growing polarization of occupational and income structures has, in part, given rise to greater urban income inequality in all regions of the world. This, in turn, has given rise to urban areas with stark contrasts between areas of wealth and poverty, with escalating crime levels fuelling the desire by the wealthy to spatially separate themselves from the poor. Thus, income inequality and spatial fragmentation are mutually reinforcing, leading to segregated and violent cities. Women, children and the aged feel the brunt of these processes. The challenges for planning in addressing this issue are particularly difficult, as urban planning cannot counter market forces. Rather, planning has to seek ways to promote social integration and cohesion, perhaps through a quality public space system.

■ Cultural diversity

Growing volumes of global migration has meant that cities and towns in all parts of the world have become much more multicultural. People from very different ethnic and religious backgrounds now live together in cities. This is making participatory processes around planning issues far more difficult. Cultural diversity has important implications for how built environments are managed. Planners need to seek the right balance between cultural groups attempting to preserve their identity in cities and the need to avoid extreme forms of segregation and urban fragmentation. Cultural mix also raises new demands on planners to mediate between conflicting lifestyles and expressions of culture. Conflicts around religious buildings, burial arrangements, ritual animal slaughter and building aesthetics are the new issues which planners have to increasingly tackle. There is also a growing demand for planners to play a role in preserving built environment heritage and historically

---

In responding to the impacts of climate change, urban areas need to take action of two kinds. ... mitigation and adaptation

Cultural mix also raises new demands on planners to mediate between conflicting lifestyles and expressions of culture

valuable urban areas, and protecting them from insensitive conversion or invasion by incompatible uses.

Urban planning issues in developing countries

While developing countries are affected by the issues discussed in the previous section, they are also affected by a range of issues that are specific to these regions of the world. These are highlighted below.

■ Urban informality

Urban growth in the developing regions of the world is distinctive in that much of the new settlement and new job creation is informal, reflecting severe levels of poverty and inequality. This is particularly the case in African urban areas, where urbanization is taking place amidst relatively low levels of economic growth. This raises a particular challenge in that conventional urban planning approaches are not designed to engage with informality and, by contrast, actively seek to formalize the informal sector. This formalization process frequently destroys livelihoods and shelter, and serves to exacerbate exclusion, marginalization and poverty. The notion that the poor have to step outside of the law in order to survive in cities is an appropriate one, as is the suggestion that conventional planning laws have often served to create informality and illegality, and have been used in eviction and land grabs. An important task for planning is to devise new forms of regulation that serve to protect both the rich and the poor, while at the same time guiding urban growth in efficient and sustainable directions.

■ Urban growth

This Global Report has emphasized the impact which urban growth will have upon towns and cities in the developing world, particularly in Africa and Asia. This growth is opening up challenges as well as opportunities for cities, and planning needs to be able to identify and respond to both of these. The need to deliver urban land at scale, linked to networks of public infrastructure, in ways which address both the mitigation and adaptation demands of environmental change is probably the biggest issue that planning is facing in these parts of the world. Significantly, earlier predictions of exploding megacities appear to have been off the mark, and much of this growth is taking place in smaller cities. For instance, most urban dwellers in Africa reside in cities of less than 500,000 people. This, in turn, increases the scale of the demand for urban professionals and managers.

■ Income inequality and poverty

This issue has been identified earlier as critical in urban areas in all parts of the world. However, it is a particularly important issue for urban planning in developing countries, given suggestions that the planning systems there often neglect the poor or even worsen their situation. Inequality is high in Latin America and Africa, while the latter, in addition, experiences high levels of poverty and prevalence of slums. In some countries, the solution to this is seen as excluding poor people from cities by implementing anti-

urban policies, or focusing on rural poverty in the hope that this will discourage people from migrating to cities.[1] However, no country in the world has ever managed to stop urbanization through either of these measures. The solution is to accept that urbanization will occur, and to use planning to address both the problems and opportunities that it presents.

■ The 'youth bulge'

An important demographic trend in developing cities and towns is the increasing proportion of young people (aged 15 to 29) relative to the adult population. While the youth can form the most energetic and innovative segment of the population, where they also comprise the bulk of the unemployed, they can be a source of social unrest and deviance, including crime. Planning for a youthful population places particular demands on urban development – in terms of the need for education and training facilities, and sport and recreational investments. It also raises demands to cope with the negative side of the youth bulge through a focus on safe public spaces and movement networks.

■ The peri-urban areas

The bulk of new growth in rapidly urbanizing cities is taking place on the urban edge, and in some parts is linking up existing settlements to form extended urban corridors. This form of growth presents a host of new planning issues in that much of this new settlement is informal, un-serviced, fragmented, has a mix of tenure systems and is beyond the boundaries of municipal governments. These areas are extremely difficult and expensive to service in the conventional way. New and incremental approaches to service and infrastructure delivery, in partnership with local communities, will have to be found. The opportunity here is that the more distributed service networks and alternative technologies (solar or wind energy) may be the most appropriate way to service these areas.

A further issue is whether the planning of peri-urban areas calls for local or regional planning action, and which level of government is best placed to deal with such areas. A combination of regional and local planning approaches may well be required.

■ Linking the green and brown agendas

This is an issue that is relevant to cities in all parts of the world, but is a particular challenge in developing countries where the development imperative is often seen as more important that achieving sustainability. However, the pace and form of urban growth in developing contexts puts even greater pressure on ecosystems. An important role for planning in these contexts is to mediate the conflicts between these often different agendas. This requires new participatory processes and partnerships, new institutional arrangements for planning, and new ways of linking planning to other relevant professionals, particularly engineers.

■ Institutional and professional capacity

In many developing countries, the decentralization agenda has not progressed very far, and many urban planning

Urban growth in the developing regions of the world is distinctive in that much of the new settlement and new job creation is informal

An important demographic trend in developing cities and towns is the increasing proportion of young people

decisions are still taken by central government. In a context of rapid urban growth, the centre cannot cope, and the planning and land development system becomes slow, bureaucratic and unresponsive to local needs. This is often justified by citing the lack of trained planning and urban professionals to staff municipal planning offices. Some developing countries (e.g. China) have accelerated the training of urban professionals to address these growing needs; but in other parts, there is a serious shortage of supply (particularly of professionals trained to address current urban issues) and this is a hindrance to effective urban planning. The issue of planner/urban professional training, along with decentralization of decision-making, is a key one.

Planning capacity at the local level is also dependent upon the strength of civil society as this forms a critical source of input and knowledge to the planning process. In some parts of the developing world, such as Latin America, civil society has been successfully mobilized around planning and urban development issues; but in others it is weak and fragmented. How to shift from technocratic and top-down approaches to more inclusive planning processes is an important issue.

Urban planning issues in transitional countries

Planning issues in these parts of the world tend to be a combination of those found in developed and developing regions; but the political history of these regions has also influenced their current planning concerns.

■ Slow population growth and declining cities

Slow or reduced population growth, the phenomenon of shrinking cities and ageing have presented problems of dealing with deteriorating buildings and infrastructure in a context where the local tax base in severely constrained. A rapidly ageing population places an increased demand on healthcare and other facilities relating to the needs of the elderly.

■ Urban sprawl, fragmentation and inequality

Population shrinkage has occurred along with growing demands for space and facilities by an emerging wealthy class. Urban development is now strongly driven by foreign investment, which has fuelled new property development, primarily for the wealthier groups. This new growth has focused on suburban development and upmarket inner-city neighbourhoods, raising issues for planning of sprawl containment, the preservation of heritage buildings in older inner-city areas, and dealing with rapidly increasing car ownership. At the same time, planning needs to address derelict industrial sites, deteriorating public housing estates, aged and failing infrastructure, and informal settlement on the urban edge.

■ Environmental issues

Communist-era industries were some of the worst polluters in the world, and while some of these have closed, many still remain and present serious environmental problems for

planning. The rapid growth of vehicle ownership has worsened air quality, and unconstrained private property development, particularly in the form of sprawl on the urban edge, has encroached upon many open spaces and agricultural land.

■ Decentralization of government and resource constraints

Decentralization to local governments has been strongly promoted, but has not been matched by adequate funding. Consequently, local governments have relied on privatized measures to provide and run services. Urban development has become the concern of multiple parties – the once powerful public authorities, private owners, builders, developers, non-profit organizations and various interest groups. This greatly complicates the terrain within which planning has to operate. Adding to this is the fact that urban planning has been shifted to local governments which have no previous experience in dealing with these matters. New local regulatory systems and administrative processes have had to be developed from scratch.

■ The changing legislative framework for planning

Many transitional countries have now produced new planning legislation as the effects of a lack of planning became increasingly evident. Frequently, this new legislation reinforced the conventional master planning approach; but several countries adopted strategic planning in addition to master plans at the behest of international development agencies. Strategic planning has introduced new issues of city competitiveness, economic growth, municipal financial reform, improved quality of life and citizen participation. Given that strategic plans are not legally recognized, their coexistence with master plans greatly complicates the legislative environment for planning.

Urban planning issues in developed countries

In these regions, high incomes and steady growth have helped to avoid certain urban issues experienced in developing and transitional countries, but have also brought a different set of urban planning problems.

■ Socio-spatial inequalities and urban fragmentation

City competitiveness, the desire to attract foreign investment and urban development, fuelled by a booming property market (until recently) have segregated many cities and towns into elite enclaves and sprawling middle-class suburbs. But the changing structure of labour markets has left many urban residents poor and unemployed, and deteriorated public housing estates now coexist with new urban mega-projects. Achieving integrated and equitable urban environments is a major challenge for planners.

■ Environmental issues

Urban areas in the developed regions, particularly the US,

Many transitional countries have now produced new planning legislation as the effects of a lack of planning became increasingly evident

Communist-era industries were some of the worst polluters in the world, many still remain and present serious environmental problems for planning have the largest ecological footprints in the world. High levels of resource consumption and car dependence, large-scale waste generation, and low-density suburban sprawl eroding agricultural land are all serious planning issues. Urban sprawl in the US has been a particularly problematic feature and has led to major loss of natural resources. Both mitigation and adaptation strategies in relation to environmental change will have to be mainstreamed into planning if it is to affect these patterns.

■ Population decline and shrinking cities

Migration from poorer regions means that slow population growth, ageing and shrinking cities are less extreme than transitional regions. Nonetheless, industrial restructuring and offshore relocations have left many older industrial and mining towns without a viable economic base. In such contexts, planning has to strategize for population outflow, abandoned homes and areas, and a declining support base for commercial activities and public facilities. In many cities, migrant inflow is supporting a youthful population; but this coexists with an older cohort now making increasing demands on health facilities and retirement homes.

■ Integrating sectoral policy within governments

As city governments have become increasingly complex and sophisticated entities in charge of managing large resource flows and budgets, so the problem of achieving integration between various line-function departments, and between different levels of government has increased. This is an important issue for planning as it relies on the relationships between functions and tiers in order to achieve spatial coherence and integration on the ground. Potentially, planning can play an important role in encouraging sectoral alignment and coordination if the function is correctly positioned within governance structures.

THE MAIN FINDINGS AND CONCLUSIONS OF THE REPORT

While Chapters 2 to 10 have considered different aspects of urban planning, there are some important common principles or positions that cut across these chapters. These can be summarized as follows.

The task of reviewing current systems of urban planning and considering revised approaches must be informed by the particularities of urban contexts. These contexts differ significantly from one part of the world to another. The Global Report concludes that a failure to appreciate this in the past partly underlies the failure of planning systems in different parts of the world. New challenges that will affect towns and cities in all parts of the world, but particularly those in developing and transitional regions, require an approach to urban planning which is inclusive and pro-poor, which sees the value of working with informal systems rather than against them, which accepts the process of urbanization as inevitable but also potentially positive, and

which recognizes and addresses current major environmental and resource issues. Achieving these outcomes will, in turn, require reconsideration of planning processes and institutional arrangements: urban planning is undertaken most effectively in partnership with civil society and the market, and through institutional structures that facilitate the integrative abilities of planning, bringing together decision-making around infrastructure, public services, natural systems and the formal and informal economy in spatially coherent and developmental ways.

Diversity of urban contexts

Urban contexts vary remarkably across the world in terms of the nature and scale of growth and socio-spatial patterning of settlements. Local economies, culture and local political and institutional systems are also highly variable. At the same time, there are also continuities across contexts, and it is clear that some of the major challenges of the 21st century will affect urban areas in different ways and to varying degrees. The key regional differences which are of relevance for planning are as follows:

- Levels of urbanization are high in the developed and transitional countries, and in Latin America, but much lower in Africa. Conversely, *rates of urbanization* are low for Europe, North America and Latin America, but much higher in sub-Saharan Africa and Asia. The implication of these levels and rates of urbanization is that most new urban growth will be taking place in the poorer regions of Africa and Asia, where the planning systems and public institutions are least equipped to deal with the challenges of rapid urbanization.
- Much of future population growth will be taking place in smaller and middle-sized cities rather than the mega-cities, which are predicted to grow more slowly. This demands that governments will have to pay greater attention to small- and medium-sized cities, especially in developing countries where planning often focuses on larger cities. The phenomenon of shrinking cities is to be found in many parts of the world in response to regional economic and demographic change, but is most prevalent in the developed and transitional countries. Shrinkage also demands new planning responses.
- Informality is a dominant phenomenon in developing countries in terms of both income generation and shelter. In the developing world, informal workers comprise some two-fifths of the economically active population, but many countries have figures much higher than this. The peri-urban fringe holds a significant proportion of the urban population in developing countries and is often the fastest growing area. For example, up to 40 per cent of China's urban growth to 2025 is expected to occur in peri-urban areas. Closely related to this is the emergence of urban mega-regions.
- The current global recession will affect cities across the world in various ways. In the case of developing countries, the economic meltdown is likely to exacerbate current levels of poverty, unemployment,

Urban sprawl in the US has been a particularly problematic feature and has led to major loss of natural resources

Urban contexts vary remarkably across the world in terms of the nature and scale of growth and socio-spatial patterning of settlements inequality, the prevalence of slums and the ability of these countries to implement urban development programmes, achieve the Millennium Development Goals (MDGs) and address key environmental issues such as climate change.

The emergence and spread of contemporary urban planning

Urban settlements have been planned since the dawn of civilization. As outlined in Chapter 3, 'modern' urban planning emerged in the latter part of the 19th century. This was largely in response to the appearance, as a result of the Industrial Revolution, of rapidly growing, chaotic and polluted cities in the industrializing world. From here, this approach to planning spread throughout the world and still remains influential. However, new and innovative approaches to planning have been emerging and provide important lessons. Key points in this chapter are:

Urban settlements have been planned since the dawn of civilization

- Urban planning systems in all parts of the world have been shaped by 19th-century Western European planning, commonly known as master planning. This approach to planning carried with it particular spatial models, approaches to land classification, road layouts, specifications of built form and building materials, tenure systems, and processes of plan formulation. Western planning models can therefore be understood as culture specific, as they emerged in response to particular political systems, cultures and sets of values.
- The diffusion of Western European planning approaches occurred through a number of different mechanisms: colonialism, market expansion and intellectual exchange. Professional bodies and international aid and development agencies also played an important role in the spread of these ideas. Frequently, these imported ideas were used for political, ethnic or racial domination and exclusion rather than in the interests of good planning. This was particularly the case with colonialism, where planning was frequently bound up with its 'modernizing' and 'civilizing' mission and with control of the location and movement of the indigenous urbanizing population.

Urban planning activity is inherently a form of governance, and is therefore inevitably part of a wider set of processes aimed at shaping urban development with the future in mind

- In many developed countries, approaches to planning have changed significantly during recent decades in response to the emergence of new forms of governance and a reduced role of the state relative to the market. However, in many developing countries, the older forms of master planning have persisted. In these countries, master planning is still found to be useful, sometimes due to the very rapid rate of state-directed city-building, and sometimes as it serves the interests of elites who wish to emulate modern Western cities and whose actions inevitably marginalize the poor and the informal in cities.
- The most obvious problem with modernist planning is that it completely fails to accommodate the way of life of the majority of inhabitants in rapidly growing, and largely poor and informal, cities, thereby contributing to

social and spatial marginalization. Furthermore, it fails to take into account the important challenges facing cities in the 21st century and, to a large extent, fails to acknowledge the need to meaningfully involve communities and other stakeholders in the planning and management of urban areas.
- The newer approaches to urban planning tend to be more strategic, flexible, action and implementation oriented, and linked to budgets and larger infrastructural elements. Many of the newer approaches are particularly concerned with new institutional processes, and they seek new forms of community and stakeholder engagement, and new ways of integrating planning with other activities and departments in local government. Generally, they attempt to fit more closely with the concept of 'governance'. Many have been initiated by international agencies, and these often attempt to introduce specific concerns into the planning process – for example, environment, safety or gender issues. In many countries, aims to achieve global positioning of cities, attraction of foreign investment and urban regeneration have shaped planning efforts.
- A major weakness of the new approaches is that they tend to focus more on process often at the expense of outcomes. They also place much emphasis on the directive aspect of the planning system and neglect the underlying regulatory system and how this links to directive plans. Planning is also weak in terms of how to deal with the major issues of the 21st century, such as climate change, resource depletion, rapid urbanization and informality.

THE INSTITUTIONAL AND REGULATORY FRAMEWORK

Urban planning activity is inherently a form of governance, or collective action, and is therefore inevitably part of a wider set of processes aimed at shaping urban development with the future in mind. In its concern with physical structures and spatial arrangements, it is deeply intertwined with land and property development rights and responsibilities.

Both the governance systems and planning systems vary with geographical context. They depend upon the nature of the political, institutional and legal systems in place, the relative roles of the public, private and community sectors in development activity, institutional capabilities and professional cultures. These, in turn, can come together differently in different cities and towns. The common goal of planning systems is to manage conflicts over the use of land and to direct urban development in ways that promote human welfare and environmental sustainability, emphasizing principles of geographic, and intra- and inter-generational equity.

Key points regarding institutional and regulatory frameworks that emerged from Chapter 4 are as follows:

- Many countries and regions are attempting to reconfigure their formal government structures, and the urban planning systems operating within them, to make them more relevant to the dynamics of contemporary circumstances. These initiatives emphasize decentralization, less hierarchical and more interactive ways of working, and greater involvement of non-state actors. Legal systems underpinning planning are also being made more flexible; but new rigidities are being introduced through national and international initiatives in environmental and human rights law.

- The presence of large-scale land and property developers, some working on a global scale, has been expanding substantially. These create challenges for national and local planning practices that are seeking to promote greater equity and environmental sensitivity in urban development. The functional dynamics of larger urban areas now operate at a much wider scale than is encompassed by administrative boundaries, making the coordination of equitable and sustainable urban development far more difficult. This requires that planners work with other actors to implement plans and projects in interactive and collaborative ways.

- The institutional context for urban planning has a significant effect on the forms and outcomes of planning. The configuration of agencies and responsibilities, as well as the systems and practices within these are important. Planning can be used for both positive and negative ends. Therefore, in the design and reconfiguration of planning systems, careful attention needs to be given to identifying opportunities that can be built on, as well as pressures which could lead to the subversion and corruption of planning institutions.

- Urban planning can play a significant role in overcoming governance fragmentation in decision-making and policy formulation, both within local government and between tiers of government. It can do this most effectively through building horizontal and vertical relationships using place and territory as loci for linking planning with the activities of other policy sectors, such as infrastructure provision. Thus, regulatory power needs to be combined with investment power.

- The regulation of land and property development activity is a vitally important role of the planning system. However, it is sustained not just by formal law, but also by social and cultural norms. In designing planning systems, all forms of land and property development activity, formal and informal, must be taken into account. Drawing informal practices into the realm of formal law can be damaging to them, and it is often necessary to work 'between' legal systems and traditions to achieve overall public benefits.

- Regulation has an important proactive as well as protective dimension. Statutory plans and permit-giving regulate the balance between public and private rights in any development project, as well as providing the authority for conserving important community assets. Urban land development can take on a chaotic and exploitative form when it occurs outside of the framework of planning and land management. This is well illustrated in the peri-urban areas of Jakarta.[2]

Participatory planning

Chapter 5 showed that one of the most important shifts in urban planning during the last century has been from an expert-driven technocratic activity to one that is inclusive of relevant stakeholders and communities. This has come about largely as a result of the shift to the notion of governance as well as strong pressures on governments to strengthen democracy and decentralization. If urban planning is a form of collective action, then it follows that planning processes should be opened up to include wider policy communities and stakeholders. However, there has been much debate on how to do this, with some arguing that processes can also be disempowering and that the aim of reaching consensus is idealistic. Some key points emerging from Chapter 5 are:

- There are several important reasons for supporting participatory planning processes: they offer an important learning process for communities and stakeholders, as well as planners, and the enriched exchange of knowledge and ideas leads to better plans; communities are more likely to 'take ownership' of planning outcomes, which is important for their long-term sustainability; participation can help to avoid or reduce conflicts between and within stakeholders and communities and with government; and forms of direct and participatory democracy are necessary to complement formal democracy in order to consolidate democratic practice. Steering processes towards achieving consensus amongst a wider group of stakeholders, rather than a small group of policy elites, has become an important part of planners' toolkits.

- Experience shows that a number of preconditions need to be in place for participation to occur. The most important is the existence of a political system that allows and encourages active citizenship. There also needs to be the legal basis for participation which incorporates requirements for participation and how it will affect planning; processes must be timely, fair and transparent and involve all relevant stakeholders; planning professionals must have the commitment and skills to incorporate participation; local governments must have sufficient resources and responsibility to make participation worthwhile; and stakeholders and communities must be sufficiently organized and informed.

- Achieving participation that is meaningful, socially inclusive and contributes to improving spatial planning requires certain measures. Socially marginalized groups should have a voice in both representative politics and participatory processes; elected political representatives should also be involved to avoid the sense that they are being undermined by participatory processes; civil society organizations should be supported and recognized; and participation at the city-wide level should also be promoted using referendums or advisory councils.

- The outcome of interactive processes amongst wider networks may lead in different directions. Some policy community members may become defensive of their own policy territory and competencies and, hence,

The institutional context for urban planning has a significant effect on the forms and outcomes of planning

One of the most important shifts in urban planning has been from an expert-driven technocratic activity to one that is inclusive of relevant stakeholders and communities withdraw from the network or act against it. Or it may lead to the emergence of new and innovative ideas and solutions for urban problems. Inclusive processes do not necessarily result in consensus. While the enlarged network of social relations enhances planners' access to knowledge resources, new ideas and human and social capital, it may also generate tensions and conflicts over power and responsibilities.

- Even if spaces for participation are provided, this does not mean that all people have equal voice. They may be part of wider social groups with cultural norms and expectations that may constrain their ability to voice their views. Women, in particular, may be affected in this way.

Empowerment and self-mobilization is of little value to poor communities if it is not part of a wider redistributive project

- Empowerment and self-mobilization is of little value to poor communities if it is not part of a wider redistributive project. If the political commitment to redistribution is not there, then the only way for the poor to achieve change is through wider social movements.

- There is a major difference between periodic and intensive participatory exercises, when plans are being prepared or revised, as well as continuing engagement in agenda-setting, monitoring, policy review and decision-making. What may be feasible on a periodic basis is not necessarily feasible or appropriate on an ongoing basis. Sustaining direct democracy alongside representative democracy depends upon ongoing support from elected representatives and institutionalizing participatory channels.

Integrating the green and brown agendas

Integrating the green and brown agendas serves to reduce the ecological footprint from land and resources while enhancing the ecological base of the city

The goal of a sustainable city is to reduce its ecological footprint from consumption of the natural systems used by the city, while simultaneously enabling human systems to be optimized for improving the quality of urban life. Thus, integrating the green and brown agendas serves to reduce the ecological footprint from land and resources while enhancing the ecological base of the city. Chapter 6 concluded that achieving this objective requires a revised role for planning, in relation to the following:

- Urban areas can be powered by renewable energy techniques and technologies, from the region to the building level. Renewable energy enables a city to reduce its ecological footprint and, if using biological fuels, can be part of a city's enhanced ecological functions. Integrating the green and brown agenda will require strategies to progressively tap local resources. This will involve recognizing renewable resources in and around a city as part of the capital base of the city and establishing ordinances on buildings that facilitate the application of renewable energy.

- Carbon-neutral cities are able to reduce their ecological footprint through energy efficiency and replacing fossil fuels, and by creating offsets in the bioregion. This can be enforced through planning schemes that mandate standards for significant reductions in carbon in all development and offset CO_2 emissions through purchasing of carbon credits, especially through tree planting.

- Cities can shift from large centralized power and water systems to small-scale and neighbourhood-based systems, including expansion of 'green infrastructure'. The distributed use of power and water in a city can enable a city to reduce its ecological footprint, as power and water can be more efficiently provided and used. Incentive packages can be created for technologies such as photovoltaic cells, grey water systems and water tanks within the context of local plans for the governance of community-based systems, as well as region-wide strategies for recycling sewage.

- Eco-efficiency strategies link industries to achieve fundamental changes in the industrial metabolism of cities and move cities from a 'linear' to a 'closed-loop' metabolic system. Producing energy and materials from waste is one example of this.

- A green infrastructure strategy, which includes wetlands, forests, parklands etc., can enhance the green agenda across the city through biofuel, food, fibre, biodiversity and recreation pursuits. Intensive greening of cities can create biodiversity corridors, provide biofuels and biomass energy, reduce run-off and feed aquifers, and can be linked to local urban agriculture projects.

- A place-based strategy should ensure that the human dimension is driving all others. It recognizes that human well-being is a central element of a sustainability strategy. The focus of this approach is making cities more self-sufficient in a range of different ways, from job creation and food production to energy production. This strategy also aims at reflecting the uniqueness of 'place' in all urban developments, as opposed to faddish copying of plans and architecture from elsewhere.

- Cities, neighbourhoods and regions can be designed to use energy sparingly by offering walkable, transit-oriented options for all, supplemented by renewably powered electric plug-in vehicles. A sustainable urban transport strategy incorporates an integrated, efficient and affordable public transport system (which may need to link formal and informal providers); a non-motorized transport system (cycling and pedestrian infrastructure), and a curb on car-dependent suburbs.

- Cities without slums can be achieved through concerted action at the local, national and international levels to meet the specific targets of the MDGs on slums, drinking water and sanitation. This requires innovative approaches that can enable slums to be upgraded on the basis of sustainability principles. In this context, attention must be paid to environmental safety, human rights and the economic productivity concerns of slum dwellers. In the short-term, however, cities and national governments must address, comprehensively and vigorously, the most pressing brown and green agenda challenges of poor access to safe drinking water and sanitation, adequate housing, and degrading environmental conditions – which are all interrelated.

Urban informality

Many governments consider informal housing and economic activities to be a sign of their failure and, hence, something to be removed. This is most unfortunate, as informality is often the only way in which the poor in many cities can survive. This was recognized in the Plan of Action of the first United Nations Conference on Human Settlements, held in Vancouver (Canada) in 1976, which stated that the 'informal sector' had proved its ability to meet the needs of the less advantaged in many parts of the world, despite the lack of public recognition and assistance. If one purpose of revisiting urban planning is to see how it can promote more inclusive and equitable cities, then a central focus of this must be to seek ways to plan with informality. Key points on this that emerged from Chapter 7 of this Global Report are as follows:

- The nature of urban development processes and limitations on the resources available to even the best endowed governments mean that public agencies must work in conjunction with private actors. Planners therefore need to base their activities on a sound understanding of the processes of urban expansion and change, in particular the motives and actions of actors in private property development processes, both large and small scale, formal and informal. It is important to note that informality occurs in various forms throughout most cities, and not just in slums or informal settlements. Furthermore, it is not only poor people who live or work informally. Informality is, therefore, found in many different types of urban areas and within a range of income and social groups.
- It is important to consider all forms of land and property development activity, and not just those located in the 'formal' sector, when considering how development in an urban area is being produced and what mechanisms are available to 'regulate' it to achieve public realm benefits. Drawing 'informal' practices into the purview of formal law may have some benefits; but it could also have damaging effects, especially on the poorest, if there is 'over-regulation'.
- Many approaches to planning and development regulation are ineffective or produce results that exclude and marginalize the urban poor and the informal sector. Sometimes they produce illegality, as those who cannot afford to comply attempt to circumvent them. Plans and regulations may not be sensitive to the different needs and priorities of the 'informal sector'. Planning can learn from practices in the informal sector, identifying and building on their strengths, and addressing their weaknesses.
- Very often, formal planning and regulation systems impose demands that poor groups cannot meet, as well as imposing cultural attitudes to land and tenure that may conflict with beliefs and social practices. Such regulations can produce major bottlenecks in the urban land supply system.[3] The Enugu case described in Chapter 7 demonstrates how the informal system of land supply has been meeting needs, but has drawn on elements of the formal legal system in order to secure protection of rights in land. This suggests ways of combining elements of both the formal and informal land delivery systems.
- In many countries, governments have limited resources and limited legitimacy. They need to be more innovative in determining how limited resources can be used most effectively and how they can build public support for regulation. Only when land administration is streamlined, and there is public acceptance of the need for restrictions on property rights, will the wide enforcement of development controls be feasible.
- Peri-urban areas are some of the fastest expanding areas of cities in the developing world, as the urban poor move to the urban edge in search of cheaper and more flexible land and shelter. Settlement processes, outside of municipal jurisdictions, may occur through customary tenure systems, private land sale or both. Conflicts are frequent. These processes are giving rise to extensive and fragmented areas of informal settlements, where the public provision of infrastructure and services is very difficult. New approaches to planning and service provision are required in such areas.
- The concentration of trunk infrastructure and services in defined areas can attract settlement to particular parts of the urban fringe. Incremental *in situ* upgrading can improve quality of life, as long as it does not displace households through the imposition of costs and controls. Guided land development ahead of informal settlement can avoid many later problems. Creating public–private partnerships in land development can help land pooling and rationalization.
- Planning in peri-urban areas needs to combine approaches from regional, rural and urban planning. A wider range of planning tools than is conventionally the case needs to be used. These include more appropriate forms of appraisal, engagement, action and implementation, as well as consolidation.

Spatial structure of cities and provision of infrastructure

Studies of urban growth show the massive expansion in the spatial footprint of cities over the past decades. The 'unbundling' of infrastructure development through forms of corporatization, privatization, developer-driven growth and the dominance of urban mega-projects has contributed to this. The spatial structure and degree of densification of the built environment also has a major impact upon urban efficiency, sustainability and spatial equity. Current trends in urban development towards sprawl, fragmented development and car domination have increased social marginalization. As shown in Chapter 8, planning has an important role to play in shaping city growth and structure through the strategic location and development of trunk infrastructure:

- The compact mixed-use and public transport-based city is generally more environmentally sustainable, efficient

Many governments consider informal housing and economic activities to be a sign of their failure and, hence, something to be removed

The spatial structure and degree of densification of the built environment also has a major impact upon urban efficiency, sustainability and spatial equity and equitable. More compact urban forms have made some contribution to managing peripheral urban growth; the importance of inner-city development, the usefulness of some smart growth principles and the role of transit-oriented development have been noted. At a local scale, the development of healthy and inclusive cities involves planning of environments offering a range of services, facilities and amenities, and which recognize the needs of various groups, including those of women, and which support the livelihoods of the urban poor. Pedestrian movement systems, particularly for lower-income groups, also require recognition.

- Traditional approaches to planning attempted to align land-use planning with infrastructure provision through a comprehensive master planning approach, and through the public provision of infrastructure. Thus, infrastructure provision was intended to follow spatial planning. This has not happened, as urban development has increasingly been driven by private-sector property developers and informal settlement processes. Where the urban planning function has been sidelined, urban development has also been shaped by public investments in transport and water treatment infrastructure.

- Strategic spatial plans linked to infrastructure development can promote more compact forms of urban expansion focused around public transport, as well as improve urban services, environmental conditions, economic opportunities and livelihoods on the existing urban periphery and in new development. Linking major infrastructure investment projects and mega-projects to strategic planning is also crucial. Spatial planning needs to work more closely with the planning of infrastructure at both a city-wide and more localized level if it is to have an impact upon the way in which cities develop, and their sustainability, efficiency and inclusiveness.

- A growing number of cities are including an infrastructure plan as a key element of a strategic spatial plan. Although several plans attempt to coordinate investment and development across a range of sectors, it is argued that transport–land-use links are crucial, and that other forms of infrastructure can follow. The involvement of a wide range of stakeholders is critical to the development of a shared and consistent approach; but the plan itself also needs to be based on credible analysis and understanding of trends and forces.

- In many cities, growth is occurring across municipal boundaries, and regional structures will often be required to manage growth and to develop appropriate planning strategies. Planning in these contexts should provide a framework for the coordination of urban policies and major projects, and an avenue for public discussion on these issues.

Monitoring and evaluation of urban plans

Monitoring and evaluation have considerable potential to enhance decision-making capacity in urban planning organizations. Monitoring and evaluation methods can assess plan impacts and outcomes, and thereby permit the evaluation of plan performance. Evaluation findings can be used to demonstrate the utility of urban planning to stakeholders and decision-makers, to inform and guide planning practice, and to make informed decisions. To date, evaluation has not been of central interest to planners and local or metropolitan authorities; but for the above reasons, there is a growing interest in evidence-based decision-making and programme evaluation. Chapter 9 made a number of important observations on this issue:

- *Ex ante* evaluation has a long history in planning as a way of assessing the appropriate choice of plan alternatives. The usual technique of cost–benefit analysis is now considered too restrictive and has been complemented with more sophisticated models. Formative and summative (*ex post*) evaluations consider the quality of the output of processes and plans. These, in turn, may evaluate plan 'conformance' (were the goals of the plan realized?) or plan 'performance' (the qualitative outcomes and impacts of the plan and the process).

- There is extensive debate over the indicators for monitoring and evaluation; but at least some should be spatially referenced, assessing the distribution of services, facilities and impacts of plans. Planning evaluators caution against the use of too many indicators and suggest a focus on those where information is easy to collect. There is a temptation to complicate these processes and they can become expensive and time consuming. The time element is important – it may take five to ten years before a planning impact can be measured.

- Technical analysis is a necessary but insufficient condition for successful plan evaluation. Participation by stakeholders can enhance plan quality and effectiveness through the contribution of insights, intelligence and perspectives that might not have been captured by the formal plan-making process. They can help to evaluate the effectiveness of a plan and to position successive plans by offering critiques of plan performance.

- Tools such as cost–benefit analysis, cost-effectiveness analysis and fiscal impact assessment will continue to be relevant, given the realities of local government resource constraints. Greater interest in performance measurement, return on investment and results-based management principles also means that these quantitative tools have a strong role in planning practice. There is a place for both qualitative and quantitative research tools in evaluation practice.

- The outcomes and impacts of long-range plans are difficult to evaluate because of the myriad of influences and factors that are at play. However, site plans, subdivision plans and neighbourhood plans may be more conducive to monitoring and evaluation because these tend to be more tangible types of plans. Similarly, it should be easier to design and manage monitoring and evaluation processes, and indicators, in smaller places, in places where the database is sound, and in municipalities where little change occurs over time.

Monitoring and evaluation have considerable potential to enhance decision-making capacity in urban planning organizations

To date, evaluation has not been of central interest to planners and local or metropolitan authorities

- There is no single approved method and the quality of indicators is more important than the number of indicators. There is generally no need to collect and analyse excessive amounts of information; but there should be clarity about the purpose of the evaluation, the knowledge sought and the role of indicators in that context. Leadership is critical and such processes require a champion to promote them as credible and important.

Urban planning education

Chapter 10 examined whether urban planning education and planning schools worldwide have the capabilities needed to lead the next generation of planning practice in light of the challenges facing urban settlements. The chapter undertook an inventory of planning schools and curricula worldwide, and concluded as follows:

- There are major regional differences in the nature of planning education across the globe, and in many countries there is no university-level training in urban planning. Two-thirds of schools surveyed for this Global Report teach both physical design and policy approaches; but the rest tend to emphasize one or the other.
- Planning curricula updating and reform are required in many transitional and developing countries where curricula have not been revised to keep up with current challenges and issues. Some planning schools in developed countries do not educate students to work in different contexts, thus limiting their mobility. The 'one-world' approach to planning education is an attempt to remedy this. The few schools that emphasize only one facet of the profession rather than both physical design and policy/social science perspectives may need to broaden their curricula in order to prepare professionals for the diverse demands in developing and transitional countries.
- A more widespread diffusion of innovative planning ideas into educational curricula is called for, particularly the ability to engage in participatory planning, understanding the implications of rapid urbanization, especially in developing and transitional regions, and the ability to bring climate change considerations into planning concerns.
- It is now recognized that planning is not a technical or 'value-neutral' profession – hence, the inculcation of necessary values needs to occur in the educational process. The promotion of social equity, sustainability and a recognition and respect for societal difference are all key values. Effective planning cannot be done without skills to assist in understanding the perspectives of disenfranchised and underserved populations and in finding equitable solutions to their needs.
- Planning schools in developing and transitional countries would be stronger if a larger proportion of their academic staff held doctoral degrees. Programmes to encourage the earning of doctorates by current

faculty and requirements for upgrading entry credentials would be important improvements.
- Planning schools, especially in developing and transitional regions, need resources to access published scholarship and to interact with professional and scholarly networks. Many planning schools are poorly linked to national and international educational and professional networks, and with accrediting bodies. Libraries are often woefully inadequate in some parts of the world, as is access to information and communication technology.

MAIN ELEMENTS OF A REVISED ROLE FOR URBAN PLANNING

This section draws on insights that cut across the chapters – which are summarized above. The first part of this section offers some overarching elements of a revised role for urban planning, and the second part some more specific aspects of this role.

Overarching aspects of a new role for urban planning

There are a number of overarching, or broad, elements that need to be recognized if urban planning is to play a significant and positive role in developing cities that are environmentally liveable, economically productive and socially inclusive. These range from acceptance of the need to revise or reform urban planning, through the ways in which innovative approaches and practices in urban planning are implemented, to how the relationship between urban planning and the market is addressed.

■ The need to revisit urban planning

A major conclusion of this Global Report is that urban planning systems and approaches in many parts of the world are not equipping governments with the necessary tools to deal with key urban issues of the 21st century. The nature and scale of current and impending urban problems are of such a magnitude that government and civil society interventions to manage urban change will be imperative. Earlier ideas that the 'market' would resolve all urban inefficiencies and externalities now seem much less supportable, although it is clear that the market has an important role to play in partnership with government and civil society. While planning in some parts of the world has been less effective, it nonetheless remains the central tool available to society to effect change. For planning to be an effective tool, urban planning systems in many parts of the world will need to be revised.

■ Planning innovations must be shaped by the context in which they occur

Following on from a realization of the need to revisit urban planning, an important conclusion of this report is that there is no one model or system of urban planning that can be

Planning curricula updating and reform are required in many transitional and developing countries

The nature and scale of current and impending urban problems are of such a magnitude that government and civil society interventions to manage urban change will be imperative

applied in all parts of the world. A central insight from the report is the great diversity of urban conditions which exists across the globe. The Global Report finds that one important reason underlying the failure of urban planning in developing countries is, in part, the importation of 'foreign' models and approaches. Usually, these models are based on assumptions regarding the institutional context of planning (including the form of political system, as well as state effectiveness and capacity), the demographic and economic context within which planning has to operate, and the nature of civil society, which do not hold in the importing country. When this occurs, the result is ineffective and inappropriate planning. While it is certainly possible to generalize about urban planning ideas and concepts, the way in which these might be used will be highly dependent upon contextual factors.

■ Embedding innovative ideas

This Global Report emphasizes that planning is a form of governance, or collective action, and is therefore inevitably part of a wider set of processes. The review of attempts to change planning systems shows that, very often, new approaches are simply 'bolted on' as an additional and parallel process to conventional practices and regulations, leaving the underlying system to continue with business as usual. And where there is a clash between the norms and values driving innovative planning ideas, and those affected by such ideas, then there is a tendency to selectively ignore or use new ideas and combine them in various ways with conventional practices. Innovative planning ideas will only have an effect if they articulate closely with the institutional arrangements, and cultural values and norms of the context in which this is taking place.

■ Urbanization as a positive phenomenon

The statistics showing rates and levels of urban growth and the demands associated with these can be very daunting. It would be unfortunate if the emphasis on these dynamics in the report gave rise to the impression that urbanization is a negative process and should in some way be curbed or halted by governments. History shows that this is simply not possible. Even the most severe of anti-urbanization measures from an earlier period of Chinese history, or from the South African apartheid era, were not able to stem the flow of people to the cities in the long term. Similarly, the effects of rapid urbanization in the form of informal settlement and job creation should not simply be viewed as negative features of cities to be removed or hidden.

Urbanization should be seen as a positive phenomenon and a precondition for improving access to services, economic and social opportunities, and a better quality of life for a country's population. In most countries, cities generate the bulk of gross domestic product (GDP); they are the 'engines of economic growth' and centres of innovation. This suggests that capitalizing on the positive potentials of urban growth should be placed high on the agenda of governments, and national urban development plans should be developed as a framework for regional and local urban planning.

Seeing urbanization as a positive force also implies that all urban citizens should be made to feel 'at home' in the city.[4] This implies an acceptance and appreciation of the many different ways in which urban communities conduct their daily lives. New roles for planning involve paying attention to urban social and economic diversity, and finding ways to harmonize their coexistence. It also involves the identification and expression of social identity, such that a 'sense of place' is encouraged in urban areas rather than simply copying globally branded urban and architectural forms.

■ The environmental challenge

Over the next decades, cities and towns in all parts of the world will have to make adjustments that may be more profound than at any other time in their history. These will be in response to climate change and resource depletion; but these factors are also likely to create social conflict. Coastal settlements will face the challenge of responding to different coastlines and sea levels, some settlements will face new water shortages, while others will need to find ways of dealing with the effects of flooding – and all urban places will have to change their dependence upon oil as an energy source. Reconfiguring cities from car dependent to public transport-based and non-motorized movement systems may be the most significant spatial change that has to be faced.

What these changes imply is that governments will have to return to an interventionist role in cities not seen since the post-war period in the developed world, and perhaps never seen in parts of the developing world. Those countries which have adopted the model of the 'developmental state' will be best positioned to deal with these changes, assuming that they have the capacity and will to implement this model. Those urban governments that fail to intervene, or do not have the capacity to do so, could be left with devastated cities and depleted populations. Environmental change will place demands on a range of urban professionals and urban planners. But unless the institutional and legal frameworks are in place, and far greater numbers of planners are appropriately trained, then this significant mechanism for urban change will not be available.

■ Relationship of urban planning to the market

New approaches to planning have also recognized the need to redefine the relationship between the planning system and the economy (the market). One important implication of rapid urbanization and city growth has been an escalation in urban land prices (excluding countries where land is under public ownership) and urban development driven increasingly by land speculation and developer-led projects. This is placing unforeseen demands on urban infrastructure, as well as resulting in fragmented and inefficient urban growth and negative social and environmental impacts. The urban planning system is potentially an important tool for governments to better manage these forces; but to do this, the system needs to change.

Planning has traditionally been perceived as simply 'red tape', stifling economic progress. Unless the planning system can be seen to provide an efficient and useful service

Environmental change will place demands on a range of urban professionals and urban planners

Urbanization should be seen as a positive phenomenon and a precondition for improving access to services, economic and social opportunities, and a better quality of life

for the private sector (directing infrastructure to where it is needed and delivering commercial land speedily), it will always be subjected to attempts to bypass, subvert or corrupt it. The other side of this coin, however, is that the planning system must be firm enough to deal with the externalities of private development and to extract public financial gain (betterment, value capture, exaction and development taxes) where it is due. The degree of flexibility within any planning process may therefore vary: very firm decisions may need to be made by public authorities about environmental protection and socio-spatial exclusion; but a more flexible approach might be needed with regard to the form and direction of private-sector activity – formal and informal.

Related to the foregoing is a need to recognize that land-use regulations are generally quite good at preventing development and the protection of areas, but are not very good at making development happen. This is where the directive planning system is crucial, playing a role in directing public budgets, shaping projects, coordinating sectoral spending and negotiating with the private sector.

Specific aspects of a new role for urban planning

The previous section has set out some overarching aspects of a new role for planning. This section considers some more specific aspects of this new role, related to guiding planning values, planning processes and products, planning tools and its institutional location.

■ The guiding values of planning

There is now broad agreement within the planning field that planning is a value-driven activity and not just a technical one. Planning systems need to shift away from what were often their original objectives – using land to entrench privilege and exclusion, and controlling the location and nature of the living environments of the poor. This may well imply shifting away from objectives that have to do with aesthetics, global positioning, and ambitions of local elites to replicate American or European lifestyles, to the far more demanding objectives of achieving inclusive, productive, equitable and sustainable cities. It is necessary to recognize that such values are unlikely to be universal in the sense that they are equally important or have the same meaning everywhere. Unless planning values articulate closely with the values of the society in which it is taking place, urban planning is unlikely to be socially and institutionally embedded to the extent required for it to be effective.

■ Shifts in the form of plans

In the mid 20th century, many thought that the best way to undertake urban development was to prepare a plan, which then was expected to be followed by all those 'producing' the city. Accordingly, physical outcomes would be as shown in the plan. However, over time, it has been realized that planning agencies usually lacked sufficient power and/or stability to exercise such control over all the agencies involved in urban development. Instead, plan-makers have had to give more attention to the way in which other agencies operate, and recognize the limits of their ability to predict future development trajectories. Essentially, the purpose of planning is not just to produce planning documents, but to set in motion processes that will improve the quality of life of urban residents.

A key shift in thinking about planning activity in both developing and developed countries has been to advocate a more proactive, flexible approach to intervening in urban development trajectories than was promoted by the so-called 'master planners'. However, in some circumstances, precisely specified designs for the future may be useful, and in cases where natural environments have to be protected or avoided, then firmness and not flexibility may be required. What is important is to find the mix of agencies and instruments to maintain careful attention to promoting and safeguarding what is considered to be in the collective interest. Urban planning needs to concern itself with the qualities of space and place: the form, scale and identity of urban places which people will experience on a daily basis.

■ Shifts in planning processes

In some parts of the world, parallel with the shift away from rigid master plans has been a change in thinking about how plans are produced and who should be involved in their production and implementation. There is now widespread acceptance that effective plans cannot be produced only by trained professionals (planners), but require the input, involvement and support from communities and stakeholders. Research and experience in both the planning and development studies fields have shown the value of participatory approaches in planning, but have also shown the great difficulties and pitfalls involved in such processes. It is important to recognize that planning is inevitably political, and is usually at the heart of conflicts over land and resources. A central role for planning is the mediation of these conflicts. There is also the recognition that planners are not the only professionals to be involved in planning: a wide range of professionals in related, and often specialist, fields also need to be involved.

■ Shifts in urban form

There is some agreement that an equitable and sustainable city will have the following spatial features: higher densities but low rise; mixed uses; public transport based; spatial integration; a defined and protected open space system; and an urban edge to prevent sprawl. At the same time, there is an awareness that this spatial model may be far easier to achieve in developed countries. In developing countries, municipal governments may not have the capacity to bring about compliance with these ideas, and an urban edge may negatively affect the poor by raising urban land values and removing the possibility of settlement in a peri-urban belt beyond the edge. However, achieving these principles in different contexts remains a worthwhile goal. Promoting the 'compact city' requires a close link between planners and engineers involved with urban infrastructure, and an infrastructure plan needs to be a central element in the spatial plan. It would also benefit from a sound monitoring and

The planning system must be firm enough to deal with the externalities of private development and to extract public financial gain ... where it is due

There is now widespread acceptance that effective plans ... require the input, involvement and support from communities and stakeholders

evaluation process so that the benefits and costs of these spatial aspects could be tested.

■ 'Urban modernism' as a problematic built form model

Most cities in the world have, in part, been shaped by early 20th-century urban modernist thinking. This promotes a belief that the 'good modern city' is spacious, uncluttered, efficient, clean, ordered, offers grand views (particularly of state and civic buildings), and does not contain informal activities. This 'good city' is also assumed to have high-rise buildings, wide roads prioritizing cars, and the separation of different land uses. Currently, this urban vision takes the form of mega-projects delivering commodified versions of waterfronts, theme parks, and retail and leisure centres. This image of a desirable city is usually strongly promoted by property developers and architects, and in developing countries, by politicians who believe that this demonstrates an ability to modernize. However, this model of built form cannot produce cities that are sustainable, equitable and inclusive. In fact, it promotes the opposite by excluding the poor and encouraging unsustainable consumption patterns. Various chapters in this Global Report have pointed to alternative built forms that are more likely to achieve the new and important goals of sustainable urban development.

■ Planning with and for informality

This report has emphasized that in developing countries, many urban inhabitants secure livelihoods and shelters informally. Informality will shape the bulk of new urbanization in Africa and Asia. This report has also argued that inappropriate planning regulations have created informality and illegality, as the poor are forced to step outside of these laws in order to survive. A central challenge for planning is devising ways of supporting, protecting and including the poor and the informal in urban areas, while at the same time being careful not to destroy their livelihoods and shelters with excessively stringent legal and process requirements. Creative ideas have begun to emerge: developing new or innovative forms of tenure and land delivery that articulate with customary laws; the provision and servicing of land ahead of informal settlement; ways of retrofitting services within informally settled areas; and providing public spaces and infrastructure for informal trade.

■ Revisiting both directive and regulatory aspects of the planning system

Many efforts at planning reform in the past have focused on planning processes while ignoring planning outcomes, and have focused on the *directive planning* aspect of the system while ignoring the regulatory or land-use management aspect. Hence, attempts to introduce strategic and participatory planning processes as a way of replacing technocratic and comprehensive master planning have usually left untouched the underlying legal framework of planning. Consequently, these new ideas have simply been 'added on' as a parallel set of activities to the conventional master planning and regulatory process, while the latter has continued to operate as usual. Evidence from the transitional countries, Latin America and Africa confirms this observation.

Experience from various parts of the world shows that it is often not too difficult to change the nature of directive plans; but it is far more difficult to change the regulatory system as this usually affects people's rights in land, and sometimes requires compensation if rights are abrogated. Besides, politicians are often reluctant to change the regulatory system for a variety of reasons. Consequently, the regulatory system often contradicts the directive plan, making the latter impossible to implement. It is also more difficult to change planning outcomes as the status quo may be supported by the property development industry and individual or community views on a desirable lifestyle. Nonetheless, necessary changes to land-use management or zoning systems include allowing for a greater mix of land uses and urban forms; permitting more flexible land-use categorizations that include informal settlements; and allowing for performance-based criteria rather than use-based criteria for approving land-use change. In some developing countries, it is also important to find new ways of linking the regulatory planning system with indigenous forms of land rights and use.[5]

■ Planning and institutional integration

As urban governments become more complex and specialized, there has been a growing awareness of the need to achieve sectoral integration within government and between levels of government. One potential role of planning is to provide a mechanism for sectoral integration since all sectoral policies and programmes have spatial implications. Such a role is also important in terms of plan production and implementation as it encourages planners to work together with other urban professionals and benefit from their areas of expertise.

Different ways of achieving this have been covered in this Global Report. The South African integrated development planning approach is intended to link the work of sectoral departments to each other and to the municipal budgeting process, and to align the plan with the actions of other levels of government. Participatory budgeting processes also serve as a way of linking the work of departments to particular areas and action plans. Municipal programmes such as the Localizing Agenda 21 Programme, the Safer Cities Programme, the Healthy Cities Programme, the Sustainable Cities Programme and the Urban Management Programme have all served to link urban planning to wider urban issues and, hence, to encourage integration. Processes such as the drawing up of a CDS help to integrate the sectoral work of municipalities. Introducing cross-cutting issues, such as dealing with the MDGs, also requires different departments, professionals and levels of government to work together.

■ Planning scales

While the focus in this Global Report has been on urban planning, it is clear that planning at the urban or local scale cannot operate in isolation from planning at the regional, national or even supra-national scales. Certain urban

---

A central challenge for planning is devising ways of supporting, protecting and including the poor and the informal in urban areas, while at the same time being careful not to destroy their livelihoods and shelters with excessively stringent legal and process requirements

One potential role of planning is to provide a mechanism for sectoral integration since all sectoral policies and programmes have spatial implications

problems can only be dealt with at the regional or national scale, and certain elements of the environment and infrastructure require planning attention above the level of the urban. Achieving coordination across scales and the correct allocation of legal powers and functions at the various levels is important for urban planning. Many cities now extend well beyond their municipal boundaries and include adjacent municipalities and rural areas as well. The concept of the city-region, which has important economic potential and attractiveness, is now recognized in many parts of the world as requiring coordinated and integrated spatial planning and management.

CONTEXTUAL AND INSTITUTIONAL CHANGES NEEDED TO MAKE URBAN PLANNING MORE EFFECTIVE

A number of preconditions are necessary for achieving more effective urban planning in various parts of the world. Obviously, these preconditions will vary from region to region, and the ideas presented here are highly generalized.

Prioritizing an urban policy at the national scale

In some regions of the world, particularly in Africa and parts of Asia, there is, unfortunately, some ambiguity about the importance of urbanization, some aversion to the urbanization process, and sometimes mistaken assumptions that urban problems can be addressed mainly through increased attention to rural development. There are even international donor and aid agencies that reinforce this belief.

However, some countries have recognized the futility of this position and have moved ahead to integrate urban policy at the national scale and to highlight the importance of cities. Brazil provides a good example through the establishment of the Ministry of Cities. A major UN-Habitat objective is to have urban issues reflected in national development strategies, poverty reduction strategies and United Nations Development Assistance Frameworks.[6] A national urban policy should set out a framework for urban settlements and urbanization policy that can serve to coordinate and align national sectoral policies, and an overall set of normative criteria which can guide urban planning and development.

National constitutions and preambles to national legislation need to contain a commitment to basic principles of social and environmental justice and sustainability, and an acknowledgement of the importance of rights to access urban opportunities. For example, the Brazilian Ministry of Cities aims 'to fight social inequalities, transforming the cities into more humanized spaces, and extending the access of the population to housing, sanitation and transport'.[7] A national urban policy should also set out a national spatial perspective that considers the long-term balance between

urban and rural, and between different kinds and locations of urban settlements. The European Spatial Development Perspective is one example of such a perspective, but at a continental scale.

Planning legislation

In some parts of the world, national planning legislation is very dated and is still strongly shaped by colonial planning legislation. Yet, as this Global Report has argued, urban areas have changed significantly in recent decades and are now very different places from those that gave rise to earlier planning legislation. Moreover, in the coming decades, a set of new urban challenges will have to be faced, and governments need to be positioned to address these. An important precondition for more effective urban planning is that national legislation is up to date and is responsive to current urban issues.

An important aspect of planning legislation is that it should consider the different planning tasks and responsibilities which need to be allocated to various levels of government and administration. In some parts of the world, the planning function is highly centralized in national government, requiring even minor urban planning decisions to be approved at national level. This leads to top-down bureaucratized planning, little chance for communities and stakeholders to become involved in planning issues, and huge backlogs in the decision-making process. Depending upon issues such as the size of territory, it is likely that there will be a need for certain planning decisions to be made at a regional scale as well as the urban scale.

Decentralization of urban planning functions

Ideally, decisions on urban planning issues should be made as close as possible to those affected by them. This implies the decentralization of urban planning decisions to the urban level of government, which is also an important precondition for opening up planning debates to urban communities and stakeholders. The decentralization of urban planning decisions requires effective local governments, greater capacity in terms of urban planning professionals, and more resources at the local level. It may also require a reconsideration of municipal boundaries in areas where urban development has outgrown older administrative limits.

The urban planning function within municipalities

In many parts of the world, urban planning forms a separate department within municipalities, giving rise to the problem of achieving integration between planning and other line-function departments. Where there is poor coordination between spatial planning and other departments involved in the location of infrastructure and facilities, then urban space can become highly fragmented and inefficient. It has also been argued in this Global Report that there needs to be a much higher level of integration between spatial plans and infrastructure plans. At a municipal level, a CDS can set out

An important precondition for more effective urban planning is that national legislation is up to date and is responsive to current urban issues

Where there is poor coordination between spatial planning and other departments involved in the location of infrastructure and facilities, then urban space can become highly fragmented and inefficient an overall vision to guide the work of all sectoral departments and political representatives. Within municipalities, coordinating structures and forums need to be set up to ensure communication between departments, between levels of government and with communities and stakeholders.

Monitoring and evaluation of urban plans

This Global Report has pointed to the important role that can be played by the monitoring and evaluation of plans and planning processes, which is to assess the impact of plans and to indicate to the broader public how planning affects urban development. Yet, the use of monitoring and evaluation in planning is not widespread, partly due to a lack of capacity and the time-consuming nature of these exercises. Current research in this field points to the importance of monitoring and evaluation, even if relatively few indicators are used and there is a reliance on existing information.

Urban research and data

Planners are sometimes accused of producing unrealistic plans that do not connect with the complex realities of social, economic and spatial change in cities. One reason for this is often a lack of research and information, particularly information on spatial characteristics of cities. Frequently, useful information may be held by international agencies and research departments, but is not consolidated and made available in ways that can be accessed by professional planners. The idea of an urban observatory[8] is a useful mechanism for collating this information, as are national state of the cities reports.[9]

Research and publication on plans and planning is taking place; but it is skewed in terms of where it is being produced and there are bottlenecks in its distribution. Most planning research occurs in well-resourced universities and institutions, primarily in the developed countries, and focuses on planning issues in this part of the world. Far fewer researchers in developed countries do planning research that is relevant to developing countries, and poorly resourced universities in developing countries manage to do far less. Language is an important barrier to the dissemination and sharing of this research, particularly since most publication in planning occurs through English-language journals. For example, 31 developed countries, mostly Anglophone, account for 98 per cent of the most cited papers in planning.[10]

City planning networks for sharing information and experience

Strong international networks, websites and regular conferences are important for any profession to share information and experience, to build the profile of the profession and to encourage students to join the profession. In the case of planning, however, these networking channels are not well developed, even in developed regions. Some networks that have been functioning – for example, the International

Society of City and Regional Planners has strong representation in some regions but not in others. The Global Planners Network (GPN) is a professional network that emerged subsequent to the 2006 World Urban Forum, and is an indication of the readiness of planners to link with each other. However, these networks still need building and support, must reach to those parts of the world which do not yet have strong representation, and need to begin the process of debating planning values and approaches. Regular international professional planning conferences and websites would assist this process.

Planning education

In many developing and transitional countries, planning curricula, just like planning legislation, have not been updated for a long time and are unable to produce planning professionals that are able to address current and future urban challenges effectively. Accreditation and other quality assurance processes are uneven regionally. In many developing and transitional countries, the annual production of new planning graduates is very small, leading to major capacity constraints. China has been successful in increasing the production of new planners, since planning has taken on a central role in the development of new urban areas. Planning professionals are also increasingly mobile internationally; but their training is often highly specific to the country in which they have been educated.

Recently, planning schools have been active in building new international networks. Nine regional planning associations are now linked through the Global Planning Education Association Network (GPEAN) and hold global planning conferences every five years. Yet, capacity within the associations is uneven, relying largely on volunteer work. A strong planning schools network able to compare and debate planning education is an important precondition for more effective urban planning.

CONCLUDING REMARKS

This chapter has summarized the main findings and insights from the previous chapters in this Global Report, and has drawn on these to consider a new role for urban planning, and the requirements needed to make this new role possible.

The central argument in this report is that planning systems in many parts of the world are not up to the task of dealing with the major urban challenges of the 21st century, and need to be revisited. In some parts of the world, planning systems have contributed to the problems of spatial marginalization and exclusion of the poor. However, there is no one model planning system or approach that can be applied in all parts of the world to solve these problems. Revised planning systems must be shaped by, and be responsive to, the contexts from which they arise, and must be institutionally 'embedded' within the practices and norms of their locale. At the same time, there are common global issues to which these revised planning systems must address.

This Global Report has pointed to the important role that can be played by the monitoring and evaluation of plans and planning processes

A strong planning schools network able to compare and debate planning education is an important precondition for more effective urban planning

Many parts of the world are facing rapid urban growth and change, often under conditions of poverty and unemployment. Cities in all parts of the world are facing the challenges of climate change; more recently, all are facing these issues within the context of global economic crisis. As the growth and strength of the private sector become less certain, governments are increasingly being expected to take on a more central role, to lead development initiatives and to ensure that basic needs are met. Urban planning has an important role to play in assisting governments and civil society to meet these challenges.

If urban planning is to play a more effective role, certain preconditions are necessary. Countries need to develop a national perspective on the role of urban areas, articulated in some form of national urban policy. As the world moves to a situation in which urban populations dominate numerically, it is imperative that governments view urbanization as a positive phenomenon and a precondition for improving access to services, economic and social opportunities, and a better quality of life. This, in turn, requires that urban planning is institutionally located in a way that allows it to play a key role in creating urban opportunities through responsive and collaborative processes. Urban planning can play a crucial integrating role in terms of coordinating the actions of different functions, tiers of government and stakeholders; but this requires careful institutional design. Finally, planning requires strengthening through stronger professional organizations and networks, more effective planning education, better urban databases and more robust planning research.

Countries need to develop a national perspective on the role of urban areas, articulated in some form of national urban policy

NOTES

1 UN Millennium Project, 2005.
2 Rakodi and Firman, 2008.
3 See the case of Enugu (Ikejiofor, 2008).

4 UN Millennium Project, 2005.
5 Ikejiofor, 2008.
6 UN-Habitat, 2007b.
7 Irazábal, 2008a.

8 UN-Habitat Urban Observatory Programme: http://ww2.unhabitat.org/programmes/guo/.
9 Currently encouraged by UN-Habitat, which publishes *The*

State of the World's Cities report every two years.
10 King (2004) in Stiftel and Mukhopadhyay (2007).

PART VI
STATISTICAL ANNEX

GENERAL DISCLAIMER

The designations employed and presentation of the data do not imply
the expression of any opinion whatsoever on the part of the Secretariat
of the United Nations concerning the legal status of any country,
city or area or of its authorities, or concerning the delimitation of
its frontiers or boundaries.

TECHNICAL NOTES

The Statistical Annex comprises 16 tables covering such broad statistical categories as demography, households, housing, economic and social indicators. The annex is divided into three sections presenting data at the regional, country and city levels. Tables A.1 to A.6 present regional-level data grouped by selected criteria of economic and development achievements, as well as geographic distribution. Tables B.1 to B.7 contain country-level data and Tables C.1 to C.3 are devoted to city-level data. Data have been compiled from various international sources, from national statistical offices and from the United Nations.

EXPLANATION OF SYMBOLS

The following symbols have been used in presenting data throughout the Statistical Annex:

category not applicable ..
data not available ...
magnitude zero –

COUNTRY GROUPINGS AND STATISTICAL AGGREGATES

World major groupings

More developed regions: All countries and areas of Europe and Northern America, as well as Australia, Japan and New Zealand.

Less developed regions: All countries and areas of Africa, Latin America, Asia (excluding Japan) and Oceania (excluding Australia and New Zealand).

Least developed countries: Afghanistan, Angola, Bangladesh, Benin, Bhutan, Burkina Faso, Burundi, Cambodia, Cape Verde, Central African Republic, Chad, Comoros, Democratic Republic of the Congo, Djibouti, Equatorial Guinea, Eritrea, Ethiopia, Gambia, Guinea, Guinea-Bissau, Haiti, Kiribati, Lao People's Democratic Republic, Lesotho, Liberia, Madagascar, Malawi, Maldives, Mali, Mauritania, Mozambique, Myanmar, Nepal, Niger, Rwanda, Samoa, São Tomé and Príncipe, Senegal, Sierra Leone, Solomon Islands, Somalia, Sudan, Timor-Leste, Togo, Tuvalu, Uganda, United Republic of Tanzania, Vanuatu, Yemen, Zambia.

Small Island Developing States:[1] American Samoa, Anguilla, Antigua and Barbuda, Aruba, Bahamas, Bahrain, Barbados, Belize, British Virgin Islands, Cape Verde, Comoros, Cook Islands, Cuba, Dominica, Dominican Republic, Fiji, French Polynesia, Grenada, Guam, Guinea-Bissau, Guyana, Haiti, Jamaica, Kiribati, Maldives, Marshall Islands, Mauritius, Micronesia (Federated States of), Montserrat, Nauru, Netherlands Antilles, New Caledonia, Niue, Northern Mariana Islands, Palau, Papua New Guinea, Puerto Rico, Saint Kitts and Nevis, Saint Lucia, Saint Vincent and the Grenadines, Samoa, São Tomé and Príncipe, Seychelles, Solomon Islands, Suriname, Timor-Leste, Tonga, Trinidad and Tobago, Tuvalu, United States Virgin Islands, Vanuatu.

Sub-Saharan Africa: Angola, Benin, Botswana, Burkina Faso, Burundi, Cameroon, Cape Verde, Central African Republic, Chad, Comoros, Congo, Côte d'Ivoire, Democratic Republic of the Congo, Djibouti, Egypt, Equatorial Guinea, Eritrea, Ethiopia, Gabon, Gambia, Ghana, Guinea, Guinea-Bissau, Kenya, Lesotho, Liberia, Madagascar, Malawi, Mali, Mauritania, Mauritius, Morocco, Mozambique, Namibia, Niger, Nigeria, Réunion, Rwanda, Saint Helena, São Tomé and Príncipe, Senegal, Seychelles, Sierra Leone, Somalia, South Africa, Sudan, Swaziland, Togo, Uganda, United Republic of Tanzania, Zambia, Zimbabwe.

Countries in the Human Development Index (HDI) aggregates[2]

High human development (HDI 0.800 and above): Albania, Antigua and Barbuda, Argentina, Australia, Austria, Bahamas, Bahrain, Barbados, Belarus, Belgium, Bosnia and Herzegovina, Brazil, Brunei Darussalam, Bulgaria, Canada, Chile, Hong Kong SAR of China, Costa Rica, Croatia, Cuba, Cyprus, Czech Republic, Democratic People's Republic of Korea, Denmark, Estonia, Finland, France, Germany, Greece, Hungary, Iceland, Ireland, Israel, Italy, Japan, Kuwait, Latvia, Libyan Arab Jamahiriya, Lithuania, Luxembourg, Malaysia, Malta, Mauritius, Mexico, Netherlands, New Zealand, Norway, Oman, Panama, Poland, Portugal, Qatar, Romania, Russian Federation, Saint Kitts and Nevis, Saudi Arabia, Seychelles, Singapore, Slovakia, Slovenia, Spain, Sweden, Switzerland, The former Yugoslav Republic of Macedonia, Tonga, Trinidad and Tobago, United Arab Emirates, United Kingdom, United States of America, Uruguay.

Medium human development (HDI 0.500–0.799): Algeria, Armenia, Azerbaijan, Bangladesh, Belize, Bhutan, Bolivia, Botswana, Cambodia, Cameroon, Cape Verde, China, Colombia, Comoros, Congo, Djibouti, Dominica, Dominican Republic, Ecuador, Egypt, El Salvador, Equatorial Guinea, Fiji, Gabon, Gambia, Georgia, Ghana, Grenada, Guatemala, Guyana, Haiti, Honduras, India, Indonesia, Iran (Islamic Republic of), Jamaica, Jordan, Kazakhstan, Kenya, Kyrgyzstan, Lao Peoples Democratic Republic, Lebanon, Lesotho, Madagascar, Maldives, Mauritania, Moldova, Mongolia, Morocco, Myanmar, Namibia, Nepal, Nicaragua, Occupied Palestinian, Pakistan, Papua New Guinea, Paraguay, Peru, Philippines, Saint Lucia, Saint Vincent and the Grenadines, Samoa, São Tomé and Príncipe, South Africa, Sudan, Solomon Islands, Sri Lanka, Suriname, Swaziland, Syrian Arab Republic, Tajikistan, Thailand, Timor-Leste, Togo, Tunisia, Turkey, Turkmenistan, Uganda, Ukraine, Uzbekistan, Vanuatu, Venezuela (Bolivarian Republic of), Viet Nam, Yemen, Zimbabwe.

Low human development (HDI 0.500 and below): Angola, Benin, Burkina Faso, Burundi, Central African Republic, Chad, Côte d'Ivoire, Democratic Republic of the Congo, Eritrea, Ethiopia, Guinea, Guinea-Bissau, Malawi, Mali, Mozambique, Niger, Nigeria, Rwanda, Senegal, Sierra Leone, United Republic of Tanzania, Zambia.

Countries in the income aggregates[3]

The World Bank classifies all member economies and all other economies with populations of more than 30,000. In the 2009 *World Development Report*, economies are divided among income groups according to 2007 gross national income (GNI) per capita, calculated using the World Bank Atlas method. The groups are as follows.

High income: Andorra, Antigua and Barbuda, Aruba, Australia, Austria, Bahamas, Bahrain, Barbados, Belgium, Bermuda, Brunei Darussalam, Canada, Cayman Islands, Channel Islands, Cyprus, Czech Republic, Denmark, Equatorial Guinea, Estonia, Faeroe Islands, Finland, France, French Polynesia, Germany, Greece, Greenland, Guam, Hong Kong SAR of China, Hungary, Iceland, Ireland, Isle of Man, Israel, Italy, Japan, Kuwait, Liechtenstein, Luxembourg, Macao SAR of China, Malta, Monaco, Netherlands Antilles, Netherlands, New Caledonia, New Zealand, Northern Mariana Islands, Norway, Oman, Portugal, Puerto Rico, Qatar, Republic of Korea, San Marino, Saudi Arabia, Singapore, Slovakia, Slovenia, Spain, Sweden, Switzerland, Trinidad and Tobago, United Arab Emirates, United Kingdom, United States of America, United States Virgin Islands.

Upper-middle income: American Samoa, Argentina, Belarus, Belize, Botswana, Brazil, Bulgaria, Chile, Costa Rica, Croatia, Cuba, Dominica, Fiji, Gabon, Grenada, Jamaica, Kazakhstan, Latvia, Lebanon, Libyan Arab Jamahiriya, Lithuania, Malaysia, Mauritius, Mayotte, Mexico, Montenegro, Palau, Panama, Poland, Romania, Russian Federation, Serbia, Seychelles, South Africa, Saint Kitts and Nevis, Saint Lucia, Saint Vincent and the Grenadines, Suriname, Turkey, Uruguay, Venezuela.

Lower-middle income: Albania, Algeria, Angola, Armenia, Azerbaijan, Bhutan, Bolivia, Bosnia and Herzegovina, Cameroon, Cape Verde, China, Colombia, Congo, Djibouti, Dominican Republic, Ecuador, Egypt, El Salvador, Georgia, Guatemala, Guyana, Honduras, India, Indonesia, Iran (Islamic Republic of), Iraq, Jordan, Kiribati, Lesotho, Maldives, Marshall Islands, Micronesia (Federated States of), Moldova, Mongolia, Morocco, Namibia, Nicaragua, Occupied Palestinian Territory, Paraguay, Peru, Philippines, Samoa, Sri Lanka, Sudan, Swaziland, Syrian Arab Republic, The former Yugoslav Republic of Macedonia, Thailand, Timor-Leste, Tonga, Tunisia, Turkmenistan, Ukraine, Vanuatu.

Low income: Afghanistan, Bangladesh, Benin, Burkina Faso, Burundi, Cambodia, Central African Republic, Chad, Comoros, Côte d'Ivoire, Democratic Peoples Republic of Korea, Democratic Republic of the Congo, Eritrea, Ethiopia, Gambia, Ghana, Guinea, Guinea-Bissau, Haiti, Kenya, Kyrgyzstan, Lao Peoples Democratic Republic, Liberia, Madagascar, Malawi, Mali, Mauritania, Mozambique, Myanmar, Nepal, Niger, Nigeria, Pakistan, Papua New Guinea, Rwanda, São Tomé and Príncipe, Senegal, Sierra Leone, Solomon Islands, Somalia, Tajikistan, Tanzania, Togo, Uganda, Uzbekistan, Viet Nam, Yemen, Zambia, Zimbabwe.

Sub-regional aggregates

■ Africa

Eastern Africa: Burundi, Comoros, Djibouti, Eritrea, Ethiopia, Kenya, Madagascar, Malawi, Mauritius, Mozambique, Réunion, Rwanda, Seychelles, Somalia, Uganda, United Republic of Tanzania, Zambia, Zimbabwe.
Middle Africa: Angola, Cameroon, Central African Republic, Chad, Congo, Democratic Republic of the Congo, Equatorial Guinea, Gabon, São Tomé and Príncipe.
Northern Africa: Algeria, Egypt, Libyan Arab Jamahiriya, Morocco, Sudan, Tunisia, Western Sahara.
Southern Africa: Botswana, Lesotho, Namibia, South Africa, Swaziland.
Western Africa: Benin, Burkina Faso, Cape Verde, Côte d'Ivoire, Gambia, Ghana, Guinea, Guinea-Bissau, Liberia, Mali, Mauritania, Niger, Nigeria, Saint Helena, Senegal, Sierra Leone, Togo.

■ Asia

Eastern Asia: China, Hong Kong SAR of China, Macao SAR of China, Democratic People's Republic of Korea, Japan, Mongolia, Republic of Korea.
South-Central Asia: Afghanistan, Bangladesh, Bhutan, India, Iran (Islamic Republic of), Kazakhstan, Kyrgyzstan, Maldives, Nepal, Pakistan, Sri Lanka, Tajikistan, Turkmenistan, Uzbekistan.
South-Eastern Asia: Brunei Darussalam, Cambodia, Indonesia, Lao People's Democratic Republic, Malaysia, Myanmar, Philippines, Singapore, Thailand, Timor-Leste, Viet Nam.

Western Asia: Armenia, Azerbaijan, Bahrain, Cyprus, Georgia, Iraq, Israel, Jordan, Kuwait, Lebanon, Occupied Palestinian Territory, Oman, Qatar, Saudi Arabia, Syrian Arab Republic, Turkey, United Arab Emirates, Yemen.

■ Europe

Eastern Europe: Belarus, Bulgaria, Czech Republic, Hungary, Moldova, Poland, Romania, Russian Federation, Slovakia, Ukraine.
Northern Europe: Channel Islands, Denmark, Estonia, Faeroe Islands, Finland, Iceland, Ireland, Isle of Man, Latvia, Lithuania, Norway, Sweden, United Kingdom.
Southern Europe: Albania, Andorra, Bosnia and Herzegovina, Croatia, Gibraltar, Greece, Holy See, Italy, Malta, Montenegro, Portugal, San Marino, Serbia, Slovenia, Spain, The former Yugoslav Republic of Macedonia.
Western Europe: Austria, Belgium, France, Germany, Liechtenstein, Luxembourg, Monaco, Netherlands, Switzerland.

■ Latin America and the Caribbean

Caribbean: Anguilla, Antigua and Barbuda, Aruba, Bahamas, Barbados, British Virgin Islands, Cayman Islands, Cuba, Dominica, Dominican Republic, Grenada, Guadeloupe, Haiti, Jamaica, Martinique, Montserrat, Netherlands Antilles, Puerto Rico, Saint Kitts and Nevis, Saint Lucia, Saint Vincent and the Grenadines, Trinidad and Tobago, Turks and Caicos Islands, United States Virgin Islands.
Central America: Belize, Costa Rica, El Salvador, Guatemala, Honduras, Mexico, Nicaragua, Panama.
South America: Argentina, Bolivia, Brazil, Chile, Colombia, Ecuador, Falkland Islands (Malvinas), French Guiana, Guyana, Paraguay, Peru, Suriname, Uruguay, Venezuela (Bolivarian Republic of).

■ Northern America

Bermuda, Canada, Greenland, Saint-Pierre-et-Miquelon, United States of America.

■ Oceania

Australia/New Zealand: Australia, New Zealand.
Melanesia: Fiji, New Caledonia, Papua New Guinea, Solomon Islands, Vanuatu.
Micronesia: Guam, Kiribati, Marshall Islands, Micronesia (Federated States of), Nauru, Northern Mariana Islands, Palau.
Polynesia: American Samoa, Cook Islands, French Polynesia, Niue, Pitcairn, Samoa, Tokelau, Tonga, Tuvalu, Wallis and Futuna Islands.

NOMENCLATURE AND ORDER OF PRESENTATION

Tables A.1 to A.6 contain regional data, grouped in income, human development and geographic aggregates. Tables B.1 to B.7 and C.1 to C.3 contain country- and city-level data, respectively. In these tables, the countries or areas are listed in English alphabetical order within the macro-regions of Africa, Asia, Europe, Latin America, Northern America and Oceania. Countries or area names are presented in the form commonly used within the United Nations Secretariat for statistical purposes. Due to space limitations, the short name is used – for example, the United Kingdom of Great Britain and Northern Ireland is referred to as 'United Kingdom'.

DEFINITION OF TERMS

Access to electricity: percentage of households which, within their housing unit, are connected to electricity.

Access to piped water: percentage of households which, within their housing unit, are connected to piped water.

Access to sewerage: percentage of households which, within their housing unit, are connected to sewerage.

Access to telephone: percentage of households which, within their housing unit, are connected to telephone.

Gini index: the extent to which the distribution of income (or, in some cases, consumption expenditure) or assets (such as land) among individuals or households within an economy deviates from a perfectly equal distribution. A Lorenz curve plots the cumulative percentages of total income received against the cumulative number of recipients, starting with the poorest individual or household. The Gini index measures the area between the Lorenz curve and a hypothetical line of absolute equality, expressed as a percentage of the maximum area under the line. Thus, a Gini index of 0 represents perfect equality, while an index of 1 implies absolute inequality.

Gross national income: the sum of value added by all resident producers plus any product taxes (less subsidies) not included in the valuation of output plus net receipts of primary income (compensation of employees and property income) from abroad. Data are in current US dollars converted using the World Bank Atlas method.

Gross national income per capita: gross national income (GNI) divided by mid-year population. GNI per capita in US dollars is converted using the World Bank Atlas method.

Gross national income PPP: gross national income converted to international dollars using purchasing power parity (PPP) rates. An international dollar has the same purchasing power over GNI as a US dollar has in the United States of America.

Household: the concept of household is based on the arrangements made by persons, individually or in groups, for providing themselves with food or other essentials for living. A household may be either:

1 A one-person household: a person who makes provision for his or her own food or other essentials for living without combining with any other person to form a part of a multi-person household.
2 A multi-person household: a group of two or more persons living together who make common provision for

food or other essentials for living. The persons in the group may pool their incomes and may, to a greater or lesser extent, have a common budget; they may be related or unrelated persons or constitute a combination of persons both related and unrelated. This concept of household is known as the 'housekeeping' concept. It does not assume that the number of households and housing units is equal. Although the concept of housing unit implies that it is a space occupied by one household, it may also be occupied by more than one household or by a part of a household (e.g. two nuclear households that share one housing unit for economic reasons or one household in a polygamous society routinely occupying two or more housing units).

Household connection to improved drinking water: percentage of households which, within their housing unit, are connected to any of the following types of water supply for drinking: piped water, public tap, borehole or pump, protected well, protected spring or rainwater.

Improved drinking water coverage: percentage of people using improved drinking water sources or delivery points. Improved drinking water technologies are more likely to provide safe drinking water than those characterized as unimproved. **Improved drinking water sources**: piped water into dwelling, plot or yard; public tap/standpipe; tube well/borehole; protected dug well; protected spring; rainwater collection. **Unimproved drinking water sources**: unprotected dug well; unprotected spring; cart with small tank/drum; bottled water;[4] tanker-truck; surface water (river, dam, lake, pond, stream, canal, irrigation channels).

Improved sanitation coverage: percentage of people using improved sanitation facilities. Improved sanitation facilities are more likely to prevent human contact with human excreta than unimproved facilities.

International poverty line: based on nationally representative primary household surveys conducted by national statistical offices or by private agencies under the supervision of government or international agencies and obtained from government statistical offices and World Bank country departments. **Population below US$1 a day** and **Population below US$2 a day**: percentages of the population living on less than US$1.08 a day and US$2.15 a day at 1993 international prices (equivalent to US$1 and US$2 in 1985 prices, adjusted for purchasing power parity).

Level of urbanization: percentage of the population residing in places classified as urban. Urban and rural settlements are defined in the national context and vary among countries (the definitions of urban are generally national definitions incorporated within the latest census).

Motor vehicles: includes cars, buses and freight vehicles but not two-wheelers.

National poverty line: based on the World Bank's country poverty assessments.

Persons in housing units: number of persons resident in housing units.

Population, rural: mid-year estimates and projections (medium variant) of the population residing in human settlements classified as rural (see also '**Population, urban**' below).

Population, total: mid-year population estimates and projections for the world, region, countries or areas. The Population Division of the United Nations Department of Economic and Social Affairs updates, every two years, population estimates and projections by incorporating new data, new estimates and new analyses of data on population, fertility, mortality and international migration. Data from new population censuses and/or demographic surveys are used to verify and update old estimates of population or demographic indicators, or to make new ones and to check the validity of the assumptions made in the projections. Population rate of change (calculated by UN-Habitat) refers to the average annual percentage change of population during the indicated period for each country, major regions and global totals. The formula used throughout the annex is as follows: $r = [(1/t) \times \ln(A2/A1)] \times 100$, where 'A1' is a value at any given year; 'A2' is a value at any given year later than the year of 'A1'; 't' is the year interval between 'A1' and 'A2'; and 'ln' is the natural logarithm function.

Population, urban: mid-year population of areas defined as urban in each country and reported to the United Nations. Estimates of the world's urban population would change significantly if China, India and a few other populous nations were to change their definition of urban centres. According to China's State Statistical Bureau, by the end of 1996 urban residents accounted for about 43 per cent of China's population, while in 1994 only 20 per cent of the population was considered urban. In addition to the continuous migration of people from rural to urban areas, one of the main reasons for this shift was the rapid growth in the hundreds of towns reclassified as cities in recent years. Because the estimates in the table are based on national definitions of what constitutes a city or metropolitan area, cross-country comparisons should be made with caution.

Population density: mid-year population divided by land area in square kilometres.

Railways: length of railway route available for train service, irrespective of the number of parallel tracks. Passengers carried by railway are the number of passengers transported by rail multiplied by kilometres travelled. Goods hauled by railway are the volume of goods transported by railway, measured in metric tonnes multiplied by kilometres travelled.

Roads: motorways, highways, main or national roads, and secondary or regional roads. A motorway is a road specially designed and built for motor vehicles that separates the traffic flowing in opposite directions. **Total road network**: includes motorways, highways and main or national roads, secondary or regional roads, and all other roads in a country. **Paved roads:** roads surfaced with crushed stone (macadam) and hydrocarbon binder or bitumized agents, with concrete or with cobblestones, as a percentage of all of the country's roads measured in length. Goods hauled by road are the volume of goods transported by road vehicles, measured in millions of metric tonnes multiplied by kilometres travelled.

Survey year: the year in which the underlying data were collected.

Urban poverty rate: percentage of the urban population living below the national urban poverty line.

Urban slum dwellers: individuals residing in housing with one or more of the following conditions: inadequate drinking water; inadequate sanitation; poor structural quality/durability of housing; overcrowding; and insecurity of tenure.

Urban agglomerations and capital cities: the term 'urban agglomeration' refers to the population contained within the contours of a contiguous territory inhabited at urban density levels without regard to administrative boundaries. It usually incorporates the population in a city or town plus that in the suburban areas lying outside of, but being adjacent to, the city boundaries. Whenever possible, data classified according to the concept of urban agglomeration are used. However, some countries do not produce data according to the concept of urban agglomeration, but use instead that of the metropolitan area or city proper. If possible, such data are adjusted to conform to the concept of urban agglomeration. When sufficient information is not available to permit such an adjustment, data based on the concept of city proper or metropolitan area are used. The sources listed online indicate whether data were adjusted to conform to the urban agglomeration concept or whether a different concept was used. Table C.1 contains revised estimates and projections for all urban agglomerations comprising 750,000 or more inhabitants.

SOURCES OF DATA

The Statistical Tables have been compiled from the following UN-Habitat databases:

UN-Habitat (United Nations Human Settlements Programme), Household Projections Project, 2002;
UN-Habitat (United Nations Human Settlements Programme), Urban Info 2006;
UN-Habitat (United Nations Human Settlements Programme), Urban Info 2008.

In addition, various statistical publications from the United Nations and other international organizations have been used. These include:

United Nations Department of Economic and Social Affairs, Population Division (2008) *World Urbanization Prospects: The 2007 Revision*, United Nations, New York;
United Nations Development Programme (2007) *Human Development Report 2007/2008*, New York, http://unstats.un.org/unsd/Demographic/products/dyb/dyb2006.htm
United Nations Statistics Division, Demographic and Social Statistics (2008) *Demographic Yearbook 2006*, United Nations, New York;
World Bank (2002) *World Development Indicators 2002*, World Bank, Washington, DC;
World Bank (2006) *World Development Indicators 2006*, World Bank, Washington, DC;
World Bank (2007) *World Development Indicators 2007*, World Bank, Washington, DC;
World Bank (2008) *World Development Indicators 2008*, World Bank, Washington, DC;
World Bank (2009) *World Development Report 2009*, World Bank, Washington, DC;
World Health Organization (WHO) and United Nations Children's Fund (UNICEF) Joint Monitoring Programme for Water Supply and Sanitation (JMP) (2008) *Progress on Drinking Water and Sanitation: Special Focus on Sanitation 2008*, WHO and UNICEF, Geneva and New York, www.who.int/water_sanitation_health/monitoring/jmp2008/en/index.html

NOTES

1 As classified by United Nations Department of Economic and Social Affairs (UNDESA); see www.sidsnet.org/sids_list.html for detail.

2 As classified by the United Nations Development Programme (UNDP); see *Human Development Report 2007/2008* for detail.

3 As classified by the United Nations Development Programme; see *World Development Report 2009* for detail.

4 Bottled water is considered improved only when the household uses water from an improved source for cooking and personal hygiene.

DATA TABLES

TABLE A.1 – REGIONAL AGGREGATES

Total Population Size, Rate of Change and Population Density

	Estimates and projections ('000)				Rate of change (%)			Population density (people/km²)	
	2000	2010	2020	2030	2000–2010	2010–2020	2020–2030	2000	2030
WORLD	6,124,123	6,906,558	7,667,090	8,317,707	1.20	1.04	0.81	45	61
World Major Aggregates									
More Developed Regions	1,194,199	1,232,457	1,253,852	1,260,770	0.32	0.17	0.06	22	24
Less Developed Regions	4,929,924	5,674,101	6,413,238	7,056,937	1.41	1.22	0.96	59	85
Least Developed Countries	679,447	863,394	1,075,104	1,300,634	2.40	2.19	1.90	33	63
Other Less Developed Countries	4,250,477	4,810,707	5,338,134	5,756,303	1.24	1.04	0.75	68	91
Less Developed Regions, excluding China	3,652,859	4,314,679	4,983,415	5,589,441	1.67	1.44	1.15	50	76
Small Island Developing States	53,319	60,411	67,231	73,556	1.25	1.07	0.90	22	30
Sub-Saharan Africa	679,873	866,948	1,081,029	1,308,461	2.43	2.21	1.91	28	54
Human Development Index Aggregates									
High Human Development	1,603,973	1,708,347	1,787,387	1,840,035	0.63	0.45	0.29	24	27
Medium Human Development	3,976,617	4,501,420	5,004,032	5,410,334	1.24	1.06	0.78	85	115
Low Human Development	445,468	578,023	731,817	897,105	2.60	2.36	2.04	32	64
Income Aggregates									
High Income	987,435	1,053,630	1,101,399	1,134,496	0.65	0.44	0.30	28	32
Middle Income	4,014,851	4,459,928	4,866,822	5,173,586	1.05	0.87	0.61	52	67
Upper-middle income	788,894	847,129	895,683	929,078	0.71	0.56	0.37	19	23
Lower-middle income	3,225,957	3,612,799	3,971,139	4,244,508	1.13	0.95	0.67	91	120
Low Income	1,120,061	1,390,855	1,696,423	2,007,007	2.17	1.99	1.68	51	92
Geographic Aggregates									
Africa	820,959	1,032,013	1,270,528	1,518,310	2.29	2.08	1.78	27	50
Eastern Africa	257,294	332,107	419,782	511,524	2.55	2.34	1.98	40	80
Middle Africa	97,765	129,583	169,062	214,994	2.82	2.66	2.40	15	33
Northern Africa	174,435	206,295	239,526	268,296	1.68	1.49	1.13	20	31
Southern Africa	51,950	56,592	59,254	61,788	0.86	0.46	0.42	19	23
Western Africa	239,515	307,436	382,903	461,709	2.50	2.20	1.87	39	75
Asia	3,704,838	4,166,308	4,596,189	4,930,983	1.17	0.98	0.70	116	155
Eastern Asia	1,476,295	1,562,576	1,631,368	1,662,797	0.57	0.43	0.19	126	141
South-Central Asia	1,516,156	1,777,379	2,032,724	2,246,028	1.59	1.34	1.00	141	208
South-Eastern Asia	519,996	594,214	658,591	710,602	1.33	1.03	0.76	116	158
Western Asia	192,390	232,139	273,506	311,556	1.88	1.64	1.30	40	64
Europe	728,501	730,478	722,060	706,908	0.03	-0.12	-0.21	32	31
Eastern Europe	304,870	290,755	275,701	258,344	-0.47	-0.53	-0.65	16	14
Northern Europe	94,341	98,353	102,008	104,973	0.42	0.36	0.29	52	58
Southern Europe	145,801	152,912	153,896	152,292	0.48	0.06	-0.10	111	116
Western Europe	183,489	188,458	190,455	191,299	0.27	0.11	0.04	166	173
Latin America and the Caribbean	523,048	593,697	659,562	712,841	1.27	1.05	0.78	25	35
Caribbean	38,617	42,300	45,664	48,357	0.91	0.77	0.57	165	206
Central America	135,587	153,657	172,095	187,152	1.25	1.13	0.84	55	75
South America	348,844	397,740	441,803	477,332	1.31	1.05	0.77	20	27
Northern America	315,672	348,574	379,270	405,429	0.99	0.84	0.67	14	19
Oceania	31,106	35,489	39,482	43,236	1.32	1.07	0.91	4	5
Australia/New Zealand	22,993	25,647	28,033	30,182	1.09	0.89	0.74	3	4
Melanesia	7,003	8,588	10,058	11,536	2.04	1.58	1.37	13	21
Micronesia	497	575	648	717	1.46	1.20	1.01	160	231
Polynesia	613	679	743	801	1.02	0.90	0.75	73	95

Sources: United Nations Department of Economic and Social Affairs, Population Division (2008) *World Urbanization Prospects: The 2007 Revision*, United Nations, New York; United Nations Statistics Division, Demographic and Social Statistics: *Demographic Yearbook 2006*. Figures in regional, income or development aggregates are calculated on the basis of country/area level data from Table B.1.

Note: Lists of countries/areas in aggregates are presented in the Technical Notes.

TABLE A.2

Urban and Rural Population Size and Rate of Change

	Urban population							Rural population						
	Estimates and projections ('000)				Rate of change (%)			Estimates and projections ('000)				Rate of change (%)		
	2000	2010	2020	2030	2000–2010	2010–2020	2020–2030	2000	2010	2020	2030	2000–2010	2010–2020	2020–2030
WORLD	2,853,909	3,494,607	4,209,669	4,965,081	2.03	1.86	1.65	3,270,214	3,411,951	3,457,421	3,352,627	0.42	0.13	-0.31
World Major Aggregates														
More Developed Regions	872,925	924,702	972,322	1,015,630	0.58	0.50	0.44	321,274	307,755	281,530	245,141	-0.43	-0.89	-1.38
Less Developed Regions	1,980,984	2,569,905	3,237,347	3,949,451	2.60	2.31	1.99	2,948,940	3,104,196	3,175,891	3,107,486	0.51	0.23	-0.22
Least Developed Countries	168,625	254,111	376,042	539,448	4.10	3.92	3.61	510,822	609,283	699,062	761,186	1.76	1.37	0.85
Other Less Developed Countries	1,812,359	2,315,794	2,861,305	3,410,002	2.45	2.12	1.75	2,438,118	2,494,913	2,476,829	2,346,300	0.23	-0.07	-0.54
Less Developed Regions, excluding China	1,519,518	1,954,765	2,472,444	3,060,484	2.52	2.35	2.13	2,133,341	2,359,914	2,510,972	2,528,957	1.01	0.62	0.07
Small Island Developing States	27,813	33,451	39,468	45,700	1.85	1.65	1.47	25,120	26,501	27,235	27,266	0.54	0.27	0.01
Sub-Saharan Africa	222,733	323,525	458,187	630,351	3.73	3.48	3.19	457,139	543,423	622,842	678,110	1.73	1.36	0.85
Human Development Index Aggregates														
High Human Development	1,185,121	1,307,876	1,417,927	1,511,730	0.99	0.81	0.64	294,473	283,859	262,569	232,884	-0.37	-0.78	-1.20
Medium Human Development	1,458,099	1,895,282	2,389,249	2,908,099	2.62	2.32	1.97	2,555,842	2,621,409	2,608,333	2,477,813	0.25	-0.05	-0.51
Low Human Development	135,150	203,556	298,266	421,367	4.10	3.82	3.46	378,767	456,112	527,171	576,685	1.86	1.45	0.90
Income Aggregates														
High Income	749,818	823,936	888,801	945,537	0.94	0.76	0.62	253,585	244,734	226,128	200,584	-0.36	-0.79	-1.20
Middle Income	1,780,349	2,209,423	2,667,114	3,118,150	3.77	3.20	2.58	2,234,101	2,250,048	2,199,180	2,054,849	-0.53	-1.08	-1.85
Upper-middle income	564,839	635,928	700,504	753,851	1.19	0.97	0.73	209,097	195,441	178,456	158,086	-0.68	-0.91	-1.21
Lower-middle income	1,215,510	1,573,495	1,966,610	2,364,299	2.58	2.23	1.84	2,025,004	2,054,607	2,020,724	1,896,763	0.15	-0.17	-0.63
Low Income	321,813	458,901	651,067	898,462	3.55	3.50	3.22	798,254	931,946	1,045,357	1,108,545	1.55	1.15	0.59
Geographic Aggregates														
Africa	295,131	412,190	566,229	759,402	3.34	3.18	2.94	525,828	619,823	704,299	758,909	1.64	1.28	0.75
Eastern Africa	53,369	78,786	117,253	172,529	3.90	3.98	3.86	203,925	253,321	302,529	338,994	2.17	1.78	1.14
Middle Africa	36,348	55,636	83,115	118,897	4.26	4.01	3.58	61,416	73,947	85,947	96,097	1.86	1.50	1.12
Northern Africa	84,431	107,312	134,654	164,519	2.40	2.27	2.00	90,004	98,984	104,872	103,777	0.95	0.58	-0.10
Southern Africa	27,979	33,264	37,792	42,484	1.73	1.28	1.17	23,971	23,329	21,463	19,304	-0.27	-0.83	-1.06
Western Africa	93,004	137,194	193,415	260,973	3.89	3.43	3.00	146,512	170,242	189,488	200,736	1.50	1.07	0.58
Asia	1,372,686	1,769,616	2,211,851	2,669,175	2.54	2.23	1.88	2,332,152	2,396,692	2,384,338	2,261,808	0.27	-0.05	-0.53
Eastern Asia	596,765	757,180	911,420	1,037,539	2.38	1.85	1.30	879,530	805,395	719,948	625,258	-0.88	-1.12	-1.41
South-Central Asia	446,597	571,987	745,666	966,262	2.47	2.65	2.59	1,069,560	1,205,392	1,287,058	1,279,766	1.20	0.66	-0.06
South-Eastern Asia	206,683	286,579	365,769	439,465	3.27	2.44	1.84	313,314	307,636	292,822	271,137	-0.18	-0.49	-0.77
Western Asia	122,641	153,870	188,995	225,909	2.27	2.06	1.78	69,748	78,269	84,510	85,647	1.15	0.77	0.13
Europe	520,270	530,248	539,752	550,287	0.19	0.18	0.19	208,231	200,230	182,308	156,621	-0.39	-0.94	-1.52
Eastern Europe	208,075	198,951	192,987	188,923	-0.45	-0.30	-0.21	96,795	91,803	82,714	69,421	-0.53	-1.04	-1.75
Northern Europe	78,697	83,050	87,590	91,933	0.54	0.53	0.48	15,644	15,303	14,418	13,040	-0.22	-0.60	-1.00
Southern Europe	95,325	103,170	108,430	113,089	0.79	0.50	0.42	50,476	49,742	45,466	39,203	-0.15	-0.90	-1.48
Western Europe	138,173	145,077	150,744	156,341	0.49	0.38	0.36	45,316	43,381	39,711	34,958	-0.44	-0.88	-1.27
Latin America and the Caribbean	394,099	471,177	542,804	603,385	1.79	1.42	1.06	128,949	122,519	116,758	109,456	-0.51	-0.48	-0.65
Caribbean	23,787	28,288	32,669	36,527	1.73	1.44	1.12	14,830	14,013	12,995	11,830	-0.57	-0.75	-0.94
Central America	93,130	110,136	128,480	145,427	1.68	1.54	1.24	42,457	43,520	43,614	41,725	0.25	0.02	-0.44
South America	277,182	332,753	381,654	421,431	1.83	1.37	0.99	71,662	64,986	60,149	55,900	-0.98	-0.77	-0.73
Northern America	249,824	286,316	320,859	351,430	1.36	1.14	0.91	65,847	62,258	58,410	53,999	-0.56	-0.64	-0.79
Oceania	21,899	25,059	28,175	31,401	1.35	1.17	1.08	9,207	10,430	11,308	11,835	1.25	0.81	0.46
Australia/New Zealand	19,984	22,754	25,291	27,608	1.30	1.06	0.88	3,009	2,893	2,743	2,573	-0.39	-0.53	-0.64
Melanesia	1,337	1,622	2,081	2,851	1.93	2.49	3.15	5,666	6,966	7,977	8,686	2.07	1.36	0.85
Micronesia	326	391	455	524	1.82	1.52	1.41	171	184	193	193	0.73	0.48	0.00
Polynesia	251	293	348	418	1.55	1.72	1.83	362	386	395	383	0.64	0.23	-0.31

Sources: United Nations Department of Economic and Social Affairs, Population Division (2008) *World Urbanization Prospects: The 2007 Revision*, United Nations, New York. Figures in regional, income or development aggregates are calculated on the basis of country/area level data from Table B.2.

Note: Lists of countries/areas in aggregates are presented in the Technical Notes.

TABLE A.3

Urbanization

	Level of urbanization						
	Estimates and projections (%)				Rate of change (%)		
	2000	**2010**	**2020**	**2030**	**2000–2010**	**2010–2020**	**2020–2030**
WORLD	46.6	50.6	54.9	59.7	0.82	0.82	0.84
World Major Aggregates							
More Developed Regions	73.1	75.0	77.5	80.6	0.26	0.33	0.38
Less Developed Regions	40.2	45.3	50.5	56.0	1.20	1.08	1.03
Least Developed Countries	24.8	29.4	35.0	41.5	1.71	1.73	1.70
Other Less Developed Countries	42.6	48.1	53.6	59.2	1.21	1.07	1.00
Less Developed Regions, excluding China	41.6	45.3	49.6	54.8	0.85	0.91	0.99
Small Island Developing States	52.2	55.4	58.7	62.1	0.60	0.58	0.57
Sub-Saharan Africa	32.8	37.3	42.4	48.2	1.30	1.27	1.28
Human Development Index Aggregates							
High Human Development	73.9	76.6	79.3	82.2	0.36	0.36	0.35
Medium Human Development	36.7	42.1	47.7	53.8	1.38	1.26	1.18
Low Human Development	30.3	35.2	40.8	47.0	1.49	1.46	1.42
Income Aggregates							
High Income	75.9	78.2	80.7	83.3	0.29	0.31	0.32
Middle Income	44.3	49.5	54.8	60.3	1.11	1.01	0.95
Upper-middle income	71.6	75.1	78.2	81.1	0.47	0.41	0.37
Lower-middle income	37.7	43.6	49.5	55.7	1.45	1.28	1.18
Low Income	28.7	33.0	38.4	44.8	1.38	1.51	1.54
Geographic Aggregates							
Africa	35.9	39.9	44.6	50.0	1.05	1.10	1.15
Eastern Africa	20.7	23.7	27.9	33.7	1.34	1.63	1.89
Middle Africa	37.2	42.9	49.2	55.3	1.44	1.35	1.18
Northern Africa	48.4	52.0	56.2	61.3	0.72	0.78	0.87
Southern Africa	53.9	58.8	63.8	68.8	0.87	0.82	0.75
Western Africa	38.8	44.6	50.5	56.5	1.39	1.24	1.12
Asia	37.1	42.5	48.1	54.1	1.37	1.25	1.18
Eastern Asia	40.4	48.5	55.9	62.4	1.81	1.42	1.11
South-Central Asia	29.5	32.2	36.7	43.0	0.88	1.31	1.59
South-Eastern Asia	39.7	48.2	55.5	61.8	1.93	1.41	1.08
Western Asia	63.7	66.3	69.1	72.5	0.39	0.42	0.48
Europe	71.4	72.6	74.8	77.8	0.16	0.29	0.41
Eastern Europe	68.3	68.4	70.0	73.1	0.03	0.23	0.44
Northern Europe	83.4	84.4	85.9	87.6	0.12	0.17	0.20
Southern Europe	65.4	67.5	70.5	74.3	0.31	0.43	0.53
Western Europe	75.3	77.0	79.1	81.7	0.22	0.28	0.32
Latin America and the Caribbean	75.3	79.4	82.3	84.6	0.52	0.36	0.28
Caribbean	61.6	66.9	71.5	75.5	0.82	0.67	0.54
Central America	68.7	71.7	74.7	77.7	0.43	0.41	0.40
South America	79.5	83.7	86.4	88.3	0.52	0.32	0.22
North America	79.1	82.1	84.6	86.7	0.37	0.30	0.24
Oceania	70.4	70.6	71.4	72.6	0.03	0.11	0.18
Australia/New Zealand	86.9	88.7	90.2	91.5	0.21	0.17	0.14
Melanesia	19.1	18.9	20.7	24.7	-0.11	0.91	1.78
Micronesia	65.6	68.0	70.2	73.1	0.36	0.32	0.40
Polynesia	40.9	43.2	46.8	52.2	0.52	0.82	1.08

Sources: United Nations Department of Economic and Social Affairs, Population Division (2008) *World Urbanization Prospects: The 2007 Revision*, United Nations, New York. Figures in regional, income or development aggregates are calculated on the basis of country/area level data from Table B.3.

Note: Lists of countries/areas in aggregates are presented in the Technical Notes.

TABLE A.4

Total Number of Households and Rate of Change

	Estimates and projections ('000)				Rate of change (%)			10-year increment ('000)		
	2000	2010	2020	2030	2000–2010	2010–2020	2020–2030	2000–2010	2010–2020	2020–2030
World	1,575,277	1,941,303	2,304,623	2,656,033	2.09	1.72	1.42	366,026	363,320	351,410
World Major Aggregates										
More Developed Regions	466,938	520,095	557,913	581,850	1.08	0.70	0.42	53,157	37,818	23,937
Less Developed Regions	1,108,339	1,421,207	1,746,710	2,074,182	2.49	2.06	1.72	312,868	325,503	327,472
Least Developed Countries	110,570	145,875	190,937	249,569	2.77	2.69	2.68	35,305	45,062	58,632
Other Less Developed Countries	997,768	1,275,332	1,555,773	1,824,612	2.45	1.99	1.59	277,564	280,441	268,839
Less Developed Regions, excluding China	747,357	957,588	1,178,073	1,406,550	2.48	2.07	1.77	210,231	220,485	228,477
Small Island Developing States	12,483	15,143	17,830	20,430	1.93	1.63	1.36	2,660	2,687	2,600
Sub-Saharan Africa	126,782	176,773	234,496	310,953	3.35	2.85	2.84	49,991	57,723	76,457
Human Development Index Aggregates										
High Human Development	550,287	627,439	688,816	734,865	1.31	0.93	0.65	77,152	61,377	46,049
Medium Human Development	873,581	1,116,763	1,360,775	1,593,928	2.46	1.98	1.58	243,182	244,012	233,153
Low Human Development	80,169	110,674	149,783	202,353	3.22	3.03	3.01	30,505	39,109	52,570
Income Aggregates										
High Income	372,396	415,394	451,520	478,475	1.09	0.83	0.58	42,998	36,126	26,955
Middle Income	974,332	1,221,976	1,457,558	1,671,231	2.26	1.76	1.37	247,644	235,582	213,673
Upper-middle income	235,769	288,822	328,961	363,151	2.03	1.30	0.99	53,053	40,139	34,190
Lower-middle income	738,563	933,154	1,128,596	1,308,079	2.34	1.90	1.48	194,591	195,442	179,483
Low Income	191,820	259,470	339,134	437,787	3.02	2.68	2.55	67,650	79,664	98,653
Geographic Aggregates										
Africa	173,413	234,177	307,452	399,054	3.00	2.72	2.61	60,764	73,275	91,602
Eastern Africa	48,064	62,954	83,329	111,114	2.70	2.80	2.88	14,890	20,375	27,785
Middle Africa	19,827	27,777	40,628	58,425	3.37	3.80	3.63	7,950	12,851	17,797
Northern Africa	29,941	38,530	47,112	55,488	2.52	2.01	1.64	8,589	8,582	8,376
Southern Africa	13,540	20,595	23,067	25,930	4.19	1.13	1.17	7,055	2,472	2,863
Western Africa	45,637	66,384	89,270	118,537	3.75	2.96	2.84	20,747	22,886	29,267
Asia	854,709	1,077,203	1,297,511	1,501,651	2.31	1.86	1.46	222,494	220,308	204,140
Eastern Asia	433,207	545,220	656,290	759,556	2.30	1.85	1.46	112,013	111,070	103,266
South-Central Asia	265,877	335,957	404,196	465,710	2.34	1.85	1.42	70,080	68,239	61,514
South-Eastern Asia	120,017	150,005	179,027	204,700	2.23	1.77	1.34	29,988	29,022	25,673
Western Asia	35,607	46,020	57,996	71,685	2.57	2.31	2.12	10,413	11,976	13,689
Europe	289,735	317,623	332,310	336,942	0.92	0.45	0.14	27,888	14,687	4,632
Eastern Europe	120,697	135,647	141,560	142,162	1.17	0.43	0.04	14,950	5,913	602
Northern Europe	39,964	44,082	47,875	50,638	0.98	0.83	0.56	4,118	3,793	2,763
Southern Europe	51,149	53,956	54,924	54,529	0.53	0.18	-0.07	2,807	968	-395
Western Europe	77,923	83,936	87,950	89,612	0.74	0.47	0.19	6,013	4,014	1,662
Latin America and the Caribbean	127,263	160,886	194,494	226,703	2.34	1.90	1.53	33,623	33,608	32,209
Caribbean	10,194	12,282	14,296	16,169	1.86	1.52	1.23	2,088	2,014	1,873
Central America	30,239	38,830	47,905	56,416	2.50	2.10	1.64	8,591	9,075	8,511
South America	86,829	109,773	132,292	154,117	2.34	1.87	1.53	22,944	22,519	21,825
Northern America	119,986	139,193	158,467	175,169	1.48	1.30	1.00	19,207	19,274	16,702
Oceania	10,169	12,219	14,387	16,511	1.84	1.63	1.38	2,050	2,168	2,124
Australia/New Zealand	8,696	10,357	12,066	13,689	1.75	1.53	1.26	1,661	1,709	1,623
Melanesia	1,346	1,708	2,134	2,605	2.38	2.23	1.99	362	426	471
Micronesia	37	42	49	53	1.29	1.57	0.76	5	7	4
Polynesia	89	111	136	162	2.15	2.07	1.74	22	25	26

Source: UN-Habitat, Household Projections Project, 2002. Figures in regional, income or development aggregates are calculated on the basis of country/area level data from Table B.4.

Note: List of countries/areas in aggregates presented in the Technical Notes.

TABLE A.5

Access to Drinking Water and Sanitation

	Improved drinking water coverage						Household connection to improved drinking water						Improved sanitation coverage					
	Total (%)		Urban (%)		Rural (%)		Total (%)		Urban (%)		Rural (%)		Total (%)		Urban (%)		Rural (%)	
	1990	2006	1990	2006	1990	2006	1990	2006	1990	2006	1990	2006	1990	2006	1990	2006	1990	2006
WORLD	77.0	87.0	95.0	96.0	63.0	78.0	48.0	54.0	79.0	78.0	24.0	31.0	54.0	62.0	78.0	79.0	36.0	45.0
World Major Aggregates																		
More Developed Regions	98.0	99.0	100.0	100.0	95.0	97.0	91.0	93.0	98.0	98.0	73.0	78.0	99.0	99.0	100.0	100.0	96.0	96.0
Less Developed Regions	71.0	84.0	93.0	94.0	59.0	76.0	36.0	46.0	69.0	70.0	19.0	27.0	41.0	53.0	66.0	71.0	28.0	39.0
Least Developed Countries	56.3	64.6	78.7	82.3	48.3	56.3	11.4	14.2	33.6	35.5	3.6	4.2	26.7	35.9	44.6	51.4	21.1	27.3
Other Less Developed Countries	63.8	77.6	82.9	85.8	52.8	70.4	34.5	44.6	64.7	66.5	18.5	26.6	37.6	49.4	60.3	65.9	25.3	36.3
Less Developed Regions, excluding China	73.4	73.9	70.6	74.0	73.7	73.4	61.7	61.0	66.9	69.0	45.1	42.8	67.0	69.4	74.0	74.0	56.7	62.3
Small Island Developing States	86.2	86.4	93.7	92.9	83.9	83.3	50.9	50.7	80.1	74.5	37.5	40.0	78.3	73.8	87.5	84.4	76.1	70.4
Sub-Saharan Africa	49.0	58.0	82.0	81.0	35.0	46.0	16.0	16.0	46.0	35.0	4.0	5.0	26.0	31.0	40.0	42.0	20.0	24.0
Human Development Index Aggregates																		
High Human Development	96.5	98.6	98.4	99.4	92.0	95.7	87.1	91.4	94.3	96.4	72.8	80.3	94.8	95.3	97.3	97.1	89.3	91.8
Medium Human Development	72.8	81.4	90.0	91.7	62.2	72.9	37.8	43.6	65.0	66.3	18.7	25.9	53.3	60.1	70.6	71.1	43.1	51.3
Low Human Development	48.4	48.4	75.4	0.0	38.9	83.8	8.5	2.7	29.8	0.0	1.3	31.9	21.1	41.2	34.4	59.3	15.5	11.3
Income Aggregates																		
High Income	99.3	99.9	99.8	99.8	97.5	99.7	97.1	97.6	99.5	99.0	90.6	92.5	99.3	99.7	99.7	99.8	98.4	99.3
Middle Income	85.8	92.3	94.1	96.5	76.3	84.7	59.4	73.8	81.0	86.5	37.1	54.6	73.7	79.2	85.7	86.5	61.6	70.2
Upper-middle income	92.7	96.3	96.2	98.1	84.9	89.3	70.3	83.5	87.5	91.9	47.4	65.2	81.7	82.9	89.1	88.1	70.9	76.5
Lower-middle income	78.8	88.3	92.1	94.9	67.7	80.1	48.6	64.2	74.6	81.1	26.7	44.1	65.8	75.5	82.3	85.0	52.4	64.0
Low Income	54.9	65.4	82.1	84.6	45.9	57.2	12.5	16.8	37.3	39.6	4.0	7.1	25.2	35.6	42.0	49.7	19.4	29.1
Geographic Aggregates																		
Africa	...	...	...	...	...	...	...	...	...	...	...	...	...	...	...	...	...	...
Eastern Africa	57.2	64.0	87.9	86.8	49.9	54.1	20.0	20.8	47.1	47.4	11.5	9.1	33.5	38.0	37.9	44.3	36.8	35.6
Middle Africa	46.4	63.1	70.2	79.6	33.5	45.9	7.2	16.7	22.3	27.2	0.3	3.7	24.5	33.7	42.5	43.0	16.0	25.2
Northern Africa	88.0	92.0	95.0	96.0	82.0	87.0	58.0	78.0	83.0	91.0	34.0	63.0	62.0	76.0	82.0	90.0	44.0	59.0
Southern Africa	77.0	84.0	98.7	95.8	64.0	77.4	29.3	39.6	58.0	66.2	11.5	23.6	39.7	45.4	65.7	59.8	26.3	35.4
Western Africa	49.9	64.9	69.8	84.9	40.6	53.3	10.6	15.2	27.8	31.3	2.0	4.5	18.3	24.7	32.9	39.7	10.8	15.3
Asia	...	...	...	...	...	...	...	...	...	...	...	...	...	...	...	...	...	...
Eastern Asia	68.0	88.0	97.0	98.0	55.0	81.0	51.0	73.0	82.0	87.0	37.0	62.0	48.0	65.0	61.0	74.0	43.0	59.0
South-Central Asia	83.1	79.7	95.4	91.5	78.8	75.3	33.3	26.3	64.1	59.3	18.4	13.3	53.3	62.8	75.2	76.9	46.9	57.8
South-Eastern Asia	73.0	86.0	92.0	92.0	64.0	81.0	16.0	32.0	41.0	53.0	4.0	14.0	50.0	67.0	74.0	78.0	40.0	58.0
Western Asia	86.0	90.0	95.0	95.0	70.0	80.0	69.0	80.0	82.0	93.0	50.0	57.0	79.0	84.0	93.0	94.0	56.0	64.0
Europe	...	...	...	...	...	...	...	...	...	...	...	...	...	...	...	...	...	...
Eastern Europe	95.0	96.8	98.6	99.2	89.9	93.6	80.3	79.8	93.6	92.0	60.3	62.8	93.4	91.3	97.0	94.9	86.9	85.6
Northern Europe	99.9	99.9	100.0	100.0	99.4	99.4	94.0	94.6	97.3	98.2	86.6	87.2	99.0	95.5	99.2	96.3	98.8	94.2
Southern Europe	98.3	99.2	99.6	99.6	97.0	98.6	95.4	91.0	98.0	97.5	90.8	83.5	97.6	96.0	99.0	98.0	95.8	93.7
Western Europe	100.0	100.0	100.0	100.0	100.0	100.0	99.4	99.8	100.0	100.0	96.3	99.0	100.0	100.0	100.0	100.0	100.0	100.0
Latin America and the Caribbean	...	...	...	...	...	...	...	...	...	...	...	...	...	...	...	...	...	...
Caribbean	91.9	93.8	95.8	96.4	89.4	91.3	66.3	72.6	86.2	87.5	52.3	61.6	87.3	87.2	91.6	90.4	86.1	86.8
Central America	75.6	89.7	93.6	96.4	64.3	80.1	56.2	79.6	83.9	91.8	38.2	63.7	63.3	76.4	78.7	82.9	44.8	64.9
South America	81.8	91.1	92.5	97.0	59.7	75.6	62.9	78.5	82.0	89.0	22.3	49.5	70.6	79.3	83.3	86.5	42.9	60.3
Northern America	...	...	...	...	...	...	...	...	...	...	...	...	...	...	...	...	...	...
Oceania	...	...	...	...	...	...	...	...	...	...	...	...	...	...	...	...	...	...
Australia/New Zealand	98.5	100.0	100.0	100.0	91.0	100.0	...	...	100.0	100.0	...	...	100.0	100.0	100.0	100.0	94.0	100.0
Melanesia	54.3	52.3	79.5	75.0	50.3	49.3	19.3	15.3	62.3	56.3	10.0	4.0	47.0	49.3	84.0	84.0	38.0	38.0
Micronesia	86.7	89.2	89.2	89.8	85.7	87.6	24.0	36.0	69.5	49.0	13.0	22.0	68.2	63.6	74.8	79.2	60.2	56.0
Polynesia	95.8	96.0	98.3	97.0	94.9	94.4	98.0	98.0	99.5	99.5	97.5	97.5	94.3	97.2	96.7	98.3	85.0	93.6

Source: WHO (World Health Organization) and UNICEF (United Nations Children's Fund) Joint Monitoring Programme for Water Supply and Sanitation (JMP), *Progress on Drinking Water and Sanitation: Special Focus on Sanitation 2008*, WHO and UNICEF, Geneva. Figures in regional, income or development aggregates are calculated on the basis of country/area level data from Table B.5.

Note: List of countries/areas in aggregates presented in the Technical Notes.

TABLE A.6

Number of Urban Agglomerations

	Estimates and projections ('000)			Distribution of urban population by size of agglomerations (%)			Population Estimates and projections ('000)		
	2000	2010	2020	2000	2010	2020	2000	2010	2020
WORLD									
10 million or more	16	20	24	8.0	8.8	9.4	228,726	307,776	393,619
5 to 10 million	28	33	43	6.9	6.7	7.2	195,724	235,469	303,898
1 to 5 million	334	414	495	22.3	23.5	23.6	636,646	820,652	992,137
500,000 to 1 million	399	477	521	9.7	9.5	8.7	276,268	331,978	365,330
Fewer than 500,000	...	...	...	53.1	51.5	51.2	1,516,545	1,798,732	2,154,686
World Major Aggregates									
More Developed Regions									
10 million or more	5	5.0	6.0	9.8	9.7	10.5	85,290	90,139	102,155
5 to 10 million	5	8.0	9.0	4.2	6.0	5.9	36,455	55,430	57,796
1 to 5 million	98	101	104	22.4	22.0	21.4	195,966	203,344	208,048
500,000 to 1 million	116	123	127	9.0	9.0	8.9	78,293	83,441	86,273
Fewer than 500,000	...	...	...	54.6	53.2	53.3	476,921	492,348	518,050
Less Developed Regions									
10 million or more	11	15	18	7.2	8.5	9.0	143,436	217,637	291,464
5 to 10 million	23	25	34	8.0	7.0	7.6	159,269	180,039	246,101
1 to 5 million	236	313	391	22.2	24.0	24.2	440,680	617,308	784,088
500,000 to 1 million	283	354	394	10.0	9.7	8.6	197,975	248,537	279,057
Fewer than 500,000	...	...	...	52.5	50.8	50.6	1,039,625	1,306,384	1,636,636
Least Developed Countries									
10 million or more	1	1	2	6.1	5.8	8.9	10,285	14,796	33,296
5 to 10 million	1	3	6	3.3	7.6	9.9	5,485	19,249	37,139
1 to 5 million	21	28	39	22.3	21.8	20.0	37,650	55,279	75,359
500,000 to 1 million	18	28	38	7.1	8.0	6.8	11,909	20,339	25,742
Fewer than 500,000	...	...	...	61.3	56.8	54.4	103,296	144,448	204,506
Other Less Developed Countries									
10 million or more	10	14	16	7.3	8.8	9.0	133,151	202,841	258,168
5 to 10 million	22	22	28	8.5	6.9	7.3	153,784	160,790	208,962
1 to 5 million	215	285	352	22.2	24.3	24.8	403,029	562,028	708,729
500,000 to 1 million	265	326	356	10.3	9.9	8.9	186,066	228,198	253,315
Fewer than 500,000	...	...	...	51.7	50.2	50.1	936,329	1,161,937	1,432,130
Less Developed Regions, excluding China									
10 million or more	10	13	15	8.6	9.7	10.0	130,193	190,106	247,973
5 to 10 million	16	19	26	7.2	6.8	7.5	109,947	133,359	186,372
1 to 5 million	158	211	260	19.6	21.2	21.1	297,727	415,188	522,006
500,000 to 1 million	190	247	297	8.7	8.8	8.4	132,328	171,464	207,360
Fewer than 500,000	...	...	...	55.9	53.4	52.9	849,324	1,044,648	1,308,733
Sub-Saharan Africa									
10 million or more	—	1	2	—	3.3	6.1	—	10,572	28,009
5 to 10 million	2	2	4	5.7	4.4	5.4	12,718	14,238	24,685
1 to 5 million	29	41	55	23.7	26.2	25.5	52,832	84,710	116,941
500,000 to 1 million	31	51	59	9.8	10.7	9.2	21,788	34,624	42,223
Fewer than 500,000	...	...	...	60.8	55.4	53.8	135,395	179,382	246,329
Geographic Aggregates									
Africa									
Eastern Africa									
10 million or more	—	—	—	—	—	—	—	—	—
5 to 10 million	—	—	1	—	—	4.3	—	—	5,083
1 to 5 million	9	9	14	26.3	25.1	26.3	14,049	19,815	30,783
500,000 to 1 million	4	12	11	4.5	11.2	7.0	2,392	8,815	8,155
Fewer than 500,000	...	...	...	69.2	63.7	62.5	36,927	50,157	73,232
Middle Africa									
10 million or more	—	—	1	—	—	16.7	—	—	13,875
5 to 10 million	1	1	1	15.1	16.3	8.6	5,485	9,052	7,153
1 to 5 million	4	8	9	17.1	27.6	21.3	6,220	15,370	17,684
500,000 to 1 million	8	8	13	14.9	9.8	11.0	5,420	5,429	9,166
Fewer than 500,000	...	...	...	52.9	46.3	42.4	19,223	25,785	35,237
Northern Africa									
10 million or more	1	1	1	12.5	11.7	10.7	10,534	12,503	14,451
5 to 10 million	—	1	2	—	4.8	9.1	—	5,185	12,227
1 to 5 million	6	7	9	19.8	16.5	13.9	16,731	17,708	18,673
500,000 to 1 million	8	14	20	6.7	8.7	10.1	5,690	9,372	13,657
Fewer than 500,000	...	...	...	61.0	58.3	56.2	51,476	62,544	75,646
Southern Africa									
10 million or more	—	—	—	—	—	—	—	—	—
5 to 10 million	—	—	—	—	—	—	—	—	—
1 to 5 million	5	7	7	40.1	49.8	47.5	11,227	16,560	17,968
500,000 to 1 million	2	1	2	6.6	1.8	3.1	1,855	606	1,187
Fewer than 500,000	...	...	...	53.2	48.4	49.3	14,897	16,098	18,637
Western Africa									
10 million or more	—	1	1	—	7.7	7.3	—	10,572	14,134
5 to 10 million	1	—	1	7.8	—	2.8	7,233	—	5,432
1 to 5 million	10	17	24	18.7	24.0	25.6	17,387	32,966	49,444
500,000 to 1 million	17	25	27	13.0	12.3	10.0	12,120	16,835	19,349
Fewer than 500,000	...	...	...	60.5	56.0	54.3	56,264	76,821	105,056

TABLE A.6
continued

	Estimates and projections ('000)			Distribution of urban population by size of agglomerations (%)			Population Estimates and projections ('000)		
	2000	2010	2020	2000	2010	2020	2000	2010	2020
Asia									
Eastern Asia									
10 million or more	3	4	5	9.9	9.9	10.0	58,858	74,961	91,259
5 to 10 million	8	7	9	9.9	7.5	7.6	59,239	56,443	69,467
1 to 5 million	92	117	148	29.1	31.0	32.6	173,804	235,022	297,520
500,000 to 1 million	110	124	113	12.9	11.8	9.1	76,782	89,235	83,063
Fewer than 500,000	...	...	...	38.2	39.8	40.6	228,082	301,518	370,111
South-Central Asia									
10 million or more	5	5	5	13.9	14.1	13.4	61,888	80,511	99,586
5 to 10 million	5	8	10	6.7	9.2	10.1	29,941	52,609	75,658
1 to 5 million	42	58	73	15.5	17.0	17.5	69,046	97,488	130,800
500,000 to 1 million	50	68	92	8.0	8.1	8.3	35,904	46,246	62,089
Fewer than 500,000	...	...	...	55.9	51.6	50.6	249,818	295,132	377,533
South-Eastern Asia									
10 million or more	—	1	2	—	4.1	7.0	—	11,662	25,581
5 to 10 million	3	3	4	11.9	7.8	7.2	24,680	22,343	26,498
1 to 5 million	14	17	23	15.4	13.0	12.0	31,863	37,281	44,053
500,000 to 1 million	14	23	28	4.4	5.5	5.0	9,157	15,807	18,339
Fewer than 500,000	...	...	...	68.2	69.6	68.7	140,984	199,485	251,299
Western Asia									
10 million or more	—	1	1	—	6.8	6.2	—	10,530	11,695
5 to 10 million	2	1	2	11.4	3.8	7.0	13,944	5,891	13,212
1 to 5 million	18	24	30	26.4	31.3	31.8	32,390	48,225	60,114
500,000 to 1 million	18	24	29	10.0	11.1	10.5	12,216	17,049	19,916
Fewer than 500,000	...	...	...	52.3	46.9	44.5	64,091	72,175	84,058
Europe									
Eastern Europe									
10 million or more	1	1	1	4.8	5.3	5.5	10,016	10,495	10,526
5 to 10 million	—	—	—	—	—	—	—	—	—
1 to 5 million	23	19	19	16.4	15.0	15.5	34,043	29,787	29,818
500,000 to 1 million	29	34	33	8.9	11.5	11.5	18,564	22,814	22,237
Fewer than 500,000	...	...	...	69.9	68.3	67.6	145,452	135,855	130,405
Northern Europe									
10 million or more	—	—	—	—	—	—	—	—	—
5 to 10 million	1	1	1	10.5	10.4	9.8	8,225	8,607	8,618
1 to 5 million	7	8	8	13.3	14.3	13.9	10,496	11,837	12,198
500,000 to 1 million	9	9	9	8.4	7.6	7.4	6,618	6,272	6,440
Fewer than 500,000	...	...	...	67.8	67.8	68.9	53,358	56,334	60,335
Southern Europe									
10 million or more	—	—	—	—	—	—	—	—	—
5 to 10 million	1	2	2	5.3	10.5	10.3	5,045	10,821	11,117
1 to 5 million	9	8	8	24.2	18.2	17.6	23,089	18,793	19,132
500,000 to 1 million	18	18	20	12.4	11.6	12.2	11,826	11,998	13,201
Fewer than 500,000	...	...	...	58.1	59.7	59.9	55,365	61,557	64,980
Western Europe									
10 million or more	—	—	1	—	—	6.7	—	—	10,031
5 to 10 million	1	1	—	7.0	6.9	—	9,692	9,958	—
1 to 5 million	10	12	12	11.6	12.9	12.7	15,997	18,764	19,166
500,000 to 1 million	18	17	18	8.8	7.7	7.9	12,185	11,106	11,880
Fewer than 500,000	...	...	...	72.6	72.5	72.8	100,299	105,250	109,667
Latin America and the Caribbean									
Caribbean									
10 million or more	—	—	—	—	—	—	—	—	—
5 to 10 million	—	—	—	—	—	—	—	—	—
1 to 5 million	4	4	4	33.3	33.3	32.7	7,932	9,424	10,687
500,000 to 1 million	1	3	3	2.4	6.4	6.2	580	1,810	2,027
Fewer than 500,000	...	...	...	64.2	60.3	61.1	15,275	17,054	19,955
Central America									
10 million or more	1	1	1	19.4	17.7	16.1	18,022	19,485	20,695
5 to 10 million	—	—	—	—	—	—	—	—	—
1 to 5 million	11	16	19	19.8	25.0	26.9	18,446	27,544	34,539
500,000 to 1 million	22	24	25	16.4	15.5	14.4	15,262	17,031	18,506
Fewer than 500,000	...	...	...	44.5	41.8	42.6	41,401	46,076	54,739
South America									
10 million or more	3	3	3	14.3	13.5	12.6	39,749	44,842	47,956
5 to 10 million	3	4	4	6.8	8.6	8.2	18,747	28,516	31,371
1 to 5 million	27	35	37	20.2	22.4	22.7	55,967	74,667	86,656
500,000 to 1 million	32	31	34	8.1	6.6	6.6	22,316	22,044	25,351
Fewer than 500,000	...	...	...	50.7	48.9	49.9	140,403	162,684	190,320
Northern America									
10 million or more	2	2	2	11.9	11.3	10.5	29,659	32,214	33,831
5 to 10 million	2	4	6	5.4	9.1	11.9	13,494	26,043	38,061
1 to 5 million	37	42	45	34.1	33.2	30.4	85,310	95,068	97,435
500,000 to 1 million	39	40	42	11.0	9.9	9.2	27,380	28,427	29,561
Fewer than 500,000	...	...	...	37.6	36.5	38.0	93,981	104,565	121,971

TABLE A.6

continued

	Estimates and projections ('000)			Distribution of urban population by size of agglomerations (%)			Population Estimates and projections ('000)		
	2000	2010	2020	2000	2010	2020	2000	2010	2020
Oceania									
10 million or more	—	—	—	—	—	—	—	—	—
5 to 10 million	—	—	—	—	—	—	—	—	—
1 to 5 million	6	6	6	57.8	57.2	54.9	12,652	14,334	15,467
500,000 to 1 million	—	2	2	—	4.3	4.3	—	1,081	1,206
Fewer than 500,000	...	...	...	42.2	38.5	40.8	9,246	9,645	11,502
Australia/New Zealand									
10 million or more	—	—	—	—	—	—	—	—	—
5 to 10 million	—	—	—	—	—	—	—	—	—
1 to 5 million	6	6	6	63.3	63.0	61.2	12,652	14,334	15,467
500,000 to 1 million	—	2	2	—	4.8	4.8	—	1,081	1,206
Fewer than 500,000	...	...	...	36.7	32.3	34.1	7,332	7,339	8,618
Melanesia									
10 million or more	—	—	—	—	—	—	—	—	—
5 to 10 million	—	—	—	—	—	—	—	—	—
1 to 5 million	—	—	—	—	—	—	—	—	—
500,000 to 1 million	—	—	—	—	—	—	—	—	—
Fewer than 500,000	...	...	...	100.0	100.0	100.0	1,337	1,622	2,081
Micronesia									
10 million or more	—	—	—	—	—	—	—	—	—
5 to 10 million	—	—	—	—	—	—	—	—	—
1 to 5 million	—	—	—	—	—	—	—	—	—
500,000 to 1 million	—	—	—	—	—	—	—	—	—
Fewer than 500,000	...	...	...	100.0	100.0	100.0	326	391	455
Polynesia									
10 million or more	—	—	—	—	—	—	—	—	—
5 to 10 million	—	—	—	—	—	—	—	—	—
1 to 5 million	—	—	—	—	—	—	—	—	—
500,000 to 1 million	—	—	—	—	—	—	—	—	—
Fewer than 500,000	...	...	...	100.0	100.0	100.0	251	293	348

Sources: United Nations Department of Economic and Social Affairs, Population Division (2008) *World Urbanization Prospects: The 2007 Revision*, United Nations, New York. The figures in regional aggregates are not consistent with city data in table C.1.

Notes: Lists of countries/areas in aggregates are presented in the Technical Notes.

TABLE B.1 – COUNTRY LEVEL DATA

Total Population Size, Rate of Change and Population Density

	Estimates and projections ('000)				Rate of change (%)			Population density (people/km²)	
	2000	2010	2020	2030	2000–2010	2010–2020	2020–2030	2000	2030
AFRICA									
Algeria	30,506	35,423	40,630	44,726	1.49	1.37	0.96	13	19
Angola	13,930	18,493	24,169	30,652	2.83	2.68	2.38	11	25
Benin	7,227	9,872	12,874	16,076	3.12	2.66	2.22	64	143
Botswana	1,729	1,953	2,165	2,358	1.22	1.03	0.85	3	4
Burkina Faso	11,882	16,097	21,034	26,505	3.04	2.68	2.31	43	97
Burundi	6,668	9,553	13,062	17,232	3.60	3.13	2.77	240	619
Cameroon	15,861	19,662	23,352	26,892	2.15	1.72	1.41	33	57
Cape Verde	451	567	690	808	2.29	1.96	1.58	112	200
Central African Republic	3,864	4,592	5,434	6,214	1.73	1.68	1.34	6	10
Chad	8,465	11,715	15,336	19,799	3.25	2.69	2.55	7	15
Comoros[1]	699	902	1,112	1,325	2.55	2.09	1.75	313	593
Congo	3,203	4,011	4,907	5,824	2.25	2.02	1.71	9	17
Côte d'Ivoire	17,049	20,375	24,315	28,088	1.78	1.77	1.44	53	87
Democratic Republic of the Congo	50,689	69,010	93,375	122,734	3.09	3.02	2.73	22	52
Djibouti	730	877	1,027	1,197	1.83	1.58	1.53	31	52
Egypt	66,529	79,537	92,578	104,070	1.79	1.52	1.17	66	104
Equatorial Guinea	431	545	693	854	2.35	2.40	2.09	15	30
Eritrea	3,684	5,323	6,937	8,433	3.68	2.65	1.95	31	72
Ethiopia	69,388	89,566	112,896	137,052	2.55	2.31	1.94	63	124
Gabon	1,182	1,390	1,599	1,791	1.62	1.40	1.13	4	7
Gambia	1,384	1,845	2,301	2,770	2.88	2.21	1.86	123	245
Ghana	20,148	24,890	29,672	34,234	2.11	1.76	1.43	84	144
Guinea	8,203	10,028	12,966	16,170	2.01	2.57	2.21	33	66
Guinea-Bissau	1,370	1,853	2,513	3,358	3.02	3.05	2.90	38	93
Kenya	31,252	40,645	51,691	62762	2.63	2.40	1.94	54	108
Lesotho	1,601	2,044	2,163	2,252	2.44	0.57	0.40	62	74
Liberia	3,071	4,311	5,849	7,797	3.39	3.05	2.87	28	70
Libyan Arab Jamahiriya	5,346	6,530	7,656	8,447	2.00	1.59	0.98	3	5
Madagascar	16,187	21,299	27,005	32,931	2.74	2.37	1.98	28	56
Malawi	11,623	15,037	19,150	23,550	2.58	2.42	2.07	98	199
Mali	10,004	13,506	18,034	23,250	3.00	2.89	2.54	8	19
Mauritania	2,566	3,363	4,153	4,944	2.70	2.11	1.74	3	5
Mauritius[2]	1,186	1,291	1,374	1,430	0.85	0.62	0.40	581	701
Morocco	28,827	32,381	36,200	39,259	1.16	1.11	0.81	65	88
Mozambique	18,194	22,635	26,809	31,117	2.18	1.69	1.49	23	39
Namibia	1,879	2,157	2,428	2,678	1.38	1.18	0.98	2	3
Niger	11,124	15,791	22,222	30,842	3.50	3.42	3.28	9	24
Nigeria	124,773	158,313	193,099	226,855	2.38	1.99	1.61	135	246
Réunion	724	836	926	999	1.44	1.02	0.76	289	398
Rwanda	8,176	10,601	13,731	16,646	2.60	2.59	1.93	310	632
Saint Helena[3]	6	7	7	8	1.54	0.00	1.34	49	66
São Tomé and Príncipe	140	165	197	234	1.64	1.77	1.72	145	242
Senegal	10,334	13,311	16,442	19,554	2.53	2.11	1.73	53	99
Seychelles	81	88	92	96	0.83	0.44	0.43	178	212
Sierra Leone	4,521	6,185	7,747	9,592	3.13	2.25	2.14	63	134
Somalia	7,055	9,486	12,291	15,193	2.96	2.59	2.12	11	24
South Africa	51,950	56,592	59,254	61,788	0.86	0.46	0.42	37	44
Sudan	33,349	41,230	50,027	58,446	2.12	1.93	1.56	13	23
Swaziland	1,058	1,160	1,218	1,264	0.92	0.49	0.37	61	73
Togo	5,403	7,122	8,984	10,856	2.76	2.32	1.89	95	191
Tunisia	9,564	10,664	11,712	12,529	1.09	0.94	0.67	58	77
Uganda	24,690	34,040	46,749	61,548	3.21	3.17	2.75	102	255
United Republic of Tanzania	33,849	43,542	54,479	65,516	2.52	2.24	1.84	36	69
Western Sahara	315	530	723	819	5.20	3.11	1.25	1	3
Zambia	10,451	12,625	15,193	17,870	1.89	1.85	1.62	14	24
Zimbabwe	12,656	13,760	15,258	16,628	0.84	1.03	0.86	32	43
ASIA									
Afghanistan	20,737	30,389	40,993	53,252	3.82	2.99	2.62	32	82
Armenia	3,082	2,987	2,955	2,838	-0.31	-0.11	-0.40	103	95
Azerbaijan	8,143	8,671	9,307	9,599	0.63	0.71	0.31	94	111
Bahrain	650	792	917	1,025	1.98	1.47	1.11	937	1,477
Bangladesh	139,434	166,638	193,333	217,932	1.78	1.49	1.20	968	1,513
Bhutan	559	684	780	851	2.02	1.31	0.87	12	18
Brunei Darussalam	333	414	491	561	2.18	1.71	1.33	58	97
Cambodia	12,780	15,224	18,102	18,102	1.75	1.73	0.00	71	115
China[4]	1,269,962	1,351,512	1,421,260	1,458,421	0.62	0.50	0.26	132	152
China, Hong Kong SAR[5]	6,662	7,419	8,040	8,532	1.08	0.80	0.59	6,062	7,764
China, Macao SAR[6]	441	490	523	543	1.05	0.65	0.38	16,964	20,869
Cyprus	786	882	975	1,056	1.15	1.00	0.80	85	114
Democratic People's Republic of Korea	22,946	24,015	24,838	25,434	0.46	0.34	0.24	190	211
Georgia	4,720	4,301	4,063	3,807	-0.93	-0.57	-0.65	68	55
India	1,046,235	1,220,182	1,379,198	1,505,748	1.54	1.23	0.88	318	458
Indonesia	211,693	239,600	261,868	279,666	1.24	0.89	0.66	111	147
Iran (Islamic Republic of)	66,125	74,276	84,244	91,155	1.16	1.26	0.79	40	55
Iraq	25,052	30,688	39,161	47,376	2.03	2.44	1.90	57	108
Israel	6,084	7,272	8,269	9,160	1.78	1.28	1.02	275	414
Japan	127,034	127,758	124,489	118,252	0.06	-0.26	-0.51	336	313
Jordan	4,799	6,453	7,469	8,554	2.96	1.46	1.36	54	96

TABLE B.I

continued

	Estimates and projections ('000)				Rate of change (%)			Population density (people/km²)	
	2000	2010	2020	2030	2000–2010	2010–2020	2020–2030	2000	2030
Kazakhstan	14,954	15,759	16,723	17,142	0.52	0.59	0.25	5	6
Kuwait	2,228	3,051	3,690	4,273	3.14	1.90	1.47	125	240
Kyrgyzstan	4,946	5,497	6,024	6,343	1.06	0.92	0.52	25	32
Lao People's Democratic Republic	5,224	6,173	7,223	8,142	1.67	1.57	1.20	22	34
Lebanon	3,772	4,227	4,616	4,925	1.14	0.88	0.65	363	474
Malaysia	23,274	27,920	32,020	35,270	1.82	1.37	0.97	71	107
Maldives	273	323	383	434	1.68	1.70	1.25	916	1,457
Mongolia	2,470	2,707	2,997	3,204	0.92	1.02	0.67	2	2
Myanmar	45,884	50,051	53,780	56,681	0.87	0.72	0.53	68	84
Nepal	24,419	29,898	35,868	41,742	2.02	1.82	1.52	166	284
Occupied Palestinian Territory	3,149	4,409	5,806	7,320	3.37	2.75	2.32	523	1,216
Oman	2,402	2,767	3,339	3,865	1.41	1.88	1.46	8	12
Pakistan	144,360	173,351	208,315	240,276	1.83	1.84	1.43	181	302
Philippines	76,213	93,001	108,748	122,388	1.99	1.56	1.18	254	408
Qatar	617	885	1,040	1,161	3.61	1.61	1.10	56	106
Republic of Korea	46,780	48,673	49,221	48,411	0.40	0.11	-0.17	470	486
Saudi Arabia	20,807	26,416	32,089	37,314	2.39	1.95	1.51	10	17
Singapore	4,017	4,592	4,965	5,202	1.34	0.78	0.47	5,882	7,616
Sri Lanka	18,714	19,576	20,229	20,249	0.45	0.33	0.01	285	309
Syrian Arab Republic	16,511	21,428	25,573	29,294	2.61	1.77	1.36	89	158
Tajikistan	6,173	7,062	8,342	9,434	1.35	1.67	1.23	43	66
Thailand	60,666	65,125	67,990	69,218	0.71	0.43	0.18	118	135
Timor-Leste	819	1,271	1,749	2,284	4.39	3.19	2.67	55	154
Turkey	68,158	77,703	86,070	92,468	1.31	1.02	0.72	87	118
Turkmenistan	4,502	5,163	5,811	6,270	1.37	1.18	0.76	9	13
United Arab Emirates	3,247	4,732	5,774	6,753	3.77	1.99	1.57	39	81
Uzbekistan	24,724	28,580	32,481	35,199	1.45	1.28	0.80	55	79
Viet Nam	79,094	90,845	101,656	110,429	1.39	1.12	0.83	238	333
Yemen	18,182	24,475	32,390	40,768	2.97	2.80	2.30	34	77
EUROPE									
Albania	3,080	3,245	3,430	3,519	0.52	0.55	0.26	107	122
Andorra	66	75	75	73	1.28	0.00	-0.27	142	157
Austria	8,111	8,442	8,575	8,643	0.40	0.16	0.08	97	103
Belarus	10,052	9,529	9,529	8,346	-0.53	0.00	-1.33	48	40
Belgium	10,193	10,522	10,684	10,780	0.32	0.15	0.09	334	353
Bosnia and Herzegovina	3,787	3,942	3,833	3,653	0.40	-0.28	-0.48	74	71
Bulgaria	8,003	7,471	6,873	6,224	-0.69	-0.83	-0.99	72	56
Channel Islands[7]	147	150	151	151	0.20	0.07	0.00	752	776
Croatia	4,506	4,532	4,369	4,168	0.06	-0.37	-0.47	80	74
Czech Republic	10,220	10,175	10,043	9,728	-0.04	-0.13	-0.32	130	123
Denmark	5,335	5,473	5,544	5,602	0.26	0.13	0.10	124	130
Estonia	1,370	1,321	1,278	1,224	-0.36	-0.33	-0.43	30	27
Faeroe Islands	46	50	53	55	0.83	0.58	0.37	33	39
Finland[8]	5,176	5,323	5,434	5,469	0.28	0.21	0.06	15	16
France	59,187	62,507	64,825	66,605	0.55	0.36	0.27	107	121
Germany	82,309	82,365	81,161	79,348	0.01	-0.15	-0.23	231	222
Gibraltar	29	29	29	29	0.00	0.00	0.00	4,563	4,844
Greece	10,975	11,215	11,274	11,179	0.22	0.05	-0.08	83	85
Holy See[9]	1	1	1	1	0.00	0.00	0.00	1,789	1,739
Hungary	10,214	9,940	9,621	9,259	-0.27	-0.33	-0.38	110	100
Iceland	281	308	329	344	0.92	0.66	0.45	3	3
Ireland	3,804	4,526	4,526	5,475	1.74	0.00	1.90	54	78
Isle of Man	77	78	78	78	0.13	0.00	0.00	134	136
Italy	57,692	59,032	58,601	57,519	0.23	-0.07	-0.19	191	191
Latvia	2,379	2,243	2,134	2,012	-0.59	-0.50	-0.59	37	31
Liechtenstein	33	36	39	42	0.87	0.80	0.74	205	260
Lithuania	3,503	3,336	3,188	3,023	-0.49	-0.45	-0.53	54	46
Luxembourg	437	483	538	601	1.00	1.08	1.11	169	232
Malta	389	411	426	434	0.55	0.36	0.19	1,231	1,373
Moldova	4,145	3,707	3,580	3,388	-1.12	-0.35	-0.55	122	100
Monaco	32	33	34	36	0.31	0.30	0.57	21,483	24,027
Montenegro	670	600	611	613	-1.10	0.18	0.03	49	44
Netherlands	15,924	16,502	16,760	17,141	0.36	0.16	0.22	383	413
Norway[10]	4,489	4,785	5,079	5,366	0.64	0.60	0.55	12	14
Poland	38,433	37,902	37,079	35,353	-0.14	-0.22	-0.48	119	109
Portugal	10,227	10,725	10,790	10,607	0.48	0.06	-0.17	111	115
Romania	22,138	21,147	20,079	18,860	-0.46	-0.52	-0.63	93	79
Russian Federation	147,423	140,318	132,407	123,915	-0.49	-0.58	-0.66	9	7
San Marino	27	31	33	33	1.38	0.63	0.00	442	545
Serbia	10,131	9,925	9,981	9,915	-0.21	0.06	-0.07	115	112
Slovakia	5,388	5,396	5,366	5,217	0.01	-0.06	-0.28	110	106
Slovenia	1,984	2,001	1,972	1,901	0.09	-0.15	-0.37	98	94
Spain	40,229	45,108	46,445	46,682	1.14	0.29	0.05	80	92
Sweden	8,868	9,242	9,652	10,012	0.41	0.43	0.37	20	22
Switzerland	7,263	7,567	7,838	8,104	0.41	0.35	0.33	176	196
TFYR Macedonia[11]	2,009	2,041	2,025	1,966	0.16	-0.08	-0.30	78	76
Ukraine	48,854	45,170	41,679	38,053	-0.78	-0.80	-0.91	81	63
United Kingdom	58,868	61,517	64,033	66,162	0.44	0.40	0.33	242	272

TABLE B.1

continued

	Estimates and projections ('000)				Rate of change (%)			Population density (people/km²)	
	2000	2010	2020	2030	2000–2010	2010–2020	2020–2030	2000	2030
LATIN AMERICA AND THE CARIBBEAN									
Anguilla	11	13	15	16	1.67	1.43	0.65	123	177
Antigua and Barbuda	77	88	97	104	1.34	0.97	0.70	174	235
Argentina	36,896	40,738	44,486	47,534	0.99	0.88	0.66	13	17
Aruba	90	103	106	108	1.35	0.29	0.19	502	598
Bahamas	303	343	381	412	1.24	1.05	0.78	22	30
Barbados	271	286	297	303	0.54	0.38	0.20	666	701
Belize	245	306	363	413	2.22	1.71	1.29	11	18
Bolivia	8,317	10,031	11,638	13,034	1.87	1.49	1.13	8	12
Brazil	174,161	198,982	219,992	236,480	1.33	1.00	0.72	20	28
British Virgin Islands	21	23	26	27	0.91	1.23	0.38	136	181
Cayman Islands	40	49	54	57	2.03	0.97	0.54	152	216
Chile	15,412	17,134	18,639	19,778	1.06	0.84	0.59	20	26
Colombia	41,683	47,890	53,238	57,577	1.39	1.06	0.78	37	51
Costa Rica	3,929	4,665	5,276	5,795	1.72	1.23	0.94	77	113
Cuba	11,142	11,257	11,248	11,126	0.10	-0.01	-0.11	101	100
Dominica	68	67	68	69	-0.15	0.15	0.15	91	92
Dominican Republic	8,744	10,191	11,557	12,709	1.53	1.26	0.95	180	262
Ecuador	12,306	13,775	15,376	16,679	1.13	1.10	0.81	43	59
El Salvador	6,195	7,142	8,077	8,935	1.42	1.23	1.01	294	425
Falkland Islands (Malvinas)	3	3	3	3	0.00	0.00	0.00	0	0
French Guiana	165	217	267	319	2.74	2.07	1.78	2	4
Grenada	100	105	107	107	0.49	0.19	0.00	292	312
Guadeloupe	421	454	474	484	0.75	0.43	0.21	247	284
Guatemala	11,229	14,377	18,091	21,691	2.47	2.30	1.81	103	199
Guyana	734	731	700	660	-0.04	-0.43	-0.59	3	3
Haiti	8,573	10,060	11,584	12,994	1.60	1.41	1.15	309	468
Honduras	6,196	7,533	9,005	10,298	1.95	1.78	1.34	55	92
Jamaica	2,589	2,756	2,872	2,924	0.63	0.41	0.18	236	266
Martinique	386	402	405	400	0.41	0.07	-0.12	350	363
Mexico	99,735	110,293	120,559	128,125	1.01	0.89	0.61	51	65
Montserrat	5	6	6	7	1.82	0.00	1.54	49	66
Netherlands Antilles	181	199	207	206	0.95	0.39	-0.05	226	257
Nicaragua	5,108	5,832	6,696	7,407	1.33	1.38	1.01	39	57
Panama	2,950	3,509	4,027	4,488	1.74	1.38	1.08	39	59
Paraguay	5,349	6,460	7,533	8,483	1.89	1.54	1.19	13	21
Peru	25,663	28,894	32,540	35,564	1.19	1.19	0.89	20	28
Puerto Rico	3,834	4,056	4,252	4,383	0.56	0.47	0.30	432	494
Saint Kitts and Nevis	46	52	59	64	1.23	1.26	0.81	176	244
Saint Lucia	153	171	188	201	1.11	0.95	0.67	283	373
Saint Vincent and the Grenadines	116	122	125	124	0.50	0.24	-0.08	299	319
Suriname	436	465	480	481	0.64	0.32	0.02	3	3
Trinidad and Tobago	1,301	1,348	1,393	1,400	0.35	0.33	0.05	254	273
Turks and Caicos Islands	19	26	29	31	3.14	1.09	0.67	44	72
United States Virgin Islands	110	111	109	103	0.09	-0.18	-0.57	318	298
Uruguay	3,318	3,374	3,495	3,590	0.17	0.35	0.27	19	21
Venezuela (Bolivarian Republic of)	24,402	29,045	33,415	37,149	1.74	1.40	1.06	27	41
NORTHERN AMERICA									
Bermuda	63	65	66	66	0.31	0.15	0.00	1,186	1,243
Canada	30,689	33,752	36,588	39,105	0.95	0.81	0.67	3	4
Greenland	56	59	63	64	0.52	0.66	0.16	0	0
Saint-Pierre-et-Miquelon	6	6	6	6	0.00	0.00	0.00	26	27
United States of America	284,857	314,692	342,547	366,187	1.00	0.85	0.67	30	38
OCEANIA									
American Samoa	57	71	83	96	2.20	1.56	1.46	287	482
Australia[12]	19,139	21,362	23,418	25,287	1.10	0.92	0.77	2	3
Cook Islands	16	13	11	11	-2.08	-1.67	0.00	68	48
Fiji	802	854	888	918	0.63	0.39	0.33	44	50
French Polynesia	236	273	306	330	1.46	1.14	0.76	59	82
Guam	155	180	201	220	1.50	1.10	0.90	283	401
Kiribati	84	100	115	131	1.74	1.40	1.30	116	180
Marshall Islands	52	63	75	83	1.92	1.74	1.01	288	457
Micronesia (Federated States of)	107	113	120	129	0.55	0.60	0.72	153	184
Nauru	10	10	11	11	0.00	0.95	0.00	478	528
New Caledonia	215	253	287	317	1.63	1.26	0.99	12	17
New Zealand	3,854	4,285	4,616	4,895	1.06	0.74	0.59	14	18
Niue	2	1	1	1	-6.93	0.00	0.00	7	5
Northern Mariana Islands	69	88	104	104	2.43	1.67	0.00	149	257
Palau	19	21	22	24	1.00	0.47	0.87	42	53
Papua New Guinea	5,381	6,708	7,937	9,183	2.20	1.68	1.46	12	20
Pitcairn	0	0	0	0	0.0	0.0	0.0	12	11
Samoa	177	192	204	217	0.81	0.61	0.62	63	77
Solomon Islands	415	531	647	762	2.46	1.98	1.64	14	26
Tokelau	2	1	1	1	-6.93	0.00	0.00	126	117
Tonga	98	102	108	115	0.40	0.57	0.63	151	177
Tuvalu	10	11	11	12	0.95	0.00	0.87	392	449
Vanuatu	190	243	299	356	2.46	2.07	1.74	16	29
Wallis and Futuna Islands	15	16	17	17	0.65	0.61	0.00	74	86

Sources: United Nations Department of Economic and Social Affairs, Population Division (2008) *World Urbanization Prospects: The 2007 Revision*, United Nations, New York; United Nations Statistics Division, Demographic and Social Statistics: *Demographic Yearbook 2006*.

TABLE B.1

continued

Notes:

(1) Including the island of Mayotte.

(2) Including Agalega, Rodrigues and Saint Brandon.

(3) Including Ascension and Tristan da Cunha.

(4) For statistical purposes, the data for China do not include Hong Kong and Macao Special Administrative Regions (SAR) of China.

(5) As of 1 July 1997, Hong Kong became a Special Administrative Region (SAR) of China.

(6) As of 20 December 1999, Macao became a Special Administrative Region (SAR) of China.

(7) Including the islands of Guernsey and Jersey.

(8) Including Åland Islands.

(9) Refers to the Vatican City State.

(10) Including Svalbard and Jan Mayen islands.

(11) The former Yugoslav Republic of Macedonia.

(12) Including Christmas Island, Cocos (Keeling) Islands and Norfolk Island.

Statistical annex

TABLE B.2

Urban and Rural Population Size and Rate of Change

	Urban population							Rural population						
	Estimates and projections ('000)				Rate of change (%)			Estimates and projections ('000)				Rate of change (%)		
	2000	2010	2020	2030	2000-2010	2010-2020	2020-2030	2000	2010	2020	2030	2000-2010	2010-2020	2020-2030
AFRICA														
Algeria	18,246	23,555	29,193	34,096	2.55	2.15	1.55	12,260	11,868	11,436	10,630	-0.32	-0.37	-0.73
Angola	6,824	10,819	15,961	21,953	4.61	3.89	3.19	7,106	7,674	8,208	8,698	0.77	0.67	0.58
Benin	2,770	4,151	6,081	8,639	4.05	3.82	3.51	4,457	5,722	6,793	7,437	2.50	1.72	0.91
Botswana	920	1,194	1,463	1,714	2.61	2.03	1.58	809	759	702	644	-0.64	-0.78	-0.86
Burkina Faso	1,971	3,286	5,424	8,640	5.11	5.01	4.66	9,911	12,811	15,609	17,865	2.57	1.98	1.35
Burundi	552	1,051	1,929	3,410	6.44	6.07	5.70	6,116	8,502	11,133	13,822	3.29	2.70	2.16
Cameroon	7,908	11,482	15,288	19,090	3.73	2.86	2.22	7,953	8,180	8,064	7,802	0.28	-0.14	-0.33
Cape Verde	241	346	465	586	3.62	2.96	2.31	210	221	225	222	0.51	0.18	-0.13
Central African Republic	1,454	1,788	2,308	3,010	2.07	2.55	2.66	2,409	2,804	3,126	3,205	1.52	1.09	0.25
Chad	1,979	3,236	5,203	8,165	4.92	4.75	4.51	6,486	8,479	10,133	11,633	2.68	1.78	1.38
Comoros[1]	196	254	343	484	2.59	3.00	3.44	503	648	769	841	2.53	1.71	0.90
Congo	1,868	2,492	3,256	4,128	2.88	2.67	2.37	1,335	1,520	1,652	1,697	1.30	0.83	0.27
Côte d'Ivoire	7,423	10,217	13,771	17,632	3.19	2.99	2.47	9,626	10,157	10,544	10,456	0.54	0.37	-0.08
Democratic Republic of Congo	15,126	24,304	39,244	60,333	4.74	4.79	4.30	35,563	44,706	54,131	62,401	2.29	1.91	1.42
Djibouti	608	773	931	1,101	2.40	1.86	1.68	122	104	97	96	-1.60	-0.70	-0.10
Egypt	28,364	34,041	41,684	51,950	1.82	2.03	2.20	38,165	45,496	50,894	52,120	1.76	1.12	0.24
Equatorial Guinea	167	216	300	422	2.57	3.29	3.41	263	329	393	432	2.24	1.78	0.95
Eritrea	655	1,149	1,905	2,900	5.62	5.06	4.20	3,029	4,174	5,032	5,533	3.21	1.87	0.95
Ethiopia	10,339	15,722	24,369	37,484	4.19	4.38	4.31	59,050	73,844	88,527	99,568	2.24	1.81	1.18
Gabon	948	1,196	1,419	1,623	2.32	1.71	1.34	235	194	179	168	-1.92	-0.80	-0.63
Gambia	680	1,073	1,496	1,967	4.56	3.32	2.74	705	772	804	803	0.91	0.41	-0.01
Ghana	8,856	12,811	17,336	22,145	3.69	3.02	2.45	11,292	12,079	12,337	12,090	0.67	0.21	-0.20
Guinea	2,547	3,546	5,373	7,865	3.31	4.16	3.81	5,656	6,482	7,594	8,304	1.36	1.58	0.89
Guinea-Bissau	407	556	825	1,297	3.12	3.95	4.52	964	1,297	1,688	2,062	2.97	2.63	2.00
Kenya	6,167	9,015	13,735	20,739	3.80	4.21	4.12	25,085	31,630	37,956	42,022	2.32	1.82	1.02
Lesotho	377	550	747	954	3.78	3.06	2.45	1,509	1,495	1,416	1,298	-0.09	-0.54	-0.87
Liberia	1,666	2,652	3,972	5,746	4.65	4.04	3.69	1,405	1,659	1,877	2,051	1.66	1.23	0.89
Libyan Arab Jamahiriya	4,082	5,086	6,147	7,001	2.20	1.89	1.30	1,263	1,444	1,509	1,446	1.34	0.44	-0.43
Madagascar	4,390	6,430	9,412	13,629	3.82	3.81	3.70	11,797	14,869	17,593	19,302	2.31	1.68	0.93
Malawi	1,764	2,973	4,887	7,634	5.22	4.97	4.46	9,859	12,064	14,263	15,916	2.02	1.67	1.10
Mali	2,787	4,503	7,207	11,022	4.80	4.70	4.25	7,217	9,003	10,827	12,228	2.21	1.84	1.22
Mauritania	1,026	1,393	1,887	2,557	3.06	3.04	3.04	1,540	1,969	2,265	2,387	2.46	1.40	0.52
Mauritius[2]	506	549	624	730	0.82	1.28	1.57	680	741	751	700	0.86	0.13	-0.70
Morocco	15,375	18,374	22,068	25,883	1.78	1.83	1.59	13,452	14,007	14,132	13,376	0.40	0.09	-0.55
Mozambique	5,584	8,699	12,404	16,708	4.43	3.55	2.98	12,610	13,935	14,405	14,409	1.00	0.33	0.00
Namibia	608	819	1,078	1,379	2.98	2.75	2.46	1,271	1,338	1,349	1,299	0.51	0.08	-0.38
Niger	1,801	2,633	4,208	7,301	3.80	4.69	5.51	9,323	13,158	18,014	23,541	3.45	3.14	2.68
Nigeria	53,048	78,845	109,772	144,246	3.96	3.31	2.73	71,725	79,468	83,328	82,609	1.03	0.47	-0.09
Réunion	651	786	886	962	1.88	1.20	0.82	73	50	40	37	-3.78	-2.23	-0.78
Rwanda	1,126	1,999	3,105	4,703	5.74	4.40	4.15	7,050	8,602	10,626	11,943	1.99	2.11	1.17
Saint Helena[3]	2	3	3	4	4.05	0.00	2.88	4	4	4	4	0.00	0.00	0.00
São Tomé and Príncipe	75	103	136	173	3.17	2.78	2.41	65	62	61	61	-0.47	-0.16	0.00
Senegal	4,200	5,710	7,743	10,403	3.07	3.05	2.95	6,134	7,601	8,698	9,152	2.14	1.35	0.51
Seychelles	41	48	56	64	1.58	1.54	1.34	40	39	36	32	-0.25	-0.80	-1.18
Sierra Leone	1,605	2,375	3,318	4,702	3.92	3.34	3.49	2,916	3,810	4,429	4,890	2.67	1.51	0.99
Somalia	2,346	3,553	5,288	7,576	4.15	3.98	3.60	4,709	5,934	7,004	7,617	2.31	1.66	0.84
South Africa	25,827	30,405	34,134	37,969	1.63	1.16	1.06	19,571	18,873	17,146	15,267	-0.36	-0.96	-1.16
Sudan	12,034	18,646	26,612	35,468	4.38	3.56	2.87	21,315	22,584	23,415	22,978	0.58	0.36	-0.19
Swaziland	247	296	369	468	1.81	2.20	2.38	811	865	849	796	0.64	-0.19	-0.64
Togo	1,974	3,094	4,534	6,220	4.49	3.82	3.16	3,429	4,028	4,451	4,636	1.61	1.00	0.41
Tunisia	6,066	7,175	8,342	9,417	1.68	1.51	1.21	3,497	3,489	3,370	3,111	-0.02	-0.35	-0.80
Uganda	2,983	4,525	7,449	12,653	4.17	4.98	5.30	21,707	29,514	39,300	48,895	3.07	2.86	2.18
United Republic of Tanzania	7,551	11,487	17,316	25,330	4.20	4.10	3.80	26,297	32,054	37,163	40,185	1.98	1.48	0.78
Western Sahara	264	434	606	704	4.97	3.34	1.50	51	96	116	115	6.33	1.89	-0.09
Zambia	3,637	4,507	5,913	7,990	2.14	2.72	3.01	6,814	8,118	9,280	9,880	1.75	1.34	0.63
Zimbabwe	4,273	5,264	6,702	8,432	2.09	2.42	2.30	8,384	8,496	8,556	8,196	0.13	0.07	-0.43
ASIA														
Afghanistan	4,413	7,532	12,163	19,294	5.35	4.79	4.61	16,324	22,857	28,830	33,958	3.37	2.32	1.64
Armenia	2,006	1,903	1,926	1,960	-0.53	0.12	0.17	1,076	1,084	1,029	878	0.07	-0.52	-1.59
Azerbaijan	4,169	4,526	5,129	5,764	0.82	1.25	1.17	3,974	4,145	4,178	3,835	0.42	0.08	-0.86
Bahrain	574	702	820	929	2.01	1.55	1.25	76	90	97	96	1.69	0.75	-0.10
Bangladesh	32,893	46,770	65,523	89,448	3.52	3.37	3.11	106,541	119,868	127,810	128,484	1.18	0.64	0.05
Bhutan	142	252	372	478	5.74	3.89	2.51	417	432	408	373	0.35	-0.57	-0.90
Brunei Darussalam	237	313	389	462	2.78	2.17	1.72	96	101	101	99	0.51	0.00	-0.20
Cambodia	2,161	3,470	5,355	7,678	4.74	4.34	3.60	10,619	11,753	12,747	13,082	1.01	0.81	0.26
China[4]	454,362	607,230	756,340	879,892	2.90	2.20	1.51	815,599	744,282	664,920	578,529	-0.92	-1.13	-1.39
China, Hong Kong SAR[5]	6,662	7,419	8,040	8,532	1.08	0.80	0.59	—	—	—	—	—	—	—
China, Macao SAR[6]	441	490	523	543	1.05	0.65	0.38	—	—	—	—	—	—	—
Cyprus	540	620	712	807	1.38	1.38	1.25	247	262	264	249	0.59	0.08	-0.58
Democratic People's Republic of Korea	13,809	15,219	16,849	18,404	0.97	1.02	0.88	9,137	8,797	7,989	7,030	-0.38	-0.96	-1.28
Georgia	2,486	2,277	2,256	2,291	-0.88	-0.09	0.15	2,234	2,024	1,807	1,516	-0.99	-1.13	-1.76
India	289,438	366,858	472,561	611,407	2.37	2.53	2.58	756,797	853,324	906,638	894,341	1.20	0.61	-0.14
Indonesia	88,918	128,634	163,850	192,805	3.69	2.42	1.63	122,774	110,965	98,018	86,861	-1.01	-1.24	-1.21
Iran (Islamic Republic of)	42,452	51,620	62,376	70,972	1.96	1.89	1.29	23,673	22,656	21,868	20,183	-0.44	-0.35	-0.80
Iraq	16,993	20,375	26,338	33,389	1.82	2.57	2.37	8,059	10,313	12,823	13,987	2.47	2.18	0.87

TABLE B.2

continued

	Urban population							Rural population						
	Estimates and projections ('000)				Rate of change (%)			Estimates and projections ('000)				Rate of change (%)		
	2000	2010	2020	2030	2000-2010	2010-2020	2020-2030	2000	2010	2020	2030	2000-2010	2010-2020	2020-2030
Israel	5,563	6,670	7,626	8,524	1.81	1.34	1.11	521	602	643	637	1.45	0.66	-0.09
Japan	82,847	85,385	86,420	86,304	0.30	0.12	-0.01	44,187	42,373	38,069	31,948	-0.42	-1.07	-1.75
Jordan	3,755	5,067	5,958	7,012	3.00	1.62	1.63	1,043	1,386	1,510	1,542	2.84	0.86	0.21
Kazakhstan	8,416	9,220	10,415	11,457	0.91	1.22	0.95	6,538	6,539	6,308	5,685	0.00	-0.36	-1.04
Kuwait	2,188	3,001	3,637	4,218	3.16	1.92	1.48	40	49	53	55	2.03	0.78	0.37
Kyrgyzstan	1,751	2,014	2,419	2,928	1.40	1.83	1.91	3,196	3,482	3,606	3,415	0.86	0.35	-0.54
Lao People's Democratic Republic	1,148	2,048	3,192	4,322	5.79	4.44	3.03	4,076	4,124	4,030	3,821	0.12	-0.23	-0.53
Lebanon	3,244	3,688	4,091	4,435	1.28	1.04	0.81	528	539	525	491	0.21	-0.26	-0.67
Malaysia	14,424	20,150	25,130	28,994	3.34	2.21	1.43	8,849	7,770	6,889	6,276	-1.30	-1.20	-0.93
Maldives	76	131	200	264	5.44	4.23	2.78	197	192	183	170	-0.26	-0.48	-0.74
Mongolia	1,397	1,555	1,820	2,104	1.07	1.57	1.45	1,072	1,152	1,177	1,100	0.72	0.21	-0.68
Myanmar	12,860	16,973	22,025	27,427	2.78	2.61	2.19	33,024	33,077	31,754	29,254	0.02	-0.41	-0.82
Nepal	3,280	5,447	8,582	12,776	5.07	4.55	3.98	21,140	24,451	27,286	28,966	1.46	1.10	0.60
Occupied Palestinian Territory	2,251	3,177	4,301	5,653	3.45	3.03	2.73	898	1,232	1,505	1,668	3.16	2.00	1.03
Oman	1,719	1,984	2,449	2,951	1.43	2.11	1.86	683	783	890	914	1.37	1.28	0.27
Pakistan	47,884	64,192	89,070	119,652	2.93	3.28	2.95	96,476	109,158	119,245	120,624	1.24	0.88	0.11
Philippines	44,621	61,731	78,595	93,860	3.25	2.42	1.77	31,592	31,270	30,153	28,528	-0.10	-0.36	-0.55
Qatar	586	848	1,004	1,125	3.70	1.69	1.14	31	37	37	36	1.77	0.00	-0.27
Republic of Korea	37,247	39,881	41,428	41,759	0.68	0.38	0.08	9,533	8,792	7,793	6,651	-0.81	-1.21	-1.58
Saudi Arabia	16,614	21,681	27,022	32,178	2.66	2.20	1.75	4,193	4,735	5,067	5,135	1.22	0.68	0.13
Singapore	4,017	4,592	4,965	5,202	1.34	0.78	0.47	—	—	—	—			
Sri Lanka	2,940	2,962	3,419	4,333	0.07	1.43	2.37	15,774	16,614	16,810	15,917	0.52	0.12	-0.55
Syrian Arab Republic	8,524	11,754	15,080	18,746	3.21	2.49	2.18	7,987	9,674	10,494	10,549	1.92	0.81	0.05
Tajikistan	1,636	1,874	2,405	3,219	1.36	2.49	2.92	4,537	5,188	5,938	6,215	1.34	1.35	0.46
Thailand	18,893	22,118	26,456	31,682	1.58	1.79	1.80	41,772	43,007	41,534	37,536	0.29	-0.35	-1.01
Timor-Leste	199	357	582	911	5.84	4.89	4.48	620	914	1,168	1,373	3.88	2.45	1.62
Turkey	44,126	54,119	63,658	71,874	2.04	1.62	1.21	24,032	23,584	22,412	20,594	-0.19	-0.51	-0.85
Turkmenistan	2,064	2,556	3,172	3,789	2.14	2.16	1.78	2,438	2,607	2,639	2,480	0.67	0.12	-0.62
United Arab Emirates	2,527	3,693	4,618	5,568	3.79	2.24	1.87	720	1,039	1,157	1,186	3.67	1.08	0.25
Uzbekistan	9,212	10,557	12,993	16,244	1.36	2.08	2.23	15,512	18,022	19,488	18,955	1.50	0.78	-0.28
Viet Nam	19,204	26,191	35,230	46,123	3.10	2.96	2.69	59,891	64,655	66,426	64,306	0.77	0.27	-0.32
Yemen	4,776	7,784	12,371	18,487	4.88	4.63	4.02	13,406	16,691	20,019	22,281	2.19	1.82	1.07
EUROPE														
Albania	1,286	1,556	1,864	2,134	1.91	1.81	1.35	1,794	1,689	1,566	1,385	-0.60	-0.76	-1.23
Andorra	61	66	64	62	0.79	-0.31	-0.32	5	9	11	11	5.88	2.01	0.00
Austria	5,337	5,703	6,028	6,376	0.66	0.55	0.56	2,774	2,739	2,547	2,267	-0.13	-0.73	-1.16
Belarus	7,029	7,076	7,000	6,773	0.07	-0.11	-0.33	3,023	2,453	1,974	1,574	-2.09	-2.17	-2.26
Belgium	9,899	10,252	10,440	10,562	0.35	0.18	0.12	294	270	244	218	-0.85	-1.01	-1.13
Bosnia and Herzegovina	1,637	1,916	2,115	2,253	1.57	0.99	...	2,150	2,025	1,719	1,401	-0.60	-1.64	-2.05
Bulgaria	5,510	5,356	5,144	4,865	-0.28	-0.40	-0.56	2,492	2,115	1,729	1,359	-1.64	-2.02	-2.41
Channel Islands[7]	45	47	52	59	0.43	1.01	1.26	102	103	100	92	0.10	-0.30	-0.83
Croatia	2,505	2,618	2,689	2,774	0.44	0.27	0.31	2,001	1,915	1,680	1,394	-0.44	-1.31	-1.87
Czech Republic	7,562	7,483	7,535	7,584	-0.11	0.07	0.06	2,659	2,692	2,508	2,143	0.12	-0.71	-1.57
Denmark	4,540	4,772	4,951	5,089	0.50	0.37	0.27	795	701	593	514	-1.26	-1.67	-1.43
Estonia	951	918	906	903	-0.35	-0.13	-0.03	419	403	372	321	-0.39	-0.80	-1.47
Faeroe Islands	17	21	26	30	2.11	2.14	1.43	30	29	27	25	-0.34	-0.71	-0.77
Finland[8]	3,164	3,402	3,672	3,927	0.73	0.76	0.67	2,012	1,920	1,761	1,542	-0.47	-0.86	-1.33
France	44,838	48,616	52,020	55,197	0.81	0.68	0.59	14,349	13,891	12,805	11,409	-0.32	-0.81	-1.15
Germany	60,141	60,826	61,386	62,163	0.11	0.09	0.13	22,168	21,539	19,775	17,185	-0.29	-0.85	-1.40
Gibraltar	27	29	29	29	0.71	0.00	0.00	—	—	—	—			
Greece	6,556	6,888	7,301	7,746	0.49	0.58	0.59	4,419	4,327	3,974	3,432	-0.21	-0.85	-1.47
Holy See[9]	1	1	1	1	0.00	0.00	0.00	—	—	—	—			
Hungary	6,596	6,790	6,954	7,045	0.29	0.24	0.13	3,618	3,149	2,667	2,214	-1.39	-1.66	-1.86
Iceland	259	285	305	321	0.96	0.68	0.51	22	24	24	23	0.87	0.00	-0.43
Ireland	2,250	2,804	3,312	3,820	2.20	1.67	1.43	1,554	1,723	1,744	1,655	1.03	0.12	-0.52
Isle of Man	40	40	40	42	0.00	0.00	0.49	37	39	38	36	0.53	-0.26	-0.54
Italy	38,782	40,354	41,558	42,881	0.40	0.29	0.31	18,910	18,677	17,043	14,638	-0.12	-0.92	-1.52
Latvia	1,619	1,529	1,489	1,468	-0.57	-0.27	-0.14	760	714	645	544	-0.62	-1.02	-1.70
Liechtenstein	5	5	6	8	0.00	1.82	2.88	28	31	33	34	1.02	0.63	0.30
Lithuania	2,346	2,240	2,206	2,191	-0.46	-0.15	-0.07	1,156	1,096	982	832	-0.53	-1.10	-1.66
Luxembourg	366	397	443	505	0.81	1.10	1.31	71	86	95	96	1.92	1.00	0.10
Malta	359	389	409	419	0.80	0.50	0.24	30	22	17	15	-3.10	-2.58	-1.25
Moldova	1,848	1,529	1,491	1,567	-1.89	-0.25	0.50	2,297	2,178	2,089	1,821	-0.53	-0.42	-1.37
Monaco	32	33	34	36	0.31	0.30	0.57	—	—	—	—			
Montenegro	392	357	359	380	-0.94	0.06	0.57	278	243	251	233	-1.35	0.32	-0.74
Netherlands	12,229	13,674	14,492	15,184	1.12	0.58	0.47	3,694	2,828	2,268	1,956	-2.67	-2.21	-1.48
Norway[10]	3,415	3,714	4,014	4,365	0.84	0.78	0.84	1,074	1,071	1,065	1,001	-0.03	-0.06	-0.62
Poland	23,719	23,177	23,141	23,351	-0.23	-0.02	0.09	14,714	14,725	13,939	12,003	0.01	-0.55	-1.50
Portugal	5,564	6,510	7,164	7,576	1.57	0.96	0.56	4,664	4,215	3,626	3,031	-1.01	-1.51	-1.79
Romania	11,842	11,556	11,657	11,907	-0.24	0.09	0.21	10,296	9,591	8,422	6,954	-0.71	-1.30	-1.92
Russian Federation	108,135	102,153	97,742	94,685	-0.57	-0.44	-0.32	39,288	38,165	34,666	29,230	-0.29	-0.96	-1.71
San Marino	25	30	31	32	1.82	0.33	0.32	2	2	2	2	0.00	0.00	0.00
Serbia	5,179	5,199	5,574	6,067	0.04	0.70	0.85	4,952	4,726	4,407	3,848	-0.47	-0.70	-1.36
Slovakia	3,031	3,064	3,208	3,376	0.11	0.46	0.51	2,357	2,332	2,158	1,841	-0.11	-0.78	-1.59
Slovenia	1,007	959	944	986	-0.49	-0.16	0.44	977	1,041	1,028	915	0.63	-0.13	-1.16
Spain	30,680	34,912	36,861	38,242	1.29	0.54	0.37	9,550	10,196	9,584	8,440	0.65	-0.62	-1.27

TABLE B.2

continued

	Urban population							Rural population					
	Estimates and projections ('000)				Rate of change (%)			Estimates and projections ('000)				Rate of change (%)		
	2000	2010	2020	2030	2000-2010	2010-2020	2020-2030	2000	2010	2020	2030	2000-2010	2010-2020	2020-2030
Sweden	7,451	7,826	8,281	8,743	0.49	0.57	0.54	1,417	1,416	1,371	1,268	-0.01	-0.32	-0.78
Switzerland	5,326	5,570	5,894	6,310	0.45	0.57	0.68	1,938	1,996	1,944	1,793	0.29	-0.26	-0.81
TFYR Macedonia[11]	1,264	1,386	1,467	1,507	0.92	0.57	0.27	745	656	557	459	-1.27	-1.64	-1.94
Ukraine	32,803	30,766	29,116	27,771	-0.64	-0.55	-0.47	16,051	14,404	12,563	10,282	-1.08	-1.37	-2.00
United Kingdom	52,600	55,451	58,337	60,974	0.53	0.51	0.44	6,268	6,066	5,696	5,188	-0.33	-0.63	-0.93
LATIN AMERICA AND THE CARIBBEAN														
Anguilla	11	13	15	16	1.67	1.43	0.65	—	—	—	—			
Antigua and Barbuda	25	27	31	40	0.77	1.38	2.55	52	61	65	64	1.60	0.64	-0.16
Argentina	33,252	37,640	41,726	44,990	1.24	1.03	0.75	3,643	3,098	2,761	2,544	-1.62	-1.15	-0.82
Aruba	42	48	52	57	1.34	0.80	0.92	48	55	54	51	1.36	-0.18	-0.57
Bahamas	249	289	328	362	1.49	1.27	0.99	54	55	53	50	0.18	-0.37	-0.58
Barbados	104	121	141	161	1.51	1.53	1.33	182	176	162	140	-0.34	-0.83	-1.46
Belize	117	161	211	263	3.19	2.70	2.20	128	145	152	150	1.25	0.47	-0.13
Bolivia	5,143	6,675	8,265	9,799	2.61	2.14	1.70	3,174	3,356	3,373	3,235	0.56	0.05	-0.42
Brazil	141,404	172,177	196,896	215,492	1.97	1.34	0.90	32,756	26,805	23,095	20,988	-2.00	-1.49	-0.96
British Virgin Islands	8	10	12	14	2.23	1.82	1.54	12	14	14	13	1.54	0.00	-0.74
Cayman Islands	40	49	54	57	2.03	0.97	0.54	—	—	—	—			
Chile	13,246	15,250	16,958	18,245	1.41	1.06	0.73	2,166	1,884	1,681	1,532	-1.39	-1.14	-0.93
Colombia	30,043	35,951	41,549	46,610	1.80	1.45	1.15	11,640	11,939	11,689	10,967	0.25	-0.21	-0.64
Costa Rica	2,318	3,001	3,656	4,277	2.58	1.97	1.57	1,611	1,664	1,621	1,518	0.32	-0.26	-0.66
Cuba	8,423	8,525	8,657	8,828	0.12	0.15	0.20	2,719	2,732	2,591	2,298	0.05	-0.53	-1.20
Dominica	49	50	53	56	0.20	0.58	0.55	20	17	15	13	-1.63	-1.25	-1.43
Dominican Republic	5,459	7,182	8,801	10,170	2.74	2.03	1.45	3,285	3,010	2,756	2,539	-0.87	-0.88	-0.82
Ecuador	7,420	9,222	11,153	12,813	2.17	1.90	1.39	4,885	4,553	4,223	3,866	-0.70	-0.75	-0.88
El Salvador	3,618	4,378	5,252	6,206	1.91	1.82	1.67	2,577	2,764	2,825	2,730	0.70	0.22	-0.34
Falkland Islands (Malvinas)	2	3	3	3	4.05	0.00	0.00	0	0	0	0	0.00	0.00	0.00
French Guiana	124	165	210	259	2.86	2.41	2.10	41	51	57	59	2.18	1.11	0.34
Grenada	31	33	37	43	0.63	1.14	1.50	69	73	70	64	0.56	-0.42	-0.90
Guadeloupe	414	446	466	477	0.74	0.44	0.23	7	8	8	7	1.34	0.00	-1.34
Guatemala	5,067	7,111	9,893	13,152	3.39	3.30	2.85	6,162	7,267	8,198	8,538	1.65	1.21	0.41
Guyana	210	208	218	244	-0.10	0.47	1.13	524	523	482	416	-0.02	-0.82	-1.47
Haiti	3,052	4,988	7,027	8,833	4.91	3.43	2.29	5,521	5,072	4,557	4,161	-0.85	-1.07	-0.91
Honduras	2,748	3,680	4,885	6,214	2.92	2.83	2.41	3,447	3,854	4,119	4,083	1.12	0.66	-0.09
Jamaica	1,342	1,481	1,643	1,822	0.99	1.04	1.03	1,248	1,275	1,229	1,102	0.21	-0.37	-1.09
Martinique	378	394	398	393	0.41	0.10	-0.13	8	8	7	6	0.00	-1.34	-1.54
Mexico	74,524	85,839	97,265	106,689	1.41	1.25	0.92	25,210	24,454	23,294	21,436	-0.30	-0.49	-0.83
Montserrat	1	1	1	1	0.00	0.00	0.00	4	5	5	5	2.23	0.00	0.00
Netherlands Antilles	163	186	192	196	1.32	0.52	0.00	18	14	11	9	-2.51	-2.41	-2.01
Nicaragua	2,796	3,343	4,086	4,873	1.79	2.01	1.76	2,312	2,489	2,611	2,534	0.74	0.48	-0.30
Panama	1,941	2,624	3,233	3,752	3.01	2.09	1.49	1,009	884	794	736	-1.32	-1.07	-0.76
Paraguay	2,960	3,973	5,051	6,103	2.94	2.40	1.89	2,389	2,488	2,482	2,380	0.41	-0.02	-0.42
Peru	18,141	20,700	23,944	27,219	1.32	1.46	1.28	7,522	8,194	8,596	8,345	0.86	0.48	-0.30
Puerto Rico	3,629	4,007	4,229	4,365	0.99	0.54	0.32	205	49	23	19	-14.31	-7.56	-1.91
Saint Kitts and Nevis	15	17	21	26	1.25	2.11	2.14	31	35	38	37	1.21	0.82	-0.27
Saint Lucia	43	48	58	73	1.10	1.89	2.30	110	123	130	129	1.12	0.55	-0.08
Saint Vincent and the Grenadines	52	58	66	72	1.09	1.29	0.87	64	64	59	51	0.00	-0.81	-1.46
Suriname	315	352	379	394	1.11	0.74	0.39	122	113	101	86	-0.77	-1.12	-1.61
Trinidad and Tobago	141	187	252	332	2.82	2.98	2.76	1,160	1,161	1,141	1,068	0.01	-0.17	-0.66
Turks and Caicos Islands	16	24	28	30	4.05	1.54	0.69	3	2	1	1	-4.05	-6.93	0.00
United States Virgin Islands	102	106	105	100	0.38	-0.09	-0.49	8	5	4	3	-4.70	-2.23	-2.88
Uruguay	3,031	3,122	3,269	3,387	0.30	0.46	0.35	287	251	226	203	-1.34	-1.05	-1.07
Venezuela (Bolivarian Republic of)	21,891	27,315	32,032	35,872	2.21	1.59	1.13	2,511	1,731	1,383	1,277	-3.72	-2.24	-0.80
NORTHERN AMERICA														
Bermuda	63	65	66	66	0.31	0.15	0.00	—	—	—	—			
Canada	24,391	27,198	30,005	32,848	1.09	0.98	0.91	6,298	6,554	6,583	6,257	0.40	0.04	-0.51
Greenland	46	50	54	57	0.83	0.77	0.54	10	9	9	8	-1.05	0.00	-1.18
Saint Pierre and Miquelon	6	6	6	6	0.00	0.00	0.00	1	1	1	1	0.00	0.00	0.00
United States of America	225,319	258,998	290,729	318,454	1.39	1.16	0.91	59,538	55,694	51,818	47,733	-0.67	-0.72	-0.82
OCEANIA														
American Samoa	51	66	79	92	2.58	1.80	1.52	6	5	4	4	-1.82	-2.23	0.00
Australia[12]	16,682	19,035	21,226	23,228	1.32	1.09	0.90	2,457	2,327	2,192	2,059	-0.54	-0.60	-0.63
Cook Islands	10	10	10	10	0.00	0.00	0.00	6	3	2	1	-6.93	-4.05	-6.93
Fiji	387	456	522	591	1.64	1.35	1.24	414	398	366	327	-0.39	-0.84	-1.13
French Polynesia	124	141	164	194	1.28	1.51	1.68	112	132	141	136	1.64	0.66	-0.36
Guam	144	168	188	208	1.54	1.12	1.01	11	12	13	13	0.87	0.80	0.00
Kiribati	36	44	54	68	2.01	2.05	2.31	48	56	61	62	1.54	0.86	0.16
Marshall Islands	36	45	56	65	2.23	2.19	1.49	16	18	18	18	1.18	0.00	0.00
Micronesia (Federated States of)	24	26	30	39	0.80	1.43	2.62	83	87	90	90	0.47	0.34	0.00
Nauru	10	10	11	11	0.00	0.95	0.00	—	—	—	—			
New Caledonia	133	166	199	233	2.22	1.81	1.58	82	87	88	84	0.59	0.11	-0.47
New Zealand	3,302	3,718	4,065	4,381	1.19	0.89	0.75	552	567	551	514	0.27	-0.29	-0.70
Niue	1	1	1	1	0.00	0.00	0.00	1	1	1	1	0.00	0.00	0.00
Northern Mariana Islands	62	81	96	111	2.67	1.70	1.45	7	8	8	8	1.34	0.00	0.00
Palau	13	17	20	22	2.68	1.63	0.95	6	4	2	2	-4.05	-6.93	0.00
Papua New Guinea	711	840	1,119	1,669	1.67	2.87	4.00	4,671	5,868	6,818	7,514	2.28	1.50	0.97

TABLE B.2

continued

	Urban population							Rural population						
	Estimates and projections ('000)				Rate of change (%)			Estimates and projections ('000)				Rate of change (%)		
	2000	2010	2020	2030	2000-2010	2010-2020	2020-2030	2000	2010	2020	2030	2000-2010	2010-2020	2020-2030
Pitcairn	—	—	—	—	—	—	—	0	0	0	0	0.00	0.00	0.00
Samoa	39	45	55	72	1.43	2.01	2.69	139	147	149	145	0.56	0.14	-0.27
Solomon Islands	65	98	149	223	4.11	4.19	4.03	350	432	498	539	2.10	1.42	0.79
Tokelau	—	—	—	—	—	—	—	2	1	1	1	-6.93	0.00	0.00
Tonga	23	26	32	43	1.23	2.08	2.95	75	76	75	73	0.13	-0.13	-0.27
Tuvalu	5	5	6	7	0.00	1.82	1.54	5	5	5	4	0.00	0.00	-2.23
Vanuatu	41	62	93	135	4.14	4.05	3.73	149	181	206	220	1.95	1.29	0.66
Wallis and Futuna Islands	—	—	—	—	—	—	—	15	16	17	17	0.65	0.61	0.00

Source: United Nations Department of Economic and Social Affairs, Population Division (2008) *World Urbanization Prospects: The 2007 Revision*, United Nations, New York.

Notes:

(1) Including Mayotte.

(2) Including Agalega, Rodrigues, and Saint Brandon.

(3) Including Ascension, and Tristan da Cunha.

(4) For statistical purposes, the data for China do not include Hong Kong and Macao, Special Administrative Regions (SAR) of China.

(5) As of 1 July 1997, Hong Kong became a Special Administrative Region (SAR) of China.

(6) As of 20 December 1999, Macao became a Special Administrative Region (SAR) of China.

(7) Refers to Guernsey, and Jersey.

(8) Including Åland Islands.

(9) Refers to the Vatican City State.

(10) Including Svalbard and Jan Mayen Islands.

(11) The former Yugoslav Republic of Macedonia.

(12) Including Christmas Island, Cocos (Keeling) Islands, and Norfolk Island.

TABLE B.3

Urbanization and Urban Slum Dwellers

	Level of urbanization							Slum population	
	Estimates and projections (%)				Rate of change (%)			Estimate ('000)	Share of urban population (%)
	2000	2010	2020	2030	2000–2010	2010–2020	2020–2030	2005	2005
AFRICA									
Algeria	59.8	66.5	71.9	76.2	1.06	0.78	0.58	...	...
Angola	49.0	58.5	66.0	71.6	1.77	1.21	0.81	4,678	86.5
Benin	38.3	42.0	47.2	53.7	0.92	1.17	1.29	2,427	71.8
Botswana	53.2	61.1	67.6	72.7	1.38	1.01	0.73	...	...
Burkina Faso	16.6	20.4	25.8	32.6	2.06	2.35	2.34	1,438	59.5
Burundi	8.3	11.0	14.8	19.8	2.82	2.97	2.91	485	64.3
Cameroon	49.9	58.4	65.5	71.0	1.57	1.15	0.81	4,224	47.4
Cape Verde	53.4	61.1	67.4	72.5	1.35	0.98	0.73	...	...
Central African Republic	37.6	38.9	42.5	48.4	0.34	0.89	1.30	1,446	94.1
Chad	23.4	27.6	33.9	41.2	1.65	2.06	1.95	2,247	91.3
Comoros[1]	28.1	28.2	30.8	36.5	0.04	0.88	1.70	204	68.9
Congo	58.3	62.1	66.3	70.9	0.63	0.65	0.67	1,285	53.4
Côte d'Ivoire	43.5	50.1	56.6	62.8	1.41	1.22	1.04	4,589	56.2
Democratic Republic of the Congo	29.8	35.2	42.0	49.2	1.67	1.77	1.58	14,115	76.4
Djibouti	83.3	88.1	90.6	92.0	0.56	0.28	0.15	...	...
Egypt	42.6	42.8	45.0	49.9	0.05	0.50	1.03	5,405	17.1
Equatorial Guinea	38.8	39.7	43.3	49.4	0.23	0.87	1.32	130	66.3
Eritrea	17.8	21.6	27.5	34.4	1.93	2.41	2.24	...	...
Ethiopia	14.9	17.6	21.6	27.4	1.67	2.05	2.38	10,118	81.8
Gabon	80.1	86.0	88.8	90.6	0.71	0.32	0.20	447	38.7
Gambia	49.1	58.1	65.0	71.0	1.68	1.12	0.88	371	45.4
Ghana	44.0	51.5	58.4	64.7	1.57	1.26	1.02	4,805	45.4
Guinea	31.0	35.4	41.4	48.6	1.33	1.57	1.60	1,418	45.7
Guinea-Bissau	29.7	30.0	32.8	38.6	0.10	0.89	1.63	390	83.1
Kenya	19.7	22.2	26.6	33.0	1.19	1.81	2.16	3,897	54.8
Lesotho	20.0	26.9	34.5	42.4	2.96	2.49	2.06	118	35.1
Liberia	54.3	61.5	67.9	73.7	1.25	0.99	0.82	...	...
Libyan Arab Jamahiriya	76.4	77.9	80.3	82.9	0.19	0.30	0.32	...	...
Madagascar	27.1	30.2	34.9	41.4	1.08	1.45	1.71	4,022	80.6
Malawi	15.2	19.8	25.5	32.4	2.64	2.53	2.39	1,468	66.4
Mali	27.9	33.3	40.0	47.4	1.77	1.83	1.70	2,715	65.9
Mauritania	40.0	41.4	45.4	51.7	0.34	0.92	1.30	...	...
Mauritius[2]	42.7	42.6	45.4	51.1	-0.02	0.64	1.18	...	...
Morocco	53.3	56.7	61.0	65.9	0.62	0.73	0.77	2,422	13.1
Mozambique	30.7	38.4	46.3	53.7	2.24	1.87	1.48	5,430	79.5
Namibia	32.4	38.0	44.4	51.5	1.59	1.56	1.48	242	33.9
Niger	16.2	16.7	18.9	23.7	0.30	1.24	2.26	1,938	82.6
Nigeria	42.5	49.8	56.8	63.6	1.59	1.32	1.13	41,664	65.8
Réunion	89.9	94.0	95.7	96.3	0.45	0.18	0.06	...	...
Rwanda	13.8	18.9	22.6	28.3	3.14	1.79	2.25	1,251	71.6
Saint Helena[3]	39.2	39.5	43.4	49.8	0.08	0.94	1.38	...	...
São Tomé and Príncipe	53.4	62.2	69.0	74.0	1.53	1.04	0.70	...	...
Senegal	40.6	42.9	47.1	53.2	0.55	0.93	1.22	1,846	38.1
Seychelles	51.0	55.3	61.1	66.6	0.81	1.00	0.86	...	...
Sierra Leone	35.5	38.4	42.8	49.0	0.79	1.08	1.35	2,180	97.0
Somalia	33.2	37.4	43.0	49.9	1.19	1.40	1.49	2,838	73.5
South Africa	56.9	61.7	66.6	71.3	0.81	0.76	0.68	8,077	28.7
Sudan	36.1	45.2	53.2	60.7	2.25	1.63	1.32	13,914	94.2
Swaziland	23.3	25.5	30.3	37.0	0.90	1.72	2.00	...	...
Togo	36.5	43.4	50.5	57.3	1.73	1.52	1.26	1,529	62.1
Tunisia	63.4	67.3	71.2	75.2	0.60	0.56	0.55	...	...
Uganda	12.1	13.3	15.9	20.6	0.95	1.79	2.59	2,420	66.7
United Republic of Tanzania	22.3	26.4	31.8	38.7	1.69	1.86	1.96	6,157	66.4
Western Sahara	83.9	81.8	83.9	85.9	-0.25	0.25	0.24	...	...
Zambia	34.8	35.7	38.9	44.7	0.26	0.86	1.39	2,336	57.2
Zimbabwe	33.8	38.3	43.9	50.7	1.25	1.36	1.44	835	17.9
ASIA									
Afghanistan	21.3	24.8	29.7	36.2	1.52	1.80	1.98	4,629	...
Armenia	65.1	63.7	65.2	69.1	-0.22	0.23	0.58	...	...
Azerbaijan	51.2	52.2	55.1	60.1	0.19	0.54	0.87	...	...
Bahrain	88.4	88.6	89.4	90.6	0.02	0.09	0.13	...	...
Bangladesh	23.6	28.1	33.9	41.0	1.75	1.88	1.90	25,184	70.8
Bhutan	25.4	36.8	47.7	56.2	3.71	2.59	1.64	49	...
Brunei Darussalam	71.1	75.7	79.3	82.3	0.63	0.46	0.37	...	...
Cambodia	16.9	22.8	29.6	37.0	2.99	2.61	2.23	2,309	78.9
China[4]	35.8	44.9	53.2	60.3	2.26	1.70	1.25	174,745	32.9
China, Hong Kong SAR[5]	100.0	100.0	100.0	100.0	0.00	0.00	0.00	...	...
China, Macao SAR[6]	100.0	100.0	100.0	100.0	0.00	0.00	0.00	...	...
Cyprus	68.6	70.3	73.0	76.4	0.24	0.38	0.46	...	...
Democratic People's Republic of Korea	60.2	63.4	67.8	72.4	0.52	0.67	0.66	...	...
Georgia	52.7	52.9	55.5	60.2	0.04	0.48	0.81	...	...
India	27.7	30.1	34.3	40.6	0.83	1.31	1.69	110,225	34.8
Indonesia	42.0	53.7	62.6	68.9	2.46	1.53	0.96	28,159	26.3
Iran (Islamic Republic of)	64.2	69.5	74.0	77.9	0.79	0.63	0.51	14,581	30.3

TABLE B.3

continued

	Level of urbanization							Slum population	
	Estimates and projections (%)				Rate of change (%)			Estimate ('000)	Share of urban population (%)
	2000	2010	2020	2030	2000–2010	2010–2020	2020–2030	2005	2005
Iraq	67.8	66.4	67.3	70.5	-0.21	0.13	0.46	9,692	52.8
Israel	91.4	91.7	92.2	93.0	0.03	0.05	0.09	...	...
Japan	65.2	66.8	69.4	73.0	0.24	0.38	0.51	...	...
Jordan	78.3	78.5	79.8	82.0	0.03	0.16	0.27	719	15.8
Kazakhstan	56.3	58.5	62.3	66.8	0.38	0.63	0.70	...	...
Kuwait	98.2	98.4	98.6	98.7	0.02	0.02	0.01	...	...
Kyrgyzstan	35.4	36.6	40.1	46.2	0.33	0.91	1.42	...	...
Lao People's Democratic Republic	22.0	33.2	44.2	53.1	4.12	2.86	1.83	969	79.3
Lebanon	86.0	87.2	88.6	90.0	0.14	0.16	0.16	1,757	53.1
Malaysia	62.0	72.2	78.5	82.2	1.52	0.84	0.46	...	...
Maldives	27.7	40.5	52.1	60.7	3.80	2.52	1.53	...	...
Mongolia	56.6	57.5	60.7	65.7	0.16	0.54	0.79	869	57.9
Myanmar	28.0	33.9	41.0	48.4	1.91	1.90	1.66	7,062	45.6
Nepal	13.4	18.2	23.9	30.6	3.06	2.72	2.47	2,595	60.7
Occupied Palestinian Territory	71.5	72.1	74.1	77.2	0.08	0.27	0.41	...	...
Oman	71.6	71.7	73.3	76.4	0.01	0.22	0.41	1,461	...
Pakistan	33.2	37.0	42.8	49.8	1.08	1.46	1.51	26,613	47.5
Philippines	58.5	66.4	72.3	76.7	1.27	0.85	0.59	22,768	43.7
Qatar	94.9	95.8	96.5	96.9	0.09	0.07	0.04	...	...
Republic of Korea	79.6	81.9	84.2	86.3	0.28	0.28	0.25	...	...
Saudi Arabia	79.8	82.1	84.2	86.2	0.28	0.25	0.23	4,070	18.0
Singapore	100.0	100.0	100.0	100.0	0.00	0.00	0.00	...	...
Sri Lanka	15.7	15.1	16.9	21.4	-0.39	1.13	2.36	345	...
Syrian Arab Republic	51.6	54.9	59.0	64.0	0.62	0.72	0.81	982	10.5
Tajikistan	26.5	26.5	28.8	34.1	0.00	0.83	1.69	...	...
Thailand	31.1	34.0	38.9	45.8	0.89	1.35	1.63	2,061	26.0
Timor-Leste	24.3	28.1	33.2	39.9	1.45	1.67	1.84	...	...
Turkey	64.7	69.6	74.0	77.7	0.73	0.61	0.49	7,635	15.5
Turkmenistan	45.8	49.5	54.6	60.4	0.78	0.98	1.01	...	...
United Arab Emirates	77.8	78.0	80.0	82.4	0.03	0.25	0.30	...	...
Uzbekistan	37.3	36.9	40.0	46.1	-0.11	0.81	1.42	...	...
Viet Nam	24.3	28.8	34.7	41.8	1.70	1.86	1.86	9,192	41.3
Yemen	26.3	31.8	38.2	45.3	1.90	1.83	1.70	...	67.2
EUROPE									
Albania	41.7	48.0	54.3	60.6	1.41	1.23	1.10	...	...
Andorra	92.4	88.0	84.9	85.1	-0.49	-0.36	0.02	...	...
Austria	65.8	67.6	70.3	73.8	0.27	0.39	0.49	...	...
Belarus	69.9	74.3	78.0	81.1	0.61	0.49	0.39	...	...
Belgium	97.1	97.4	97.7	98.0	0.03	0.03	0.03	...	...
Bosnia and Herzegovina	43.2	48.6	55.2	61.7	1.18	1.27	1.11	...	...
Bulgaria	68.9	71.7	74.8	78.2	0.40	0.42	0.44	...	...
Channel Islands[7]	30.5	31.4	34.2	39.1	0.29	0.85	1.34	...	...
Croatia	55.6	57.8	61.6	66.5	0.39	0.64	0.77	...	...
Czech Republic	74.0	73.5	75.0	78.0	-0.07	0.20	0.39	...	...
Denmark	85.1	87.2	89.3	90.8	0.24	0.24	0.17	...	...
Estonia	69.4	69.5	70.9	73.8	0.01	0.20	0.40	...	...
Faeroe Islands	36.3	42.5	48.5	55.0	1.58	1.32	1.26	...	...
Finland[8]	61.1	63.9	67.6	71.8	0.45	0.56	0.60	...	...
France	75.8	77.8	80.2	82.9	0.26	0.30	0.33	...	...
Germany	73.1	73.8	75.6	78.3	0.10	0.24	0.35	...	...
Gibraltar	100.0	100.0	100.0	100.0	0.00	0.00	0.00	...	...
Greece	59.7	61.4	64.8	69.3	0.28	0.54	0.67	...	...
Holy See[9]	100.0	100.0	100.0	100.0	0.00	0.00	0.00	...	...
Hungary	64.6	68.3	72.3	76.1	0.56	0.57	0.51	...	...
Iceland	92.2	92.3	92.7	93.3	0.01	0.04	0.06	...	...
Ireland	59.1	61.9	65.5	69.8	0.46	0.57	0.64	...	...
Isle of Man	51.8	50.6	51.2	53.9	-0.23	0.12	0.51	...	...
Italy	67.2	68.4	70.9	74.6	0.18	0.36	0.51	...	...
Latvia	68.1	68.2	69.8	73.0	0.01	0.23	0.45	...	...
Liechtenstein	15.1	14.2	15.2	18.6	-0.61	0.68	2.02	...	...
Lithuania	67.0	67.2	69.2	72.5	0.03	0.29	0.47	...	...
Luxembourg	83.8	82.2	82.4	84.1	-0.19	0.02	0.20	...	...
Malta	92.4	94.7	96.0	96.6	0.25	0.14	0.06	...	...
Moldova	44.6	41.2	41.7	46.3	-0.79	0.12	1.05	...	...
Monaco	100.0	100.0	100.0	100.0	0.00	0.00	0.00	...	...
Montenegro	58.5	59.5	58.9	62.0	0.17	-0.10	0.51	...	...
Netherlands	76.8	82.9	86.5	88.6	0.76	0.43	0.24	...	...
Norway[10]	76.1	77.6	79.0	81.4	0.20	0.18	0.30	...	...
Poland	61.7	61.2	62.4	66.0	-0.08	0.19	0.56	...	...
Portugal	54.4	60.7	66.4	71.4	1.10	0.90	0.73	...	...
Romania	53.5	54.6	58.1	63.1	0.20	0.62	0.83	...	...
Russian Federation	73.4	72.8	73.8	76.4	-0.08	0.14	0.35	...	...
San Marino	93.4	94.3	94.9	95.5	0.10	0.06	0.06	...	...
Serbia	51.1	52.4	55.8	61.2	0.25	0.63	0.92	...	...
Slovakia	56.3	56.8	59.8	64.7	0.09	0.51	0.79	...	...

TABLE B.3

continued

	Level of urbanization							Slum population	
	Estimates and projections (%)				Rate of change (%)			Estimate ('000)	Share of urban population (%)
	2000	2010	2020	2030	2000–2010	2010–2020	2020–2030	2005	2005
Slovenia	50.8	48.0	47.9	51.8	-0.57	-0.02	0.78	...	...
Spain	76.3	77.4	79.4	81.9	0.14	0.26	0.31	...	...
Sweden	84.0	84.7	85.8	87.3	0.08	0.13	0.17	...	...
Switzerland	73.3	73.6	75.2	77.9	0.04	0.22	0.35	...	...
TFYR Macedonia[11]	62.9	67.9	72.5	76.6	0.76	0.66	0.55	...	...
Ukraine	67.1	68.1	69.9	73.0	0.15	0.26	0.43	...	...
United Kingdom	89.4	90.1	91.1	92.2	0.08	0.11	0.12	...	...
LATIN AMERICA AND THE CARIBBEAN									
Anguilla	100.0	100.0	100.0	100.0	0.00	0.00	0.00	4	36.7
Antigua and Barbuda	32.1	30.3	32.5	38.4	-0.58	0.70	1.67	1	4.8
Argentina	90.1	92.4	93.8	94.6	0.25	0.15	0.08	9,343	26.2
Aruba	46.7	46.9	48.8	52.5	0.04	0.40	0.73	...	...
Bahamas	82.0	84.1	86.1	87.9	0.25	0.24	0.21	...	...
Barbados	36.3	40.8	46.6	53.4	1.17	1.33	1.36	...	...
Belize	47.8	52.7	58.0	63.7	0.98	0.96	0.94	61	47.3
Bolivia	61.8	66.5	71.0	75.2	0.73	0.65	0.57	2,972	50.4
Brazil	81.2	86.5	89.5	91.1	0.63	0.34	0.18	45,509	29.0
British Virgin Islands	39.4	41.0	45.2	51.6	0.40	0.98	1.32	...	...
Cayman Islands	100.0	100.0	100.0	100.0	0.00	0.00	0.00	...	...
Chile	85.9	89.0	91.0	92.3	0.35	0.22	0.14	1,270	9.0
Colombia	72.1	75.1	78.0	81.0	0.41	0.38	0.38	5,920	17.9
Costa Rica	59.0	64.3	69.3	73.8	0.86	0.75	0.63	290	10.9
Cuba	75.6	75.7	77.0	79.3	0.01	0.17	0.29	...	...
Dominica	71.1	74.6	78.1	81.3	0.48	0.46	0.40	...	...
Dominican Republic	62.4	70.5	76.2	80.0	1.22	0.78	0.49	1,043	17.6
Ecuador	60.3	66.9	72.5	76.8	1.04	0.80	0.58	1,808	21.5
El Salvador	58.4	61.3	65.0	69.5	0.48	0.59	0.67	1,166	28.9
Falkland Islands (Malvinas)	85.8	92.9	95.4	96.3	0.80	0.27	0.09	...	...
French Guiana	75.1	76.4	78.6	81.4	0.17	0.28	0.35	15	10.5
Grenada	31.0	31.0	34.2	40.5	0.00	0.98	1.69	2	6.0
Guadeloupe	98.4	98.2	98.3	98.5	-0.02	0.01	0.02	24	5.4
Guatemala	45.1	49.5	54.7	60.6	0.93	1.00	1.02	2,550	42.9
Guyana	28.6	28.5	31.2	37.0	-0.04	0.91	1.70	72	33.7
Haiti	35.6	49.6	60.7	68.0	3.32	2.02	1.14	2,316	70.1
Honduras	44.4	48.8	54.3	60.3	0.94	1.07	1.05	1,169	34.9
Jamaica	51.8	53.7	57.2	62.3	0.36	0.63	0.85	852	60.5
Martinique	97.8	98.0	98.2	98.4	0.02	0.02	0.02	6	1.6
Mexico	74.7	77.8	80.7	83.3	0.41	0.37	0.32	11,686	14.4
Montserrat	11.0	14.3	16.9	21.6	2.62	1.67	2.45	...	...
Netherlands Antilles	90.2	93.2	94.7	95.5	0.33	0.16	0.08	...	...
Nicaragua	54.7	57.3	61.0	65.8	0.46	0.63	0.76	1,473	45.5
Panama	65.8	74.8	80.3	83.6	1.28	0.71	0.40	430	23.0
Paraguay	55.3	61.5	67.1	71.9	1.06	0.87	0.69	634	17.6
Peru	70.7	71.6	73.6	76.5	0.13	0.28	0.39	7,329	36.1
Puerto Rico	94.6	98.8	99.5	99.6	0.43	0.07	0.01	...	...
Saint Kitts and Nevis	32.8	32.4	35.4	41.6	-0.12	0.89	1.61	...	...
Saint Lucia	28.0	28.0	30.6	36.1	0.00	0.89	1.65	6	11.9
Saint Vincent and the Grenadines	44.4	47.8	52.6	58.6	0.74	0.96	1.08	...	...
Suriname	72.1	75.6	79.0	82.0	0.47	0.44	0.37	13	3.9
Trinidad and Tobago	10.8	13.9	18.1	23.7	2.52	2.64	2.70	247	24.7
Turks and Caicos Islands	84.6	93.3	96.5	97.4	0.98	0.34	0.09	...	...
United States Virgin Islands	92.6	95.3	96.5	97.0	0.29	0.13	0.05	...	...
Uruguay	91.3	92.5	93.5	94.3	0.13	0.11	0.09	...	...
Venezuela (Bolivarian Rep. of)	89.7	94.0	95.9	96.6	0.47	0.20	0.07	7,521	32.0
NORTHERN AMERICA									
Bermuda	100.0	100.0	100.0	100.0	0.00	0.00	0.00	...	...
Canada	79.5	80.6	82.0	84.0	0.14	0.17	0.24	...	...
Greenland	81.6	84.0	86.1	87.9	0.29	0.25	0.21	...	...
Saint-Pierre-et-Miquelon	88.9	89.3	90.2	91.3	0.04	0.10	0.12	...	...
United States of America	79.1	82.3	84.9	87.0	0.40	0.31	0.24	...	...
OCEANIA									
American Samoa	88.8	93.0	94.8	95.6	0.46	0.19	0.08	...	...
Australia[12]	87.2	89.1	90.6	91.9	0.22	0.17	0.14	...	...
Cook Islands	63.9	76.3	83.6	87.3	1.77	0.91	0.43	...	...
Fiji	48.3	53.4	58.8	64.4	1.00	0.96	0.91	...	...
French Polynesia	52.4	51.6	53.8	58.8	-0.15	0.42	0.89	...	...
Guam	93.1	93.2	93.5	94.2	0.01	0.03	0.07	...	...
Kiribati	43.0	44.0	46.9	52.3	0.23	0.64	1.09	...	...
Marshall Islands	68.4	71.8	75.3	78.8	0.49	0.48	0.45	...	...
Micronesia (Fed. States of)	22.3	22.7	25.1	30.3	0.18	1.01	1.88	...	...
Nauru	100.0	100.0	100.0	100.0	0.00	0.00	0.00	...	...
New Caledonia	61.9	65.5	69.4	73.5	0.57	0.58	0.57	...	...
New Zealand	85.7	86.8	88.1	89.5	0.13	0.15	0.16	...	...
Niue	33.7	39.9	46.7	53.7	1.69	1.57	1.40	...	...

TABLE B.3

continued

	Level of urbanization							Slum population	
	Estimates and projections (%)				Rate of change (%)			Estimate ('000)	Share of urban population (%)
	2000	2010	2020	2030	2000–2010	2010–2020	2020–2030	2005	2005
Northern Mariana Islands	90.2	91.3	92.4	93.3	0.12	0.12	0.10	...	...
Palau	69.9	82.7	89.0	91.6	1.68	0.73	0.29	...	...
Papua New Guinea	13.2	12.5	14.1	18.2	-0.54	1.20	2.55	...	...
Pitcairn	0.0	0.0	0.0	0.0	...	...	...	...	...
Samoa	21.9	23.4	27.1	33.2	0.66	1.47	2.03	...	...
Solomon Islands	15.7	18.6	23.0	29.2	1.70	2.12	2.39	...	...
Tokelau	0.0	0.0	0.0	0.0	...	...	...	...	...
Tonga	23.2	25.3	30.1	36.9	0.87	1.74	2.04	...	...
Tuvalu	46.0	50.4	55.6	61.5	0.91	0.98	1.01	...	...
Vanuatu	21.7	25.6	31.0	38.0	1.65	1.91	2.04	...	...
Wallis and Futuna Islands	0.0	0.0	0.0	0.0	...	...	...	...	...

Sources: United Nations Department of Economic and Social Affairs, Population Division (2008) *World Urbanization Prospects: The 2007 Revision*, United Nations, New York; UN-Habitat, Urban Info 2008.

Notes:

(1) Including Mayotte.

(2) Including Agalega, Rodrigues, and Saint Brandon.

(3) Including Ascension, and Tristan da Cunha.

(4) For statistical purposes, the data for China do not include Hong Kong and Macao, Special Administrative Regions (SAR) of China.

(5) As of 1 July 1997, Hong Kong became a Special Administrative Region (SAR) of China.

(6) As of 20 December 1999, Macao became a Special Administrative Region (SAR) of China.

(7) Refers to Guernsey, and Jersey.

(8) Including Åland Islands.

(9) Refers to the Vatican City State.

(10) Including Svalbard and Jan Mayen Islands.

(11) The former Yugoslav Republic of Macedonia.

(12) Including Christmas Island, Cocos (Keeling) Islands, and Norfolk Island.

TABLE B.4

Total Number of Households and Rate of Change

	Estimates and projections ('000)				Rate of change (%)			10-year increment ('000)		
	2000	2010	2020	2030	2000–2010	2010–2020	2020–2030	2000–2010	2010–2020	2020–2030
AFRICA										
Algeria	4,966	6,437	7,931	9,345	2.59	2.09	1.64	1,471	1,494	1,413
Angola	...	...	...	...	...	...	...	...	...	...
Benin	1,054	1,494	2,035	2,747	3.49	3.09	3.00	440	540	711
Botswana	367	441	526	635	1.84	1.76	1.89	74	84	109
Burkina Faso	1,632	1,960	2,431	3,004	1.83	2.15	2.12	327	470	573
Burundi	1,530	2,087	2,911	3,984	3.10	3.33	3.14	556	823	1,073
Cameroon	3,359	4,875	6,889	9,735	3.72	3.46	3.46	1,515	2,014	2,845
Cape Verde	91	124	167	213	3.15	2.92	2.45	33	42	46
Central African Republic	751	984	1,298	1,738	2.70	2.77	2.92	232	314	439
Chad	1,112	1,387	1,753	2,202	2.20	2.34	2.28	274	365	449
Comoros	97	138	183	238	3.43	2.86	2.61	40	45	54
Congo	702	1,039	1,589	2,385	3.92	4.24	4.06	337	549	796
Côte d'Ivoire	2,856	3,788	4,972	6,561	2.82	2.72	2.77	931	1,184	1,588
Democratic Republic of the Congo	10,796	15,105	22,904	33,749	3.36	4.16	3.88	4,309	7,799	10,845
Djibouti	133	166	218	282	2.19	2.74	2.55	32	52	63
Egypt	13,410	17,736	21,935	25,754	2.80	2.12	1.61	4,326	4,198	3,818
Equatorial Guinea	103	146	209	293	3.50	3.60	3.35	43	63	83
Eritrea	726	1,070	1,499	2,061	3.88	3.37	3.18	344	429	561
Ethiopia	12,302	16,506	23,145	32,602	2.94	3.38	3.43	4,203	6,639	9,457
Gabon	309	402	531	699	2.62	2.78	2.76	92	128	168
Gambia	164	232	308	396	3.46	2.85	2.50	67	76	87
Ghana	4,163	6,004	8,396	11,422	3.66	3.35	3.08	1,841	2,391	3,026
Guinea	1,115	1,413	1,870	2,445	2.37	2.80	2.68	298	457	574
Guinea-Bissau	138	175	219	279	2.34	2.22	2.41	36	43	59
Kenya	7,238	10,298	13,361	17,159	3.53	2.60	2.50	3,059	3,062	3,798
Lesotho	411	514	647	827	2.22	2.30	2.46	102	133	180
Liberia	306	714	953	1,437	8.45	2.89	4.10	407	239	483
Libyan Arab Jamahiriya	788	974	1,087	1,300	2.12	1.09	1.79	186	112	212
Madagascar	3,280	4,286	5,895	7,600	2.68	3.19	2.54	1,006	1,609	1,704
Malawi	1,742	1,633	1,773	2,395	-0.65	0.82	3.01	-109	140	621
Mali	1,826	2,423	3,327	4,535	2.83	3.17	3.10	596	904	1,208
Mauritania	372	473	597	740	2.38	2.33	2.14	100	124	142
Mauritius	279	312	343	365	1.12	0.97	0.61	33	31	21
Morocco	5,390	6,720	8,034	9,344	2.21	1.79	1.51	1,330	1,313	1,310
Mozambique	3,227	3,472	3,815	4,651	0.73	0.94	1.98	245	343	835
Namibia	321	378	421	502	1.64	1.08	1.76	57	42	81
Niger	1,306	1,640	2,096	2,595	2.27	2.46	2.13	333	456	498
Nigeria	28,008	42,406	57,072	75,706	4.15	2.97	2.83	14,397	14,666	18,634
Réunion	197	242	289	329	2.05	1.75	1.31	45	46	40
Rwanda	1,468	2,616	3,473	4,632	5.78	2.83	2.88	1,148	857	1,158
Saint Helena	...	...	...	...	...	...	...	...	...	...
São Tomé and Príncipe	...	...	...	...	...	...	...	...	...	...
Senegal	928	1,255	1,708	2,270	3.02	3.08	2.84	326	452	562
Seychelles	...	...	...	...	...	...	...	...	...	...
Sierra Leone	...	...	...	...	...	...	...	...	...	...
Somalia	1,270	1,855	2,663	3,894	3.79	3.61	3.80	585	807	1,230
South Africa	12,227	18,909	20,984	23,324	4.36	1.04	1.06	6,681	2,075	2,339
Sudan	3,314	4,091	5,167	6,422	2.11	2.33	2.18	777	1,075	1,255
Swaziland	212	352	487	639	5.07	3.25	2.71	140	135	151
Togo	956	1,326	1,887	2,653	3.27	3.53	3.41	369	561	766
Tunisia	2,023	2,504	2,879	3,228	2.13	1.39	1.15	480	374	349
Uganda	3,987	5,253	7,556	10,805	2.76	3.64	3.58	1,265	2,303	3,248
United Republic of Tanzania	5,977	7,200	8,826	10,785	1.86	2.04	2.00	1,222	1,625	1,959
Western Sahara	...	...	...	...	...	...	...	...	...	...
Zambia	1,664	2,053	2,647	3,403	2.10	2.54	2.51	388	594	756
Zimbabwe	2,939	3,760	4,723	5,923	2.46	2.28	2.26	820	963	1,199
ASIA										
Afghanistan	...	...	...	...	...	...	...	...	...	...
Armenia	679	695	695	692	0.23	0.00	-0.04	16	0	-2
Azerbaijan	1,561	1,772	1,953	2,066	1.27	0.97	0.56	211	181	113
Bahrain	100	118	134	139	1.69	1.28	0.37	18	16	5
Bangladesh	24,135	31,899	37,654	43,883	2.79	1.66	1.53	7,764	5,754	6,228
Bhutan	370	501	685	912	3.02	3.14	2.86	130	184	227
Brunei Darussalam	54	63	70	71	1.57	1.01	0.18	9	6	1
Cambodia	2,209	3,024	3,969	4,945	3.14	2.72	2.20	814	944	976
China	360,981	463,619	568,637	667,631	2.50	2.04	1.60	102,637	105,017	98,994
China, Hong Kong SAR	1,979	2,517	2,786	2,923	2.40	1.02	0.48	538	269	136
China, Macao SAR	154	211	252	279	3.17	1.79	1.01	57	41	26
Cyprus	199	222	232	233	1.08	0.41	0.08	22	9	1
Democratic People's Republic of Korea	...	...	...	...	...	...	...	...	...	...
Georgia	1,342	1,317	1,358	1,392	-0.19	0.31	0.25	-25	41	34
India	185,929	230,024	273,302	308,338	2.13	1.72	1.21	44,095	43,278	35,036
Indonesia	52,040	63,642	74,483	83,481	2.01	1.57	1.14	11,602	10,840	8,997
Iran (Islamic Republic of)	15,153	21,161	26,332	31,218	3.34	2.19	1.70	6,007	5,171	4,886
Iraq	2,722	3,356	4,302	5,653	2.09	2.48	2.73	634	945	1,351
Israel	1,661	2,064	2,390	2,637	2.17	1.47	0.98	403	325	246

TABLE B.4

continued

	Estimates and projections ('000)				Rate of change (%)			10-year increment ('000)		
	2000	2010	2020	2030	2000– 2010	2010– 2020	2020– 2030	2000– 2010	2010– 2020	2020– 2030
Japan	48,520	52,921	55,069	56,049	0.87	0.40	0.18	4,401	2,147	980
Jordan	651	916	1,254	1,658	3.41	3.14	2.79	265	337	403
Kazakhstan	5,709	6,462	7,342	8,270	1.24	1.28	1.19	752	880	927
Kuwait	260	367	422	457	3.43	1.41	0.80	106	55	35
Kyrgyzstan	935	1,018	1,143	1,251	0.84	1.16	0.90	82	125	107
Lao People's Democratic Republic	982	1,342	1,838	2,446	3.12	3.14	2.86	360	495	608
Lebanon	...	...	...	...	...	...	...	...	...	...
Malaysia	4,748	6,153	7,801	9,146	2.59	2.37	1.59	1,405	1,648	1,344
Maldives	40	57	76	99	3.52	2.86	2.63	17	19	23
Mongolia	532	684	794	879	2.51	1.49	1.02	151	109	85
Myanmar	9,892	12,120	13,808	15,430	2.03	1.30	1.11	2,228	1,688	1,621
Nepal	4,265	5,796	7,641	9,734	3.07	2.76	2.42	1,530	1,844	2,093
Occupied Palestinian Territory	...	...	...	...	...	...	...	...	...	...
Oman	358	494	654	878	3.21	2.80	2.94	135	159	223
Pakistan	15,609	21,383	28,843	37,058	3.15	2.99	2.51	5,774	7,459	8,215
Philippines	15,660	20,951	27,130	33,319	2.91	2.58	2.05	5,290	6,179	6,188
Qatar	105	118	122	123	1.12	0.37	0.04	12	4	0
Republic of Korea	14,180	16,571	18,659	20,375	1.56	1.19	0.88	2,391	2,087	1,716
Saudi Arabia	2,898	3,807	4,949	6,330	2.73	2.62	2.46	908	1,142	1,381
Singapore	727	755	764	722	0.37	0.12	-0.57	27	8	-42
Sri Lanka	3,867	4,515	4,987	5,418	1.55	0.99	0.83	648	471	431
Syrian Arab Republic	2,550	3,593	4,555	5,636	3.43	2.37	2.13	1,043	961	1,081
Tajikistan	1,104	1,302	1,545	1,801	1.65	1.71	1.53	198	243	255
Thailand	15,839	18,817	21,033	23,006	1.72	1.11	0.90	2,977	2,216	1,972
Timor-Leste	...	...	...	...	...	...	...	...	...	...
Turkey	15,779	20,186	24,505	28,529	2.46	1.94	1.52	4,407	4,318	4,024
Turkmenistan	604	681	798	951	1.20	1.59	1.74	76	117	152
United Arab Emirates	828	977	1,041	1,066	1.65	0.64	0.24	148	64	25
Uzbekistan	4,223	5,110	5,919	6,661	1.91	1.47	1.18	886	809	741
Viet Nam	17,677	22,906	27,858	31,834	2.59	1.96	1.33	5,229	4,951	3,975
Yemen	3,152	5,057	8,236	12,713	4.73	4.88	4.34	1,905	3,178	4,477
EUROPE										
Albania	652	685	766	829	0.50	1.11	0.79	33	80	62
Andorra	...	...	...	...	...	...	...	...	...	...
Austria	3,317	3,645	3,846	3,896	0.94	0.54	0.13	327	201	50
Belarus	3,133	3,318	3,290	3,264	0.57	-0.08	-0.08	184	-27	-26
Belgium	4,258	4,569	4,792	4,887	0.70	0.48	0.20	310	222	95
Bosnia and Herzegovina	...	...	...	...	...	...	...	...	...	...
Bulgaria	3,284	3,366	3,321	3,235	0.25	-0.13	-0.26	81	-44	-86
Channel Islands	...	...	...	...	...	...	...	...	...	...
Croatia	1,623	1,703	1,704	1,687	0.48	0.01	-0.10	79	1	-16
Czech Republic	4,375	4,618	4,693	4,638	0.54	0.16	-0.12	243	74	-55
Denmark	2,469	2,591	2,737	2,786	0.48	0.55	0.18	121	145	49
Estonia	581	612	607	606	0.52	-0.08	-0.02	31	-5	-1
Faeroe Islands	...	...	...	...	...	...	...	...	...	...
Finland	2,247	2,450	2,599	2,680	0.86	0.59	0.30	202	149	80
France	24,175	26,431	28,114	29,330	0.89	0.62	0.42	2,255	1,683	1,216
Germany	35,888	37,900	38,901	38,814	0.55	0.26	-0.02	2,011	1,001	-86
Gibraltar	...	...	...	...	...	...	...	...	...	...
Greece	3,902	4,278	4,392	4,370	0.92	0.26	-0.05	376	113	-21
Holy See	...	...	...	...	...	...	...	...	...	...
Hungary	3,977	4,046	4,052	3,945	0.17	0.01	-0.27	69	5	-106
Iceland	110	130	151	170	1.67	1.48	1.19	20	20	19
Ireland	1,225	1,449	1,631	1,828	1.68	1.18	1.14	224	182	196
Isle of Man	...	...	...	...	...	...	...	...	...	...
Italy	22,542	23,548	23,891	23,473	0.44	0.14	-0.18	1,005	343	-417
Latvia	871	876	850	839	0.06	-0.29	-0.14	4	-25	-11
Liechtenstein	...	...	...	...	...	...	...	...	...	...
Lithuania	1,305	1,436	1,500	1,527	0.96	0.43	0.18	131	63	27
Luxembourg	165	190	207	217	1.39	0.89	0.47	24	17	9
Malta	131	152	167	179	1.45	0.94	0.70	20	14	12
Moldova	1,249	1,384	1,454	1,520	1.02	0.49	0.45	134	69	66
Monaco	...	...	...	...	...	...	...	...	...	...
Montenegro	...	...	...	...	...	...	...	...	...	...
Netherlands	6,814	7,490	8,059	8,293	0.95	0.73	0.29	676	568	234
Norway	1,987	2,215	2,467	2,652	1.09	1.08	0.72	228	251	184
Poland	13,051	14,105	14,345	14,362	0.78	0.17	0.01	1,053	239	17
Portugal	3,649	3,880	4,021	4,072	0.62	0.36	0.13	231	140	51
Romania	7,955	8,457	8,423	8,288	0.61	-0.04	-0.16	501	-33	-135
Russian Federation	65,781	76,793	81,556	81,906	1.55	0.60	0.04	11,012	4,762	349
San Marino	...	...	...	...	...	...	...	...	...	...
Serbia	...	...	...	...	...	...	...	...	...	...
Slovakia	2,032	2,248	2,349	2,396	1.01	0.44	0.20	215	101	46
Slovenia	723	770	773	755	0.64	0.03	-0.23	47	2	-17
Spain	12,692	13,119	13,039	12,713	0.33	-0.06	-0.25	426	-80	-325
Sweden	4,284	4,738	5,157	5,361	1.01	0.85	0.39	453	418	204
Switzerland	3,303	3,709	4,028	4,171	1.16	0.82	0.35	406	318	142
TFYR Macedonia[1]	546	614	669	724	1.17	0.86	0.78	67	55	54

TABLE B.4

continued

	Estimates and projections ('000)				Rate of change (%)			10-year increment ('000)		
	2000	2010	2020	2030	2000–2010	2010–2020	2020–2030	2000–2010	2010–2020	2020–2030
Ukraine	15,855	17,307	18,072	18,603	0.88	0.43	0.29	1,452	764	530
United Kingdom	24,880	27,580	30,171	32,184	1.03	0.90	0.65	2,699	2,590	2,013
LATIN AMERICA AND THE CARIBBEAN										
Anguilla	...	...	...	...	...	...	...	...	...	...
Antigua and Barbuda	...	...	...	...	...	...	...	...	...	...
Argentina	10,556	12,736	15,011	17,324	1.88	1.64	1.43	2,179	2,275	2,312
Aruba	...	...	...	...	...	...	...	...	...	...
Bahamas	70	77	84	88	1.00	0.88	0.46	7	7	4
Barbados	85	95	104	110	1.14	0.86	0.60	10	8	6
Belize	48	64	87	108	2.95	2.98	2.21	16	22	21
Bolivia	1,616	2,051	2,596	3,165	2.39	2.36	1.98	435	545	568
Brazil	45,227	56,629	66,577	75,944	2.25	1.62	1.32	11,402	9,947	9,367
British Virgin Islands	...	...	...	...	...	...	...	...	...	...
Cayman Islands	...	...	...	...	...	...	...	...	...	...
Chile	4,133	5,276	6,572	7,861	2.44	2.20	1.79	1,143	1,296	1,288
Colombia	8,776	11,510	14,615	17,660	2.71	2.39	1.89	2,734	3,104	3,044
Costa Rica	1,026	1,454	1,880	2,329	3.49	2.57	2.14	428	425	448
Cuba	4,052	4,737	5,361	5,829	1.56	1.24	0.84	684	623	468
Dominica	...	...	...	...	...	...	...	...	...	...
Dominican Republic	2,089	2,677	3,268	3,789	2.48	2.00	1.48	587	591	521
Ecuador	3,106	4,218	5,408	6,573	3.06	2.48	1.95	1,112	1,189	1,165
El Salvador	1,677	2,271	2,972	3,748	3.03	2.69	2.32	593	701	776
Falkland Islands (Malvinas)	...	...	...	...	...	...	...	...	...	...
French Guiana	...	...	...	...	...	...	...	...	...	...
Grenada	...	...	...	...	...	...	...	...	...	...
Guadeloupe	139	165	191	212	1.72	1.43	1.02	26	25	20
Guatemala	1,791	2,349	3,070	3,852	2.71	2.68	2.27	558	720	782
Guyana	182	199	216	228	0.90	0.81	0.56	17	16	12
Haiti	1,582	2,082	2,584	3,203	2.74	2.16	2.15	499	501	619
Honduras	1,186	1,693	2,314	2,959	3.56	3.13	2.46	506	621	644
Jamaica	506	535	566	586	0.55	0.56	0.36	28	30	20
Martinique	126	145	162	176	1.37	1.13	0.81	18	17	13
Mexico	22,970	28,887	34,767	39,857	2.29	1.85	1.37	5,917	5,880	5,090
Montserrat	...	...	...	...	...	...	...	...	...	...
Netherlands Antilles	67	81	97	110	1.89	1.72	1.24	14	15	12
Nicaragua	833	1,202	1,700	2,263	3.67	3.47	2.86	369	498	562
Panama	707	907	1,112	1,297	2.49	2.04	1.53	199	205	184
Paraguay	1,164	1,699	2,356	3,127	3.77	3.27	2.83	534	657	771
Peru	5,650	7,162	8,649	9,979	2.37	1.89	1.43	1,511	1,486	1,330
Puerto Rico	1,177	1,342	1,513	1,680	1.31	1.20	1.05	164	171	167
Saint Kitts and Nevis	...	...	...	...	...	...	...	...	...	...
Saint Lucia	...	...	...	...	...	...	...	...	...	...
Saint Vincent and the Grenadines	...	...	...	...	...	...	...	...	...	...
Suriname	103	118	138	154	1.29	1.56	1.12	14	19	16
Trinidad and Tobago	295	341	362	381	1.45	0.59	0.50	46	20	18
Turks and Caicos Islands	...	...	...	...	...	...	...	...	...	...
United States Virgin Islands	...	...	...	...	...	...	...	...	...	...
Uruguay	1,023	1,146	1,290	1,441	1.13	1.18	1.11	122	143	151
Venezuela (Bolivarian Rep. of)	5,288	7,024	8,859	10,656	2.84	2.32	1.85	1,735	1,834	1,797
NORTHERN AMERICA										
Bermuda	...	...	...	...	...	...	...	...	...	...
Canada	12,690	15,449	18,171	20,692	1.97	1.62	1.30	2,759	2,721	2,520
Greenland	...	...	...	...	...	...	...	...	...	...
Saint-Pierre-et-Miquelon	...	...	...	...	...	...	...	...	...	...
United States of America	107,296	123,743	140,296	154,477	1.43	1.26	0.96	16,447	16,553	14,180
OCEANIA										
American Samoa	...	...	...	...	...	...	...	...	...	...
Australia	7,268	8,671	10,107	11,470	1.76	1.53	1.27	1,402	1,436	1,363
Cook Islands	...	...	...	...	...	...	...	...	...	...
Fiji	156	190	222	251	2.00	1.52	1.23	34	31	29
French Polynesia	53	66	79	90	2.12	1.77	1.32	12	12	11
Guam	37	42	49	53	1.29	1.57	0.76	5	7	3
Kiribati	...	...	...	...	...	...	...	...	...	...
Marshall Islands	...	...	...	...	...	...	...	...	...	...
Micronesia (Federated States of)	...	...	...	...	...	...	...	...	...	...
Nauru	...	...	...	...	...	...	...	...	...	...
New Caledonia	55	67	79	89	1.88	1.69	1.22	11	12	10
New Zealand	1,427	1,686	1,958	2,218	1.66	1.50	1.25	258	272	259
Niue	...	...	...	...	...	...	...	...	...	...
Northern Mariana Islands	...	...	...	...	...	...	...	...	...	...
Palau	...	...	...	...	...	...	...	...	...	...
Papua New Guinea	1,027	1,306	1,643	2,025	2.40	2.30	2.09	278	337	381
Pitcairn	...	...	...	...	...	...	...	...	...	...
Samoa	35	44	57	72	2.21	2.51	2.31	8	12	14
Solomon Islands	72	101	136	175	3.30	2.97	2.53	28	34	39
Tokelau	...	...	...	...	...	...	...	...	...	...
Tonga	...	...	...	...	...	...	...	...	...	...

TABLE B.4

continued

	Estimates and projections ('000)				Rate of change (%)			10-year increment ('000)		
	2000	2010	2020	2030	2000–2010	2010–2020	2020–2030	2000–2010	2010–2020	2020–2030
Tuvalu	...	...	...	...	...	...	...	...	...	...
Vanuatu	34	43	53	63	2.40	2.11	1.70	9	10	9
Wallis and Futuna Islands	...	...	...	...	...	...	...	...	...	...

Source: UN-Habitat, Household Projections Project, 2002.

Note:
(1) The former Yugoslav Republic of Macedonia.

TABLE B.5

Access to Drinking Water and Sanitation

	Improved drinking water coverage						Household connection to improved drinking water						Improved sanitation coverage					
	Total (%)		Urban (%)		Rural (%)		Total (%)		Urban (%)		Rural (%)		Total (%)		Urban (%)		Rural (%)	
	1990	2006	1990	2006	1990	2006	1990	2006	1990	2006	1990	2006	1990	2006	1990	2006	1990	2006
AFRICA																		
Algeria	94	85	99	87	88	81	68	72	87	81	48	55	88	94	99	98	77	87
Angola	39	51	37	62	40	39	1	15	3	27	0	1	26	50	55	79	9	16
Benin	63	65	73	78	57	57	7	11	18	25	1	2	12	30	32	59	2	11
Botswana	93	96	100	100	88	90	24	48	40	62	13	28	38	47	60	60	22	30
Burkina Faso	34	72	62	97	29	66	4	5	26	27	1	0	5	13	23	41	2	6
Burundi	70	71	97	84	68	70	3	6	32	46	1	1	44	41	41	44	44	41
Cameroon	49	70	76	88	31	47	12	15	26	26	2	2	39	51	47	58	34	42
Cape Verde	...	...	...	...	...	...	...	...	...	...	...	...	...	...	...	...	...	...
Central African Republic	58	66	78	90	47	51	2	2	6	6	0	0	11	31	21	40	5	25
Chad	...	48	...	71	16	40	2	5	8	16	0	1	5	9	19	23	1	4
Comoros	93	85	98	91	91	81	31	13	50	30	23	3	18	35	34	49	12	26
Congo	...	71	...	95	...	35	...	27	...	43	...	3	...	20	...	19	...	21
Côte d'Ivoire	67	81	71	98	65	66	22	35	49	62	5	13	20	24	39	38	8	12
Democratic Republic of the Congo	43	46	90	82	25	29	22	9	79	27	0	1	15	31	53	42	1	25
Djibouti	76	92	79	98	68	54	57	71	69	81	21	8	...	67	...	76	...	11
Egypt	94	98	97	99	92	98	61	89	89	99	39	82	50	66	68	85	37	52
Equatorial Guinea	43	43	45	45	42	42	4	6	12	16	0	0	51	51	60	60	46	46
Eritrea	43	60	62	74	39	57	6	8	40	42	0	0	3	5	20	14	0	3
Ethiopia	13	42	74	96	4	31	0	9	1	50	0	1	4	11	19	27	2	8
Gabon	...	87	95	95	...	47	...	45	...	52	...	8	...	36	...	37	...	30
Gambia	...	86	...	91	...	81	...	30	...	51	2	5	...	52	...	50	...	55
Ghana	56	80	86	90	39	71	16	20	40	37	2	4	6	10	11	15	3	6
Guinea	45	70	72	91	35	59	10	9	34	26	1	1	13	19	19	33	10	12
Guinea-Bissau	...	57	...	82	...	47	...	10	...	30	0	1	...	33	...	48	...	26
Kenya	41	57	90	85	30	49	20	19	58	47	11	12	39	42	18	19	44	48
Lesotho	...	78	...	93	...	74	5	15	19	59	2	5	...	36	...	43	30	34
Liberia	57	64	85	72	34	52	11	1	21	1	3	0	40	32	59	49	24	7
Libyan Arab Jamahiriya	71	...	72	...	68	...	54	...	54	...	55	...	97	97	97	97	96	96
Madagascar	39	47	80	76	27	36	7	5	28	14	1	2	8	12	15	18	6	10
Malawi	41	76	92	96	34	72	7	7	43	28	2	2	46	60	50	51	46	62
Mali	33	60	50	86	28	48	2	8	8	22	0	2	35	45	53	59	30	39
Mauritania	37	60	30	70	41	54	11	23	19	35	5	14	20	24	33	44	11	10
Mauritius	100	100	100	100	100	100	100	100	100	100	100	100	94	94	95	95	94	94
Morocco	75	83	94	100	58	58	41	58	75	87	9	15	52	72	80	85	25	54
Mozambique	...	42	...	71	...	26	...	7	...	17	...	2	...	31	...	53	...	19
Namibia	57	93	98	99	42	90	33	43	84	69	13	28	26	35	73	66	8	18
Niger	41	42	59	91	38	32	4	...	21	37	1	...	3	7	16	27	1	3
Nigeria	50	47	80	65	34	30	14	4	33	7	4	2	26	30	33	35	22	25
Réunion	...	...	...	...	...	...	...	...	...	...	...	...	...	...	...	...	...	...
Rwanda	65	65	94	82	63	61	2	5	32	22	0	1	29	23	31	34	29	20
Saint Helena	...	...	...	...	...	...	...	...	...	...	...	...	...	...	...	...	...	...
São Tomé and Príncipe	...	86	...	88	...	83	...	26	...	32	...	17	...	24	...	29	...	18
Senegal	67	77	91	93	51	65	22	43	50	78	4	18	26	28	52	54	9	9
Seychelles	...	...	100	100	...	...	...	...	100	100	...	...	...	...	...	...	100	100
Sierra Leone	...	53	...	83	...	32	...	9	...	20	1	1	...	11	...	20	...	5
Somalia	...	29	...	63	...	10	1	16	3	45	0	0	...	23	...	51	...	7
South Africa	81	93	98	100	62	82	55	67	89	84	18	42	55	59	64	66	45	49
Sudan	64	70	85	78	57	64	34	27	75	46	19	13	33	35	53	50	26	24
Swaziland	...	60	...	87	...	51	...	25	...	57	...	15	...	50	...	64	...	46
Togo	49	59	79	86	36	40	4	5	14	12	0	0	13	12	25	24	8	3
Tunisia	82	94	95	99	62	84	62	75	87	94	26	39	74	85	95	96	44	64
Uganda	43	64	78	90	39	60	2	2	18	11	0	1	29	33	27	29	29	34
United Republic of Tanzania	49	55	90	81	39	46	8	14	31	45	3	4	35	33	29	31	36	34
Western Sahara	...	...	...	...	...	...	...	...	...	...	...	...	...	...	...	...	...	...
Zambia	50	58	86	90	27	41	23	16	53	41	3	2	42	52	49	55	38	51
Zimbabwe	78	81	99	98	70	72	33	35	95	87	7	6	44	46	65	63	35	37
ASIA																		
Afghanistan	...	22	...	37	...	17	...	3	...	11	...	0	...	30	...	45	...	25
Armenia	...	98	99	99	...	96	86	89	97	97	64	74	...	91	94	96	...	81
Azerbaijan	68	78	82	95	51	59	43	48	66	76	16	19	...	80	...	90	...	70
Bahrain	...	...	100	100	...	...	...	...	100	100	...	...	...	...	100	100	...	...
Bangladesh[1]	78	80	88	85	76	78	6	5	30	20	0	0	26	36	56	48	18	32
Bhutan	...	81	...	98	...	79	...	14	...	54	...	9	...	52	...	71	...	50
Brunei Darussalam	...	...	...	...	...	...	...	...	...	...	...	...	...	...	...	...	...	...
Cambodia	...	65	...	80	...	61	...	13	...	43	...	5	...	28	...	62	...	19
China	67	88	97	98	55	81	49	72	81	87	37	62	48	65	61	74	43	59
China, Hong Kong SAR	...	...	...	...	...	...	...	...	...	...	...	...	...	...	...	...	...	...
China, Macao SAR	...	...	...	...	...	...	...	...	...	...	...	...	...	...	...	...	...	...
Cyprus	100	100	100	100	100	100	100	100	100	100	100	100	100	100	100	100	100	100
Democratic People's Republic of Korea	...	100	100	100	...	100	...	77	...	81	...	71	...	...	...	...	...	...
Georgia	76	99	91	100	58	97	55	64	81	87	22	38	94	93	96	94	91	92
India	71	89	90	96	65	86	18	21	52	49	7	10	14	28	44	52	4	18
Indonesia	72	80	92	89	63	71	9	20	26	34	2	7	51	52	73	67	42	37
Iran (Islamic Republic of)	92	...	99	99	84	...	84	...	96	96	69	...	83	...	86	...	78	...
Iraq	83	77	99	88	46	56	...	73	...	86	...	48	...	76	75	80	...	69
Israel	100	100	100	100	100	100	100	100	100	100	98	98	...	...	100	100	...	...

TABLE B.5

continued

	Improved drinking water coverage						Household connection to improved drinking water						Improved sanitation coverage					
	Total (%)		Urban (%)		Rural (%)		Total (%)		Urban (%)		Rural (%)		Total (%)		Urban (%)		Rural (%)	
	1990	2006	1990	2006	1990	2006	1990	2006	1990	2006	1990	2006	1990	2006	1990	2006	1990	2006
Japan	100	100	100	100	100	100	93	97	97	99	86	94	100	100	100	100	100	100
Jordan	97	98	99	99	91	91	94	93	97	96	87	81	...	85	...	88	...	71
Kazakhstan	96	96	99	99	91	91	66	58	93	83	31	24	97	97	97	97	96	98
Kuwait	...	...	...	...	...	...	...	...	...	...	...	...	...	...	...	...	...	...
Kyrgyzstan	...	89	97	99	...	83	44	52	75	87	25	33	...	93	...	94	...	93
Lao People's Democratic Republic	...	60	...	86	...	53	...	21	...	69	...	8	...	48	...	87	...	38
Lebanon	100	100	100	100	100	100	...	...	100	100	...	...	...	...	100	100	...	...
Malaysia	98	99	100	100	96	96	...	95	98	98	...	87	...	94	95	95	...	93
Maldives	96	83	100	98	95	76	20	23	77	76	0	0	...	59	100	100	...	42
Mongolia	64	72	97	90	21	48	29	22	51	35	0	6	...	50	...	64	...	31
Myanmar	57	80	86	80	47	80	5	6	18	16	1	2	23	82	47	85	15	81
Nepal	72	89	97	94	70	88	7	17	44	49	3	11	9	27	36	45	6	24
Occupied Palestinian Territory	...	89	...	90	...	88	...	78	...	84	...	64	...	80	...	84	...	69
Oman	81	...	85	...	73	...	26	...	35	...	8	...	85	...	97	97	61	...
Pakistan	86	90	96	95	81	87	21	29	52	48	8	19	33	58	76	90	14	40
Philippines	83	93	92	96	75	88	22	53	37	69	8	24	58	78	71	81	46	72
Qatar	100	100	100	100	100	100	...	...	100	100	...	...	100	100	100	100	100	100
Republic of Korea	...	...	97	97	...	...	...	...	96	96	...	...	...	...	...	...	...	...
Saudi Arabia	89	...	97	97	63	...	88	...	97	97	60	...	...	...	100	100	...	...
Singapore	...	...	100	100	...	...	...	...	100	100	...	...	...	...	100	100	...	...
Sri Lanka	67	82	91	98	62	79	10	7	36	32	4	3	71	86	85	89	68	86
Syrian Arab Republic	83	89	96	95	70	83	72	81	93	93	51	68	81	92	94	96	69	88
Tajikistan	...	67	...	93	...	58	...	37	...	81	...	23	...	92	...	95	...	91
Thailand	95	98	98	99	94	97	32	51	78	84	13	35	78	96	92	95	72	96
Timor Leste	...	62	...	77	...	56	...	16	...	28	...	11	...	41	...	64	...	32
Turkey	85	97	92	98	74	95	60	93	70	97	46	86	85	88	96	96	69	72
Turkmenistan	...	...	...	...	...	...	...	...	...	...	...	...	...	...	...	...	...	...
United Arab Emirates	100	100	100	100	100	100	...	78	...	80	...	70	97	97	98	98	95	95
Uzbekistan	90	88	97	98	85	82	57	49	86	85	37	28	93	96	97	97	91	95
Viet Nam	52	92	87	98	43	90	8	22	38	59	1	8	29	65	62	88	21	56
Yemen	...	66	...	68	...	65	...	20	...	57	...	6	28	46	79	88	14	30
EUROPE																		
Albania	...	97	100	97	...	97	...	81	98	92	...	72	...	97	97	98	...	97
Andorra	100	100	100	100	100	100	...	...	100	100	...	...	100	100	100	100	100	100
Austria	100	100	100	100	100	100	100	100	100	100	100	100	100	100	100	100	100	100
Belarus	100	100	100	100	100	99	...	87	...	94	...	68	...	93	...	91	...	97
Belgium	...	...	100	100	...	...	100	...	100	100	90	...	...	...	...	...	...	...
Bosnia and Herzegovina	97	99	99	100	96	98	...	82	96	94	...	72	...	95	99	99	...	92
Bulgaria	99	99	100	100	97	97	88	...	96	96	72	...	99	99	100	100	96	96
Channel Islands	...	...	...	...	...	...	...	...	...	...	...	...	...	...	...	...	...	...
Croatia	99	99	100	100	98	98	...	85	95	95	...	71	99	99	99	99	98	98
Czech Republic	100	100	100	100	100	100	...	95	97	97	...	91	100	99	100	100	98	98
Denmark	100	100	100	100	100	100	100	100	100	100	100	100	100	100	100	100	100	100
Estonia	100	100	100	100	99	99	80	90	92	97	51	75	95	95	96	96	94	94
Faeroe Islands	...	...	...	...	...	...	...	...	...	...	...	...	...	...	...	...	...	...
Finland	100	100	100	100	100	100	92	...	96	100	85	...	100	100	100	100	100	100
France	...	100	100	100	...	100	99	100	100	100	95	100	...	...	...	...	...	...
Germany	100	100	100	100	100	100	99	99	100	100	97	97	100	100	100	100	100	100
Gibraltar	...	...	...	...	...	...	...	...	...	...	...	...	...	...	...	...	...	...
Greece	96	100	99	100	91	99	92	100	99	100	82	99	97	98	100	99	93	97
Holy See	...	...	...	...	...	...	...	...	...	...	...	...	...	...	...	...	...	...
Hungary	96	100	98	100	91	100	86	94	94	95	72	93	100	100	100	100	100	100
Iceland	100	100	100	100	100	100	100	100	100	100	100	100	100	100	100	100	100	100
Ireland	...	...	100	100	...	...	98	98	99	99	96	96	...	...	...	...	...	...
Isle of Man	...	...	...	...	...	...	...	...	...	...	...	...	...	...	...	...	...	...
Italy	...	...	100	100	...	...	99	99	100	100	96	96	...	...	...	...	...	...
Latvia	99	99	100	100	96	96	...	82	...	93	...	59	...	78	...	82	...	71
Liechtenstein	...	...	...	...	...	...	...	...	...	...	...	...	...	...	...	...	...	...
Lithuania	...	...	...	...	...	...	76	81	89	93	49	57	...	...	...	...	...	...
Luxembourg	100	100	100	100	100	100	100	100	100	100	98	98	100	100	100	100	100	100
Malta	100	100	100	100	100	100	100	100	100	100	96	96	...	...	100	100	...	...
Moldova	...	90	98	96	...	85	...	43	...	79	...	12	...	79	...	85	...	73
Monaco	...	...	100	100	...	...	...	...	100	100	...	...	...	...	100	100	...	...
Montenegro	...	98	...	100	...	96	...	83	...	98	...	66	...	91	...	96	...	86
Netherlands	100	100	100	100	100	100	98	100	100	100	95	100	100	100	100	100	100	100
Norway	100	100	100	100	100	100	100	100	100	100	100	100	...	...	...	...	...	...
Poland	...	...	100	100	...	...	88	98	97	99	73	96	...	...	...	...	...	...
Portugal	96	99	98	99	94	100	87	99	95	99	80	99	92	99	97	99	88	98
Romania	76	88	93	99	55	76	49	50	85	86	7	8	72	72	88	88	52	54
Russian Federation	94	97	97	100	86	88	76	82	86	93	49	52	87	87	93	93	70	70
San Marino	...	...	...	...	...	...	...	...	...	...	...	...	...	...	...	...	...	...
Serbia	...	99	...	99	...	98	...	81	...	97	...	63	...	92	...	96	...	88
Slovakia	100	100	100	100	100	100	95	94	100	94	89	94	100	100	100	100	99	99
Slovenia	...	...	...	...	...	...	...	...	...	...	...	...	...	...	...	...	...	...
Spain	100	100	100	100	100	100	99	99	99	99	100	100	...	100	...	100	100	100
Sweden	100	100	100	100	100	100	100	100	100	100	100	100	100	100	100	100	100	100
Switzerland	100	100	100	100	100	100	100	100	100	100	99	99	100	100	100	100	100	100

TABLE B.5

continued

	Improved drinking water coverage						Household connection to improved drinking water						Improved sanitation coverage					
	Total (%)		Urban (%)		Rural (%)		Total (%)		Urban (%)		Rural (%)		Total (%)		Urban (%)		Rural (%)	
	1990	2006	1990	2006	1990	2006	1990	2006	1990	2006	1990	2006	1990	2006	1990	2006	1990	2006
TFYR Macedonia[2]	...	100	...	100	...	99	...	92	...	96	...	84	...	89	...	92	...	81
Ukraine	...	97	100	97	...	97	...	75	...	87	...	51	96	93	98	97	93	83
United Kingdom	100	100	100	100	100	100	100	100	100	100	98	98	...	...	...	...	...	...
LATIN AMERICA AND THE CARIBBEAN																		
Anguilla	...	...	...	...	...	...	...	...	...	...	...	...	...	...	99	99	...	...
Antigua and Barbuda	...	...	95	95	...	...	...	...	...	...	...	...	...	...	98	98	...	...
Argentina	94	96	97	98	72	80	69	79	76	83	22	45	81	91	86	92	45	83
Aruba	100	100	100	100	100	100	100	100	100	100	100	100	...	...	...	...	...	...
Bahamas	...	...	98	98	...	...	...	...	...	...	...	...	100	100	100	100	100	100
Barbados	100	100	100	100	100	100	...	...	98	100	...	...	100	99	99	99	100	100
Belize	...	100	100	100	...	...	...	...	92	100	...	...	...	...	...	...	...	...
Bolivia	72	86	91	96	49	69	53	75	78	91	22	45	33	43	47	54	15	22
Brazil	83	91	93	97	54	58	66	77	85	88	8	17	71	77	82	84	37	37
British Virgin Islands	98	98	98	98	98	98	97	97	97	97	97	97	100	100	100	100	100	100
Cayman Islands	...	...	...	...	...	...	...	...	...	...	...	...	...	...	...	...	...	...
Chile	91	95	99	98	49	72	84	92	97	98	22	46	84	94	91	97	48	74
Colombia	89	93	98	99	68	77	76	87	94	96	36	63	68	78	81	85	39	58
Costa Rica	...	98	...	99	88	96	...	97	...	99	74	95	94	96	96	96	92	95
Cuba	...	91	95	95	...	78	65	74	77	82	31	49	98	98	99	99	95	95
Dominica	...	...	100	100	...	...	...	...	98	98	...	...	...	...	...	...	...	...
Dominican Republic	84	95	98	97	66	91	63	82	85	92	35	62	68	79	77	81	57	74
Ecuador	73	95	82	98	61	91	52	81	72	91	27	65	71	84	88	91	50	72
El Salvador	69	84	90	94	48	68	45	62	74	78	16	38	73	86	88	90	59	80
Falkland Islands (Malvinas)	...	...	...	...	...	...	...	...	...	...	...	...	...	...	...	...	...	...
French Guiana	...	...	...	...	...	...	...	...	...	...	...	...	...	...	...	...	...	...
Grenada	...	...	97	97	...	...	...	...	...	...	...	...	97	97	96	96	97	97
Guadeloupe	...	...	98	98	...	...	...	...	98	98	...	...	...	...	...	...	...	...
Guatemala	79	96	89	99	72	94	49	78	70	91	34	67	70	84	87	90	58	79
Guyana	...	93	...	98	...	91	...	67	...	81	...	61	...	81	...	85	...	80
Haiti	52	58	62	70	48	51	9	11	27	21	2	4	29	19	49	29	20	12
Honduras	72	84	91	95	60	74	58	79	82	93	42	67	45	66	68	78	29	55
Jamaica	92	93	98	97	86	88	61	70	89	90	33	47	83	83	82	82	83	84
Martinique	...	...	...	...	...	...	...	...	...	...	...	...	...	...	...	...	...	...
Mexico	88	95	94	98	72	85	76	91	87	96	47	73	56	81	74	91	8	48
Montserrat	100	100	100	100	100	100	...	...	98	98	...	...	96	96	96	96	96	96
Netherlands Antilles	...	...	...	...	...	...	...	...	...	...	...	...	...	...	...	...	...	...
Nicaragua	70	79	91	90	46	63	53	61	85	84	16	27	42	48	59	57	23	34
Panama	...	92	100	96	...	81	...	89	97	93	...	79	...	74	...	78	...	63
Paraguay	52	77	78	94	28	52	29	62	60	84	0	29	60	70	88	89	34	42
Peru	75	84	88	92	46	63	56	77	74	90	16	44	55	72	73	85	15	36
Puerto Rico	...	...	...	...	...	...	...	...	...	...	...	...	...	...	...	...	...	...
Saint Kitts and Nevis	99	99	99	99	99	99	...	...	...	...	...	...	96	96	96	96	96	96
Saint Lucia	98	98	98	98	98	98	...	...	...	...	...	...	...	...	...	...	...	...
Saint Vincent and the Grenadines	...	...	...	...	...	...	...	...	...	...	...	...	...	...	...	...	96	96
Suriname	...	92	99	97	...	79	...	71	...	80	...	46	82	90	89	...	...	60
Trinidad and Tobago	88	94	92	97	88	93	69	74	81	86	68	72	93	92	93	92	93	92
Turks and Caicos Islands	100	100	100	100	100	100	...	...	...	...	...	...	...	...	98	98	...	...
United States Virgin Islands	...	...	...	...	...	...	...	...	...	...	...	...	...	...	...	...	...	...
Uruguay	100	100	100	100	100	100	...	96	...	97	...	84	100	100	100	100	99	99
Venezuela (Bolivarian Republic of)	89	...	93	...	70	...	81	...	87	...	48	...	83	...	90	...	47	...
NORTHERN AMERICA																		
Bermuda	...	...	...	...	...	...	...	...	...	...	...	...	...	...	...	...	...	...
Canada	100	100	100	100	99	99	85	88	100	100	38	38	100	100	100	100	99	99
Greenland	...	...	...	...	...	...	...	...	...	...	...	...	...	...	...	...	...	...
Saint-Pierre-et-Miquelon	...	...	...	...	...	...	...	...	...	...	...	...	...	...	...	...	...	...
United States of America	99	99	100	100	94	94	84	87	97	97	46	46	100	100	100	100	99	99
OCEANIA																		
American Samoa	...	...	...	...	...	...	...	...	...	...	...	...	...	...	...	...	...	...
Australia	100	100	100	100	100	100	...	...	...	...	...	...	100	100	100	100	100	100
Cook Islands	94	95	99	98	87	88	...	...	...	...	...	...	96	100	100	100	91	100
Fiji	48	47	43	43	51	51	17	20	32	32	7	7	68	71	87	87	55	55
French Polynesia	100	100	100	100	100	100	98	98	99	99	96	96	98	98	99	99	97	97
Guam	100	100	100	100	100	100	...	...	...	...	...	...	99	99	99	99	98	98
Kiribati	48	65	76	77	33	53	24	36	46	49	13	22	22	33	26	46	20	20
Marshall Islands	96	...	95	...	97	...	...	...	...	...	...	...	75	...	88	...	51	...
Micronesia (Federated States of)	88	94	93	95	86	94	...	...	...	...	...	...	29	25	54	61	20	14
Nauru	...	...	...	...	...	...	...	...	...	...	...	...	...	...	...	...	...	...
New Caledonia	...	...	...	...	...	...	...	...	...	...	...	...	...	...	...	...	...	...
New Zealand	97	...	100	100	82	...	...	...	100	100	...	...	...	...	...	...	88	...
Niue	100	100	100	100	100	100	...	...	100	100	...	...	100	100	100	100	100	100
Northern Mariana Islands	98	98	98	98	100	97	...	...	...	93	...	...	84	94	85	94	78	96
Palau	90	89	73	79	98	94	...	...	...	...	...	...	61	67	76	96	54	52
Papua New Guinea	39	40	88	88	32	32	11	12	61	61	4	4	44	45	67	67	41	41
Pitcairn	...	...	...	...	...	...	...	...	...	...	...	...	...	...	...	...	...	...
Samoa	91	88	99	90	89	87	...	...	...	...	...	...	98	100	100	100	98	100
Solomon Islands	69	70	94	94	65	65	11	14	76	76	1	1	29	32	98	98	18	18

TABLE B.5

continued

	Improved drinking water coverage						Household connection to improved drinking water						Improved sanitation coverage					
	Total (%)		Urban (%)		Rural (%)		Total (%)		Urban (%)		Rural (%)		Total (%)		Urban (%)		Rural (%)	
	1990	2006	1990	2006	1990	2006	1990	2006	1990	2006	1990	2006	1990	2006	1990	2006	1990	2006
Tokelau	...	...	...	...	94	88	...	...	...	...	...	...	...	...	...	...	39	78
Tonga	100	100	100	100	100	100	...	...	...	...	...	...	96	96	98	98	96	96
Tuvalu	90	93	92	94	89	92	...	...	...	...	...	...	78	89	83	93	74	84
Vanuatu	61	...	93	...	53	...	38	...	80	...	28	...	...	...	...	...	...	...
Wallis and Futuna Islands	...	...	...	...	100	100	...	...	...	...	99	99	...	...	...	...	...	...

Source: WHO (World Health Organization) and UNICEF (United Nations Children's Fund) Joint Monitoring Programme for Water Supply and Sanitation (JMP), *Progress on Drinking Water and Sanitation: Special Focus on Sanitation 2008,* WHO and UNICEF, Geneva.

Notes:

(1) The figures for Bangladesh have been adjusted for arsenic contamination levels based on the national surveys conducted and approved by the Government.

(2) The former Yugoslav Republic of Macedonia.

TABLE B.6

Poverty and Inequality

| | Gross national income PPP $/capita | | Inequality | | | | National poverty line | | | | International poverty line | | | | | | |
| | | | Income / consumption[2] | | Land | | | | | | | | | | | | |
	2000	2007	Survey year	Gini index	Survey year	Gini index	Survey year	Rural %	Urban %	Total %	Survey year	Rural %	Urban %	Total %	Survey year	Below US$1/day	Below US$1/day
AFRICA																	
Algeria	5,040[l]	7,640[l]	1995[c]	0.35		...	1995	30.3	14.7	22.6	1998	16.6	7.3	12.2	1995	<2	15.1
Angola	1,180[l]	4,400		...							...						...
Benin	980	1,310	2003[c]	0.37		...	1995	25.2	28.5	26.5	1999	33.0	23.3	29.0	2003	30.9	73.7
Botswana	7,170	12,420	1993[c]	0.61		...		...	...	...		...	...	...	1993	28.0	55.5
Burkina Faso	970[l]	1,120	2003[c]	0.40	1993	0.42	1998	61.1	22.4	54.6	2003	52.4	19.2	46.4	2003	27.2	71.8
Burundi	580[l]	330	1998[c]	0.42			1990	36.0	43.0	36.4					1998	54.6	87.6
Cameroon	1,590	2,120	2001[c]	0.45		...	1996	59.6	41.4	53.3	2001	49.9	22.1	40.2	2001	17.1	50.6
Cape Verde	...	2,940															
Central African Republic	1,160[l]	740	1993[c]	0.61		...									1993	66.6	84.0
Chad	870	1,280		...		...	1995-96	67.0	63.0	64.0							...
Comoros	...	1,150		...													...
Congo	570	2,750		...													...
Côte d'Ivoire	1,500	1,590	2002[c]	0.45		...									2002	14.8	48.8
Democratic Republic of the Congo	...	290		...													...
Djibouti	...	2,260		...													...
Egypt	3,670	5,400	2000[c]	0.34	1990	0.65	1995-96	23.3	22.5	22.9	1999-2000	...	...	16.7	1999-2000	3.1	43.9
Equatorial Guinea	...	21,230		...													...
Eritrea	960	520[l]		...			1993-94	...	...	53.0							...
Ethiopia	660	780	1999-2000[c]	0.30	2001	0.47	1995-96	47.0	33.3	45.5	1999-2000	45.0	37.0	44.2	1999-2000	23.0	77.8
Gabon	5,360	13,080															...
Gambia	1,620[l]	1,140	1998[c]	0.50			1992	...	...	64.0	1998	61.0	48.0	57.6	1998	59.3	82.9
Ghana	1,910[l]	1,330	1998-99[c]	0.41		...	1992	...	...	50.0	1998-99	49.9	18.6	39.5	1998-99	44.8	78.5
Guinea	1,930	1,120	2003[c]	0.39		...	1994	...	...	40.0							...
Guinea-Bissau	710	470	1993[c]	0.47	1988	0.62		...	...	...							...
Kenya	1,010	1,540	1997[c]	0.43		...	1994	47.0	29.0	40.0	1997	53.0	49.0	52.0	1997	22.8	58.3
Lesotho	2,590[l]	1,890	1998[c]	0.63	1989-90	0.49											...
Liberia	...	290		...													...
Libyan Arab Jamahiriya	...	14,710[l]		...													...
Madagascar	820	920	2001[c]	0.48		...	1997	76.0	63.2	73.3	1999	76.7	52.1	71.3	2001	61.0	85.1
Malawi	600	750	2004-05[c]	0.39	1993	0.52	1990-91	...	...	54.0	1997-98	66.5	54.9	65.3	2004-05	20.8	62.9
Mali	780	1,040	2001[c]	0.40		...					1998	75.9	30.1	63.8	2001	36.1	72.1
Mauritania	1,630	2,010	2000[c]	0.39			1996	65.5	30.1	50.0	2000	61.2	25.4	46.3	2000	25.9	63.1
Mauritius	9,940	11,390															...
Morocco	3,450	3,990	1999[c]	0.40	1996	0.62	1990-91	18.0	7.6	13.1	1998-99	27.2	12.0	19.0	1998-99	<2	14.3
Mozambique	800[l]	690	2002-03[c]	0.47		...	1996-97	71.3	62.0	69.4					2002-03	36.2	74.1
Namibia	6,410[l]	5,120	1993[y]	0.74	1997	0.36									1993	34.9	55.8
Niger	740[l]	630	1995[c]	0.51		...	1989-93	66.0	52.0	63.0					1995	60.6	85.8
Nigeria	800	1,770	2003[c]	0.44			1985	49.5	31.7	43.0	1992-93	36.4	30.4	34.1	2003	70.8	92.4
Réunion	...	...		...													...
Rwanda	930	860	2000[c]	0.47			1993	...	...	51.2	1999-2000	65.7	14.3	60.3	2000	60.3	87.8
Saint Helena	...	...															
São Tomé and Príncipe	...	1,630															...
Senegal	1,480	1,640	2001[c]	0.41	1998	0.50	1992	40.4	23.7	33.4					2001	17.0	56.2
Seychelles	...	15,450[l]															
Sierra Leone	480	660	1989[c]	0.63			1989	...	...	82.8	2003-04	79.0	56.4	70.2	1989	57.0	74.5
Somalia	...	...															
South Africa	9,160[l]	9,560	2000[c]	0.58		...									2000	10.7	34.1
Sudan	1,520	1,880		...													...
Swaziland	4,600	4,930															...
Togo	1,410	800		...		...	1987-89	...	...	32.3							...
Tunisia	6,070	7,130	2000[c]	0.40	1993	0.70	1990	13.1	3.5	7.4	1995	13.9	3.6	7.6	2000	<2	6.6
Uganda	1,210[l]	920	2002[c]	0.46	1991	0.59	1999-2000	37.4	9.6	33.8	2002-03	41.7	12.2	37.7			
United Republic of Tanzania	520	1,200	2000-01[c]	0.35		...	1991	40.8	31.2	38.6	2000-01	38.7	29.5	35.7	2000-01	57.8	89.9
Western Sahara	...	...		...													...
Zambia	750	1,220	2004[c]	0.51			1998	83.1	56.0	72.9	2004	78.0	53.0	68.0	2004	63.8	87.2
Zimbabwe	2,550	...	1995-96[c]	0.50		...	1990-91	35.8	3.4	25.8	1995-96	48.0	7.9	34.9	1995-96	56.1	83.0
ASIA																	
Afghanistan	...	...		...													
Armenia	2,580	5,900	2003[c]	0.34		...	1998-99	50.8	58.3	55.1	2001	48.7	51.9	50.9	2003	<2	31.1
Azerbaijan	2,740	6,370	2001[c]	0.37			1995	...	...	68.1	2001	42.0	55.0	49.8	2001	3.7	33.4
Bahrain	...	34,310		...													
Bangladesh	1,590	1,340	2000[c]	0.33	1996	0.62	1995-96	55.2	29.4	51.0	2000	53.0	36.6	49.8	2000	41.3	84.0
Bhutan	...	4,980															
Brunei Darussalam	...	49,900		...													
Cambodia	1,440	1,690	2004[c]	0.42			1997	40.1	21.1	36.1	2004	38.0	18.0	35.0	1997	34.1	77.7
China	3,920	5,370	2004[y]	0.47			1996	7.9	<2	6.0	1998	4.6	<2	4.6	2004	9.9	34.9
China, Hong Kong SAR	25,590	44,050		...													
China, Macao SAR	...	...		...													
Cyprus	...	26,370		...													
Democratic People's Republic of Korea	...	...		...													
Georgia	2,680	4,770	2003[c]	0.40		...	2002	55.4	48.5	52.1	2003	52.7	56.2	54.5	2003	6.5	25.3
India	2,340	2,740	2004-05[c]	0.37		...	1993-94	37.3	32.4	36.0	1999-2000	30.2	24.7	28.6	2004-05	33.5	80.0
Indonesia	2,830	3,580	2000[c]	0.34	1993	0.46	1996	...	...	15.7	1999	34.4	16.1	27.1	2002	7.5	52.4
Iran (Islamic Republic of)	5,910	10,800	1998[c]	0.43		...		...	...	...		...	...	...	1998	<2	7.3

TABLE B.6

continued

	Gross national income PPP $/capita		Inequality — Income/consumption²		Inequality — Land		National poverty line				International poverty line						
	2000	2007	Survey year	Gini index	Survey year	Gini index	Survey year	Rural %	Urban %	Total %	Survey year	Rural %	Urban %	Total %	Survey year	Below US$1/day	Below US$1/day
Iraq	...	...	...	...	...	...	...	...	...	...	...	...	...	...	...	...	...
Israel	19,330	25,930	2001[y]	0.39	...	...	...	...	...	...	...	...	...	...	...	...	...
Japan	27,080	34,600	1993[y]	0.25	1995	0.59	...	...	...	...	...	...	...	...	...	...	...
Jordan	3,950	5,160	2002-03[c]	0.39	1997	0.78	1997	27.0	19.7	21.3	2002	18.7	12.9	14.2	2002-03	<2	7.0
Kazakhstan	5,490	9,700	2003[c]	0.34	...	...	1996	39.0	30.0	34.6	...	...	...	...	2003	<2	16.0
Kuwait	18,690	49,970	...	...	...	...	...	...	...	...	...	...	...	...	...	...	...
Kyrgyzstan	2,540	1,950	2003[c]	0.30	...	...	2001	51.0	41.2	47.6	2003	...	...	41.0	2003	<2	21.4
Lao People's Democratic Republic	1,540[i]	1,940	1998[c]	0.35	1999	0.39	1993	48.7	33.1	45.0	1997-98	41.0	26.9	38.6	2002	27.0	74.1
Lebanon	4,550	10,050	...	...	...	...	...	...	...	...	...	...	...	...	...	...	...
Malaysia	8,330	13,570	1997[y]	0.49	...	...	1989	...	...	15.5	...	...	...	...	1997	<2	9.3
Maldives	...	5,040	...	...	...	...	...	...	...	...	...	...	...	...	...	...	...
Mongolia	1,760	3,160	2002[c]	0.33	...	...	1998	32.6	39.4	35.6	2002	43.4	30.3	36.1	2002	10.8	44.6
Myanmar	...	...	...	...	...	...	...	...	...	...	...	...	...	...	...	...	...
Nepal	1,370	...	2003-04[c]	0.47	1992	0.45	1995-96	43.3	21.6	41.8	2003-04	34.6	9.6	30.9	2003-04	24.1	68.5
Occupied Palestinian Territory	...	...	...	...	...	...	...	...	...	...	...	...	...	...	...	...	...
Oman	...	19,740	...	...	...	...	...	...	...	...	...	...	...	...	...	...	...
Pakistan	1,860	2,570	2002[c]	0.31	1990	0.57	1993	33.4	17.2	28.6	1998-99	35.9	24.2	32.6	2002	17.0	73.6
Philippines	4,220	3,730	2003[c]	0.45	1991	0.55	1994	53.1	28.0	40.6	1997	50.7	21.5	36.8	2002	14.8	43.0
Qatar	...	...	...	...	...	...	...	...	...	...	...	...	...	...	...	...	...
Republic of Korea	17,300	24,750	1998[y]	0.32	1990	0.34	...	...	...	...	...	...	...	...	1998	<2	<2
Saudi Arabia	11,390	22,910	...	...	...	...	...	...	...	...	...	...	...	...	...	...	...
Singapore	24,910	48,520	1998[y]	0.43	...	...	...	...	...	...	...	...	...	...	...	...	...
Sri Lanka	3,460	4,210	2002[c]	0.40	...	...	1990-91	22.0	15.0	20.0	1995-96	27.0	15.0	25.0	2002	5.6	41.6
Syrian Arab Republic	3,340	4,370	...	...	...	...	...	...	...	...	...	...	...	...	...	...	...
Tajikistan	1,090	1,710	2003[c]	0.33	...	...	...	...	...	...	...	...	...	...	2003	7.4	42.8
Thailand	6,320	7,880	2002[c]	0.42	1993	0.47	1994	...	...	9.8	1998	...	...	13.6	2002	<2	25.2
Timor-Leste	...	3,080[i]	...	...	...	...	...	...	...	...	...	...	...	...	...	...	...
Turkey	7,030	12,090	2003[c]	0.44	1991	0.61	1994	...	...	28.3	2002	34.5	22.0	27.0	2003	3.4	18.7
Turkmenistan	3,800	4,350[i]	1998[c]	0.41	...	...	...	...	...	...	...	...	...	...	...	...	...
United Arab Emirates	...	...	...	...	...	...	...	...	...	...	...	...	...	...	...	...	...
Uzbekistan	2,360	2,430[i]	2003[c]	0.37	...	...	2000	30.5	22.5	27.5	...	...	...	...	2003	<2	<2
Viet Nam	2,000	2,550	2004[c]	0.34	1994	0.53	1998	45.5	9.2	37.4	2002	35.6	6.6	28.9	...	...	...
Yemen	770	2,200	1998[c]	0.33	...	...	1998	45.0	30.8	41.8	...	...	...	...	1998	15.7	45.2
EUROPE																	
Albania	3,600	6,580	2004[c]	0.31	1998	0.84	...	...	...	...	2002	29.6	19.8	25.4	2004	<2	10.0
Andorra	...	...	...	...	...	...	...	...	...	...	...	...	...	...	...	...	...
Austria	26,330	38,090	2000[y]	0.29	1999-2000	0.59	...	...	...	...	...	...	...	...	...	...	...
Belarus	7,550	10,740	2002[c]	0.30	...	...	...	...	...	...	2000	...	...	41.9	2002	<2	<2
Belgium	27,470	35,110	2000[y]	0.33	1999-2000	0.56	...	...	...	...	...	...	...	...	...	...	...
Bosnia and Herzegovina	...	7,280	2001[c]	0.26	...	...	...	...	...	...	2002	19.9	13.8	19.5	...	...	...
Bulgaria	5,560	11,180	2003[c]	0.29	...	...	1997	...	...	36.0	2001	...	...	12.8	2003	<2	6.1
Channel Islands	...	...	...	...	...	...	...	...	...	...	...	...	...	...	...	...	...
Croatia	7,960	15,050	2001[c]	0.29	...	...	...	...	...	...	...	...	...	...	2001	<2	<2
Czech Republic	13,780	21,820	1996[y]	0.25	2000	0.92	...	...	...	...	...	...	...	...	1996	<2	<2
Denmark	27,250	36,740	1997[y]	0.25	1999-2000	0.51	...	...	...	...	...	...	...	...	...	...	...
Estonia	9,340	19,680	2003[c]	0.36	2001	0.79	1995	14.7	6.8	8.9	...	...	...	...	2003	<2	7.5
Faeroe Islands	...	...	...	...	...	...	...	...	...	...	...	...	...	...	...	...	...
Finland	24,570	35,270	2000[y]	0.27	1999-2000	0.27	...	...	...	...	...	...	...	...	...	...	...
France	24,420	33,470	1995[y]	0.33	1999-2000	0.58	...	...	...	...	...	...	...	...	...	...	...
Germany	24,920	33,820	2000[y]	0.28	1999-2000	0.63	...	...	...	...	...	...	...	...	...	...	...
Gibraltar	...	...	...	...	...	...	...	...	...	...	...	...	...	...	...	...	...
Greece	16,860	32,520	2000[c]	0.34	1999-2000	0.58	...	...	...	...	...	...	...	...	...	...	...
Holy See	...	...	...	...	...	...	...	...	...	...	...	...	...	...	...	...	...
Hungary	11,990	17,430	2002[c]	0.27	...	...	1993	...	...	14.5	1997	...	...	17.3	2002	<2	<2
Iceland	...	34,060	...	...	...	...	...	...	...	...	...	...	...	...	...	...	...
Ireland	25,520	37,040	...	...	...	...	...	...	...	...	...	...	...	...	...	...	...
Isle of Man	...	33,750[i]	...	...	...	...	...	...	...	...	...	...	...	...	...	...	...
Italy	23,470	29,900	2000[y]	0.36	1999-2000	0.73	...	...	...	...	...	...	...	...	...	...	...
Latvia	7,070	16,890	2003[c]	0.38	2001	0.58	...	...	...	...	...	...	...	...	2003	<2	4.7
Liechtenstein	...	...	...	...	...	...	...	...	...	...	...	...	...	...	...	...	...
Lithuania	6,980	17,180	2003[c]	0.36	...	...	...	...	...	...	...	...	...	...	2003	<2	7.8
Luxembourg	...	64,400	...	...	1999-2000	0.48	...	...	...	...	...	...	...	...	...	...	...
Malta	...	20,990	...	...	...	...	...	...	...	...	...	...	...	...	...	...	...
Moldova	2,230	2,930	2001[c]	0.36	...	...	2001	64.1	58.0	62.4	2002	67.2	42.6	48.5	2003	<2	20.8
Monaco	...	...	...	...	...	...	...	...	...	...	...	...	...	...	...	...	...
Montenegro	...	10,290	...	...	...	...	...	...	...	...	...	...	...	...	...	...	...
Netherlands	25,850	39,500	1999[y]	0.31	1999-2000	0.57	...	...	...	...	...	...	...	...	...	...	...
Norway	29,630	53,690	2000[y]	0.26	1999	0.18	...	...	...	...	...	...	...	...	...	...	...
Poland	9,000	15,590	2002[c]	0.35	2002	0.69	1993	...	...	23.8	...	...	...	...	2002	<2	<2
Portugal	16,990	20,640	1997[y]	0.39	1999-2000	0.74	...	...	...	...	...	...	...	...	1994	<2	<2
Romania	6,360	10,980	2003[c]	0.31	...	...	1994	27.9	20.4	21.5	...	...	...	...	2003	<2	12.9
Russian Federation	8,010	14,400	2002[c]	0.40	...	...	1994	...	...	30.9	...	...	...	...	2002	<2	12.1
San Marino	...	37,080[i]	...	...	...	...	...	...	...	...	...	...	...	...	...	...	...
Serbia	...	10,220	2003[c3]	0.30	...	...	...	...	...	...	...	...	...	...	...	...	...
Slovakia	11,040	19,330	1996[y]	0.26	...	...	...	...	...	...	...	...	...	...	1996	<2	2.9

TABLE B.6

continued

	Gross national income PPP $/capita		Inequality				National poverty line				International poverty line						
			Income / consumption[2]		Land												
	2000	2007	Survey year	Gini index	Survey year	Gini index	Survey year	Rural %	Urban %	Total %	Survey year	Rural %	Urban %	Total %	Survey year	Below US$1/day	Below US$1/day
Slovenia	17,310	26,640	1998[c]	0.28	1991	0.62		...	...	...		...	...	...	1998	<2	<2
Spain	19,260	30,110	2000[y]	0.35	1999-2000	0.77		...	...	...		...	...	...		...	...
Sweden	23,970	35,840	2000[y]	0.25	1999-2000	0.32		...	...	...		...	...	...		...	...
Switzerland	30,450	43,080	2000[y]	0.38	1999	0.50		...	...	...		...	...	...		...	...
TFYR Macedonia[4]	5,020	8,510	2003[c]	0.39		...	2002	25.3	...	21.4	2003	22.3	...	21.7	2003	<2	<2
Ukraine	3,700	6,810	2003[c]	0.28		...	2000	34.9	...	31.5	2003	28.4	...	19.5	2003	<2	4.9
United Kingdom	23,550	34,370	1999[y]	0.36	1999-2000	0.66		...	...	...		...	...	...		...	...
LATIN AMERICA AND THE CARIBBEAN																	
Anguilla	...	...	...		...											...	...
Antigua and Barbuda	...	17,620[i]	...		...											...	...
Argentina	12,050	12,990	2004[y]	0.51	1988	0.83	1995	...	28.4	...	1998	...	29.9	...	2004	6.6	17.4
Aruba	...	...	...		...											...	...
Bahamas	...	...														...	...
Barbados	...	16,140[i]	...													...	...
Belize	...	6,200[i]														...	...
Bolivia	2,360	4,140	2002[y]	0.60		...	1997	77.3	53.8	63.2	1999	81.7	50.6	62.7	2002	23.2	42.2
Brazil	7,300	9,370	2004[y]	0.57	1996	0.85	1998	51.4	14.7	22.0	2002-03	41.0	17.5	21.5	2004	7.5	21.2
British Virgin Islands	...	...														...	...
Cayman Islands	...	...	...													...	...
Chile	9,100	12,590	2003[y]	0.55		...	1996	...	...	19.9	1998	...	...	17.0	2003	<2	5.6
Colombia	6,060	6,640	2003[y]	0.59	2001	0.80	1995	79.0	48.0	60.0	1999	79.0	55.0	64.0	2003	7.0	17.8
Costa Rica	7,980	10,700[i]	2003[y]	0.50		...	1992	25.5	19.2	22.0		...	...	...	2003	3.3	9.8
Cuba	...	...	...		...			...	...	...		...	...	...		...	...
Dominica	...	7,410[i]														...	...
Dominican Republic	5,710	6,340[i]	2004[y]	0.52		...	2000	45.3	18.2	27.7	2004	55.7	34.7	42.2	2004	2.8	16.2
Ecuador	2,910	7,040	1998[y]	0.54			1995	56.0	19.0	34.0	1998	69.0	30.0	46.0	1998	17.7	40.8
El Salvador	4,410	5,640[i]	2002[y]	0.52			1995	64.8	38.9	50.6	2002	49.8	28.5	37.2	2002	19.0	40.6
Falkland Islands (Malvinas)	...	...														...	...
French Guiana	...	...														...	...
Grenada	...	6,910[i]	...													...	...
Guadeloupe	...	...														...	...
Guatemala	3,770	4,520[i]	2002[y]	0.55			1989	71.9	33.7	57.9	2000	74.5	27.1	56.2	2002	13.5	31.9
Guyana	...	2,880[i]														...	...
Haiti	1,470[i]	1,150[i]	2001[y]	0.59			1987	...	...	65.0	1995	66.0	...	...	2001	53.9	78.0
Honduras	2,400	3,620[i]	2003[y]	0.54	1993	0.66	1998-99	71.2	28.6	52.5	2004	70.4	29.5	50.7	2003	14.9	35.7
Jamaica	3,440	6,210	2004[c]	0.46			1995	37.0	18.7	27.5	2000	25.1	12.8	18.7	2004	<2	14.4
Martinique	...	...														...	...
Mexico	8,790	12,580	2004[c]	0.46			2000	42.4	12.6	24.2	2004	27.9	11.3	17.6	2004	3.0	11.6
Montserrat	...	...														...	...
Netherlands Antilles	...	...	...													...	...
Nicaragua	2,080[i]	2,520[i]	2001[c]	0.43	2001	0.72	1993	76.1	31.9	50.3	1998	68.5	30.5	47.9	2001	45.1	79.9
Panama	5,680[i]	10,610[i]	2003[y]	0.56	2001	0.52	1997	64.9	15.3	37.3		...	...	...	2003	7.4	18.0
Paraguay	4,450[i]	4,380	2003[y]	0.58	1991	0.93	1991	28.5	19.7	21.8		...	...	...	2003	13.6	29.8
Peru	4,660	7,240	2003[y]	0.52	1994	0.86	2001	77.1	42.0	54.3	2004	72.1	42.9	53.1	2003	10.5	30.6
Puerto Rico	...	...	...		...											...	...
Saint Kitts and Nevis	...	13,320[i]														...	...
Saint Lucia	...	9,430[i]	...													...	...
Saint Vincent and the Grenadines	...	7,170[i]	...													...	...
Suriname	...	7,640[i]	...													...	...
Trinidad and Tobago	8,220	22,490	1992[y]	0.39			1992	20.0	24.0	21.0		...	...	...	1992	12.4	39.0
Turks and Caicos Islands	...	...														...	...
United States Virgin Islands	...	...														...	...
Uruguay	8,880	11,040	2003[y]	0.45	2000	0.79	1994	...	20.2	...	1998	...	24.7	...	2003	<2	5.7
Venezuela (Bolivarian Republic of)	5,740	11,920	2003[y]	0.48	1996-1997	0.88	1989	...	...	31.3		...	...	...	2003	18.5	40.1
NORTHERN AMERICA																	
Bermuda	...	...	...		...											...	...
Canada	27,170[i]	35,310	2000[y]	0.33	1991	0.64		...	...	...		...	...	...		...	...
Greenland	...	...	...													...	...
Saint-Pierre-et-Miquelon	...	...														...	...
United States of America	34,100	45,850	2000[y]	0.41	1997	0.76		...	...	...		...	...	...		...	...
OCEANIA																	
American Samoa	...	...	...													...	...
Australia	24,970	33,340	1994[y]	0.35		...										...	...
Cook Islands	...	...	...													...	...
Fiji	...	4,370														...	...
French Polynesia	...	...														...	...
Guam	...	...														...	...
Kiribati	...	2,240[i]														...	...
Marshall Islands	...	...														...	...
Micronesia (Federated States of)	...	3,270[i]														...	...
Nauru	...	...														...	...
New Caledonia	...	...														...	...
New Zealand	18,530	26,340	1997[y]	0.36												...	...
Niue	...	...														...	...
Northern Mariana Islands	...	...	...													...	...

TABLE B.6

continued

	Gross national income PPP $/capita		Inequality				National poverty line				International poverty line					
			Income / consumption[2]		Land												
	2000	2007	Survey year	Gini index	Survey year	Gini index	Survey year	Rural %	Urban %	Total %	Survey year	Rural %	Urban %	Total %	Survey year	Below US$1/day	Below US$1/day
Palau	...	...	...			...	...	...	...	...	...	...	...		...	...
Papua New Guinea	2,180[1]	1,870[1]	1996[c]	0.51		...	1996	41.3	16.1	37.5	...	...	...		...	...
Pitcairn	...	...	...			...	...	...	...	...	...	...	...		...	...
Samoa	...	3,930[1]	...			...	...	...	...	...	...	...	...		...	...
Solomon Islands	...	1,680[1]	...			...	...	...	...	...	...	...	...		...	...
Tokelau	...	...	...			...	...	...	...	...	...	...	...		...	...
Tonga	...	3,650[1]	...			...	...	...	...	...	...	...	...		...	...
Tuvalu	...	...	...			...	...	...	...	...	...	...	...		...	...
Vanuatu	...	3,410[1]	...			...	...	...	...	...	...	...	...		...	...
Wallis and Futuna Islands	...	...	...			...	...	...	...	...	...	...	...		...	...

Sources: World Bank (2002) *World Development Indicators 2002*, World Bank, Washington, DC; World Bank (2007) *World Development Indicators 2007*, World Bank, Washington, DC; World Bank (2009) *World Development Report 2009*, World Bank, Washington, DC.

Notes:

(1) Estimate is based on regression; others are extrapolated from the latest International Comparison Program benchmark estimates.

(2) "c" indicates that data refer to consumption inequality, "y" indicates that data refer to income inequality. The inequality data for Argentine and Uruguay in this table refers to urban.

(3) Data for Serbia includes Montenegro.

(4) The former Yugoslav Republic of Macedonia.

TABLE B.7

Transport Infrastructure

	Roads[1]				Motor vehicles		Railways[1]		
	Total (km)	Paved (%)	Passengers (m-p-km)	Goods hauled (m-t-km)	Number per 1000 population		Route (km)	Passengers (m-p-km)	Goods hauled (m-t-km)
	2000–05	2000–05	2000–05	2000–05	1990	2005	2000–06	2000–06	2000–06
AFRICA									
Algeria	108,302	70.2	...	...	55	91	3,572	929	1,471
Angola	51,429	10.4	166,045	4,709	19	...	2,761	...	...
Benin	19,000	9.5	...	...	3	...	578	66	86
Botswana	24,455	33.2	...	...	18	113	888	171	842
Burkina Faso	92,495	4.2	...	...	4	7	622	...	...
Burundi	12,322	10.4	...	...	...	...	...	...	...
Cameroon	50,000	10.0	...	...	10	11	1,016	357	1,076
Cape Verde	...	...	...	...	...	...	...	...	...
Central African Republic	24,307	...	...	...	1	...	...	...	...
Chad	33,400	0.8	...	...	2	...	...	...	...
Comoros	...	...	...	...	...	...	...	...	...
Congo	17,289	5.0	...	...	18	...	795	135	231
Côte d'Ivoire	80,000	8.1	...	...	24	...	639	10	129
Democratic Republic of the Congo	153,497	1.8	...	...	...	...	3,641	140	444
Djibouti	...	...	...	...	...	...	...	...	...
Egypt	92,370	81.0	...	...	29	...	5,150	40,837	3,917
Equatorial Guinea	...	...	...	...	...	...	...	...	...
Eritrea	4,010	21.8	...	...	1	...	306	...	...
Ethiopia	37,018	13.4	219,113	2,456	1	2	...	...	...
Gabon	9,170	10.2	...	...	32	...	810	95	2,219
Gambia	3,742	19.3	16	...	...	7	...	...	...
Ghana	57,613	17.9	...	...	8	21	977	85	242
Guinea	44,348	9.8	...	...	4	14	1,115	...	...
Guinea-Bissau	3,455	27.9	...	...	...	...	...	...	...
Kenya	63,265	14.1	...	22	12	18	1,917	226	1,399
Lesotho	5,940	18.3	...	...	11	...	...	...	...
Liberia	10,600	6.2	...	...	14	...	490	...	...
Libyan Arab Jamahiriya	83,200	57.2	...	...	165	257	2,757	...	...
Madagascar	49,827	11.6	...	...	6	...	732	10	12
Malawi	15,451	45.0	...	...	4	...	710	26	38
Mali	18,709	18.0	...	...	3	...	733	196	189
Mauritania	7,660	11.3	...	...	10	...	717	...	...
Mauritius	2,015	100.0	...	...	59	130	...	...	...
Morocco	57,626	61.9	...	1,256	37	59	1,907	2,987	5,919
Mozambique	30,400	18.7	...	...	4	...	3,070	172	768
Namibia	42,237	12.8	47	591	71	85	...	...	...
Niger	18,423	20.6	...	...	6	5	...	...	...
Nigeria	193,200	15.0	...	...	30	...	3,528	174	77
Réunion	...	...	...	...	...	...	...	...	...
Rwanda	14,008	19.0	...	...	2	3	...	...	...
Saint Helena	...	...	...	...	...	...	...	...	...
São Tomé and Príncipe	...	...	...	...	...	...	...	...	...
Senegal	13,576	29.3	...	...	11	14	906	88	265
Seychelles	...	...	...	...	...	...	...	...	...
Sierra Leone	11,300	8.0	...	...	...	4	...	...	...
Somalia	22,100	11.8	...	...	2	...	...	...	...
South Africa	364,131	17.3	...	434	139	143	20,247	991	109,721
Sudan	11,900	36.3	...	...	9	...	5,478	40	766
Swaziland	3,594	30.0	...	...	66	84	301	...	11,394
Togo	7,520	31.6	...	...	24	...	568	...	...
Tunisia	19,232	65.8	...	16,611	48	95	1,909	1,319	2,067
Uganda	70,746	23.0	...	...	2	5	259	...	218
United Republic of Tanzania	78,891	8.6	...	...	5	...	4,582[2]	946[2]	1,990[2]
Western Sahara	...	...	...	...	...	...	...	...	...
Zambia	91,440	22.0	...	...	14	...	1,273	183	...
Zimbabwe	97,267	19.0	...	...	32	...	...	...	...
ASIA									
Afghanistan	38,782	23.7	...	...	...	...	...	...	...
Armenia	7,515	90.0	2,131	231	5	...	711	27	654
Azerbaijan	59,141	49.4	10,892	7,536	52	61	2,122	878	10,067
Bahrain	...	...	...	...	...	...	...	...	...
Bangladesh	239,226	9.5	...	...	1	1	2,855	4,164	817
Bhutan	...	...	...	...	...	...	...	...	...
Brunei Darussalam	...	...	...	...	...	...	...	...	...
Cambodia	38,257	6.3	201	3	...	36	650	45	92
China	1,930,544	81.6	929,210	869,320	5	24	62,200	666,200	2,170,700
China, Hong Kong SAR	1,955	100.0	...	...	66	72	...	...	...
China, Macao SAR	...	...	...	...	...	...	...	...	...
Cyprus	...	...	...	...	...	...	...	...	...
Democratic People's Republic of Korea	31,200	6.4	...	...	...	...	5,214	...	...
Georgia	20,247	39.4	5,200	570	...	71	1,515	720	6,127
India	3,383,344	47.4	...	...	4	12	63,465	575,702	407,398
Indonesia	372,929	55.3	...	...	16	109	...	14,345	4,430
Iran (Islamic Republic of)	179,388	67.4	...	...	34	...	7,131	11,149	19,127
Iraq	45,550	84.3	...	...	14	...	1,963	570	1,682
Israel	17,589	100.0	...	...	210	293	899	1,618	1,149

TABLE B.7

continued

	Roads[1]				Motor vehicles		Railways[1]		
	Total (km)	Paved (%)	Passengers (m-p-km)	Goods hauled (m-t-km)	Number per 1000 population		Route (km)	Passengers (m-p-km)	Goods hauled (m-t-km)
	2000–05	2000–05	2000–05	2000–05	1990	2005	2000–06	2000–06	2000–06
Japan	1,177,278	77.7	947,562	327,632	469	586	20,052	245,957	22,632
Jordan	7,601	100.0	...	...	60	115	293	...	1,024
Kazakhstan	90,800	83.0	91,651	47,100	76	116	14,205	12,129	191,200
Kuwait	5,749	85.0	...	...	...	422	...	...	...
Kyrgyzstan	18,500	91.1	5,874	1,336	...	39	424	50	561
Lao People's Democratic Republic	31,210	14.4	...	...	9	57	...	...	...
Lebanon	6,970	...	...	...	321	...	401	...	...
Malaysia	98,721	81.3	...	...	124	272	1,667	1,181	1,178
Maldives	...	...	...	...	...	...	...	...	...
Mongolia	49,250	3.5	557	242	21	43	1,810	1,228	8,857
Myanmar	27,966	11.4	...	...	2	5	...	...	...
Nepal	17,280	56.9	...	...	...	...	59	...	...
Occupied Palestinian Territory	4,996	100.0	...	...	...	36	...	...	...
Oman	34,965	27.7	...	...	130	...	...	...	...
Pakistan	258,340	64.7	209,959	...	6	14	7,791	24,237	5,013
Philippines	200,037	9.9	...	...	10	34	491	144	1
Qatar	...	...	...	...	...	...	...	...	...
Republic of Korea	102,293	16.8	91,665	12,545	79	319	3,392	31,004	10,108
Saudi Arabia	152,044	29.9	...	...	165	...	1,020	393	1,192
Singapore	3,234	100.0	...	...	130	137	...	...	...
Sri Lanka	97,286	81.0	21,067	...	21	42	1,200	4,358	135
Syrian Arab Republic	94,890	20.1	589	...	26	36	1,888	607	2,256
Tajikistan	27,767	...	...	...	3	...	616	50	1,117
Thailand	57,403	98.5	...	...	46	...	4,044	9,195	4,037
Timor-Leste	...	...	...	...	...	...	...	...	...
Turkey	426,914	...	182,152	166,831	50	117	8,697	6,183	9,078
Turkmenistan	24,000	81.2	...	...	...	...	2,529	1,286	8,670
United Arab Emirates	4,030	100.0	...	...	121	...	...	...	...
Uzbekistan	81,600	87.3	...	1,200	...	...	4,014	2,012	10,007
Viet Nam	222,179	...	...	...	...	8	2,671	4,558	2,928
Yemen	71,300	8.7	...	...	34	...	...	...	...
EUROPE									
Albania	18,000	39.0	197	2,200	11	85	447	73	26
Andorra	...	...	...	...	...	...	...	...	...
Austria	133,928	100.0	69,000	26,411	421	599	5,690	8,470	17,036
Belarus	94,797	88.6	9,231	15,055	61	...	5,498	13,568	43,559
Belgium	150,567	78.0	126,680	54,856	423	529	3,542	9,150	8,130
Bosnia and Herzegovina	21,846	52.3	...	300	114	...	1,000	53	1,173
Bulgaria	44,033	99.0	14,401	6,840	163	360	4,154	2,389	5,164
Channel Islands	...	...	...	...	...	...	...	...	...
Croatia	28,472	84.4	3,403	9,328	...	349	2,726	1,266	2,835
Czech Republic	127,781	100.0	90,055	46,600	246	394	9,513	6,631	14,385
Denmark	72,257	100.0	70,635	11,058	368	437	2,212	5,459	2,030
Estonia	57,016	22.7	3,190	7,641	211	477	959	248	10,311
Faeroe Islands	...	...	...	...	...	...	...	...	...
Finland	78,821	65.0	70,300	27,800	441	531	5,732	3,478	9,706
France	950,985	100.0	771,000	193,000	494	596	29,286	76,159	41,898
Germany	...	100.0	1,062,700	237,609	405	585	34,218	72,554	88,022
Gibraltar	...	...	...	...	...	...	...	...	...
Greece	117,533	91.8	18,360	248	497	2,576	1,854	613	...
Holy See	...	...	...	...	...	...	...	...	...
Hungary	159,568	43.9	13,300	12,505	212	316	7,730	6,953	8,537
Iceland	...	...	...	...	...	...	...	...	...
Ireland	96,602	100.0	...	15,900	270	447	1,919	1,781	303
Isle of Man	...	...	...	...	...	...	...	...	...
Italy	484,688	100.0	97,560	192,700	529	667	16,225	46,144	20,131
Latvia	69,829	100.0	2,869	2,767	135	377	2,375	894	17,921
Liechtenstein	...	...	...	...	...	...	...	...	...
Lithuania	79,497	78.2	38,484	15,908	160	467	1,772	428	12,457
Luxembourg	...	...	...	...	...	...	...	...	...
Malta	...	...	...	...	...	...	...	...	...
Moldova	12,737	86.3	1,640	1,577	53	94	1,075	355	2,980
Monaco	...	...	...	...	...	...	...	...	...
Montenegro[3]	...	...	...	...	...	...	...	...	...
Netherlands	126,100	90.0	...	77,100	405	486	2,813	14,730	4,331
Norway	92,864	77.5	58,247	14,966	458	546	4,087	2,440	9,568
Poland	423,997	69.7	29,314	119,740	168	386	19,507	16,742	45,438
Portugal	78,470	86.0	...	23,187	222	507	2,839	3,412	2,422
Romania	198,817	30.2	9,438	37,220	72	185	10,844	7,960	16,032
Russian Federation	537,289	...	...	25,200	87	174	85,245	177,639	1,950,900
San Marino	...	...	...	...	...	...	...	...	...
Serbia[3]	45,290	62.4	3,865	3,100	137	199	3,809	852	3,482
Slovakia	43,000	87.3	32,214	18,517	194	256	3,659	2,166	9,326
Slovenia	38,485	100.0	848	11,033	306	523	1,228	777	3,245
Spain	666,292	99.0	397,117	132,868	360	550	14,484	21,047	11,586
Sweden	425,383	31.5	112,010	39,373	464	513	9,867	5,673	13,120
Switzerland	71,296	100.0	97,996	15,753	491	563	3,011	13,830	8,571

TABLE B.7

continued

	Roads[1]				Motor vehicles		Railways[1]		
	Total (km)	Paved (%)	Passengers (m-p-km)	Goods hauled (m-t-km)	Number per 1000 population		Route (km)	Passengers (m-p-km)	Goods hauled (m-t-km)
	2000–05	2000–05	2000–05	2000–05	1990	2005	2000–06	2000–06	2000–06
TFYR Macedonia[4]	13,182	...	842	4,100	132	163	699	94	441
Ukraine	169,323	97.4	51,820	23,895	63	128	22,001	52,655	223,980
United Kingdom	388,008	100.0	736,000	163,000	400	517	15,810	43,200	22,110
LATIN AMERICA AND THE CARIBBEAN									
Anguilla	...	...	...	...	...	...	...	...	...
Antigua and Barbuda	...	...	...	...	...	...	...	...	...
Argentina	51,429	30.0	...	...	181	...	...	...	...
Aruba	...	...	...	...	...	...	...	...	...
Bahamas	...	...	...	...	...	...	...	...	...
Barbados	...	...	...	...	...	...	...	...	...
Belize	...	...	...	...	...	...	...	...	...
Bolivia	62,479	7.0	...	...	41	49	...	...	...
Brazil	1,751,868	5.5	...	...	88	170	...	...	...
British Virgin Islands	...	...	...	...	...	...	...	...	...
Cayman Islands	...	...	...	...	...	...	...	...	...
Chile	79,604	20.2	...	...	81	135	2,035	737	1,241
Colombia	164,257	...	157	38,199	39	59	2,137	...	7,751
Costa Rica	35,330	24.4	...	...	87	198	...	...	...
Cuba	60,856	49.0	...	...	37	...	...	...	...
Dominica	...	...	...	...	...	...	...	...	...
Dominican Republic	12,600	49.4	...	...	75	115	1,743	...	...
Ecuador	43,197	15.0	10,641	5,453	35	55	966	...	...
El Salvador	10,029	19.8	...	...	33	...	283	...	...
Falkland Islands (Malvinas)	...	...	...	...	...	...	...	...	...
French Guiana	...	...	...	...	...	...	...	...	...
Grenada	...	...	...	...	...	...	...	...	...
Guadeloupe	...	...	...	...	...	...	...	...	...
Guatemala	14,095	34.5	...	...	21	68	886	...	...
Guyana	...	...	...	...	...	...	...	...	...
Haiti	4,160	24.3	...	...	8	...	...	...	...
Honduras	13,600	20.4	...	...	22	67	699	...	...
Jamaica	21,532	73.9	...	...	52	...	272	...	...
Martinique	...	...	...	...	...	...	...	...	...
Mexico	355,796	37.0	422,915	204,217	119	208	...	...	...
Montserrat	...	...	...	...	...	...	...	...	...
Netherlands Antilles	...	...	...	...	...	...	...	...	...
Nicaragua	18,669	11.4	...	...	19	46	6	...	...
Panama	11,643	34.6	...	...	75	103	355	...	...
Paraguay	29,500	50.8	...	...	27	85	441	...	...
Peru	78,829	14.4	...	...	...	47	...	...	...
Puerto Rico	25,645	95.0	...	10	295	...	96	...	...
Saint Kitts and Nevis	...	...	...	...	...	...	...	...	...
Saint Lucia	...	...	...	...	...	...	...	...	...
Saint Vincent and the Grenadines	...	...	...	...	...	...	...	...	...
Suriname	...	...	...	...	...	...	...	...	...
Trinidad and Tobago	8,320	51.1	...	...	117	...	...	...	...
Turks and Caicos Islands	...	...	...	...	...	...	...	...	...
United States Virgin Islands	...	...	...	...	...	...	...	...	...
Uruguay	77,732	10.0	...	...	138	176	3,003	12	331
Venezuela (Bolivarian Republic of)	96,155	33.6	...	...	93	...	336	...	54
NORTHERN AMERICA									
Bermuda	...	...	...	...	...	...	...	...	...
Canada	1,408,900	39.9	493,814	184,774	...	582	67,346	1,430	445,689
Greenland	...	...	...	...	...	...	...	...	...
Saint-Pierre-et-Miquelon	...	...	...	...	...	...	...	...	...
United States of America	6,544,257	65.3	7,814,575	2,116,532	756[5]	814[5]	153,787	47,717	2,589,349[5]
OCEANIA									
American Samoa	...	...	...	...	...	...	...	...	...
Australia	812,972	...	290,280	168,630	530	671	9,528	1,290	46,164
Cook Islands	...	...	...	...	...	...	...	...	...
Fiji	...	...	...	...	...	...	...	...	...
French Polynesia	...	...	...	...	...	...	...	...	...
Guam	...	...	...	...	...	...	...	...	...
Kiribati	...	...	...	...	...	...	...	...	...
Marshall Islands	...	...	...	...	...	...	...	...	...
Micronesia (Federated States of)	...	...	...	...	...	...	...	...	...
Nauru	...	...	...	...	...	...	...	...	...
New Caledonia	...	...	...	...	...	...	...	...	...
New Zealand	93,460	64.9	...	...	524	720	...	...	4,078
Niue	...	...	...	...	...	...	...	...	...
Northern Mariana Islands	...	...	...	...	...	...	...	...	...
Palau	...	...	...	...	...	...	...	...	...
Papua New Guinea	19,600	3.5	...	...	27	...	...	...	...
Pitcairn	...	...	...	...	...	...	...	...	...
Samoa	...	...	...	...	...	...	...	...	...
Solomon Islands	...	...	...	...	...	...	...	...	...

TABLE B.7

continued

	Roads[1]				Motor vehicles		Railways[1]		
	Total (km)	Paved (%)	Passengers (m-p-km)	Goods hauled (m-t-km)	Number per 1000 population		Route (km)	Passengers (m-p-km)	Goods hauled (m-t-km)
	2000–05	2000–05	2000–05	2000–05	1990	2005	2000–06	2000–06	2000–06
Tokelau	...	...	...	...	...	...	...	...	...
Tonga	...	...	...	...	...	...	...	...	...
Tuvalu	...	...	...	...	...	...	...	...	...
Vanuatu	...	...	...	...	...	...	...	...	...
Wallis and Futuna Islands	...	...	...	...	...	...	...	...	...

Source: World Bank (2008) *World Development Indicators 2008,* World Bank, Washington, DC.

Notes:

(1) Data are for the latest year available in the period shown.
(2) includes Tazara railway.
(3) Data for Serbia includes Montenegro.
(4) The former Yugoslav Republic of Macedonia.
(5) Data are from the US Federal Highway Administration.

TABLE C.I – CITY LEVEL DATA

Urban Agglomerations with 750,000 Inhabitants or More: Population Size and Rate of Change in Selected Cities

		Estimates and projections ('000)			Annual rate of change (%)		Share in national urban population (%)		
		2000	2010	2020	2000–2010	2010–2020	2000	2010	2020
AFRICA									
Algeria	El Djazaïr (Algiers)	2,754	3,574	4,235	2.61	1.70	15.1	15.2	14.5
Algeria	Wahran (Oran)	706	852	1,030	1.88	1.90	3.9	3.6	3.5
Angola	Huambo	578	1,035	1,567	5.83	4.15	8.5	9.6	9.8
Angola	Luanda	2,591	4,775	7,153	6.11	4.04	38.0	44.1	44.8
Benin	Cotonou	642	841	1,196	2.70	3.52	23.2	20.3	19.7
Burkina Faso	Ouagadougou	828	1,324	2,111	4.69	4.67	42.0	40.3	38.9
Cameroon	Douala	1,432	2,108	2,721	3.87	2.55	18.1	18.4	17.8
Cameroon	Yaoundé	1,192	1,787	2,312	4.05	2.58	15.1	15.6	15.1
Chad	N'Djaména	711	1,127	1,753	4.61	4.42	35.9	34.8	33.7
Congo	Brazzaville	986	1,505	1,938	4.23	2.53	52.8	60.4	59.5
Côte d'Ivoire	Abidjan	3,032	4,175	5,432	3.20	2.63	40.8	40.9	39.4
Democratic Republic of the Congo	Kananga	557	879	1,383	4.56	4.53	3.7	3.6	3.5
Democratic Republic of the Congo	Kinshasa	5,485	9,052	13,875	5.01	4.27	36.3	37.2	35.4
Democratic Republic of the Congo	Lubumbashi	1,004	1,544	2,406	4.30	4.44	6.6	6.4	6.1
Democratic Republic of the Congo	Mbuji-Mayi	932	1,489	2,330	4.69	4.48	6.2	6.1	5.9
Egypt	Al-Iskandariyah (Alexandria)	3,600	4,421	5,210	2.05	1.64	12.7	13.0	12.5
Egypt	Al-Qahirah (Cairo)	10,534	12,503	14,451	1.71	1.45	37.1	36.7	34.7
Ethiopia	Addis Ababa	2,493	3,453	5,083	3.26	3.87	24.1	22.0	20.9
Ghana	Accra	1,674	2,332	3,041	3.32	2.65	18.9	18.2	17.5
Ghana	Kumasi	1,187	1,826	2,393	4.31	2.70	13.4	14.3	13.8
Guinea	Conakry	1,219	1,645	2,393	3.00	3.75	47.9	46.4	44.5
Kenya	Mombasa	686	985	1,453	3.62	3.89	11.1	10.9	10.6
Kenya	Nairobi	2,233	3,363	4,881	4.09	3.73	36.2	37.3	35.5
Liberia	Monrovia	836	1,185	1,753	3.49	3.92	50.2	44.7	44.1
Libyan Arab Jamahiriya	Banghazi	945	1,271	1,505	2.96	1.69	23.2	25.0	24.5
Libyan Arab Jamahiriya	Tarabulus (Tripoli)	1,877	2,322	2,713	2.13	1.56	46.0	45.7	44.1
Madagascar	Antananarivo	1,361	1,877	2,642	3.21	3.42	31.0	29.2	28.1
Mali	Bamako	1,110	1,708	2,633	4.31	4.33	39.8	37.9	36.5
Morocco	Dar-el-Beida (Casablanca)	3,043	3,267	3,716	0.71	1.29	19.8	17.8	16.8
Morocco	Fès	870	1,060	1,243	1.98	1.59	5.7	5.8	5.6
Morocco	Marrakech	755	923	1,085	2.01	1.62	4.9	5.0	4.9
Morocco	Rabat	1,507	1,793	2,083	1.74	1.50	9.8	9.8	9.4
Mozambique	Maputo	1,096	1,621	2,235	3.91	3.21	19.6	18.6	18.0
Niger	Niamey	680	1,027	1,580	4.12	4.31	37.8	39.0	37.5
Nigeria	Abuja	832	1,994	2,971	8.74	3.99	1.6	2.5	2.7
Nigeria	Benin City	975	1,302	1,755	2.89	2.99	1.8	1.7	1.6
Nigeria	Ibadan	2,236	2,835	3,752	2.37	2.80	4.2	3.6	3.4
Nigeria	Ilorin	653	835	1,123	2.46	2.96	1.2	1.1	1.0
Nigeria	Kaduna	1,220	1,560	2,083	2.46	2.89	2.3	2.0	1.9
Nigeria	Kano	2,658	3,393	4,487	2.44	2.79	5.0	4.3	4.1
Nigeria	Lagos	7,233	10,572	14,134	3.80	2.90	13.6	13.4	12.9
Nigeria	Maiduguri	758	969	1,301	2.46	2.95	1.4	1.2	1.2
Nigeria	Ogbomosho	798	1,031	1,386	2.56	2.96	1.5	1.3	1.3
Nigeria	Port Harcourt	863	1,104	1,479	2.46	2.92	1.6	1.4	1.3
Nigeria	Zaria	752	963	1,293	2.47	2.95	1.4	1.2	1.2
Rwanda	Kigali	497	947	1,413	6.45	4.00	44.2	47.4	45.5
Senegal	Dakar	2,029	2,856	3,726	3.42	2.66	48.3	50.0	48.1
Sierra Leone	Freetown	688	894	1,200	2.62	2.94	42.9	37.6	36.2
Somalia	Muqdisho (Mogadishu)	1,201	1,500	2,142	2.22	3.56	51.2	42.2	40.5
South Africa	Cape Town	2,715	3,357	3,627	2.12	0.77	10.5	11.0	10.6
South Africa	Durban	2,370	2,839	3,070	1.81	0.78	9.2	9.3	9.0
South Africa	Ekurhuleni (East Rand)	2,326	3,157	3,427	3.05	0.82	9.0	10.4	10.0
South Africa	Johannesburg	2,732	3,618	3,916	2.81	0.79	10.6	11.9	11.5
South Africa	Port Elizabeth	958	1,053	1,150	0.95	0.88	3.7	3.5	3.4
South Africa	Pretoria	1,084	1,409	1,544	2.62	0.91	4.2	4.6	4.5
South Africa	Vereeniging	897	1,127	1,236	2.28	0.92	3.5	3.7	3.6
Sudan	Al-Khartoum (Khartoum)	3,949	5,185	7,017	2.72	3.03	32.8	27.8	26.4
Togo	Lomé	1,023	1,669	2,410	4.89	3.67	51.8	53.9	53.2
Uganda	Kampala	1,097	1,597	2,506	3.76	4.51	36.8	35.3	33.6
United Republic of Tanzania	Dar es Salaam	2,116	3,319	4,804	4.50	3.70	28.0	28.9	27.7
Zambia	Lusaka	1,073	1,421	1,797	2.81	2.35	29.5	31.5	30.4
Zimbabwe	Harare	1,379	1,663	2,037	1.87	2.03	32.3	31.6	30.4
ASIA									
Afghanistan	Kabul	1,963	3,768	5,836	6.52	4.38	44.5	50.0	48.0
Armenia	Yerevan	1,111	1,102	1,102	-0.08	0.00	55.4	57.9	57.2
Azerbaijan	Baku	1,806	1,931	2,097	0.67	0.82	43.3	42.7	40.9
Bangladesh	Chittagong	3,308	5,012	6,688	4.15	2.88	10.1	10.7	10.2
Bangladesh	Dhaka	10,285	14,796	19,422	3.64	2.72	31.3	31.6	29.6
Bangladesh	Khulna	1,285	1,699	2,294	2.79	3.00	3.9	3.6	3.5
Bangladesh	Rajshahi	678	887	1,208	2.69	3.09	2.1	1.9	1.8
Cambodia	Phnum Pénh (Phnom Penh)	1,160	1,651	2,457	3.53	3.98	53.7	47.6	45.9
China	Anshan, Liaoning	1,552	1,703	2,029	0.93	1.75	0.3	0.3	0.3
China	Anshun	763	896	1,085	1.61	1.91	0.2	0.1	0.1
China	Anyang	763	948	1,156	2.17	1.98	0.2	0.2	0.2
China	Baoding	890	1,206	1,482	3.04	2.06	0.2	0.2	0.2
China	Baotou	1,655	2,209	2,691	2.89	1.97	0.4	0.4	0.4
China	Beijing	9,782	11,741	13,807	1.83	1.62	2.2	1.9	1.8
China	Bengbu	805	944	1,142	1.59	1.90	0.2	0.2	0.2
China	Benxi	979	1,046	1,249	0.66	1.77	0.2	0.2	0.2

TABLE C.1

continued

		Estimates and projections ('000)			Annual rate of change (%)		Share in national urban population (%)		
		2000	2010	2020	2000–2010	2010–2020	2000	2010	2020
China	Changchun	2,730	3,400	4,082	2.19	1.83	0.6	0.6	0.5
China	Changde	1,341	1,543	1,852	1.40	1.83	0.3	0.3	0.2
China	Changsha, Hunan	2,091	2,832	3,443	3.03	1.95	0.5	0.5	0.5
China	Changzhou, Jiangsu	1,068	1,445	1,772	3.02	2.04	0.2	0.2	0.2
China	Chengdu	3,919	4,266	5,014	0.85	1.62	0.9	0.7	0.7
China	Chifeng	1,148	1,348	1,625	1.61	1.87	0.3	0.2	0.2
China	Chongqing	6,037	6,690	7,823	1.03	1.56	1.3	1.1	1.0
China	Dalian	2,858	3,335	3,971	1.54	1.75	0.6	0.5	0.5
China	Dandong	776	921	1,117	1.71	1.93	0.2	0.2	0.1
China	Daqing	1,366	1,842	2,252	2.99	2.01	0.3	0.3	0.3
China	Datong, Shanxi	1,518	2,038	2,488	2.95	2.00	0.3	0.3	0.3
China	Dongguan, Guangdong	3,770	4,850	5,808	2.52	1.80	0.8	0.8	0.8
China	Foshan	754	1,027	1,265	3.09	2.08	0.2	0.2	0.2
China	Fushun, Liaoning	1,433	1,516	1,800	0.56	1.72	0.3	0.3	0.2
China	Fuxin	631	839	1,036	2.85	2.11	0.1	0.1	0.1
China	Fuyang	609	840	1,038	3.22	2.12	0.1	0.1	0.1
China	Fuzhou, Fujian	2,096	2,834	3,445	3.02	1.95	0.5	0.5	0.5
China	Guangzhou, Guangdong	7,388	9,447	11,218	2.46	1.72	1.6	1.6	1.5
China	Guilin	795	1,075	1,323	3.02	2.08	0.2	0.2	0.2
China	Guiyang	2,929	3,980	4,818	3.07	1.91	0.6	0.7	0.6
China	Haerbin	3,444	3,753	4,421	0.86	1.64	0.8	0.6	0.6
China	Handan	1,321	1,775	2,171	2.95	2.01	0.3	0.3	0.3
China	Hangzhou	2,411	3,269	3,967	3.04	1.94	0.5	0.5	0.5
China	Hefei	1,637	2,214	2,700	3.02	1.98	0.4	0.4	0.4
China	Hengyang	873	1,087	1,324	2.19	1.97	0.2	0.2	0.2
China	Heze	1,277	1,388	1,655	0.83	1.76	0.3	0.2	0.2
China	Huai'an	1,198	1,315	1,571	0.93	1.78	0.3	0.2	0.2
China	Huaibei	733	995	1,227	3.06	2.10	0.2	0.2	0.2
China	Huainan	1,353	1,515	1,812	1.13	1.79	0.3	0.3	0.2
China	Hohhot	1,389	1,878	2,295	3.02	2.01	0.3	0.3	0.3
China	Huzhou	1,141	1,288	1,545	1.21	1.82	0.3	0.2	0.2
China	Jiamusi	853	1,099	1,345	2.53	2.02	0.2	0.2	0.2
China	Jiaozuo	742	915	1,115	2.10	1.98	0.2	0.2	0.1
China	Jiaxing	877	1,047	1,268	1.77	1.92	0.2	0.2	0.2
China	Jilin	1,928	2,606	3,171	3.01	1.96	0.4	0.4	0.4
China	Jinan, Shandong	2,625	2,914	3,453	1.04	1.70	0.6	0.5	0.5
China	Jining, Shandong	1,044	1,260	1,525	1.88	1.91	0.2	0.2	0.2
China	Jinxi, Liaoning	1,908	2,658	3,248	3.32	2.00	0.4	0.4	0.4
China	Jinzhou	858	1,009	1,221	1.62	1.91	0.2	0.2	0.2
China	Jixi, Heilongjiang	908	1,006	1,208	1.02	1.83	0.2	0.2	0.2
China	Kaifeng	793	918	1,110	1.46	1.90	0.2	0.2	0.1
China	Kaohsiung	1,469	1,595	1,899	0.82	1.74	0.3	0.3	0.3
China	Kunming	2,594	3,095	3,694	1.77	1.77	0.6	0.5	0.5
China	Langfang	711	861	1,048	1.91	1.97	0.2	0.1	0.1
China	Lanzhou	2,071	2,785	3,387	2.96	1.96	0.5	0.5	0.4
China	Leshan	1,118	1,197	1,427	0.68	1.76	0.2	0.2	0.2
China	Lianyungang	682	865	1,060	2.38	2.03	0.2	0.1	0.1
China	Liaoyang	725	835	1,009	1.41	1.89	0.2	0.1	0.1
China	Linfen	719	891	1,087	2.14	1.99	0.2	0.1	0.1
China	Linyi, Shandong	1,932	2,177	2,594	1.19	1.75	0.4	0.4	0.3
China	Liuan	1,553	1,771	2,120	1.31	1.80	0.3	0.3	0.3
China	Liupanshui	989	1,329	1,632	2.95	2.05	0.2	0.2	0.2
China	Liuzhou	1,201	1,629	1,995	3.05	2.03	0.3	0.3	0.3
China	Luoyang	1,481	1,830	2,212	2.12	1.90	0.3	0.3	0.3
China	Luzhou	1,208	1,673	2,047	3.26	2.02	0.3	0.3	0.3
China	Mianyang, Sichuan	1,152	1,509	1,842	2.70	1.99	0.3	0.2	0.2
China	Mudanjiang	1,004	1,355	1,662	3.00	2.04	0.2	0.2	0.2
China	Nanchang	1,822	2,585	3,168	3.50	2.03	0.4	0.4	0.4
China	Nanchong	1,712	2,364	2,881	3.23	1.98	0.4	0.4	0.4
China	Nanjing, Jiangsu	3,477	3,813	4,492	0.92	1.64	0.8	0.6	0.6
China	Nanning	1,743	2,357	2,873	3.02	1.98	0.4	0.4	0.4
China	Nantong	759	1,031	1,269	3.06	2.08	0.2	0.2	0.2
China	Nanyang, Henan	1,512	2,115	2,581	3.36	1.99	0.3	0.3	0.3
China	Neijiang	1,388	1,525	1,819	0.94	1.76	0.3	0.3	0.2
China	Ningbo	1,551	2,092	2,553	2.99	1.99	0.3	0.3	0.3
China	Pingdingshan, Henan	904	854	1,006	-0.57	1.64	0.2	0.1	0.1
China	Pingxiang, Jiangxi	775	1,047	1,289	3.01	2.08	0.2	0.2	0.2
China	Qingdao	2,698	2,977	3,521	0.98	1.68	0.6	0.5	0.5
China	Qinhuangdao	805	1,092	1,344	3.05	2.08	0.2	0.2	0.2
China	Qiqihaer	1,535	1,712	2,043	1.09	1.77	0.3	0.3	0.3
China	Quanzhou	1,158	1,592	1,950	3.18	2.03	0.3	0.3	0.3
China	Shanghai	13,243	15,789	18,466	1.76	1.57	2.9	2.6	2.4
China	Shangqiu	1,349	1,907	2,331	3.46	2.01	0.3	0.3	0.3
China	Shantou	1,255	1,756	2,158	3.36	2.06	0.3	0.3	0.3
China	Shaoxing	617	846	1,045	3.16	2.11	0.1	0.1	0.1
China	Shenyang	4,599	4,952	5,808	0.74	1.59	1.0	0.8	0.8
China	Shenzhen	6,069	8,114	9,654	2.90	1.74	1.3	1.3	1.3
China	Shijiazhuang	1,947	2,628	3,198	3.00	1.96	0.4	0.4	0.4
China	Suining, Sichuan	1,352	1,481	1,766	0.91	1.76	0.3	0.2	0.2
China	Suzhou, Anhui	1,509	2,137	2,607	3.48	1.99	0.3	0.4	0.3

TABLE C.1

continued

		Estimates and projections ('000)			Annual rate of change (%)		Share in national urban population (%)		
		2000	2010	2020	2000–2010	2010–2020	2000	2010	2020
China	Suzhou, Jiangsu	1,326	1,795	2,195	3.03	2.01	0.3	0.3	0.3
China	Taian, Shandong	1,534	1,696	2,022	1.00	1.76	0.3	0.3	0.3
China	Taichung	930	1,151	1,400	2.13	1.96	0.2	0.2	0.2
China	Tainan	725	791	951	0.87	1.84	0.2	0.1	0.1
China	Taipei	2,640	2,651	3,104	0.04	1.58	0.6	0.4	0.4
China	Taiyuan, Shanxi	2,521	3,104	3,725	2.08	1.82	0.6	0.5	0.5
China	Tangshan, Hebei	1,703	1,977	2,367	1.49	1.80	0.4	0.3	0.3
China	Tianjin	6,722	7,468	8,745	1.05	1.58	1.5	1.2	1.2
China	Tianmen	1,609	1,777	2,118	0.99	1.76	0.4	0.3	0.3
China	Tianshui	1,143	1,279	1,533	1.12	1.81	0.3	0.2	0.2
China	Tongliao	790	935	1,133	1.69	1.92	0.2	0.2	0.2
China	Ürümqi (Wulumqi)	1,730	2,340	2,851	3.02	1.98	0.4	0.4	0.4
China	Weifang	1,372	1,646	1,985	1.82	1.87	0.3	0.3	0.3
China	Wenzhou	1,845	2,556	3,111	3.26	1.97	0.4	0.4	0.4
China	Wuhan	6,662	7,542	8,837	1.24	1.58	1.5	1.2	1.2
China	Wuhu, Anhui	692	868	1,061	2.27	2.01	0.2	0.1	0.1
China	Wuxi, Jiangsu	1,410	1,903	2,326	3.00	2.01	0.3	0.3	0.3
China	Xiamen	1,977	2,739	3,331	3.26	1.96	0.4	0.5	0.4
China	Xi'an, Shaanxi	3,725	4,178	4,931	1.15	1.66	0.8	0.7	0.7
China	Xiangfan, Hubei	855	1,164	1,431	3.09	2.07	0.2	0.2	0.2
China	Xiantao	1,470	1,618	1,930	0.96	1.76	0.3	0.3	0.3
China	Xianyang, Shaanxi	946	1,212	1,480	2.48	2.00	0.2	0.2	0.2
China	Xingyi, Guizhou	715	868	1,056	1.94	1.96	0.2	0.1	0.1
China	Xining	849	1,142	1,404	2.96	2.07	0.2	0.2	0.2
China	Xinxiang	770	968	1,182	2.29	2.00	0.2	0.2	0.2
China	Xinyang	1,195	1,677	2,052	3.39	2.02	0.3	0.3	0.3
China	Xinyu	772	981	1,199	2.40	2.01	0.2	0.2	0.2
China	Xuanzhou	823	899	1,079	0.88	1.83	0.2	0.1	0.1
China	Xuzhou	1,648	2,284	2,792	3.26	2.01	0.4	0.4	0.4
China	Yancheng, Jiangsu	677	914	1,127	3.00	2.09	0.1	0.2	0.1
China	Yantai	1,684	2,301	2,805	3.12	1.98	0.4	0.4	0.4
China	Yibin	805	954	1,157	1.70	1.93	0.2	0.2	0.2
China	Yichang	704	953	1,174	3.03	2.09	0.2	0.2	0.2
China	Yichun, Heilongjiang	816	785	928	-0.39	1.67	0.2	0.1	0.1
China	Yichun, Jiangxi	917	1,025	1,231	1.11	1.83	0.2	0.2	0.2
China	Yinchuan	795	1,079	1,328	3.05	2.08	0.2	0.2	0.2
China	Yingkou	694	847	1,032	1.99	1.98	0.2	0.1	0.1
China	Yiyang, Hunan	1,223	1,425	1,714	1.53	1.85	0.3	0.2	0.2
China	Yongzhou	976	1,032	1,231	0.56	1.76	0.2	0.2	0.2
China	Yuci	660	921	1,141	3.33	2.14	0.1	0.2	0.2
China	Yueyang	918	821	961	-1.12	1.57	0.2	0.1	0.1
China	Yulin, Guangxi	909	1,227	1,507	3.00	2.06	0.2	0.2	0.2
China	Zaozhuang	1,990	2,242	2,670	1.19	1.75	0.4	0.4	0.4
China	Zhangjiakou	897	1,120	1,364	2.22	1.97	0.2	0.2	0.2
China	Zhanjiang	1,340	1,709	2,076	2.43	1.95	0.3	0.3	0.3
China	Zhaotong	724	855	1,038	1.66	1.94	0.2	0.1	0.1
China	Zhengzhou	2,472	2,738	3,243	1.02	1.69	0.5	0.5	0.4
China	Zhenjiang, Jiangsu	688	930	1,147	3.01	2.10	0.2	0.2	0.2
China	Zhuhai	809	1,114	1,371	3.20	2.08	0.2	0.2	0.2
China	Zhuzhou	868	1,176	1,445	3.04	2.06	0.2	0.2	0.2
China	Zibo	2,806	3,209	3,812	1.34	1.72	0.6	0.5	0.5
China	Zigong	1,049	1,149	1,375	0.91	1.80	0.2	0.2	0.2
China	Zunyi	679	924	1,140	3.08	2.10	0.1	0.2	0.2
China, Hong Kong SAR	Hong Kong[1]	6,662	7,419	8,040	1.08	0.80	100.0	100.0	100.0
Democratic People's Rep. of Korea	Hamhung	732	788	851	0.74	0.77	5.3	5.2	5.1
Democratic People's Rep. of Korea	N'ampo	1,020	1,148	1,232	1.18	0.71	7.4	7.5	7.3
Democratic People's Rep. of Korea	P'yongyang	3,117	3,346	3,537	0.71	0.56	22.6	22.0	21.0
Georgia	Tbilisi	1,100	1,108	1,114	0.07	0.05	44.2	48.7	49.4
India	Agra	1,293	1,705	2,118	2.77	2.17	0.4	0.5	0.4
India	Ahmadabad	4,427	5,726	6,989	2.57	1.99	1.5	1.6	1.5
India	Aligarh	653	864	1,083	2.80	2.26	0.2	0.2	0.2
India	Allahabad	1,035	1,279	1,592	2.12	2.19	0.4	0.3	0.3
India	Amritsar	990	1,299	1,619	2.72	2.20	0.3	0.4	0.3
India	Asansol	1,065	1,425	1,776	2.91	2.20	0.4	0.4	0.4
India	Aurangabad	868	1,200	1,499	3.24	2.22	0.3	0.3	0.3
India	Bangalore	5,567	7,229	8,795	2.61	1.96	1.9	2.0	1.9
India	Bareilly	722	869	1,087	1.85	2.24	0.2	0.2	0.2
India	Bhiwandi	603	860	1,081	3.55	2.29	0.2	0.2	0.2
India	Bhopal	1,426	1,845	2,288	2.58	2.15	0.5	0.5	0.5
India	Bhubaneswar	637	913	1,147	3.60	2.28	0.2	0.2	0.2
India	Kolkata (Calcutta)	13,058	15,577	18,707	1.76	1.83	4.5	4.2	4.0
India	Chandigarh	791	1,051	1,314	2.84	2.23	0.3	0.3	0.3
India	Jammu	588	859	1,079	3.79	2.28	0.2	0.2	0.2
India	Chennai (Madras)	6,353	7,559	9,170	1.74	1.93	2.2	2.1	1.9
India	Coimbatore	1,420	1,810	2,243	2.43	2.14	0.5	0.5	0.5
India	Delhi	12,441	17,015	20,484	3.13	1.86	4.3	4.6	4.3
India	Dhanbad	1,046	1,330	1,656	2.40	2.19	0.4	0.4	0.4
India	Durg-Bhilainagar	905	1,174	1,465	2.60	2.21	0.3	0.3	0.3
India	Faridabad	1,018	1,512	1,887	3.96	2.22	0.4	0.4	0.4
India	Ghaziabad	928	1,464	1,830	4.56	2.23	0.3	0.4	0.4

TABLE C.1

continued

		Estimates and projections ('000)			Annual rate of change (%)		Share in national urban population (%)		
		2000	**2010**	**2020**	**2000–2010**	**2010–2020**	**2000**	**2010**	**2020**
India	Guwahati (Gauhati)	797	1,054	1,318	2.79	2.24	0.3	0.3	0.3
India	Gwalior	855	1,040	1,298	1.96	2.22	0.3	0.3	0.3
India	Hubli-Dharwad	776	948	1,184	2.00	2.22	0.3	0.3	0.3
India	Hyderabad	5,445	6,761	8,224	2.16	1.96	1.9	1.8	1.7
India	Indore	1,597	2,176	2,696	3.09	2.14	0.6	0.6	0.6
India	Jabalpur	1,100	1,369	1,703	2.19	2.18	0.4	0.4	0.4
India	Jaipur	2,259	3,136	3,867	3.28	2.10	0.8	0.9	0.8
India	Jalandhar	694	918	1,150	2.80	2.25	0.2	0.3	0.2
India	Jamshedpur	1,081	1,389	1,729	2.51	2.19	0.4	0.4	0.4
India	Jodhpur	842	1,062	1,327	2.32	2.23	0.3	0.3	0.3
India	Kanpur	2,641	3,369	4,141	2.43	2.06	0.9	0.9	0.9
India	Kochi (Cochin)	1,340	1,612	1,999	1.85	2.15	0.5	0.4	0.4
India	Kota	692	885	1,108	2.46	2.25	0.2	0.2	0.2
India	Kozhikode (Calicut)	875	1,008	1,257	1.41	2.21	0.3	0.3	0.3
India	Lucknow	2,221	2,877	3,546	2.59	2.09	0.8	0.8	0.8
India	Ludhiana	1,368	1,762	2,186	2.53	2.16	0.5	0.5	0.5
India	Madurai	1,187	1,367	1,697	1.41	2.16	0.4	0.4	0.4
India	Meerut	1,143	1,496	1,862	2.69	2.19	0.4	0.4	0.4
India	Moradabad	626	847	1,062	3.02	2.26	0.2	0.2	0.2
India	Mumbai (Bombay)	16,086	20,072	24,051	2.21	1.81	5.6	5.5	5.1
India	Mysore	776	943	1,179	1.95	2.23	0.3	0.3	0.2
India	Nagpur	2,089	2,611	3,219	2.23	2.09	0.7	0.7	0.7
India	Nashik	1,117	1,590	1,981	3.53	2.20	0.4	0.4	0.4
India	Patna	1,658	2,325	2,879	3.38	2.14	0.6	0.6	0.6
India	Pune (Poona)	3,655	5,010	6,135	3.15	2.03	1.3	1.4	1.3
India	Raipur	680	944	1,184	3.28	2.27	0.2	0.3	0.3
India	Rajkot	974	1,359	1,696	3.33	2.22	0.3	0.4	0.4
India	Ranchi	844	1,120	1,400	2.83	2.23	0.3	0.3	0.3
India	Salem	736	933	1,168	2.37	2.25	0.3	0.3	0.2
India	Solapur	853	1,135	1,417	2.86	2.22	0.3	0.3	0.3
India	Srinagar	954	1,218	1,518	2.44	2.20	0.3	0.3	0.3
India	Surat	2,699	4,174	5,142	4.36	2.09	0.9	1.1	1.1
India	Thiruvananthapuram	885	1,008	1,256	1.30	2.20	0.3	0.3	0.3
India	Tiruchirappalli	837	1,011	1,262	1.89	2.22	0.3	0.3	0.3
India	Vadodara	1,465	1,875	2,324	2.47	2.15	0.5	0.5	0.5
India	Varanasi (Benares)	1,199	1,434	1,781	1.79	2.17	0.4	0.4	0.4
India	Vijayawada	999	1,209	1,505	1.91	2.19	0.3	0.3	0.3
India	Visakhapatnam	1,309	1,628	2,020	2.18	2.16	0.5	0.4	0.4
Indonesia	Bandar Lampung	743	937	1,172	2.32	2.24	0.8	0.7	0.7
Indonesia	Bandung	2,138	2,568	3,156	1.83	2.06	2.4	2.0	1.9
Indonesia	Bogor	751	1,003	1,257	2.89	2.26	0.8	0.8	0.8
Indonesia	Jakarta	8,390	9,703	11,689	1.45	1.86	9.4	7.5	7.1
Indonesia	Malang	757	857	1,065	1.24	2.17	0.9	0.7	0.7
Indonesia	Medan	1,912	2,264	2,786	1.69	2.07	2.2	1.8	1.7
Indonesia	Padang	716	931	1,166	2.63	2.25	0.8	0.7	0.7
Indonesia	Palembang	1,459	1,903	2,361	2.66	2.16	1.6	1.5	1.4
Indonesia	Semarang	1,427	1,462	1,792	0.24	2.04	1.6	1.1	1.1
Indonesia	Surabaya	2,611	3,035	3,715	1.50	2.02	2.9	2.4	2.3
Indonesia	Pekan Baru	588	891	1,128	4.16	2.36	0.7	0.7	0.7
Indonesia	Ujung Pandang	1,051	1,374	1,713	2.68	2.21	1.2	1.1	1.0
Iran (Islamic Republic of)	Ahvaz	867	1,056	1,252	1.97	1.70	2.0	2.0	2.0
Iran (Islamic Republic of)	Esfahan	1,382	1,743	2,071	2.32	1.72	3.3	3.4	3.3
Iran (Islamic Republic of)	Karaj	1,087	1,585	1,952	3.77	2.08	2.6	3.1	3.1
Iran (Islamic Republic of)	Kermanshah	729	837	981	1.38	1.59	1.7	1.6	1.6
Iran (Islamic Republic of)	Mashhad	2,073	2,654	3,151	2.47	1.72	4.9	5.1	5.1
Iran (Islamic Republic of)	Qom	841	1,035	1,230	2.08	1.73	2.0	2.0	2.0
Iran (Islamic Republic of)	Shiraz	1,115	1,300	1,521	1.54	1.57	2.6	2.5	2.4
Iran (Islamic Republic of)	Tabriz	1,264	1,484	1,736	1.60	1.57	3.0	2.9	2.8
Iran (Islamic Republic of)	Tehran	7,128	8,221	9,404	1.43	1.34	16.8	15.9	15.1
Iraq	Al-Basrah (Basra)	759	923	1,143	1.96	2.14	4.5	4.5	4.3
Iraq	Al-Mawsil (Mosul)	1,056	1,447	1,891	3.15	2.68	6.2	7.1	7.2
Iraq	Baghdad	5,200	5,891	7,345	1.25	2.21	30.6	28.9	27.9
Iraq	Irbil (Erbil)	757	1,009	1,305	2.87	2.57	4.5	5.0	5.0
Israel	Hefa (Haifa)	888	1,043	1,159	1.61	1.05	16.0	15.6	15.2
Israel	Tel Aviv-Yafo (Tel Aviv-Jaffa)	2,752	3,256	3,600	1.68	1.00	49.5	48.8	47.2
Japan	Fukuoka-Kitakyushu	2,716	2,816	2,834	0.36	0.06	3.3	3.3	3.3
Japan	Hiroshima	2,044	2,045	2,046	0.00	0.00	2.5	2.4	2.4
Japan	Kyoto	1,806	1,804	1,804	-0.01	0.00	2.2	2.1	2.1
Japan	Nagoya	3,122	3,267	3,295	0.45	0.09	3.8	3.8	3.8
Japan	Osaka-Kobe	11,165	11,337	11,368	0.15	0.03	13.5	13.3	13.2
Japan	Sapporo	2,508	2,556	2,565	0.19	0.04	3.0	3.0	3.0
Japan	Sendai	2,184	2,272	2,288	0.40	0.07	2.6	2.7	2.6
Japan	Tokyo	34,450	36,094	36,399	0.47	0.08	41.6	42.3	42.1
Jordan	Amman	1,007	1,106	1,268	0.94	1.37	26.8	21.8	21.3
Kazakhstan	Almaty	1,142	1,240	1,355	0.82	0.89	13.6	13.5	13.0
Kuwait	Al Kuwayt (Kuwait City)	1,499	2,305	2,790	4.30	1.91	68.5	76.8	76.7
Kyrgyzstan	Bishkek	770	869	1,011	1.21	1.51	44.0	43.1	41.8
Lebanon	Bayrut (Beirut)	1,487	1,941	2,119	2.66	0.88	45.8	52.6	51.8
Malaysia	Johore Bharu	630	999	1,294	4.61	2.59	4.4	5.0	5.2
Malaysia	Klang	631	1,128	1,503	5.81	2.87	4.4	5.6	6.0

TABLE C.1

continued

		Estimates and projections ('000)			Annual rate of change (%)		Share in national urban population (%)		
		2000	2010	2020	2000–2010	2010–2020	2000	2010	2020
Malaysia	Kuala Lumpur	1,306	1,519	1,820	1.51	1.81	9.1	7.5	7.2
Mongolia	Ulaanbaatar	763	919	1,044	1.86	1.28	54.6	59.1	57.4
Myanmar	Mandalay	810	1,034	1,308	2.44	2.35	6.3	6.1	5.9
Myanmar	Nay Pyi Taw	...	1,024	1,321	...	2.55	...	6.0	6.0
Myanmar	Yangon	3,553	4,348	5,361	2.02	2.09	27.6	25.6	24.3
Nepal	Kathmandu	644	1,029	1,578	4.69	4.28	19.6	18.9	18.4
Pakistan	Faisalabad	2,140	2,833	3,755	2.81	2.82	4.5	4.4	4.2
Pakistan	Gujranwala	1,224	1,643	2,195	2.94	2.90	2.6	2.6	2.5
Pakistan	Hyderabad	1,221	1,581	2,112	2.58	2.90	2.6	2.5	2.4
Pakistan	Islamabad	594	851	1,148	3.60	2.99	1.2	1.3	1.3
Pakistan	Karachi	10,019	13,052	16,922	2.64	2.60	20.9	20.3	19.0
Pakistan	Lahore	5,448	7,092	9,275	2.64	2.68	11.4	11.0	10.4
Pakistan	Multan	1,263	1,650	2,203	2.67	2.89	2.6	2.6	2.5
Pakistan	Peshawar	1,066	1,415	1,893	2.83	2.91	2.2	2.2	2.1
Pakistan	Quetta	614	836	1,128	3.09	3.00	1.3	1.3	1.3
Pakistan	Rawalpindi	1,519	2,015	2,683	2.83	2.86	3.2	3.1	3.0
Philippines	Cebu	721	862	1,062	1.79	2.09	1.6	1.4	1.4
Philippines	Davao	1,152	1,523	1,910	2.79	2.26	2.6	2.5	2.4
Philippines	Manila	9,958	11,662	13,892	1.58	1.75	22.3	18.9	17.7
Philippines	Zamboanga	605	856	1,098	3.47	2.49	1.4	1.4	1.4
Republic of Korea	Goyang	744	960	1,012	2.55	0.53	2.0	2.4	2.4
Republic of Korea	Bucheon	763	907	948	1.73	0.44	2.0	2.3	2.3
Republic of Korea	Incheon	2,464	2,580	2,607	0.46	0.10	6.6	6.5	6.3
Republic of Korea	Gwangju	1,346	1,474	1,507	0.91	0.22	3.6	3.7	3.6
Republic of Korea	Busan	3,673	3,421	3,383	-0.71	-0.11	9.9	8.6	8.2
Republic of Korea	Seongnam	911	954	971	0.46	0.18	2.4	2.4	2.3
Republic of Korea	Seoul	9,917	9,762	9,738	-0.16	-0.02	26.6	24.5	23.5
Republic of Korea	Suweon	932	1,130	1,178	1.93	0.42	2.5	2.8	2.8
Republic of Korea	Daegu	2,478	2,455	2,458	-0.09	0.01	6.7	6.2	5.9
Republic of Korea	Daejon	1,362	1,507	1,544	1.01	0.24	3.7	3.8	3.7
Republic of Korea	Ulsan	1,011	1,080	1,102	0.66	0.20	2.7	2.7	2.7
Saudi Arabia	Al-Madinah (Medina)	795	1,105	1,364	3.29	2.11	4.8	5.1	5.0
Saudi Arabia	Ar-Riyadh (Riyadh)	3,567	4,856	5,866	3.08	1.89	21.5	22.4	21.7
Saudi Arabia	Ad-Dammam	639	903	1,119	3.46	2.14	3.8	4.2	4.1
Saudi Arabia	Jiddah	2,509	3,239	3,906	2.55	1.87	15.1	14.9	14.5
Saudi Arabia	Makkah (Mecca)	1,168	1,486	1,806	2.41	1.95	7.0	6.9	6.7
Singapore	Singapore	4,017	4,592	4,965	1.34	0.78	100.0	100.0	100.0
Syrian Arab Republic	Dimashq (Damascus)	2,044	2,675	3,293	2.69	2.08	24.0	22.8	21.8
Syrian Arab Republic	Halab (Aleppo)	2,222	2,968	3,649	2.89	2.07	26.1	25.3	24.2
Syrian Arab Republic	Hims (Homs)	809	1,095	1,365	3.03	2.20	9.5	9.3	9.1
Thailand	Krung Thep (Bangkok)	6,332	6,918	7,807	0.89	1.21	33.5	31.3	29.5
Turkey	Adana	1,123	1,362	1,557	1.93	1.34	2.5	2.5	2.4
Turkey	Ankara	3,179	3,908	4,403	2.06	1.19	7.2	7.2	6.9
Turkey	Antalya	595	839	969	3.44	1.44	1.3	1.6	1.5
Turkey	Bursa	1,180	1,589	1,817	2.98	1.34	2.7	2.9	2.9
Turkey	Gaziantep	844	1,109	1,274	2.73	1.39	1.9	2.1	2.0
Turkey	Istanbul	8,744	10,530	11,695	1.86	1.05	19.8	19.5	18.4
Turkey	Izmir	2,216	2,724	3,085	2.06	1.24	5.0	5.0	4.8
Turkey	Konya	734	978	1,126	2.87	1.41	1.7	1.8	1.8
United Arab Emirates	Dubayy (Dubai)	938	1,516	1,894	4.80	2.23	37.1	41.0	41.0
Uzbekistan	Tashkent	2,135	2,247	2,636	0.51	1.60	23.2	21.3	20.3
Viet Nam	Hai Phòng	1,704	2,129	2,752	2.23	2.57	8.9	8.1	7.8
Viet Nam	Hà Noi	3,752	4,723	6,036	2.30	2.45	19.5	18.0	17.1
Viet Nam	Thành Pho Ho Chí Minh (Ho Chi Minh City)	4,621	5,723	7,293	2.14	2.42	24.1	21.9	20.7
Yemen	Al-Hudaydah	457	951	1,528	7.33	4.74	9.6	12.2	12.4
Yemen	Sana'a'	1,365	2,345	3,636	5.41	4.39	28.6	30.1	29.4
Yemen	Ta'izz	465	902	1,437	6.63	4.66	9.7	11.6	11.6
EUROPE									
Austria	Wien (Vienna)	2,158	2,385	2,476	1.00	0.37	40.4	41.8	41.1
Belarus	Minsk	1,700	1,846	1,883	0.82	0.20	24.2	26.1	26.9
Belgium	Antwerpen	912	920	920	0.09	0.00	9.2	9.0	8.8
Belgium	Bruxelles-Brussel	1,733	1,744	1,744	0.06	0.00	17.5	17.0	16.7
Bulgaria	Sofia	1,128	1,212	1,236	0.72	0.20	20.5	22.6	24.0
Czech Republic	Praha (Prague)	1,172	1,160	1,159	-0.10	-0.01	15.5	15.5	15.4
Denmark	København (Copenhagen)	1,077	1,087	1,095	0.09	0.07	23.7	22.8	22.1
Finland	Helsinki	1,019	1,139	1,195	1.11	0.48	32.2	33.5	32.6
France	Bordeaux	763	817	853	0.68	0.43	1.7	1.7	1.6
France	Lille	1,007	1,059	1,102	0.50	0.40	2.2	2.2	2.1
France	Lyon	1,362	1,443	1,495	0.58	0.35	3.0	3.0	2.9
France	Marseille-Aix-en-Provence	1,357	1,418	1,469	0.44	0.35	3.0	2.9	2.8
France	Nice-Cannes	894	941	980	0.51	0.41	2.0	1.9	1.9
France	Paris	9,692	9,958	10,031	0.27	0.07	21.6	20.5	19.3
France	Toulouse	778	863	900	1.04	0.42	1.7	1.8	1.7
Germany	Berlin	3,384	3,423	3,436	0.11	0.04	5.6	5.6	5.6
Germany	Hamburg	1,710	1,777	1,792	0.38	0.08	2.8	2.9	2.9
Germany	Köln (Cologne)	963	1,037	1,061	0.74	0.23	1.6	1.7	1.7
Germany	München (Munich)	1,202	1,300	1,318	0.78	0.14	2.0	2.1	2.1
Greece	Athínai (Athens)	3,179	3,256	3,300	0.24	0.13	48.5	47.3	45.2
Greece	Thessaloniki	797	837	865	0.49	0.33	12.2	12.2	11.9
Hungary	Budapest	1,787	1,664	1,655	-0.71	-0.05	27.1	24.5	23.8

TABLE C.1

continued

		Estimates and projections ('000)			Annual rate of change (%)		Share in national urban population (%)		
		2000	2010	2020	2000–2010	2010–2020	2000	2010	2020
Ireland	Dublin	989	1,098	1,257	1.05	1.35	43.9	39.2	37.9
Italy	Milano (Milan)	2,985	2,940	2,938	-0.15	-0.01	7.7	7.3	7.1
Italy	Napoli (Naples)	2,232	2,253	2,254	0.09	0.00	5.8	5.6	5.4
Italy	Palermo	855	865	869	0.12	0.05	2.2	2.1	2.1
Italy	Roma (Rome)	3,385	3,333	3,330	-0.15	-0.01	8.7	8.3	8.0
Italy	Torino (Turin)	1,694	1,647	1,645	-0.28	-0.01	4.4	4.1	4.0
Netherlands	Amsterdam	1,005	1,044	1,078	0.38	0.32	8.2	7.6	7.4
Netherlands	Rotterdam	991	1,014	1,046	0.23	0.31	8.1	7.4	7.2
Norway	Oslo	774	858	909	1.03	0.58	22.7	23.1	22.7
Poland	Kraków (Cracow)	756	755	755	-0.01	0.00	3.2	3.3	3.3
Poland	Lódz	799	745	735	-0.70	-0.14	3.4	3.2	3.2
Poland	Warszawa (Warsaw)	1,666	1,724	1,736	0.34	0.07	7.0	7.4	7.5
Portugal	Lisboa (Lisbon)	2,672	2,890	3,058	0.78	0.57	48.0	44.4	42.7
Portugal	Porto	1,254	1,380	1,476	0.96	0.67	22.5	21.2	20.6
Romania	Bucuresti (Bucharest)	1,949	1,947	1,949	-0.01	0.01	16.5	16.8	16.7
Russian Federation	Chelyabinsk	1,082	1,088	1,085	0.06	-0.03	1.0	1.1	1.1
Russian Federation	Yekaterinburg	1,303	1,319	1,324	0.12	0.04	1.2	1.3	1.4
Russian Federation	Kazan	1,096	1,119	1,122	0.21	0.03	1.0	1.1	1.1
Russian Federation	Krasnoyarsk	911	930	935	0.21	0.05	0.8	0.9	1.0
Russian Federation	Moskva (Moscow)	10,016	10,495	10,526	0.47	0.03	9.3	10.3	10.8
Russian Federation	Nizhniy Novgorod	1,331	1,269	1,262	-0.48	-0.06	1.2	1.2	1.3
Russian Federation	Novosibirsk	1,426	1,376	1,366	-0.36	-0.07	1.3	1.3	1.4
Russian Federation	Omsk	1,136	1,129	1,125	-0.06	-0.04	1.1	1.1	1.2
Russian Federation	Perm	1,014	1,003	1,007	-0.11	0.04	0.9	1.0	1.0
Russian Federation	Rostov-na-Donu (Rostov-on-Don)	1,061	1,047	1,044	-0.13	-0.03	1.0	1.0	1.1
Russian Federation	Samara	1,173	1,126	1,119	-0.41	-0.06	1.1	1.1	1.1
Russian Federation	Sankt Peterburg (Saint Petersburg)	4,729	4,508	4,477	-0.48	-0.07	4.4	4.4	4.6
Russian Federation	Saratov	878	831	822	-0.55	-0.11	0.8	0.8	0.8
Russian Federation	Ufa	1,049	1,000	987	-0.48	-0.13	1.0	1.0	1.0
Russian Federation	Volgograd	1,010	973	965	-0.37	-0.08	0.9	1.0	1.0
Russian Federation	Voronezh	854	840	838	-0.17	-0.02	0.8	0.8	0.9
Serbia	Beograd (Belgrade)	1,127	1,096	1,132	-0.28	0.32	21.8	21.1	20.3
Spain	Barcelona	4,560	5,057	5,182	1.03	0.24	14.9	14.5	14.1
Spain	Madrid	5,045	5,764	5,934	1.33	0.29	16.4	16.5	16.1
Spain	Valencia	795	816	841	0.26	0.30	2.6	2.3	2.3
Sweden	Stockholm	1,206	1,285	1,326	0.63	0.31	16.2	16.4	16.0
Switzerland	Zürich (Zurich)	1,078	1,119	1,150	0.37	0.27	20.2	20.1	19.5
Ukraine	Dnipropetrovs'k	1,077	1,045	1,042	-0.30	-0.03	3.3	3.4	3.6
Ukraine	Donets'k	1,026	978	972	-0.48	-0.06	3.1	3.2	3.3
Ukraine	Kharkiv	1,484	1,457	1,455	-0.18	-0.01	4.5	4.7	5.0
Ukraine	Kyiv (Kiev)	2,606	2,748	2,772	0.53	0.09	7.9	8.9	9.5
Ukraine	Odesa	1,037	977	970	-0.60	-0.07	3.2	3.2	3.3
Ukraine	Zaporizhzhya	822	778	772	-0.55	-0.08	2.5	2.5	2.7
United Kingdom	Birmingham	2,285	2,291	2,315	0.03	0.10	4.3	4.1	4.0
United Kingdom	Glasgow	1,171	1,164	1,187	-0.06	0.20	2.2	2.1	2.0
United Kingdom	Liverpool	818	815	836	-0.04	0.25	1.6	1.5	1.4
United Kingdom	London	8,225	8,607	8,618	0.45	0.01	15.6	15.5	14.8
United Kingdom	Manchester	2,243	2,235	2,258	-0.04	0.10	4.3	4.0	3.9
United Kingdom	Newcastle upon Tyne	880	887	908	0.08	0.23	1.7	1.6	1.6
United Kingdom	West Yorkshire	1,495	1,539	1,565	0.29	0.17	2.8	2.8	2.7
LATIN AMERICA AND THE CARIBBEAN									
Argentina	Buenos Aires	11,847	13,089	13,653	1.00	0.42	35.6	34.8	32.7
Argentina	Córdoba	1,348	1,494	1,606	1.03	0.72	4.1	4.0	3.8
Argentina	Mendoza	838	918	993	0.91	0.79	2.5	2.4	2.4
Argentina	Rosario	1,152	1,233	1,326	0.68	0.73	3.5	3.3	3.2
Argentina	San Miguel de Tucumán	722	832	902	1.42	0.81	2.2	2.2	2.2
Bolivia	La Paz	1,390	1,692	2,027	1.97	1.81	27.0	25.3	24.5
Bolivia	Santa Cruz	1,054	1,551	1,876	3.86	1.90	20.5	23.2	22.7
Brazil	Baixada Santista[2]	1,468	1,810	2,031	2.09	1.15	1.0	1.1	1.0
Brazil	Belém	1,748	2,335	2,639	2.90	1.22	1.2	1.4	1.3
Brazil	Belo Horizonte	4,659	5,941	6,597	2.43	1.05	3.3	3.5	3.4
Brazil	Brasília	2,746	3,938	4,463	3.61	1.25	1.9	2.3	2.3
Brazil	Campinas	2,264	3,003	3,380	2.82	1.18	1.6	1.7	1.7
Brazil	Campo Grande	654	830	943	2.38	1.28	0.5	0.5	0.5
Brazil	Cuiabá	686	857	972	2.23	1.26	0.5	0.5	0.5
Brazil	Curitiba	2,494	3,320	3,735	2.86	1.18	1.8	1.9	1.9
Brazil	Florianópolis	734	1,142	1,328	4.42	1.51	0.5	0.7	0.7
Brazil	Fortaleza	2,875	3,599	4,011	2.25	1.08	2.0	2.1	2.0
Brazil	Goiânia	1,608	2,189	2,482	3.08	1.26	1.1	1.3	1.3
Brazil	Grande São Luís	876	1,106	1,252	2.33	1.24	0.6	0.6	0.6
Brazil	Grande Vitória	1,398	1,829	2,067	2.69	1.22	1.0	1.1	1.1
Brazil	João Pessoa	827	1,012	1,142	2.02	1.21	0.6	0.6	0.6
Brazil	Maceió	952	1,281	1,460	2.97	1.31	0.7	0.7	0.7
Brazil	Manaus	1,392	1,898	2,156	3.10	1.27	1.0	1.1	1.1
Brazil	Natal	910	1,161	1,316	2.44	1.25	0.6	0.7	0.7
Brazil	Norte/Nordeste Catarinense[3]	815	1,059	1,205	2.62	1.29	0.6	0.6	0.6
Brazil	Pôrto Alegre	3,505	4,096	4,517	1.56	0.98	2.5	2.4	2.3
Brazil	Recife	3,230	3,831	4,236	1.71	1.00	2.3	2.2	2.2
Brazil	Rio de Janeiro	10,803	12,171	13,179	1.19	0.80	7.6	7.1	6.7
Brazil	Salvador	2,968	3,695	4,114	2.19	1.07	2.1	2.1	2.1

Statistical annex

TABLE C.1

continued

		Estimates and projections ('000)			Annual rate of change (%)		Share in national urban population (%)		
		2000	2010	2020	2000–2010	2010–2020	2000	2010	2020
Brazil	São Paulo	17,099	19,582	21,124	1.36	0.76	12.1	11.4	10.7
Brazil	Teresina	789	958	1,082	1.94	1.22	0.6	0.6	0.5
Chile	Santiago	5,275	5,879	6,224	1.08	0.57	39.8	38.6	36.7
Chile	Valparaíso	803	880	956	0.92	0.83	6.1	5.8	5.6
Colombia	Barranquilla	1,531	1,907	2,157	2.20	1.23	5.1	5.3	5.2
Colombia	Bucaramanga	855	1,073	1,223	2.27	1.31	2.8	3.0	2.9
Colombia	Cali	1,950	2,378	2,675	1.98	1.18	6.5	6.6	6.4
Colombia	Cartagena	737	948	1,086	2.52	1.36	2.5	2.6	2.6
Colombia	Medellín	2,724	3,524	3,975	2.57	1.20	9.1	9.8	9.6
Colombia	Bogotá	6,356	8,320	9,299	2.69	1.11	21.2	23.1	22.4
Costa Rica	San José	1,032	1,374	1,627	2.86	1.69	44.5	45.8	44.5
Cuba	La Habana (Havana)	2,187	2,159	2,150	-0.13	-0.04	26.0	25.3	24.8
Dominican Republic	Santo Domingo	1,854	2,298	2,722	2.15	1.69	34.0	32.0	30.9
Ecuador	Guayaquil	2,077	2,690	3,154	2.59	1.59	28.0	29.2	28.3
Ecuador	Quito	1,357	1,846	2,189	3.08	1.70	18.3	20.0	19.6
El Salvador	San Salvador	1,233	1,520	1,776	2.09	1.56	34.1	34.7	33.8
Guatemala	Ciudad de Guatemala (Guatemala City)	908	1,104	1,481	1.95	2.94	17.9	15.5	15.0
Haiti	Port-au-Prince	1,653	2,209	3,012	2.90	3.10	54.2	44.3	42.9
Honduras	Tegucigalpa	793	1,022	1,317	2.54	2.54	28.8	27.8	27.0
Mexico	Aguascalientes	734	927	1,050	2.33	1.25	1.0	1.1	1.1
Mexico	Chihuahua	683	841	949	2.08	1.21	0.9	1.0	1.0
Mexico	Ciudad de México (Mexico City)	18,022	19,485	20,695	0.78	0.60	24.2	22.7	21.3
Mexico	Ciudad Juárez	1,225	1,396	1,544	1.31	1.01	1.6	1.6	1.6
Mexico	Culiacán	749	837	928	1.11	1.03	1.0	1.0	1.0
Mexico	Guadalajara	3,703	4,408	4,847	1.74	0.95	5.0	5.1	5.0
Mexico	León de los Aldamas	1,290	1,573	1,758	1.98	1.11	1.7	1.8	1.8
Mexico	Mérida	848	1,017	1,139	1.82	1.13	1.1	1.2	1.2
Mexico	Mexicali	770	935	1,051	1.94	1.17	1.0	1.1	1.1
Mexico	Monterrey	3,266	3,901	4,298	1.78	0.97	4.4	4.5	4.4
Mexico	Puebla	1,907	2,318	2,578	1.95	1.06	2.6	2.7	2.7
Mexico	Querétaro	795	1,032	1,172	2.61	1.27	1.1	1.2	1.2
Mexico	Saltillo	643	802	907	2.21	1.23	0.9	0.9	0.9
Mexico	San Luis Potosí	858	1,050	1,181	2.02	1.18	1.2	1.2	1.2
Mexico	Tijuana	1,287	1,666	1,881	2.58	1.21	1.7	1.9	1.9
Mexico	Toluca de Lerdo	1,417	1,584	1,743	1.11	0.96	1.9	1.8	1.8
Mexico	Torreón	1,014	1,201	1,339	1.69	1.09	1.4	1.4	1.4
Nicaragua	Managua	887	944	1,104	0.62	1.57	31.7	28.2	27.0
Panama	Ciudad de Panamá (Panama City)	1,072	1,379	1,653	2.52	1.81	55.3	52.5	51.1
Paraguay	Asunción	1,507	2,030	2,506	2.98	2.11	50.9	51.1	49.6
Peru	Arequipa	705	862	984	2.01	1.32	3.9	4.2	4.1
Peru	Lima	7,116	8,375	9,251	1.63	0.99	39.2	40.5	38.6
Puerto Rico	San Juan	2,237	2,758	2,803	2.09	0.16	61.7	68.8	66.3
Uruguay	Montevideo	1,561	1,504	1,515	-0.37	0.07	51.5	48.2	46.4
Venezuela (Bolivarian Republic of)	Barquisimeto	947	1,184	1,356	2.23	1.36	4.3	4.3	4.2
Venezuela (Bolivarian Republic of)	Caracas	2,864	3,098	3,482	0.79	1.17	13.1	11.3	10.9
Venezuela (Bolivarian Republic of)	Maracaibo	1,725	2,200	2,501	2.43	1.28	7.9	8.1	7.8
Venezuela (Bolivarian Republic of)	Maracay	899	1,060	1,214	1.65	1.36	4.1	3.9	3.8
Venezuela (Bolivarian Republic of)	Valencia	1,370	1,900	2,172	3.27	1.34	6.3	7.0	6.8
NORTHERN AMERICA									
Canada	Calgary	953	1,182	1,304	2.15	0.98	3.9	4.3	4.3
Canada	Edmonton	924	1,112	1,217	1.85	0.90	3.8	4.1	4.1
Canada	Montréal	3,471	3,781	4,014	0.86	0.60	14.2	13.9	13.4
Canada	Ottawa-Gatineau	1,079	1,182	1,274	0.91	0.75	4.4	4.3	4.2
Canada	Toronto	4,607	5,447	5,827	1.67	0.67	18.9	20.0	19.4
Canada	Vancouver	1,959	2,219	2,380	1.25	0.70	8.0	8.2	7.9
United States of America	Atlanta	3,542	4,695	5,035	2.82	0.70	1.6	1.8	1.7
United States of America	Austin	913	1,216	1,329	2.87	0.89	0.4	0.5	0.5
United States of America	Baltimore	2,083	2,322	2,508	1.09	0.77	0.9	0.9	0.9
United States of America	Boston	4,049	4,597	4,919	1.27	0.68	1.8	1.8	1.7
United States of America	Bridgeport-Stamford	894	1,056	1,154	1.67	0.89	0.4	0.4	0.4
United States of America	Buffalo	977	1,046	1,142	0.68	0.88	0.4	0.4	0.4
United States of America	Charlotte	769	1,044	1,144	3.06	0.91	0.3	0.4	0.4
United States of America	Chicago	8,333	9,211	9,756	1.00	0.57	3.7	3.6	3.4
United States of America	Cincinnati	1,508	1,687	1,831	1.12	0.82	0.7	0.7	0.6
United States of America	Cleveland	1,789	1,944	2,104	0.83	0.79	0.8	0.8	0.7
United States of America	Columbus, Ohio	1,138	1,314	1,431	1.44	0.85	0.5	0.5	0.5
United States of America	Dallas-Fort Worth	4,172	4,955	5,300	1.72	0.67	1.9	1.9	1.8
United States of America	Dayton	706	800	878	1.25	0.93	0.3	0.3	0.3
United States of America	Denver-Aurora	1,998	2,396	2,590	1.82	0.78	0.9	0.9	0.9
United States of America	Detroit	3,909	4,203	4,499	0.73	0.68	1.7	1.6	1.5
United States of America	El Paso	678	780	856	1.40	0.93	0.3	0.3	0.3
United States of America	Hartford	853	942	1,031	0.99	0.90	0.4	0.4	0.4
United States of America	Honolulu	720	813	891	1.21	0.92	0.3	0.3	0.3
United States of America	Houston	3,849	4,609	4,936	1.80	0.69	1.7	1.8	1.7
United States of America	Indianapolis	1,228	1,491	1,623	1.94	0.85	0.5	0.6	0.6
United States of America	Jacksonville, Florida	886	1,023	1,119	1.44	0.90	0.4	0.4	0.4
United States of America	Kansas City	1,365	1,514	1,645	1.04	0.83	0.6	0.6	0.6
United States of America	Las Vegas	1,335	1,917	2,085	3.62	0.84	0.6	0.7	0.7
United States of America	Los Angeles-Long Beach-Santa Ana	11,814	12,773	13,461	0.78	0.52	5.2	4.9	4.6
United States of America	Louisville	866	980	1,071	1.24	0.89	0.4	0.4	0.4
United States of America	Memphis	976	1,118	1,221	1.36	0.88	0.4	0.4	0.4

TABLE C.1

continued

		Estimates and projections ('000)			Annual rate of change (%)		Share in national urban population (%)		
		2000	2010	2020	2000–2010	2010–2020	2000	2010	2020
United States of America	Miami	4,946	5,755	6,141	1.51	0.65	2.2	2.2	2.1
United States of America	Milwaukee	1,311	1,429	1,553	0.86	0.83	0.6	0.6	0.5
United States of America	Minneapolis-St Paul	2,397	2,695	2,905	1.17	0.75	1.1	1.0	1.0
United States of America	Nashville-Davidson	755	912	999	1.89	0.91	0.3	0.4	0.3
United States of America	New Orleans	1,009	982	1,002	-0.27	0.20	0.4	0.4	0.3
United States of America	New York-Newark	17,846	19,441	20,370	0.86	0.47	7.9	7.5	7.0
United States of America	Oklahoma City	748	813	891	0.83	0.92	0.3	0.3	0.3
United States of America	Orlando	1,165	1,401	1,526	1.84	0.85	0.5	0.5	0.5
United States of America	Philadelphia	5,160	5,630	6,003	0.87	0.64	2.3	2.2	2.1
United States of America	Phoenix-Mesa	2,934	3,687	3,964	2.28	0.72	1.3	1.4	1.4
United States of America	Pittsburgh	1,755	1,889	2,044	0.74	0.79	0.8	0.7	0.7
United States of America	Portland	1,595	1,946	2,110	1.99	0.81	0.7	0.8	0.7
United States of America	Providence	1,178	1,318	1,435	1.12	0.85	0.5	0.5	0.5
United States of America	Richmond	822	944	1,033	1.38	0.90	0.4	0.4	0.4
United States of America	Riverside-San Bernardino	1,516	1,808	1,962	1.76	0.82	0.7	0.7	0.7
United States of America	Rochester	696	781	856	1.15	0.92	0.3	0.3	0.3
United States of America	Sacramento	1,402	1,662	1,805	1.70	0.83	0.6	0.6	0.6
United States of America	Salt Lake City	890	998	1,091	1.15	0.89	0.4	0.4	0.4
United States of America	San Antonio	1,333	1,522	1,655	1.33	0.84	0.6	0.6	0.6
United States of America	San Diego	2,683	3,002	3,231	1.12	0.74	1.2	1.2	1.1
United States of America	San Francisco-Oakland	3,236	3,544	3,803	0.91	0.71	1.4	1.4	1.3
United States of America	San Jose	1,543	1,720	1,865	1.09	0.81	0.7	0.7	0.6
United States of America	Seattle	2,727	3,174	3,415	1.52	0.73	1.2	1.2	1.2
United States of America	St Louis	2,081	2,260	2,441	0.83	0.77	0.9	0.9	0.8
United States of America	Tampa-St Petersburg	2,072	2,389	2,581	1.42	0.77	0.9	0.9	0.9
United States of America	Tucson	724	854	936	1.65	0.92	0.3	0.3	0.3
United States of America	Virginia Beach	1,397	1,535	1,667	0.94	0.82	0.6	0.6	0.6
United States of America	Washington, DC	3,949	4,464	4,778	1.23	0.68	1.8	1.7	1.6
OCEANIA									
Australia	Adelaide	1,102	1,167	1,258	0.57	0.75	6.6	6.1	5.9
Australia	Brisbane	1,603	1,970	2,170	2.06	0.97	9.6	10.3	10.2
Australia	Melbourne	3,433	3,851	4,137	1.15	0.72	20.6	20.2	19.5
Australia	Perth	1,373	1,598	1,746	1.52	0.89	8.2	8.4	8.2
Australia	Sydney	4,078	4,427	4,716	0.82	0.63	24.4	23.3	22.2
New Zealand	Auckland	1,063	1,321	1,441	2.17	0.87	32.2	35.5	35.4

Source: United Nations Department of Economic and Social Affairs, Population Division (2008) *World Urbanization Prospects: The 2007 Revision*, United Nations, New York.

Notes:

(1) As of 1 July 1997, Hong Kong became a Special Administrative Region (SAR) of China.

(2) Including Santos.

(3) Including Joinville.

TABLE C.2

Population of Capital Cities (2007)

AFRICA

Country	Capital	('000)
Algeria	El Djazaïr (Algiers)	3,355
Angola	Luanda	4,007
Benin[1]	Cotonou	762
Botswana	Gaborone	224
Burkina Faso	Ouagadougou	1,148
Burundi	Bujumbura	430
Cameroon	Yaoundé	1,610
Cape Verde	Praia	125
Central African Republic	Bangui	672
Chad	N'Djaména	987
Comoros	Moroni	46
Congo	Brazzaville	1,332
Côte d'Ivoire[2]	Abidjan	3,801
Côte d'Ivoire[2]	Yamoussoukro	669
Democratic Republic of the Congo	Kinshasa	7,851
Djibouti	Djibouti	583
Egypt	Al-Qahirah (Cairo)	11,894
Equatorial Guinea	Malabo	96
Eritrea	Asmera	600
Ethiopia	Addis Ababa	3,102
Gabon	Libreville	576
Gambia	Banjul	407
Ghana	Accra	2,120
Guinea	Conakry	1,494
Guinea-Bissau	Bissau	330
Kenya	Nairobi	3,011
Lesotho	Maseru	212
Liberia	Monrovia	1,165
Libyan Arab Jamahiriya	Tarabulus (Tripoli)	2,188
Madagascar	Antananarivo	1,697
Malawi	Lilongwe	732
Mali	Bamako	1,494
Mauritania	Nouakchott	673
Mauritius	Port Louis	150
Morocco	Rabat	1,705
Mozambique	Maputo	1,445
Namibia	Windhoek	313
Niger	Niamey	915
Nigeria	Abuja	1,579
Réunion	Saint-Denis	143
Rwanda	Kigali	852
Saint Helena	Jamestown	1
São Tomé and Principe	São Tomé	58
Senegal	Dakar	2,603
Seychelles	Victoria	26
Sierra Leone	Freetown	826
Somalia	Muqdisho (Mogadishu)	1,450
South Africa[3]	Bloemfontein	417
South Africa[3]	CapeTown	3,211
South Africa[3]	Pretoria	1,336
Sudan	Al-Khartum (Khartoum)	4,762
Swaziland[4]	Lobamba	...
Swaziland[4]	Mbabane	78
Togo	Lomé	1,451
Tunisia	Tunis	746
Uganda	Kampala	1,420
United Republic of Tanzania	Dodoma	183
Western Sahara	El Aaiún	200
Zambia	Lusaka	1,328
Zimbabwe	Harare	1,572

ASIA

Country	Capital	('000)
Afghanistan	Kabul	3,324
Armenia	Yerevan	1,102
Azerbaijan	Baku	1,892
Bahrain	Al-Manamah (Manama)	157
Bangladesh	Dhaka	13,476
Bhutan	Thimphu	83
Brunei Darussalam	Bandar Seri Begawan	22
Cambodia	Phnum Pénh (Phnom Penh)	1,465
China	Beijing	11,108
China, Hong Kong SAR[5]	Hong Kong	7,206
China, Macao SAR[6]	Macao	481
Cyprus	Lefkosia (Nicosia)	233
Democratic People's Republic of Korea	P'yongyang	3,301
Georgia	Tbilisi	1,099
India[7]	Delhi	15,915
Indonesia	Jakarta	9,143
Iran (Islamic Republic of)	Tehran	7,875
Iraq	Baghdad	5,500
Israel	Jerusalem	736
Japan	Tokyo	35,670
Jordan	Amman	1,064
Kazakhstan	Astana	594
Kuwait	Al Kuwayt (Kuwait City)	2,061
Kyrgyzstan	Bishkek	837
Lao People's Democratic Republic	Vientiane	746
Lebanon	Bayrut (Beirut)	1,857
Malaysia[8]	Kuala Lumpur	1,448
Maldives	Male	111
Mongolia	Ulaanbaatar	884
Myanmar	Nay Pyi Taw	418
Nepal	Kathmandu	895
Occupied Palestinian Territory	Ramallah	68
Oman	Masqat	621
Pakistan	Islamabad	780
Philippines	Manila	11,103
Qatar	Ad-Dawhah (Doha)	386
Republic of Korea	Seoul	9,799
Saudi Arabia	Ar-Riyadh (Riyadh)	4,462
Singapore	Singapore	4,436
Sri Lanka[9]	Colombo	656
Sri Lanka[9]	Sri Jayewardenepura Kotte	120
Syrian Arab Republic	Dimashq (Damascus)	2,467
Tajikistan	Dushanbe	553
Thailand	Krung Thep (Bangkok)	6,706
Timor-Leste	Dili	159
Turkey	Ankara	3,715
Turkmenistan	Ashgabat	744
United Arab Emirates	Abu Zaby (Abu Dhabi)	604
Uzbekistan	Tashkent	2,184
Viet Nam	Hà Noi	4,377
Yemen	Sana'a'	2,008

EUROPE

Country	Capital	('000)
Albania	Tiranë (Tirana)	406
Andorra	Andorra la Vella	24
Austria	Wien (Vienna)	2,315
Belarus	Minsk	1,806
Belgium	Bruxelles-Brussel	1,743
Bosnia and Herzegovina	Sarajevo	377
Bulgaria	Sofia	1,186
Channel Islands[10]	St Helier	29
Channel Islands[10]	St Peter Port	17
Croatia	Zagreb	689
Czech Republic	Praha (Prague)	1,162
Denmark	København (Copenhagen)	1,086
Estonia	Tallinn	397
Faeroe Islands	Tórshavn	20
Finland	Helsinki	1,115
France	Paris	9,902
Germany	Berlin	3,405
Gibraltar	Gibraltar	29
Greece	Athínai (Athens)	3,242
Holy See	Vatican City	1
Hungary	Budapest	1,675
Iceland	Reykjavík	192
Ireland	Dublin	1,060
Isle of Man	Douglas	26
Italy	Roma (Rome)	3,340
Latvia	Riga	722
Liechtenstein	Vaduz	5
Lithuania	Vilnius	543
Luxembourg	Luxembourg-Ville	84
Malta	Valletta	199
Moldova	Chisinau	592
Monaco	Monaco	33
Montenegro	Podgorica	142
Netherlands[11]	Amsterdam	1,031
Norway	Oslo	834
Poland	Warszawa (Warsaw)	1,707
Portugal	Lisboa (Lisbon)	2,811
Romania	Bucuresti (Bucharest)	1,940
Russian Federation	Moskva (Moscow)	10,471
San Marino	San Marino	4
Serbia	Beograd (Belgrade)	1,100
Slovakia	Bratislava	424
Slovenia	Ljubljana	244
Spain	Madrid	5,567
Sweden	Stockholm	1,264
Switzerland	Bern	337
TFYR Macedonia[12]	Skopje	480
Ukraine	Kyiv (Kiev)	2,705
United Kingdom	London	8,566

LATIN AMERICA AND THE CARIBBEAN

Country	Capital	('000)
Anguilla	The Valley	1
Antigua and Barbuda	St. John's	26
Argentina	Buenos Aires	12,792
Aruba	Oranjestad	32
Bahamas	Nassau	240
Barbados	Bridgetown	116
Belize	Belmopan	16
Bolivia[13]	La Paz	1,590
Bolivia[13]	Sucre	243
Brazil	Brasília	3,594
British Virgin Islands	Road Town	9
Cayman Islands	George Town	28
Chile	Santiago	5,719
Colombia	Bogotá	7,764
Costa Rica	San José	1,284
Cuba	La Habana (Havana)	2,178
Dominica	Roseau	14
Dominican Republic	Santo Domingo	2,154
Ecuador	Quito	1,697
El Salvador	San Salvador	1,433
Falkland Islands (Malvinas)	Stanley	2
French Guiana	Cayenne	63
Grenada	St.George's	32
Guadeloupe	Basse-Terre	12
Guatemala	Ciudadde Guatemala (GuatemalaCity)	1,025
Guyana	Georgetown	133
Haiti	Port-au-Prince	2,002
Honduras	Tegucigalpa	947
Jamaica	Kingston	581
Martinique	Fort-de-France	92
Mexico	Ciudad de México (MexicoCity)	19,026
Montserrat[14]	Brades Estate	1
Montserrat[14]	Plymouth	—
Netherlands Antilles	Willemstad	120
Nicaragua	Managua	920
Panama	Ciudadde Panamá (Panama City)	1,280
Paraguay	Asunción	1,870
Peru	Lima	8,007
Puerto Rico	SanJuan	2,689
Saint Kitts and Nevis	Basseterre	13
Saint Lucia	Castries	14
Saint Vincent and the Grenadines	Kingstown	26
Suriname	Paramaribo	252
Trinidad and Tobago	Port of Spain	54
Turks and Caicos Islands	Grand Turk	6
United States Virgin Islands	Charlotte Amalie	53
Uruguay	Montevideo	1,514
Venezuela (Bolivarian Republic of)	Caracas	2,986

TABLE C.2

continued

		('000)			('000)			('000)
NORTHERN AMERICA								
Bermuda	Hamilton	11	Canada[15]	Ottawa-Gatineau	1,143	United States of America	Washington, DC	4,338
Greenland	Nuuk (Godthåb)	15	Saint-Pierre-et-Miquelon	Saint-Pierre	6			
OCEANIA								
American Samoa	Pago Pago	58	Micronesia (Fed. States of)	Palikir	7	Pitcairn	Adamstown	0
Australia	Canberra	378	Nauru	Nauru	10	Samoa	Apia	43
Cook Islands[16]	Rarotonga	10	New Caledonia	Nouméa	156	Solomon Islands	Honiara	66
Fiji	Greater Suva	224	New Zealand	Wellington	366	Tokelau[19]		
French Polynesia	Papeete	131	Niue	Alofi	1	Tonga	Nuku'alofa	25
Guam	Hagåtña	149	Northern Mariana Islands[18]	Saipan	76	Tuvalu	Funafuti	5
Kiribati[17]	Tarawa	42	Palau	Koror	12	Vanuatu	Port Vila	40
Marshall Islands	Majuro	28	Papua New Guinea	Port Moresby	299	Wallis and Futuna Islands	Matu-Utu	1

Source: United Nations Department of Economic and Social Affairs, Population Division (2008) *World Urbanization Prospects: The 2007 Revision*, United Nations, New York.

Notes:

(1) Porto-Novo is the constitutional capital, Cotonou is the seat of government.

(2) Yamoussoukro is the capital, Abidjan is the seat of government.

(3) Pretoria is the administrative capital, Cape Town is the legislative capital and Bloemfontein is the judicial capital.

(4) Mbabane is the administrative capital, Lobamba is the legislative capital.

(5) As of 1 July 1997, Hong Kong became a Special Administrative Region (SAR) of China.

(6) As of 20 December 1999, Macao became a Special Administrative Region (SAR) of China.

(7) The capital is New Delhi, included in the urban agglomeration of Delhi. The population of New Delhi was estimated at 294,783 in the year 2001.

(8) Kuala Lumpur is the financial capital, Putrajaya is the administrative capital.

(9) Colombo is the commercial capital, Sri Jayewardenepura Kotte is the administrative and legislative capital.

(10) Refers to Guernsey, and Jersey. St Helier is the capital of the Bailiwick of Jersey and St Peter Port is the capital of the Bailiwick of Guernsey.

(11) Amsterdam is the capital, 's-Gravenhage is the seat of government.

(12) The former Yugoslav Republic of Macedonia.

(13) La Paz is the capital and the seat of government; Sucre is the legal capital and the seat of the judiciary.

(14) Due to volcanic activity, Plymouth was abandoned in 1997. The government premises have been established at Brades Estate.

(15) The capital is Ottawa.

(16) The capital is Avarua, located on the island of Rarotonga; the estimated population refers to the island of Rarotonga. Population estimates for Avarua have not been made available.

(17) The capital is Bairiki, located on the island of Tarawa; the estimated population refers to the island of South Tarawa. Population estimates for Bairiki have not been made available.

(18) The capital is Garapan, located on the island of Saipan; the estimated population refers to the island of Saipan. The population of Garapan was estimated at 3588 in the year 2000.

(19) There is no capital in Tokelau. Each atoll (Atafu, Fakaofo and Nukunonu) has its own administrative capital.

TABLE C.3

Access to Services in Selected Cities

		Percentage of households with											
		Access to piped water			Access to sewerage			Access to electricity			Access to telephone		
		1990	2000	2003	1990	2000	2003	1990	2000	2003	1990	2000	2003
AFRICA													
Angola	Luanda	...	...	13.1	...	...	20.4	...	...	36.2	...	...	...
Benin	Djougou	56.4	47.5	47.5	0.0	0.0	0.1	2.6	37.5	47.9	1.5	2.9	5.1
Benin	Porto-Novo	45.8	51.3	59.5	3.4	6.7	11.7	12.2	52.4	69.6	5.4	10.9	19.0
Burkina Faso	Ouagadougou	25.6	31.9	33.8	0.4	9.8	12.7	25.7	47.5	54.1	10.1	19.3	22.1
Cameroon	Yaounde	35.5	33.9	33.5	20.7	25.1	26.4	81.7	98.2	98.2	9.4	9.4	9.4
Côte d'Ivoire	Abidjan	57.9	72.4	76.7	19.2	36.1	41.2	59.8	94.1	94.1	13.2	13.2	13.3
Democratic Republic of the Congo	Kinshasa	...	...	64.0	...	...	6.7	...	...	...	...	...	11.2
Democratic Republic of the Congo	Butembo	...	...	14.4	...	...	0.0	...	...	...	...	...	6.2
Egypt	Cairo	93.0	98.1	99.6	47.1	66.2	71.9	98.7	99.8	99.8	...	54.1	73.4
Egypt	Alexandria	94.5	97.6	98.5	59.9	75.1	79.7	98.6	99.7	99.7	...	44.0	65.7
Egypt	Port Said	94.5	96.0	96.4	62.9	81.9	87.6	96.4	99.4	99.4	...	63.6	78.3
Egypt	Suez	94.9	98.4	99.5	60.6	71.5	74.8	99.4	99.5	99.5	...	46.1	66.6
Egypt	Assyut	85.2	96.2	99.6	28.8	21.8	19.8	95.3	98.2	99.1	...	19.5	44.5
Egypt	Aswan	80.9	96.3	96.3	17.5	35.8	41.3	96.8	99.1	99.8	...	45.5	56.9
Egypt	Beni Suef	...	99.3	99.3	4.1	45.2	57.5	93.4	98.3	99.8	...	41.9	56.9
Ethiopia	Addis Ababa	...	...	60.8	...	...	4.2	...	...	97.1	...	...	20.6
Ethiopia	Nazret	...	...	16.0	...	...	0.3	...	...	79.7	...	...	5.3
Gambia	Banjul	...	...	45.4	...	...	30.5	...	...	...	...	...	...
Ghana	Accra	63.3	57.3	55.5	12.7	31.1	36.6	93.0	88.0	86.4	3.8	21.8	27.2
Guinea	Conakry	...	...	39.2	...	...	11.2	...	...	71.4	...	...	7.2
Lesotho	Maseru	...	...	42.0	...	...	5.5	...	...	18.1	...	...	...
Mali	Bamako	...	35.4	49.0	9.8	18.0	30.2	7.1	51.4	64.6	8.5	13.3	20.5
Morocco	Casablanca	78.2	81.9	83.1	48.6	78.6	87.6	56.4	87.0	96.1	28.5	44.7	68.9
Morocco	Rabat	77.6	86.2	88.8	68.6	88.6	94.6	80.3	93.7	97.7	30.8	58.6	66.9
Morocco	Fes	...	...	93.8	...	...	89.1	...	...	97.7	...	...	57.9
Morocco	Marrakech	...	...	88.8	...	...	88.1	...	...	98.3	...	...	...
Morocco	Tangier	...	...	84.5	...	...	96.2	...	...	89.4	...	...	77.4
Morocco	Meknès	...	...	85.6	...	...	90.1	...	...	97.3	...	...	68.4
Mozambique	Maputo	...	...	65.4	...	...	22.1	...	...	39.2	...	...	6.9
Nigeria	Lagos	...	...	...	...	...	...	96.7	99.1	99.8	14.1	14.1	31.8
Nigeria	Ibadan	...	...	...	...	...	...	49.7	49.7	98.9	3.7	3.7	14.8
Nigeria	Ogbomosho	...	...	...	...	...	...	99.1	95.5	94.4	31.9	19.8	16.2
Nigeria	Zaria	...	...	...	...	...	...	81.1	95.6	95.6	2.7	6.6	12.4
Nigeria	Akure	...	...	...	...	...	...	76.8	91.2	95.5	4.0	7.3	8.3
Rwanda	Kigali	27.8	33.4	35.1	10.2	4.5	2.8	34.0	44.4	47.5	8.6	8.6	8.6
Senegal	Dakar	51.2	89.2	89.2	...	33.6	40.0	62.3	87.9	95.6	...	...	...
South Africa	Johannesburg	...	...	87.1	...	...	87.5	...	...	84.9	...	...	47.7
South Africa	Cape Town	...	...	95.7	...	...	93.8	...	...	92.0	...	...	45.2
South Africa	Durban	...	...	...	...	...	37.9	...	...	...	...	...	24.5
South Africa	Pretoria	...	...	87.1	...	...	87.5	...	...	84.9	...	...	47.7
South Africa	Port Elizabeth	...	...	...	...	...	28.4	...	...	...	...	...	17.6
South Africa	West Rand	...	...	84.5	...	...	78.8	...	...	78.2	...	...	41.5
Sudan	Khartoum	...	...	...	...	...	1.0	...	...	54.2	...	...	...
Sudan	Wad Medani	...	...	...	...	...	...	...	...	73.1	...	...	...
Sudan	Port Sudan	...	...	...	...	...	...	...	...	35.1	...	...	...
Sudan	Waw	...	...	...	...	...	...	...	...	6.3	...	...	...
Sudan	Nyala	...	...	...	...	...	...	...	...	26.5	...	...	...
Sudan	Juba	...	...	...	...	...	...	...	...	30.0	...	...	...
Sudan	Kassala	...	...	...	...	...	...	...	...	39.4	...	...	...
Uganda	Kampala	11.9	14.4	15.1	2.0	11.0	13.6	44.5	54.2	57.1	11.7	17.4	26.0
United Republic of Tanzania	Dar es Salaam	63.3	62.3	62.0	3.6	4.2	4.4	28.6	51.0	57.7	...	...	...
United Republic of Tanzania	Arusha	35.2	24.0	24.0	0.6	0.4	0.4	19.0	36.1	41.3	...	...	...
Zambia	Ndola	52.6	63.9	67.3	53.7	68.3	72.7	51.2	52.6	53.0	16.8	16.8	16.8
Zambia	Chingola	78.8	75.1	74.0	62.1	81.0	86.7	80.6	76.5	75.2	3.0	3.0	3.1
Zimbabwe	Harare	96.3	91.7	90.3	57.8	94.5	94.5	68.6	83.4	87.8	20.9	20.9	20.9
ASIA													
Armenia	Yerevan	...	...	99.2	...	...	93.0	...	...	99.1	...	...	...
Azerbaijan	Baku	...	...	81.6	...	...	64.8	...	...	96.0	...	...	...
Bangladesh	Dhaka	...	...	52.0	...	...	60.1	...	...	88.2	...	...	...
Bangladesh	Rajshahi	...	...	...	...	...	38.9	...	...	57.8	...	...	...
Cambodia	Phnom Penh	...	...	76.4	...	...	81.1	...	...	97.6	...	...	...
Cambodia	Siem Reab	...	...	...	...	...	29.0	...	...	55.7	...	...	...
China	Shanghai	...	...	99.3	...	...	66.2	...	...	...	...	...	...
China	Beijing	...	...	97.7	...	...	47.6	...	...	...	...	...	...
China	Guangzhou	...	...	86.3	...	...	45.5	...	...	...	...	...	...
China	Harbin	...	...	65.9	...	...	31.7	...	...	...	...	...	...
China	Zhengzhou	...	...	66.8	...	...	32.6	...	...	...	...	...	...
China	Lanzhou	...	...	69.1	...	...	44.3	...	...	...	...	...	...
China	Xuzhou	...	...	34.6	...	...	12.4	...	...	...	...	...	...
China	Yulin	...	...	17.3	...	...	9.6	...	...	...	...	...	...
China	Yiyang	...	...	23.8	...	...	9.8	...	...	...	...	...	...
China	Yueyang	...	...	30.5	...	...	16.5	...	...	...	...	...	...
China	Datong	...	...	63.3	...	...	22.7	...	...	...	...	...	...
China	Leshan	...	...	31.5	...	...	13.0	...	...	...	...	...	...
China	Yongzhou	...	...	20.4	...	...	6.7	...	...	...	...	...	...
China	Chifeng	...	...	33.4	...	...	10.3	...	...	...	...	...	...
China	Huaibei	...	...	30.7	...	...	12.7	...	...	...	...	...	...

TABLE C.3

continued

		Percentage of households with											
		Access to piped water			Access to sewerage			Access to electricity			Access to telephone		
		1990	2000	2003	1990	2000	2003	1990	2000	2003	1990	2000	2003
China	Hegang	...	...	71.3	...	...	18.5	...	...	...	...	...	...
China	Dandong	...	...	51.3	...	...	25.6	...	...	...	...	...	...
China	Dezhou	...	...	20.6	...	...	7.2	...	...	...	...	...	...
China	Anqing	...	...	21.7	...	...	10.5	...	...	...	...	...	31.6
China	Shaoguan	...	...	52.4	...	...	10.8	...	...	...	...	...	25.6
China	Changzhi	...	...	49.3	...	...	12.6	...	...	...	...	...	45.4
India	Mumbai	68.0	78.9	82.2	30.3	38.6	41.1	87.6	99.0	99.0	...	...	29.7
India	Kolkota	30.5	36.2	37.9	42.7	43.7	44.0	78.6	97.6	97.6	...	...	9.0
India	Delhi	70.8	83.3	87.1	53.6	84.0	93.1	95.4	98.1	99.0	...	...	18.9
India	Hyderabad	65.5	93.0	93.0	54.6	50.8	49.6	89.8	97.7	97.7	...	...	28.5
India	Pune (Poona)	59.2	54.2	52.7	46.5	22.2	15.0	91.0	92.6	93.1	...	...	19.1
India	Kanpur	56.5	46.2	43.1	47.4	27.9	22.0	80.4	97.2	97.2	...	...	35.3
India	Jaipur	88.1	82.6	80.9	87.0	61.5	53.9	96.6	98.4	98.9	...	...	13.2
India	Coimbatore	36.7	35.8	35.5	44.7	51.7	53.8	86.1	90.4	91.7	...	...	39.0
India	Kochi (Cochin)	28.2	27.3	27.1	86.1	27.5	27.5	82.4	88.5	90.3	...	...	20.3
India	Vijayawada	41.0	38.7	38.1	46.0	50.2	51.4	84.3	96.8	96.8	...	...	19.6
India	Amritsar	65.5	90.0	97.4	86.6	87.4	87.6	98.6	99.1	99.1	...	...	19.6
India	Srinagar	78.2	90.4	94.0	51.3	70.5	76.3	99.7	99.2	99.1	...	...	13.0
India	Jodhpur	77.9	83.0	84.5	67.2	77.3	80.3	93.1	98.4	98.4	...	...	27.0
India	Akola	59.2	76.7	81.9	30.3	50.2	56.2	80.6	99.2	99.2	...	...	15.0
India	Rajahmundry	23.0	39.1	44.0	31.3	41.6	44.7	82.8	88.0	89.6	...	...	35.7
India	Yamunanagar	50.3	62.0	65.5	48.5	71.9	78.9	95.9	98.9	99.8	...	...	25.9
India	Kharagpur	...	46.8	56.3	33.3	77.7	91.0	60.9	88.1	96.3	...	...	34.0
India	Hisar	48.0	77.6	86.5	32.9	85.0	85.0	92.1	99.0	99.0	...	...	18.9
India	Jalna	...	...	25.1	...	...	44.6	...	...	90.4	...	...	17.6
India	Karnal	...	...	72.9	...	...	62.1	...	...	95.5	...	...	20.1
India	Agartala	22.9	25.6	26.4	32.0	47.7	52.4	86.1	91.5	93.1	...	...	44.8
India	Gadag-Betigeri	62.4	75.6	79.5	49.3	65.4	70.2	89.6	97.0	99.3	...	...	69.3
India	Krishnanagar	32.9	32.7	32.7	49.2	69.7	75.8	68.7	84.6	89.4	...	...	...
Indonesia	Jakarta	27.2	32.1	35.6	44.4	66.0	59.5	99.1	99.8	99.9	...	...	...
Indonesia	Bandung	53.5	44.1	41.3		58.4	71.2	97.6	98.3	98.5	...	...	...
Indonesia	Surabaja	95.6	42.3	26.3	36.5	57.7	64.1	99.1	99.9	99.9	...	...	...
Indonesia	Medan	71.9	47.8	40.5	78.9	77.9	77.5	96.9	94.0	93.2	...	...	64.5
Indonesia	Palembang	73.5	64.8	62.3	41.3	78.9	90.1	95.2	97.4	98.0	...	...	39.9
Indonesia	Ujung Pandang	45.9	34.6	31.2	44.3	80.4	91.2	95.3	99.3	99.3	...	...	16.8
Indonesia	Bogor	10.8	29.3	40.4	...	68.6	86.0	92.5	99.1	99.8	...	...	...
Indonesia	Surakarta	55.8	...	...	45.3	61.2	66.0	99.6	99.5	99.5	...	...	...
Indonesia	Pekan Baru	77.2	...	...	69.2	70.0	70.3	94.3	97.2	98.1	...	...	...
Indonesia	Denpasar	39.4	48.5	51.2	52.1	86.3	96.5	98.5	99.5	99.8	...	...	...
Indonesia	Jambi	79.4	49.6	40.6		67.2	58.2	98.3	96.3	95.7	...	...	...
Indonesia	Purwokerto	...	19.6	25.0	32.9	52.7	58.6	90.6	96.6	98.4	...	...	...
Indonesia	Kediri	...	26.2	33.8		53.8	70.7	91.2	98.9	99.7	...	...	...
Indonesia	Palu	46.5	29.6	24.6	41.8	59.7	65.0	84.0	95.8	99.3	...	...	...
Indonesia	Bitung	38.4	54.2	58.9		71.4	84.6	93.2	97.3	98.5	...	...	...
Indonesia	Jaya Pura	23.1	61.1	61.1	43.2	66.0	72.8	61.3	99.5	99.5	...	...	...
Indonesia	Dumai	14.8	11.6	10.6		58.8	74.0	65.7	92.4	97.2	...	...	...
Iraq	Baghdad	...	...	97.2	...	...	96.7	...	...	...	...	...	...
Iraq	Mosul	...	...	99.6	...	...	95.1	...	...	...	...	...	...
Iraq	Amara	...	...	88.3	...	...	75.0	...	...	...	...	...	...
Kazakhstan	Shimkent	...	...	76.9	...	...	60.9	...	...	99.6	...	...	...
Kazakhstan	Zhezkazgan	...	...	100.0	...	...	99.5	...	...	100.0	...	...	...
Mongolia	Ulan Bator	...	...	49.4	...	...	49.1	...	...	99.0	...	...	...
Myanmar	Yangon	...	...	36.8	...	...	31.3	...	...	...	...	...	...
Pakistan	Karachi	...	...	77.4	...	...	90.0	...	...	96.8	...	...	60.7
Pakistan	Faisalabad	...	...	78.1	...	...	87.2	...	...	98.7	...	...	44.9
Pakistan	Islamabad	...	...	80.3	...	...	70.3	...	...	97.8	...	...	28.5
Philippines	Metro Manila	67.8	71.8	72.9	50.7	73.5	80.4	97.6	98.7	99.0	37.3	55.3	42.6
Philippines	Cebu	19.1	52.9	63.0	50.7	58.4	60.8	85.0	88.3	89.3	8.5	36.5	81.5
Philippines	Cagayan de Oro	86.5	...	...	...	79.2	79.2	90.0	76.8	72.9	3.8	21.1	79.2
Philippines	Bacolod	...	47.2	54.2	42.8	63.3	69.5	72.9	85.5	89.3	6.8	31.9	45.5
Tajikistan	Dushanbe	...	...	93.3	...	...	69.6	...	...	99.0	...	...	89.9
Turkey	Istanbul	86.6	86.6	86.6	91.4	98.7	98.7	100.0	100.0	100.0	75.6	80.9	...
Turkey	Ankara	97.4	95.7	95.2	91.8	99.0	99.0	100.0	100.0	100.0	82.1	92.3	...
Turkey	Izmir	98.2	95.3	94.4	93.4	99.2	99.2	100.0	100.0	100.0	62.4	89.4	...
Turkey	Bursa	97.7	88.8	85.0	95.9	85.2	80.7	100.0	100.0	100.0	65.4	87.0	...
Turkey	Adana	94.9	96.8	96.8	81.9	83.7	84.2	100.0	100.0	100.0	37.8	80.0	...
Turkey	Gaziantep	96.8	93.3	90.9	79.1	91.6	95.4	100.0	100.0	100.0	48.0	79.3	82.5
Turkey	Kahramanmaras	...	95.7	95.7	...	24.3	34.8	100.0	100.0	100.0	28.6	100.0	95.4
Turkey	Antakya	99.4	82.0	74.6	...	...	...	100.0	100.0	100.0	73.9	85.7	97.5
Turkey	Aksaray	...	...	40.5	...	...	21.4	...	...	...	...	...	93.5
Uzbekistan	Tashkent	...	...	98.7	...	...	79.4	...	...	...	...	...	92.7
Viet Nam	Ho Chi Minh City	90.3	89.0	88.7	83.9	92.9	95.6	99.6	99.7	99.8	12.3	60.7	88.8
Viet Nam	Ha Noi	...	64.7	78.8	...	74.6	95.1	100.0	100.0	100.0	16.8	60.5	100.0
Viet Nam	Hai Phong	46.4	87.4	99.6	...	73.9	95.1	100.0	100.0	100.0	12.9	26.0	89.2
Viet Nam	Da Nang	53.8	82.9	91.7	69.1	93.6	93.6	100.0	100.0	100.0	40.7	60.4	69.0
Yemen	Sana'a	...	...	78.7	...	...	24.8	...	...	98.8	...	...	...
Yemen	Aden	...	...	93.3	...	...	83.1	...	...	95.6	...	...	...
Yemen	Taiz	...	...	84.0	...	...	39.9	...	...	95.2	...	...	...

TABLE C.3

continued

		Percentage of households with										
		Access to piped water			Access to sewerage			Access to electricity			Access to telephone		
		1990	2000	2003	1990	2000	2003	1990	2000	2003	1990	2000	2003
LATIN AMERICA AND THE CARIBBEAN													
Brazil	Rio de Janeiro	...	...	88.5	...	...	63.3	98.9	99.1	99.1	34.7	50.4	55.1
Brazil	Sao Paolo	...	...	93.8	...	...	79.9	98.7	99.0	99.1	28.7	67.5	79.2
Brazil	Belo Horizonte	...	...	84.4	...	...	78.9	98.8	99.3	99.4	31.2	81.0	95.9
Brazil	Fortaleza	...	...	76.8	...	...	19.8	95.4	99.1	99.1	20.6	54.9	65.1
Brazil	Curitiba	...	...	84.2	...	...	55.4	97.3	99.2	99.8	45.1	73.5	82.0
Brazil	Brasilia	...	...	89.8	...	...	69.0	97.3	98.9	99.4	40.1	75.3	85.9
Brazil	Goiânia	...	...	93.4	...	...	73.8	99.5	99.1	99.0	25.5	67.6	80.2
Brazil	São José dos Campos	...	...	...	...	...	...	99.1	99.2	99.2	28.7	54.5	62.3
Brazil	Nova Iguaçu	...	...	...	...	...	...	...	...	99.5	...	...	23.7
Brazil	Ribeirão Preto	...	...	...	...	...	...	99.0	99.5	99.6	40.8	74.8	85.0
Brazil	Vitoria	...	...	90.4	...	...	82.1	...	...	99.4	...	...	69.3
Brazil	Guarujá	...	...	...	...	...	...	98.7	99.5	99.8	13.7	43.6	52.5
Brazil	Rondonópolis	...	...	...	...	...	...	93.8	96.9	97.9	17.8	41.3	48.3
Chile	Santiago	...	...	...	...	...	...	...	...	...	93.0	91.7	91.3
Chile	Chillan	...	...	...	...	...	...	...	...	...	26.1	43.4	48.6
Colombia	Bogotá	...	...	100.0	...	...	100.0	...	...	99.8	...	...	...
Colombia	Medellín	...	...	100.0	...	...	99.5	...	...	99.9	...	...	...
Colombia	Neiva	...	...	100.0	...	...	95.4	...	...	98.7	...	...	...
Colombia	Valledupar	...	...	99.6	...	...	98.7	...	...	99.6	...	...	...
Ecuador	Guayaquil	...	...	...				...	...	...	23.8	39.9	44.8
Guatemala	Guatemala City	...	...	52.7	...	...	65.3	...	...	91.0	...	...	31.9
Mexico	Mexico	...	...	...	...	...	...	...	...	...	...	...	57.1
Mexico	Guadalajara	...	...	...	...	...	...	...	...	...	...	...	67.9
Mexico	Tijuana	...	...	...	...	...	...	...	...	...	...	...	61.7
Mexico	León	...	...	...	...	...	...	...	...	...	...	...	44.8
Mexico	Culiacán	...	...	...	...	...	...	...	...	...	...	...	59.6
Mexico	Hermosillo	...	...	...	...	...	...	...	...	...	...	...	55.6
Mexico	Villahermosa	...	...	...	...	...	...	...	...	...	...	...	48.8
Venezuela (Bolivarian Republic of)	Caracas	...	...	...	...	...	...	...	...	...	48.3	53.9	55.6
Venezuela (Bolivarian Republic of)	Maracaibo	...	...	...	...	...	...	...	...	...	31.3	41.9	45.1
Venezuela (Bolivarian Republic of)	Valencia	...	...	...	...	...	...	...	...	...	28.5	43.0	47.4

Source: UN-Habitat, Urban Info 2006.

REFERENCES

Abbott, C. (2001) *Greater Portland: Urban Life and Landscape in the Pacific Northwest*, University of Pennsylvania Press, Philadelphia

Abers, R. (1998) 'Learning democratic practice: Distributing government resources through popular participation in Porto Alegre, Brazil', in M. Douglass and J. Friedmann (eds) *Cities for Citizens*, Wiley, London, pp39–66

Abramson, D. (2005) 'The "studio abroad" as a mode of transcultural engagement in urban planning education: A reflection on ten years of Sino-Canadian collaboration', *Journal of Planning Education and Research* **25**: 89–102

ABS-CBN News (2009) 'UAE halts building projects worth $582B', www.abs-cbnnews.com/business/02/05/09/uae-halts-building-projects-worth-582b-study

Adams, F. J. and G. Hodge (1965) 'City planning instruction in the United States: The pioneering days, 1900–1930', *Journal of the American Planning Association* **31**(1): 43–51

ADB (Asian Development Bank) (1998) *Resettlement Policy and Practice in South–East Asia and the Pacific*, www.adb.org/Documents/Conference/Resettlement/default.asp

Africapolis (2008) *Urban Dynamics in West Africa, 1950–2020: Geo-Statistical Approach*, http://e-geopolis.eu/ecrire/upload/DRAFT_1_-_SUMMARY_AFRICAPOLIS_REPORT.pdf

Afshar, F. (2001) 'Preparing planners for a globalizing world: The planning school at the University of Guelph', *Journal of Planning Education and Research* **20**(3): 339–352

Aguilar, A. G. (2008) 'Peri-urbanization, illegal settlements and environmental impact in Mexico City', *Cities* **25**: 133–145

Aguilar, A. G., P. M. Ward and C. B. Smith (2003) 'Globalization, regional development and mega-city expansion in Latin America: Analyzing Mexico City's peri-urban hinterland', *Cities* **20**(1): 3–21

Al-Asad, M. (undated) 'The contemporary built environment in the Arab Middle East', in *The Middle East Institute Viewpoints: Architecture and Urbanism in the Middle East,* Middle East Institute, Washington, DC, www.mideasti.org/files/architecture-and-urbanism.pdf

Albrechts, L. (2001a) 'From traditional land use planning to strategic spatial planning: The case of Flanders', in L. Albrechts, J. Alden and A. da Rosa Pires (eds) *The Changing Institutional Landscape of Planning*, Ashgate, Aldershot, pp83–108

Albrechts, L. (2001b) 'In pursuit of new approaches to strategic spatial planning: A European perspective', *International Planning Studies* **6**(3): 293–310

Albrechts, L., P. Healey and K. Kunzmann (2003) 'Strategic spatial planning and regional governance in Europe', *Journal of the American Planning Association* **69**: 113–129

Allen, A. (2003) 'Environmental planning and management of the peri-urban interface: Perspectives on an emerging field', *Environment and Urbanization* **15**(1): 135–148

Allen, A. and N. You (2002) *Sustainable Urbanisation: Building the Green and Brown Agenda*, Development Planning Unit, London

Allmendinger, P. and M. Tewdwr-Jones (2002) *Planning Futures: New Directions for Planning Theory*, Routledge, New York

Allmendinger, P. and H. Thomas (eds) (1998) *Urban Planning and the British New Right*, Routledge, London

Alonso, W. (1986) 'The unplanned paths of planning schools', *The Public Interest* **82** (winter): 58–71

Alterman, R. (ed) (1988) *Private Supply of Public Services: Evaluation of Real Estate Exactions, Linkage, and Alternative Land Policies*, New York University Press, New York

Alterman, R. and D. Macrae Jr. (1983) 'Planning and policy analysis: Converging or diverging trends', *Journal of the American Planning Association* **49**(2): 200–215

Altshuler, A. (1966) *The City Planning Process: A Political Analysis*, Cornell University Press, Ithaca, NY

American Society of Planning Officials (1941) *Report of the Committee on Education for Planners*, Chicago, IL

Amis, P. (2004) 'Regularising the informal sector: Voice and bad governance' in N. Devas, P. Amis, J. Beall, U. Grant, D. Mitlin, F. Nunan and C. Rakodi (eds) *Urban Governance, Voice and Poverty in the Developing World*, Earthscan, London, pp145–163

Angel, S. (2008) 'An arterial grid of dirt roads', *Cities*, **25**(3): 146–162

Angel, S., S. C. Sheppard and D. L. Civco, with R. Buckley, A. Chabaeva, L. Gitlin, A. Kraley, J. Parent and M. Perlin (2005) *The Dynamics of Global Urban Expansion*, World Bank, Washington, DC

Ansari, J. (2004) 'Time for a new approach in India', *Habitat Debate* **10**(4): 15

Ansari, J. H. (2008) 'Revisiting urban planning in Southern Asia', Unpublished regional study prepared for the *Global Report on Human Settlements 2009*, www.unhabitat.org/grhs/2009

Archer, E. (1996) 'Land management for integrated urban development in Asian cities: Implementing the formula L+P+F+NI=SUD', in K. Singh, F. Steinberg and N. von Einsiedel (eds) *Integrated Urban Infrastructure Development in Asia*, IT Publications, London, pp395–415

Arief, A. (1998) 'The urban metabolism of Ciliwung River settlements: Squatters vs resettlement', PhD thesis, ISTP, Murdoch University, Perth, Australia

Arimah, B. and D. Adeagbo (2000) 'Compliance with urban development and planning regulations in Ibadan, Nigeria', *Habitat International* **24**(3): 279–294

Aristizabal, N. and A. O. Gomez (2002) 'Are services more important than titles in Bogota?', in G. Payne (ed) *Land, Rights and Innovation: Improving Tenure Security for the Poor*, ITDG Publishing, London, pp100–113

Arnstein, S. A. (1969) 'A ladder of citizen participation', *Journal of the American Institute of Planners* **35**(4): 216–224

Ashworth, W. (1954) *Genesis of Modern Britain Town Planning,* Routledge and Kegan, London

Attahi, K., A. Kouame and H.-M. Daniel (2008) 'Revisiting urban planning in Sub-Saharan Africa "francophone" countries', Unpublished regional study prepared for the *Global Report on Human Settlements 2009,* www.unhabitat.org/grhs/2009

Auckland Regional Council (2006) *Review of Overseas Metropolitan Infrastructure Planning,* SGS Economics and Planning on behalf of Auckland Regional Council, Auckland

Augustinus, C. and M. Barry (2004) 'Strategic action planning in post conflict societies', Paper presented at the United Nations/Federation Internationale des Geometres (FIG) Commission 7 Symposium on Land Administration in Post-Conflict Areas, Geneva, 29–30 April 2004, www.fig.net/commission7/geneva _2004/papers/lapca_02_augustinus.pdf

Australian Government (2009) *Population Flows: Immigration Aspects, 2007–08 Edition,* Department of Immigration and Citizenship, Belconnen, www.immi.gov.au/media/publications/statistics/ popflows2007-08/PopFlows_09_chp1.pdf

Avritzer, L. (2006) 'New public spheres in Brazil: Local democracy and deliberative politics', *International Journal of Urban and Regional Research* **30**(3): 623–637

Ayataç, H. (2007) 'The international diffusion of planning ideas: The case of Istanbul, Turkey', *Journal of Planning History* **6**(2): 114–137

Babjanian, B. (2005) 'Bottom up and top down? Community development in post-Soviet Armenia', *Social Policy and Administration* **39**(4): 448–462

Baer, W. C. (1997) 'General plan evaluation criteria: An approach to making better plans', *Journal of the American Planning Association* **63**(3): 329–344

Bailey, N. (2009) 'Managing the metropolis: Economic change, institutional reform and spatial planning in London', in S. Davoudi and I. Strange (eds) *Space and Place in Strategic Spatial Planning,* Routledge, London, pp181–207

Baiocchi, G. (2003) 'Participation, activism and politics: The Porto Alegre experiment', in A. Fung and E. O. Wright (eds) *Deepening Democracy: Institutional Innovation and Empowered Participatory Governance,* Verso, London, pp45–76

Ball, M. (1983) *Housing Policy and Economic Power: The Political Economy of Owner Occupation,* Methuen, London

Banfield, E. C. (1955) 'Note on a conceptual scheme', in E. C. Banfield and M. Meyerson (eds) *Politics, Planning and the Public Interest,* Free Press, Glencoe, IL, pp303–329

Banfield, E. C. (1959) 'Ends and means in planning', *International Social Science Journal* **11**(3): 361–368

Barras, R. (1987) 'Technical change and the urban development cycle', *Urban Studies* **24**(1): 5–30

Barter, P. (2000) 'Transport dilemmas in dense urban areas: Examples from Eastern Asia', in M. Jenks and R. Burgess (eds) *The Compact City: Sustainable Urban Forms for Developing Countries,* Spon Press, London, pp231–244

Barter, P., J. Kenworthy and F. Laube (2003) 'Lessons from Asia on sustainable urban transport' in N. Low and B. Gleeson (eds) *Making Urban Transport Sustainable,* Palgrave Macmillan, New York, pp252–270

Batey, P. (1985) 'Postgraduate planning education in Britain – its purpose, content and organization', *Town Planning Review* **56**(4): 407–420

Batley, R. (1993) 'Political control of urban planning and management', in N. Devas and C. Rakodi (eds) *Managing Fast Growing Cities: New Approaches to Urban Planning and Management in the Developing World,* Longman Scientific and Technical, Essex, pp176–206

Batley, R. (1996) 'Public–private relationships and performance in service delivery', *Urban Studies* **33**(4–5): 723–751

Batty, M. (1984) *Information Technology in Planning Education,* Papers in Planning Research, 80, UWIST Department of Town Planning, Cardiff

Baum, H. (1996) 'Why the rational paradigm persists: Tales from the field', *Journal of Planning Education and Research* **15**(2): 127–135

Baum, S., Y. Van Gellecum and T. Yigitcanlar (2004) 'Wired communities in the city: Sydney, Australia', *Australian Geographical Studies* **42**(2): 175–192

Bayat, A. (2004) 'Globalization and the politics of the informals in the global South', in A. Roy and N. Alsayyad (eds) *Urban Informality: Transnational Perspectives from the Middle East, Latin America and South Asia,* Lexington Books, Lanham

BBC News (2000) 'China begins massive census', http://news.bbc.co.uk/1/hi/world/asia-pacific/ 1000357.stm

BBC News (2009a) 'Global house prices drop further', http://news.bbc.co.uk/2/hi/business/8079169.stm

BBC News (2009b) 'Eurozone unemployment rises again', http://news.bbc.co.uk/2/hi/business/ 7976286.stm

Beall, J. (2002) 'Globalization and social exclusion in cities: Framing the debate with lessons from Africa and Asia', *Environment and Urbanization* **14**(1): 41–51

Beatley, T. (2005) *Native to Nowhere,* Island Press, Washington, DC

Beatley, T. and K. Manning (1997) *The Ecology of Place,* Island Press, Washington, DC

Beauchemin, C. and P. Bocquier (2004) 'Migration and urbanisation in Francophone West Africa: An overview of the recent empirical evidence', *Urban Studies* **41**(11): 2245–2272

Behrens, R. (2005) 'Accommodating walking as a travel mode in South African cities: Towards improved neighbourhood movement network design practices', *Planning Practice and Research* **20**(2): 163–182

Behrens, R. and V. Watson (1996) *Making Urban Places: Principles and Guidelines for Layout Planning,* University of Cape Town Press, Cape Town

Bell, G. and R. Packard (1976) 'Human settlements education: A survey of programs in the less developed countries', *Ekistics* **41**(246): 263–270

Belzer, D. and G. Autler (2002) 'Transit oriented development: Moving from rhetoric to reality', Paper for the Brookings Institution Center on Urban and Metropolitan Policy and The Great American Station Foundation, Washington, DC

Benedict, M. and E. McMahon (2006) *Green Infrastructure: Linking Landscapes and Communities,* Island Press, Washington, DC

Benevolo, L. (1967) *The Origins of Modern Town Planning* (translated by Judith Landry from 1963 Italian original), MIT Press, Cambridge, MA

Benjamin, S. (2000) 'Governance, economic settings and poverty in Bangalore', *Environment and Urbanization,* **12**(1), 35–56

Berrisford, S. and M. Kihato (2006) 'The role of planning law in evictions in sub-Saharan Africa', *South African Review of Sociology* **37**(1): 20–34

Bertaud, A. (2002) 'Notes on transportation and spatial structure', http://alain-bertaud.com

Bertaud, A. (2004) 'The spatial organisation of cities: Deliberate outcome or unforeseen consequences', http://alain-bertaud.com

Bertolini, L. (2007) 'Evolutionary urban transportation: An exploration', *Environment and Planning A*, **39**: 1998–2019

Bertolini, L., F. Le Clercq, and L. Kapoen (undated) *Transport and Land Use Concepts for the Emerging Urban Region*, Unpublished manuscript

Bhattachatya, S. (2003) 'European heat wave caused 35,000 deaths', *New Scientist* **10**, October, www.newscientist.com/article/dn4259-european-heatwave-caused-35000-deaths.html

Biderman, C., M. O. Smolka and A. Sant'Anna (2008) 'Urban housing informality: Does building and land use regulation matter?', *Land Lines* **20**(3): 14–19

Biermann, S. (2000) 'Bulk engineering services: Costs and densities', in M. Jenks and R. Burgess (eds) (2000) *Compact Cities: Sustainable Urban Forms for Developing Countries*, Spon Press, London, pp295–310

Biermann, S., M. van Ryneveld and C. Venter (2004) *Cost-Benefit Comparative Assessment of Low Income Housing Development Localities: Case Studies from Johannesburg and Ethekwini*, Unpublished report, Housing Finance Resource Programme, Pretoria

Birch, E. L. (1980) 'Advancing the art and science of planning: Planners and their organizations 1909–1980', *Journal of the American Planning Association* **46**(1): 22–49

Block, A. (1954) 'Soviet housing: Some town planning problems', *Soviet Studies* **6**(1): 1–15

Bloom, D. E and T. Khanna (2007) 'The urban revolution', *Finance & Development*, September: 9–14

Boarnet, M. and A. Haughwout (2000) 'Do highways matter? Evidence and policy implications of highways' influence on metropolitan development', Discussion paper for the Brookings Institution Center for Urban and Metropolitan Policy, Washington DC

Bolay, J.-C. and A. Rabinnovich (2004) 'Intermediate cities in Latin America risk and opportunities of coherent urban development', *Cities* **21**(5): 407–421

Boonyabancha, S. (2005) 'Baan Mankong: Going to scale with "slum" and squatter upgrading in Thailand', *Environment and Urbanization* **17**(1): 21–46

Boonyabancha, S. (2008) 'Land for housing the poor – by the poor: Experiences from the Baan Mankong nation-wide slum upgrading program in Thailand', Paper presented at the Land Meeting, 27–28 November 2008, International Institute for Environment and Development, London

Booth, P. (2005) 'The nature of difference: Traditions of law and government and their effects on planning in Britain and France', in B. Sanyal (ed) *Comparative Planning Cultures*, Routledge, New York, pp259–284

Borja, J. and M. Castells (1997) *Local and Global: Management of Cities in the Information Age*, Earthscan, London

Boyce, D. (1970) 'Toward a framework for defining and applying urban indicators in plan-making', *Urban Affairs Quarterly* **6**(2): 145–171

Bracken, I. (1981) *Urban Planning Methods: Research and Policy Analysis*, Methuen, New York

Breetzke, K. (2008) 'From conceptual frameworks to quantitative models: Spatial planning in the Durban metropolitan area, South Africa – the link to housing and infrastructure planning', Unpublished case study prepared for the *Global Report on Human Settlements 2009*, www.unhabitat.org/grhs/2009

Breheny, M. (1995) 'The compact city and transport energy consumption', *Transactions of the Institute of British Geographers* **20**: 81–101

Breitenbach, E. (2006) *Gender Statistics: An Evaluation*, Working Paper Series 51, Equality and Human Rights Commission, Manchester

Brenner, N. (1999) 'Globalization as re-territorialization: The re-scaling of urban governance in the European Union', *Urban Studies* **36**(3): 431–451

Brenner, N. (2000) 'Building Euro-regions: Locational politics and the political geography of neoliberalism in post-unification Germany', *European Urban and Regional Studies* **7**(4): 319–345

Briggs, J. and D. Mwamfupe (2000) 'Peri-urban development in an era of structural adjustment in Africa: The city of Dar es Salaam, Tanzania', *Urban Studies* **37**(4): 797–809

Bromley, R. (1978) 'Introduction: the urban informal sector: Why is it worth discussing?', *World Development* **6**(9/10): 1034–1035

Brooks, M. P. (1988) 'Four critical junctures in the history of the urban planning profession: An exercise in hindsight', *Journal of the American Planning Association* **54**(2): 117–131

Brown, A. (ed) (2006) *Contested Space: Street Trading, Public Space and Livelihoods in Developing Cities*, ITDG Publishing, London

Brown, A. and T. Lloyd-Jones (2002) 'Spatial planning, access and infrastructure', in C. Rakodi and T. Lloyd-Jones (eds) *Urban Livelihoods: A People-Centred Approach to Reducing Poverty*, Earthscan, London, pp188–204

Brown, A. and C. Rakodi (2006) 'Enabling the street economy', in A. Brown (ed) *Contested Space: Street Trading, Public Space and Livelihoods in Developing Cities*, ITDG Publishing, London, pp197–211

Bryant, N. (2009) 'Australia hard hit by mining slump', http://news.bbc.co.uk/2/hi/business/7973008.stm

Buccus, I., D. Hemron, J. Hicks and L. Piper (2008) 'Community development and engagement with local governance in South Africa', *Community Development Journal*, **43**(3), 297–311

Buckley, R. M. and J. Kalarickal (2005) 'Housing policy in developing countries: Conjectures and refutations', *World Bank Research Observer* **20**(2): 233–257

Bulkleley, H. and K. Kern (2006) 'Local government and the governing of climate change in Germany and the UK', *Urban Studies* **43**(12): 2237–2259

Burayidi, M. (1993) 'Dualism and universalism: Competing paradigms in planning education?' *Journal of Planning Education and Research* **12**(3): 223–229

Burchell, R. W., D. Listokin, and C. G. Galley (2000) 'Smart growth: More than a ghost of urban policy past, less than a bold new horizon', *Housing Policy Debate* **11**(4): 821–878

Bureau of Labor Statistics (2009) *The Unemployment Situation: March 2009*, United States Labor Department; Washington, DC www.bls.gov/news.release/pdf/empsit.pdf

Burwell, D. (2005) 'Way to go! Three simple rules to make transportation a positive force in the public realm', *Making Places*, June, www.pps.org

Cabannes, Y. (2004a) 'Participatory budgeting: A significant contribution to participatory democracy', *Environment and Urbanization* **16**(1): 27–46

Cabannes, Y. (2004b) *Participatory Budgeting: Conceptual Framework and Analysis of Its Contribution to Urban Governance and the Millennium Development Goals*, UN-Habitat Urban Management Programme, Regional Office for Latin America, Quito, Ecuador

Cabannes, Y. (2006) 'Les budgets participatifs en Amérique Latine', *Mouvements* **47**: 127–138

Caldeira, T. and J. Holston (2005) 'State and urban space in Brazil: From modernist planning to democratic interventions', in M. Keiner, M. Koll-Schretzenmayr and W. A. Schmid (eds) *Managing Urban Futures: Sustainability and Growth in Developing Countries*, Ashgate, Aldershot, pp143–164

Calthorpe, P. (1993) *The Next American Metropolis: Ecology, Community and the American Dream*, Princeton Architectural Press, New York

Campbell, H. and J. Henneberry (2005) 'Planning obligations, the market orientation of planning and planning professionalism', *Journal of Property Research* **22**(1): 37–59

Candiracci, S. (undated) *Facing Poverty by Improving Non-Motorised Transport: Kibera Bicycle Transport Project*, UN-Habitat Energy and Transport Brochure 19, UN-Habitat, Nairobi

Carmin, J. (2003) 'Non-governmental organizations and public participation in local environmental decision-making in the Czech Republic', *Local Environment* **8**(5): 541–552

Cars, G., P. Healey, A. Madanipour, and C. de Magalhaes (eds) (2002) *Urban Governance, Institutional Capacity and Social Milieux*, Ashgate, Aldershot

Cascetta, E. and F. Pagliara (2008) 'Integrated railways-based policies: The Regional Metro System (RMS) project of Naples and Campania', *Transport Policy* **15**: 81–93

CEC (Commission of the European Communities) (1997) *The EU Compendium of Spatial Planning Systems and Policies*, Office for the Official Publications of the European Communities, Luxembourg

CEC (1999) *European Spatial Development Perspective: Towards a Balanced and Sustainable Development of the Territory of the European Union*, Office for the Official Publications of the European Communities, Luxembourg

Centre on Housing Rights and Evictions (2006) *Global Survey on Forced Evictions: Violations of Human Rights 2003–2006*, Centre on Housing Rights and Evictions, Geneva

Cerruti, M. and R. Bertoncello, (2003) 'Urbanization and internal migration patterns in Latin America', Paper prepared for the conference on African Migration in Comparative Perspective, Johannesburg, South Africa, 4–7 June

Cervero, R. (2004) 'Transit and the metropolis: Finding harmony', in S. Wheeler and T. Bentley (eds) *The Sustainable Urban Development Reader*, Routledge, London, pp89–103

Cervero, R. (2008) *Effects of TOD on Housing, Parking and Travel*, Transit Cooperative Research Program Report 128, Federal Transit Administration, Washington, DC

Chafe, Z. (2007) 'Reducing natural risk disasters in cities', in *2007 State of the World: Our Urban Future*, Worldwatch Institute, Washington, DC

Chambers, R. (1994a) 'The origins and practice of participatory rural appraisal', *World Development* **24**(9): 953–969

Chambers, R. (1994b) 'Participatory rural appraisal (PRA): A review of experience', *World Development* **22**(9): 1253–1268

Chambers, R. (1994c) 'Participatory rural appraisal (PRA): Challenges, potential and paradigm', *World Development* **22**(10): 1437–1454

Chen, H., B. Jia, and S. Lau (2008) 'Sustainable urban form for Chinese compact cities: Challenges of a rapidly urbanising economy', *Habitat International* **32**: 28–40

Chen, S. and M. Ravallion (2007) 'Absolute poverty measures for the developing world, 1981–2004', in

Proceedings of the National Academy of Sciences, www.pnas.org/content/104/43/16757.full.pdf+html.

Chen, X. (2008) 'Monitoring and evaluation in China's urban planning system: A case study of Xuzhou', Unpublished case study prepared for the *Global Report on Human Settlements 2009*, www.unhabitat.org/grhs/2009

Cherry, G. (1979) 'The town planning movement and the late Victorian city', *Transactions of the Institute of British Geographers*, New series, **4**(2): 306–319

Cheru, F. (2005) *Globalization and Uneven Development in Africa: The Limits to Effective Urban Governance in the Provision of Basic Services*, UCLA Globalization Research Centre-Africa, www.globalization-africa.org/papers/57.pdf

Chettiparamb, A. (2007) 'Dealing with complexity: An autopoietic view of the People's Planning Campaign, Kerala', *Planning Theory and Practice* **8**(4): 489–508

Chevériat, C. (2000) 'Natural disasters in Latin America and the Caribbean: An overview of risk', Working Paper 434, Inter-American Development Bank, Research Department, Washington, DC

Choe, S. C. (1998) 'Urban corridors in Pacific Asia' in F. C. Lo and Y. M. Yeung (eds) *Globalization and the World of Large Cities*, UNU Press, Tokyo, pp155–173

Christopher, A. J. (1984) *Colonial Africa*, Routledge, New York

Cities Alliance (2005) *City Development Strategy (CDS)*, www.citiesalliance.com/activities-output/topics/cds/cds-work-with-ca.html#essentials_of_a_cds

City of Malmö (2005) 'Sustainable city of tomorrow: Experiences of a Swedish housing exposition', Swedish Research Council for Environment, Agricultural Sciences and Spatial Planning, Stockholm

Clapham, D., J. Hegedüs, K. Kintrea, I. Tosics and H. Kay (1996) *Housing Privatization in Eastern Europe*, Greenwood Press, Westport, CT

Cohen, B. (2006) 'Urbanization in developing countries: Current trends, future projections and key challenges for sustainability', *Technology in Society* **28**: 63–80

Cohen, M. (2005) 'Present at the creation: Reflections on the Urban Management Programme', *Habitat Debate* **11**(4): 5

Colic-Peisker, V. and F. Tilbury (2008) 'Being black in Australia: A case study of intergroup relations', *Race and Class* **49**(4): 38–56

Commission for Social Development (2009) 'The current global crises and their impact on social development', www.un.org/esa/socdev/csd/2009/documents/crp2.pdf

Confederation of EU Rectors' Conferences and the Association of European Universities (CRE) (1999) *The Bologna Declaration on European Higher Education: An Explanation*, http://ec.europa.eu/education/policies/educ/bologna/bologna.pdf, accessed 20 January 2009

Cooke, B. and U. Kothari (2001) 'The case for participation as tyranny', in B. Cooke and U. Kothari (eds) *Participation: The New Tyranny?*, Zed Books, London, pp1–15

Cornwall, A. (2008) 'Unpacking participation: Models, meanings and practices', *Community Development Journal* **43**(3): 269–283

Cox, W. (2009) 'Examining sprawl in Europe and America: Europeans are moving to the suburb too', www.reason.org/commentaries/cox_20090116.shtml

Cross, C., L. Luckin, T. Mzimela and C. Clark (1996) 'On the edge: Poverty, livelihoods and natural resources in rural KwaZulu-Natal', in M. Lipton, F. Ellis and M. Lipton (eds) *Land, Labour and Livelihoods in Rural South Africa*, Indicator Press, Durban, pp173–214

Crot, L. (2008) 'The characteristics and outcomes of participatory budgeting: Buenos Aires, Argentina', Unpublished case study prepared for the *Global Report on Human Settlements 2009*, www.unhabitat.org/grhs/2009

Crow, S. (1996) 'Development control: The child that grew up in the cold,' *Planning Perspectives* **11**(4): 399–411

Cullingworth, B. and R. Caves (2003) *Planning in the USA: Policies, Issues, and Processes*, Routledge, London

Cullingworth, J. (1993) *The Political Culture of Planning: American Land Use in Comparative Perspective*, Routledge, London and New York

Curry, A, T. Hodgson, R. Kelnar and A. Wilson (2006) *Intelligent Infrastructure Futures, the Scenarios – Towards 2055*, Foresight Directorate, Office of Science and Technology, UK Government, London

Curtis, C. (2005) 'Creating liveable streets: Developing traffic management guidelines for Western Australia', in K. Williams (ed) *Spatial Planning, Urban Form and Sustainable Transport*, Ashgate, Aldershot, pp183–202

Daher, R. (undated) 'Global capital, urban regeneration and heritage conservation in the Levant', in *Architecture and Urbanism in the Middle East*, Middle East Institute, Washington, DC, www.mideasti.org/files/architecture-and-urbanism.pdf

Dalton, L. C. (1986) 'Why the rational paradigm persists – The resistance of professional education and practice to alternative forms of planning', *Journal of Planning Education and Research* **5**: 147–153

Davidoff, P. (1965) 'Advocacy and pluralism in planning', *Journal of the American Institute of Planners* **31**: 103–115

Davies, H. W. E., D. Edwards, A. Hooper and J. Punter (1989) *Development Control in Western Europe*, HMSO, London

Davis, M. (2004) 'Planet of slums', *New Left Review* **26** (March/April): 1–23

Davoudi, S. (2005) 'Towards a conceptual framework for the evaluation of governance relations in polycentric urban regions of Europe', in D. Miller and D. Patassini (eds) *Beyond Benefit and Cost Analysis: Accounting for Non Market Values in Planning Evaluation*, Ashgate, Aldershot, pp275–277

Davoudi, S. (2008) 'Conceptions of the city-region, a critical review', *Journal of Planning and Urban Design* **161**(2): 51–60

Davoudi, S. and P. Ellison (2006) *Implications of the Bologna Process for Planning Education in Europe: Results of the 2006 Survey*, Association of European Schools of Planning, www.aesop-planning.com/Documents/2006_Bologna_Survey.pdf

Davoudi, S. and N. Evans (2005) 'The challenge of governance in regional waste planning', *Environment and Planning C* **23**(4): 493–519

Day, D. (1997) 'Citizen participation in the planning process: An essentially contested concept?', *Journal of Planning Literature* **11**(3): 421–434

D'Cruz, C. and D. Satterthwaite (2005) *Building Homes, Changing Official Approaches: The Work of Urban Poor Organizations and their Federations and their Contributions to Meeting the Millenium Development Goals in Urban Areas*, Poverty Reduction in Urban Areas Series 16, IIED, London

de Soto, H. (2000) *The Mystery of Capital: Why Capitalism Triumphs in the West and Fails Everywhere Else*, Black Swan, London

Demographia (undated) 'Urban population and economic growth: International context', www.demographia.com/db-19502000.pdf

Devas, N. (1993) 'Evolving approaches', in N. Devas and C. Rakodi (eds) *Managing Fast Growing Cities: New Approaches to Urban Planning and Management in the Developing World*, Longman Scientific and Technical, Essex, pp63–101

Devas, N. (2001) 'Does city governance matter for the urban poor?' *International Planning Studies* **6**(4): 393–408

Diaw, K., T. Nnkya and V. Watson (2002) 'Planning education in sub-Saharan Africa: Responding to the demands of a changing context', *Planning Practice and Research* **17**(3): 337–348

Diaz Barriga, M. (1996) 'Necesidad: Notes on the discourses of urban politics in the Ajusco foothills of Mexico City', *American Ethnologist* **23**(2): 291–310

Dieleman, F. and M. Wegener (2004) 'Compact city and urban sprawl', *Built Environment* **30**(4): 308–323

DiGaetano, A. and E. Strom (2003) 'Comparative urban governance: An integrated approach', *Urban Affairs Review* **38**(3): 356–395

Dillinger, W. (1994) *Decentralization and Its Implications for Urban Service Delivery*, Urban Management Programme Discussion Paper 16, World Bank, Washington, DC

Dingding, X. (2008) 'Blueprint of railways development', *China Daily*, 17 November

The Dominion Post (2008) 'Costly year for natural disasters' *The Dominion Post*, 3 May, www.stuff.co.nz/4507602a11.html

Douglass, M. (2005) 'Globalization, mega-projects and the environment: Urban form and water in Jakarta', Paper presented to the International Dialogic conference on Global Cities: Water, Infrastructure and the Environment, the UCLA Globalization Research Center – Africa, Los Angeles, May, www.globalization-africa.org/papers/58.pdf

Douglass, M. (2008) 'Civil society for itself and in the public sphere: Comparative research on globalization, cities and civic space in Pacific Asia', in M. Douglass, K. C. Ho and G. L. Ooi (eds) *Globalization, the City and Civil Society in Pacific Asia: The Social Production of Civic Spaces*, Routledge, London, pp27–49

Drakakis-Smith, D. (2000) *Third World Cities*, 2nd edition, Routledge, London

Droege, P. (2006) *The Renewable City*, Wiley, Chichester

Duffy, G. (2007) 'Brazil's homeless and landless unite', BBC News, http://news.bbc.co.uk/2/hi/americas/6563359.stm

Dummet, M. (2009) 'Bangladesh migrant workers suffer', BBC News, http://news.bbc.co.uk/2/hi/south_asia/7993337.stm

Dupont, V. (2007) 'Conflicting stakes and governance in the peripheries of large Indian metropolises: An introduction', *Cities* **24**(2): 89–94

Duquennois, A. N. and P. Newman (2008) 'Linking the green and brown agendas: A case study on Cairo, Egypt', Unpublished case study prepared for the *Global Report on Human Settlements 2009*, www.unhabitat.org/grhs/2009

Durand-Lasserve, A., A. Bagre, M. Gueye and J. Tonato (2002) 'Current changes and trends: Benin, Burkina Faso and Senegal', in G. Payne (ed) *Land, Rights and Innovation: Improving Tenure Security for the Poor*, ITDG Publishing, London, pp114–135

Dutch Architects (undated) 'Herman, Karsten Thomas', www.dutcharchitects.eu/k/73, accessed 28 June 2008

Dyrberg, T. B. (1997) *The Circular Structure of Power*, Verso, London

EBRD (2006) *What Drives Growth in Transition Countries*, London, www.ebrd.com/pubs/econo/15anni.htm

Ecology.com (undated) 'The industrial revolution', www.ecology.com/archived-links/industrial-revolution/index.html

ECON Analysis and Centre for Local Government (2005) *The Impacts of City Development Strategies*, ECON Analysis and University of Technology, for Cities Alliance, Oslo and Sydney

Economic Times (2009) 'ILO: Unemployment, social crisis looms in Asia', *Economic Times*, 22 April 2009, http://economictimes.indiatimes.com/articleshow/4435645.cms

EEA (European Environment Agency) (2006) *Urban Sprawl in Europe: The Ignored Challenge*, EEA Report No 10/2006, European Commission Joint Research Centre/European Environment Agency, Copenhagen, Denmark

Environmental News Service (2005) 'Global wind map shows best wind farm locations', 17 May, www.ens-newswire.com

Etzioni, A. (1967) 'Mixed-scanning: A "third" approach to decision making', *Public Administration Review* **27**(5): 385–392

Ewing, R. (1997) 'Is LA style sprawl desirable?', *Journal of the American Planning Association* **63**(1): 107–125

Ewing, R., K. Bartholomew, S. Winkelman, J. Walters, D. Chen, B. McCann and D. Goldberg (2007) *Growing Cooler: The Evidence on Urban Development and Climate Change*, October, Urban Land Institute, Washington, DC

Fainstein, S. (2000) 'New directions in planning theory', *Urban Affairs Review* **35**(4): 451–478

Faludi, A. and B. Waterhout (eds) (2002) *The Making of the European Spatial Development Perspective*, Routledge, London

Farmer, A. and A. Farmer (2001) 'Developing sustainability: Environmental non-governmental organization in former Soviet Central Asia', *Sustainable Development* **9**: 136–148

Farrelly, E. (2005) 'Attack of common sense hits planners', *Sydney Morning Herald*, 26 April

Ferguson, B. and J. Navarrete (2003) 'New approaches to progressive housing in Latin America: A key to habitat programme and policy', *Habitat International* **27**(2): 309–323

Fernandes, E. (2001) 'Land and the production of urban illegality', *Land Lines* **13**(3): 1–4

Fernandes, E. (2003) 'Illegal housing: Law, property rights and urban space', in P. Harrison, M. Huchzermeyer and M. Mayekiso (eds) *Confronting Fragmentation: Housing and Urban Development in a Democratising Society*, University of Cape Town Press, Cape Town, pp228–243

Fernandes, E. and A. Varley (eds) (1998) *Illegal Cities: Law and Urban Change in Developing Countries*, Zed Books, London

Fernando, A., S. Russell, A. Wilson and E. Vidler (1999) *Urban Governance, Partnership and Poverty in Colombo*, School of Public Policy, International Development Department, University of Birmingham, Birmingham

Firman, T. and C. Rakodi (2008) 'An extended metropolitan region in Asia: Jakarta, Indonesia' Unpublished case study prepared for the *Global Report on Human Settlements 2009*, www.unhabitat.org/grhs/2009

Fischoff, B. (1996) 'Public values in risk research', *Annals of the American Academy of Political and Social Scientists* **545**: 75–84

Flyvberg, B. (2007) 'Megaproject policy and planning: Problems, causes, concerns', Institut for Samfundsudvikling og Planlægning, Aalborg Universitet, Aalborg

Forester, J. (1993) *Critical Theory, Public Policy and Planning Practice: Toward a Critical Pragmatism*, State University of New York Press, Albany, NY

Frank, A. (2006) 'Three decades of thought on planning education', *Journal of Planning Literature* **21**: 15–67

Frank, A. I. and I. Mironowicz (2008) 'Planning education in Poland', Unpublished case study prepared for the *Global Report on Human Settlements 2009*, www.unhabitat.org/grhs/2009

Freestone, R. (1998) 'An imperial aspect: The Australian town planning tour of 1914–15', *Australian Journal of Politics and History* **44**(2): 159–176

Friedmann, J. (1992) *Empowerment: The Politics of Alternative Development*, Blackwell, Cambridge

Friedmann, J. (2005a) 'Globalization and the emerging culture of planning', *Progress in Planning* **64**: 183–234

Friedmann, J. (2005b) *China's Urban Transition*, University of Minnesota Press, Minneapolis, MN

Gandy, M. (2006) 'Planning, anti-planning and the urban infrastructure crisis facing metropolitan Lagos', *Urban Studies* **43**(2): 371–396

Garau, P. (2008) 'Revisiting urban planning in developed countries', Unpublished regional study prepared for the *Global Report on Human Settlements 2009*, www.unhabitat.org/grhs/2009

Garau, P., E. D. Sclar and G. Y. Carolini (2005) *A Home in the City, UN Millennium Project*, Task Force on Improving the Lives of Slum Dwellers, Earthscan, London

Garcia, R. B. (1993) *Changing Paradigms of Professional Practice, Education and Research in Academe: A History of Planning Education in the United States*, Dissertation prepared at the University of Pennsylvania, Department of City and Regional Planning, Philadelphia

Gasparini, L. (2003) 'Different lives: Inequality in Latin America and the Caribbean', in D. De Ferranti, G. E. Perry, F. H. G. Ferreira, M. Walton, D. Coady, W. Cunningham, L. Gasparini, J. Jacobsen, Y. Matsuda, J. Robinson, K. Sokoloff and Q. Wodon (eds) *Inequality in Latin America and the Caribbean: Breaking with History?*, World Bank, Washington, DC.

Gatabaki-Kamau, R. and S. Karirah-Gitau (2004) 'Actors and interests: the development of an informal settlement in Nairobi, Kenya', in K. T. Hansen and M. Vaa (eds) *Reconsidering Informality: Perspectives from Urban Africa*, Nordiska Afrikainstitutet, Uppsala, pp158–175

GCIM.org (undated) 'Migration at a glance', Global Commission on International Migration, www.gcim.org/attachements/Migration%20at%20a%20glance.pdf

Geertz, C. (1983) *Local Knowledge*, Basic Books, New York

Gehl, J. and L. Gemzoe (2000) *New City Spaces*, the Danish Architectural Press, Copenhagen

Gehl, J., L. Gemzoe, S. Kirknaes and B. Søndergaard (2006) *New City Life*, the Danish Architectural Press, Copenhagen

GHK (2000) *City Development Strategies (CDSs): Taking Stock and Signposting the Way Forward: A Discussion Report for DFID (UK) and the World Bank*, GHK London

Giddings, B. and B. Hopwood (2006) 'From evangelist bureaucrat to visionary developer: The changing character of the master plan in Britain', *Planning Practice and Research* **21**(3): 337–348

Gilbert, A. (1998) *The Latin American City*, 2nd edition, Latin America Bureau, London

Gilbert, A. (2002) 'On the mystery of capital and the myths of Hernando de Soto: What difference does legal title make?', *International Development Planning Review* **24**(1): 1–20

Gilbert, A. and P. Healey (1985) *The Political Economy of Land: Urban Development in an Oil Economy*, Gower, Aldershot

Girardet, H. (2000) *The Gaia Atlas of Cities*, Gaia Books, London

Girouard, M. (1985) *Cities and People*, Yale University Press, Boston

Glenn, H. P. (2007) *Legal Traditions of the World: Sustainable Diversity in Law*, 3rd edition, Oxford University Press, Oxford

Godschalk, D. (2000) 'Smart growth efforts around the nation', *Popular Government* **66**(1) (fall): 12–20

Goldblum, C. and T. Wong (2000) 'Growth, crisis and spatial change: Haphazard urbanization in Jakarta, Indonesia', *Land Use Policy* **17**: 29–37

Goldstein, H., S. Bollens, E. Feser, and C. Silver (2006) 'An experiment in the internationalization of planning education: The NEURUS program', *Journal of Planning Education and Research* **25**: 349–363

Golobic, M. and I. Marusic (2007) 'Developing an integrated approach for public participation: A case of land-use planning in Slovenia', *Environment and Planning B: Planning and Design* **34**(6): 993–1010

Goodman, R. (1971) *After the Planners*, Touchstone, New York

Gordon, P. and H. Richardson (1997) 'Are compact cities a desirable planning goal?', *Journal of the American Planning Association* **63**(1): 95–109

Gordon, R. (2005) 'Boulevard of dreams', *SFGate*, 8 September, www.sfgate.com

Gospodini, A. and P. Skayannis (2005) 'Towards an "integration model" of planning education programmes in a European and international context: The contribution of recent Greek experience', *Planning Theory and Practice* **6**(3): 355–382

Gounden, K. (1999) *Distant Decentralised Office Parks: A Case Study of La Lucia Ridge Office Estate*, MSc thesis, University of Natal, Durban

Grabow, S. and A. Heskin (1973) 'Foundations for a radical concept of planning', *Journal of the American Planning Association* **39**(2): 106–114

Graham, S. (2002) 'Bridging urban digital divides? New technologies and urban polarisation', *Urban Studies* **39**(1): 33–56

Graham, S. and S. Marvin (1999) 'Planning cyber-cities? Integrating telecommunications into urban planning', *Town Planning Review* **70**(1): 89–104

Graham, S. and S. Marvin (2001) *Splintering Urbanism: Networked Infrastructures, Technological Mobilities and the Urban Condition*, Routledge, London

Grant, J. (2005) 'Mixed use in theory and practice: Canadian experience with implementing and planning principle' in B. Stiftel and V. Watson (eds) *Dialogues in Urban and Regional Planning, Vol 1*, Routledge, London, pp15–36

Grant, J. (2006) *Planning the Good Community: New Urbanism in Theory and Practice*, Routledge, London and New York

Grant, R. and J. Nijman (2006) 'Globalization and the corporate geography of cities in the less-developed world', in N. Brenner and R. Keil (eds) *The Global Cities Reader*, Routledge, London and New York

Greed, C. and D. Reeves (2005) 'Mainstreaming equality into strategic spatial policy making: Are planners losing sight of gender?', *Construction Management and Economics* **23**: 1059–1070

Guha-Khasnobis, B., R. Kanbur and E. Ostrom (2006) 'Beyond formality and informality', in B. Guha-Khasnobis, R. Kanbur and E. Ostrom (eds) *Linking the Formal and Informal Economy: Concepts and Policies*, Oxford University Press, Oxford, pp1–19

Gulyani, S. and E. M. Bassett (2007) 'Retrieving the baby from the bathwater: Slum upgrading in Sub Saharan Africa', *Environment and Planning C* **25**: 486–515

Gunder, M. and T. Fookes (1997) 'Planning school programs in Australia and New Zealand', *Australian Planner* **14**(1): 54–61

Hague, C., P. Wakely, J. Crespin, and C. Jasko (eds) (2006) *Making Planning Work: A Guide to Approaches and Skills*, Intermediate Technology Publications Ltd, Burton on Dunsmore, UK

Hall, P. (1988) *Cities of Tomorrow*, Blackwell, Oxford

Hall, P. and U. Pfeiffer (2000) *Urban Future 21: A Global Agenda for Twenty-First Century Cities*, E & FN Spon, London

Halla, F. (2002) 'Preparation and implementation of a general planning scheme in Tanzania: Kahama strategic urban development planning framework', *Habitat International* **26**(2): 281–293

Halla, F. (2005) 'Critical elements in sustaining participatory planning: Bagamoyo strategic urban development planning framework in Tanzania', *Habitat International* **29**(1): 137–162

Halweil, B. and D. Nierenberg (2007) 'Farming cities', in M. Sheehnan (ed) *State of the World, 2007*, Worldwatch Institute, Washington, DC

Hamdi, N. (2004) *Small Change*, Earthscan, London

Hamdi, N. and R. Goethert (1996) *Action Planning for Cities: A Guide for Community Practice*, Wiley, Chichester

Handy, S. (2005) 'Smart growth and the transportation–land use connection: What does the research tell us?', *International Regional Science Review* **28**(2): 146–167

Hansen, K. T. (2004) 'Who rules the streets? The politics of vending space in Lusaka', in K. T. Hansen and M. Vaa (eds) *Reconsidering Informality: Perspectives from Urban Africa*, Nordiska Afrikainstitutet, Uppsala, pp62–80

Hardoy, J. (1992) 'Theory and practice of urban planning in Europe, 1850–1930: Its transfer to Latin America', in R. M. Morse and J. Hardoy (eds), *Rethinking the Latin American City*, Woodrow Wilson Center Press, Washington, DC, pp20–49

Hardoy, J., D. Mitlin and D. Satterthwaite (2001) *Environmental Problems in an Urbanizing World*, Earthscan, London

Hargrove, C. and M. Smith (2006) *The Natural Advantage of Nations*, Earthscan, London

Harris, B. (1967) 'The limits of science and humanism in planning', *Journal of the American Institute of Planners* **33**: 324–335

Harris, N. (1983) 'Metropolitan planning in developing countries: Tasks for the 1980s', *Habitat International* **7**(3/4): 5–17

Harris, N. and H. Thomas (2009) 'Making Wales: Spatial strategy-making in devolved context', in S. Davoudi and I. Strange (eds) *Space and Place in Strategic Spatial Planning*, Routledge, London, pp43–71

Harrison, P. (2001) 'The genealogy of South Africa's integrated development plan', *Third World Planning Review* **23**(2): 175–193

Harrison, P., A. Todes and V. Watson (2008) *Planning and Transformation: Learning from the Post-Apartheid Experience*, Routledge, London and New York

Hart, K. (1973) 'Informal income opportunities and urban employment in Ghana', *Journal of Modern African Studies* **11**(1): 61–89

Hartz-Karp, J. and P. Newman (2006) 'The participative route to sustainability', in S. Paulin (ed) *Communities Doing It for Themselves: Creating Space for Sustainability*, University of Western Australia Press, Perth, pp28–42

Harvey, D. (1985) *The Urbanisation of Capital*, Blackwell, Oxford

Haughton, G., P. Allmendinger, D. Counsell and G. Vigar (forthcoming) *The New Spatial Planning*, Routledge, London

Hawken, P., A. Lovins and H. Lovins (1999) *Natural Capitalism: The Next Industrial Revolution*, Earthscan, London

Hayden, D. (1980) 'What would a non-sexist city be like? Speculations on housing, urban design, and human work', *Journal of Women in Culture and Society* **5**(3): 170–187

Healey, P. (1980) 'The development of planning education in the UK and its relevance as a model for other countries', *Ekistics* **47**(285): 416–420

Healey, P. (1992) 'The reorganization of state and market in planning', *Urban Studies* **29**(3/4): 411–434

Healey, P. (1997) *Collaborative Planning: Shaping Places in Fragmented Societies*, Macmillan, Basingstoke

Healey, P. (1998) 'Regulating property development and the capacity of the development industry', *Journal of Property Research* **15**(3): 211–228

Healey, P. (2004) 'The treatment of space and place in the new strategic spatial planning in Europe', *International Journal of Urban and Regional Research* **28**(1): 45–67

Healey, P. (2007) *Urban Complexity and Spatial Strategies: Towards a Relational Planning for our Times*, Routledge, London

Healey, P. (2008) 'Developing neighbourhood management capacity in Kobe, Japan: Interactions between civil society and formal planning institutions', Unpublished case study prepared for the *Global Report on Human Settlements 2009*, www.unhabitat.org/grhs/2009

Healey, P. and O. Samuels (1981) *British Planning Education in the 1970s and 1980s*, Social Science Research Council, London

Healey, P., M. Purdue, and F. Ennis (1995) *Negotiating Development*, Spon, London

Healey, P., A. Khakee, A. Motte and B. Needham (eds) (1997) *Making Strategic Spatial Plans: Innovation in Europe*, UCL Press Ltd, London

Heller, P., K. N. Harilal and S. Chaudhuri (2007) 'Building local democracy: Evaluating the impact of decentralization in Kerala, India', *World Development* **35**(4): 626–648

Hemmens, G. (1988) 'Thirty years of planning education', *Journal of Planning Education and Research* **7**(2): 85–91

Herbert, M. (1999) 'A city in good shape: Town planning and public health', *Town Planning Review*, **70**(4): 433–453

Hill, M. (1968) 'A goals achievement matrix for evaluating alternative plans', *Journal of the American Institute of Planners* **324**(1): 19–29

Hill, M. (1985) 'Can multiple-objective evaluation methods enhance rationality in planning?', in M. Breheny and A. Hooper (eds) *Rationality in Planning: Critical Essays on the Role of Rationality in Urban and Regional Planning*, Pion, London, pp166–182

Hillier, J. and P. Healey (eds) (2008) *Critical Essays in Planning Theory, Volumes 1, 2 and 3*, Ashgate, Aldershot

Hinojosa, R. C., T. S. Lyons, and F. D. Zinn (1992) 'The relevance of North American planning education for overseas practice: A survey of graduates', *Journal of Planning Education and Research* **12**(1): 32–38

Hirt, S. (2005) 'Planning the post-Communist city: Experiences from Sofia', *International Planning Studies* **10**(3–4): 219–240

Hirt, S. and K. Stanilov (2008) 'Revisiting urban planning in the transitional countries', Unpublished regional study prepared for the *Global Report on Human Settlements 2009*, www.unhabitat.org/grhs/2009

HM Treasury (2006) *Short Executive Summary: Stern Review on the Economics of Climate Change*, Cambridge University Press, Cambridge, www.hm-treasury.gov.uk

Ho, G. (2002) *International Sourcebook on Environmentally Sound Technologies for Wastewater and Stormwater Management*, UNEP/IETC, International Water Association Publishing, London

Ho, G. (2003) 'Small water and wastewater systems: Pathways to sustainable development?', *Water Science and Technology* **48**(11/12): 7–14

Hoernig, H. and M. Seasons (2005) 'Understanding indicators', in R. Philips (ed) *Community Indicators Measuring Systems*, Ashgate, Burlington, VT, pp3–31

Home, R. K. (1997) *Of Planting and Planning: The Making of British Colonial Cities*, Spon Press, London

Hopkins, L. (2001) *Urban Development: The Logic of Making Plans*, Island Press, Washington, DC

Houtzager, P. (2003) 'Introduction: From polycentrism to the polity?', in P. Houtzager and M. Moore (eds) *Changing Paths: The New Politics of Inclusion*, University of Michigan Press, Ann Arbor, pp1–31, http://unstats.un.org/unsd/demographic/products/dyb/dybsets/2006%20DYB.pdf

Hull, R. W. (1976) *African Cities and Towns before the European Conquest*, W. W. Norton and Company, London and New York

Hunt, J. and R. Brouwers (2003) *Review of Gender and Evaluation: OECD-DAC Network on Development Evaluation*, Final report to DAC Network on Development Evaluation OECD, Paris, www.oecd.org/LongAbstract/0,3425,en_2649_34435_37881391_119829_1_1_1,00.htm, accessed 2 January 2009

Iacono, M., D. Levinson, and A. El-Geneidy (2007) *Models of Transportation and Land Use Change: A Guide to the Territory*, Unpublished manuscript

IFAD (International Fund for Agricultural Development) (2002) *A Guide for Project Monitoring and Evaluation*, IFAD, Rome, www.ifad.org/evaluation/guide/index.htm, accessed 2 January 2009

IFRCRCS (International Federation of Red Cross and Red Crescent Societies) (2003) *World Disasters Report 2003*, IFRC, Geneva

IFRCRCS (2008) 'Plan 2009–2010: Central Europe and Southern Caucasus regional programmes: Executive summary', International Federation of Red Cross and Red Crescent Societies, www.ifrc.org/docs/appeals/annual09/MAA6600109p.pdf

IGE (2007) *Development Actions and the Rising Incidence of Disasters*, World Bank, Washington, DC

Ikejiofor, U. C. (2006) 'Integrative strategies or functional interface? Emerging trends in land administration in contemporary Enugu, Nigeria', *International Development Planning Review* **28**(2): 37–58

Ikejiofor, U. C. (2008) 'Planning within a context of informality: Issues and trends in land delivery in Enugu, Nigeria', Unpublished case study prepared for the *Global Report on Human Settlements 2009*, www.unhabitat.org/grhs/2009

ILO (International Labour Organization) (1972) *Incomes, Employment and Equality in Kenya*, International Labour Office, Geneva

ILO (2009) *Global Employment Trends*, ILO, Geneva, www.ilo.org/wcmsp5/groups/public/---dgreports/---dcomm/documents/publication/wcms_101461.pdf

IMF (International Monetary Fund) (2009) *World Economic Outlook Update April 2009: Crisis and Recovery*, IMF, Washington, DC, www.imf.org/external/pubs/ft/weo/2009/01/pdf/supptbls.pdf

Inkoom, D. K. B. (2008) 'Planning education in Ghana', Unpublished case study prepared for the *Global Report on Human Settlements 2009*, www.unhabitat.org/grhs/2009

Innes, J. (1995) 'Planning theory's emerging paradigm: Communicative action and interactive practice', *Journal of Planning Education and Research* **14**(4): 183–189

Innes, J. and D. Booher (2000) 'Indicators for sustainable communities: A strategy building on complexity theory and distributed intelligence', *Planning Theory and Practice* **1**(2): 173–186

Iracheta, A. C. (ed) (2004) *Mercado de suelo para la vivienda de interes social en ciudades seleccionadas. Indicatores y orientactiones bàsicas [Land Market for Social Interest Housing in Selected Cities: Basic Indicators and Orientations]*, PROURBA, El Colegio Mexiquense, A. C. Proyecto Fondo Sectorial CONAFOVI–CONACYT [National Housing Development Commission/National Council for Science and Technology Sectoral Project Fund], Zinacantepec

Iracheta, A. C. and M. O. Smolka (undated) 'Access to serviced land for the urban poor: The regularization paradox in Mexico', Unpublished paper

Irazábal, C. (2006) *City Making and Urban Governance in the Americas: Curitiba and Portland*, Ashgate, Aldershot

Irazábal, C. (2008a) 'Revisiting urban planning in Latin America and the Caribbean', Unpublished regional study prepared for the *Global Report on Human Settlements 2009*, www.unhabitat.org/grhs/2009

Irazábal, C. (ed) (2008b) *Ordinary Places, Extraordinary Events: Citizenship, Democracy and Public Space in Latin America*, Routledge, Taylor and Francis, London

Irazábal, C. and J. Foley (2008) 'Venezuela's communal councils and the role of planners', *Progressive Planning*, **174**: 30–33

IRIN (Integrated Regional Information Networks) (2008) 'Humanitarian news and analysis', UN Office for the Coordination of Humanitarian Affairs, www.irinnews.org/Report.aspx?ReportId=73996

ISDR (International Strategy for Disaster Reduction) (2004) *Living with Risk: A Review of Global Disaster Reduction Initiatives*, www.unisdr.org/eng/about_isdr/bd-lwr-2004-eng.htm

Istituto Nazionale di Urbanistica (2006) *Rapporto dal Territorio 2005*, INU Edizioni srl, Rome

Jacobi, P. (1999) *Challenging Traditional Participation in Brazil: The Goals of Participatory Budgeting*, Woodrow Wilson International Center for Scholars, No. 32, Washington, DC

Jacobs, J. (1963) *The Death and Life of Great American Cities*, Vintage, New York

Jacobs, J. (1984) *Cities and the Wealth of Nations*, Vintage, New York

Jain, A. K. (2008) *The Delhi Metro*, Delhi Development Authority, Delhi

Jenkins, P. (2000) 'Urban management, urban poverty and urban governance: Planning and land management in Maputo', *Environment and Urbanization* **12**(1): 137–152

Jenkins, P. (2004) 'Beyond the formal/informal dichotomy: Access to land in Maputo, Mozambique', in K. T. Hansen and M. Vaa (eds) *Reconsidering Informality: Perspectives from Urban Africa*, Nordiska Afrikainstitutet, Uppsala, pp210–226

Jenkins, P., H. Smith, and Y. P. Wang (2007) *Planning and Housing in the Rapidly Urbanising World*, Routledge, London

Jenks, M. (2000) 'The appropriateness of compact city concepts to developing countries', in M. Jenks and R. Burgess (eds) *Compact Cities: Sustainable Urban Forms for Developing Countries*, Spon Press, London, pp343–350

Jenks, M. and R. Burgess (eds) (2000) *Compact Cities. Sustainable Urban Forms for Developing Countries*, Spon Press, London

Jenks, M., E. Burton, and K. Williams (eds) (1996) *The Compact City: A Sustainable Urban Form?*, E&FN Spon, London

Jessop, B. (1997) 'Governance of complexity and the complexity of governance: Preliminary remarks on some problems and limits of economic guidance', in A. Amin and J. Hausner (eds) *Beyond Market and Hierarchy: Interactive Governance and Social Complexity*, Edward Elgar, Cheltenham, pp95–108

Jessop, B. (2000) 'Governance failure', in G. Stoker (ed) *The New Politics of British Local Governance*, Macmillan, London, pp11–32

Jha, S., Rao, V., & Woolcock, M. (2007) 'Governance in the gullies: democratic responsiveness and leadership in Delhi's slums', *World Development* **35**(2), 230–246

Jhabvala, R. (2007) 'A bottom-up approach in India (SEWA)', *Habitat Debate* **13**(2): 14

Jiron, P. (2008) *Mobility on the Move: Examining Daily Mobility Practices in Santiago de Chile*, PhD thesis, London School of Economics and Political Sciences, London

Johnson, C. (ed) (2008) *Connecting Cities: India*, Publication for Metropolis Congress, Sydney

Johnston, R., Poulsen, M. and Forrest, J. (2005). 'Ethnic residential segregation across an urban system: The Maori in New Zealand, 1991–2001', *The Professional Geographer*, **57**(1): 115–129

Jones, G. W. and R. A. Pisa (2000) 'Public–private partnerships for urban land development in Mexico: A victory for hope versus expectation?', *Habitat International* **24**: 1–18

Jun, M. (2004) 'The effects of Portland's urban growth boundary on urban development patterns and commuting', *Urban Studies* **41**(7): 1333–1348

Kagawa, A. and J. Turkstra, (2002) 'The process of urban land tenure formalization in Peru', in G. Payne (ed) *Land, Rights and Innovation: Improving Tenure Security for the Poor*, ITDG Publishing, London, pp57–77

Kalabamu, F. T. (2006) 'The limitations of state regulation of land delivery processes in Gaborone, Botswana', *International Development Planning Review* **28**(2): 209–234

Kamete, A. (2004) 'Home industries and the formal city in Harare, Zimbabwe', in K. T. Hansen and M. Vaa (eds) *Reconsidering Informality: Perspectives from Urban Africa*, Nordiska Afrikainstitutet, Uppsala, pp120–138

Kamete, A. Y. (2007) 'Cold-hearted, negligent and spineless? Planning, planners and the (r)ejection of "filth" in urban Zimbabwe', *International Planning Studies* **12**(2): 153–171

Kane, L. and R. Behrens (2002) 'Transport planning models: An historical and critical overview', Paper presented to the 21st Southern African Transport Conference, Towards Building Capacity and Accelerating Delivery, Pretoria, July

Karki, T. K. (2004) 'Implementation experiences of land pooling projects in Kathmandu Valley', *Habitat International* **28**(1): 67–88

Kazimbaya-Senkwe, B. M. (2004) 'Home based enterprises in a period of economic restructuring in Zambia', in K. T. Hansen and M. Vaa (eds) *Reconsidering Informality: Perspectives from Urban Africa*, Nordiska Afrikainstitutet, Uppsala, pp99–119

Kenworthy, J. (2008) 'An international review of the significance of rail in developing more sustainable urban transport systems in higher income cities', *World Transport Policy and Practice* **14**(2): 21–37

Kenworthy J. and Laube F. (2001) *The Millennium Cities Database for Sustainable Transport*, UITP, Brussels

Kenworthy J., F. Laube, P. Newman, P. Barter, T. Raad, C. Poboon and B. Guia (1999) *An International Sourcebook of Automobile Dependence in Cities, 1960–1990*, University Press of Colorado, Boulder, CO

Kessides, C. (2006) *The Urban Transition in Sub-Saharan Africa: Implications for Economic Growth and Poverty Reduction*, Cities Alliance, Sida and the World Bank, Washington, DC

Khosa, M. (2001) *Empowerment through Economic Transformation*, Human Sciences Research Council, Pretoria

King, A. (1980) 'Exporting planning: The colonial and neo-colonial experience', in G. E. Cherry (ed) *Shaping an Urban World*, St Martin's Press, New York, pp203–226

King, D. A. (2004) 'The scientific impact of nations: What different countries get for their research spending', *Nature* **430**: 311–316

Kipfer, S. and R. Keil (2002) 'Toronto Inc? Planning the competitive city in the new Toronto', *Antipode* **34**(3): 227–264

Kironde, J. M. L. (2006) 'The regulatory framework, unplanned development and urban poverty: Findings from Dar es Salaam', *Land Use Policy* **23**(4): 460–472

Klosterman, R. E. (1985) 'Arguments for and against planning', *Town Planning Review* **56**(1): 5–20

Klosterman, R. E. (1994) 'An introduction to the literature on large scale urban models', *Journal of the American Planning Association* **60**(1): 41–44

Kombe, W. J. (2001) 'Institutionalising the concept of environmental planning and management (EPM): Successes and challenges in Dar es Salaam', *Development in Practice* **11**(2/3): 190–207

Kooy, M. and K. Bakker (2008) 'Splintered networks: The colonial and contemporary waters of Jakarta', *Geoforum* **39**(6): 1843–1858, doi:10.1016/j.geoforum.2008.07.012

Korten, D. (1999) *The Post-Corporate World: Life after Capitalism,* Kumarian Press, West Hartford

Kostoff, S. (1991) *The City Shaped*, Thames and Hudson, London

Kovàcs, Z. and I. Tosics (forthcoming) 'Urban sprawl on the Danube: The impacts of suburbanization in Budapest', in K. Stanilov and L. Skora (eds) *Confronting Suburbanization: Urban Decentralization in Post-Socialist Central and Eastern Europe*, Blackwell, Oxford

Krueckeberg, D. (1985) 'The tuition of American planning: From dependency toward self-reliance', *Town Planning Review* **56**(4): 421–441

Krumholz, N. and J. Forester (1990) *Making Equity Planning Work*, Temple University Press, Philadelphia

Kundu, A. (2002) 'Tenure security, housing investment and environmental improvement: The cases of Delhi and Ahmedabad, India', in G. Payne (ed) *Land, Rights and Innovation: Improving Tenure Security for the Poor*, ITDG Publishing, London, pp136–157

Kunzmann, K. (2004) 'Unconditional surrender: The gradual demise of European diversity in planning', Paper presented at the Congress of the Association of European Schools of Planning, 3 July, www.planum.net/topics/documents/kunzmann_epp_01.pdf

Kusek, J. Z. and R. C. Rist (2003) *Ten Steps to a Results-Based Monitoring and Evaluation System*, World Bank, Washington, DC

Kusiima, A. (2008) 'A review of planning education at Makerere University, Uganda', Paper prepared for the workshop on the Revitalization of Planning Education in Africa, 13–15 October, Cape Town

Kyessi, A. (2005) 'Community-based urban water management in fringe neighbourhoods: The case of Dar es Salaam, Tanzania', *Habitat International*, **29**: 1–25

Laquian, A. A. (2007) 'The planning and governance of Asia's mega-urban regions', in United Nations Department for Economic and Social Affairs (UNDESA) (ed) *United Nations Expert Group Meeting on Population Distribution, Urbanization, Internal Migration and Development*, New York, 21–23 January 2008, UNDESA, Population Division, New York

Le Clercq, F. and L. Bertolini (2003) 'Achieving sustainable accessibility: An evaluation of policy measures in the Amsterdam area', *Built Environment* **29**(1): 36–47

Le Galès, P. (1998) 'Regulation and governance in European cities', *International Journal of Urban and Regional Research* **22**(3): 482–506

Le Galès, P. (2006). 'Cities are back in town: The US/Europe Comparison', Cahier Européen numéro 05/06 du Pôle Ville/Métropolis/Cosmopolis, Centre d'Etudes Européennes de Sciences Po (Paris), www.portedeurope.org/IMG/pdf/cahierville0606.pdf

Leaf, M. (1999) 'Vietnam's urban edge: The administration of urban development in Hanoi', *Third World Planning Review* **21**(3): 297–315

Leaf, M. (2002) 'A tale of two villages – globalization and peri-urban change in China and Vietnam', *Cities* **19**(1), 23–31

Leaf, M. (2005a) 'Modernity confronts tradition: The professional planner and local corporatism in the rebuilding of China's cities', in B. Sanyal (ed) *Comparative Planning Cultures*, Routledge, London, pp91–111

Leaf, M. (2005b) 'A question of boundaries: Planning and Asian urban transitions', in M. Keiner, M. Koll-Schretzenmayr and W. A. Schmid (eds) *Managing Urban Futures: Sustainability and Urban Growth in Developing Countries*, Ashgate, Aldershot, pp89–102

Leaf, M. and L. Hou (2006) 'The "third spring" of urban planning in China: The resurrection of professional planning in the post-Mao era', *China Information* **20**(3): 553–585

Lecroart, P. (2008) 'The urban regeneration of Plaine Saint-Denis, Paris region, 1985–2020: Integrated planning in a large "urban project"', Unpublished case study prepared for the *Global Report on Human Settlements 2009*, www.unhabitat.org/grhs/2009

Leduka, R. C. (2006a) 'Chiefs, civil servants and city council: State–society relationships in evolving land delivery processes in Maseru, Lesotho', *International Development Planning Review* **28**(2): 181–208

Leduka, R. C. (2006b) 'Explaining informal land delivery processes and institutions in African cities:

Conceptual framework and emerging evidence', *South African Review of Sociology* **37**(1): 1–19

Lee, D. (1973) 'Requiem for large-scale urban models', *Journal of the American Institute of Planners* **39**(2): 163–178

Lees, A. and L. H. Lees (2007) *Cities and the Making of Modern Europe, 1750–1914*, Cambridge University Press, Cambridge, MA

Lerch, D. (2007) *Post Carbon Cities: Planning for Energy and Climate Uncertainty*, Post Carbon Press, Portland, OR

Levin, M. (1976) 'Why can't Johnny plan?' *Planning* **42**(8): 21–23

Li, T. (2008) 'The Chengzhongcun land market in China: Boon or bane? A perspective on property rights', *International Journal of Urban and Regional Research* **32**(2): 282–304

Lichfield, N. and H. Darin-Drabkin (1980) *Land Policy and Planning*, George, Allen and Unwin, London

Lichfield, N., P. Kettle and M. Whitehead (1975) *Evaluation in the Planning Process*, Pergamon, Oxford

Lipietz, B. (2008) 'Building a vision for the post-apartheid city: What role for participation in Johannesburg's City Development Strategy?', *International Journal of Urban and Regional Research* **32**(1): 135–163

Lipton, M. (1984) 'Family, fungibility and formality: Rural advantages of informal non-farm enterprise versus the urban–formal state', in S. Amin (ed) *Human Resources, Employment and Development: Vol 5, Developing Countries*, Macmillan for International Economic Association, London, pp189–242

Liu, Y. and F. Wu (2006) 'Urban poverty neighbourhoods: Typology and spatial concentration under China's market transition, a case study of Nanjing', *Geoforum* **37**(4): 610–626

Lloyd Jones, T. (2000) 'Compact city policies for megacities: Core areas and metropolitan regions', in M. Jenks and R. Burgess (eds) *Compact Cities: Sustainable Urban Forms for Developing Countries*, Spon Press, London, pp37–52

Logan, M. (2002) 'Progress in planning – has there been any? The case of the cities of East Asia', *Progress in Planning* **57**(3–4): 239–260

Lourenco-Lindell, I. (2004) 'Trade and the politics of informalisation in Bissau, Guinea–Bissau', in K. T. Hansen and M. Vaa (eds) *Reconsidering Informality: Perspectives from Urban Africa*, Nordiska Afrikainstitutet, Uppsala, pp84–98

Lu, D. (2006) 'Travelling urban form: The neighbourhood unit in China', *Planning Perspectives* **21**: 369–392

Lyons, M. (2001) 'Participation, empowerment and sustainability: (How) do the links work?' *Urban Studies* **38**(8): 1233–1251

Lyons, M. and B. Mbiba (2003) *Good Practice Manual for Development and Formalisation of Markets and Street Trading in Africa*, Peri-Urban Unit, Urban and Environmental Studies, South Bank University, London

Mabin, A. and A. Todes (2008) 'A review of planning education at University of the Witwatersrand, Johannesburg', Paper prepared for the workshop on The Revitalization of Planning Education in Africa, 13–15 October, Cape Town

Mabogunje, A. L. (1990) 'Urban planning and the post-colonial state in Africa: A research overview', *African Studies Review* **33**(2): 121–203

Macionis, J. J. and Parrillo, V. N. (2004) *Cities and Urban Life*, 3rd edition, Pearson/Prentice Hall, Upper Saddle River, NJ

Mackenzie, S. and D. Rose (1983) 'Industrial change, the domestic economy and home life', in J. Anderson, S. Duncan and R. Hudson (eds) *Redundant Spaces in Cities and Regions? Studies in Industrial Decline and Social Change*, Academic Press, London

Magalhaes, F. and E. Rojas (2007) *Facing the Challenge of Informal Settlements in Urban Centers*, Inter-American Development Bank, www.iadb.org/publications/search.cfm?countries=andtopics=AG

Maier, K. (1994) 'Planning and an education in planning in the Czech Republic', *Journal of Planning Education and Research* **13**: 263–269

Majale, M. (2008) 'Developing participatory planning practices in Kitale, Kenya', Unpublished case study prepared for the *Global Report on Human Settlements 2009*, www.unhabitat.org/grhs/2009

Majoor, S. (2008) *Disconnected Innovations: New Urbanity in Large-Scale Development Projects*, Uitgeverij Eburon, Delft

Marcuse, P. (2006) 'Space in the globalizing city', in N. Brenner and R. Keil (eds) *The Global Cities Reader*, Routledge, London and New York

Marsh, D. and R. A. W. Rhodes (1992) *Policy Networks in British Government*, Oxford University Press, Oxford

Marshall, T. (2000) 'Urban planning and governance: Is there a Barcelona Model?', *International Planning Studies* **5**(3): 299–319

Marshall, T. (2004) *Transforming Barcelona: The Renewal of a European Metropolis*, Routledge, London

Matovu, G. (2006) 'Capacity building for participatory planning and budgeting in Africa: Initiatives and strategic perspectives', Presentation to the Pan African Conference of Ministers of Local Government, Maseru, Lesotho

Mattingly, M. (1993) 'Urban management intervention in land markets', in N. Devas and C. Rakodi (eds) *Managing Fast Growing Cities: New Approaches to Urban Planning and Management in the Developing World*, Longman Scientific and Technical, Essex, pp102–131

Mattingly, M. (2001) *Spatial Planning for Urban Infrastructure Planning and Investment, A Guide to Training and Practice*, Development Planning Unit, University College London

Mattingly, M. and H. Winarso (2000) 'Urban spatial planning and public capital investments: The experience of Indonesia's Integrated Urban Infrastructure Investment Programme', *Development Planning Unit Working Paper 113*, University College London

Mayor of London (2004) *The London Plan*, Greater London Authority, London

Mazmanian, D. and J. Nienaber (1979) *Can Organizations Change? Environmental Protection, Citizen Participation, and the Corps of Engineers*, Brookings Institution, Washington, DC

Mazza, L. (2004) *Prove parziali di riforma urbanistica*, FrancoAngeli, Milan

Mazziotti, D. (1974) 'The underlying assumptions of advocacy: Pluralism and reform', *Journal of the American Institute of Planners* **36**: 12–21

Mbiba, B. and M. Huchzermeyer (2002) 'Contentious development: Peri-urban studies in sub-Saharan Africa', *Progress in Development Studies* **2**(2): 113–131

McAuslan, P. (1993) 'The role of law in urban planning', in N. Devas and C. Rakodi (eds) *Managing Fast Growing Cities: New Approaches to Urban Planning and Management in the Developing World*, Longman Scientific and Technical, Essex, pp236–264

McDonald, D. and J. Pape (2002) *Cost Recovery and the Crisis of Service Delivery in South Africa*, HSRC Press, Cape Town

McDonaugh, W. and M. Braungart (2002) *Cradle to Cradle: Remaking the Way We Make Things*, North Point Press, New York

McGee, T. (1991) 'The emergence of *desakota* regions in Asia: Expanding a hypothesis', in N. Ginsburg, B. Keppel and T. G. McGee (eds) *The Extended Metropolis: Settlement Transition in Asia*, University of Hawaii Press, Honolulu, pp1–25

McGranahan, G., D. Balk and D. Anderson (2007) 'The rising tide: Assessing the risks of climate change and human settlements in low elevation coastal zones', *Environment and Urbanization* 19(1): 17–37

McLoughlin, J. B. (1970) *Urban and Regional Planning: A systems approach*, Faber and Faber, London

Meagher, K. (2005) 'Social capital or analytical liability? Social networks and African informal economies', *Global Networks* 5(3): 217–238

Mean, M. and C. Tims (2005) *People Make Places: Growing the Public Life of Cities*, Demos, London

Medvekov, Y. and O. Medvekov (2007) 'Upscale housing in post-Soviet Moscow and its environs', in K. Stanilov (ed) *The Post-Socialist City: Urban Form and Space Transformations in Central and Eastern Europe After Socialism*, Springer, Dordrecht, pp245–265

Mehta, D. (2005) 'Our common past: The contribution of the Urban Management Programme', *Habitat Debate*, 11(4): 6–7

Meyerson, M. (1956) 'Building the middle range bridge for comprehensive planning', *Journal of the American Institute of Planners* 22: 58–64

Meyerson, M. and E. Banfield (1955) *Politics, Planning and the Public Interest: The Case of Public Housing in Chicago*, The Free Press, New York

Middle East Youth Initiative (undated) 'Employment', www.shababinclusion.org/section/topics/employment

Millennium Ecosystem Assessment (2005) *Ecosystems and Human Well Being,* Millennium Ecosystem Assessment, World Resources Institute, Island Press, Washington, DC

Mindali, O., A. Rowe, and I. Salomon (2004) 'Urban density and energy consumption: A new look at old statistics', *Transport Research Part A* 38: 243–262

Mitchell, D. (2003) *The Right to the City: Social Justice and the Fight for Public Space*, Guilford Press, New York

Mitlin, D. (2004) 'Civil society organizations: Do they make a difference to urban poverty?' in N. Devas, P. Amis, J. Beall, U. Grant, D. Mitlin, F. Nunan and C. Rakodi (eds) *Urban Governance, Voice and Poverty in the Developing World*, London, Earthscan, pp123–144

Mitlin, D. (2008) 'With and beyond the state: Co-production as a route to political influence, power and transformation for grassroots organizations', *Environment and Urbanization* 20(2): 339–360

Mitlin, D. and D. Satterthwaite (1994) *Cities and Sustainable Development: Background Paper for Global Forum '94,* Unpublished paper, IIED, London

Mohammed, A. (2001) 'Afloat in the Atlantic: A search for relevant models of planning education and accreditation in the English-speaking Caribbean', *Third World Planning Review* 23(2): 195–211

Mohit, R. S. (2002) 'A level playing field: Security of tenure and the urban poor in Bangkok, Thailand', in G. Payne (ed) *Land, Rights and Innovation: Improving Tenure Security for the Poor*, ITDG Publishing, London, pp278–299

Moser, C. (1978) 'Informal sector or petty commodity production: Dualism or dependence in urban development?', *World Development* 6(9–10): 1041–1064

Moser, C. (1993) *Gender Planning and Development: Theory, Practice and Training*, Routledge, London

Motte, A. (2007) *Les Agglomerations Françaises Face aux Defis Metropolitaines*, Economica/Anthropos, Paris

Moulaert, F. with P. Delladetsima, J.-C. Delvainquière, C. Demazière, S. Vicari and M. Martinez (2000) *Globalisation and Integrated Area Development in European Cities*, Oxford University Press, Oxford

Mtani, A. (2002) 'The women's perspective: The case of Manzese, Dar es Salaam, Tanzania', in *Proceedings of the First International Seminar on Safety for Women and Girls*, Montreal, May, www.femmesetvilles.org/seminar/english/set_intro_en.htm

Murphy, C. (1999) 'Cultivating Havana: Urban agriculture and food security in the years of crisis', *Development Report No 12*, Food First, Institute for Food and Development Policy, Oakland, CA

Musyoka, R. (2006) 'Non-compliance and formalisation: Mutual accommodation in land subdivision processes in Eldoret, Kenya', *International Development Planning Review* 28(2): 235–261

Myerson, G. and Y. Rydin (1996) 'Sustainable development: The implications of the global debate for land use planning', in S. Buckingham-Hatfield and B. Evans (eds) *Environmental Planning and Sustainability*, John Wiley and Sons, Chichester, pp19–34

Mykhnenko, V. and I. Turok (2007) *Cities in Transition: East European Urban Trajectories 1960–2005*, Working Paper No 4, Centre for Public Policy for Regions, University of Glasgow, Scotland

Nadin, V. (2007) 'The emergence of the spatial planning approach in England', *Planning Practice and Research* 22(1): 43–62

Nassar, M. M. (2008) 'Revisiting urban planning in North Africa and the Middle East', Unpublished regional study prepared for the *Global Report on Human Settlements 2009*, www.unhabitat.org/grhs/2009

National Commission for Women (2005) *Report of the National Workshop and Public Hearing on Women's Right to Adequate Housing, Land and Livelihood*, Organized by National Commission for Women in co-operation with Mahila Samakhya Allahabad and Consult for Women and Land Rights Co Supported by Action Aid India, Indo Global Social Service Society Allahabad, India, 26–27 May 2005

National Research Council (2003) *Cities Transformed: Demographic Change and Its Implications in the Developing World*, The National Academies Press, Washington, DC

Naudé, W. (2009) *The Financial Crisis of 2008 and the Developing Countries*, Discussion Paper No 2009/01, World Institute for Development Economics Research, Helsinki

Nedovic-Budic, Z. and B. Cavric (2006) 'Waves of planning: A framework for studying the evolution of planning systems and empirical insights from Serbia and Montenegro', *Planning Perspectives* 21: 393–425

Needham, B., P. Koenders and B. Kruijt (1993) *Urban Land and Property Markets in the Netherlands*, UCL Press, London

Needleman, M. L. and C. E. Needleman (1974) *Guerrillas in the Bureaucracy*, John Wiley and Sons, New York

Neto, F., Y. Ha and A. Weliwita (2007) 'The urban informal economy – new policy approaches', *Habitat Debate* 13(2): 4–5

New Zealand (2009) *Monitoring Tools, Indicators and Data Management*, Quality Planning: The RMA Resource, www.qualityplanning.org.nz/monitoring/monitor-tools.php

Newman, P. and I. Jennings (2008) *Cities as Sustainable Ecosystems,* Island Press, Washington, DC

Newman, P. and J. Kenworthy (1996) 'The land use–transport connection: An overview', *Land Use Policy* **13**(1): 1–22

Newman, P. and J. Kenworthy (1999) *Sustainability and Cities: Overcoming Automobile Dependence*, Island Press, Washington, DC

Newman, P. and J. Kenworthy (2000) 'Sustainable urban form: The big picture', in K. Williams, E. Burton and M. Jenks (eds) (2000) *Achieving Sustainable Urban Form*, E&FN Spon, London, pp109–120

Newman, P. and J. Kenworthy (2007) 'Greening urban transport' in *State of the World, 2007*, Worldwatch Institute, Washington, DC

Newman, P. and A. Thornley (1996) *Urban Planning in Europe: International Competition, National Systems and Planning Project*, Routledge, London and New York

Newman, P., T. Beatley and H. Boyer (2009) *Resilient Cities: Responding to Peak Oil and Climate Change*, Island Press, Washington, DC

New Zealand Yearbook (2006) 'Ethnicity (Grouped total responses) by main urban areas census of population and dwellings', www.stats.govt.nz/urban-rural-profiles/main-urban-areas/people.htm

Nientied, P. (1998) 'The question of town and regional planning in Albania', *Habitat International* **22**(1): 41–47

Njoh, A. (1999) *Urban Planning, Housing and Spatial Structures in Sub-Saharan Africa,* Ashgate, Aldershot

Njoh, A. J. (2003a) 'Urbanization and development in sub-Saharan Africa', *Cities*, **20**(3): 167–174

Njoh, A. (2003b) *Planning in Contemporary Africa: The State, Town Planning and Society in Cameroon,* Ashgate, Aldershot

Njoh, A. (2008a) 'Community-based and non-governmental organizations in urban development in Mexico City: The case of San Miguel Teotongo', Unpublished case study prepared for the *Global Report on Human Settlements 2009*, www.unhabitat.org/grhs/2009

Njoh, A. (2008b) 'New urbanism, an alternative to traditional urban design: The case of Celebration, Florida, USA', Unpublished case study prepared for the *Global Report on Human Settlements 2009*, www.unhabitat.org/grhs/2009

Njoh, A. (2008c) 'Self-help, a viable non-conventional urban public service delivery strategy: Lessons from Cameroon', Unpublished case study prepared for the *Global Report on Human Settlements 2009*, www.unhabitat.org/grhs/2009

Njoh, A. (2008d) 'The state as enabler in urban policy-making in Colombo, Sri Lanka', Unpublished case study prepared for the *Global Report on Human Settlements 2009*, www.unhabitat.org/grhs/2009

Nkurunziza, E. (2006) 'Two states, one city? Conflict and accommodation in land delivery in Kampala, Uganda', *International Development Planning Review* **28**(2): 159–180

Nnkya, T. J. (1996) *Planning in Practice and Democracy in Tanzania*, Institute of Town and Landscape Planning, Royal Danish Academy of Fine Arts, Copenhagen

Nnkya, T. J. (1999) 'Land use planning practice under the public land ownership policy in Tanzania', *Habitat International* **23**(1): 135–155

Nnkya, T. J. (2006a) 'Collaborative turn in planning practice? A case', Paper presented to Planning Africa 2006 Conference, Cape Town, www.saplanners.org.za

Nnkya, T. J. (2006b) 'An enabling framework? Governance and street trading in Dar es Salaam, Tanzania', in A. Brown (ed) *Contested Space: Street Trading, Public Space and Livelihoods in Developing Cities*, ITDG Publishing, London, pp79–98

Nnkya, T. J. and J. Lupala (2008) 'A review of planning education at School of Urban and Regional Planning, Ardhi University, Dar es Salaam', Paper prepared for the workshop on the Revitalization of Planning Education in Africa, 13–15 October, Cape Town

Nocks, B. C. (1974) 'Case studies: A decade of planning education at three schools', in D. R. Godschalk (ed) (1995) *Planning in America: Learning from Turbulence*, American Institute of Planners, Washington, DC, pp206–226

Nolan, R. B. and L. L. Lem (2001) *A Review of the Evidence for Induced Travel and Changes in Transportation and Environmental Policy in the United States and the United Kingdom*, Centre for Transport Studies, Imperial College London

Odendaal, N. and J. Duminy (2008) 'Does technology shape our cities? Understanding the relationship between digital technologies and urban change in eThekwini, 1992–2007', Paper presented to the Planning Africa Conference: Shaping Futures, Johannesburg

OECD (Organisation for Economic Co-operation and Development) (2002) *Glossary of Key Terms in Evaluation*, OECD, Paris, www.oecd.org/findDocument/0,2350,en_2649_34435_1_119678_1_1_1,00.htm, accessed 2 January 2009

OECD (2008) *Growing Unequal? Income Distribution and Poverty in OECD Countries*, OECD, Paris

OECD (2009) *World Economic Outlook: Interim Report*, OECD, Paris

Office of the Deputy Prime Minister (2004) *Planning Policy Statement 11: Regional Spatial Strategies*, Office of the Deputy Prime Minister, London

Office of the Deputy Prime Minister (2005) *Diversity and Equality in Planning: A Good Practice Guide*, Office of the Deputy Prime Minister, London

Okpala, D. (2008) 'Revisiting urban planning in sub-Saharan Africa "Anglophone" countries', Unpublished regional study prepared for the *Global Report on Human Settlements 2009*, www.unhabitat.org/grhs/2009

Ontario (2008) *Development Permit System: A Handbook for Municipal Implementation*, Ministry of Municipal Affairs and Housing, Ontario, www.mah.gov.on.ca/Page5911.aspx

Oranje, M. (2008) 'A review of planning education at University of Pretoria', Paper prepared for the workshop on The Revitalization of Planning Education in Africa, 13–15 October, Cape Town

Owens, C. (2008) 'Challenges in evaluating livability in Vancouver, Canada', Unpublished case study prepared for the *Global Report on Human Settlements 2009*, www.unhabitat.org/grhs/2009

Owens, S. and R. Cowell (2002) *Land and Limits: Interpreting Sustainability in the Planning Process*, Routledge, London

Ozawa, C. P. (ed) (2004) *The Portland Edge: Challenges and Successes in Growing Communities,* Island Press, Washington, DC

Pagonis, T. and A. Thornley (2000) 'Urban development projects in Moscow: Market/state relations in the new Russia', *European Planning Studies* **8**(6): 751–766

Pal, L. (2006) *Beyond Policy Analysis*, 3rd edition, Thomson Nelson, Toronto

Papayanis, N. (2006) 'César Daly, Paris and the emergence of modern urban planning', *Planning Perspectives* **21**: 325–346

Parlevliet, J. and T. Xenogiani (2008) *Report on Informal Employment in Romania*, Working Paper 271, OECD Development Centre, Paris

Parnell, S. and J. Robinson (2006) 'Development and urban policy: Johannesburg's City Development Strategy', *Urban Studies* **43**(2): 337–355

Patel, S. and D. Mitlin (2004) 'Grassroots-driven development: The alliance of SPARC, the National Slum Dwellers Federation and Mahila Milan', in D. Mitlin and D. Satterthwaite (eds) *Empowering Squatter Citizen: Local Government, Civil Society and Urban Poverty Reduction*, Earthscan, London, pp216–243

Pawłowski, K. K. (1973) 'Narodziny miasta nowoczesnego', *Sztuka drugiej połowy XIX w*. Materiały sesji Stowarzyszenia Historyków Sztuki, Łódź

Payne, G. (1997) *Urban Land Tenure and Property Rights in Developing Countries: A Review*, Intermediate Technology Publications, London

Payne, G. (2001) 'Urban land tenure policy options: Titles or rights?', *Habitat International* **25**: 415–429

Payne, G. (2005) 'Getting ahead of the game: A twin-track approach to improving existing slums and reducing the need for future slums', *Environment and Urbanisation* **17**(1): 133–145

Payne, G. and M. Majale (2004) *The Urban Housing Manual: Making Regulatory Frameworks Work for the Poor*, Earthscan, London

Payne, G., A. Durand-Lasserve and C. Rakodi (2007) 'Urban land titling programmes', in M. E. Brother and J. A. Solberg (eds) *Legal Empowerment – A Way out of Poverty*, Norwegian Ministry of Foreign Affairs, Issue 3, Oslo, pp11–41

Peel, D. and A. Frank (2008) 'The internationalization of planning education: Issues, perceptions, and priorities for action', *Town Planning Review* **79**(1): 757–776

Perloff, H. (1957) *Education for Planning: City, State and Regional*, Johns Hopkins University Press, Baltimore

Perry, G. (2007) *Informality: Exit and Exclusion*, World Bank, Washington, DC http://siteresources.worldbank.org/INTLAC/Resources/CH1.pdf

Peterson, J. (1979) 'The impact of sanitary reform upon American urban planning', *Journal of Social History*, **13**: 84–89

Peterson, P. (2008) 'Civic engagement and urban reform in Brazil', *Planning Theory and Practice* **9**(3): 406–410

Pezzoli, K. and D. Howe (2001) 'Planning pedagogy and globalization: A content analysis of syllabi', *Journal of Planning Education and Research* **20**: 365–375

Phillips, T. (2006) 'Brazil's roofless reclaim the cities', *The Guardian*, www.guardian.co.uk/world/2006/jan/23/brazil.uknews1

Plummer, J. (2000) *Municipalities and Community Participation: A Sourcebook for Capacity Building*, Earthscan, London

Porio, E., C. S. Crisol, N. F. Magno, D. Cid and E. N. Paul (2004) 'The Community Mortgage Programme: An innovative social housing programme in the Philippines and its outcomes', in D. Mitlin and D. Satterthwaite (eds) *Empowering Squatter Citizen: Local Government, Civil Society and Urban Poverty Reduction*, Earthscan, London, pp54–81

Porter, L. and A. Hecht (undated) *Canada Module Urban/Economic*, www.geographie.uni-marburg.de/vgt/english/canada/module/m2/U11.htm

Posselthwyte, C. (1986) *Reuniting the Divided City: Working Mothers in a Planned Environment*, MSc thesis, University of Cape Town, Cape Town

Potts, D. (2007) *The State and the Informal in Sub-Saharan African Urban Economies: Revisiting Debates on Dualism*, Crisis States Research Centre Working Paper 18, Development Studies Institute, London School of Economics, London

Pretty, J. (1995) 'Participatory learning for sustainable agriculture', *World Development* **23**(8): 1247–1263

Puig, J. (2008) 'Barcelona and the power of solar ordinances: Political will, capacity building and people's participation', in Droege, P. (ed) *Urban Energy Transition: From Fossil Fuels to Renewable Power*, Elsevier Publishers, Amsterdam, pp433–450

PUKAR (Partners for Urban Knowledge Action and Research) (2005) *The Gender and Space Project at PUKAR*, www.pukar.org.in/genderandspace/gender-space.html

Punter, J. (2003) *The Vancouver Achievement*, UBC Press, Vancouver, BC

Puri, V. K. (2007) *Master Plan for Delhi*, JBA Publishers, Delhi

Putnam, R. (1993) *Making Democracy Work: Civic Traditions of Modern Italy*, Princeton Architectural Press, Princeton, NJ

Putnam, R. D. (2000) *Bowling Alone: The Collapse and Revival of American Community*, Simon & Schuster, New York

Qadeer, M. A. (1986) *The Purpose of Studying 'Planning in the Third World' in Western Universities*, Queen's University, Kingston, Ontario

Qadeer, M. A. (1988) 'Planning in the third world in western universities', *Ekistics* **328**: 64–68

Qadeer, M. (1999) 'Urbanisation of everybody', institutional imperatives and social transformation in Pakistan', *The Pakistan Development Review* **38**(4): 1193–1210

Qadeer, M. (2004) 'Guest editorial: Urbanization by implosion', *Habitat International* **28**(1): 1–12

Quang, N. and H. Detlef Kammeier (2002) 'Changes in the political economy of Vietnam and their impacts on the built environment of Hanoi', *Cities* **19**(6): 373–388

Rabinovitch, J. and J. Leitman (2004) 'Urban planning in Curitiba', in S. Wheeler and T. Bentley (eds) *The Sustainable Urban Development Reader*, Routledge, London, pp236–249

Rabinovitz, F. (1969) *City Politics and Planning*, Atherton Press, New York

Rakodi, C. (2004) 'Urban politics: exclusion or empowerment?', in N. Devas, P. Amis, J. Beall, U. Grant, D. Mitlin, F. Nunan and C. Rakodi (eds) *Urban Governance, Voice and Poverty in the Developing World*, Earthscan, London, pp68–94

Rakodi, C. (2006) 'Social agency and state authority in land delivery processes in African cities: Compliance, conflict and cooperation', *International Development Planning Review* **28**(2): 263–285

Rakodi, C. (2008) 'Cardiff, UK: The politics of urban regeneration', Unpublished case study prepared for the *Global Report on Human Settlements 2009*, www.unhabitat.org/grhs/2009

Rakodi, C. and T. Firman (2008) 'An extended metropolitan region in Asia: Jakarta, Indonesia', Unpublished case study prepared for the *Global Report on Human Settlements 2009*, www.unhabitat.org/grhs/2009

Ramnath, A. (2007) *A Process for a Synchronised Synergy between Integrated Development Plans and Regional Water Plans*, MSc thesis, University of KwaZulu-Natal, Durban

Rao, M. and A. Sharma (1990) 'The role of non-motorised urban travel', in H. Dimitriou (ed) *Transport Planning for Third World Cities*, Routledge, London, pp117–143

Ratha, D., S. Mohapatra and Z. Xu (2008) 'Outlook for remittance flows 2008–2010: Growth expected to moderate significantly, but flows to remain resilient', in *Migration and Development Brief*, No 8, World Bank, Washington, DC

Reeves, D. (2003) *Gender Equality and Plan Making: The Gender Mainstreaming Toolkit*, RTPI, www.rtpi.org.uk

Reeves, D. and B. Parfitt, with C. Archer (2009) 'Gender and urban planning', Unpublished thematic study prepared for the *Global Report on Human Settlements 2009*, www.unhabitat.org/grhs/2009

RERC (Real Estate Research Corporation) (1974) *The Cost of Sprawl: Environmental and Economic Costs of Alternative Residential Development Patterns at the Urban Fringe*, Volume 1, Executive Summary, US Government Printers, Washington, DC

Revkin, A. (2008) 'Car-free, solar city in Gulf could set a new standard for green design', *The New York Times*, 5 February

Rhodes, R. A. W. (1997) *Understanding Governance: Policy Networks, Governance, Reflexivity and Accountability*, Open University Press, Buckingham

Richardson, H., C. Bae, and M. Baxamusa (2000) 'Compact cities in developing countries: Assessment and implications', in M. Jenks and R. Burgess (eds) (2000) *Compact Cities: Sustainable Urban Forms for Developing Countries*, Spon Press, London, pp25–36

Rieniets, T. (2005) 'Shrinking cities – growing domain for urban planning?', http://aarch.dk/fileadmin/grupper/institut_ii/PDF/paper_presentation_EURA2005.pdf

Rodwin, L. (1980) 'Training for urban studies in third world countries', *Ekistics* **47**(285): 404–410

Roever, S. (2005) *Enforcement and Compliance in Lima's Street Markets: The Origins and Consequences of Policy Incoherence toward Informal Traders*, World Institute for Development Economics Research of the United Nations University (UNU–WIDER), www.wider.unu.edu/publications/working-papers/research-papers/2005/en_GB/rp2005–16/

Rojas, E. (2006) 'The metropolitan regions of Latin America: Problems of governance and development', in E. Rojas, J. R. Cuadrado-Roura and J. M. F. Guiell (eds) *Governing the Metropolis*, Inter-American Development Bank, Washington, DC

Rojas, F. and M. Smolka (1998) 'New Colombian law implements value capture', *Land Lines* **10**(2): 1–2

Rolnick, R. (1999) *Territorial Exclusion and Violence: The Case of Sao Paulo, Brazil*, Project on Urbanisation, Population, Environment and Security, Woodrow Wilson International Centre, Washington, DC

Rosen, G. (1993) *A History of Public Health*, The Johns Hopkins University Press, Baltimore, MD

Rossi, P. H., H. Freeman and M. Lipsey (eds) (1999) *Evaluation: A Systematic Approach*, 6th edition, Sage, Thousand Oaks, CA

RTPI (Royal Town Planning Institute) (2003) *Gender Equality and Plan Making*, the Gender Mainstreaming Toolkit, www.rtpi.org.uk/download/3187/GenderEquality-PlanMaking.pdf

RTPI (2007) *Gender and Spatial Planning*, RTPI Good Practice Note 7, www.rtpi.org.uk/download/3322/GPN7.pd

RTPI, UCL (University College London) and Deloitte (2007) *Effective Practice in Spatial Planning*, RTPI, London

Rubin, J. (2008) *Delays Will Tighten Global Oil Markets*, CIBC World Markets Occasional Report, no 65, 10 January 2008, http://research.cibcwm.com/economic_public/download/occrept65.pdf

Russia Today (2009) 'January sees Russian unemployment rate climb to 4-year high', *Russia Today*, www.russiatoday.com/Business/2009-02-19/January_sees_Russian_unemployment_rate_climb_to_4_year_high_.html

Rutherford, J. (2005) 'Networks in cities, cities in networks: Territory and globalisation intertwined in telecommunications infrastructure development in Europe', *Urban Studies* **42**(13): 2389–2406

Sager, T. (1997) 'Planning and the liberal paradox: A democratic dilemma in social choice', *Journal of Planning Literature* **12**(1): 16–29

Salet, W. and E. Gualini (eds) (2007) *Framing Strategic Urban Projects: Learning from Current Experiences in European Urban Regions*, Routledge, London

Salet, W., A. Thornley and A. Kreukels (eds) (2003) *Metropolitan Governance and Spatial Planning: Comparative Studies of European City-Regions*, E&FN Spon, London

Sandercock, L. (1998) *Towards Cosmopolis: Planning for Multicultural Cities*, John Wiley, Chichester

Sandercock, L. (2005) 'An anatomy of civic ambition in Vancouver', *Harvard Design Magazine* **22** (spring/summer): 36–43

Sanyal, B. (1989) 'Poor countries' students in rich countries' universities: Possibilities of planning education for the twenty-first century', *Journal of Planning Education and Research* **8**(3): 139–155

Sarbib, J. L. (1983) 'The University of Chicago program in planning: A retrospective look', *Journal of Planning Education and Research* **2**(2): 77–81

Sawin, J. L. and K. Hughes (2007) 'Energizing cities' in M. Sheehnan (ed) *State of the World, 2007*, Worldwatch Institute, Washington, DC

Schenk, H. (2002) 'Urban fringes in Asia: Market versus plans – Cases from Bangalore and Hanoi', in I. S. A. Baud and J. Post (eds) *Realigning Actors in an Urbanizing World: Governance and Institutions from a Development Perspective*, Ashgate, Aldershot, pp119–136

Scheurer, J. (2003) *Urban Ecology, Innovations in Housing Policy and the Future of Cities: Towards Sustainability in Neighbourhood Communities*, PhD thesis, ISTP Murdoch University, Perth, Australia

Scheurer, J. and P. Newman (2008) 'Vauban: A European model bridging the green and brown agendas', Unpublished case study prepared for the *Global Report on Human Settlements 2009*, www.unhabitat.org/grhs/2009

Schneider, F. (2007) 'Measuring the size of the informal economy', *Habitat Debate* **13**(2): 19

Scholz, B. (2002) 'Crushed homes, crushed lives', *Habitat Debate* **8**(4): 14–15

Schönleitner, G. (2004) 'Can public deliberation democratise state action? Municipal health councils and local democracy in Brazil' in J. Harriss, K. Stokke and O. Tørnqvist (eds) *Politicising Democracy: The New Local Politics of Democratisation*, Palgrave Macmillan, Basingstoke, pp75–106

Schoonraad, M. (2000) 'Cultural and institutional obstacles to compact cities in South Africa', in M. Jenks and R. Burgess (eds) *Compact Cities: Sustainable Urban Forms for Developing Countries,* Spon Press, London, pp219–230

Scriven, M. (1991) *Evaluation Thesaurus*, 4th edition, Sage, Newbury Park

Seaforth, W. (2002) 'Towards woman-friendly cities', *Habitat Debate* **8**(4): 1–3

Selee, A. (2003) *Deliberative Approaches to Governance in Latin America*, Woodrow Wilson Center, Washington, DC, www.deliberative-democracy.net/index.php?option=com_content&view=article&id=45:deliberative-governance&catid=47:contributions%Itemid=89

Shatkin, G. (2006) '"Fourth world" cities in the global economy: The case of Phnom Penh, Cambodia', in N. Brenner and R. Keil (eds) *The Global City Reader*, Routledge, London and New York, pp210–216

Sheikh, K. and S. Rao (2007) 'Participatory city planning in Chhattisgarh: A civil society initiative', *Environment and Urbanization* **19**(2): 563–581

Shen, Q., C. Liu, J. Liao, F. Zhang and C. Dorney (2007) 'Changing urban growth patterns in a pro-smart growth state: The case of Maryland 1973–2002', Paper for the Lincoln Institute for Land Policy, Cambridge, MA

Sheuya, S. (2008) 'Improving the health and lives of people living in slums', *Annals of the New York Academy of Science* **1136**: 1–9

Siddiqui, K. and S. A. Siddiqui (2004) 'Karachi' in K. Siddiqui (ed) *Mega City Governance in South Asia*, The Universal Press Limited, Dhaka, pp274–352

Silas, J. (1993) *Surabaya 1293–1993: City of Partnership*, Municipal Government of Surabaya, Indonesia

Simmonds, D. and D. Coombe (2000) 'The transport implications of alternative urban form', in K. Williams, E. Burton and M. Jenks (eds) *Achieving Sustainable Urban Form*, E&FN Spon, London, pp121–130

Simone, A. (1999) 'Thinking about African urban management in an era of globalisation', *African Sociological Review* **3**(2): 69–98

Sindzingre, A. (2006) 'The relevance of the concepts of formality and informality: A theoretical appraisal', in B. Guha-Khasnobis, R. Kanbur and E. Ostrom (eds) *Linking the Formal and Informal Economy: Concepts and Policies*, Oxford University Press, Oxford, pp58–74

Singh, K. and F. Steinberg (1996) 'Multi-sectoral investment planning approach for integrated development of urban services', in K. Singh, F. Steinberg and N. von Einsiedel (eds) *Integrated Urban Infrastructure Development in Asia*, IT Publications, London, pp17–32

Sintomer, Y., C. Herzberg and A. Rocke (2008) 'Participatory budgeting in Europe: Potentials and challenges', *International Journal of Urban and Regional Research* **32**(1): 164–178

Sirolli, E. (1999) *Ripples from the Zambezi: Passion, Entrepreneurship, and the Rebirth of Local Economies*, New Society Publishers, Vancouver, BC

Sivam, A. and D. Evans (2001) 'Improving the flow of serviced land in the formal housing markets of less developed countries', *Third World Planning Review* **23**(4): 367–386

Sivaramakrishan, K. and L. Green (1986) *Metropolitan Management: The Asian Experience*, Oxford University Press, London

Skinner, C. (2008) 'The struggle for the streets: Processes of exclusion and inclusion of street traders in Durban, South Africa', *Development Southern Africa* **25**(2): 227–242

Skinner, C. and R. Dobson (2007) 'Bringing the informal economy into urban plans – Warwick Junction, South Africa', *Habitat Debate* **13**(2): 11

Slater, B. (2008) 'Towns disappear as urban sprawl grows', *The Australian*, www.theaustralian.news.com.au/story/0,25197,23436441-5016345,00.html

Sorensen, A. (2002) *The Making of Urban Japan: Cities and Planning from Edo to the Twenty-first Century*, Nissan Institute/Routledge, New York

South African Cities Network (2004) *State of the Cities Report 2004*, South African Cities Network, Johannesburg

Souza, C. (2001) 'Participatory budgeting in Brazilian cities: Limits and possibilities in building democratic institutions', *Environment and Urbanization* **13**(1): 159–184

Souza, C. (2007) 'Local democratization in Brazil: Strengths and dilemmas of deliberative democracy', *Development* **50**(1): 90–95

Souza, M. (2003) 'Alternative urban planning and management in Brazil: Instructive examples for other countries in the South?', in P. Harrison, M. Huchzermeyer and M. Mayekiso (eds) *Confronting Fragmentation: Housing and Urban Development in a Democratizing Society*, University of Cape Town Press, Cape Town, pp190–208

Spiegel, A., V. Watson and P. Wilkinson (1996) 'Domestic diversity and fluidity among some African households in Greater Cape Town', *Social Dynamics* **21**(2): 7–30

Standing Advisory Committee on Trunk Road Assessment (1994) *Trunk Roads and the Generation of Traffic*, UK Department of Transport, London

Starrs, T. (2005) 'The SUV in our pantry', *Solar Today*, July/August

Statistics New Zealand (2001) 'Historical context: New Zealand, 2001', www.stats.govt.nz/urban-rural-profiles/historical-context/default.htm.

Statistics New Zealand (2009) *Household Labour Force Survey: December 2008 Quarter*, www.stats.govt.nz/NR/rdonlyres/5F30AA35-03D6-4FE5-925E 49BD36 173656/0/householdlabourforcesurveydec08 qtrhotprevised.pdf

Steinberg, F. (2005) 'Strategic urban planning in Latin America: Experiences of building and managing the future', *Habitat International* **29**(1): 69–93

Stiftel, B. (2000) 'Planning theory', in R. Pelaseyed (ed) *The National AICP Examination Course Guidebook 2000*, American Institute of Certified Planners, Washington, DC, pp4–16

Stiftel, B. (2009) 'Planning the paths for planning schools', Paper presented at the Symposium on Planning Education, held at the University of South Australia, 13 February, www.unisa.edu.au/nbe/Planning60/programme.asp

Stiftel, B. and C. Mukhopadhyay (2007) 'Thoughts on Anglo-American hegemony in planning scholarship: Do we read each others work?' *Town Planning Review* **78**(5): 545–572

Stiftel, B. and V. Watson (2005) *Dialogues in Urban and Regional Planning, Volume 1*, Routledge, London

Stiftel, B., V. Watson and H. Acselrad (2006a) 'Introduction: Global commonality and regional specificity', in B. Stiftel, V. Watson and H. Acselrad (eds) *Dialogues in Urban and Regional Planning, Volume 2*, Routledge, London, pp1–24

Stiftel, B., V. Watson, and H. Ascelrad (2006b) *Dialogues in Urban and Regional Planning, Volume 2*, Routledge, London

Stiftel, B., A. Forsyth, L. Dalton and F. Steiner (2009) 'Assessing planning school performance: Multiple paths, multiple measures', *Journal of Planning Education and Research* **28**: 323–335

Stoker, G. (2000) 'Urban political science and the challenge of urban governance', in J. Pierre (ed)

Debating Governance, Oxford University Press, Oxford, pp91–109

Strobel, R. (2003) 'From "cosmopolitan fantasies" to "national traditions": Socialist realism in East Berlin', in J. Nasr and M. Volait (eds) *Urbanism Imported or Exported? Native Aspirations and Foreign Plans*, Wiley-Academy, Chichester

Swyngedouw, E. (2005) 'Governance innovation and the citizen: The Janus Face of governance-beyond-the-state', *Urban Studies* **42**(11): 1991–2006

Swyngedouw, E., F. Moulaert and A. Rodriguez (2002) 'Neoliberal urbanization in Europe: Large-scale urban development projects and the new urban policy', *Antipode* **34**(3): 542–577

Talen, E. (1996) 'After the plans: Methods to evaluate the implementation success of plans', *Journal of Planning Education and Research* **16**: 79–91

Talen, E. (1997) 'Do plans get implemented? A review of evaluation in planning', *Journal of Planning Literature* **10**(3): 248–259

Talukder, S. (2004) *Metropolitan Governance: Case Study of Dhaka,* ISTP, PhD thesis, Murdoch University, Perth, Australia

Taniguchi, M. and T. Ikeda (2005) 'The compact city as a means of reducing reliance on the car: A model-based analysis for sustainable urban layout', in K. Williams (ed) *Spatial Planning, Urban Form and Sustainable Transport*, Ashgate, Aldershot, pp139–150

Tapales, P. D. (1996) 'The Philippines', in P. L. McCarney (ed) *The Changing Nature of Local Government in Developing Countries*, Centre for Urban and Community Studies, University of Toronto, Toronto, pp197–219

Taylor, N. (1998) *Urban Planning Theory since 1945*, Sage Publications, London

Teitz, M. (1968) 'Cost effectiveness: A systems approach to analysis of urban services', *Journal of the American Institute of Planners* **34**(5): 303–311

Tempesta, T. and M. Thiene (1997) 'Agricultural land values and urban growth', *Land Reform* **2**, www.fao.org/sd/Ltdirect/LR972/w6728t04.htm

Thomson, J. (1977) *Great Cities and their Traffic*, Penguin, London

Tibaijuka, A. K. (2005) *Report of the Fact-Finding Mission to Zimbabwe to Assess the Scope and Impact of Operation Murambatsvina by the UN Special Envoy on Human Settlements Issues in Zimbabwe*, UN-Habitat, Nairobi, www.unhabitat.org/downloads/docs/1664_96507_Zi mbabweReport.pdf

Todes, A. (2003) 'Housing, integrated urban development and the compact city', in P. Harrison, M. Huchzmeyer and M. Mayekiso (eds) *Confronting Fragmentation: Housing and Urban Development in a Democratising Society*, Juta, Cape Town, pp109–121

Todes, A., N. Malaza and A. Williamson (2008) 'Good practice in planning with gender in the Commonwealth', Paper for the Commonwealth Association of Planners, presented at the World Urban Forum, Nanjing

Tripp, A. M. (2003) 'Non-formal institutions, informal economies and the politics of inclusion', in S. Kayizzi-Mugerwa (ed) *Reforming Africa's Institutions: Ownership, Incentives and Capabilities*, United Nations University (UNU) Press, Tokyo, pp301–321

Tugwell, R.G. (1939) 'The fourth power', *Planning and Civic Comment*, AIP and Civic Association, April–June

UCL Deloitte (2006) *Delivering Tomorrow's Places: Effective Practice in Spatial Planning*, Draft Report for the RTPI, DCLG, GLA and Joseph Rowntree Foundation

UN (United Nations) (1999) *1999 World Survey on the Role of Women in Development: Globalization, Gender and Work*, Report of the Secretary General to the UN General Assembly (Document A/54/227), New York

UN (2005) *World Urbanization Prospects: The 2005 Revision*, Washington, DC

UN (2006a) *Economic, Social and Cultural Rights – Women and Adequate Housing*, www2.ohchr.org/english/issues/housing/women.htm

UN (2006b) *World Migrant Stock: The 2005 Revision Database*, http://esa.un.org/migration

UN (2007) *The Millennium Development Goals Report 2007*, New York, NY, www.un.org/millenniumgoals/pdf/mdg2007.pdf

UN (2008) *World Urbanization Prospects: The 2007 Revision*, Population Division, Department of Economic and Social Affairs, New York, www.un.org/esa/population/publications/wup2007/2 007WUP_Highlights_web.pdf

UN (2009) *People Matter: Civic Engagement in Public Governance: World Public Sector Report 2008*, UN, New York

UN Millennium Project (2005) *A Home in the City*, United Nations Millennium Project, Task Force on Improving the Lives of Slum Dwellers, Earthscan, London, www.unmillenniumproject.org/ documents/slumdwellers-complete.pdf

UNCHS (United Nations Centre for Human Settlements (Habitat)) (1993) *The Urban Poor as Agents of Development: Community Action Planning in Sri Lanka*, United Nations Centre for Human Settlements, Nairobi

UNCHS (1995) *A Reappraisal of the Urban Planning Process*, UNCHS, Nairobi

UNCHS (1996) *An Urbanising World: Global Report on Human Settlements 1996*, Oxford University Press for UNCHS, Oxford, www.unhabitat.org/grhs/1996

UNCHS (1997) *The Istanbul Declaration and the Habitat Agenda*, UNCHS, Nairobi

UNCHS (2000) 'UNCHS (Habitat) – the Global Campaign for Good Governance', *Environment and Urbanization* **12**: 197–202

UNCHS (2001a) *Cities in a Globalizing World: Global Report on Human Settlements 2001*, Earthscan, London, www.unhabitat.org/grhs/2001

UNCHS (2001b) *Tools to Support Participatory Urban Decision Making*, UNCHS, Nairobi, www.unhabitat.org/pmss/getPage.asp?page= bookView&book=1122

UNDESA (United Nations Department of Economic and Social Affairs) and IASIA (International Association of Schools and Institutes of Administration) (2008) *Standards of Excellence for Public Administration Education and Training*, Task Force on Standards of Excellence for Public Administration Education and Training, New York and Brussels, www.iias-iisa.org/ iasia/f/standards_excellence/Documents/IASIA_UN% 20Standards%20of%20Excellence.pdf

UNEP (United Nations Environment Programme) (2002) *Global Environment Outlook 3: Past, Present and Future Perspectives*, Earthscan, London

UNEP (2007) *Global Environmental Outlook: Environment for Development (GEO4)*, Progress Press Ltd, Valleta, Malta, www.unep.org/geo/geo4/ report/GEO-4_Report_Full_en.pdf.

UNESCAP (United Nations Economic and Social Council for Asia Pacific) (2003) *Promoting the Millennium Development Goals in Asia and the Pacific*, United Nations, Bangkok www.eclac.org/publicaciones/ xml/6/32606/LCG2356B_1.pdf

UNFPA (United Nations Population Fund) (2007) *State of the World Population 2007: Unleashing the Potential of Urban Growth*, UNFPA, New York, NY

UN-Habitat (United Nations Human Settlements Programme) (2002a) *The Global Campaign on Urban Governance, A Concept Paper*, Nairobi, www.unhabitat.org/downloads/docs/2099_24326_concept_paper.doc

UN-Habitat (2002b) *Local Democracy and Decentralization in East and Southern Africa: Experiences from Uganda, Kenya, Botswana, Tanzania and Ethiopia*, UN-Habitat, Nairobi

UN-Habitat (2002c) *International Instruments on Housing Rights*, UNHRP Report No 2, UN-Habitat, Nairobi, www.unhabitat.org/list.asp?typeid=48&catid=282&subMenuID=58

UN-Habitat (2002d) 'Tools to enhance women's participation in urban governance', *Habitat Debate* **8**(4): 5

UN-Habitat (2003) *The Challenge of Slums: Global Report on Human Settlements 2003*, Earthscan, London, www.unhabitat.org/grhs/2003

UN-Habitat (2004a) *The State of the World's Cities 2004/2005: Globalization and Urban Culture*, UN-Habitat and Earthscan, London

UN-Habitat (2004b) *Urban Land for All*, UN-Habitat, Nairobi

UN-Habitat (2005) *The Legacy of the Urban Management Programme*, UN-Habitat, Nairobi

UN-Habitat (2006a) 'Displaced people's rights to the city: Planning for slum prevention', *Urban Planning in a State of Flux Series*, Brochure 3, UN-Habitat, Nairobi

UN-Habitat (2006b) *Enabling Shelter Strategies: Review of Experience from Two Decades of Implementation*, UN-Habitat, Nairobi

UN-Habitat (2006c) 'Introducing (spatial) planning in post-conflict situations: The case of Somali cities', *Urban Planning in a State of Flux Series*, Brochure 6, UN-Habitat, Nairobi

UN-Habitat (2006d) 'No more master plans: Strategic urban development planning in Dar es Salaam', *Urban Planning in a State of Flux Series*, Brochure 1, UN-Habitat, Nairobi

UN-Habitat (2006e) 'Paving the way for sustainable development in a post disaster situation: The case of the tsunami damaged village of Xaafun, North East Somalia', *Urban Planning in a State of Flux Series*, Brochure 5, UN-Habitat, www.unhabitat.org/pmss/getPage.asp?page=promoView&promo=2295

UN-Habitat (2006f) *The State of The World's Cities 2006/2007: The Millennium Development Goals and Urban Sustainability,* UN-Habitat and Earthscan, London

UN-Habitat (2006g) 'Urban trialogues: Visions, projects, co-productions. Localising Agenda 21', *Urban Planning in a State of Flux Series*, Brochure 4, UN-Habitat, Nairobi

UN-Habitat (2006h) *Innovative Policies for the Urban Informal Economy*, UN-Habitat, Nairobi

UN-Habitat (2006i) *Urban Planning in a State of Flux*, UN-Habitat, Nairobi

UN-Habitat (2007a) *Forced Evictions – Towards Solutions? Second Report of the Advisory Group on Forced Evictions to the Executive Director of UN-HABITAT*, Advisory Group on Forced Evictions (AGFE), Nairobi, www.unhabitat.org/pmss/getPage.asp?page=bookView&?book=2353

UN-Habitat (2007b) *Enhancing Urban Safety and Security: Global Report on Human Settlements 2007*, Earthscan, London, www.unhabitat.org/grhs/2007

UN-Habitat (2007c) *Medium Term Strategic and Institutional Plan for UN-Habitat for the Period 2008–2013,* Nairobi

UN-Habitat (2008a) *Secure Land Rights for All*, UN-Habitat, Nairobi

UN-Habitat (2008b) *The State of The World's Cities 2008/2009*, UN-Habitat, Nairobi

UN-Habitat (2008c) *Gender Mainstreaming in Local Authorities*, UN-Habitat, Nairobi

UN-Habitat (2009) *Women's Safety Audits: What Works and Where?* UN-Habitat, Nairobi

UN-Habitat and Department for International Development (DFID) (2002) *Sustainable Urbanization: Achieving Agenda 21*, United Nations Human Settlements Programme, Nairobi.

UN-Habitat and EcoPlan (2005) *Promoting Local Economic Development through Strategic Planning*, United Nations Human Settlements Programme, Nairobi

UN-Habitat and OHCHR (Office of the United Nations High Commission on Human Rights) (2002) *Housing Rights Legislation*, UNHRP Report No 1, UN-Habitat and OHCHR, Nairobi, www.unhabitat.org/list.asp?typeid=48&catid=282&subMenuID=58

Universalia (2006) *Independent Evaluation of the Cities Alliance: Volume I: Final Report*, Universalia for Cities Alliance, Canada

Urban Transportation Monitor (1999) 'Summary information from Texas Transportation Institute Annual Mobility Report 1999', *Urban Transportation Monitor* **13**(22), Lawley Publications, Burke, Virginia

Urry, J. (1981) *The Anatomy of Civil Society: The Economy, Civil Society and the State*, Macmillan, London

Van Grusven, L. (2000) 'Singapore: The changing residential landscape in a winner city', in P. Marcuse and R. van Kempen (eds) *Globalizing Cities: A New Spatial Order?*, Blackwell, Malden, MA, pp95–126

Varley, A. (2007) 'Gender and property formalization: conventional and alternative approaches', *World Development* **35**(10): 1739–1758

Vidal, A. C., J. Hutchinson, R. Putnam, I. Light, X. de Souza Briggs, W. M. Rohe, J. Gress and M. Woolcock (2004) 'Using social capital to help integrate planning theory, research, and practice: Preface', *Journal of the American Planning Association* **70**(2): 142–192

Vigar, G. and P. Healey (1999) 'Territorial integration and "plan-led" planning', *Planning Practice and Research* **14**(2): 153–170

Vigar, G., P. Healey, A. Hull, and S. Davoudi (2000) *Planning, Governance and Spatial Strategy in Britain: An Institutionalist Analysis*, Macmillan, London

Vujovic, S. and M. Petrovic (2007) 'Belgrade's post-socialist urban evolution: Reflections by the actors in the development process', in S. Tsenkova and Z. Nedovìc-Budìc (eds) *The Urban Mosaic of Post-Socialist Europe: Space, Institutions and Policy*, Springer and Physica-Verlag, Heidelberg, pp361–384

Wacquant, L. (2008) *Urban Outcasts: A Comparative Sociology of Advanced Marginality*, Polity Press, Cambridge

Waibel, M. (2008) 'Mega-urban growth, informality and the issue of governability: Towards theorising specific informal dynamics in a wider context' in I. C. Stiftung (ed) *8th Berlin Roundtables on Transnationality. Urban Planet: Collective Identities, Governance and Empowerment in Megacities*, Berlin, 11–17 June, www.irmgard-coninx-stiftung.de

Walton, J. (1998) 'Urban conflict and social movements in poor countries: Theory and evidence of collective action', *International Journal of Urban and Regional Research* **22**(3): 460–481

Ward, P. and S. Chant (1987) 'Community leadership and self-help housing', *Progress in Planning* **27**(2): 69–136

Ward, S. V. (2002) *Planning the Twentieth-Century City: The Advanced Capitalist World*, John Wiley & Sons, Chichester

Watson, V. (2003) 'Conflicting rationalities: Implications for planning theory and practice', *Planning Theory and Practice* **4**(4): 395–407

Watson, V. (2007) *Revisiting the Role of Urban Planning: Concept Paper for the 2009 Global Report on Human Settlements*, University of Cape Town, Cape Town

Webster, C. and L. W.-C. Lai (2003) *Property Rights, Planning and Markets: Managing Spontaneous Cities*, Edward Elgar, Cheltenham, UK

Webster, D. and L. Muller (2004) 'The challenge of peri-urban growth in East Asia: The case of China Hangzhou–Ningbo corridor', in M. Freire and B. Yuen (eds) *Enhancing Urban Management in East Asia*, Ashgate, Aldershot, pp23–54

Weiss, C. (1998) *Evaluation*, 2nd edition, Prentice-Hall, Upper Saddle River, NJ

Wekwete, K. H. (1997) 'Urban management: The recent experience', in C. Rakodi (ed) *The Urban Challenge in Africa: Growth and the Management of Large Cities*, United Nations University Press, Tokyo

Welsh Assembly Government (2003) *People, Places, Futures: The Wales Spatial Plan*, Welsh Assembly Government, Cardiff

Went, A., P. Newman and W. James (2008) *CUSP Discussion Paper 2008/1 Renewable Transport: How Renewable Energy and Electric Vehicles using Vehicle to Grid Technology Can Make Carbon Free Urban Development*, Curtin University Sustainability Policy (CUSP) Institute, Perth

White, S. (1996) 'Depoliticising development: The uses and abuses of participation', *Development in Practice* **6**(1): 6–15

WHO-Europe (2007) *Threats and Challenges to Health Security in the WHO European Region: Natural Disasters and Emergencies on the Increase*, Fact Sheet EURO/03/07, Copenhagen, Rome, 2 April 2007, www.euro.who.int/Document/Mediacentre/fs0307e.pdf

Wigle, S. J. (2006) *Land, Shelter and Livelihoods: Exploring the Linkages in Mexico City*, PhD thesis, University of Toronto, Toronto

Wildavsky, A. (1973) 'If planning is everything, maybe it's nothing', *Policy Sciences* **4**: 127–153

Wiley-Schwartz, A. (2006) 'A revolutionary change in transportation planning: The slow road movement', *New York Times*, 10 July

Wilkinson, P. (2002) 'Integrated planning at the local level? The problematic intersection of integrated development planning and integrated transport planning in contemporary South Africa', Paper presented to Planning Africa Conference 2002, Durban

Wilkinson, P. (2006) 'Transit oriented development: A strategic instrument for spatial restructuring and public transport system enhancement in South African cities?', Paper presented at 25th Southern African Transport Conference, Pretoria, July

Williams, K., E. Burton and M. Jenks (eds) (2000) *Achieving Sustainable Urban Form*, E&FN Spon, London

Williams, R. H. (1989) 'Internationalizing planning education, 1992 and the European ERASMUS program', *Journal of Planning Education and Research* **10**(1): 75–78

Women's International News (2003) *Reports from Around the World: Americas, Recife, Brazil: Gender and the Participatory Budget*, INBRIEF, Bridge, Institute of Development Studies, University of Sussex, Brighton, UK

Wong, C. (1995) 'Developing quantitative indicators for urban and regional policy analysis', in R. Hambleton and H. Thomas (eds) *Urban Policy Evaluation: Challenge and Change*, Paul Chapman Publishing, London, pp111–122

World Bank (1997) *World Development Report 1997: The State in a Changing World*, World Bank, Washington, DC

World Bank (1998) *Fortifying Rio's Resurgence: A Report to the Mayor*, Unpublished report, World Bank, Washington, DC

World Bank (2002) *World Development Report 2002: Building Institutions for Markets*, Oxford University Press for the World Bank, New York, NY

World Bank (2004) *Involuntary Resettlement Sourcebook: Planning and Implementation in Development Projects: Volume 1*, World Bank, Washington, DC, www-wds.worldbank.org/servlet/WDSContentServer/WDSP/IB/2004/10/04/000012009_20041004165645/Rendered/PDF/301180v110PAPE1ettlement0sourcebook.pdf

World Bank (2007a) *Doing Business*, World Bank, Washington, DC, www.doingbusiness.org/Downloads/

World Bank (2007b) *Making the Most of Scarcity: Accountability for Better Water Management Results in the Middle East and North Africa*, World Bank, Washington, DC

World Commission on Environment and Development (1987) *Our Common Future*, Oxford University Press, Oxford

Yahya, S. (2002) *The Origins of Participatory Planning in Kenya*, Intermediate Technology Development Group-Eastern Africa, Nairobi

Yeung, Y. M. and F. C. Lo (1998) 'Globalization and world city formation in Pacific Asia', in F. C. Lo and Y. M. Yeung (eds) *Globalization and the World of Large Cities*, United Nations University Press (UNU), Tokyo, pp132–154

Yiftachel, O. (2003) 'Control, resistance and informality: Jews and Arabs in the Beer-Sheva Region, Israel', in N. Al-Sayyad and A. Roy (eds) *Urban Informality in the Era of Liberalization: A Transnational Perspective*, Lexington Books, Boulder, CO, pp111–133

Yuen, B. (2008) 'Revisiting urban planning in East Asia, Southeast Asia and the Pacific', Unpublished regional study prepared for the *Global Report on Human Settlements 2009*, www.unhabitat.org/grhs/2009

Zérah, M.-H. (2008) 'Splintering urbanism in Mumbai: Contrasting trends in a multilayered society', *Geoforum* **39**(6): 1922–1932, doi:10.1016/j.geoforum.2008.02.001

Zhang, X. (2000) 'High-rise and high-density compact urban form: The development of Hong Kong', in M. Jenks and R. Burgess (eds) *Compact Cities: Sustainable Urban Forms for Developing Countries*, Spon Press, London, pp245–254

Zillman, K. (2000) 'Rethinking the compact city: Informal urban development in Caracas', M. Jenks and R. Burgess (eds) *Compact Cities: Sustainable Urban Forms for Developing Countries*, Spon Press, London, pp193–206

INDEX